MONTHLY ENTRIES *for the* **Spiritual**
but not **Religious** *through the* **Year**

MONTHLY ENTRIES *for the* **Spiritual** *but not* **Religious** *through the* **Year**

Texts, Reflections, Journal/Meditations,
and Prayers for the Spiritual but not Religious

MARK G. BOYER

WIPF & STOCK · Eugene, Oregon

MONTHLY ENTRIES FOR THE SPIRITUAL BUT NOT RELIGIOUS THROUGH THE YEAR
Texts, Reflections, Journal/Meditations, and Prayers for the Spiritual but Not Religious

Copyright © 2022 Mark G. Boyer. All rights reserved. Except for brief quotations in critical publications or reviews, no part of this book may be reproduced in any manner without prior written permission from the publisher. Write: Permissions, Wipf and Stock Publishers, 199 W. 8th Ave., Suite 3, Eugene, OR 97401.

Wipf & Stock
An Imprint of Wipf and Stock Publishers
199 W. 8th Ave., Suite 3
Eugene, OR 97401

www.wipfandstock.com

PAPERBACK ISBN: 978-1-6667-4767-6
HARDCOVER ISBN: 978-1-6667-4768-3
EBOOK ISBN: 978-1-6667-4769-0

JULY 14, 2022 8:58 AM

The Scripture quotations contained herein are from the New Revised Standard Version Bible, copyright © 1989 by the Division of Christian Education of the National Council of the Churches of Christ in the U.S.A., and are used by permission. All rights reserved.

Dedicated to

Michael J. King,
friend, intellectual, traveler, SBNR.

"Your whole life is a spiritual practice."
—JOSEFA RANGEL

"The goal of spiritual practice is to know the essence and enjoy its delights."
—RAMI SHAPIRO

"We are moving toward a completely religionless time; people as they are now simply cannot be religious anymore. . . . It is also a sign of a new openness to [Dietrich] Bonhoeffer's 'religionless Christianity' that many people now call themselves 'spiritual but not religious.'"
—THOMAS CATHCART

"The new reformation will focus on the God experience itself, not on the explanations of ancient people's God experiences, explanations that fail to speak to modern humans."
—JARMO TARKKI

". . . '[T]he sacred' is not an article of belief, but an element of experience."
—MARCUS J. BORG

". . . [E]*very* space is sacred space. . . . This place is Holy. That spot is Holy. Every object, every form, every inch of space is Holy."
—PHILIP GOLDBERG

"There is more to being nonreligious than what you don't believe."
—TOM KRATTENMAKER

Contents

Introduction — xv

1 | The Month of *January*

New Year's Day (January 1) — 1
Ninth Day of Christmas: Fireplace (January 2) — 2
Tenth Day of Christmas: Candy Canes (January 3) — 3
Eleventh Day of Christmas: The Grinch (January 4) — 4
Twelfth Day of Christmas: Frosty the Snowman (January 5) — 5
Epiphany: Christmas Day 3 (January 6) — 6
National Law Enforcement Appreciation Day (January 9) — 8
World Religion Day (Third Sunday) — 10
Martin Luther King, Jr., Day (Third Monday) — 11
National Religious Freedom Day (January 16) — 13
Inauguration Day (January 20) — 14
National Sanctity of Human Life Day (January 22) — 15
International Holocaust Remembrance Day (January 27) — 17

2 | The Month of *February*

Groundhog Day (February 2) — 20
International Day of Human Fraternity (February 4) — 21
Super Bowl Sunday (First Sunday) — 24
Abraham Lincoln's Birthday (February 12) — 25
World Radio Day (February 13) — 26
Valentine's Day (February 14) — 28
President's Day (Washington's Birthday) (Third Monday) — 29
National Random Acts of Kindness Day (February 17) — 31
Chinese New Year (Jan. 21 – Feb. 20) — 32
World Day for Social Justice (February 20) — 34
National Love Your Pet Day (February 20) — 36

Tooth Fairy Day (February 28) — 37

Mardi Gras (Carnival) (Tuesday before Ash Wednesday) — 39

3 | The Month of March

World Wildlife Day (March 3) — 41

International Women's Day (March 8) — 42

Daylight Saving Time Begins (Second Sunday) — 44

St. Patrick's Day (March 17) — 45

Spring Begins (March 19–21) — 46

International Day of Happiness (March 20) — 47

International Day for the Elimination of Racial Discrimination (March 21) — 49

World Poetry Day (March 21) — 51

International Day of Forests (March 21) — 53

World Water Day (March 22) — 54

Passover (Begins Any Evening Between March 21 and April 20) — 55

National Doctors Day and National Physicians Week (March 30 and March 25–31) — 57

4 | The Month of April

April Fool's (Fools') Day (April 1) — 60

International Day of Conscience (April 5) — 61

National Beer Day (April 7) — 64

World Health Day (April 7) — 66

National Former Prisoner(s) of War Recognition Day (April 9) — 68

National Pet Day (April 11) — 72

Easter Sunday (March 22–April 25) — 73

Thomas Jefferson's Birthday (April 13) — 75

Income Tax Day (April 15) — 77

Patriots' Day (Third Monday) — 78

American Revolutionary War Began (April 19) — 79

World Creativity and Innovation Day (April 21) — 80

Earth Day (April 22) — 83

English Language Day (April 23) — 84

Administrative Professionals Week and Administrative Professionals Day (Last Full Week of April and Wednesday of the Last Full Week of April) ... 86

Arbor Day (Last Friday) ... 88

Ramadan (Any Month from One Sighting of a Crescent Moon to the Next) ... 89

5 | THE MONTH OF *May*

May Day (May 1) ... 91

International Workers' Day (May 1) ... 92

Loyalty Day (May 1) ... 94

National Teacher Appreciation Week and National Teacher Appreciation Day (First Full Week of May, Tuesday of the First Full Week of May) ... 95

World Press Freedom Day (May 3) ... 96

International Firefighters' Day (May 4) ... 98

Cinco de Mayo (May 5) ... 100

National Day of Prayer (First Thursday) ... 102

National Nurses Day, National Student Nurses' Day, and International Nurses Day (May 6–12) ... 103

World Laughter Day (First Sunday) ... 104

V-E Day (May 8) ... 105

Mother's Day (Second Sunday) ... 107

International Day of Families (May 15) ... 108

Peace Officers Memorial Day and Police Week (May 15) ... 110

Armed Forces Week and Day (Second Saturday to Third Sunday and Third Saturday) ... 114

World Bee Day (May 20) ... 115

World Day for Cultural Diversity for Dialogue and Development (May 21) ... 117

National Wine Day (May 25) ... 120

Red Nose Day (Last Thursday) ... 121

Memorial Day (Last Monday) ... 122

CONTENTS

6 | THE MONTH OF *June*

D-Day (Normandy Landings) (June 6)	125
World Food Safety Day (June 7)	127
World Ocean Day (June 8)	128
World Day Against Child Labor (June 12)	130
Flag Day (June 14)	132
Father's Day (Third Sunday)	134
Juneteenth National Independence Day (June 19)	136
Summer Solstice (June 20–22)	138
World Refugee Day (June 20)	139
National American Eagle Day (June 20)	141

7 | THE MONTH OF *July*

Canada Day (July 1)	144
National Postal Workers Day, National U.S. Postage Stamp Day (July 1)	146
Independence Day (July 4)	148
National Tattoo Day (July 17)	150
Nelson Mandela International Day (Mandela Day) (July 18)	152
First Manned Moon Landing (Apollo 11) (July 20–21)	153
Parents' Day (Fourth Sunday)	155
World War I Began (July 28)	156
International Day of Friendship (Friendship Day) (July 30)	158
World Day Against Trafficking in Persons (July 30)	160

8 | THE MONTH OF *August*

International Day of the World's Indigenous Peoples (August 9)	162
International Youth Day (August 12)	163
Panama Canal Opened (August 15)	165
World Humanitarian Day (August 19)	166
National Aviation Day (August 19)	168
National Senior Citizen's Day (August 21)	173
Women's Equality Day (August 26)	174
School Begins (August—September)	176

9 | THE MONTH OF *September*

World Day of Prayer for the Care of Creation (September 1)	178

CONTENTS

World War II Began (September 1)	179
Victory Over Japan Day (V-J Day) (September 2)	181
International Day of Charity (September 5)	182
Labor Day (First Monday)	183
National Grandparents Day (Sunday after Labor Day)	184
National Pet Memorial Day (Second Sunday)	186
Patriot Day and National Day of Service and Remembrance (September 11)	187
The Star-Spangled Banner Written (September 14)	189
National Stepfamily Day (September 16)	190
Constitution Day and Citizenship Day (September 17)	192
National POW/MIA Recognition Day (Third Friday)	194
International Day of Peace (September 21)	199
Autumnal Equinox (September 22–23)	200
Native American Day (Fourth Friday)	201
National Good Neighbor Day (September 26)	202
International Day for the Total Elimination of Nuclear Weapons (September 26)	204
World Tourism Day (September 27)	206
National Coffee Day, International Coffee Day (September 29, October 1)	208

10 | THE MONTH OF *October*

International Day for Older Persons (October 1)	211
World Teachers' Day (October 5)	213
Leif Erikson Day (October 9)	215
World Mental Health Day (October 10)	218
Columbus Day (Second Monday)	220
National Farmer's Day (October 12)	221
White Cane Safety Day, Blind Americans Equality Day (October 15)	222
World Food Day (October 16)	226
National Boss's Day (October 16)	227
International Day for the Eradication of Poverty (October 17)	229
Missouri Day (Third Wednesday)	230

xi

CONTENTS

Sweetest Day (Third Saturday)	233
United Nations Day (October 24)	235
National Mother-in-Law Day (Fourth Sunday)	237
National Chocolate Day (October 28)	238
World Cities Day (October 31)	241
Reformation Day (October 31)	243
Halloween 1 (October 31)	245
Halloween 2 (October 31)	246

11 | The Month of *November*

All Saints' Day (November 1)	249
All Souls' Day (November 2)	250
Election Day (Tuesday after the First Monday)	251
Daylight Saving Time Ends (First Sunday)	252
World Freedom Day (November 9)	253
Veterans Day (November 11)	256
National Philanthropy Day (November 15)	258
America Recycles Day (November 15)	261
World Philosophy Day (Third Thursday)	264
Gettysburg Address Anniversary (November 19)	265
International Men's Day (November 19)	267
World Toilet Day (November 19)	268
World (Universal, International) Children's Day (November 20)	270
National Children's Day 1 (November 20)	273
National Children's Day 2 (November 20)	275
National Child's Day 1 (November 20)	277
National Child's Day 2 (November 20)	280
Great American Smokeout (Third Thursday)	284
World Television Day (November 21)	286
Thanksgiving Day (Fourth Thursday)	288
Black Friday (Friday after Thanksgiving)	291
Small Business Saturday (Saturday after Thanksgiving)	292
Cyber Monday (Monday after Thanksgiving)	294
Giving Tuesday (Tuesday after Thanksgiving)	296

12 | The Month of *December*

World AIDS Day (December 1)	299
International Day of Disabled Persons: Part 1 (December 3)	302
International Day of Disabled Persons: Part 2 (December 3)	306
International Volunteer Day for Economic and Social Development (December 5)	310
St. Nicholas Day (December 6)	313
National Pearl Harbor Remembrance Day (December 7)	315
Green Monday (Second Monday)	317
Human Rights Day (December 10)	318
Human Rights Week (December 10–17)	321
International Mountain Day (December 11)	326
Bill of Rights Day (December 15)	328
International Migrants Day (December 18)	332
International Human Solidarity Day (December 20)	335
Super Saturday (Saturday before Christmas)	338
Winter Solstice (December 21–22)	339
Festivus (December 23)	341
Christmas Eve (December 24)	342
Twelve Days of Christmas (Christmas Day 1, December 25)	343
Christmas Day 2 (December 25)	346
Kwanzaa Begins (December 26 (to January 1)	348
Third Day of Christmas: Christmas Tree (December 27)	351
Fourth Day of Christmas: Charlie Brown Christmas Tree (December 28)	352
Fifth Day of Christmas: Candles (December 29)	354
Sixth Day of Christmas: Reindeer (December 30)	355
New Year's Eve (December 31)	357
Bibliography	361
Index	387
Recent Books by Mark G. Boyer published by Wipf & Stock	361

Introduction

General Spirituality

This is a book about spirituality. Howard Rice says, "Spirituality is the pattern by which we shape our lives in response to our experience of God as a very real presence in and around us."[1] First, we experience God, consciously or unconsciously. According to Rami Shapiro, we are in God. Known as panentheism, we already exist in the divine. Thus, spirituality is being in harmony with the universe and everyone and everything in it. Once we are aware—consciously or unconsciously (intuition)—we nourish that connection in the way or ways that fill us the best. For some people, Bible reading, Bible study, other study, pottery making, dance, volunteering, cooking, caring for a pet, singing, sewing, etc. is both an experience of God (spirituality) and a means of nourishing personal spirituality. Divine Spirit and human spirit connect. To illustrate this point, Shapiro narrates a parable from the Zohar, the bible of Jewish mysticism: "There was once a cave-dwelling ascetic who ate nothing but raw wheat. Curious about life outside his cave, he visited a city and tasted thick black bread, cake, and honey-dipped pastry. 'What are these made of?' he asked. 'Wheat flour' he was told. 'Then I am master of all of them,' he scoffed, 'for I eat the essence of them all—wheat.'"[2] Then, Shapiro explains: "Commenting on the parable, the Zohar says, 'This ascetic was a fool; focusing solely on the essence, he never learned to enjoy the delights that flow from it.'"[3]

Knowing the essence, knowing the Divine, is knowing the universe and everyone and everything in it. If all is in God, then all is filled with God, and all can nourish spirituality. We pattern our lives on such sublime experiences that are brought to us by way of the ordinary. Then, we delight in them. The historical Jesus called such experiences the delight of God's kingdom, reign, empire, etc. Being in harmony with the universe is disrupted by chaos. Chaos, the daily pull to disorder or non-patterned life, keeps us out of harmony. It disrupts, invades, and provokes disharmony. Each person must discover and use what works for him or her to bring him or her out of chaos and back to harmony with himself or herself and with all that exists. Commonly

---

1. Maher, "Soul and Spirit," 10.
2. Shapiro, "Roadside Assistance," 11.
3. Shapiro, "Roadside Assistance," 11.

called prayer, the practice is to reunite the broken pieces of life into a harmonious whole through reading, study, gardening, walking, painting. etc. Philip Goldberg writes, "Exquisite architecture can evoke awe and transcendence every bit as much as a mountain range or a field of wildflowers."[4] He writes about feeling the energy in "a library especially if you value books . . . . 'Libraries are like mountains or meadows or creeks: sacred space.' A park bench can be sacred space. So can a puddle-sized pond, a pier, an empty ball field, a quiet museum gallery, an unused room in an office building, a hospital chapel, or a lonesome tree. . . ."[5] Goldberg states: ". . . Divine Presence is everywhere, but it is, to most of us mortals, more discernable in some places than in others. . . . [T]he Divine will reveal itself in surprising places, even in a kitchen. . . ."[6] While saying words—what most people think prayer is—is important, those who practice spirituality know more is needed to transform chaos into harmony. The transformation is done by God to whom we connect through all else. Because we exist in the very One—no matter what name we give—all is done in the divine presence, and we are transformed in the process. We engage in this process over and over and over again throughout our lives, hopefully to finish on the other side of death basking in the divine presence as a transformed self. It makes no difference if we awaken to the divine presence in whom we live and more and have our being. Transformation occurs because we cooperate with God, whether we are aware of it or not. God transforms over and over again into the divine. And we are not alone in this ongoing process. "Transformed people transform people," states Vaillancourt Murphy.[7] Richard Rohr adds, "We transform people to the degree we have been transformed."[8] Shapiro emphasizes that "spirituality is progressive" and, thus, he speaks "of a maturing rather than a mature spirituality. . . . The individual person journeys to the self where he or she knows all is God."[9] Philip Sheldrake says, ". . . [S]pirituality involves a process of transformation that seeks to enable us to move from less adequate values and ways of life to what is more adequate and, indeed, fulfilling in an ultimate sense."[10] Marianne Williamson states, "God works through each of us to the extent to which we make ourselves receptive."[11] All human experience is spiritual, no matter how one limits it with descriptive adjectives, like civil, awesome, secular, religious, etc. According to Rohr: "We may begin by making little connections with other people, with nature and animals, then grow into deeper connectedness with people. Finally, we can experience

4. Goldberg, "Holy Places," 24.
5. Goldberg, "Holy Places," 24.
6. Goldberg, "Holy Places," 24–5.
7. Hendler-Voss, "Restore Justice," 37.
8. Rohr, "God."
9. Shapiro, "Roadside Assistance: Holy Land," 47.
10. Sheldrake, *Spiritual Way*, xi.
11. Kiesling, "New American," 67.

full connectedness as union with God."[12] Even though we may feel alone, we are not. We are in God. According to Shapiro, spirituality is "a progressive stripping away of the conditioning that blinds [us] to the truest fact of [our] existence: [we] are a happening of God, YHVH, . . . the Happening happening as all happening."[13] Thomas Cathcart, quoting Ken Wilber, states, "A mystic is not one who sees God as an object, but one who is immersed in God as an atmosphere."[14] Echoing Rohr, Shapiro states, "Spirituality isn't fixed but fluid, not a final 'aha' but a recurring 'wow.'"[15] In other words, spirituality is a lifetime process.

While "we live and move and have our being" in God,[16] we are also traveling throughout our lives into God. Poust states: "Life itself is a pilgrimage . . . to the core of [one's] being, to that destination in [one's] heart where God resides."[17] Keith Kachtick reminds us that the "French philosopher Voltaire said, 'God is a circle with no circumference whose center is everywhere.'"[18] Rohr writes: "When we love something, we grant it soul, we see its soul, and we let its soul touch ours. We must love something deeply to know its soul (anima)." Then, he adds, "Before the resonance of love, we are largely blind to the meaning, value, and power of ordinary things to 'save' us and help us live in union with the source of all being. In fact, until we can appreciate and even delight in the soul of other things, even trees and animals, we probably haven't discovered our own souls either. Soul knows soul through love, which is why it's the great commandment (Matthew 22:36)."[19] Shapiro states, ". . . Jesus was a Jewish mystic who came to know what all mystics know, namely, that all things are a part of God and nothing is apart from God."[20] Michael Casey writes, ". . . [O]ur world is in constant communication with the spiritual world and with God, who stands at its center."[21] This leads Thomas Hubl to state, ". . . [N]othing is not spiritual."[22] Likewise, Rohr states: "I know myself and all others to be a part of God. . . . And with this sense of wholeness comes a sense of holiness, a sense of love from and for all beings."[23] Williamson explains, "Mature spirituality extends beyond the confines of the narrow self. . . . It's a global and universal phenomenon. . . . But you can't ever evolve beyond a connection

12. Rohr, "Community."
13. Shapiro, "Roadside Assistance: Holy Land," 47.
14. Cathcart, *There is no God*, 43–44.
15. Shapiro, "Roadside Assistance: Holy Land," 47.
16. NRSV: Acts 17:28.
17. Poust, *Everyday Divine*, 149.
18. Kachtick, "Circles," 27.
19. Rohr, "Communion."
20. Shapiro, "Roadside Assistance: Holy Land," 48.
21. Casey, *Balaam's Donkey*, 325.
22. Hubl, "Lean."
23. Rohr, "A Big Experiment."

to God himself."[24] Commenting on the word *namaste*, which means "I honor the divinity with you," Goldberg writes: "It's an everyday acknowledgment that we all share the same divine essence at the core of our being . . . . In short, my essential nature is infinite, eternal Spirit, and so is yours, and so is everyone else's. . . . [W]e are one another."[25] According to Sheldrake, "Christian spiritual traditions all embody a sense of transcendence . . . and point toward a final eternal endpoint for human existence."[26]

Title: Monthly Entries for the Spiritual but not Religious through the Year

Monthly Entries

For each of the twelve months of the year a number of entries ranging from ten to twenty-five are presented. The number of monthly entries depends on the national and international days being marked during each month of the year. Each entry consists of a (1) title, (2) date of observance, (3) text, (4) reflection, (5) journal/meditation question, and (6) prayer.

Title: The title names the national or international day being celebrated. Thus, the first entry for the month of January is New Year's Day. The first entry for the month of February is Groundhog Day.

Date of Observance: Under the title, in most entries, is the exact date of the month when the nation and/or the world celebrates the event. Thus, New Year's Day is marked on January 1, Groundhog Day on February 2. However, there are occasions when the celebration occurs on the first Thursday of the month, the second Saturday of the month, or the last Monday of the month. Because these are moveable commemorations, the reader will need to consult a calendar to determine when those days occur.

Text: While a few entries begin with a biblical text, most begin with a text from a United States Public Law, a presidential proclamation, a United Nations declaration, etc. These are the new sacred texts of our own time and place. Before documents—such as laws, prophecies, regal declarations, prayers, etc.—were collected and declared to be biblical, they were the ordinary texts of biblical culture. Since this book is for the spiritual but not religious, it is of utmost importance that modern sacred texts—those documents our culture considers to be holy—are used here. Glynn Cardy presents some appropriate words of John Shelby Spong: "I treasure the Bible. I live in it and work on it all the time. But it is not the word of God. It's the tribal story of a particular people, and the best thing about that story is that the story keeps growing

---

24. Kiesling, "New American," 64.
25. Goldberg, "Namaste," 13.
26. Sheldrake, *Spiritual Way*, xi.

INTRODUCTION

and evolving."[27] Likewise, Jarmo Tarkki writes, "If the Jesus experience is going to be relevant in the twenty-first century, we must speak the language of our time, just as the authors of the gospels and the inventors of church dogmas did in their own time."[28] Modern texts are worthy of reflection.

Reflection: This book presents reflections based on the text. As a noun, the word, *reflections*, refers to expressing something in the hope that one will think seriously, carefully, and relatively calmly about it. The author gleans the spirituality from the text in his reflective words. Sometimes he presents historical background on the day being celebrated. At other times he quotes from presidential proclamations, statements made by others, messages, or words that shed more light on what is being celebrated. This means that some reflections are short, some are medium, and some are long. The length of the reflection is determined by the resources available. The truth about the celebration is revealed through the reflection. Grasping the truth is a spiritual experience. By reading the texts and reflections presented here and contemplating their words, the reader enters into meditation, the inner process of reflecting on the wisdom of others.

Journal/Meditation: The reflection is followed by a question for personal journaling and/or meditation. The question functions as a guide for personal appropriation of the text and reflection, thus leading the reader into personal prayer. The journal/meditation question is designed to foster a process of actively applying the reflection to one's life and further development of it. The question gets one started; where the journal/meditation goes cannot be predetermined. It may be a single statement or an idea with which one lingers for a few minutes, a few hours, or a few days. Such contemplation has no end; the reader decides when he or she has finished his or her exploration because he or she needs to attend to other things. People who like to journal—written or electronic—will find the question appropriate for that activity.

According to Annmarie Scobey: "Meditation involves quieting the mind and heart. It is a time of focusing our attention on a . . . word or on our breath; a time of letting our thoughts pass by, without holding onto them or entering into them. It is a time of deep awareness. . . . A common theme . . . is silence and stillness. Contemplation, a cousin of meditation, was explained by St. Gregory the Great in the sixth century as 'resting in God.' St. Gregory went on to explain that in this 'resting,' the mind and heart are not so much seeking God as beginning to experience God's actual presence. The reduction of action and thought, according to St. Gregory, allows the person practicing contemplation to sustain [his or her] consent to God's presence. In other words—without action and thought, less gets in the way of experiencing God."[29]

---

27. Cardy, "When," 10.
28. Tarkki, "John Shelby Spong."
29. Scobey, "Keep Prayer in Mind," 43–44.

Introduction

In *Rosarium Virginis Mariae*, Pope St. John Paul II states, "Listening and mediation are nourished by silence."[30] He continues: "A discovery of the importance of silence is one of the secrets of practicing contemplation and mediation. One drawback of a society dominated by technology and the mass media is the fact that silence becomes increasingly difficult to achieve."[31] It is best to pause frequently after reading the text and the reflection so that the mind can focus on what is being read. Michael Hansen writes about journaling and meditation/contemplation. A spiritual journal helps "to discern the different spirits stirring in . . . prayer, reflections, spiritual conversations, and daily life. . . . The good running through [one's] life will shine through even in times of suffering. . . . [S]piritual journals are the keepers of consolations and truth. They are source springs for gratitude."[32] According to Hansen: "Contemplative prayer is silent love. It is the gift of union in God. It is possible for anyone—for such is the generosity of God's love."[33] One method of contemplation "is a natural movement in . . . reading that leads to contemplation. It moves from my head to my heart, from recollection to quiet, from desire to gift."[34] Another method uses a prayer word; a person "repeats the prayer word interiorly, in a slow and rhythmical manner, with the syllables equally stressed." The contemplator merely "allows the prayer word to be present."[35] According to Shapiro, ". . . [C]ontemplation reveals the unity of all things in, with, and as God."[36]

Prayer: A prayer concludes the entry and summarizes the title, which was illustrated by the text, explored in the reflection, and served as the foundation for the journal/meditation exercise.

Title: For the Spiritual but not Religious

The term *spiritual but not religious* became popular in the 1990s and early 2000s. According to Thomas Cathcart, there is "an innate, human dimension, a spiritual dimension, that is fundamental to our existence."[37] He sees the spiritual but not religious as "a more contemporary faith, . . . an affirmation of our ultimate concern and an acceptance of the power to live it out."[38] According to Cathcart, "Religion, as such,

---

30. "*Rosarium*," par. 31.
31. "*Rosarium*," par. 31.
32. Hansen, *First*, 349–50.
33. Hansen, *First*, 337.
34. Hansen, *First*, 337.
35. Hansen, *First*, 338.
36. Shapiro, "Roadside," 11.
37. Cathcart, *There is no God*, 7.
38. Cathcart, *There is no God*, 18.

has lost its power to grasp many of us where we live."[39] Thus, the *spiritual but not religious* phrase is used to identify a practice of spirituality that does not regard organized religion as a valuable means to further interior spiritual growth of the individual. Barna research states that the spiritual but not religious "shirk definition." It adds, "For them there is truth in all religions, and they refuse to believe any single religion has a monopoly on ultimate reality."[40] Amy Hollywood writes: ". . . [S]pirituality has to do with the heart, feeling, and experience. The spiritual person has an immediate and spontaneous experience of the divine or of some higher power. She [or he] does not subscribe to beliefs handed to her [or him] by existing religious traditions, nor does she [or he] engage in the ritual life of any particular institution."[41] Robin Young and Karyn Miller-Medzon argue that "the concept of spirituality . . . has to do with how we interact with others, with living more contemplatively, and with appreciating nature and the natural world."[42] Referring to Krista Tippett, Young writes that Tippett has been "noticing the emergence of a powerful secular spirituality."[43] Later, Young writes that to Tippett, "part of the key is that mind, body, and spirit are not separate; . . . the spirituality she pursues is about connecting [one's] inner and outer self, making space for discernment and authenticity. It's about 'constantly coming back, looking inward, getting re-centered, looking beyond ourselves,' she says."[44]

In the United States, "[a]bout a quarter of . . . adults (27 percent) now say they think of themselves as spiritual but not religious . . . ,"[45] writes Michael Lipka and Claire Gecewicz for the Pew Research Center. This "rapidly rising 'spiritual but not religious' segment of American adults . . . are religiously unaffiliated" (37 percent), state Lipka and Gecewicz.[46] Frederic and Mary Ann Brussat, reviewing Linda A. Mercadante's *Belief Without Borders,* state that the spiritual but not religious are "those unaffiliated with any religion."[47] They "are among the one in five Americans who don't identify with any religion according to a 2012 report from Pew Research Center's Forum on Religion and Public Life," state the Brussats.[48] Mercadante writes that those "who self-identify as 'spiritual but not religious'" represent "the influence of America's increasing religious diversity [which] is evident in the burgeoning world of alternative spiritualities."[49] Those who identify themselves as spiritual but not religious are

---

39. Cathcart, "There is no God, 128.
40. "Meet."
41. Hollywood, "Spiritual."
42. Young and Miller-Medzon, "Can Spirituality Exist?"
43. Young and Miller-Medzon, "Can Spirituality Exist?"
44. Young and Miller-Medzon, "Can Spirituality Exist?"
45. Lipka and Gecewicz, "More."
46. Lipka and Gecewicz, "More."
47. Brussat and Brussat, Review of *Belief Without Borders.*
48. Brussat and Brussat, Review of *Belief Without Borders.*
49. Mercadante, "Are the Spiritual?"

characterized differently by those collecting and interpreting the data. Mercadante, a professor of Historical Theology at the Methodist Theological School in Ohio, who has written extensively about the spiritual but not religious, presents what she calls common themes she has surfaced from her research: "a 'detraditioning' or shift in the locus of authority to the individual; a rejection of the doctrine of sin or being 'born bad'; nature as a source or mediator of spiritual feelings; a therapeutic orientation of spiritual practices; a rejection of exclusivism; ethical objections to the behavior of believers; acceptance of the idea that all religions teach the same thing; a yen for mixing and matching of beliefs and practices; an overhaul of ideas and images of God; a disavowal of an oppressively authoritarian religious tradition; an abandonment of the interventionist, personal, caring God; human beings as inherently good—even divine; the righteousness of not belonging; doing good in the world; rejection of heaven and hell; and replacing afterlife with reincarnation, karma, and expanding consciousness."[50]

While every researcher will not agree with all of those common themes, Mercadante contends that "many SBNRs [(spiritual but not religious)] are creating a particularly American spiritual mix, borrowing, adapting, and adjusting from many sources."[51] She identifies the key ingredients of the mix as being individualistic, "detraditioning," therapeutic, and the freedom to pick and choose ideas, adapting them to the American context.

Individualistic

First, this new spirituality does not give community any kind of top priority. "For the spiritual," writes Hollywood, "religion is inert, arid, and dead. . . . ."[52] Barna's research has isolated two types of irreligious spirituality; one type, those who "consider themselves 'spiritual,' . . . say their religious faith is not very important in their life;" the other type consists of "those who do not claim any faith at all."[53] Burton echoes this research, writing that some of the spiritual but not religious "maintain a connection to some sort of organized faith tradition, even if they do not practice it regularly" and "still identify with a religious tradition, even if they are less likely to attend services or say religion is important in their lives."[54] The approach to organized religion, according to Burton, has been replaced with all types of other practices; nevertheless, "spirituality, in some sense, is beneficial to [the spiritual but not religious], even if they see that spirituality as opposed to organized religion."[55] Likewise, Lipka and Gecewicz

50. Brussat and Brussat, Review of *Belief Without Borders*.
51. Mercadante, "Are the Spiritual?"
52. Hollywood, "Spiritual."
53. "Meet."
54. Burton, "Spiritual."
55. Burton, "Spiritual."

report that among the spiritual but not religious are those who "have low levels of religious observance, saying they seldom or never attend religious services" and those who "appear to be quite observant."[56] Lipka and Gecewicz report that while 37 percent of American adults are "religiously unaffiliated, . . . most actually do identify with a religious group, including 35 percent who say they are Protestant, 14 percent who are Catholic, and 11 percent who are members of other faiths, such as Judaism, Islam, Buddhism, or Hinduism."[57] Barna contends: "The broader cultural resistance to institutions is a response to the view that they are oppressive, particularly in their attempts to define reality. Seeking autonomy from this kind of religious authority seems to be the central task of the 'spiritual but not religious' and very likely the reason for their religious suspicion."[58] Spiritual curiosity characterizes those who identify themselves as spiritual but not religious. According to Caroline Kitchener, "identity captured by the term 'spirituality' . . . is seen as a larger, freer arena to explore big questions."[59]

Being individualistic does not automatically rule out having a higher power or believing in God. Kitchener reports that while the spiritual but not religious may reject organized religion, they "maintain a belief in something larger than themselves. That 'something' can range from Jesus to art, music, and poetry. There is often yoga involved."[60] Burton says that the spiritual but not religious "reported feeling a connection to 'something much larger than' themselves and 'felt particularly connected to the world around' them and to a 'higher purpose.'"[61] Young and Miller-Medzon report that Brene Brown proposes "spiritual belief of inextricable connection. How am I connected to you in a way this is bigger and more primal than our politics."[62] Some of the spiritual but not religious refer to the higher power as God. Burton reports that Ava Lee Scott, one of her interviewees "believes in a higher power—something some people might call God—but believes that such a power transcends individual traditions' dogmas. 'Whatever name you call your higher power,' she [said], 'we are all connected.'"[63] Barna reports that the spiritual but not religious "hold unorthodox views about God or diverge from traditional viewpoints." Some "believe that God represents a state of higher consciousness that a person may reach . . . . They are just as likely to be polytheistic . . . as monotheistic . . . and significantly fewer agree that God is everywhere . . . . [T]heir God is more abstract than embodied, more likely to occupy minds than the heavens and the earth."[64] Glynn Cardy presents John Shelby Spong's

---

56. Lipka and Gecewicz, "More."
57. Lipka and Gecewicz, "More."
58. "Meet."
59. Kitchener, "What."
60. Kitchener, "What."
61. Burton, "Spiritual."
62. Young and Miller-Medzon, "Can Spirituality Exist?"
63. Burton, "Spiritual."
64. "Meet."

words, which illustrate this understanding of God, quoting, "God is not a Christian, God is not a Jew, or a Muslin, or a Hindu, or a Buddhist. All of those are human systems which human beings have created to try to help us walk into the mystery of God. I honor my tradition. I walk through my tradition, but I don't think my tradition defines God, I think it only points me to God."[65] Later in his tribute to Spong, Cardy quotes him again, writing, "I think that anything that begins to give people a sense of their own worth and dignity is God."[66] Likewise, Robert Jones, in presenting what he considers to be the twelve theses of Spong, writes that Spong advocated non-personal images for the experience of God, wind, love, rock, among them. Then, he quotes Spong as stating, "I cannot say who God is, but I can tell you how I believe I experience God, realizing I may be deluded."[67] Stephen J. Patterson summarizes this higher power or God belief stating: "To believe in God is to believe in a transcendent reality running through and beyond all things, a fundamental reality in which existence itself is grounded. Faith in God is an act of trusting in this reality, and risking a life that is oriented to it."[68] Kitchener quotes Matthew Hedstrom, a professor of religion at the University of Virginia, as telling his students "that the 'spiritual-but-not-religious' designation is about 'seeking,' rather than 'dwelling:' searching for something you believe in, rather than accepting something that, while comfortable and familiar, doesn't feel quite right. In the process of traveling around, reading books, and experimenting with new rituals, he says, 'you can find your identity out there.'"[69]

Detraditioning

While we have already touched on some detraditioning that the spiritual but not religious have done, Mercadante states: "Now, the source of spiritual authority has shifted from 'out there' to 'in here.' In other words, many feel they must rely primarily on their own spiritual judgment rather than looking to an authoritative figure of tradition as many religions advocate."[70] Quoting Kenneth Pargament, Kitchener writes that the word *spiritual* has "positive connotations of having a life with meaning, a life with some sacredness to it—you have some depth to who you are as a human being." Kitchener adds, ". . . [Y]ou're not blindly accepting a faith passed down from your parents, but you're also not completely rejecting the possibility of a higher power."[71] The Brussats refer to this as "a 're-sacralization' of the world." Then, they quote Mercadante: "They want to see and experience the sacred in more areas of life. They want a

---

65. Cardy, "When," 10.
66. Cardy, "When," 23.
67. Jones, "Twelve."
68. Patterson, "Dirt," 198.
69. Kitchener, "What."
70. Mercadante, "Are the Spiritual?"
71. Kitchener, "What."

spirituality which is vital and personal."[72] In its research, Barna refers to this as "the private experience of God within."[73] What Barna discovered is "that what counts as 'God' for the spiritual but not religious is contested among them, and that's probably just the way they like it. Valuing the freedom to define their own spirituality is what characterizes this segment."[74] As already noted above, "to be religious is to be institutional . . . , but to be spiritual but not religious is to possess a deeply personal and private spirituality, . . . a spirituality divorced from religion [that] looks within."[75] The spiritual but not religious "have primarily rejected religion and prefer instead to define their own boundaries for spirituality," according to Barna's research, "often mixing beliefs and practices from a variety of religions and traditions" and displaying "an uncommon inclination to think beyond the material and to experience the transcendent."[76] This means, as Burton states, "spiritual experience can come from unlikely places."[77] She mentions "artistic practice" replacing "an approach to organized religion;" "nature and herbs" being "the magic healers of the earth [that connect] to the spiritual;" "meditation, yoga, and personal ritualistic acts [that provide a] feeling of transcendence." She quotes Megan Ribar, writing, "The practices I consider spiritual are the things I do to care for myself in a deep way, to calm myself when I'm distressed, to create meaning out of the experiences of my life."[78] Other spiritual experiences come from dog walking and photography. Hollywood notes that the spiritual but not religious prefer "feeling, enthusiasm, and experience."[79] She critiques that as "an attempt to identify an independent realm of experience that is irreducible to other forms of experience,"[80] and rightly so, because when the spiritual but not religious "speak about spirituality" they mean the "interior life." The spiritual but not religious are suspicious "of the particular form such practices [as meditation, prayer, and devotional reading] take within Christianity and other religious traditions."[81] She adds: ". . . [M]any who consider themselves spiritual understand their spirituality in terms of an attunement with nature or spirit—something that is bigger than and lies beyond the boundaries of themselves. . . . [T[here is a keen desire for this experience to be one's own."[82]

72. Brussat and Brussat, Review of *Belief Without Borders*.
73. "Meet."
74. "Meet."
75. "Meet."
76. "Meet."
77. Burton, "Spiritual."
78. Burton, "Spiritual."
79. Hollywood, "Spiritual."
80. Hollywood, "Spiritual."
81. Hollywood, "Spiritual."
82. Hollywood, "Spiritual."

INTRODUCTION

Therapeutic

Mercadante's third key ingredient of the spiritual but not religious' spiritual mix is the therapeutic. The focus is "on becoming whole and healthy," she writes, "not just physically, but emotionally and spiritually. . . . [T]his new American spirituality often promotes this as primary."[83] According to Young and Miller-Medzon: "In 2018, scientists at Yale University and Columbia University found the 'spiritual part of the brain'—an area they're calling the 'neurobiological home' of spirituality. It's an area that lights up during more traditional religious experiences of feeling in touch with God, but more broadly also when that 'transcendence' involves communion with nature or humanity, the research finds."[84] Referring to Tippett's comments, Young and Miller-Medzon discovered "those who use nature to experience the spiritual." They call this "the notion of 'awe.'" Quoting Tippett, they write: "[A]we is a life-giving, health-giving thing. . . . [H]umans can experience awe through the natural world."[85] The Brussats echo Young and Miller-Medzon, noting that the spiritual but not religious place "their emphasis on mystery and awe, finding the sacred in the ordinary, caring for the earth, and becoming more open to pluralism and the interplay between science and spirituality."[86] Burton quotes Ribar as stating, "I do not often believe that there's a divine order to things, and practices like [meditation, yoga, and personal ritualistic acts] can be a way to create beauty out of the chaos I often feel I'm surrounded by."[87] For the spiritual but not religious, both science and spirituality are means to total wholeness.

Pick and Choose

Mercadante's fourth key ingredient of the spiritual but not religious' spiritual mix deals with "the freedom to pick and choose ideas, adapting them to the American context. There seems little felt obligation to take the whole religious package of any particular tradition."[88] In this new American spirituality, writes Mercadante, the spiritual but not religious borrow, adapt, and adjust what they find attractive or compelling in the culturally and religiously diverse world increasingly around them; they feel "they must keep their options open on the journey of spiritual growth."[89] As already noted above, some believe in God, some do not. Some study the teachings of Jesus, some do not. They live "their spirituality in the absence of the institutional church," states Barna. "But they still take part in a set of spiritual practices, albeit a mish-mash

83. Mercadante, "Are the Spiritual?"
84. Young and Miller-Medzon, "Can Spirituality Exist?"
85. Young and Miller-Medzon, "Can Spirituality Exist?"
86. Brussat and Brussat, Review of *Belief Without Borders*.
87. Burton, "Spiritual."
88. Mercadante, "Are the Spiritual?"
89. Mercadante, "Are the Spiritual?"

of them. Somewhat unsurprisingly, they are very unlikely to take part in the most religious practices like scripture reading . . . , prayer . . . , and even groups or retreats . . . . Their spiritual nourishment is found in more informal practices like yoga . . . , meditation . . . , and silence and/or solitude . . . . But their most common spiritual practice is spending time in nature for reflection."[90] A common practice seems to be meditation. However, Burton discovered "that the single greatest spiritual experience for this group was not prayer or meditation but music."[91] Many have "a desire for community, one thing their more solitary ritual practices [hasn't] been able to give them," states Burton. They are "shy of organized spiritual community."[92] The Brussats state that Mercadante writes that "meaning-making" now occurs in "popularly mediated gathering places, such as the internet, social media, self-help literature, television, and film."[93] In this new spiritual milieu, where the spiritual but not religious group of Americans "are more highly educated than the general public"[94] and "are, generally, happier than nonspiritual people,"[95] we have a group who value curiosity, progressive intellectual freedom, an experimental approach to spirituality, a mystical hunger, and are impatient with organized religion and its piety in established churches. Some writers see this development related to the cultural trends of deinstitutionalization, individualization, and globalization. For the spiritual but not religious, spirituality refers to a person's relationship with God, but there is a deeper level; it also involves a person's self-identity, a feeling loved by God, for those who believe in God. As Burton points out, ". . . [R]eligious identity (i.e., religious community participants see themselves as belonging to), religious observance (i.e., actually attending services and participating in religious life), and spiritual experiences are three distinct categories, which sometimes overlap but do not automatically track onto one another."[96]

Categories

In her book, *Belief without Borders*, Mercadante divides the spiritual but not religious into five types, which may help to summarize this section of the introduction and reveal for whom this book is written. First, there are the dissenters, who stay away from organized and institutional religions. Second, there are those focused on therapeutic spirituality that centers on the individual person's wellbeing. Named the casuals, they see religious and/or spiritual practice as merely functional. Third, explorers are those who seek novel spiritual practices; they are curious, spiritual tourists. Fourth, there

---

90. "Meet."
91. Burton, "Spiritual."
92. Burton, "Spiritual."
93. Brussat and Brussat, Review of *Belief Without Borders*.
94. Lipka and Gecewicz, "More."
95. Burton, "Spiritual."
96. Burton, "Spiritual."

are the seekers, who are looking for a new religious identity, an alternative spiritual group, or a new spiritual home, maybe even recovering some earlier religious or spiritual identity. Immigrants, people who have discovered themselves in a new spiritual realm, form the fifth type of spiritual but not religious. These are the people who are trying to adjust to their newfound identity, trying on new spiritual clothes.

Title: Through the Year

There are from ten to twenty-five entries for every month of the year. Selections have been made from the 194 days honored by the United Nations. In the United States, there are sixty-four days that come with presidential proclamations, twenty weeks, and fifty-five months; selections have been made from the days. Only a few weekly celebrations have been noted because they coincide with a specific day embedded within the week; no monthly commemorations have been covered. Furthermore, there are various lists of holidays in the United States; there are lists of twenty, twenty-four, thirty, and ninety-eight. The National Day Calendar states that there are over 1,500 national days. Some days in one of the many online calendars do not cohere with the same days in other online calendars. From all the many celebrations, the author has chosen 189 entries. When it comes to presenting material from presidential proclamations, the cut-off point is December 31, 2021. Also, because they are so numerous, when a president issued a proclamation every year he was in office—four or eight—the author has quoted only from the first proclamation made. To read others, the website, https:www.presidency.ucsb.edu, makes all such documents easy to find.

Subtitle: Texts, Reflections, Journal/Meditations, and Prayers for the SBNR

The subtitle of this book states its contents. The texts that have been chosen are footnoted, so that the reader can locate them if he or she wants more information. The Bibliography at the back of the book gives the website address where the text can be found in its entirely. Likewise, quoted material in the reflections is footnoted. When someone else explains or presents something worthy of reflection, the source is documented. The Bibliography gives the website address from where the material is taken. The Journal/Meditations were created by the author, as were the Prayers. The audience for this book is anyone who identifies as a SNBR, a **S**piritual **B**ut **N**ot **R**eligious, but others will find a year's worth of spiritual material worth their time and effort. It is the author's hope that this book of entries will foster the spirituality of the spiritual but not religious and anyone else who chooses to read it for spiritual nourishment.

INTRODUCTION

A Few Notes

Bible

The Bible used in this book is the *New Revised Standard Version* (NRSV). In notating biblical texts, the first number refers to the chapter in the book, and the second number refers to the verse within the chapter. Thus, Isaiah 7:11 means that the quotation comes from Isaiah, chapter 7, verse 11. Mark 6:2 means that the quotation comes from Mark's Gospel, chapter 6, verse 2. When more than one sentence appears in a verse, the letters a, b, c, etc. indicate the sentence being referenced in the verse. Thus, 2 Kings 1:6a means that the quotation comes from the Second Book of Kings, chapter 1, verse 6, sentence 1. Also, poetry, such as the Psalms and sections of Judith, Proverbs, and Isaiah, may be noted using the letters a, b, c, etc. to indicate the lines being used. Thus, Psalm 16:4a refers to the first line of verse 4 of Psalm 16; there are two more lines of verse 4: b and c.

In the Hebrew Bible (Old Testament) the reader often sees LORD (note all capital letters). Because God's name (Yahweh or YHWH or YHVH, referred to as the Tetragrammaton) is not to be pronounced, the name Adonai (meaning *Lord*) is substituted for Yahweh when a biblical text is read. When a biblical text is translated and printed, LORD (see Genesis 2:4) is used to alert the reader to what the text actually states: Yahweh. Furthermore, when the biblical author writes Lord Yahweh, printers present Lord GOD (note all capital letters for GOD; see Genesis 15:2) to avoid the printed ambiguity of LORD LORD. When the reference is to Jesus, the word printed is Lord (note capital L and lower-case letters; see Luke 11:1). When writing about a lord (note all lower-case letters (cf. Matt 18:25) with servants, no capital L is used.

Abbreviations

To avoid as much confusion as possible, the reader will encounter no abbreviations for biblical books. The name of the book in the Bible is printed in full after its source, NRSV (New Revised Standard Version).

When a printed book has no page numbers, the footnote will display n.p. (not paginated). When a printed magazine has no date, n.d. appears in the Bibliography.

BCE means *Before the Common Era*. It is the same as BC, meaning Before Christ. Likewise, CE means *Common Era*; it is the same as AD, meaning *Anno Domini* in Latin, translated as In the Year of the Lord.

Cf. (cf.) is the abbreviation for *confer/conferatur* in Latin, meaning *compare* to other material listed. E.g. (e.g.) is the abbreviation for *exempli gratia* in Latin, meaning *for example*. Ca. (ca.) is the abbreviation for *circa* in Latin, meaning *about* a certain time or *around* a certain time. Par. (par.) is the abbreviation for *paragraph*; it is followed by a number. Some documents contain numbered paragraphs (pars.), and they are noted by a paragraph number instead of page number.

Introduction

Throughout this book, United States is abbreviated U.S., and United Nations is abbreviated U.N. Other abbreviations used are mentioned in the reflection before being used in the rest of the text that follows.

1

The Month of *January*

NEW YEAR'S DAY
January 1

Text: "The LORD said to Moses and Aaron in the land of Egypt: This month shall mark for you the beginning of months; it shall be the first month of the year for you."[1]

Reflection: The first day of January is known as New Year's Day. At midnight revelers blow horns, raise glasses of alcohol, toast each other, and wish each other a happy new year. The thirty-one-day month named January gets its name from the Roman Janus, the god of beginnings, of the past and the future, and of gates, doorways, and bridges. He displays his function in his usual depiction: He has two faces looking in opposite directions. As such, the first day of January is a day of transition; one walks through the gate, door, or over the bridge; the previous year is left behind, and a new year looms ahead. In other words, one solar cycle of time has ended, and a new solar cycle of time has begun. We are in the process of change, usually associated with the chaos of the past, but looking into the order that will, hopefully, characterize the future. With his two faces, Janus can look back at the past and forward to the future simultaneously, just like we can. Thus, this transition day is perfect for making a new year's resolution.

    A new year's resolution is a decision to begin something new in one's life or a decision to stop something old in one's life. While a resolution is usually announced on New Year's Day, there are other transitions where a resolution is appropriate. A marriage or anniversary presents the opportunity for a resolution to cooperate more. The birth of a child to parents is an occasion to make and announce a resolution to stop smoking, drinking alcohol, or driving too fast. Even the death of a loved one can be the occasion for a resolution to handle finances in a new way. Growth in spirituality takes place by viewing the beginning of anything new as an opportunity to make a

---

1. NRSV: Exodus 12:1–2.

resolution to change a small part or aspect of our lives by beginning something new or stopping something old. Every day we pass from what is old to what is new. Even the football games featured on the television this day may serve as the transition from the old activities of the previous evening to the new winning team of today's game.

Journal/Meditation: What new year's resolution are you making? What passage from old to new will you need to make?

Prayer: This day marks the beginning of a new year for me, O LORD. Grant me the grace to keep the resolution I have made, as I pass from old to new before you today, tomorrow, and forever. Amen.

Ninth Day of Christmas: Fireplace

January 2

Text: "The stockings were hung by the chimney with care, / In hopes that St. Nicholas soon would be there; / . . . He spoke not a word, but went straight to his work, / And filled all the stockings; then turned with a jerk, / And laying his finger aside of his nose, / And giving a nod, up the chimney he rose."[2]

Reflection: While Clement Clarke Moore refers to the fireplace as a chimney, the chimney is technically the hollow vertical structure made of brick or steel rising above the roof of a home that allows gas, smoke, or steam from a fire to escape into the atmosphere. For Moore, it is also the portal for St. Nicholas to enter and to leave the home! Another part of a fireplace is the hearth, the floor that extends into the room where it is located. Likewise, most fireplaces have a mantel, an ornamental frame made of stone, brick, or wood that focuses attention on the fireplace inside the house. In the not too far past, the fireplace served as the center of the house for the family. Heat for the house was generated by the fire burning in it over which cooking was done. People thought of it as the sign of their home and the life of the family members who lived in it. While it is seldom used for heat and modern kitchens have taken away its function as a place to cook food, the fireplace remains the center of a home; indeed, it is still found in the center of many living rooms, family rooms, and dens today; natural gas or propane logs have replaced many coal-burning and wood-burning fireplaces. Its modern adaptation consists of fire pits—made of metal or stone and burning wood, natural gas, or propane—found in back yards today, or virtual fireplaces displayed on computer or television screens with the sound effects of a crackling fire and drafts caused by the flames!

    At Christmastime, the fireplace inside the home is exaggerated with decorations. Evergreen garland with white or multi-colored lights may outline the mantel. Red candles may be grouped before, placed behind, or intertwined with the garland.

---

2. Moore, "A Visit."

Statues of Santa Clause may also sit on the mantel, with an empty place to leave a plate of cookies and a glass of milk for St. Nicholas on Christmas Eve. Individual families may have other special mementos that are displayed on the mantel only during Christmastime. And, of course, as Moore notes, individual stockings or socks filled by St. Nicholas—often with a person's name on each one—are hung from it in the hope of finding a treat in it on Christmas morning. At the time of Moore's writing (early nineteenth century), most children's gifts fit into a sock; today, of course, socks serve only a decorative purpose. Nevertheless, on this ninth day of Christmas, spend some time in front of the fireplace in your home.

Journal/Meditation: How is the fireplace in your home a sign of your family members who live there? What events of Christmastime take place near it? If you do not have a fireplace in your home, where is Christmas celebrated? How is that place decorated?

Prayer: You have often revealed yourself in fire, O God, so that people could be aware of your presence. May all who gather in my home recognize you in the flames of our fireplace (firepit or hearts). Amen.

Tenth Day of Christmas: Candy Canes

January 3

Text: "Even though I walk through the darkest valley, I fear no evil; for you [, LORD,] are with me; your rod and your staff—they comfort me."[3]

Reflection: Most people would not associate candy canes with the rod and staff mentioned in Psalm 23. God is presented using the image for a king in the ancient world: shepherd. The word connotes leadership and providence for his subjects. The staff was a clublike weapon used for warding off sheep predators. The staff with its familiar crook was used to discipline wandering sheep. It could encircle a sheep's neck or belly and pull it out of a gully or brambles or closer to the rest of the flock. A candy cane is in the form of a shepherd's staff. It is traditionally white with red stripes and flavored with peppermint. Today, a candy cane comes in multiple flavors, colors, and sizes. Candy canes can be eaten, used as Christmas tree ornaments, stocking stuffers, intertwined with bows, used in holiday creations, gift baskets, table place settings, and more. There are three basic theories as to the origin of this Christmastime sweet.

First, candy canes are thought to have originated in Cologne, Germany, in 1670, when a choirmaster asked the candymaker to develop a long-lasting sweet treat to keep noisy children occupied during Christmas services. The hook on the staff was designed to remind children of the shepherds who were first to visit the baby Jesus in Luke's Gospel. Because candy canes were also used on St. Nicholas Day, December 6, they were associated with the pastoral staff (crosier) and its crook carried by the

---

3. NRSV: Psalm 23:4.

bishop of Myra. Because Jesus, in John's Gospel, identified himself as the good shepherd, the red stripe came to represent his blood shed on the cross, and the white came to represent his pure or sinless life. If turned upside down, the candy cane forms the letter J, which stands for Jesus, whose birth is celebrated at Christmastime. National Candy Cane day is marked on December 26.

Reflection/Meditation: Whom do you shepherd? For each person you shepherd identify the ways you shepherd him or her. Who shepherds you? How does he or she do it?

Prayer: Good Shepherd, I know that even though I walk through the darkest valley, I fear no evil; for you are with me; your rod and your staff comfort me. Grant that I may be like you, when I shepherd those entrusted to my care. Amen.

Eleventh Day of Christmas: The Grinch
January 4

Text: "The Grinch hated Christmas! The whole Christmas season! Now, please don't ask why. No one quite knows the reason. It could be his head wasn't screwed on just right. It could be, perhaps, that his shoes were too tight. But I think that the most likely reason of all may have been that his heart was two sizes too small."[4]

Reflection: The Grinch, a children's story character created by Dr. Seuss, is a grouchy, solitary creature who attempts to bring Christmas to an end by stealing all the gifts and decorations from the homes of the town of Whoville on Christmas Eve. He is depicted as an avocado green, hairy, pot-bellied, pear-shaped, snub-nosed creature with a catlike face. He lives in seclusion in a cave on the cliff overlooking Whoville; his only companion is Max, his unloved but loyal dog. After disguising himself as Santa Clause with Max disguised as a reindeer, the Grinch rides a sleigh down the mountain to Whoville, where he stops at the homes and steals Christmas gifts, trees and decorations, and food. After getting to the top of Mount Crumpit, from where he intends to dump the sleigh full of things he has stolen, he stops, expecting to hear bitter and sorrowful cries from the Whoville citizens. Instead, he hears them singing joyous Christmas songs. He reaches the conclusion that Christmas must mean more than gifts, trees and decorations, and food. That awareness makes his heart grow three sizes bigger, and he returns all he stole to the Whoville citizens, even joining them for their Christmas feast.

The Grinch has been transformed. The goal of all spiritual practice is transformation or change in perspective. The transfigured Grinch becomes an anti-icon of Christmas commercialization and holiday season extravagance. He becomes a sign of those who despise the twelve days of Christmas because of the economy's focus on propagating a greedy attitude through pre- and post-Christmas sales and the

---

4. Geisel, *How the Grinch*, n.p.

commercialization battles they precipitate. By the eleventh day of Christmas, some people may be playing the role of the Grinch. It takes only a few moments of meditation on its meaning for the citizens of Whoville to spark the enlargement of the Grinch's heart. Maybe the Grinch's enlarged heart can spark the growth of our two-sizes-too-small heart.

Journal/Meditation: Are there any overlaps between the Grinch's attitude toward Christmas and yours? If so, what are they? If not, how has your heart expanded during this current twelve-days-of-Christmas season.

Prayer: Give me a heart large enough for Christmas with those I love, O God. Remove any greed that may exist within me. I sing your praises today, tomorrow, and forever. Amen.

Twelfth Day of Christmas: Frosty the Snowman
January 5

Text: ". . . [A] whistling wind brought an old black top hat! And that was the right fit. What [Sally and Joe] did not know was that the hat was a magic hat. With the hat, to the kids' astonishment, the snowman came to life! 'Is it alive?' asked one of the puzzled kids. 'Yes,' replied the snowman, 'very much so. I am Frosty the Snowman.'"[5]

Reflection: Magic is the art of conjuring tricks and illusions that make apparently impossible things seem to happen; magic is usually performed as entertainment. According to Basab Ghosh, the author of "The Legend of Frosty the Snowman," Billy and Sally, who were sledding on newly fallen snow on a hillside, marshal their siblings to create the largest snowman they had ever seen. After rolling three balls of snow—large, medium, and small—and stacking them on the ground in the order in which they rolled them, they, according to the "Frosty the Snowman" song, written by Walter Rollins and Steve Nelson and first recorded by Gene Autry and the Cass County Boys in 1950, gave the snowman two eyes made of pieces of coal, a nose made with a button, and they stuck a corncob pipe where his mouth should have been. They put red boots where his feet should have been, and they placed a broom in his stick arms. According to the legend, the wind sent them an old black top hat, while the song states that they found it. The magic was in the old silk hat; once they put it on the snowman's head, he came alive and began to move! The children follow him down the hill, and, with his help, they build a snow-block house; then, they go ice skating on a nearby lake. While on a shopping trip underneath the winter sun, a warm wind blows away Frosty's hat. He runs after it, while the kids wait for him. When he does not return, the kids searched for him, finding a pile of snow with a top hat on it. A policeman explains to the children that Frosty will return on a cold day when it snows.

5. Ghosh, "The Legend."

As both the legend and the song make clear, this is a fictional tale about a snowman brought to life by a magic silk hat. At the time when the song was written, a silk top hat was part of the equipment of most magicians. The tall cylindrical hat with a flat top and a narrow brim was worn as part of formal dress, but magicians used it as a hiding place for pigeons, scarves, and flowers. The legend and the song indicate that there is magic in the Christmas Season for children that seems to fade away for adults. The children declare that the snowman was alive, that he could laugh, and that he could play. Adults, of course, readily dismiss such claims. The hot sun brings both children and adults back to reality; all of us melt away. And yet we hope that those we love—children and adults—will be seen again someday. In other words, the magic of life gives way to the stark reality of death, in whose presence we hope for more life in the future.

Journal/Meditation: On this twelfth day of Christmas, what magic of living are you enjoying and celebrating? When has the reality of melting (death) touched you? What hope was given to you?

Prayer: O God, for you life is changed, not ended. Give me hope through the death and resurrection of your Son, Jesus, and give me the magic of children to play and dance before you forever. Amen.

Epiphany: Christmas Day 3

January 6

Text: "In the time of King Herod, after Jesus was born in Bethlehem of Judea, wise men from the East came to Jerusalem, asking, 'Where is the child who has been born king of the Jews? For we observed his star at its rising, and have come to pay him homage.' When King Herod heard this, he was frightened, and all Jerusalem with him; and calling together all the chief priests and scribes of the people, he inquired of them where the Messiah was to be born. They told him, 'In Bethlehem of Judea . . . .' Then Herod secretly called for the wise men and learned from them the exact time when the star had appeared. Then he sent them to Bethlehem . . . . [T]hey set out; and there ahead of them, went the star that they had seen at its rising, until it stopped over the place where the child was. When they saw that the star had stopped, they were overwhelmed with joy. On entering the house, they saw the child with Mary his mother; and they knelt down and paid him homage. Then, opening their treasure chests, they offered him gifts of gold, frankincense, and myrrh. And having been warned in a dream not to return to Herod, they left for their own country by another road."[6]

Reflection: January 6, the last day of Christmas, is called the Epiphany. The word *epiphany* means the appearance of a god or the manifestation of a god. Augustus

---

6. NRSV: Matthew 2:1–5, 8–12.

Caesar, who was the Roman Emperor when Jesus was born, was supposed to be the son of the god Apollo; before his birth there had been an omen predicting the birth of a new emperor. Once Julius Caesar was deified, his adopted son, Augustus, assumed the title of son of god. Indeed, when Julius died, a comet had appeared in the sky which was interpreted as his divine soul ascending into heaven and indicating that the new emperor was Augustus, a name meaning majestic, exalted, venerable, sanctified, consecrated, and holy. According to Arthur George, "The Christian evangelists had to compete with this when claiming that Christ, not the emperor, was the divine one, the true Lord of heaven and earth, the bringer of real peace, and the authentic savior of all."[7] The author of Matthew's Gospel presents Jesus, conceived in his mother Mary from the Holy Spirit[8] and named Emmanuel, which means "God is with us."[9] The divine portent marking his birth is a star; it calls attention to something new and important, as decreed by divine heavenly powers. Matthew knew the story about Balaam, a type of magus, in the Hebrew Bible book of Numbers. Brought to curse the Israelites, Balaam blesses them, declaring that "a star shall come out of Jacob, and a scepter shall rise out of Israel."[10] By portraying the star over Bethlehem, the city in which King David was born, Matthew presents spiritual light coming to humankind. The star marks the birth of a new spiritual leader. The magi, Zoroastrian priests from Persia, non-Israelites, follow the spiritual light to Jerusalem, where the light goes out! Once they leave the holy city, where the divine light was supposed to be shining, the star re-emerges and leads them to Bethlehem. Matthew predicted that Isaiah's words about nations coming to Jerusalem's light,[11] about a multitude of camels bringing gold and frankincense,[12] about three kings bringing gifts and falling down before the king of Judah[13] manifested Jesus as God's Son. "His scene of the magi submitting to the baby Jesus demonstrated that eastern religions were being surpassed by Christianity."[14] To the gifts that the unidentified number of magi present to the infant Jesus, Matthew adds myrrh to turn the three gifts into funeral gifts: gold coins to put on the closed eyes, frankincense to cover the smell of death, and myrrh to perfume or anoint the dead body! In other words, the author has already informed the reader how the story will end.

Furthermore, because Matthew thinks of Jesus as a new Moses, a liberator of people, the magi account becomes the occasion to present Herod as a new Pharoah

---

7. George, *Mythology*, 201.
8. Cf. NRSV: Matthew 1:20.
9. NRSV: Matthew 1:23.
10. NRSV: Numbers 24:17b.
11. Cf. NRSV: Isaiah 60:3.
12. Cf. NRSV: Isaiah 60:6b.
13. Cf. NRSV: Isaiah 60:10; Psalm 72:10-11.
14. George, *Mythology*, 219.

killing baby boys[15] and Jesus being taken to Egypt to escape slaughter, like Moses.[16] Once Herod dies, Jesus is brought out of Egypt, like Moses led his people out of Egypt, to Nazareth.[17] All of these actions are informed by God through Joseph, a great dreamer, just like his ancestor Joseph, son of Jacob, sold into slavery in Egypt, where he becomes second in command to Pharaoh. To legitimize the magi's faith, they, too, become recipients of divine intervention. Before Matthew's story about the manifestation of the Son of God was written, Mark's narrative existed. Because there are no divine or miraculous conception tales in Mark's Gospel, Jesus is manifested as Son of God at his baptism. He hears God's voice from the heaven declare, "You are my Son, the Beloved"[18] after the Spirit has descended upon him.[19] In John's Gospel, even though he was God in the beginning,[20] his first manifestation took place at a wedding in Cana of Galilee, where his glory was revealed.[21] Other manifestations of his divinity were added to the list, such as feeding multitudes of people, but the star and the magi remained and took up residence on January 6. "The story of the magi . . . was important because . . . it was a model for pagans recognizing Jesus Christ as their savior, which is what Christians wanted pagans (gentiles) to do."[22]

Journal/Meditation: What spiritual light has shined upon you during this Christmas Season? What do you think is the meaning of the presentation of funerary gifts at a baby shower? Do you think Christians are still interested in others recognizing Jesus as their savior? Explain.

Prayer: Lord God, on this day you revealed new spiritual light to the world. Shine your light of grace upon me as I journey through life. Help me to recognize the many manifestations of your glory, and grant that I may one day behold your epiphany in heaven. Amen.

NATIONAL LAW ENFORCEMENT APPRECIATION DAY
January 9

Text: "Each person who is appointed to serve in an organization for civil defense shall, before entering upon his [or her] duties, take an oath, in writing before a person authorized to administer oaths in this state [of Missouri], which oath shall be substantially as follows: 'I, _____, do solemnly swear (or affirm) that I will support

---

15. Cf. NRSV: Matthew 2:16–18; Exodus 1:15–22.
16. Cf. NRSV: Matthew 2:13–15; Exodus 2:1–10.
17. Cf. NRSV: Matthew 2:19–23.
18. NRSV: Mark 1:11.
19. Cf. NRSV: Mark 1:10.
20. Cf. NRSV: John 1:1–2.
21. Cf. NRSV: John 2:1–11.
22. George, *Mythology*, 230.

and defend the Constitution of the United States and the Constitution of the State of Missouri, against all enemies, foreign and domestic; that I will bear true faith and allegiance to the same; that I take this obligation freely, without any mental reservation or purpose of evasion; and that I will well and faithfully discharge the duties upon which I am about to enter. And I do further swear (or affirm) that I do not advocate, nor am I a member of any political party or organization that advocates the overthrow of the government of the United States or of this state by force or violence, and that during such a time as I am a member of the (name of disaster or emergency organization), I will not advocate nor become a member of any political party or organization that advocates the overthrow of the government of the United States or of this state by force or violence.'"[23]

Reflection: The above text is the oath taken by law enforcement officers when they enter into service. In the oath, they promise to defend both the United States Constitution and the Missouri Constitution against all enemies both foreign and domestic. They also swear or affirm that they are not members of any group attempting to overthrow the federal and/or the state government by using force or violence. In other words, they promise to protect people and their rights. "Whether its civil unrest, labor strikes, huge sporting events, or just helping a cat get down from a tree, law enforcement officers are a critical part of our lives, woven into the everyday fabric of living in America. They keep our neighborhoods safe and help ensure that whatever it is [we] need to do, [we] can do [it] with peace of mind."[24] National Law Enforcement Appreciation Day presents the occasion to say thank you to those who put their lives on the line every day in public service to their communities. With over 900,000 law enforcement officers throughout the U.S. the day helps bring awareness about the difficult decisions police officers have to make each day in the best interest of the law and people on the local, state, and federal levels. While most Americans will only encounter a police officer at a routine traffic stop for some reason, law enforcement officers often find themselves facing guns, knives, and runaway suspects. On National Law Enforcement Day, we show our support for the protection we receive with a card or note of thanks to the local, county, state, or federal police officers. Other ways to demonstrate support is to wear blue clothing, install a blue porch light, and abide by the laws the officers enforce.

National Law Enforcement Appreciation Day was created in 2015 following a chain of events involving Ferguson, Missouri, police officer Darren Wilson, who shot and killed twenty-eight-year-old Michael Brown, Jr., on August 9, 2014. The event ignited much unrest in Ferguson, even though Wilson was not indicted by a grand jury and the U.S. Department of Justice cleared him of civil rights violations, concluding that Wilson shot Brown in self-defense. In order to change the negative portrayal of

---

23. Missouri Revised Statutes.
24. "National Law Enforcement Appreciation Day."

Wilson—and other police officers—into a positive one, multiple organizations—Concerns of Police Survivors, FBI National Academy Associates, Fraternal Order of Police, International Association of Chiefs of Police, Officer Down Memorial Page, Law Enforcement United, National Law Enforcement Officers Memorial Fund, International Conference of Police Chaplains, National Troopers Coalition, and more—created the day to express their gratitude for police officers. On this day citizens are encouraged to thank law enforcement officers for their services and show their support for the brave men and women who risk their lives every day to protect their communities. The International Association of Chiefs of Police sponsor a "Law Enforcement Oath of Honor," which adds to the positive view of police officers: "On my honor, I will never betray my integrity, my character, or the public trust. I will always have the courage to hold myself and others accountable for our actions. I will always maintain the highest ethical standards and uphold the values of my community, and the agency I serve."[25]

Journal/Meditation: Do you possess a positive or a negative opinion of law enforcement officers? Explain how that opinion came to be. After reading the oath in the above text and the oath of honor immediately above, what word or phrase gets your attention? What does it mean to you? Does it temper your opinion about police officers?

Prayer: Almighty God, your care embraces the world. Watch over all law enforcement officers and protect them from harm when they perform their duties to the communities they serve. Give those whose streets and homes are kept safe a greater appreciation for those who watch over them. Hear my prayer for the brave men and women who have sworn to enforce the law for the common good. Amen.

World Religion Day
Third Sunday

Text: ". . . [I]nterfaith discourse, if it is to contribute meaningfully to healing the ills that afflict a desperate humanity, must now address honestly . . . the implications of the over-arching truth . . . that God is one and that, beyond all diversity of cultural expression and human interpretation, religion is likewise one."[26]

Reflection: Initiated in 1950 in the United States, World Religion Day is celebrated world-wide by those who follow Bahaism, which was founded in Iran in 1863. The Bahai faith teaches that all religions are valuable, and that humankind is spiritually one. Thus, the day's observance on the third Sunday of January is based on the Bahai principles of oneness and revelation. Spiritual principles underling the religions of the world are harmonious, according to the Bahai faith; in that regard world religions play an important role in unifying humankind. For the Bahai, religion has been evolving

---

25. "Law Enforcement Oath of Honor."
26. Buck, "World Religion Day," 937.

progressively and continuously throughout human history. In 1968, the Universal House of Justice, an elected council that oversees Bahaism, issued a letter to the leaders of religions of the world in which it declared that interfaith discourse could only heal the ills of the world and attain world peace if leaders embraced the truth that God is one and religion is one. While there is diversity of cultural expression and human interpretation, the Bahaist is focused on the unity that could exist among practitioners of religion. Thus, World Religion Day serves as a celebration of the need for and the gradual revelation of a world religion for humanity, namely the Bahai faith itself.

Since 1950, this Bahai-inspired idea has developed into a variety of observances sponsored by independently interfaith or multi-faith organized groups which took advantage of the opportunity to focus on world peace through meetings, panels, symposia, speeches, mayoral proclamations, postage stamps, and other activities. In other words, the Bahaism ideas have been tweaked by world religions: Hinduism, Buddhism, Islam, Confucianism, Christianity, Taoism, and Judaism. Yes, there are spiritual principles that underlie all world religions and create a harmony among them that can unify humankind. Yes, religion continues evolving throughout human history. No, one does not have to be a Bahaist to see the need for the coming of a world religion for humanity that both unites and brings peace.

Journal/Meditation: What harmonious spiritual principles underlie the world's religions? What role do world religions play in world peace? About which major world religion do you know the least? Investigate it online or in a book.

Prayer: O God, you will the existence of world religions and reveal yourself to people through them. With your grace at work in various and diverse faiths, bring harmony and peace into your world today, tomorrow, and forever. Amen.

Martin Luther King, Jr., Day
Third Monday

Text: "I still have a dream. It is a dream deeply rooted in the American dream. I have a dream that one day this nation will rise up and live out the true meaning of its creed. We hold these truths to be self-evident that all men are created equal. I have a dream that one day . . . the sons of former slaves and the sons of former slaveowners will be able to sit down together at the table of brotherhood, . . . that oppression will be transformed into an oasis of freedom and justice, . . . [that we can] in a nation where [we] will not be judged by the color of [our] skin but by [our] character, . . . that little black boys and black girls will be able to join hands with little white boys and white girls as sisters and brothers."[27]

---

27. King, "Dream Speech."

Reflection: On August 28, 1963, Martin Luther King, Jr., gave what has come to be known as the "I Have a Dream" speech on the steps of the Lincoln Memorial in Washington, DC, before over 250,000 civil rights supports. The speech referenced the Emancipation Proclamation delivered by Abraham Lincoln in 1863. The proclamation freed all the slaves in the United States. Luther declared that one hundred years later, African Americans were still not free. The American civil rights activist described his dreams of freedom and equality rising from a land of slavery and hatred. In the edited portion of the speech presented above, he roots his dream in the American dream that all people are equal and entitled to be respected as brothers and sisters. He specifies that the children of former slaves and the children of former slaveowners should be able to sit at the same table and eat in the same restaurants. Oppression should be transformed into freedom and justice. Skin color should not matter in a nation where its citizens should be judged by their character. He reaches a crescendo echoing the prophet Isaiah 40:4–5, saying, "I have a dream that one day every valley shall be engulfed, every hill shall be exalted and every mountain shall be made low, the rough places will be made plains and the crooked places will be made straight and the glory of the Lord shall be revealed and all flesh shall see it together."[28] Just as Isaiah called upon his readers to bring a message of comfort to the city of Jerusalem after the Babylonian captivity of the Jews, King paints a picture of the end of slavery that denied equality in all things to those whose skin was black.

It comes as no surprise that the civil rights spoken of by King in 1963 is still a dream in many parts of the world and the U.S. King's picture of an integrated and unified America remains a dream, violated by white supremacists. King's prophetic voice was silenced in 1968 by James Earl Ray on April 4 in Memphis, Tennessee. However, King's message continues to be proclaimed on the third Monday of January every year with the federal holiday signed into law in 1983 by then-president Ronald Reagan. While the holiday can fall anywhere from January 15 to 21, King's actual birthday is January 15. His memorial, erected in Washington, DC, was dedicated in 2011. The civil rights, for which King spoke, wrote, and marched, are the rights that all citizens of the United States are supposed to have, such as the right to vote and the right to receive fair treatment from the law. The exercise of such rights is not dependent upon skin color, occupation, or academic degrees. All citizens—yellow, red, brown, black, white—have the right to a prompt, fair trial by jury, the right to run for elected office, and the freedom to pursue life, liberty, and the pursuit of happiness. Because the exercise of these rights is still not often allowed by supremacists, King's words, "I have a dream today," continue to be spoken in the hope that they will be heard.

Journal/Meditation: What civil right do you, consciously or unconsciously, deny to others? What civil right do you think is most threatened by supremacists? What do you do to make King's dream a reality?

28. King, "Dream Speech."

Prayer: Almighty God, you create all men and women and endow them with equality before you. Grant that all your children—yellow, red, brown, black, and white—will set aside their prejudices and join hands to sing, "Free at last, free at last. Thank [You,] God almighty, we are free at last." Amen.

National Religious Freedom Day

January 16

Text: "Congress shall make no law respecting an establishing of religion, or prohibiting the free exercise thereof . . . ."[29]

Reflection: On January 16, 1786, the Virginia General Assembly adopted Thomas Jefferson's Virginia Statute for Religious Freedom, which became the basis for the establishment clause of the First Amendment of the United States Constitution. The establishment clause prohibits congress from establishing a nation-wide religion, and it cannot prohibit the free exercise of religion for those who choose to practice religion. National Religious Freedom Day has been officially proclaimed by presidents of the U.S. since 1993. According to Jefferson, people have a natural right to worship God according to their consciences. Law cannot force religious profession, nor can it withhold civil rights from those who profess a different religion or no religion at all. The annual celebration of this day not only acknowledges the contribution the Virginia Statute of Religious Freedom made to our understanding and enjoyment of religious freedom today, but it recognizes the freedom that citizens have to express their religious beliefs without fear of any penalty for doing so. In other words, this day acknowledges that those who practice religion have a right to do so and a right to disagree with other religious practitioners while proclaiming their own religious truth.

For example, there is the belief in some religions that marriage is a relationship between one man and one woman, but that is not a universal religious principle; in the Bible patriarchs and kings often had more than one wife, like some Mormon groups do today. Stands against marriage between two men or between two women may not be a part of one's religious teachings, but that does not imply that people in such marriages can be discriminated. By reflecting on religious freedom, beginning with the fact that all are free, we raise our awareness and appreciation of its value in order to keep it from eroding. Religious freedom is enjoyed by our nation, and it must be protected so that citizens can maintain their religious identity and freely express it without fear of discrimination for doing so. In other words, the highest form of religious freedom is for one person to say that he or she disagrees with another but will support and maintain his or her right to do so without any fear, discrimination, or harassment. To put it simply, both parties can be right and should willingly support each other's freedom to exercise his or her religion and proclaim its truths.

29. "All Amendments," Amendment 1.

Journal/Meditation: What polarized religious issues divide our country today? In what specific ways can you support religious freedom, minimally agreeing to disagree?

Prayer: Almighty God, my country was founded on the principle that no law ever be enacted that established religion or prohibited the free exercise thereof. Give the people of this nation a full understanding of religious freedom for themselves and for all others. Amen.

Inauguration Day

(every four years: 2025, 2029, 2033, etc.)
January 20 (when a Sunday, January 21)

Text: "I do solemnly swear (or affirm) that I will faithfully execute the Office of President of the United States, and will to the best of my ability, preserve, protect, and defend the Constitution of the United States."[30]

Reflection: Unless a president dies in office and his or her successor, the vice president, needs to be sworn into office immediately, the reelected or newly-elected president begins his or her four-year term by taking the oath or affirmation of office at noon on January 20 before exercising any official power. While most presidents choose to swear, the United States Constitution provides the option to affirm that he or she will preserve, protect, and defend the constitution to the best of his or her ability. If January 20 falls on a Sunday, the oath of office takes place privately with a public ceremony held the next day, January 21. The president promises to preserve the constitution, that is, to make sure it lasts. He or she also promises to protect it, that is, to keep away anything that might cause it to change, to be harmed, or to be damaged. And the president promises to defend the constitution from attack, harm, or danger. The oath of office can be administered in one of two forms: It can be presented to the president in question form (presently disused), to which he or she answers, "I do" or "I swear." Or, it can be presented orally in phrases, which are repeated by the president verbatim. The constitution does not contain the customary concluding phrase, "So help me God," but most presidents have added it to the oath, while placing their left hand on a Bible and raising their right hand, neither of which is specified by the constitution. Likewise, while the chief justice of the supreme court usually administers the oath of office, the constitution does not indicate who does so. Following the oath, the U.S. Marine Band plays "Hail to the Chief," and a twenty-one-gun salute is fired. While the presidential term began in other months in the past, since 1937 it has been set on January 20. In addition to the general public, other attendees at the inauguration include the vice president, members of congress, supreme court justices, high-ranking military officers, former presidents, and other dignitaries. It is customary, but not

---

30. "Constitution of the U.S.," Article II, Section 1, Clause 8.

required, that the outgoing president and vice president—if there are any—attend the ceremony.

Over the years, various traditions have been added to the simple oath-taking ceremony. Because the constitution does not state where the oath of office takes place publicly, since 1801 it has been held outside at the Capitol Building—east front from 1829 to 1977, or west front from 1981 to the present—in Washington, DC. Following the taking of the oath, the president traditionally gives an inaugural address in which he or she presents his or her vision for the country and sets goals for the nation. Another tradition includes a luncheon in the U.S. Capitol for the president, vice president, and guests in Statuary Hall. Over the course of the years, prayers, poetry, parades, speeches, and balls have been added to the day's festivities to solemnize further the importance of the day.

Meditation/Journal: What does the phrase "preserve, protect, and defend the Constitution of the United States" in the presidential oath of office mean to you? In what specific ways do you "preserve, protect, and defend the Constitution of the United States"?

Prayer: O God, I ask you to keep safe my president, as he (she) preserves, protects, and defends the Constitution of the United States. Grace this nation with unity, justice, and tranquility, and shower the blessings of liberty upon all her people. Amen.

National Sanctity of Human Life Day
Near January 22

Text: "The values and freedoms we cherish as Americans rest on our fundamental commitments to the sanctity of human life. The first of the 'unalienable rights' affirmed by our Declaration of Independence is the right to life itself, a right the Declaration states has been endowed by our Creator on all human beings—whether young or old, weak or strong, healthy or handicapped."[31]

Reflection: The very first National Sanctity of Human Life Day was proclaimed by President Ronal Reagan on Sunday, January 22, 1984, in commemoration of the "tragedy of stunning dimensions that stands in sad contrast to [the] belief that each life is sacred."[32] The above text is the opening paragraph of Reagan's proclamation, in which he states that children who had died in legalized abortions "will never laugh, never sing, never experience the joy of human love; nor will they strive to heal the sick, or feed the poor, or make peace among nations."[33] He refers to the Supreme Court decision of January 22, 1973, Roe v. Wade, as "the erosion of our sense of the worth and

---

31. Reagan, "Proclamation 5147."
32. Reagan, "Proclamation 5147."
33. Reagan, "Proclamation 5147."

dignity of every individual." Later, in the proclamation, he adds, "We have been given the precious gift of human life, made more precious still by our births in or pilgrimages to a land of freedom." He called upon all citizens "in homes and places of worship to give thanks for the gift of life, and to reaffirm [their] commitment to the dignity of every human being and the sanctity of each human life."[34] He issued similar proclamations for Sunday, January 20, 1985 (Proclamation 5292); Sunday, January 19, 1986 (Proclamation 5430); Sunday, January 18, 1987 (Proclamation 5599); Sunday, January 17, 1988 (Proclamation 5761); and Sunday, January 22, 1989 (Proclamation 5931). Reagan's successor, President George Bush, continued to issue National Sanctity of Human Life Day proclamations. In his first for Sunday, January 21, 1990, he noted that the "Constitution recognizes the sanctity of life by providing that no person shall be deprived of life without the due process of law."[35] He added, ". . . [W]e thank God for the millions of Americans who work every day to affirm the sanctity of life: scientists who devote their lives to researching cures for disabling and deadly diseases; doctors and nurses who care for premature babies, the elderly, and the sick; those who inspire our youth to say 'no' to drugs and 'yes' to the full richness of life; and those who work to affirm the sanctity of life in our laws and public policy. . . . One of the key issues connected with the sanctity of life, abortion, has been a divisive issue in our nation for many years."[36] Bush urges alternatives to abortion, such as adoption, because "unborn children are persons, entitled to medical care and legal protection."[37] He issued similar proclamations for Sunday, January 20, 1992 (Proclamation 6241); Sunday, January 19, 1992 (Proclamation 6397); and Sunday, January 17, 1993 (Proclamation 6521).

In George W. Bush's first National Sanctity of Human Life Day for Sunday, January 20, 2002, he stated, "that every human being is endowed by our Creator with certain 'unalienable rights.' Chief among them is the right to life itself."[38] He continued, "That value should apply to every American, including the elderly and the unprotected, the weak and the infirm, and even to the unwanted." Repeating himself, he stated, "Life is an inalienable right, understood as given to each of us by our Creator."[39] He urged citizens to "join together in pursuit of a more compassionate society, rejecting the notion that some lives are less worthy of protection than others; whether because of age or illness, social circumstance or economic condition," he asked them to seek "a society that values life—from its very beginnings to its natural end."[40] He issued similar proclamations for Sunday, January 19, 2003 (Proclamation 7639); Sunday, January 18, 2004 (Proclamation 7752); Sunday, January 16, 2005 (Proclamation 7863); Sunday

34. Reagan, "Proclamation 5147."
35. Bush, "Proclamation 6090."
36. Bush, "Proclamation 6090."
37. Bush, "Proclamation 6090."
38. Bush, G.W., "Proclamation 7520."
39. Bush, G.W., "Proclamation 7520."
40. Bush, G.W., "Proclamation 7520."

January 22, 2006 (Proclamation 7975); Sunday, January 21, 2007 (Proclamation 8101); Sunday, January 20, 2008 (Proclamation 8217); and Sunday, January 18, 2009 (Proclamation 8339). In 2018, President Donald J. Trump issued his first proclamation of National Sanctity of Human Life Day for Monday, January 22, writing, "Today, we focus our attention on the love and protection each person, born and unborn, deserves regardless of disability, gender, appearance, or ethnicity."[41] According to Trump, the day was established "to affirm the truth that all life is sacred, that every person has inherent dignity and worth, and that no class of people should ever be discarded as 'non-human.'"[42] He urged citizens to promote the health of pregnant mothers and their unborn children along with single moms, the infirm, the disabled, orphans, foster children, those addicted to opioids, the weak, and the powerless. He sought to dispel the notion that "worth depends on the extent to which we are planned for or wanted." He noted how science and medicine have given "an even greater appreciation for the humanity of the unborn." Finally, he noted that "the fight to protect life is not yet over," and how it is important to "commit to advocating each day for all who cannot speak for themselves."[43] He issued similar proclamations for Sunday, January 20, 2019 (Proclamation 9838); Wednesday, January 22, 2020 (Proclamation 9978); and Thursday, January 22, 2021 (Proclamation 10136).

Journal/Meditation: How does your perspective on abortion influence how you read the words of United States presidents quoted above? Do you agree or disagree that every person has the right to life? What are the consequences of your position? Explain.

Prayer: Mighty God, you bestow life and human dignity on all the people you have created. Give me a greater appreciation for human differences so that disability, gender, appearance, nor ethnicity gets in my way of acknowledging that all life is sacred and valuable to you now and a forever. Amen.

International Holocaust Remembrance Day
January 27

Text: "Honoring the courage and dedication shown by the soldiers who liberated the concentration camps, reaffirming that the Holocaust, which resulted in the murder of one third of the Jewish people, along with countless members of other minorities, will forever be a warning to all people of the dangers of hatred, bigotry, racism, and prejudice, [the General Assembly] resolves that the United Nations will designate 27 January as an annual International Day of Commemoration in memory of the victims of the Holocaust."[44]

41. Trump, "Proclamation 9691."
42. Trump, "Proclamation 9691."
43. Trump, "Proclamation 9691."
44. United Nations General Assembly, A/RES/60/7.

Reflection: On January 27, 1945, the Red Army liberated the Auschwitz concentration camp in Poland. On November 1, 2005, fifty years later, the General Assembly of the United Nations declared January 27 International Holocaust Remembrance Day. It commemorates the victims of the Holocaust, namely, the genocide of six million European Jews and eleven million members of other minorities by Nazi Germany, between 1941 and 1945. The resolution contains six parts. The first part establishes the annual January 27 international day of commemoration. Part two urges United Nation members to develop educational programs to teach future generations the lessons of the Holocaust in order to help prevent future acts of genocide. Any denial of the Holocaust as an historical event is rejected in part three. Part four commends member nations to continue to preserve the sites associated with Nazi death camps, concentration camps, forced labor camps, and prisons during the Holocaust. In part five, the United Nations General Assembly condemns without reserve all manifestations of religious intolerance, incitement, harassment, or violence against persons or communities based on ethnic origin or religious belief. And part six requests the Secretary-General to establish a program of outreach on the subject of the Holocaust, as well as mobilizing civil society for its remembrance and education.

The vocabulary used in the resolution is worthy of reflection. There are four dangers mentioned. The first is hatred, a feeling of intense dislike, anger, hostility, or animosity. The second is bigotry, intolerance toward people who hold different views, especially on matters of politics, religion, or ethnicity. The third is racism, prejudice or animosity against people who belong to other races or the belief that people of different races have different qualities and abilities, and that some races are inherently superior or inferior. The fourth danger is prejudice, a preformed opinion, usually an unfavorable one, based on insufficient knowledge, irrational feelings, or inaccurate stereotypes, or the holding of opinions that are formed beforehand on the basis of insufficient knowledge; an unfounded hatred, fear, or mistrust of a person or group, especially one of a particular religion, ethnicity, nationality, or social status. All four of those dangers can lead to genocide, the systematic killing of all the people from a national, ethnic, or religious group. They can also lead to denial, a statement saying that the Holocaust did not take place. In addition to the four dangers, the resolution condemns without reserve four practices. The first is religious intolerance, refusing to accept people who are religiously different or live religiously differently. The second condemned practice is incitement, the stirring of feelings or the provoking of action, especially militancy or violence. The third condemned practice is harassment, persistently annoying, attacking, or bothering somebody. And the fourth condemned practice if violence, the use of physical force to injure somebody or damage something. According to the resolution, any of those condemned practices can be based on ethnicity, the sharing of distinctive cultural traits as a group in society, or religious belief, namely, statements, principles, or doctrine that a religious group accepts as true.

Journal/Meditation: Which one of the four dangers or of the four condemnations do you need to address in yourself? in your neighborhood? in your town or city? in the nation? in the world?

Prayer: O God, you create all people in your image and likeness, and you desire that they live together without hatred, bigotry, racism, or prejudice in your presence. Make me aware of religious intolerance, incitement, harassment, or violence against people based on ethnic origin or religious belief and show me what I can do to foster peace. Amen.

2

The Month of *February*

GROUNDHOG DAY
February 2

Text: "Divination of the weather . . . became a tradition . . . . People used various mediums to make a forecast, including animals . . . . Beginning in ancient times, people attributed magical powers to animals that changed their behavior at key points of the seasonal cycle. Most important were hibernating animals, which emerge from their winter sleep in the spring . . . . The focus on the hedgehog (or badger) for divining the weather was most pronounced in Germany . . . . Germans . . . adopted the American groundhog as the oracular animal."[1]

Reflection: Before German immigrants settled in Pennsylvania, they used the hedgehog or the badger to divine the weather. Commonly called the Pennsylvania Dutch, they brought with them to the United States from Germany the custom that they adapted to fit the groundhog. If the animal sees his shadow on February 2, it means that winter will continue for six weeks and he should return to hibernation; if he does not see his shadow because of cloudiness, it means that spring is about to come, and the animal should remain out of hibernation. Before hedgehogs and badgers became the oracular animals in Europe, bears served the same purpose. The German immigrants' superstitious practice coalesced into the annual ceremony held at Punxsutawney, Pennsylvania, where Punxsutawney Phil—not named Phil until 1961—is pretended to be a supercentenarian, who has been forecasting the weather since 1887. Today, crowds as large as 40,000 people gather on Gobbler's Knob to watch members of the Punxsutawney Groundhog Club rouse Phil out of his den to determine whether more winter or spring lies ahead.

    The groundhog's den is a type of cave, which was and continues to be a mysterious place. Leaving the sunny world, one enters a cave, liminal space, crossing from

---

1. George, *Mythology*, 44.

the everyday world into the numinous world. Throughout human history, not only animals, but humans have sought caves, in which to have spiritual experiences and receive revelations of divine knowledge. In other words, transformation occurs in caves, which are considered to be wombs, in which new life is quickened. Not only were the Greeks interested in divine knowledge arising from the cave-womb, but the prophet Elijah in the Hebrew Bible (Old Testament) spent time in a cave-womb on Mount Horeb (Sinai) seeking direction from God and hearing a tiny, whispering sound;[2] once he emerged from the cave-womb, he went about completing his mission. Likewise, Jesus, who according to tradition was born from his mother's womb in a cave, after his death on the cross descended to the cave of the underworld to free those residing there for resurrection and eternal life. Even if Phil sees his shadow on February 2 and returns to his cave, the new life of spring will follow nevertheless six weeks later.

Journal/Meditation: Where is your cave-womb (like man-caves, she-sheds, basements, etc.)? What kind of transformation has occurred in you after entering and leaving a cave-womb?

Prayer: God, you give new life to those who enter liminal space, leaving behind their old world and being born again after transformation into a new way of life. Give me the knowledge I need to change over and over again and recognize your presence on both sunny and cloudy days. Amen.

INTERNATIONAL DAY OF HUMAN FRATERNITY
February 4

Text: "Reaffirming . . . the right to freedom of thought, conscience, and religion; expressing deep concern at those acts that advocate religious hatred and thereby undermine the spirit of tolerance and respect for diversity . . . which require a global response based on unity, solidarity, and renewed multilateral cooperation; recognizing the valuable contribution of people of all religions or beliefs to humanity and the contribution that dialogue among all religious groups can make towards an improved awareness and understanding of the common values shared by all humankind; underlining the importance of raising awareness about different cultures and religions or beliefs and of education in the promotion of tolerance, which involves the acceptance by the public of and its respect for religious and cultural diversity, including with regard to religious expression, and underlining further the fact that education, in particular at school, should contribute in a meaningful way to promoting tolerance and elimination of discrimination based on religion or belief; acknowledging that tolerance, pluralistic tradition, mutual respect, and the diversity of religions and beliefs promote human fraternity; taking note . . . of the meeting between Pope Francis and

---

2. Cf. NRSV: 1 Kings 19:9–18.

the Grand Iman of Al-Azhar, Ahmad al-Tayyib, on 4 February 2019 in Abu Dhabi, which resulted in the signing of the document entitled 'Human Fraternity for World Peace and Living Together,' [the General Assembly of the United Nations] decides to proclaim 4 February as the International Day of Human Fraternity, to be observed each year beginning in 2021."[3]

Reflection: One of the more recent annual celebrations added to the United Nations' calendar is the International Day of Human Fraternity, which was passed on December 21, 2020, by the General Assembly. As is indicated in the above text, taken from the resolution establishing the annual commemoration, the day was instituted by the signing of "A Document on Human Fraternity for World Peace and Living Together" by Francis and al-Tayyib on February 4, 2019. That six-page document, itself worthy of everyone's reading and reflection, echoes the purpose of the establishment of the U.N.: ". . . to achieve international cooperation in solving international problems, including by promoting and encouraging respect for human rights and for fundamental freedoms for all without distinction as to race, sex, language, or religion."[4] According to the U.N. article about the day, "At the core of all the faith systems and traditions is the recognition that we are all in this together and that we need to love and support one another to live in harmony and peace in an environmentally sustainable world."[5] The U.N. states that all need "to recognize the valuable contribution of people of all religions, or beliefs, to humanity and the contribution that dialogue among all religious groups can make towards an improved awareness and understanding of the common values shared by all humankind."[6]

The document—"A Document on Human Fraternity for World Peace and Living Together"—upon which the U.N. bases this day's observance begins with this declaration: "Faith leads a believer to see in the other a brother or sister to be supported and loved. Through faith in God, who has created the universe, creatures, and all human beings, . . . believers are called to express this human fraternity by safeguarding creation and the entire universe and supporting all persons, especially the poorest and those most in need."[7] The two signers of the document invite "all persons who have faith in God and faith in human fraternity to unite and work together so that [the document] may serve as a guide for future generations to advance a culture of mutual respect in the awareness of the great divine grace that makes all human beings brothers and sisters."[8] After a series of "in the name of," the document states, "In the name of human fraternity that embraces all human beings, unites them and renders

---

3. United Nations General Assembly, A/RES/75/200.
4. "International Day of Human Fraternity."
5. "International Day of Human Fraternity."
6. "International Day of Human Fraternity."
7. "Document on Human Fraternity."
8. "Document on Human Fraternity."

them equal," it advocates "the adoption of a culture of dialogue as the path; mutual cooperation as the code of conduct; [and] reciprocal understanding as the method and standard . . . to work strenuously to spread the culture of tolerance and of living together in peace."[9] It calls upon men and women in all ranks of government, intellectuals, artists, media professionals, etc. "to rediscover the values of peace, justice, goodness, beauty, human fraternity, and coexistence in order to confirm the importance of these values as anchors of salvation for all, and to promote them." It names "among the most important causes of the crises of the modern world . . . a desensitized human conscience, a distancing from religious values, and a prevailing individualism accompanied by materialistic philosophies that deify the human person and introduce worldly and material values in place of supreme and transcendental principles." It also states, ". . . [T]here exists both a moral deterioration that influences international action and a weakening of spiritual values and responsibility."[10] The signers call for a reawakening of religious awareness which corresponds to the contemporary understanding of spirituality today: ". . . [A]uthentic teachings of religions invite us to remain rooted in the values of peace; to defend the values of mutual understanding, human fraternity, and harmonious coexistence; to re-establish wisdom, justice, and love; and to reawaken religious awareness among young people so that future generations may be protected from the realm of materialistic thinking and from dangerous policies of unbridled greed and indifference that are based on the law of force and not on the force of law."[11] As has already been stated above and repeated many times in the document, dialogue is the means "to reconciliation and fraternity among all believers, indeed among believers and non-believers, and among all people of good will." Specifically, ". . . Dialogue, understanding, and the widespread promotion of a culture of tolerance, acceptance of others, and of living together peacefully would contribute significantly to reducing many economic, social, political, and environmental problems that weigh so heavily on a large part of humanity; dialogue among believers means coming together in the vast space of spiritual, human, and shared social values and, from here, transmitting the highest moral virtues that religions aim for."[12] The document ends with the expression of the hope of finding a universal peace that all can enjoy in this life.

Journal/Meditation: How important is dialogue in solving a problem in your family? What spiritual values are necessary for dialogue to take place? Where do you find mutual respect in our culture? Where do you find human fraternity in our culture?

Prayer: God, creator of the universe, all creatures, and all human beings, you invite to human fraternity all people so that a culture of mutual respect in the awareness of

9. "Document on Human Fraternity."
10. "Document on Human Fraternity."
11. "Document on Human Fraternity."
12. "Document on Human Fraternity."

your grace may lead to the declaration that all people are brothers and sisters. Grant that through dialogue, I may arrive at deepened spiritual, human, and shared values and live together peacefully with others in all our diversity. Amen.

Super Bowl Sunday

First Sunday

Text: ". . . [T]he label Super Bowl became popular. It was born unintentionally as an offhand remark by Lamar Hunt, owner of the Kansas City Chiefs, and it grew and grew—until it reached the point that there was Super Week, Super Sunday, Super Teams, Super Players, ad infinitum."[13]

Reflection: Usually held on the first Sunday of February, although it was moved to the second Sunday in 2022, the Super Bowl is the National Football League's annual championship game between the winners of the American Football Conference and the National Football Conference. Each conference consists of sixteen teams grouped into four divisions. Thus, the American Football Conference contains the Buffalo Bills, Miami Dolphins, New England Patriots, and New York Jets in the East Division; the Baltimore Ravens, Cincinnati Bengals, Cleveland Browns, and Pittsburgh Steelers in the North Division; the Houston Texans, Indianapolis Colts, Jacksonville Jaguars, and Tennessee Titans in the South Division; and the Denver Broncos, Kansas City Chiefs, Oakland Raiders, and Los Angeles Chargers in the West Division. The National Football Conference contains the Dallas Cowboys, New York Giants, Philadelphia Eagles, and Washington Commanders in the East Division; the Chicago Bears, Detroit Lions, Green Bay Packers, and Minnesota Vikings in the North Division; the Atlanta Falcons, Carolina Panthers, New Orleans Saints, and Tampa Bay Buccaneers in the South Division; and the Arizona Cardinals, Los Angeles Rams, San Francisco 49ers, and Seattle Seahawks in the West Division. Thus, the National Football League is composed of thirty-two teams. Because Super Bowl is a registered trademarked by the National Football League, the NFL prohibits any other business from using the name for profit-making ventures, which violates federal law; it also prohibits showings in churches or at other events that promote any kind of message. The NFL asks others to refer to it with the euphemism of Big Game. Thus, the first Big Game was held in 1967.

The Big Game has become an unofficial national holiday which involves families and groups of people gathering together to watch the game on television. It may accomplish in a better way what all holidays are designed to do: foster community. People gather together in front of a large-screen TV to watch the winning team of the American Football Conference and the winning team of the National Football Conference play football; in that gathering, there will most likely be fans of both teams who hope to cheer to victory their chosen team. This is one of the most-watched

13. "What to Name."

sporting events in the world. While they are eating and watching the game, many people look forward to seeing the commercials, which often only appear during the Big Game, and the half-time entertainment. Popular singers and musicians present a half-time concert. Community is also fostered through food and drink, representing the second largest food consumption event second only to Thanksgiving. On Big Game Day, diverse groups of people create communities around the nation to see who will win the Vince Lombardi Trophy.

Journal/Meditation: What community aspect is present in your Big Game Day celebration? What effect did that have on you?

Prayer: O God, guide and protector of all your people, keep all football players safe today, and keep all their fans in peace. Through our observance of this Big Game Day, draw me and my family and friends deeper into your love. Amen.

Abraham Lincoln's Birthday
February 12

Text: ". . . We cannot dedicate—we cannot consecrate—we cannot hallow—this ground. The brave men, living and dead, who struggled here, have consecrated it, far above our poor power to add or detract. . . . It is for us the living, rather, to be dedicated here to the unfinished work which they who fought here have thus far so nobly advanced. It is rather for us to be here dedicated to the great task remaining before us—that from these honored dead we take increased devotion to that cause for which they gave the last full measure of devotion—that we here highly resolve that these dead shall not have died in vain—that this nation, under God, shall have a new birth of freedom—and the government of the people, by the people, for the people, shall not perish from the earth."[14]

Reflection: Without looking at the footnote, which identifies the source of the above text, most people would not recognize that it comes from the Gettysburg Address by Abraham Lincoln, November 19, 1863. "Four score and seven years ago . . . ," its memorable beginning, would have given away its source readily. However, the words above provide several avenues for thoughtful reflection. The first is found in the three *cannot* sentences. According to Lincoln, it was not those gathered there who could dedicate, consecrate, or hallow the battle ground; it was the brave men who fought and died there who dedicated, consecrated, and hallowed the place. The Civil War battle fought at Gettysburg, Pennsylvania, and the Union victory that occurred there was a turning point to bringing the war to an end because it stopped General Robert E. Lee's second and most ambitious invasion of the North. It was the bloodiest battle

---

14. Lincoln, "Gettysburg Address."

of the Civil War. Thus, a portion of the battle field became a cemetery; the bodies of those buried there continue to dedicate, consecrate, and hallow the ground.

The second avenue of reflection is found in Lincoln's words about the task left for the living, namely, to finish the work of those who fought in the battle. That task was the new birth of freedom for the nation. Freedom is a state in which people are able to act and to live as they choose, without being subject to any undue restraints and restrictions. In particular, Lincoln was referring to the freedom that he had decreed for the slaves. Thus, the task ahead for the living was a new birth of freedom for all people living in the United States. Freedom for all could only be accomplished by maintaining a government of the people, by the people, and for the people. *Of, by,* and *for* represent the democratic ideal. A democracy fosters the free and equal right of every person to participate in a system of government, practiced by electing representatives of the people by the people and for the people. The work of democracy never ends; it is passed on from one generation to another. Lincoln's prayer was that it not perish from the earth.

Journal/Meditation: How do you participate in democracy? What freedom have you brought to birth? What is your prayer for the United States?

Prayer: All people are created equal in your sight, O God. Guide our democracy always to be in the process of new birth. Preserve our government of the people, by the people, and for the people. And grant that it shall not perish from the earth. Amen.

World Radio Day
February 13

Text: The General Assembly of the United Nations "[s]tresses that the central objective of the news services implemented by the Department of Public Information is the timely delivery of accurate, objective, and balanced news and information emanating from the United Nations system in all four mass media, namely, print, radio, television, and the internet, to the media and other audiences worldwide, with the overall emphasis on multilingualism, and reiterates its request to the Department to ensure that all news-breaking stories and news alerts are accurate, impartial, and free of bias; . . . emphasizes the importance of the Department of Public Information continuing to draw the attention of world media to stories that do not obtain prominent coverage . . . through video and audio coverage by United Nations Television and United Nations Radio; welcomes the sustained efforts of United Nations Radio, which remains one of the most effective and far-reaching traditional media available to the Department of Public Information and an important instrument in United Nations activities . . . ; [and] endorses the resolution adopted by the General Conference of the United

Nations Education, Scientific, and Cultural Organization . . . proclaiming 13 February, the day United Nations Radio was established in 1946, as World Radio Day . . . ."[15]

Reflection: On November 3, 2011, the General Conference of the United Nations Education, Scientific, and Cultural Organization (UNESCO) proclaimed February 13 each year to be World Radio Day. February 13 was chosen in recognition of the day the United Nations created United Nations Radio in 1946. In a letter dated January 26, 2012, from the Director-General of UNESCO to the U.N. Secretary General, ". . . the objectives of the day are to raise awareness in the general public and media of the value of the radio, improve international cooperation between radio broadcasters, and encourage decision makers to create and provide access to information through radio, including community radio, thus contributing to sustainable development."[16] In the original resolution adopted by UNESCO, the General Conference stated: "Mindful that the celebration of a world radio day will raise greater awareness among the public and the media of the importance of radio, and enhance networking and international cooperation among broadcasters, convinced that this event will encourage decision makers and those who work on radio broadcasting in all its forms to establish and provide access to information through radio, including community radio, and to diversify the content in order that all may enjoy the benefit; proclaims World Radio Day, to be celebrated on 13 February, the day the United Nations established United Nations Radio in 1946."[17] The General Assembly of the United Nations adopted UNESCO's resolution on December 18, 2012, in its own fifteen-page resolution, from which comes the text above.

In its resolution, the General Assembly of the U.N. urged all countries and organizations of the U.N. to reaffirm their commitment "to the principles of freedom of the press and freedom of information, as well as to those of the independence, pluralism, and diversity of the media."[18] It also asked them to aim at "[t]he creation of conditions that will enable developing counties and their media, public, private, or other, to have, by using their national and regional resources, the communications technology suited to their national needs, as well as the necessary program materials, especial for radio and television broadcasting."[19] With those and many more words, the U.N. endorsed the fact that "[r]adio is a powerful medium for celebrating humanity in all its diversity and constitutes a platform for democratic discourse."[20] According to "World Radio Day," "At the global level, radio remains the most widely consumed medium. [It] means radio can shape a society's experience of diversity, stand as an arena

---

15. United Nations General Assembly, A/RES/67/124 A-B, Sections 50, 52–4.
16. United Nations General Assembly, A/67/62.
17. United Nations General Assembly, A/67/62.
18. United Nations General Assembly, A/RES/67/124 A.
19. United Nations General Assembly, A/RES/67/124 A.
20. "World Radio Day."

for all voices to speak . . . , be represented, and heard. Radio stations . . . [offer] a wide variety of programs, viewpoints, and content, and reflect the diversity of audiences in their organizations and operations."[21] Because radio is a low-cost medium, it can reach remote communities, providing a means for people to enter the public debate no matter what their educational level. In addition, it provides emergency communication and disaster relief, bringing people together and fostering dialogue that leads to change. Since 2014, various themes have been employed to highlight the importance of the day, such as gender equality and women's empowerment; youth and radio; radio in times of emergency and disaster; radio and sports; radio and diversity; dialogue, tolerance, and peace; and evolution, innovation, and connect.

Journal/Meditation: How valuable is radio to you? What percent of information do you obtain through radio? How do you think radio celebrates humanity in all its diversity and constitutes a platform for democratic discourse?

Prayer: God, you bestowed upon people the ability to communicate with one another through speech and hearing. Grant to all radio broadcasters a variety of messages, viewpoints, and content that reflect the diversity of all you have created. Grant to all listeners the willingness to enter into positive dialogue for change. Amen.

Valentine's Day
February 14

Text: "And in a clearing on a hill of flowers / Was set this noble goddess, Nature; / Of branches were her halls and her bowers / Wrought according to her art and measure; / Nor was there any fowl she does engender / That was not seen there in her presence, / To hear her judgement, and give audience. / For this was on Saint Valentine's day, / When every fowl comes there his mate to take, / Of every species that men know, I say, / And then so huge a crowd did they make, / That earth and sea, and tree, and every lake / Was so full, that there was scarcely space / For me to stand, so full was all the place."[22]

Reflection: While February 14 marks the death day of two saints named Valentine (meaning strong, powerful, potent, or vigorous), both the bishop and priest, who were martyred in the third century CE, have been long forgotten. As is noted above in the selection from Geoffrey Chaucer's "Parliament of Fowls," the poet represents the first recorded association of Valentine's Day with romance, love, and marriage. In his dream, Chaucer presents a paradisal vision of nature in a clearing on a hill filled with blooming flowers and trees in which huge flocks of birds of every kind have gathered on Valentine's day to choose a mate. It is from Chaucer's words that we derive the

---

21. "World Radio Day."
22. Chaucer, "Parliament."

phrase *love birds*, referring to lovers, who display public affection. Chaucer's poem, written in 1382, was quickly followed in 1400 by France's Charles VI's *Charter of the Court of Love*, which describes the festivities that took place at the royal court: a feast, amorous song, poetry competitions, jousting, and dancing; at these celebrations of romance, ladies would often hear and solve lovers' disputes. By 1847 in the United States, mass-produced Valentines picked up where seventeenth-century hand-written letters and cards decorated with hearts and arrow-launching cupids, which had become traditional, left off. Embossed paper lace Valentines were sold in book and stationary stores, followed by greeting cards. In 1868, Cadbury, a British chocolate company, created heart-shaped boxes filled with chocolates, and, of course, those were quickly associated with the sign of the holiday: a red heart, pierced by Cupid's arrow. By the twentieth century, mass-printed Valentine's Day cards were available for adults and children to satisfy the fad which had become securely established in the United States. Quickly, confectioners, jewelers, and florists added their products to the holiday.

There are two points to consider when celebrating Valentine's Day. The first is displayed in Chaucer's poem. Romance occurs in the spring, when life is quickening upon the earth. Romance, love, and marriage lead to offspring, just like spring flowers, budding trees, and other signs of life stir everywhere. Second, those who observe the day bring a playfulness to it that is grounded in the universal emotion of love, signified by the red—the color of passion and life energy—heart. The unattached seek passionate attachment to another in the hope of sharing life. Those already in a relationship celebrate their bond with each other and the life that has sprung forth from it. Romance, love, and marriage are in the air for humankind and, according to Chaucer, for the love birds, too.

Journal/Meditation: To whom do you express love? How do you express the universal emotion of love? Which of your relationships are about sharing the abundance of life?

Prayer: God of love, you exist as a trinity of persons bound together in creative love. Fill all my relationships with your divine love that they may overflow with life today, tomorrow, and forever. Amen.

President's Day (Washington's Birthday)
Third Monday

Text: "No people can be found to acknowledge and adore the invisible hand, which conducts the affairs of men [and women,] more than the people of the United States. Every step, by which they have advanced to the character of an independent nation, seems to have been distinguished by some token of providential agency. And in the important revolution just accomplished in the system of the united government, the tranquil deliberations, and voluntary consent of so many distinct communities, from which the event has resulted, cannot be compared with the means by which most governments have been established, without some return of pious gratitude along with a humble anticipation of the future blessings which the past seems to presage."[23]

Reflection: George Washington was born on February 22, 1732, on his father's tobacco plantation in the Colony known as Virginia. After he grew up, he worked as a surveyor on the Virginia frontier before joining the Virginia militia and attaining the rank of major. He was selected by the Continental Congress to serve as commander in chief of the Continental Army in 1775, when the American War for Independence began between the colonies and Great Britain. After winning the war of independence, Washington oversaw the writing of the United States Constitution, and, after its ratification, he became the first president of the United States, serving two four-year terms: 1789–93, 1793–97. In his first inaugural address, a portion of which is provided above, on April 30, 1789, he acknowledges the invisible hand (God) which, by providence, has guided the people of the U.S. to becoming an independent nation. He also sees the hand of God at work in the revolution that made it possible for leaders to engage in tranquil deliberations and the voluntary consent of many distinct communities that made it possible for democracy to be established. In comparison to other nations and their way of establishing a government, people have to show gratitude, according to Washington, while anticipating future blessings, which the past blessings seem to presage. Such was the attitude of the first president of the United States, often called the father of the country.

In 1879, congress declared February 22 a federal holiday for government offices in Washington, DC. That was expanded in 1885 to include all federal offices. Washington's Birthday was the first federal holiday to honor an American president. On January 1, 1971, the holiday shifted to the third Monday in February, which created the irony that Washington's birthday always falls between February 15 and 21, but never on his real birthday! More irony followed in 1976, when the congress posthumously promoted Washington to the rank of a six-star general, ensuring that he would outrank all members of the military forever! And, while the day is often called President's Day, the location of the apostrophe determines what is being celebrated. President's Day is another name for Washington's Birthday; Richard Nixon is the president who proclaimed February 21, 1971, President's Day. Presidents' Day can refer to Washington's birthday and Lincoln's birthday marked in the same month, and it can also honor the office of the presidency; when the bill placing the holiday on the third Monday of the month was signed into law on June 28, 1968, it was called Washington's Birthday, not President's or Presidents' Day. Nevertheless, by the mid-1980s, advertisers were referring to it as Presidents' Day, and that name caught on. Washington's image is one of four U.S. presidents carved into Mount Rushmore National Memorial in South Dakota; it is also found on the one-dollar bill and the quarter-dollar coin. Of course, his name lives on the capital of the United States in Washington, DC, Washington State,

---

23. Washington, "First Inaugural Address."

and the traditional eating of cherry pie, based on the legend of the young Washington chopping down a cherry tree, on his birthday.

Journal/Meditation: Where do you see the hand of God guiding the United States today? What blessings has God bestowed on the U.S.? Make a list.

Prayer: Your hand, O God, has guided the experiment of the United States entrusted into the hands of the American people. With gratitude I thank you for the blessings of independence, revolution, and freedom, which you have bestowed on my country. In humble anticipation I await your future blessings forever and ever. Amen.

NATIONAL RANDOM ACTS OF KINDNESS DAY
February 17

Text: "The mission of The Random Acts of Kindness Foundation is to make kindness the norm in our schools, workplaces, homes, and communities. We work toward that goal by creating free content that promotes kindness toward others and teaches important social emotional learning skills to kids."[24]

Reflection: Every year in the United States, National Random Acts of Kindness Day is celebrated on February 17 by individuals, groups, and organizations to encourage random acts of kindness. However, the primary sponsor of the day is The Random Acts of Kindness Foundation (RAKF), which came into existence in 1995 in the Bay Area of San Francisco, California. According to the RAKF webpage, "It was during a summer of violence when a reporter noted that people should stop reporting on 'random acts of violence' and start practicing random acts of kindness and senseless acts of beauty."[25] After the RAFK was born, it was purchased by a private foundation and moved to Denver, Colorado. RAFK is "a small nonprofit that invests time, expertise, and resources into its mission: Make Kindness the Norm."[26] It operates from two basic principles: people connect through kindness, and kindness can be taught. RAFK does not grant money nor does it accept donations; it is privately endowed. What it does is provide digital services and resources in three focus areas—school, workplace, and home—for anyone who wants to use them at https://randomactsofkindness.org and provide volunteer (non-facilitated) opportunities for individuals to create kindness in their communities. The foundation follows a simple framework for everything it does: Inspire to Empower to Act to Reflect to Share. The "evidence-based" classroom "curriculum gives students the social and emotional skills needed to live more successful lives." The "workplace kindness calendar shows companies how easy it is to

---

24. "Random Acts of Kindness."
25. "Random Acts of Kindness," Frequently Asked Questions.
26. "Random Acts of Kindness," Frequently Asked Questions.

change workplace culture through simple kind gestures."[27] Resources for kindness at home "provide activities, challenges, and resources for households to engage in kindness together."[28] RAKF creates "a common language between schools, work, and home with all of [its] resources."[29]

Random Acts of Kindness Day, founded by Josh de Jong, began in 2004 in New Zealand, where it is marked on September 1. From New Zealand, observance of the day spread to other countries around the world. In the U.S., RAKF sponsors kindness activities along with other resources for the day in order to make kindness the norm, not only on February 17, but on every day of the year. Ideas abound for how to observe the day. For example, one can pay for the coffee or meal of the person in line in front of him or her; one can write a kind note for someone, share words of encouragement, or put skills to work for someone in need. A random act of kindness consists of dropping off food at the local food pantry, calling or sending a card to someone not spoken to in a while, sending flowers to a hospital, assisted living center, or nursing home for anyone the person at the front desk thinks needs them. Send "Thank-You" notes to the local fire department, police department, or senior citizen center. Take muffins to work, let a car into the traffic in front of you, wash a friend's car, pay the bus fare for another passenger, plant a tree, run an errand for a neighbor, leave quarters at the laundromat—almost anything done for anyone is a random act of kindness. "The positive effects of kindness are experienced in the brain of everyone who witnesses the act, improving [his or her] mood and making [him or her] significantly more likely to 'pay it forward.' This means one good deed in a crowded area can create a domino effect and improve the day of dozens of people."[30]

Journal/Meditation: What actions would you have to take to make kindness the norm in your life? When have you connected to another person through kindness? Who taught kindness to you? To whom have you taught kindness?

Prayer: LORD God, kindness flows from you to your people like an overflowing river. Through the kind grace you bestow upon me, enable me to share randomly your kindness with others. Grant that your kindness may go before me and follow after me all the days of my life that I may live in your house my whole life long. Amen.

Chinese New Year

Between January 21 and February 20

Text: ". . . [T]he beginning of Chinese New Year started with the fight against a mythical beast called Nian, who had the body of a bull and the head of a lion. It was said

27. "Random Acts of Kindness," About Us.
28. "Random Acts of Kindness," Frequently Asked Questions.
29. "Random Acts of Kindness," About Us.
30. "Random Acts of Kindness," Frequently Asked Questions.

to be a ferocious animal that lived in the mountains and hunted for a living. Towards the end of Winter when there was nothing to eat, Nian would come on the first day of the New Year to the villages to eat livestock, crops, and even villagers, especially children. To protect themselves, the villagers would put food in front of their doors at the beginning of every year. It was believed that after the Nian ate the food they prepared, it wouldn't attack any more people. . . . [O]ver time they learned that the ferocious Nian was afraid of three things: the color red, fire, and noise. So when the New Year was about to come, the villagers would hang red lanterns and red spring scrolls on windows and doors. They also used firecrackers to frighten away the Nian. From then on, Nian never came to the village again. [E]veryone had a big celebration and the ritual involved in banishing him was repeated the following year, and so the ritual was passed down from generation to generation and the custom of celebrating the New Year with firecrackers, noise, and the color red has persisted to this day."[31]

Reflection: The legend of Nian explains the three major traditions of the Chinese New Year. The first is the lighting of firecrackers, strung on a long-fused string. Each firecracker is made with gunpowder rolled in a red paper. The loud popping noise caused by the hundreds of firecrackers strung together scares away evil spirits. Before the invention of firecrackers, bamboo stems were filled with gunpowder and lit to create small explosions that were used to drive away evil spirits, like Nian. The second is noise, which is the result of the popping firecrackers. And the third is the color red, which brought fear to Nian. Not only are the firecrackers made from red paper, but red lanterns are hung, red spring scrolls are placed on windows and doors, red clothes are worn, and red envelopes, usually containing money, are given by older people to younger people. Other practices include giving the home a thorough cleaning, which sweeps away the bad luck of the preceding year and prepares the home to receive good luck in the new year; the reunion dinner, consisting of special meats (pork, chicken, fish, duck), noodles (signifying longevity), fruits (oranges, tangerines, pomelos, signifying fullness and wealth) dumplings and spring rolls (signifying wealth), and sweet rice balls (signifying family togetherness), is served to all the members of the family in either the senior members home or close by it. In the United States, a parade may be held in larger cities along with cultural festivals and music concerts.

Because Chinese New Year, also called Spring Festival and Lunar New Year, begins on the new moon that appears between January 21 and February 20, the festival can begin on any day of the week within a range of thirty-one days, usually, but not always, around February 4 or 5. Each year features a presiding animal from the twelve-year cycle of the Chinese zodiac. Thus, the years of the tiger are 2022, 2034, 2046, etc. The years of the rabbit are 2023, 2035, 2047, etc. The years of the dragon are 2024, 2036, 2048, etc. The years of the snake are 2025, 2037, 2049, etc. The years of the horse are 2026, 2038, 2050, etc. The years of the goat are 2027, 2039, 2051, etc.

31. "Chinese New Year."

The years of the monkey are 2028, 2040, 2052, etc. The years of the rooster are 2029, 2041, 2053, etc. The years of the dog are 2030, 2041, 2054, etc. The years of the pig are 2031, 2043, 2055, etc. The years of the rat are 2032, 2044, 2056, etc. The years of the ox are 2033, 2045, 2057, etc. No matter what the designated zodiac animal for the year is, those celebrating Chinese New Year wish each other prosperity, happiness, success, health, and longevity—all the while hoping that Nian never returns.

Journal/Meditation: When do you give your house a thorough (spring) cleaning? Is such a cleaning associated with a specific holiday or dinner? To whom do you wish prosperity, happiness, success, health, and longevity?

Prayer: Eternal God, the cycle of seasons and years is the way all people mark the passage of time, which for you is without beginning or end. During my short journey on earth, grant the members of my family and me prosperity, happiness, success, health, and longevity today, tomorrow, and forever. Amen.

World Day for Social Justice
February 20

Text: "Recalling the commitment to promote national and global economic systems based on the principles of justice, equity, democracy, participation, transparency, accountability, and inclusion; reaffirming the commitment . . . to full and productive employment and decent work for all, including for women and young people . . . ; recogniz[ing] that social development and social justice are indispensable for the achievement and maintenance of peace and security within and among nations and that, in turn, social development and social justice cannot be attained in the absence of peace and security or in the absence of respect for all human rights and fundamental freedoms; further recogniz[ing] that globalization and interdependence are opening new opportunities through trade, investment and capital flows, and advances in technology, including information technology, for the growth of the world economy and the development and improvement of living standards around the world, while at the same time there remain serious challenges, including serious financial crises, insecurity, poverty, exclusion, and inequality within and among societies and considerable obstacles to further integration and full participation in the global economy for developing countries as well as some countries with economies in transition; recogniz[ing] the need to consolidate further the efforts of the international community in poverty eradication and in promoting full employment and decent work, gender equality, and access to social wellbeing and justice for all; [the General Assembly of the United Nations] decides to declare . . . 20 February [to] be celebrated annually as the World Day of Social Justice."[32]

32. United Nations General Assembly, A/RES/62/10.

Reflection: On November 26, 2007, the United Nations General Assembly passed the resolution establishing February 20 as World Day of Social Justice, from which the above text is taken. The resolution recalls the U.N.'s commitment to economic systems that are grounded in the principles of justice (fairness in the way people are treated), equity (a general condition of impartiality), democracy (free representation of people), participation (having a role to play in the system), transparency (clearly recognizable for what it is), accountability (responsible to people), and inclusion (all are included). Not only are the principles lofty goals to be attained, but they are often ignored by those who have the power to control the economic system to their greater benefit. Human society, its organization, and the way people interact combined with the distribution of wealth, opportunities, and privileges, according to the U.N., are the means to achieve and maintain peace and security both within a country and among nations. Without peace and security, without respect for basic human rights and fundamental freedoms, social development and social justice cannot be achieved.

In a globalized and interdependent world, new opportunities present themselves for growth of the world economy. Trade, investment and capital flows, and advances in all forms of technology have the potential to further justice, equity, democracy, participation, transparency, accountability, and inclusion. These, in turn, develop and improve living standards around the world. However, according to the U.N., many serious challenges to the participation of all people in the world economy remain: financial crises, insecurity, poverty, exclusion, and inequality. In other words, the lofty goals represented by the principles have not been achieved everywhere. Thus, the U.N. calls upon all nations to eradicate poverty by promoting full employment, decent work, gender equality, access to social wellbeing, and justice for all. The World Day of Social Justice raises awareness of the need to promote social justice both within countries and within a global economic system to improve fair outcomes for all people.

Journal/Meditation: Which principle—justice, equity, democracy, participation, transparency, accountability, inclusion—do you think is hardest to maintain in a global economy? How would you describe the spirituality that underlies the principles of justice, equity, democracy, participation, transparency, accountability, and inclusion? Where do you find social justice lacking in the area in which you live?

Prayer: Upon all people you bestow equal human rights, O LORD, and you call upon people to treat each other with social justice. Give me the grace to recognize poverty, exclusion, gender inequality, unemployment, human rights, and social protection, and grant me the wisdom to work to change them today, tomorrow, and forever. Amen.

National Love Your Pet Day

February 20

Text: "The young man [Tobias] went out and the angel [Raphael in disguise as Azariah] went with him; and the dog came out with him and went along with them. So they both journey along, and when the first night overtook them, they camped by the Tigris River."[33]

Reflection: In the apocryphal biblical book of Tobit, the narrator tells the reader about a young man named Tobias, who is sent by his father, Tobit, from Nineveh to Media to retrieve some money. Azariah, whom Tobias has met in the marketplace, knows the way to Media and has agreed to guide Tobias there. Accompanying the two companions is the family dog. The reader finds out nothing more about the pet dog until near the end of the story, when the narrator again states, "And the dog went along behind them."[34] Dogs, domesticated wolves, have lived with people for thousands of years, receiving food and shelter in exchange for companionship. As early as the 1600s, European royalty began to keep and breed many types of dogs. Cats, too, were kept as pets, along with birds, fish, and reptiles. The first Love Your Pet Day is attributed to Johann Heinrich Zimmerman; over 5,000 people attended the first World Animal Day in Berlin, Germany, enacted by Zimmermann, a canine aficionado and a cynologist. Cynology, a word used infrequently, is the study of matters related to canines or domestic dogs. The word indicates a serious zoological approach to the study of dogs, writers on canine subjects, dog breeders, dog trainers, and dog enthusiasts. Zimmerman was a cynologist (the Greek word for dog is *kyon*, and the Greek word for study is *logia*; therefore, cynology; one who studies dogs is a cynologist). Zimmerman is also known for having sailed as a seaman on the HMS Discovery's third voyage with James Cook to the Pacific (March 12, 1776–1780) and, after keeping a journal, wrote an account of the voyage and had it published.

On National Love Your Pet Day, we remember the unconditional love that pets give us, often making a house feel more like a welcoming and inviting home. The antics of pets often cause us to smile and bring joy to us in our homes. Taking time to show our love and appreciation to our dog, cat, guinea pig, bird, fish, reptile, etc. in a way appropriate to the animal, demonstrates our human ability to love our pets. Whether we are conscious of it or not, we have a special relationship with our pet. Science has demonstrated that pets help relieve stress and lower blood pressure. So, on National Love Your Pet Day, we can reciprocate with a walk, a hike, play time, a trip to the dog park, pictures, snuggling, cuddling—whatever is appropriate to our pet and what our pet likes to do. Giving a special treat, a new toy, or undivided attention will show our affection. Washing bedding or purchasing a new bed, grooming, training

---

33. NRSV: Tobit 6:1b–2.
34. NRSV: Tobit 11:4.

and practicing commands, being sure vaccines are up to date, and maybe adopting a pet from a shelter or volunteering to serve as a foster pet parent are ways to mark this day. For anyone who does not have a pet, volunteering at the local shelter and/or making a donation and volunteering to watch a friend's or family member's pet can get non-pet owners involved. Closely associated with National Love Your Pet Day are: National Adopt a Shelter Pet Day (April 30), National Dog Mom's Day (Second Saturday in May), National Rescue Dog Day (May 20), and Responsible Dog Ownership Day (Third Saturday in September).

Journal/Meditation: Over the years, what pets have you had? Make a list of them with their names, if they had names. Which one was your favorite? Why? If you have a pet now, how do you intend to celebrate National Love Your Pet Day?

Prayer: When you created all the animals on the earth, Father, you pronounced them good. You entrusted their care to people, who have in the course of time adopted many of them into their homes as pets. Bestow upon pet owners a great respect for all animals, and bestow upon all animals an even greater love for the people who care for them. See our cooperation as praise of you forever. Amen.

Tooth Fairy Day
February 28

Text: "Many a refractory child will allow a loose tooth to be removed if he [or she] knows about the tooth fairy. If he [or she] takes his [or her] little tooth and puts it under the pillow when he [or she] goes to bed, the tooth fairy will come in the night and take it away, and in its place will leave some little gift. It is a nice plan for mothers [or fathers] to visit the five-cent counter and lay in a supply of articles to be used on such occasions."[35]

Reflection: The modern narrative concerning the Tooth Fairy appeared on the "Practical Housekeeper's Own Page" of the September 27, 1908, issue of the *Chicago Daily Tribune*. Written by Lillian Brown, the above text explains the process of exchanging a childhood tooth for a gift, and offers advice to parents to have a supply of gifts to leave when slipping their son's or daughter's tooth from under the pillow. There are other variations of this usually-oral tale, such as putting the lost baby tooth on the bedside table and getting money instead of a gift. In the United Kingdom, February 28 is Tooth Fairy Day; that is why it is placed here under February 28. A tooth is a hard whitish bony object arranged in two arched rows inside a human mouth and used for biting and chewing food. Children get a full set of twenty baby teeth by the time they are three years old, and they begin to lose those teeth around the age of five or six. Baby teeth fall out to make room for thirty-two adult teeth, which enter

35. Brown, "Tooth Fairy."

the mouth by the time children are twelve to fourteen. However, the last four, called wisdom teeth, don't emerge until the age of seventeen to twenty-one. A fairy is an imaginary supernatural being, usually resembling a small person, with magic powers. In this case, the imaginary supernatural being, who sneaks into one's room at night and confiscates a baby tooth placed under a pillow possesses the power to transform that tooth into a small amount of cash. In Middle-Ages England, children burned baby teeth to save them from hardship in the afterlife. Likewise, baby teeth had to be disposed of correctly—swallowed, buried, or burned—because they could be used by a witch to impose a curse. Because rodents were known for their strong teeth, a tooth fed to a rodent was believed to lead to the development of healthy adult teeth. Vikings paid children—often called a tooth fee—for lost teeth, and then wore them on necklaces as good luck charms in battles.

Teaching children about the tooth fairy can lead to better oral hygiene, especially if it becomes known that the tooth fairy expects them to brush their teeth. A lost tooth that has been brushed, is healthy, and without a cavity receives a larger monetary reward that one that is dirty, unhealthy, and has a cavity. To help emphasize the importance of good dental habits, the tooth fairy may give a small container into which a tooth can be placed before it goes under the pillow; the tooth fairy can exchange the tooth for a gift, a note, a coin, stickers, sugar-free gum, etc. What the tooth fairy keeps in mind is that this is a ritual of loss; it offers comfort for children experiencing fear, pain, trauma, or embarrassment. Rituals of loss vary among cultures, but, in general, baby teeth are thrown into the sun, into fire, between one's legs, onto or over the roof of the house, placed in a rodent hole, buried, hidden, placed in a tree or on a wall, or given to the mother, child, or animal to swallow. In the 1970s, Rosemary Wells, a professor teaching scientific writing in Evanston, Illinois' Northwest University's dental school, researched thoroughly the tooth fairy saga, tracking the origin of the practice and surveying Americans on their tooth fairy practices for twenty years. As a result, she began a small museum in her home dedicated to the tooth fairy. The average gift left by the tooth fairy is four dollars, because even the tooth fairy has monetary limits! Nevertheless, rituals concerning tooth loss are a part of shared human experience.

Journal/Meditation: Was there a tooth fairy when you were a child? Explain. If you had a tooth fairy in your home, how did he or she function? What other rituals of loss did you enact there? If you did not have a tooth fairy in your home, what did you do with baby teeth after they fell out?

Prayer: O God, I give all my worries and losses to you. Hear the prayers of your children around the world who desire that their loose teeth will come out soon, and give them comfort that only you can bestow now and forever. Amen.

Mardi Gras (Carnival)
Tuesday before Ash Wednesday

Text: "The European Carnival . . . was more directly a creation of the church as a lead-up to Lent. . . . For the church, the holiday also had a didactic function, showing what would happen to society if the Devil and his henchmen were to rule our lives. . . . [O]nce Christianity took hold, the Lenten season leading to Easter matched the transition into spring in timing and in spirit, and Carnival became our institutionalized pre-Lenten festival of dissolution."[36]

Reflection: Depending on where it is celebrated, Carnival (from the Latin *carne*, meaning *meat*) can begin any time after January 6 and culminates with Mardi Gras (French for *Fat Tuesday*). Both Carnival and Mardi Gras refer to the practice of not eating meat, cheese, milk, and eggs after Lent begins with Ash Wednesday. In some countries, the remaining cheese, milk, and eggs were used to make pancakes, shaped in discs like the sun to represent the lengthening days of spring. In other words, Mardi Gras used to be the last day to eat meat (fat) before Lent began the next day. Because the date for Easter changes every year—it is the first Sunday after the first full moon after the Spring Equinox—the date for Ash Wednesday changes every year, and, consequently, the date for Mardi Gras also changes every year. Thus, Mardi Gras can take place on any Tuesday, February 4 through March 10; it all depends on the date for Easter. In a few places, Mardi Gras is known as Shrove Tuesday, coming from the word *shrive*, which refers to the absolution or forgiveness of sins given to a penitent in the Sacrament of Penance (Confession); the purpose of Lent was to engage in penitential practices, like not eating meat, to demonstrate sorrow for sins.

As noted in the text above, Carnival is a dissolution festival, a celebration of transition from one phase to another. Carnival celebrates two dissolutions: winter and Christmas. Winter is gradually disappearing, and spring is gradually appearing. Christmas celebrating[37] is gradually disappearing, and Lenten abstinence is gradually appearing. In other words, Mardi Gras is like New Year's Eve. It was the last opportunity to eat the last of the preserved winter meat before it spoiled in the warmer weather. What occurs today in such places as New Orleans, Louisiana, in the United States and in some other major cities around the world is an economic festival. People travel for great distances to crowd the streets, watch parades, see people in masquerade, catch a string of beads, and contribute to the local economy through the purchase of food, drink, and motel/hotel rooms. The modern world has added another meaning to this dissolution festival: Money is gradually disappearing, and indebtedness is gradually appearing.

36. George, *Mythology*, 65.

37. In the post-Vatican II Roman Catholic liturgical calendar, the Christmas Season ends with the Feast of the Baptism of the Lord, usually the first or second Sunday of January. The weeks between the end of Christmas and the beginning of Lent are referred to as Ordinary Time.

Journal/Meditation: How do you celebrate Mardi Gras? In your life, what is disappearing, and what is appearing? What transition occurs?

Prayer: You give times and seasons to your people, O LORD, to mark transition phases in their lives. Grant me the grace to understand that it is through the gradual dissolution of some of my old life that the gradual appearance of some new life occurs today, tomorrow, and forever. Amen.

3

The Month of *March*

WORLD WILDLIFE DAY
March 3

Text: "Recognizing the important role of the Convention on International Trade in Endangered Species of Wild Fauna and Flora in ensuring that international trade does not threaten the species' survival, [the General Assembly of the United Nations] decides to proclaim 3 March, the day of the adoption of the Convention on International Trade in Endangered Species of Wild Fauna and Flora [in 1973], as World Wildlife Day [, and] invites all . . . individuals to observe and raise awareness of World Wildlife Day in an appropriate manner . . . ."[1]

Reflection: On December 20, 2013, the General Assembly of the United Nations proclaimed March 3, the international day of the adoption of the Convention on International Trade in Endangered Species of Wild Fauna and Flora (CITES), as World Wildlife Day in order to raise awareness of the "intrinsic value of wildlife and its various contributions, including its ecological, genetic, social, economic, scientific, educational, cultural, recreational, and aesthetic contributions to sustainable development and human wellbeing."[2] On December 20, 2012, CITES had "expressed deep concern about environmental crimes, including trafficking in endangered and, where applicable, protected species of wild fauna and flora, and emphasized the need to combat such crimes by strengthening international cooperation, capacity-building, criminal justice responses, and law enforcement efforts."[3] However, as early as 1973, CITES had been raising awareness about fauna and flora; in 2013, the United Nations joined in the effort. Most people are not aware of how close to extinction are the Amur Leopard, Black Rhino, Bornean Orangutan, Sumatran Tiger, Sumatran Elephant, Vaquita, and

---

1. United Nations General Assembly, A/RES/68/205.
2. United Nations General Assembly, A/RES/68/205.
3. United Nations General Assembly, A/RES/68/205.

Mountain Gorilla. Extinction means that no living members of a species or family exists, like dinosaurs. World Wildlife Day offers people the opportunity to tell others about endangered animals and to discuss the biggest threats to wildlife, such as habitat change caused by humans, over-exploitation (overhunting), illegal tracking (illegal game trade), overfishing, and deforestation.

While most states have conservation departments that regulate hunting, fishing, trapping, etc., each person is responsible to ensure that earth remains a thriving, living, breathing planet. We take care of it; we are responsible for creating a sustainable world of wildlife and wild flora conservation. Any broken link in the animal food chain causes ripples. For example, without wolves, elk herds and deer herds have little to fear and stay in place, eating plants, which may be endangered, down to their roots, which results in their deaths. Throwing trash out the car window, dumping trash in the ocean, and refusing to recycle harm wildlife. Furthermore, poaching, catching wild animals or fishing illegally on public land or while trespassing on private land, harms multiple animals and their environment that conservation efforts attempt to keep in balance. Since the first World Wildlife Day in 2014, the United Nations has presented themes about getting serious about wildlife crime, the future of wildlife, big cats, life below water, sustaining life on earth, forests, and more.

Journal/Meditation: What do you consider to be the biggest threat to wildlife where you live? If your state publishes a conservation magazine, do you subscribe to it and read it in order to become aware of threats to flora and fauna?

Prayer: God, you are the creator of all that exists, but you have made people stewards of your creation. With your Holy Spirit, direct me to support conservation efforts where I live that I may help to maintain what you have entrusted to my care. Amen.

INTERNATIONAL WOMEN'S DAY
March 8

Text: ". . . [U]nder capitalism the female half of the human race is doubly oppressed. The working woman and the peasant woman are oppressed by capital, but over and above that—they remain in 'household bondage,' they continue to be 'household slaves,' for they are overburdened with the drudgery of the most squalid backbreaking and stultifying toil in the kitchen and the family household. The second and most important step is the abolition of the private ownership of land and the factories. This and this alone opens up the way towards a complete and actual emancipation of woman, her liberation from 'household bondage' through transition from petty individual housekeeping to large-scale socialized domestic services."[4]

---

4. Cheah, "Women in Red."

Reflection: The text above is part of a speech given by Vladimir Lenin at the first Woman's Day celebration in Russia on March 8, 1917, in St. Petersburg (Petrograd). While Russian women had been marking the day since 1913, female textile workers abandoned their work in factories which led to a mass strike and chaos in the streets. Women demanded an end to World War I, an end to food shortages, and an end to czarism; this marked the beginning of the February Revolution.[5] After Tsar Nicholas II abdicated on March 15, 1917, the provisional government granted women the right to vote. In appreciation to his female Bolshevik supporters, who also helped bring about the Russian October Revolution in 1917, Lenin made International Working Women's Day a national holiday. This meant that the day was associated with far-left movements, eventually being adopted by global feminism in the 1960s. International Women's Day was adopted by the United Nations in 1977. From its beginning in Russia and its association with the Russian Revolution, it has been tweaked repeatedly, until it reached its present status: an annual holiday which commemorates the cultural, political, and socioeconomic achievements of women. It brings attention to issues of gender equality, reproductive rights, violence and abuse against women, and other issues, campaigns, or themes.

In the United States, the first National Woman's Day celebration took place in New York on February 28, 1909, organized by the Socialist Party of America; women demanded civil, social, political, and religious rights. It remained primarily a communist holiday until 1967, when feminism adopted it, and it emerged as a day of activism. In the 1970s and 1980s, women's groups were joined by labor organizations in calling for equal pay, equal economic opportunity, equal legal rights, reproductive rights, subsidized child care, and the prevention of violence against women. Thus, the United Nations began marking the day in 1975, proclaiming it International Women's Day, a holiday focused on women's rights with each year's observance centered on a particular theme or issue within women's rights. Today, women are recognized for their achievements with no regard to national, ethnic, linguistic, cultural, economic, or political achievements. It now has a global dimension for women in both developed and developing countries. Contrary to Lenin's words above, women have used capital and private ownership for emancipation from household bondage and slavery.

Journal/Meditation: Where you live what is the women's rights issue that needs the most attention? Where you live what is the achievement for which women are most recognized?

Prayer: O God, you have shown mothers, wives, sisters, and aunts the way to equality by showering them with grace. Give to all women the strength to travel on, to make a difference among women, and to conquer doubts they meet along the path to transforming the world into a place of equal rights and dignity. Amen.

---

5. According to the Julian Calendar, it was February 23.

Daylight Saving Time Begins
Second Sunday

Text: "Daylight Saving Time (DST) is a period of the year between spring and fall when clocks in most parts of the United States are set one hour ahead of standard time. The beginning . . . [date and time]—the second Sunday in March at two o'clock ante meridian . . . —[is] set in statute. . . . Only congress can change the length of the DST observance period."[6]

Reflection: Before there was Daylight Saving Time (DST), there had to be Standard Time, which was not adopted until 1883 by the United States and Canada railroads. At that time, four time zones were established: Eastern, Central, Mountain, and Pacific. In 1918, congress established five standard time zones; in addition to the four mentioned above, Alaska was added to the list. In 1966, congress amended the 1918 law to include Atlantic, Yukon, Alaska-Hawaii, Samoa, and Bering standard time zones. In 1983, Yukon was absorbed into Pacific; Alaska-Hawaii returned to Alaska; and Bearing was absorbed into the new Hawaii-Aleutian Time Zone. Now, there were eight time zones. Chamorro was added in 2000. Thus, there are nine Standard Time zones for the U.S. and its territories. From east to west these are: Atlantic (Puerto Rico, U.S. Virgin Islands), Eastern (over twenty states or parts of states), Central (over twenty states or parts of states), Mountain (fourteen states or parts of states), Pacific (five states or parts of states), Alaska (part of the state), Hawaii-Aleutian (Hawaii and part of Alaska), Samoa (America Samoa, Jarvis Island, Midway Atoll, Palmyra Atoll, Kingman Reef), and Chamorro (Guam, Northern Mariana Islands).

Daylight Saving Time is the practice of advancing clocks by one hour during the warmer months of late winter, spring, summer, and part of autumn so that darkness occurs at a later clock time. In 1966, congress put into law the statue that DST would begin at 2 a.m. on the last Sunday in April, giving that day only twenty-three hours. In 1986, the law was amended to the second Sunday of March, where it remains. The rationale behind the statute and its amendments is that all people living in a region will begin and end work earlier with an extra hour of daylight for other outdoor leisure activities, reduces traffic accidents and crime, promotes business, and saves energy. Opponents of DST argue that it disrupts human circadian rhythms, increases traffic collisions, and makes energy savings nebulous. DST is not observed in the Atlantic, Samoa, or Chamorro standard time zones, nor by Hawaii in the Hawaii-Aleutian Standard Time Zone. The effects of DST on individual spirituality have not been studied.

Journal/Meditation: What effects, if any, does Daylight Saving Time have on your spiritual practices?

---

6. Clark and Cunningham, "Daylight Saving Time." The ending of DST is covered in The Month of November, chapter 11.

Prayer: God of all time and every season, you give me years, months, and days to praise your name. You give me light and darkness that increase and decrease through every year. Grant me the grace to serve you faithfully in time that one day I may enter into timelessness with you forever. Amen.

St. Patrick's Day
March 17

Text: "I arise today, through / The strength of heaven, / The light of the sun, / The radiance of the moon, / The splendor of fire, / The speed of lighting, / The swiftness of wind, / The depth of the sea, / The stability of earth, / The firmness of rock."[7]

Reflection: The prayer known as Saint Patrick's Breastplate—the fourth section of which is presented above—is part of an eleventh-century collection of hymns. The title of the prayer comes from the Christian Bible (New Testament) letter to the Ephesians, in which the author exhorts his readers: "Stand . . . and fasten the belt of truth around your waist, and put on the breastplate of righteousness."[8] Each of the eleven sections of the prayer begins with "I arise today, through" or "I clasp unto my heart today" (in modern translations) or "I bind unto myself today" or "I join unto myself today" (in older translations). Then, the section presents a list of sources of strength that the pray-er calls on for support. Thus, in section four above, the pray-er seeks support from the strength of heaven, the light of the sun, the radiance of the moon, the splendor of fire, the speed of lighting, the swiftness of wind, the depth of the sea, the stability of the earth, and the firmness of rock. The prayer is attributed to Saint Patrick, whose feast day is celebrated on March 17, the day he died in Ireland.

Patrick (385–461) was born in Roman Britain into a wealthy family; his father was a deacon and his grandfather was a priest. At the age of sixteen, Patrick was kidnapped by Irish raiders and taken as a slave to Ireland, where he spent six years working as a shepherd; while tending the sheep, he found God. He escaped his captors and, after making his way home, was ordained a priest. Later, he returned to Ireland as a bishop—a shepherd—to convert the Irish to Christianity, spending many years evangelizing the northern part of Ireland. March 17 honors Patrick for bringing Christianity to Ireland and celebrates Irish heritage and culture. Public parades and festivals, drinking Irish whiskey, beer, or cider, along with wearing green attire or displaying shamrocks (according to tradition used by Saint Patrick to explain the Trinity), takes place around the world. Saint Patrick's Day is marked in more countries than any other festival. In the United States it has been taking place since 1601, as a celebration of Irish and Irish-American culture.

---

7. "Saint Patrick's Breastplate."
8. NRSV: Ephesians 6:14.

Journal/Meditation: How do you mark Saint Patrick's Day? What aspect of Irish heritage or culture attracts you to it? According to section four (above) from Saint Patrick's Breastplate, there are a variety of sources from which to seek support; from where do you seek support?

Prayer: "I arise today, through / God's strength to pilot me, / God's might to uphold me, / God's wisdom to guide me, / God's eye to look before me, / God's ear to hear me, / God's word to speak to me, / God's hand to guard me, / God's shield to protect me, / God's host to save me . . . ."[9] Amen.

Spring Begins
March 19–21

Text: "Earth's rotational axis [is] tilted about 23.5 degrees from the perpendicular with respect to earth's orbit around the sun. As a result, the amount that earth's axis tilts towards or away from the sun varies during the year. . . . [W]hen earth's axis neither tilts towards or away from the sun [—that is,] . . . the axis [is] . . . perpendicular to the sun resulting in a nearly equal length of day and night at all latitudes [—that is] referred to as [an] equinox (derived from two Latin words: *aequus* (equal) and *nox* (night)."[10]

Reflection: The spring equinox is also called the vernal (from the Latin *ver* for spring) equinox. It occurs seldom on March 19 and 21 and usually on March 20. At the moment the center of the visible sun is directly above the equator is the equinox. The length of day and night are approximately the same all over the planet. In other words, the center of the sun spends the same amount of time above and below the horizon. Another way to understand equinox is to see it as the time when the sun rises at one of earth's rotational poles and sets at the other; for a very brief time, both the North Pole and the South Pole are in daylight. Depending on where a person lives on the earth, the date and the day when both night and day are equally twelve hours varies before or after the equatorial equinox. As noted in the text above, this is due to the earth's axial tilt. While there are two annual equinoxes, the fall (autumnal) one will be covered in The Month of September, chapter 9. After the spring equinox, the hours of daylight continue to increase until the solstice in June.

The calendar used today is the Gregorian Calendar, begun in 1582. Before it existed, the Julian Calendar, established by Julius Caesar in 45 BCE, set the equinox at March 25. Because the Julian Calendar is about eleven minutes longer (1 day in 128 years), by 300 CE, the spring equinox was occurring on March 21. By 1580, it was occurring on March 11. Pope Gregory XIII decided to correct the calendar by deleting ten days from the Julian Calendar and by reducing the number of leap years. Gregory's

---

9. "Saint Patrick's Breastplate."
10. "Solstices and Equinoxes."

fix, nevertheless, leaves a small variation in the date and the time for the spring equinox because the length of a day is not exactly twenty-four hours; it is twenty-three hours and fifty-six minutes. For Gregory, what was important was calculating the date for the spring equinox, because that is how Easter is determined since 325 CE. Easter is the first Sunday after the first full moon after the spring equinox. In other words, after the spring equinox (March 19–21) one looks for the next full moon, and the Sunday after the full moon is Easter. That means that Easter can occur anytime between March 19 and April 25. Because of modern technology, we don't have to figure out when official spring begins, nor do we need to pay attention to the phases of the moon; we look on a calendar or listen to the local weather meteorologist tell us.

Journal/Meditation: How do the increasing minutes and hours of daylight after the spring equinox affect your spirituality? How do the decreasing minutes and hours of darkness after the spring equinox affect your spirituality?

Prayer: God of day and darkness, you created the sun to give light to the day and the moon to give light to the night. When both daylight and moonlight decrease and when both daylight and moonlight increase, draw me closer to you today, tomorrow, and forever. Amen.

INTERNATIONAL DAY OF HAPPINESS
March 20

Text: "Conscious that the pursuit of happiness is a fundamental human goal, recognizing the relevance of happiness and wellbeing as universal goals and aspirations in the lives of human beings around the world . . . , [the General Assembly of the United Nations] decides to proclaim 20 March the International Day of Happiness."[11]

Reflection: On June 28, 2012, the General Assembly of the United Nations (U.N.) proclaimed March 20 International Day of Happiness. In its resolution, the U.N. states that pursuing happiness is a fundamental human goal; thus, the aim of the day is to help people around the world realize the importance of happiness in their lives and the need to incorporate it into public policies. In its declaration, the U.N. states that there is a need for a more inclusive, equitable, and balanced approach to economic growth that promotes sustainable development, poverty eradication, happiness, and the well-being of all people. People are urged to continue to progress in what makes their lives better. They are urged to share their happiness with their family and friends because quality relationships are crucial to happiness. Confucius echoes those sentiments in *The Analects*. Writing about government, he states, "Good government obtains when those who are near are made happy, and those who are far off are attracted."[12] In his in-

---

11. United Nations General Assembly, A/RES/66/281.
12. *Analects* 13:16 (cf. 19:25).

troduction to *The Dhammapada*, Bhikku Bodhi explains that Buddhism is concerned "with establishing wellbeing and happiness in the immediately visible sphere of concrete human relations."[13] He adds, ". . . [O]ur innate sense of moral justice requires that goodness be recompensed with happiness . . . ."[14] According to Bodhi, *The Dhammapada* teaches that people seek happiness, while afraid of pain, loss, and death, and walk the delicate balance between good and evil, purity and defilement, progress and decline.[15] Likewise, *The Rig Veda* implores the gods of India to give the singers happiness[16] or health and happiness,[17] or peace and happiness,[18] to mention but a few of the over-fifty occurrences of the word *happiness*. Nine out of 17 verses of hymn 63 in book 10 of *The Rig Veda* mention happiness. The singer asks the gods "with adoration and with hymns for happiness."[19] A god is petitioned to "make . . . good and easy paths to happiness."[20] All the wise gods are asked to preserve the singers "from all sin . . . for happiness;"[21] thus, "free from defect, [they] will ascend for happiness."[22] In battles, the singers invoke the gods to give happiness.[23] "Bless us, all holy ones, that we may have your help, guard and protect us from malignant injury," begins verse 11 of hymn 63; it continues, "With fruitful invocation may we call on you, gods, who give ear to us for grace, for happiness."[24] "Keep far away from us all hatred, O you gods, and give us ample shelter for our happiness," states verse 12 of hymn 63, while verse 13 petitions a single god to lead the singers "safely through all . . . . pain and grief to happiness."[25]

While various books of the Bible mention happiness, the Hebrew Bible (Old Testament) hymnal, Psalms, uses the word *happy* the most[26]—over twenty times. The Old Testament (Apocrypha) book of Tobit uses the word *happiness* twice. In a prayer for newly-married Tobias and Sarah, Raguel, Sarah's father, says, "Be merciful to them, O Master, and keep them safe; bring their lives to fulfillment in happiness and mercy."[27] Fourteen days later, Tobias and Sarah leave "with happiness and joy."[28] The Old Testament (Apocrypha) book of Sirach also uses the word two times. The

13. Bodhi, "Introduction," 9.
14. Bodhi, "Introduction," 11.
15. Bodhi, "Introduction," 19.
16. Cf. *Rig Veda* 10:63:5.
17. Cf. *Rig Veda* 5:51:12.
18. Cf. *Rig Veda* 10:35:3.
19. *Rig Veda* 10:63:5.
20. *Rig Veda* 10:63:7.
21. *Rig Veda* 10:63:8.
22. *Rig Veda* 10:63:10; 10:63:14.
23. Cf. *Rig Veda*, 10:63:9.
24. *Rig Veda* 10:63:11.
25. *Rig Veda* 10:63:13.
26. Cf. NRSV: Psalms 1:1; 2:12b; 32:1–2; 34:8b, etc.
27. NRSV: Tobit 8:17b.
28. NRSV: Tobit 10:13a.

author states: "Do not reveal your thoughts to anyone, or you may drive away your happiness,"[29] and "Some companions rejoice in the happiness of a friend . . . ."[30] Happiness is also found in the Hebrew Bible (Old Testament) book of Lamentations[31] and in the Old Testament (Apocrypha) book of Fourth Maccabees.[32] *The Book of Mormon*, while it mentions living "after the manner of happiness,"[33] is more focused on "that happiness which is prepared for the saints."[34] The book of Mosiah states that those who keep God's commandments are considered blessed and happy. ". . . [I]if they hold out faithful to the end they are received into heaven, that thereby they may dwell with God in a state of never-ending happiness."[35] Those whom God judges to be good will enjoy "the resurrection of endless life and happiness."[36] It is "by the maintenance of the sacred word of God, to which we owe all our happiness," states Alma.[37] Thus, many of the writings of world religions recognize that the pursuit of happiness is a fundamental and human goal.

Journal/Meditation: What happiness do you pursue? Make a list and rank them in their order of importance to you. What do you notice about your list?

Prayer: Blessed are you, O God, because you bestow happiness on all people. Be merciful, O Master, and keep me safe. Bring my life to fulfilment in happiness and mercy today, tomorrow, and forever. Amen.

INTERNATIONAL DAY FOR THE ELIMINATION OF RACIAL DISCRIMINATION
March 21

Text: "Reaffirming that racial discrimination and apartheid are denials of human rights and fundamental freedoms and of justice and are offences against human dignity; recognizing that racial discrimination and apartheid, wherever they are practiced, constitute a serious impediment to economic and social development and are obstacles to international cooperation and peace; deeply concerned that racial discrimination and apartheid, despite the decisive condemnation of them by the United Nations, continue to exist in some countries and territories; convinced of the urgent necessity of further measures to attain the goal of the complete elimination of all

---

29. NRSV: Sirach 8:19.
30. NRSV: Sirach 37:4.
31. Cf. NRSV: Lamentations 3:17.
32. Cf. NRSV: 4 Maccabees 16:9.
33. *Book of Mormon*: 2 Nephi 5:27.
34. *Book of Mormon*: 2 Nephi 9:43.
35. *Book of Mormon*: Mosiah 3:41b.
36. *Book of Mormon*: Mosiah 16:11; cf. Alma 3:26; 28:12; 40:12; 41:4–5.
37. *Book of Mormon*: Alma 44:5.

forms of racial discrimination and apartheid; [the General Assembly of the United Nations] condemns, wherever they exist, all policies and practices of apartheid, racial discrimination, and segregation, including the practices of discrimination inherent in colonialism; [and] ... proclaims 21 March as International Day for the Elimination of Racial Discrimination."[38]

Reflection: On October 26, 1966, the General Assembly of the United Nations passed several resolutions dealing with forms of racial discrimination. The first of those, from which the above text is taken, begins by recalling previous resolutions dealing with racial discrimination in 1905, 1963, and 1965. March 21 was chosen for the International Day for the Elimination of Racial Discrimination because on that day in 1960 in Sharpeville, South Africa, police opened fire and killed sixty-nine people at a peaceful demonstration against apartheid. Even though the U.N. condemned racial discrimination, segregation, and apartheid in 1966, apartheid did not come to an end until after a series of negotiations from 1990 to 1993 and the election of a democratic government in 1994. The 1966 U.N. resolution called upon all members to initiate programs of action to eliminate racial discrimination and apartheid through "the promotion of equal opportunity for educational and vocational training, and guarantees for the employment, without distinction on grounds of race, color or ethnic origin, of basic human rights such as the rights to vote, to equality in the administration of justice, to equal economic opportunities, and to equal access to social services."[39] On November 15, 1979, the U.N. issued a twenty-seven point program of activities to be undertaken during the second half of the 1980s for action to combat racism and racial discrimination. In the resolution, the General Assembly of the U.N. proclaimed "that the elimination of all forms of racism and discrimination based on race ... [were] matters of high priority for the international community and ... for the United Nations."[40] In its efforts to eradicate totally racism, racial discrimination, and apartheid, the U.N. strongly condemned "the policies of apartheid, racism, and racial discrimination practiced in southern Africa and elsewhere, including the denial of the right of peoples to self-determination."[41]

The program of activities to combat racism and racial discrimination states that the objective is "the complete and final elimination of all forms of racism and racial discrimination." It states, "Every effort should be made to bring about the complete isolation of the racist regimes," and that all members of the U.N. should apply "sanctions against those regimes."[42] All collaboration is to stop, no technological assistance is to be given, no military supplies are to be manufactured, no loans or investments

---

38. United Nations General Assembly, A/RES/2142 (XXI).
39. United Nations General Assembly, A/RES/2142 (XXI).
40. United Nations General Assembly, A/RES/34/24.
41. United Nations General Assembly, A/RES/34/24.
42. United Nations General Assembly, A/RES/34/24.

are to be made, and an embargo on the supply of petroleum is to be maintained. All effort is to be made to mobilize public support for the elimination of all forms of racism. While the primary focus at the time was on South Africa, the program sought the investigation of the policies and practices that may be racially discriminatory in occupied Arab territories, discriminatory practices that violate the human rights and dignity of migrant workers, and the involvement of youth in the struggle against racial discrimination. According to the document, "A week of solidarity with the peoples struggling against racism and racial discrimination, beginning on 21 March, should be organized annually in all states." Furthermore, "All states should adopt, as a matter of high priority, measures to declare punishable by law any dissemination of ideas based on racial superiority or hatred and to prohibit organizations based on racial prejudice and hatred . . . established on the basis of racial criteria or propagating ideas of racial discrimination and apartheid."[43] As a result of the work of the U.N., not only was apartheid dismantled, but racist laws and practices have been abolished in many countries. However, that does not mean that all citizens of many countries have come to recognize that all human beings are born free and equal in dignity and rights no matter their race. Much work remains to be done.

Journal/Meditation: What forms of racial discrimination continue to exist today? What ideas do you encounter that support some form of racial superiority? What can you do to combat racial discrimination where you live?

Prayer: Father, you created all human beings in freedom, made them equal in dignity, and bestowed upon them rights that give them the potential to contribute to the well-being of society. Give me the wisdom to recognize racial discrimination, segregation, and prejudice in my life, and give me the grace to eradicate it so that difference truly becomes a source of richness and strength. Amen.

World Poetry Day
March 21

Text: "The General Conference" [of the United Nations Educational, Scientific, and Cultural Organization (UNESCO)] convinced that the initiative to hold a worldwide event in support of poetry would give fresh recognition and impetus to national, regional, and international poetry movements; mindful that this event, which responds to aesthetic needs in the present-day world, must have repercussions on the promotion of linguistic diversity, since through poetry endangered languages will have greater opportunities to express themselves within their respective communities; mindful also that a societal movement towards the recognition of ancestral values entails a return to the oral tradition and acceptance of language as a factor contributing to the

---

43. United Nations General Assembly, A/RES/34/24.

socialization and structuring of the human individual . . . ; recalling that since poetry is an art rooted both in the written text and in the spoken word, any action to promote it should be conductive to an intensification of international intercultural exchange; proclaims 21 March as World Poetry Day."[44]

Reflection: During the thirtieth session of the General Conference of the United Nations Educational, Scientific, and Cultural Organization (UNESCO), held in Paris October 26 to November 17, 1999, March 21 was declared annual World Poetry Day, as noted in the above text. The day is designed to celebrate "one of humanity's most treasured forms of cultural and linguistic expression and identity," states UNESCO's "World Poetry Day."[45] According to UNESCO, "Practiced throughout history—in every culture and on every continent—poetry speaks to our common humanity and our shared values, transforming the simplest of poems into a powerful catalyst for dialogue and peace."[46] The world-wide support the day gives to poetry fosters renewed interest in the art form. It promotes reading, writing, publishing, and teaching poetry throughout the world. It also supports "linguistic diversity through poetic expression and increasing the opportunity for endangered languages to be heard."[47] As the above text notes, poetry gives languages opportunities to express themselves within their respective communities.

Another important point that the text above makes is that oral poetry communicates ancestral values. It delivers values that aid socialization and the formation of the human individual, especially to the young. While some values are communicated through written poetry, there exists oral traditions within communities that bear values from one generation to the next in the formation of identity. Aesthetically, both the oral and written forms of poetry lead to intercultural exchange; that is, cultures recognize similar or identical values expressed in the medium. Thus, on World Poetry Day it is appropriate to honor poets, to revive oral tradition of poetry recitals, to promote the reading, writing, and teaching of poetry, to foster the convergence between poetry and other arts (such as theater, dance, music, and painting), and to raise the visibility of poetry in the media.[48]

Journal/Meditation: Who is your favorite poet? What is his or her poem that is your favorite? Find a copy and reflect on its words: What meaning does it have for you? What values does the poem communicate to you?

Prayer: O God, I seek wisdom in poetry, insight into things divine. Give my heart delight, point my feet on the straight path, and open my ears to receive poetry's

44. "World Poetry Day, 30 C/Resolution 29."
45. "World Poetry Day, UNESCO."
46. "World Poetry Day, UNESCO."
47. "World Poetry Day, UNESCO."
48. "World Poetry Day, UNESCO."

instruction. To you, who give wisdom and enable my progress, be all glory forever and ever. Amen.

INTERNATIONAL DAY OF FORESTS
March 21

Text: "Noting the useful contribution of national, regional, and international actions during the International Year [of Forests] to raising awareness at all levels in order to strengthen the sustainable management, conservation, and sustainable development of all types of forests and tress outside forests for the benefit of current and future generations, . . . [the General Assembly of the United Nations] decides to proclaim 21 March of each year the International Day of Forests . . . in order to celebrate and raise awareness of the importance of all types of forests and of trees outside forests."[49]

Reflection: As the above text states, the annual International Day of Forests, established by the General Assembly of the United Nations on December 21, 2012, was the direct result of the success of the International Year of Forests in 2011. On December 20, 2006, the General Assembly of the U.N. recognized "that forests and sustainable forest management can contribute significantly to sustainable development, poverty eradication, and the achievement of internationally agreed development goals . . . ."[50] It also emphasized "the need for sustainable management of all types of forests including fragile forest ecosystems." Furthermore, "[c]onvinced that concerted efforts should focus on raising awareness at all levels to strengthen the sustainable management, conservation, and sustainable development of all types of forests for the benefit of current and future generations, [it decided] to declare 2011 the International Year of Forests."[51] Thus, in 2012, the U.N. General Assembly invited all members to present and promote concrete activities with regard to all types of forests and trees outside forests, such as tree planting campaigns.

Raising awareness about forests begins with the fact that over 32 million acres (the size of England) of forests are lost annually. Because forests play a major role in climate change, deforestation results in about 18 percent of the world's carbon emissions; healthy forests are one of the world's primary carbon depositories. Over 60,000 species of trees form forests that cover more than 30 percent of the world's land, providing food, fiber, water, and medicine. According to "International Day of Forests:" "When we drink a glass of water, write in a notebook, take medicine for a fever, or build a house, we do not always make the connection with forests. And yet, these and many other aspects of our lives are linked to forests in one way or another."[52] Because

---

49. United Nations General Assembly, A/RES/67/200.
50. United Nations General Assembly, A/RES/61/193.
51. United Nations General Assembly, A/RES/61/193.
52. "International Day of Forests."

global deforestation continues at an alarming rate, their "sustainable management and their use of resources are key to combating climate change, and to contributing to the prosperity and wellbeing of current and future generations."[53]

Journal/Meditation: In what specific ways is your life connected to forests? What can you contribute to management, conservation, or sustainable development of forests? How can you fight climate change in your own yard?

Prayer: The trees of the forest sing for joy before you, O LORD. When the oaks hear your voice, they bend in worship. Give all people a greater awareness and respect for the forests on the earth, and grant me a greater awareness of how much I use your precious gift. Amen.

World Water Day
March 22

Text: "Considering that the extent to which water resource development contributes to economic productivity and social wellbeing is not widely appreciated . . . , considering also that, as populations and economic activities grow, many countries are rapidly reaching conditions of water scarcity or facing limits to economic development, considering further that the promotion of water conservation and sustainable management requires public awareness at local, national, regional, and international levels, [the General Assembly of the United Nations] decides to declare 22 March of each year World Day for Water."[54]

Reflection: On December 22, 1992, the General Assembly of the United Nations (U.N.) declared March 22 of every year to be World Water Day. The purpose of the day is to promote public awareness of the need to conserve and develop water resources. The U.N. recommended some means to accomplish that goal: the publication and distribution of documentaries and the organization of conferences, round tables, seminars, and expositions. In other words, the U.N. highlights the importance of fresh water for the people and animals who live on the earth. In order to provide that, it advocates for the sustainable management of freshwater resources. Since the 1992 declaration, the day has been celebrated with theatrical and musical programs along with lobbying and campaigns to raise money for water projects. The hope is that as people around the world learn more about all kinds of water-related issues, they will take action to make a difference in their time and place.

As the earth continues to warm due to climate change, water scarcity, water pollution, water supply, and sanitation are issues that shout to be addressed. Water scarcity or drought afflicts many areas of the world. Rivers, creeks, and streams are often

---

53. "International Day of Forests."
54. United Nations General Assembly, A/RES/47/193.

polluted by runoff from lawns saturated with chemicals. Floods can be reduced by restoring wetlands and reconnecting rivers to floodplains. In parts of the world, often due to pollution, freshwater has to be diverted through tunnels and pipes to supply large cities and towns. Not only is sanitation lacking in many areas of the world, but the release of inadequately treated water results in the spread of disease. However, properly treated wastewater can be reused in cooling towers and irrigation. Add to this the water-energy connection—namely, the fact that generating and transmitting energy often requires the use of water resources, specifically for hydroelectric, nuclear, and thermal energy—and it is not difficult to understand water's role in sustainable development. Not to be missed, of course, is the relationship between water and jobs; an abundance of quality water can provide jobs and change people's lives. Everyone can invest in green roofs, green infrastructure, and planting trees. As the U.N. makes clear, the goal of World Water Day is to inspire people to learn more about water and then do something about it.

Journal/Meditation: In what ways is water important to you, your home, family, livelihood, cultural practices, wellbeing, and local environment? What can you do to protect this natural resource?

Prayer: O LORD, you make springs gush forth in the valleys, and by the streams the birds of the air build their nests, while creatures small and large quench their thirst. With me you share the abundance of your fresh and life-giving water. Grant me greater appreciation for your gift and inspire me to act to protect it now and forever. Amen.

Passover

Begins Any Evening Between March 21 and April 20

Text: "The LORD said to Moses and Aaron in the land of Egypt: '. . . Tell the whole congregation of Israel that . . . they are to take a lamb for each family, a lamb for each household. Your lamb shall be without blemish, a year-old male; you may take it from the sheep or from the goats. . . . [T]hen the whole assembled congregation of Israel shall slaughter it at twilight. They shall take some of the blood and put on the two doorposts and the lintel of the houses in which they eat it. They shall eat the lamb that same night; they shall eat it roasted over the fire with unleavened bread and bitter herbs. . . . It is the passover of the LORD. For I will pass through the land of Egypt that night, and I will strike down every firstborn in the land of Egypt, both human beings and animals; on all the gods of Egypt I will execute judgments: I am the LORD. The blood shall be a sign for you on the houses where you live: when I see the blood, I will pass over you, and no plague shall destroy you when I strike the land of Egypt.'"[55]

---

55. NRSV: Exodus 12:1, 3, 5, 6b–8, 11c–14.

Reflection: Because Passover is both an annual religious and cultural festival, and because it is marked by a number of other groups,[56] it is treated here. Basically, Passover is about facing imminent death and ending alive in several layers of understanding. First, the Hebrews (later called Israelites, then Jews) face death as slaves in Egypt. Second, as the tenth of the plagues makes clear, without the lamb's blood sprinkled on the doorposts and lintel of their houses, their firstborn face death at the LORD's hands. Blood, which represents life, blocks the house's portal (door) from opening to death. Freedom, escape from slavery, exodus, depends on the death of the firstborn of the slave owners. Every year Passover, the great escape from death, is celebrated traditionally in Israel for seven days and in other parts of the world by Jews often for eight days. The spring feast, which begins on the evening preceding the first full day of Passover,[57] can occur on any evening of the week usually between March 21 and April 20 on the night of a full moon after the Spring Equinox. Because the Jewish calendar is lunar, the insertion of another month from time to time to make the lunar calendar more closely correspond to the solar calendar alters the calculation. As indicated above, at first the passover lamb was sacrificed in the home. Once the portable tabernacle was constructed in the desert after the exodus, the lamb was slaughtered before it. Then, once the first Temple was built in Jerusalem (1000–957 BCE) by King Solomon, lambs were sacrificed there, beginning in the afternoon before Passover began that evening, with the blood collected and splashed on the altar. Solomon's Temple was destroyed in 586 BCE by Nebuchadnezzar, King of Babylon. However, it was rebuilt in 516 BCE and enlarged throughout the years, until it was destroyed by the Romans in 70 CE. Because there was no place to sacrifice the lambs and no place to pour the blood, the ritual came to an end. At the annual meal (called the seder) eaten on the evening that begins Passover in remembrance of the exodus, a lamb's shank bone, in honor of the Passover lamb, is placed on the seder plate, along with bitter herbs representing the bitterness of slavery; a sweet brown mixture made from nuts, apples, cinnamon, and sweet red wine representing mortar; a vegetable dipped in salt water to represent tears, a roasted egg representing a sacrifice once offered in the Jerusalem Temple, and unleavened bread. Also, four cups of wine are drunk at various points during the seder meal.

The unleavened bread is called matzoth, a flatbread made only from flour and water. Matzoth is eaten on the first night of Passover and, often, during the entire week. "Seven days you shall eat unleavened bread," says the LORD.[58] Later, in the same chapter, the narrator states that the Egyptians urged the Hebrews to depart quickly from the land. "So the people took their dough before it was leavened, with

---

56. Passover is observed by Saint Thomas Syrian Christians, the Samaritan Religion, Quartodeciman Christians, Messianic Jews, and Sunni Moslems, to name a few.
57. The day begins with sunset the evening before.
58. NRSV: Exodus 12:15a.

their kneading bowls wrapped up in their cloaks on their shoulders."[59] Thus, matzoth reminds those celebrating Passover of their ancestors' rapid departure from Egypt; it also serves as a sign of being a slave in order to promote humility, appreciate freedom, and avoid an inflated ego represented by leavened bread. However, some scholars have pointed out that matzoth were often baked in preparation for a journey, because it preserved well and was light to carry. A third opinion states that leaven was considered to be a sign of corruption and spoiling, which is why the LORD tells Moses and Aaron, "For seven days no leaven shall be found in your house; for whoever eats what is leavened shall be cut off from the congregation of Israel, whether an alien or a native of the land."[60] Thus, before Passover begins all leaven (traditionally made from one of five types of fermented grains: wheat, barley, oats, rye, and spelt) is removed from the home. Like the blood on the doorposts once protected the home's portal from the death-wielding hand of God, the removal of leaven from the home ensures that no corruption has gotten in by the ordinary means of baking bread!

Journal/Meditation: In what situation have you faced death and ended alive? Explain. What do you consider the modern equivalent of protecting your home from evil both without and within?

Prayer: LORD, guard me from all evil both within and without. With your saving hand trace over me your grace to save me from anything that might harm me. And bring me through my final passover to life with you forever and ever. Amen.

National Doctors Day and National Physicians Week
March 30 and March 25–31

Text: "Whereas society owes a debt of gratitude to physicians for the contributions of physicians in enlarging the reservoir of scientific knowledge, increasing the number of scientific tools, and expanding the ability of health professions to use the knowledge and tools effectively in the never-ending fight against disease; and whereas society owes a debt of gratitude to physicians for the sympathy and compassion of physicians in ministering to the sick and in alleviating human suffering; now, therefore, be it resolved by the Senate and House of Representatives of the United States of America in congress assembled, that (1) March 30, 1991, is designated as 'National Doctors Day'; and (2) the President is authorized and requested to issue a proclamation calling on the people of the United States to observe the day with appropriate programs, ceremonies, and activities."[61]

---

59. NRSV: Exodus 12:34.
60. NRSV: Exodus 12:19.
61. "Public Law 101–473."

Reflection: The first Doctors Day took place on March, 30, 1933, in Winder, Georgia. Eudora Brown Almond, the wife of Doctor Charles B. Almond, decided that it was important to set aside a day to honor physicians. She did so by fostering the mailing of cards to physicians and their wives along with flowers placed on the graves of deceased doctors. The date was chosen to commemorate the first use of general anesthesia in surgery on March 30, 1842, in Jefferson, Georgia, when Doctor Crawford Long anesthetized James Venable with ether and removed a tumor from his neck. The idea of a day honoring doctors was presented to the Georgia State Medical Alliance in 1933 by Mrs. E.R. Harris of Winder, and on May 10, 1934, the resolution was adopted at the annual state meeting in Augusta, Georgia. After that, in 1935, Mrs. J. Bonar White introduced the resolution to the Women's Alliance of the Southern Medical Association, and the annual observance became an integral part of the Southern Medical Association. While a resolution commemorating Doctors Day was adopted by the U.S. House of Representatives on March 30, 1958, it was not until 1990 that legislation passed the Senate on September 28 and passed the House on October 16 that President George Bush signed it into law on October 30, 1990, creating the public law above. It designated March 30 as National Doctors Day. In the first proclamation of National Doctors Day, dated February 21, 1991, Bush quoted from a former president of the American Medical Association, Doctor Elmer Hess, who said, "The Almighty has reserved for himself the power to create life, but he has assigned to a few of us the responsibility of keeping in good repair the bodies in which this life is sustained."[62] Bush recognized the physicians of the U.S. for their leadership in the prevention and treatment of illness and injury and urged citizens to observe the day with appropriate programs and activities.

In 2017, Doctors Marion Mass, Kimberly Jackson, and Christina Lang had Doctors Day changed to National Physicians Week (NPW), March 25 to 31. After founding Physicians Working Together in 2015, Jackson began a series of articles in honor of the week, and that was followed by online conferences, which focused on physician wellbeing and advocacy. Other activities include a scholarship program for medical students and residents. Physicians Working Together unites doctors of all levels, training, and specialties to make the patient-doctor relationship central in the healing profession. It also strengthens healthy physician relationships through collaboration and genuine camaraderie. Over the past few years, the theme of the week has been devoted to highlighting the shortage of physicians in the U.S., an open forum for physicians to discuss ways to improve their practice, and the effort encouraging physicians, healthcare workers, and communities to work together to end coronavirus. Basically, National Physicians Week, which now includes National Doctors Day, focuses on advocacy and the need for citizens to support and appreciate the physician community. Traditionally, physicians are given a red carnation on National Doctors Day or at some other time during National Physicians Week.

62. "National Doctors Day."

Journal/Meditation: How do you show your appreciation to each of your doctors? Which of your physicians has been the best in keeping your body in good repair? Explain.

Prayer: Almighty God, you have entrusted the care of your people to those you have called to serve as physicians. While you reserve to yourself the power to create life, you have assigned doctors the responsibility to keep in good repair the bodies in which life is sustained. Guide the hands, the minds, and the hearts of all the doctors who keep me alive in your service, and bless them with an outpouring of your grace that strengthens them in all their work. Amen.

4

The Month of *April*

April Fool's (Fools') Day
April 1

Text: ". . . [T]he past winter, one of the mildest in living memory, . . . resulted in an exceptionally heavy spaghetti crop. . . . [A]nd the spaghetti harvest goes forward. Another reason why this may be a bumper year lies in the virtual disappearance of the spaghetti weevil, the tiny creature whose depredations have caused much concern in the past. After picking, the spaghetti is laid out to dry in the warm . . . sun. Many people are often puzzled by the fact that spaghetti is produced at such uniform length. But this is the result of many years of patient endeavor by plant breeders who've succeeded in producing the perfect spaghetti. And now, the harvest is marked by a traditional meal. . . . And it is, of course, spaghetti—picked earlier in the day, dried in the sun, and so brought fresh from garden to table at the very peak of condition. . . . [T]here is nothing like real home-grown spaghetti."[1]

Reflection: On April 1, 1957, Richard Dimbleby narrated a three-minute story—"The Swiss Spaghetti Harvest"—accompanied by video on the British Broadcasting Corporation's (BBC) news show *Panorama*. A part of the transcript of that tale, written by David Wheeler, is found above. Set in Ticino, a town on the borders of Switzerland and Italy, Dimbleby talks about the bumper spaghetti harvest taking place, while the footage of cameraman Charles de Jaeger displays a Swiss family dressed in traditional Alpine clothing pulling pasta off of spaghetti trees and placing it into baskets. Because Dimbleby had a reputation of being one of the most revered public figures in Britain, he was able to fool many of his viewers. With de Jaeger's staged video, Dimbleby was able to present the hoax in such a convincing manner that hundreds of viewers telephoned the BBC wanting to know how they could grow their own spaghetti trees! De Jaeger had used twenty pounds of moist, cooked spaghetti and hired some local girls

---

1. Dimbleby, "Swiss Spaghetti."

to hang it in some trees. Then, he filmed them climbing ladders and carrying wicker baskets they filled with picked spaghetti, which was then laid out to dry in the sun. After he had all the footage he needed, he prepared a spaghetti feast for the actors, which he also filmed. The April Fool's Day joke was kept a secret in the BBC office until the episode aired. Then, due to the number of telephone calls, the BBC broadcast a statement later in the evening in which it informed viewers of the hoax.

April Fool's Day is the name given to the first day of the month of April, when the annual custom of practical jokes and hoaxes occur. On this day, jokesters often expose their pranks by shouting, "April Fools!" at the recipient. There are multiple theories as to the origin of the day, but no one is sure where playing harmless pranks originated; all that is known is that jokes and hoaxes seem to be relatively common around the world. Nevertheless, controversy surrounds pranks. The positive view is that jokes are good for one's health because it brings forth laughter, which reduces stress. The negative view is the hoaxes can be manipulative, rude, or misinformational; genuine news or an important warning on the day can be misinterpreted and ignored. Also, stories designed to be jokes can be taken seriously, resulting in a waste of resources when the hoax presents people in some kind of danger. Both those for and against April Fool's Day pranks can learn from "The Swiss Spaghetti Harvest" story.

Journal/Meditation: Are you for or against April Fool's Day jokes, hoaxes, and pranks? What do you learn from "The Swiss Spaghetti Harvest" story?

Prayer: LORD, you created me and endowed me with wisdom and reason. Give me a discerning heart that I do not harm others in any way on this April Fool's Day. May all laughter be to your glory forever. Amen.

INTERNATIONAL DAY OF CONSCIENCE
April 5

Text: "Recalling the preamble to the Universal Declaration of Human Rights, in which it is stated that disregard and contempt for human rights have resulted in barbarous acts which have outraged the conscience of humankind, and the advent of a world in which human beings shall enjoy freedom of speech and belief and freedom from fear and want has been proclaimed as the highest aspiration of the common people . . . ; reaffirming . . . that the task of the United Nations to save future generations from the scourge of war requires transformation towards a culture of peace, which consists of values, attitudes, and behaviors that reflect and inspire social interaction and sharing based on the principles of freedom, justice, and democracy, all human rights, tolerance, and solidarity, that reject violence and endeavor to prevent conflicts by tackling their root causes to solve problems through dialogue and negotiation and that guarantee the full exercise of all rights and the means to participate fully in the development process of their society; [the General Assembly of the United Nations] declares 5 April the International Day of Conscience; [and] underlines that the International Day of Conscience constitutes a means of regularly mobilizing the efforts of the international community to promote peace, tolerance, inclusion, understanding, and solidarity, in order to build a sustainable world of peace, solidarity, and harmony."[2]

Reflection: On July 25, 2019, The General Assembly of the United Nations passed Resolution 75/329, from which the above text is taken, declaring April 5 the annual International Day of Conscience. According to International Event Day, the U.N. "acknowledges that all the crimes against humanity were motivated by the attempt to gain more control over other communities without considering the dignity of their culture, values, and the right to live the way they want . . ."[3] When that has occurred in history, the result is colonization, holocaust, massacres, and other crimes against humanity of which the world is ashamed. The U.N. thinks "that conscience stops people from committing crimes against others."[4] And that is why it recently instituted the International Day of Conscience. As is noted in the above text, "The core values that underlie this day include peace, tolerance, understanding, solidarity, and inclusion. Moreover, [the day] insists upon the global community to have a firm belief in coexistence, acceptance of different cultures, diversity, and cultural assortment. . . . [P]eace and stability in the world cannot be achieved without promoting inter-cultural harmony . . . . [C]onscience is an influential entity that obliges people to condemn evil practices like colonization, racial discrimination, social stratification, gender discrimination, religious discrimination, social injustice, human trafficking, drug smuggling, organ smuggling, and war crimes against marginalized communities, anarchic regions, and weaker/unstable countries."[5] In other words, "This day is celebrated to highlight the importance of conscience and the role of conscience in stopping people from harming others orally, physically, sexually, or mentally. . . . [It] is celebrated to highlight that everyone has self-respect and the right to live with peace and security."[6]

According to "International Day of Conscience: Commemorating the Importance of the Human Conscience," "Conscience refers to a person's moral sense of right and wrong, viewed as acting as a guide to one's behavior." It is "a built-in sense which prompts a person to act in accordance with what he or she considers to be correct, right, or morally good together with a feeling of obligation to do right or be good. The importance of conscience lies in the core of inward looking and self-reflection, so as to think and whereupon act in a way considered morally correct. . . . [T]he sense of conscience functions as a mechanism of self-examination and understanding of one's actions and their consequences. . . . [F]ailing to act in a way that is considered

2. United Nations General Assembly, A/RES/73/329.
3. "International Event Day."
4. "International Event Day."
5. "International Event Day."
6. "International Event Day."

morally good can bring to a person feelings of guilt, regret, and the inner need for self-improvement. . . . [A] well-formed conscience among individuals and societies is able to promote a culture of peace."[7] Human beings, who are highly influenced by thoughts and feelings, "are governed by conscience, and history proves that the nations who regarded conscience were just, and those who did not regard it became cruel. Morality, ethics, and virtue are guided by conscience, and conscience stops people and nations from exploiting others."[8] In a world that continues to suffer from conflicts and turbulence, which create uncertainty and encroachment on human rights, building a world of peace becomes an integral part of culture. By raising awareness of the issues involved in conscience and peace, the day reminds people to self-reflect, to follow their conscience, to act morally, and to love building a culture of peace based on the values of equality, tolerance, justice, freedom, solidarity, pluralism, and mutual understanding. According to the "International Day of Conscience" on the U.N. website, "The task of constructing a culture of peace requires comprehensive educational, cultural, social, and civic action, in which each person has something to learn and something to give and share."[9] The goal is "to make a culture of peace inseparable from culture [itself] and to take root in people's hearts and minds. Peace is not only the absence of differences and conflicts. It is a positive, dynamic, participatory process linked intrinsically to democracy, justice, and development for all by which differences are respected, dialogue is encouraged, and conflicts are constantly transformed by non-violent means into new avenues of cooperation."[10] In summary, ". . . [A] culture of peace is a set of values, attitudes, traditions and customs, modes of behavior and way of life that reflect and are directed towards respect for life for human beings and their rights, the rejection of violence in all its forms, the recognition of the equal rights of men and women, the recognition of the rights of everyone to freedom of expression, opinion, and information, attachment to the principles of democracy, freedom, justice, development for all, tolerance, solidarity, pluralism, and acceptance of differences and understanding between nations, between ethnic, religious, cultural, and other groups and between individuals."[11]

Journal/Meditation: What disregarded human right have you experienced resulting in a morally offensive act? Explain. Where do you experience someone, a group, or a nation attempting to gain control over someone else, another group, or another nation? What are the results? In your opinion, specifically what keeps the world from achieving a culture of peace?

---

7. "International Day of Conscience: Commemorating."
8. "International Event Day."
9. "International Day of Conscience."
10. "International Day of Conscience."
11. "International Day of Conscience."

Prayer: Creator God, you have given conscience to people to guide their behavior. Bestow your grace that forms and informs human conscience so that oral, physical, sexual, and mental harm are replaced with respect for equal human rights, freedom, justice, and the acceptance of differences that leads to peace among individuals, groups, and nations. Fill me with a desire to participate in this exciting and dynamic process that can change the world with conscience. Amen.

National Beer Day
April 7

Text: "The manufacturer for sale of beer, ale, porter, wine, similar fermented malt or vinous liquor, or fruit juice, containing one-half of one per centum of alcohol by volume and not more than 3.2 per centum of alcohol by weight, shall, before engaging in business, secure a permit authorizing him [or her] to engage in such manufacture, which permit shall be obtained in the same manner as permit under the National Prohibition Act, as amended and supplemented, to manufacture intoxicating liquor, and be subject to all the provisions of law relating to such a permit. Such permit may be issued to a manufacturer for sale of any such fermented malt or vinous liquor or fruit juice, containing less than one-half of one per centum of alcohol by volume . . . . Such permit shall specify a maximum alcoholic content permissible for such fermented malt or vinous liquor or fruit juice at the time of withdrawal from the factory or other disposition, which shall not be greater than 3.2 per centum of alcohol by weight, nor greater than the maximum alcoholic content permissible under the law of the state, territory, or the District of Columbia . . . ."[12]

Reflection: The above text, taken from the Cullen-Harrison Act—otherwise known as Public Law 73–3—, refined the definition of an alcoholic beverage under the Volstead Act from 0.5 percent to 3.2 percent. The eighteenth amendment to the United States Constitution had been ratified in January 1919; it established Prohibition, but it did not define what intoxicating liquors meant. A bill attempting to do so was vetoed by President Woodrow Wilson on October 27, 1919. However, the National Prohibition Act (Volstead Act) became law when Wilson's veto was overridden by the House of Representatives the same day, and by the Senate the next day. Before the eighteenth amendment was repealed by the twenty-first amendment on December 5, 1933—also cancelling the Volstead Act—President Franklin D. Roosevelt signed the five-page Public Law 73–3, from which the above text is taken, into law on March 23, 1933, the day after it had been passed by congress. That law made it legal to sell 3.2 percent beer and low-alcoholic-content wine, effective April 7, 1933. With the end of prohibition on December 5, 1933, Public Law 73–3 was abrogated. That is why National Beer Day is marked on April 7. Upon signing the bill, Roosevelt is reported to have said, "I

---

12. "Public Law 73–3."

The Month of April

think this would be a good time for a beer."[13] As demonstrated in his 1932 campaign, Roosevelt was against Prohibition, which had been meant to end alcoholism, but had instead led to lawlessness and helped foster organized crime. Thus within the first one hundred days of his presidency, he had made 3.2 percent beer and wine legal even though all of Prohibition would be repealed nine months later. National Beer Day was created by Justin Smith, a Richmond, Virginia, Craft Beer Examiner, and his friend, Mike Connolly, from Liverpool, England. Smith's Facebook page caught the attention of Colorado Beer Examiner Eli Shayotovich. And, since 2009, National Beer Day has been celebrated in the U.S. The day before, April 6, is known as New Beer's Eve.

National American Beer Day (NABD) is marked on October 27, the day in 1919 Wilson vetoed what became the National Prohibition Act (Volstead Act). NABD celebrates the storied history of beer making in America. As early as 9500 BCE beer was being made. Before the U.S. was a country, beer was being brewed by Native Americans using corn, birch sap, berries, and other ingredients. Beer is the third most widely consumed beverage after water and tea. The first national beer brand sold in the U.S. was Anheuser-Busch in St. Louis; it was begun by Eberhard Anheuser in 1860, but when his daughter married Adolphus Busch, a brewery supplier, it was renamed Anheuser-Busch. While several large beer makers remain, the majority of new breweries are small breweries and brewpubs, making craft brews. Beer styles originating in the U.S. include American pale ale, Pennsylvania porter, American IPA (India Pale Ale), steam beer, amber ale, cream ale, and Cascadian dark ale. Not only are New Beer's Eve (April 6), National Beer Day (April 7), and National American Beer Day (October 27) beer days, but this non-exhaustive list also includes National Hangover Day (January 1), Baltic Porter Day (January 18), National Beer Can Appreciation Day (January 24), World Bartender Day (February 24), International Women's Collaboration Brew Day (March 8), St. Patrick's Day (March 17), National Bock Beer Day (March 20), Orval Day (March 23), King Gambrinus Day (April 11), German Beer Day (April 23), National Homebrew Day (May 7), National Bourbon Day (June 14), National IPA Day (First Thursday in August), International Beer Day (First Friday in August), National Sour Beer Day (September 20), Crush a Can Day (September 27), National Drink a Beer Day (September 28), Barrel-Aged Beer Day (First Friday of October) National Beer and Pizza Day (October 9), Homebrewing Legalization Day (October 14), International Stout Day (First Thursday of November), Learn How to Home-brew Day (First Saturday of November), National Repeal Day (December 5), National Lager Day (December 10), and New Year's Eve (December 31), to name a few! Beer days are celebrated by visiting one of the 2,100 breweries in the U.S., drinking a glass of favorite ale or lager, touring a brewery, or visiting a bottling works. Anyone one of these beer days is a good time for a beer.

---

13. "Franklin D. Roosevelt Presidential Library."

Journal/Meditation: What is the spirituality of drinking beer? When is your favorite time to drink beer? Among drinks—like water, tea, lemonade, soda, etc.—where does beer rank for you? Why?

Prayer: O God, you have given people the knowledge to brew all types of beer from corn, berries, sap, and other ingredients. It gives joy to those who drink it. Give me the wisdom to drink beer and other alcoholic beverages responsibly. Amen.

World Health Day
April 7

Text: "Health is a state of complete physical, mental, and social wellbeing and not merely the absence of disease or infirmity. The enjoyment of the highest attainable standard of health is one of the fundamental rights of every human being without distinction of race, religion, political belief, economic, or social condition. The health of all peoples is fundamental to the attainment of peace and security and is dependent upon the fullest cooperation of individuals and states. . . . The objective of the World Health Organization shall be the attainment by all peoples of the highest possible level of health."[14]

Reflection: Every year on April 7, World Health Day is celebrated by the World Health Organization (WHO). It is a global health awareness day marked on the occasion of WHO's founding, April 7, 1948. In 1945, three U.N. delegates—one from China, Norway, and Brazil—discussed the possibility of creating an international organization under the auspices of the U.N. By July 22, 1946, WHO's constitution had been written and signed by all the members of the U.N., making it the first specialized agency of the U.N. The constitution became effective on April 7, 1948, which is why World Health Day is marked that day. After the constitution was approved and became effective, WHO's first act was to create World Health Day, first observed on July 22, the day the members of the U.N. signed the constitution, but later changed to April 7 to commemorate the establishment of WHO. Annually, World Health Day draws attention to a subject of major importance for world health by employing a specific theme since 1950. Themes have covered the heart, oral health, polio, aging, blood, mental health, antimicrobial resistance, diabetes, depression, universal health coverage, and, most recently, coronavirus. As a specialized agency of the United Nations, WHO's main objective, as noted in the above text, is the attainment by all peoples of the highest possible level of health. On World Health Day, a focus is given to an important public health issue that affects the international community. According to the "World Health Organization" U.N. page, "health is a shared responsibility, involving equitable

---

14. "Constitution of the World Health Organization."

access to essential care and collective defense against transnational threats."[15] WHO responds using a six-point agenda, which consist of two health objectives, two strategic needs, and two operational approaches. The first health objective is promoting development because "poverty continues to contribute to poor health, and poor health anchors large populations in poverty. Health development is directed by the ethical principle of equity," that is "access to life-saving or health-promoting interventions should not be denied for unfair reasons . . . ."[16] The second health objective is fostering health security; threats to health security demand collective action. "One of the greatest threats to international health security arises from outbreaks of emerging and epidemic-prone diseases." The first strategic need is the strengthening of health systems, that is, "health services must reach poor and underserved populations."[17] This requires "adequate numbers of appropriately trained staff, sufficient financing, suitable systems for collecting vital statistics, and access to appropriate technology including essential drugs."[18] The second strategic need is harnessing research, information, and evidence. "WHO generates authoritative health information, in consultation with leading experts, to set norms and standards, articulate evidence-based policy options, and monitor the evolving global heath situation."[19] The first operational approach is enhancing partnerships within U.N. agencies, international organizations, donors, civil society, and the private sector. WHO encourages partners to implement programs within countries using the best technical guidelines and practices. The second operational approach is improving performance; "WHO participates in ongoing reforms aimed at improving its efficiency and effectiveness, both at the international level and within countries. . . . [I]ts strongest asset—its staff—works in an environment that is motivating and rewarding."[20]

Only three United States presidents have endorsed the observance of World Health Day. The first was Dwight D. Eisenhower in 1959; he acknowledged that mental illness—the theme for that year—was "one of the great areas of human need which required . . . active concern working in concert with . . . neighbors in the United Nations."[21] After congress passed Public Law 99–16 on April 4, 1985, stating that "the health of a nation depends upon the health of its people" and "improvement of the health of the people of our nation contributes to world health, and world health contributes to the health of our nation,"[22] President Ronald Reagan issued a proclamation, in which he stated, ". . . [G]ood health is a priceless commodity, which all the

15. "World Health Organization."
16. "World Health Organization."
17. "World Health Organization."
18. "World Health Organization."
19. "World Health Organization."
20. "World Health Organization."
21. Eisenhower, "Statement, World Health Day."
22. "Public Law 99–16."

world's people should have the opportunity to enjoy throughout their life span."[23] As congress had indicated, Reagan proclaimed April 1–7, 1985, World Health Week, and April 7, 1985, World Health Day. After congress issued Public Law 99-268 on March 27, 1986, authorizing and requesting the president to designate April 6–12, 1986, World Health Week, and April 7, 1986, World Health Day,[24] Reagan did so. In his proclamation, Reagan wrote, ". . . [G]ood health is a priceless treasure and . . . recent advances in the sciences of medicine, nutrition, hygiene, public health, and immunology make the possession of that treasure possible for more people than ever before."[25] He added, "In recent years, health leaders and private physicians in the United States have emphasized how much each person can do to maintain good health by a regimen of good diet, proper exercise, and the avoidance of substance abuse."[26] The third president to mark World Health Day was Donald J. Trump on April 7, 2020. He issued a message about "the challenges posed by the coronavirus pandemic" and reiterated the basic guidelines people should follow to protect themselves from the spread of the virus. He paid tribute to all "doctors, nurses, health care administrators, researchers, scientists, educators, public health officials, and all of the extraordinary men and women who [were] helping diagnose, heal, inform, protect, and reassure the American people."[27]

Journal/Meditation: What is your definition of health? Do you think that health is a fundamental right of every person? Explain. What do you consider the greatest health area of human need to be today? Explain.

Prayer: Merciful God, through the work of human hands, you provide health care to all who suffer from disease around the world. Pour you blessings upon all seeking treatment, all caregivers, all medical scientists striving to find cures, and all global partners working together to improve health delivery systems. Hear my prayer of thanksgiving for your healing presence today on World Health Day, tomorrow, and forever. Amen.

National Former Prisoner(s) of War Recognition Day
April 9

Text: "Whereas thousands of members of the Armed Forces of the United States who served in . . . wars were captured by the enemy and held as prisoners of war; whereas many such prisoners of war were subjected to brutal and inhumane treatment by their

23. Reagan, "Proclamation 5316."
24. "Public Law 99-268."
25. Reagan, "Proclamation 5454."
26. Reagan, "Proclamation 5454."
27. Trump, "Message."

captors in violation of international codes and customs for the treatment of prisoners of war and died, or were disabled, as a result of such treatment; whereas these great sacrifices of former prisoners of war and their families deserve national recognition: Now, therefore, be it resolved by the Senate and the House of Representatives of the United State of America in congress assembled, that April 9, 1988, is designated as 'National Former Prisoners of War Recognition Day,' in honor of the members of the Armed Forces of the United States who have been held as prisoners of war...."[28]

Reflection: The above text, Public Law 100–269, became law on March 28, 1988. Ronald Reagan became the first U.S. president to issue a proclamation that April 9, 1988, was National Former Prisoners of War Recognition Day. The opening paragraph of his proclamation recounted the reason April 9 was chosen for the observance: "... [I]n 1942 ... U.S. forces holding out on the Bataan Peninsula in the Philippines were captured. Later, as prisoners of war, these gallant Americans were subjected to the infamous Bataan Death March and to other inhumane treatment that killed thousands of them before they could be liberated."[29] Near the end of his one and one-half page proclamation, Reagan added, "To our former prisoners of war who endured so much, we say that with your example and with God's help we will seek to meet the standards of devotion you have set; we will never forget your service or your sacrifice."[30] On April 13, 1989, Public Law 101–13, worded exactly the same as its predecessor, was issued, and George Bush issued his first National Former Prisoners of War Recognition Day. "Few Americans could appreciate [our nation's freedoms] than those who suffered capture and imprisonment during times of war," he wrote.[31] Expanding the application of the day beyond its original inception, Bush declared: "Thousands of Americans captured during World War II and the Korean and Vietnam conflicts endured starvation, disease, and physical and psychological torture, in addition to separation from loved ones. Our nation must never forget the great price these and other Americans paid so that we might live in peace and freedom."[32] On April 5, 1990, Public Law 101–266, worded exactly the same as its predecessors, was issued, and George Bush issued a proclamation, stating, "Few of us could have a more profound understanding of the value of liberty than these [prisoners of war] who once experienced the terrible reality of life without it."[33] On March 28, 1991, congressed passed Public Law 102–23, which specifically mentioned the capture of U.S. Armed Forces by the armed forces of Iraq as being held as prisoners of war and how they endured incredible hardships. It also changed the name of the day from "Former Prisoners"

28. "Public Law 100–269."
29. Reagan, "Proclamation 5788."
30. Reagan, "Proclamation 5788."
31. Bush, "Proclamation 5951."
32. Bush, "Proclamation 5951."
33. Bush, "Proclamation 6113."

to "Former Prisoner." It asked Bush to designate April 9, 1991, and April 9, 1992, as "National Former Prisoner of War Recognition Day." Bush responded on April 3, 1991, with a proclamation, writing: "While we celebrate the liberation of Kuwait [in the Persian Gulf War] and the triumphant return of our courageous troops, we also pause to remember with solemn pride and appreciation, those service members who bore heavy costs in this conflict. Among them are Americas who were held as prisoners of war."[34] He added, "Their faith in Almighty God, their love of family, and their deep sense of patriotism and self-discipline have been an inspiration to us all."[35] Bush mentioned that Americans have been prisoners of war (POW) during World War II, the Korean conflict, the Vietnam War, and other conflicts. ". . . American POWs have demonstrated an unfailing devotion to duty, honor, and country," he said. And he called upon "[a]ll Americans to join in remembering former American prisoners of war and their families, who have suffered at the hands of our enemies."[36]

On August 2, 1993, congress enacted Public Law 103–60, which, except for one paragraph and the name change (indicated above) was identical to Public Law 100–269, authorized and requested the president to issue a proclamation designating April 9, 1994, National Former Prisoner of War Recognition Day. President William J. Clinton responded with his first such proclamation, writing, "Today, we honor the particular sacrifice of the thousands of Americans who have been captured and held as prisoners of war—in Europe and the Pacific, in Korea and Vietnam, in the Persian Gulf during Operation Desert Storm, and elsewhere."[37] Clinton issued similar documents in 1995 (Proclamation 6782) and 1996 (Proclamation 6879) in response to Senate Joint Resolution 26 of January 31, 1995; in 1987 (Proclamation 6986) in response to Senate Resolution 68 of March 20, 1997; in 1988 (Proclamation 7079), 1999 (Proclamation 7182), and 2000 (Proclamation 7289). In his first of eight National Former Prisoner of War Recognition Day proclamations, George W. Bush stated, ". . . [O]ur living former prisoners of war form a living testament to the courage Americans have shown in defending liberty. . . . [P]risoners endured, in addition to separation from their loved ones, isolation, disease, and torture. . . . American troops . . . stood bravely in the face of enemy capture and returned home with honor." Later, near the end of the two-page document, he added, "We remain committed to ensuring that future generations know of their heroism in order to full appreciate their courage and resolve."[38] Bush issued similar proclamations in 2002 (Proclamation 7538), 2003 (Proclamation 7660), 2004 in response to Senate Joint Resolution 13 issued May 22, 2003 (Proclamation 7770), 2005 (Proclamation 7880), 2006 (Proclamation 7998), 2007 (Proclamation 8121) and 2008 (Proclamation 8234). "Today we honor all prisoners of war by

---

34. Bush, "Proclamation 6267."
35. Bush, "Proclamation 6267."
36. Bush, "Proclamation 6267."
37. Clinton, "Proclamation 6541."
38. Bush, G.W., "Proclamation 7421."

recognizing the tremendous sacrifices made and the hardships endured by those who fight for our freedom," stated Barack Obama in his first National Former Prisoner of War Recognition Day proclamation in 2009.[39] After recounting the April 9, 1942, surrender of about 10,000 to 12,000 U.S. military personnel and 65,000 to 76,000 Filipino soldiers on the Bataan Peninsula in the Philippines and the Bataan Death March that began on April 9, 1942, and lasted for almost two weeks, along with 1,600 American POWs in the Korean War and American POWs in the Vietnam War, Obama stated, "There are countless tales of the bravery of American prisoners of war—of the burdens borne, of the acts of heroism."[40] Obama issued seven more such proclamations in 2010 (Proclamation 8490), 2011 (Proclamation 8652), 2012 (Proclamation 8799), 2013 (Proclamation 8956), 2014 (Proclamation 9102), 2015 (Proclamation 9252), and 2016 (Proclamation 9421). In honor of the seventy-fifth anniversary of the fall of Bataan, Senate Resolution 138, issued April 25, 2017, honors "servicemen and servicewomen [who have been] held as prisoners of war [and] have endured unimaginable cruelty and unspeakable treatment at the hands of their captors" in British prison ships, tiger cages in North Vietnam, coal mines in Japan, and mind shafts in Germany.[41] In response to the three-page resolution, President Donald J. Trump issued a proclamation on April 7, 2017, stating: ". . . America honors our service men and women imprisoned during war. These patriots have moved and inspired our nation through their unyielding sacrifices and devout allegiance."[42] Before narrating the history of the day, he notes that "more than half a million Americans have been captured and interned as POWs since the American Revolution." And later he adds: "They have been stripped of liberty, and regained it. They have faced the darkness of captivity, and emerged to the warm light of freedom. These victories have no match. These triumphs ignite the flame of liberty deep within their hearts, and in ours, and make America the great nation it is today."[43] Trump issued three more such proclamations in 2018 (Proclamation 9722), 2019 (Proclamation 9861), and 2020 (Proclamation 10008). In his first proclamation of National Former Prisoner of War Recognition Day in 2021, President Joseph R. Biden noted, "Enduring with limitless dignity and determination, . . . former prisoners of war are a powerful reminder that their indomitable spirit could not be broken, even by brutal treatment in contravention of international law and morality." He added, ". . . [P]risoners of war steadfastly demonstrated their devotion to duty, honor, and country."[44] Thus, on April 9 annually, the men and women of the U.S. Armed Forces, who endured brutal treatment as prisoners of war, who suffered

---

39. Obama, "Proclamation 8360."
40. Obama, "Proclamation 8360."
41. "Senate Resolution 138."
42. Trump, "Proclamation 9591."
43. Trump, "Proclamation 9591."
44. Biden, "Proclamation 10176."

separation from family, who displayed incredible endurance and faith during captivity, are honored.

Journal/Meditation: Why do you think prisoners of war appreciate national freedoms more than most citizens? In what specific ways do prisoners of war demonstrate devotion to duty, honor, and country? How do prisoners of war form a living testament to the courage Americans have shown in defending liberty?

Prayer: God, you bestow liberty and freedom on all people. However, during times of war, enemies strip liberty and freedom from prisoners of war. Help my country to restore these precious gifts that their light may shine for all to see forever. Amen.

NATIONAL PET DAY
April 11

Text: "I believe all animals are sentient beings that deserve our love and compassion . . . even not-so-cuddly animals like reptiles and rats. No animal should ever have to suffer, especially at the hand of humans. Millions of unwanted animals perish every day, due to just that . . . being 'unwanted.' I'd like to ask animal lovers everywhere to pledge to give . . . to their favorite animal shelter or rescue to help support animals in need."[45]

Reflection: Even though National Pet Month is observed in May in the United States, National Pet Day is celebrated on April 11. It was founded in 2006 by Colleen Paige, whose words form the text above. Paige is a Pet and Family Lifestyle Expert, an animal welfare advocate, an animal behaviorist, an interior designer, a writer, a photographer, and an author.[46] She founded the day "to celebrate the joy pets bring to our lives and to create public awareness about the plight of many different kinds of animals awaiting a forever home in shelters and rescues all around the globe."[47] According to *National Today*, Paige "encouraged people who want[ed] purebred dogs and cats to contact rescue organizations instead of going to a breeder. 'Don't shop! Adopt!' has become the holiday motto."[48] Paige is also responsible for founding National Puppy Day (March 23), National Dog Day (August 26), and National Cat Day (October 29), to name but a few, in order to save millions of unwanted pets.

The most popular ten pets, beginning with the most popular, are: dog, cat, fish, bird (parakeet, cockatiel, parrot, etc.), hamster/gerbil/mouse, horse, snake, guinea pig, lizard (iguana, chameleon, gecko, etc.), and tarantula.[49] Other pets include chickens,

---

45. Paige, "National Pet Day: Life Upgraded."
46. Paige, "About Colleen."
47. "National Pet Day: Life Upgraded."
48. "National Pet Day—April 11, 2022."
49. "National Pet Day—April 11, 2022."

ferrets, rabbits, rats, and hedgehogs. People celebrate National Pet Day by buying a special treat for their pet, buying a special gift, buying a special toy, being more patient, going for a walk, or taking their pet for a drive. Many Americans are known to treat their pets like family members, watch TV and read books with them, and talk to them regularly. Some people mark the day by volunteering at the local animal shelter, adopting a pet from the local animal shelter, bringing a supply of animal food to the local animal shelter, or making a donation to the local animal shelter. According to *Days of the Year*, "National Pet Day celebrates the joy that pets bring into people's lives and encourages people to help reduce the number of animals in shelters. Bringing humans and animals together helps make the world a better place."[50] It is important to keep in mind that "[e]ncouraging adoption as a first choice is one of the main ideas behind National Pet Day," while celebrating "the unconditional love that animals give to people in their daily lives" and encouraging "people to take the time to spend time with their beloved animals."[51]

Journal/Meditation: If you own a pet, what joy does it bring to your life? How would you characterize the unconditional love it shows you? If you do not own a pet, whom do you know who does? What joy does his or her pet bring to his or her life? How would you characterize the unconditional love it shows to your friend? How do you intend to celebrate National Pet Day?

Prayer: You have entrusted the care of all animals to people, Creator God, to give them joy and unconditional love. Move more and more human hearts to recognize animals as sentient beings who deserve love and compassion and to rescue them from suffering and early death. May my care for your creatures become a sign of your care for me. Amen.

Easter Sunday
March 22–April 25

Text: "Easter celebrates the central stories on which Christianity is based, concerning the most influential figure in Western civilization, yet its mythical theme of death-and-resurrection is universal. Easter also comes at a most propitious time of the year, when springtime renewal and rebirth are in the air.... The archetypal motif of death-and-resurrection has existed all over the world since time immemorial.... Christians express Easter's meaning through its... symbols and rituals.... [R]ebirth depends on death."[52]

---

50. "National Pet Day," *Days of the Year*.
51. "National Pet Day," *Days of the Year*.
52. George, *Mythology*, 69.

Reflection: The central story of Christianity is the death of Jesus—marked on the Good Friday before Easter Sunday—and the resurrection of Jesus—marked three biblical days later on Easter. Belief in the resurrection is a matter of faith. However, one does not have to believe in order to celebrate Easter. In the ancient world before zero was invented, the first day (Friday) to the third day (Sunday) were not considered two days, but three. And three in biblical literature indicates the spiritual order; it is another way to write about the divine presence or God (spirituality). Furthermore, "The three-day motif . . . reflects lunar mythology based on the lunar cycle. Traditionally, the period in which the waning moon dies, the moon is not visible (is dead), and the waxing moon appears (is reborn) is viewed as three days. . . . Three days is the period in which mythical figures are dead or dormant before being revived," writes Arthur George.[53] In Greek, the word for Easter is *pascha*, which refers to the Jewish Passover festival and the passover lamb sacrificed on the afternoon before Passover began in commemoration of the lamb's blood sprinkled on the lintel and doorposts of Hebrew homes in Egypt to protect those within from the imminent death of the firstborn. The English word *Easter* comes from Eostre (also Eastre), a goddess of dawn, spring, and fertility. Thus, it is not difficult to see that while modern Easter Sunday remembers divine intervention raising Jesus from the grave, it is also peppered with dawn, spring, and fertility. Its very calculation—being the first Sunday after the first full moon after the Spring Equinox—indicates its connection to spring. Thus, Easter occurs on a Sunday between March 22 and April 25.

The death-and-resurrection motif is based on the seasonal agricultural cycle. In the autumn, things begin to shrivel and die. Winter pronounces the death sentence. But with the passing of winter, spring brings forth new life. The motif is echoed in spirituality; a person dies to himself or herself through divine contact in prayer, fasting, and baptism, and is born anew. To illustrate the universal theme of death-and-resurrection, a variety of signs gradually were gathered around Easter. For example, fire, which represents life, renewal, transformation, and purification—a deity itself at one time—kindled from flint and steel and not embers from an existing fire, came to represent new life, renewal, purification, and transformation from death to life. Eggs, inanimate objects that produced life, came to be understood as possessing the divine life force. Thus, they became signs of immortality, the cosmos (earth, heaven, sun, moon), the rebirth of spring, colored red to represent blood (life) or other colors to represent the colors of spring, and the tomb out of which Christ emerged. The Easter lily, which emerges from a seemingly dead bulb and produces trumpet-like blossoms, is a sign of the death-and-resurrection motif. The newness of Easter and spring came to be represented by new clothes and, for a time, Easter bonnets! The fertility dimension of Easter was captured in the Easter Bunny, who brought the Easter eggs; a rabbit can give birth to a litter every twenty-eight to thirty days! Sunrise services, held early

---

53. George, *Mythology*, 91.

on Easter Sunday morning connect the death-and-resurrection motif to dawn, the new light of every day that conquers the night.

Journal/Meditation: What is your favorite sign of Easter? How does it illustrate the death-and-resurrection motif? How does it fit into your spirituality?

Prayer: God of death and God of life, both within and without me you present your truth that my rebirth depends on death. Through the signs that surround me, help me to plumb the depths of your wisdom. And grant that I may one day pass through death to eternal life with you. Amen.

THOMAS JEFFERSON'S BIRTHDAY
April 13

Text: "We hold these truths to be self-evident, that all men [and women] are created equal, that they are endowed by their Creator with certain unalienable rights, that among these are life, liberty, and the pursuit of happiness. That to secure these rights, governments are instituted among men [and women], deriving their just powers from the consent of the governed. That whenever any form of government becomes destructive of these ends, it is the right of the people to alter or to abolish it, and to institute new government, laying its foundation on such principles and organizing its powers in such form as to them shall seem most likely to effect their safety and happiness."[54]

Reflection: The text above is taken from "The Declaration of Independence," whose principal author was Thomas Jefferson (April 13, 1743–July 4, 1826). Jefferson was an American statesman, a diplomat, a lawyer, an architect, a musician, a philosopher, and a founding father of the United States. From 1801 to 1809, he served as the third president of the U.S. (sworn in by Chief Justice John Marshall at the new Capitol Building in Washington, DC, on March 4, 1801), and before that he served as John Adams's vice president from 1797 to 1801, and before that he was George Washington's Secretary of State from 1790 to 1793. While he shunned organized religion, he was a strong proponent of democracy, republicanism, and individual rights. The ideals, values, and teachings of the Enlightenment were his guiding light, as can be found in his appeal to the "Supreme Judge of the world for the rectitude of [the Declaration's signers'] intentions . . . , in the name, and by the authority of the good people of [the thirteen united] colonies . . . . [which] . . . ought to be free and independent states [and] absolved from all allegiance to the British Crown . . . ."[55] Jefferson ends the Declaration "with a firm

---

54. "Declaration of Independence."
55. "Declaration of Independence."

reliance on the protection of divine providence" and the mutual pledge of the signers' lives, fortune, and honor to each other.[56]

Other than being the principal author of "The Declaration of Independence" signed in congress on July 4, 1776, Jefferson is remembered for his work in procuring the Louisiana Territory. After Spain, to which the French had given Louisiana in 1762, ceded ownership of the 827,987 square miles back to France in 1800, Jefferson began a search for a way to buy the land. Napoleon, who had risen to power in France, offered to sell Louisiana to the U.S. for $15 million. While Jefferson was president, he urged his negotiators to seize the opportunity and accept the offer. The treaty was signed April 30, 1803, the senate ratified the purchase on October 20, 1803, and the land doubled the size of the U.S. Jefferson persuaded congress to fund an expedition to explore and map the newly acquired territory. Thus, he appointed Meriwether Lewis and William Clark to lead the Corps of Discovery (1803–6). The Corps began its exploration in May 1804 and concluded it in September 1806, bringing home scientific and geographic reports and information about the Native American tribes living on the new frontier. Because of the Declaration of Independence, the Louisiana Purchase, and much more, on March 21, 1938, President Franklin D. Roosevelt proclaimed April 13 Jefferson's Birthday. On April 13, 1976, President Gerald R. Ford recognized Jefferson as a giant in history. Ford urged citizens to reflect on the meaning and the purpose of the Declaration and on the many other works of Jefferson. On April 11, 2007, President George W. Bush proclaimed April 13 Thomas Jefferson Day, urging citizens to reflect on Jefferson's extraordinary achievements and to learn more about his influence on U.S. history and ideals. Besides having his name used for cities and counties across the U.S., Jefferson is depicted in stone on the Mount Rushmore Memorial, and he is cast in bronze in a nineteen-foot statue inside the Jefferson Memorial in Washington, DC, dedicated in 1943, the two hundredth anniversary of his birth.

Journal/Meditation: What do the words of "The Declaration of Independence"—"all men [and women] are created equal"—mean to you? What do the words of "The Declaration of Independence"—"all men [and women] . . . are endowed by their Creator with certain unalienable rights"—mean to you? What are the responsibilities you have to exercise the rights of life, liberty, and the pursuit of happiness?

Prayer: Supreme Judge, you endowed Thomas Jefferson with the ability to proclaim and defend your gifts of life, liberty, and the pursuit of happiness to those who sought to abolish them. Grant me a deep respect for the wisdom of the third president of the United States, as I share the freedom and independence which he has entrusted to my care. All glory be to you, my Creator, now and forever. Amen.

56. "Declaration of Independence."

Income Tax Day
April 15

Text: "The congress shall have power to lay and collect taxes on incomes, from whatever source derived, without apportionment among the several states, and without regard to any census or enumeration."[57]

Reflection: Amendment 16, above, to the United States Constitution modified Article 1, Section 9, of the Constitution after it was passed by congress on July 2, 1909, and ratified on February 3, 1913. The amendment made it possible for congress to establish Income Tax Day, April 15, when individual income tax returns are due to be submitted to the federal government. While a federal income tax day on personal incomes was begun with the Revenue Act of 1861 to assist in funding the Civil War, it was repealed ten years later and determined to be unconstitutional. Likewise, the Wilson-Gorman Act of 1894, a flat rate federal income tax which taxed incomes over $4,000, was determined to be unconstitutional by the U.S. Supreme Court in 1895 because it was not apportioned according to the population of each state. Eighteen years later, in 1913, the Sixteenth Amendment repealed the "no capitation, or other direct, tax shall be laid, unless in proportion to the census or enumeration herein before directed to be taken" of the Constitution (Article 1, Section 9) and gave the congress the legal authority to tax all incomes without regard to the apportionment requirement (population) of each state. On the first year of the federal income tax, 1913, tax day was March 1. In 1918, it was changed to March 15, and in 1955 to April 15, where it continues today unless it conflicts with a weekend or another holiday. With the IRS Restructuring and Reform Act of 1998, the most comprehensive reorganization and modernization of the Internal Revenue Service took place.

The basic idea behind Income Tax Day is that at the lowest common denominator the country is composed of individual citizens who have monetary incomes. While there are various conditions and tax breaks depending on a person's situation in life, all citizens to some degree contribute to the common good, what is shared by all. In other words, individuals share in the common good of highways, libraries, government buildings—villages, towns, cities, counties, states, federal—monuments, parks, etc. For all to enjoy what all provide for each other, taxes are levied on one's income; those monies are apportioned according to a budget submitted by the president and approved by the congress, both house and senate, after fine tuning it. Then, it is sent to the president for his signature. The process is designed so that all citizens provide for the common good through Income Tax Day.

Journal/Meditation: Where do you see your income tax dollars at work in the area where you live? While many people consider Income Tax Day a negative experience, what positive experiences have you had as a result of it?

---

57. "All Amendments," Amendment 16.

Prayer: Source of all life, you create community from many individuals, and, through their mutual sharing, they provide for each other's needs. Fill me with a deeper and positive appreciation for income tax day in the human family. Grant that the sharing accomplished through income tax day may abound in good deeds for all. Amen.

Patriots' Day
Third Monday

Text: "Listen my children and you shall hear / Of the midnight ride of Paul Revere, / On the eighteenth of April, in Seventy-five; / Hardly a man is now alive / Who remembers that famous day and year."[58]

Reflection: The third Monday of April is a holiday in the states of Maine and Massachusetts, and April 19, the original Patriots' Day, in Wisconsin is a special observance day for schools. As can be inferred from the opening stanza's five-lines of Henry Wadsworth Longfellow's "Paul Revere's Ride," on April 18, 1775, the colonists were prepared for the arrival of the British to fight the first battle of the American Revolutionary War (American War of Independence). That first battle was fought in the areas of Lexington, Concord, and Menotomy (now Arlington), near Boston, Massachusetts, on April 19, 1775. Among all those remembered for the bloodshed that occurred on that date is Paul Revere, who spread the word about the British invasion during the night before the battle occurred. Massachusetts Governor Frederic T. Greenhalge is credited with beginning Patriots' Day in 1894 on April 19 to commemorate the battles that officially marked the beginning of the American Revolutionary War. Maine established the holiday in 1907. In 1938, the Massachusetts legislature passed a bill establishing Patriots' Day as an annual commemoration of the opening of the American War of Independence. In 1969, the observance was moved from April 19 to the third Monday of April. Connecticut established the observance on April 16, 2018.

Patriots' Day is marked with re-enactments of the battles that occurred in Lexington, Concord, and Menotomy (Arlington). On Monday morning, mounted re-enactors retrace Paul Revere's ride, while announcing the coming of the British all along his route. It is also marked in the Boston Marathon, which was added to the day's celebration in 1897, and, like the shift in the day's observance in 1969, also now takes place on the third Monday in April. Some people consider the Boston Marathon the most significant celebration on Patriots' Day. However, what is more significant is "the fate of a nation" that "was riding that night," shouting "a cry of defiance and not of fear,"[59] warning the colonists in Lexington, Concord, and Menotomy that the war for freedom and independence was about to begin. It was "the midnight message of

---

58. Longfellow, "Paul Revere's Ride."
59. Longfellow, "Paul Revere's Ride."

Paul Revere."⁶⁰ That message, that spirit of defiance, continues to echo in those who proudly support or defend our country and its way of life. They are known as patriots.

Journal/Meditation: What do you think is the message of Patriots' Day today? Upon what does the fate of our nation depend today?

Prayer: God of all ages, on Patriots' Day I remember when my country began to claim its place among the many nations of the world. Grant many blessings of peace to my country and continue to fill her citizens with the spirit of those first patriots, who, through war, brought freedom for all. Grant this prayer today, tomorrow, and forever. Amen.

American Revolutionary War Began
April 19

Text: "We . . . , the representatives of the United States of America, in general congress, assembled, appealing to the Supreme Judge of the world for the rectitude of our intentions, do, in the name, and by authority of the good people of these colonies, solemnly publish and declare that these United Colonies are, and of right ought to be, free and independent states; that they are absolved from all allegiance to the British Crown, and that all political connection between them and the state of Great Britain is and ought to be totally dissolved; and that as free and independent states, they have full power to levy war, conclude peace, contract alliances, establish commerce, and to do all other acts and things which independent states may of right do. And for the support of this Declaration, with a firm reliance on the protection of divine providence, we mutually pledge to each other our lives, our fortunes, and our sacred honor."⁶¹

Reflection: While fifty-six men signed their names to "The Declaration of Independence"—from which the above text is taken—on July 4, 1776, the American Revolutionary War had begun on April 19, 1775. Also known as the Revolutionary War and the American War of Independence, the first battle occurred on April 19, 1775, when the British army in Boston was attacked at Lexington and Concord by the militia from Massachusetts after having destroyed gun powder stores. The fight for independence continued until September 3, 1783, when the Treaty of Paris was signed between Great Britain and the United States. Here, there is no need to recount the events of the American Revolutionary War over eight years long, as countless history books recount them in response to Great Britain's taxation policies and lack of colonial representation. The reflection here is on the last paragraph of "The Declaration of the Independence" presented above. The representatives of the thirteen colonies that became the United States invented revolution. Not only did they overthrow the rule

---

60. Longfellow, "Paul Revere's Ride."
61. "Declaration of Independence."

of King George III, they also overthrew the British Parliament government. They set in motion in the world a process in which many other countries would participate in the future. And they did all this when they were but colonists and not yet a country. In other words, they invented the process of revolution step by step.

The fifty-six signers of "The Declaration of Independence" declared a representative form of government. It is in the name and with the authority of the people of the colonies that they declare their freedom and independence from Great Britain. They are no longer colonists; with "The Declaration of Independence" they are independent states owing no allegiance to the mother country and having no political connection. All of the past has been dissolved. They declare themselves free to make war, to make peace, to contract alliances with other countries, to establish commerce, and to do all else that independent states do. They name God the Supreme Judge of the world, and they presume that he will judge their intentions to be right, even while they rely on the protection of Divine Providence, another name for God, that indicates that they think he wills what they are enacting. The fifty-six men, representing thirteen colonies—Georgia, North Carolina, South Carolina, Maryland, Virginia, Pennsylvania, Delaware, New York, New Jersey, New Hampshire, Massachusetts, Rhode Island, Connecticut—pledge to each other their lives (because they may be killed in war, or, if Great Britain conquers their revolution, they may be hanged as traitors), their fortunes (because any funds they may have had in the mother country are now forfeited, and, if they lose the war, any money, land, and personal property they have will be confiscated), and their sacred honor (because if they win, they will be honorable heroes, and if they lose, they will die an honorable death). Thus, the first Revolutionary War was fought on the continent of North America in order for thirteen colonies to gain independence from Great Britain and a form a new nation: the United States of America.

Journal/Meditation: Where do you think revolution is needed today? Explain. What is at stake should a revolution occur? What do you think is the most difficult part of a representative form of government?

Prayer: Supreme Judge of the World, you create people to be free, and through the founders of the United Colonies established the United States in which people live in freedom. In your Divine Providence, continue to pour your blessings on my life, my fortune, my honor, and this land today, tomorrow, and forever. Amen.

World Creativity and Innovation Day
April 21

Text: "Recalling the Constitution of the United Nations Educational, Scientific, and Cultural Organization, which states that the organization, as part of its purposes and functions, will maintain, increase, and diffuse knowledge by encouraging cooperation among the nations in all branches of intellectual activity; underlining the need to focus on the importance of micro-, small-, and medium-sized enterprises in achieving the Sustainable Development Goals [Resolution 70/1 of September 25, 2015], in particular in promoting innovation, creativity, and decent work for all . . . ; acknowledging that innovation is essential for harnessing the economic potential of each nation and the importance of supporting mass entrepreneurship, creativity, and innovation, which create a new momentum for economic growth and job creation and expand opportunities for all . . . ; recalling . . . that cultural and creative industries should be part of economic growth strategies; [the General Assembly of the United Nations] decides to designate 21 April as World Creativity and Innovation Day . . . in order to raise awareness of the role of creativity and innovation in problem-solving and by extension, economic, social, and sustainable development."[62]

Reflection: On April 27, 2017, the General Assembly of the United Nations passed the resolution establishing World Creativity and Innovation Day, from which comes the above text. According to the resolution, more than fifty member nations had been commemorating the day since 2002. In the words of the resolution, they had been taking action "in global partnership to promote creative environments, processes, and products."[63] Creativity refers to the quality of being able to make things. Innovation is the act of inventing or introducing something new. Both creativity and innovation, according to the U.N., spring from the encouraged "creative multidisciplinary thinking for a sustainable future" at both the individual and group levels.[64] Critical thinking leads to the development of micro-sized, small-sized, and medium-sized enterprises, which are critical to the sustainable development agenda of the U.N. "The creative industries . . . stimulate innovation and diversification, are an important factor in the burgeoning services sector, support entrepreneurship, and contribute to cultural diversity . . . ," according to Isabelle Durant.[65] According to the U.N., "A low-cost tiny home that provides everything [one] needs. A boat made of recycled plastic and flip-flops. Land use tracked by space-based tools. Vaccine-delivery drones—[all are examples of creativity and innovation and] light up the way to a better future for all."[66] While there may not be a universal understanding of creativity, nevertheless, "[t]he concept is open to interpretation from artistic expression to problem-solving in the context of economic, social, and sustainable development. . . . World Creativity and Innovation Day . . . raise[s] the awareness of the role of creativity and innovation in all aspects of human development." Thus, these "have become the true wealth of nations

---

62. United Nations General Assembly, A/RES/71/284.
63. United Nations General Assembly, A/RES/71/284.
64. "First Ever."
65. "World Creativity."
66. "World Creativity."

in the twenty-first century."[67] According to *Merinews*, ". . . [T]he creative economy, which includes audiovisual products, design, new media, performing arts, publishing and visual arts, is a highly transformation sector of the world economy in terms of income generation, job creation, and export earnings."[68]

On World Creativity and Innovation Day, first celebrated on April 21, 2018, "the world is invited to embrace the idea that innovation is essential for harnessing the economic potential of nations. Innovation, creativity, and mass entrepreneurship can provide new momentum for economic growth and job creation. It can expand opportunities for everyone . . . . It can provide solutions to some of the most pressing problems, such as poverty eradication and the elimination of hunger . . . ."[69] The U.N. reminds us that "[c]ulture is an essential component of sustainable development and represents a source of identity, innovation, and creativity for the individual and community" while also having "a significant non-monetary value that contributes to inclusive social development, to dialogue and understanding between peoples." That means that "[c]ultural and creative industries should be a part of economic growth strategies . . . ."[70] One example of how that works is seen in the U.N.'s Creative Cities Network, which promotes "cooperation with and among cities that have identified creativity as a strategic factor for sustainable urban development. [The cities in the network] "work together towards a common objective placing creativity and cultural industries at the heart of their development plans at the local level and cooperating actively at the international level."[71] Thus, on April 21, World Creativity and Innovation Day raises awareness about the importance of creativity and innovation in problem solving within cultures around the world and how both create sustainable economic and social development and growth.

Journal/Meditation: Where do you find creativity and/or innovation in micro-sized, small-sized, or medium-sized enterprises where you live? Give three examples. How do those examples contribute to cultural diversity? What problems do those examples seem to solve in your community?

Prayer: Creator God, you share your creativity with people by giving them the ability to reason to innovation in order to solve problems, advance cultural diversity, and provide economic and social development. Grace me with the ability and willingness to use my creativity to make the world a better place at home, in my city, in my country, and in the world. Amen.

---

67. "World Creativity."
68. "First Ever."
69. "First Ever."
70. "World Creativity."
71. "World Creativity."

Earth Day

April 22

Text: "This planet is threatened with destruction, and we who live in it with death. The heavens reek, the waters below are foul, and children die in infancy, and we and the world, which is our home, live on the brink of nuclear annihilation. We are in a crisis of survival."[72]

Reflection: The text above was spoken by Barry Commoner at the very beginning of "Earth Day: A Question of Survival," a special broadcast over the CBS Television Network on April 22, 1970—the first Earth Day—and hosted by Walter Cronkite. The state of the planet, as described by Commoner, represented the earth and what its inhabitants had done to their mother. The air was polluted with smog; rivers, streams, and lakes were full of toxic chemicals; and children exposed to lead in paint often died. And if that were not enough, the world's superpowers dueled off and on with nuclear weapons. Commoner's opening comments were accurate; we were, and we remain, in a crisis of survival. His words were meant to get people to support environmental protection. That first Earth Day held in the United States became an international event twenty years later in 1990 with organized responses in 141 nations, which has since expanded to 193 countries. At the minimum, Earth Day has raised awareness around the world to the destruction of our common home. While education is a primary activity in schools, clean-ups of fields, beaches, and city blocks, along with tree planting and recycling have become common in the effort to change human behavior and policy. Other Earth Day celebrations have resulted in a greater concern for air and water pollution, protection for the ozone layer, the growing of organic food, endangered species, oil spills and cleanup, peeling lead paint, global climate change, solar energy, renewable energy, wind energy, the use of plastics, green spaces, hiking trails, etc.

All the work of countless people around the world reached a pivot point on Earth Day 2016, when the most significant climate accord in the history of the movement was signed by world leaders from 175 nations. Known as the Paris Agreement of the United Nations and signed at the opening ceremony at the U.N. Headquarters in New York, the Conference of Parties represents an international political response to climate change. The twenty-five-page document hopes to achieve a universal goal on climate: keeping global warming below two-degrees Centigrade. This document represents the first time 175 nations (with two more signing later) ever affixed their signatures—indicating their intention to be bound by the agreement—to an international agreement on a single day. Echoing the previous words of Commoner, the Paris Agreement recognizes the need for an effective and progressive response to the urgent threat of climate change and acknowledges that it is a common concern of all people. In twenty-nine articles, prepared on December 12, 2015, it presents a plan for a global

---

72. Commoner, "Earth Day," 1.

response that will prevent the destruction of Mother Earth by her many and diverse children, while fostering sustainable development. The future of the planet, our home, hangs in the balance.

Journal/Meditation: How do you celebrate Earth Day? In what specific activities do you engage to support environmental protection?

Prayer: Father God, you created all people and things in wisdom and love, and you entrusted to human kind the care of your world. Fill me with a greater respect for Mother Earth, and inspire me with actions that support and protect the environment today, tomorrow, and forever. Amen.

English Language Day
April 23

Text: "There was a quiet language that began on a small cluster of islands off the coast of Western Europe. It slowly developed and spread through a few different permutations until one day, in an explosion of colonialism, it suddenly spread across the world like wildfire. It became the language of what was once the most powerful nation in the world and has since become the language of commerce in countries all over the world. English Language Day celebrates this language, its history, and its oddities! The first origins of the English Language can be found in medieval England and takes its name from the Angles. The Angles were a West Germanic tribe that found its way to England, taking their name from the Anglia peninsula that juts out into the Baltic Sea. From its inception, it has taken on grammar, tones, and words from every language it has come into contact with. There are those who would argue that English is no longer a language of its own, but an amalgam of every language it [has] come into contact with. So powerful has English become, that it is now the *Lingua Franca* of the entire world, bringing together everyone for trade and communication, and serving as a required second language in almost every nation."[73]

Reflection: The above text, taken from the "Days of the Year Calendar," summarizes the origins of the English Language in a few sentences. Because of Great Britain's colonizing practices, English has made its way around the globe, adding to its grammar, tones, and words from all other languages with which it has come in contact, and becoming the common language between people, whose native languages are different. And while there are different variations between Canadian English, United Kingdom English, Scots English, and American English, it remains the official language of over sixty countries around the world and the second language of many more. Observed on April 23, English Language Day was established by the United Nations Department of Public Information in 2010 "to celebrate multilingualism and cultural diversity as

---

73. "English Language Day."

well as to promote equal use of all six official [U.N.] languages . . . ."[74] In addition to English, the other five languages of the United Nations are Arabic (marked on December 8, the date on which the U.N. General Assembly designated it as the sixth official language of the U.N. in 1973), French (marked on March 20, International Day of Francophonie), Russian (marked on June 6, the birthday of Aleksandr Pushkin, considered by many to be the greatest Russian poet), Spanish (marked on October 12, traditionally observed in Spanish speaking countries as the day of the Hispanic), and Chinese (marked on April 20, pays tribute to a mythical figure named Cangjie, who is presumed to have invented Chinese characters around 5,000 years ago). April 23 was the date chosen for English Language Day because it is considered the traditional birthday and death day of William Shakespeare. According to a February 19, 2010, U.N. press release, "Each of the six official languages will be celebrated by the United Nations on its designated day in new and creative ways, including with unique information materials and cultural events showcasing each language through music, art, poetry, food, theater, and film screenings."[75] The focus of English Language Day, along with its other five colanguages of the U.N., is on multilingualism, and is the outgrowth from the February 15, 2002, resolution of the General Assembly acknowledging the United Nations Educational, Scientific, and Cultural Organization's decision on November 17, 1999, to proclaim February 17 "International Mother Language Day."[76]

In resolution 56/262, the General Assembly of the U.N. recognized "that the United Nations pursues multilingualism as a means of promoting, protecting, and preserving diversity of languages and cultures globally." In the two-page document, it also recognized "that genuine multilingualism promotes unity in diversity and international understanding," while recalling its emphasis on "the importance of multilingualism in United Nations public relations and information activities."[77] On July 24, 2013, in a seven-page resolution, the General Assembly of the U.N. stated that it welcomed "the implementation within the United Nations of a day dedicated to each of the official languages in order to inform and raise awareness of their history, culture, and use."[78] It also reaffirmed "that linguistic diversity is an important element of cultural diversity," it called for the elimination of "the disparity between the use of English and the use of the five other official languages" in public information, and it reaffirmed "the need to achieve full parity among the six official languages of the United Nations websites."[79] In a fifteen-page December 29, 2014, resolution, the General Assembly again emphasized "the importance of multilingualism in the activities of the United Nations," and requested the Secretary-General "to redouble his

74. "English Language Day U.N."
75. "Department of Public Information."
76. United Nations General Assembly, A/RES/56/262.
77. United Nations General Assembly, A/RES/56/262.
78. United Nations General Assembly, A/RES/67/292.
79. United Nations General Assembly, A/RES/67/292.

efforts to ensure full parity among the six official languages in accordance with General Assembly resolution 67/292 on multilingualism . . . ."[80] The Secretary-General was asked to appoint a Coordinator for Multilingualism who would be "responsible for the overall implementation of multilingualism Secretariat-wide" and to instruct the public information department "to continue to inform the public about the importance of this principle." The resolution also reiterated its concern for "the simultaneous distribution of documents in all six official languages."[81] On September 11, 2017, the General Assembly issued a ten-page document on multilingualism indicating that it was a core value of the U.N. It repeated many words of previous resolutions, but did add that "the contribution of multilingualism in promoting international peace and security, development of human rights, through the work of the United Nations departments and offices" needed to be recognized on International Mother Language Day, February 17.[82] Thus, English Language Day is one among many means of "harmonious communication among peoples and an enabler of multilateral diplomacy. . . . By promoting dialogue, tolerance, and understanding, multilingualism [of which English is a part] ensures effective participation of all in the [U.N.'s] work, as well as greater transparency and efficiencies and better outcomes."[83]

Journal/Meditation: Do you know another language? Why do you think it is important or not important to know another language? How do you think language promotes, protects, and preserves the diversity of cultures? Why is that important?

Prayer: You speak no language and all languages, O God. Through the diversity of languages, you bring harmonious communication among peoples and enable multilateral diplomacy. Grant me the grace to promote multilingualism that through dialogue, tolerance, and understanding, I may help to make the world a more peaceable place. Amen.

Administrative Professionals Week and Administrative Professionals Day
Last Full Week of April and Wednesday of the Last Full Week of April

Text: "During the [last] week of April, . . . people all across the world will be celebrating Administrative Professionals Week. . . . The profession has changed monumentally over the last fifty years. . . . We've gone through the stages of name change: secretary, office clerk, receptionist, staff assistant, office manager . . . . These . . . names have morphed into administrative assistant, administrative professional, executive assistant, senior administrative assistant . . . . More than just dealing with phone calls, and

---

80. United Nations General Assembly, A/RES/69/250.
81. United Nations General Assembly, A/RES/69/250.
82. United Nations General Assembly, A/RES/71/328.
83. "Multilingualism."

message taking, admins have to make many decisions which require critical thinking . . . ."[84]

Reflection: In the United States, the last full week of April is designated as Administrative Professional Week. The Wednesday of that week is called Administrative Professionals Day (Secretaries Day). Both the week and the day highlight the import role of administrative professionals. The origins of a day to acknowledge secretaries began with the founding of the National Secretaries Association (NSA) in 1942 to recognize the contributions of administrative personnel to the economy and to attract more workers to the occupation. Three people associated with the holiday—first official programed by U.S. Secretary of Commerce Charles W. Sawyer for the first week of June 1952—include Mary Barrett, president of NSA; C. King Woodbridge, president of Dictaphone Corporation; and Happy F. Klemfuss and Daren Ball, account executives at Young & Rubicam. In 1952, they sought to recognize the importance and value of the secretarial position to a company or business and to management, as well as encourage more women—and men today—to become secretaries. They promoted the values and importance of the job that secretaries do and created the holiday in recognition of the importance of secretaries. As is noted in the text above, much change has taken place since 1952. In 1955, the week of observance was moved from the first week of June to the last full week of April. The National Secretaries Association changed its name to Professional Secretaries International in 1981 and to the International Association of Administrative Professions in 1998. What had been National Secretaries Week and National Secretaries Day became Professional Secretaries Week and Professional Secretaries Day. In 2000, they were renamed Administrative Professionals Week and Administrative Professionals Day. The current names are broader terms meant to encompass more positions than the original secretary career.

Today, both women and men do more than answer telephone calls and take messages. Administrators are in an on-going evolution in their positions, which often require making decisions. Administrative Professionals Week and Day provide the opportunity for showing gratitude by employers and supervisors to the people upon whom they depend, to highlight the importance of administrative professionals to organizations and businesses, and to enhance the work-related skills of employees. Flowers, cards, gift certificates, candies, and gift baskets, along with taking administrative professionals to lunch, are some of the ways administrative professionals are recognized during the week or on Wednesday's Administrative Professionals Day. In the U.S. alone, there are an estimated 4.1 million administrative professionals, many of whom use their skills to work toward management positions.

Journal/Meditation: When have you most recently encountered an administrative professional? How did she or he serve you? What decisions, if any, did she or he help you make?

84. "Skinny."

Prayer: God of mercy, you created women and men and gave them work to finish. Help me to do the work you have entrusted to me that it may be a blessing to others. Give all administrative professionals the strength to follow your way this day. Amen.

Arbor Day
Last Friday

Text: "Arbor Day (which means simply 'Tree Day') is now observed in every state in our Union—and mainly in the schools. At various times from January to December, but chiefly in this month of April, you give a day or part of a day to special exercises and perhaps to actual tree planting, in recognition of the importance of trees to us as a nation, and of what they yield in adornment, comfort, and useful products to the communities in which you live."[85]

Reflection: While the first Arbor Day in the United States was sponsored by J. Sterling Morton, a resident of Nebraska City, Nebraska, during an annual meeting of the Nebraska State Board of Agriculture held in Lincoln on April 10, 1872, with an estimated one million trees planted in Nebraska, the first proclamation of an Arbor Day was made by President Theodore Roosevelt on April 15, 1907. It was addressed to school children in the U.S. As can be noted in the text above, Roosevelt indicates that Arbor Day is being observed in all the states, but primarily in the schools, where children may have planted a tree. By the 1920s, all states in the Union had passed public laws that stipulated a certain day in the annual calendar to be observed as Arbor Day. The president's proclamation focuses on the importance of trees to the nation, and he notes that within the lifetime of the children he is addressing, the nation's need for trees will become serious.[86] He also writes that "the road to success is the right use of what we have and the improvement of present opportunity." He continues, "A people without children would face a hopeless future; a country without trees is also as hopeless."[87] Roosevelt's proclamation was due primarily to Major Israel McCreight, a Pennsylvania conservationist, who, in 1906, recommended a campaign of youth education and a national policy on conservation education. Gifford Pinchot (Pixchor), Chief of the U.S. Forest Service, embraced McCreight's recommendations and asked Roosevelt to make the proclamation. Nodding his head to Forester Pinchot (Pixchor), Roosevelt states: "A true forest is not merely a storehouse full of wood, but, as it were, a factory of wood, and at the same time a reservoir of water. When you help to preserve our forests or to plant new ones, you are acting the part of good citizens."[88]

---

85. Roosevelt, T., "Arbor Day Proclamation," 9.
86. Roosevelt, T., "Arbor Day Proclamation," 9.
87. Roosevelt, T., "Arbor Day Proclamation," 9.
88. Roosevelt, T., "Arbor Day Proclamation," 9.

The mission of Arbor Day observance is to continue to urge individuals and groups to plant trees. National Arbor Day is held the last Friday in April, when it is customary to plant a tree. In 1972, the Arbor Day Foundation was founded; as a nonprofit membership organization, it is dedicated to planting trees in neighborhoods, communities, cities, and forests throughout the world to ensure a greener and healthier future for everyone. The goal of the foundation is to help people understand that trees can serve as a solution for many of the global issues faced today, such as air quality, water quality, climate change, deforestation, etc. Through its conservation and educational programs, the foundation restores forests, improves tree cover in communities, and inspires next generation tree planters to ensure that its work continues. In "Forest Service Circular 96," issued April 2, 1907, Pinchot (Pixchor) wrote: "The lesson of Arbor Day is the use and the value of the tree in the life of the nation. . . . But the forest of trees, where wood is growing to supply material for homes, for fuel, for a hundred industries; where the forest litter is storing the waters for streams to quench . . . thirst, to irrigate . . . lands, to drive . . . mills, to fill . . . rivers deep for the vast traffic of inland navigation; in a word, the forest as producer and custodian of the necessities of life and happiness is the true message of Arbor Day."[89]

Journal/Meditation: Where can you plant a tree? How do the trees in your neighborhood offer hope to you? Where is the closest forest that promotes the necessities of life?

Prayer: O LORD, the trees of the forest sing for joy before you. Deepen my appreciation for every kind of tree that reveals your glory. You are to be praised now and forever. Amen.

Ramadan
Any Month from One Sighting of a Crescent Moon to the Next

Text: "O believers, fasting is enjoined on you as it was on those before you, so that you might become righteous. Fast a (fixed) number of days, but if someone is ill or is traveling (he should complete) the number of days (he had missed); and those who find it hard to fast should expiate by feeding a poor person. Ramadan is the month in which the Qur'an was revealed as guidance to man [and woman] and clear proof of the guidance, and criterion (of falsehood and truth). So when you see the new moon, you should fast the whole month; but a person who is ill or traveling (and fails to do so) should fast on other days, as God wishes ease and not hardship for you, so that you complete the (fixed) number (of fasts), and give glory to God for the guidance, and be grateful."[90]

---

89. Pinchot (Pixchor), "Forest Service Circular," 10–11.
90. Pelikan, *Qur'an* 2:183–184a, 185.

Reflection: The ninth month of the Islamic lunar calendar is called Ramadan, meaning *scorching heat, to become intensely hot, burning, blazing, glowing*; it is a twenty-nine- to thirty-day month devoted to fasting, prayer, reflection, and community. This annual observance, which is one of the Five Pillars of Islam, begins with the sighting of the crescent moon and lasts until the next sighting of the crescent moon. Because it is a based on a lunar calendar, the month of Ramadan begins typically on the day immediately after a new moon—when the crescent appears—and can fall in any month of the Gregorian calendar; this reflection about Ramadan is located in April because that is the month in which Ramadan was beginning when this book was written.[91] As noted in the text above, Muslims believe that all their Scripture was revealed to them during Ramadan. The holiday of Eid marks the end of Ramadan with the sighting of the next crescent moon, usually after completion of thirty days of fasting.

All healthy adult Muslims are obliged to fast from dawn to sunset unless, as noted in the text above, one is acutely or chronically ill, traveling, elderly, pregnant, breastfeeding, diabetic, or menstruating. Before sunrise, Muslins share a simple, pre-fast meal. Then, throughout the day, they fast from food and drink, tobacco, sex, and sinful behavior. After sunset, they share a feast that breaks the fast. The nightly meal begins with the eating of dates to commemorate Muhammad's practice of breaking his fast by eating three dates. Muslims believe that the spiritual rewards gained from fasting are multiplied during Ramadan, as they devote themselves to prayer, charity, self-discipline, and recitation of the *Qur'an*. Fasting redirects the heart away from worldly pursuits and towards those in need and God. According to Muslim belief, good deeds are rewarded more during this month than at any other time. The month of spiritual reflection, self-improvement, and heightened devotions and worship is comparable to a thirty-day retreat. While most Muslims continue to work during Ramadan, in some places their hours of work are shortened; however, this differs from one country to another. Muslims are encouraged to read the entire *Qur'an* during Ramadan. There are various cultural practices—such as lights in city streets, bathing in a holy spring, lighting firecrackers, and serving specific kinds of food—that differ around the world where Muslim communities are located.

Journal/Meditation: When have you most recently fasted? How long did your fast last? From what did you fast? What were the spiritual rewards of your fasting?

Prayer: O God, you wish ease and not hardship for your people, even though you impose fasting upon them to enable them to become righteous. Help me to understand the truth that fasting from some food and drink enables others to have some food and drink. I am grateful for all your gifts, and I give glory to you for your guidance. Amen.

---

91. From 2023 to 2024, Ramadan begins in March; from 2026 to 2027, it begins in February; from 2028 to 2030, it begins in January.

5

The Month of *May*

MAY DAY

May 1

Text: "Since May 1 lies about halfway between the vernal equinox and the summer solstice, it was a good time to mark the transition into summer. . . . In the colder climate of Northern Europe, May 1 was a perilous but ultimately optimistic moment of transition from the old to the new, from the winter to the summer season. . . . May Day, being halfway between the equinox and the summer solstice when the sun's waxing light and warmth is more clearly felt, *celebrates and guarantees* the full-blown forces of summer."[1]

Reflection: Because May Day comes in between March 20 (21) and June 20 (21), it quickly became a day to mark the end of spring (or winter) and the beginning of summer. Due to traces left by various cultures, the May 1 celebrations focused on fertility; by May 1, the crops had been sowed, livestock was heavy with new life, and humankind found the time ideal for conceiving. In Rome, during the Republic, a festival was held in honor of Flora, the goddess of flowers. The Greeks also held a spring festival in honor of Rhea, called the Great Mother and Queen of Heaven. In Rome, the Great Mother had a son-lover, named Attis, who was attacked by a wild boar and bled to death under a pine tree. The Great Mother believed that he had taken refuge in the pine tree for the winter and would be reborn in the spring. Thus, the Great Mother was honored by a pine tree that was cut and stripped of its branches, wrapped in linen, and decorated before being brought to the Great Mother's temple, where Attis was raised out of the tree, which was then erected before the temple and danced around by worshipers. The tree, an obvious phallus, represented longevity, life, and renewal. It also served to unite the three levels of the universe: its top reached to the heaven; its base was planted in the earth; its roots could reach to the underworld. In other words,

---

1. George, *Mythology*, 121, 125.

it united the source of all life above the earth, on the earth, and under the earth. Later, in other cultures, the tree was called a Maypole, and it represented the transition from spring planting to summer fertility.

In later cultural developments, it was common to choose a May Queen and a May King. The queen and king would be crowned at the base of the Maypole where the renewal of fertility was being celebrated by dancers around the pole holding flowers and spreading garlands as signs of summer and fertility. In the eighth century, the Catholic Church developed a May Day ceremony of crowning with flowers an image of the Blessed Virgin Mary and declaring her to be Queen of Heaven and Queen of Earth. In some places, the tradition of giving a May basket, full of sweets and flowers, to friends and neighbors became a way to mark the transition from spring to summer fertility. Nevertheless, May Day never became an important part of American culture, and its observance is confined to small communities who brought its observance with them when they immigrated to the United States. Across the U.S. modern May Day celebrations may involve cleaning the deck, putting out the wicker furniture, opening the swimming pool, lighting the grill, etc.

Journal/Meditation: How do you mark the transition from spring to summer in your family?

Prayer: God of all times, seasons, and life, raise your hand in blessing over the crops sown throughout this land. Give increase to livestock, and give children to parents who long to nurture them. Make me fruitful in all my works today, tomorrow, and forever. Amen.

INTERNATIONAL WORKERS' DAY

May 1

Text: "An eight-hour day for every workingman! That is the object of a great campaign just launched—the first in America—by the Labor Center association in New York. Millions of striking poster stamps will carry the message to all corners of the country. Every union man and union sympathizer is asked to use these stamps on all his correspondence—to spread it broadside under the eyes of his fellow-workers, employers, and the general public. With 400,000 railway employees threatening a strike unless they get the eight-hour day, and the coal miners doing the same, it is evident this campaign is to have the greatest publicity in the history of organized labor!"[2]

Reflection: The working classes' struggle to gain the eight-hour work day gave rise to the International Workers' Day. Before the eight-hour day was won, men, women, and children were forced to work long hours in miserable conditions just for subsistence living. As early as 1810, Robert Owen of England had fought for a ten-hour

---

2. "Labor Unions."

day, which was finally granted to women and children in 1847, while French workers won the twelve-hour day in 1848. In the United States, as early as 1791, Philadelphia carpenters went on strike for the ten-hour day. In 1836, the *National Laborer* declared: "We have no desire to perpetuate the ten-hour system for we believe that eight hours' daily labor is more than enough for any man to perform."[3] The 1866 General Congress of Labor in Baltimore declared: "The first and great necessity of the present, to free this country from capitalist slavery, is the passing of a law by which eight hours shall be the normal working day in all states of the American Union."[4] In 1872, 100,000 workers in New York struck and won the eight-hour day for building trades workers. The eight-hour work day continued to gain momentum until May 1, 1886, when more than 300,000 workers across the U.S. walked off their jobs in the first May Day celebration. In Chicago, 40,000 went on strike, but the ranks continued to fill until 100,000 had joined the strikers. On May 3, 1886, violence broke out at the McCormick Reaper Works between police and strikers. On May 4, a public meeting was held in Haymarket Square. When police began to move to dismiss the small crowd, a bomb was thrown into their ranks. Police fired into the crowd, leaving an estimated seven or eight civilians dead and seven police officers dead.

According to Andy McInerney: "The Haymarket incident placed the U.S. working class, especially the U.S. movement for the eight-hour day, at center stage of the world workers' movement. So when the AFL convention in 1888 announced that May 1, 1890, would be a day when labor would enforce the eight-hour day with strikes and demonstrations, the world was listening."[5] As can be seen from the text above, the eight-hour work day was still not a reality all across the nation as late as 1916. While May 1 picked up momentum around the world, it began to lose steam in the country in which it began: United States. Today, millions of workers in countries around the world mark May 1 as a day to raise the demands of the working class. On International Workers' Day, it is worth remembering that the eight-hour work day, which all workers enjoy today, is the result of the struggle of workers for over a hundred years.

Journal/Meditation: What do you think has been the most important development for the working class since the institution of the eight-hour work day? What modern refinement have you experienced concerning the eight-hour work day (such as four ten-hour work days)?

Prayer: LORD God, you have entrusted labor to the human race in order to continue your work of creation. Grant that all men and women find work that enhances their human dignity and brings glory to your name now and forever. Amen.

---

3. McInerney, "May Day," 92.
4. McInerney, "May Day," 94.
5. McInerney, "May Day," 98.

Loyalty Day
May 1

Text: "Whereas the prime requisite for retaining our freedom is unswerving devotion to the liberties embodied in our Constitution; and whereas it is fitting that a special day be set aside for solemn re-evaluation of those priceless gifts of freedom which are our heritage, to the end that we may stimulate and renew that high sense of patriotism which has signalized our glorious history as a nation; whereas the congress . . . has set aside May 1, 1955, as Loyalty Day . . . calling upon the people to observe that day by reaffirming their loyalty to our beloved country; now, therefore, I, Dwight D. Eisenhower, . . . do hereby . . . request the appropriate officials to arrange for the display of the flag of the United States upon all government buildings on that day as a manifestation of our loyalty to the nation which that flag symbolizes."[6]

Reflection: The first loyalty day observance occurred in 1921. Originally called "Americanization Day," it was intended to replace International Workers' Day. The United States congress recognized the day on April 27, 1955, and President Dwight D. Eisenhower issued its proclamation the next day, setting May 1, 1955, as noted above, as a day to reflect on the freedoms enshrined in the U.S. Constitution in order to foster patriotism by displaying the flag, a sign of loyalty to the nation. On July 18, 1958, both the U.S. Senate and the House of Representatives made Loyalty Day an annual observance "for the reaffirmation of loyalty to the United States of America and for the recognition of the heritage of American freedom . . . , calling upon officials of the government to display the flag of the United States on all government buildings on such day and inviting the people of the United States to observe such day, in schools and other suitable places, with appropriate ceremonies."[7]

On August 12, 1998, the U.S. Senate and the House of Representatives passed Public Law 105–225, "an act to revise, codify, and enact without substantive change certain general and permanent laws, related to patriotic and national observances, ceremonies, and organizations, as title 36, United States Code, 'Patriotic and National Observances, Ceremonies, and Organizations.'"[8] Among those permanent laws was Section 115. Loyalty Day. According to its stated purpose, "Loyalty Day is a special day for the reaffirmation of loyalty to the United States and for the recognition of the heritage of American freedom."[9] A person who is loyal remains faithful to his or her country; he or she possesses a feeling of duty, devotion, attachment to his or her country. In the U.S., this is demonstrated by displaying the flag and appropriate ceremonies in schools and other suitable places. Since it became a legal holiday in 1958, Loyalty

---

6. Eisenhower, "Proclamation 3091."
7. "Public Law 85-529."
8. "Public Law 105–225."
9. "Public Law 105–225," 36 U.S. Code, Section 115.

Day has been recognized every year by every president. As Eisenhower noted in the first Loyalty Day proclamation, the primary way for keeping our freedom is through devotion to the liberties embodied in our Constitution. One day a year is set aside for us solemnly to reevaluate and reflect upon our priceless gift of freedom.

Journal/Meditation: What do you consider to be your most priceless gift of freedom? In what specific ways do you demonstrate loyalty to the United States? How do you recognize the heritage of American freedom?

Prayer: God of justice, you have blessed the United States with the gift of countless freedoms. Give peace to this country, and instill loyalty in her citizens. Let your justice guide my life, as I share my freedom with other people on the earth. Amen.

NATIONAL TEACHER APPRECIATION WEEK AND NATIONAL TEACHER APPRECIATION DAY
First Full Week of May, Tuesday of the First Full Week of May

Text: "... I have seen firsthand the dedication, selflessness, and vision of our nation's educators.... They are mentors who guide with creativity and care; advocates who fight for students' needs; role models who help students dream and dare more boldly; and leaders who tirelessly support the families and communities that depend on them. ... [E]ducators build the future of our country, and we are grateful for their commitment to our shared future.... [W]e honor the service and passion and celebrate the immeasurable contributions of our nation's educators in schools from coast to coast."[10]

Reflection: As early as 1944, Ryan Krug, a teacher in Wisconsin, began correspondence with political and educational leaders about the need to establish a national day to honor teachers. In Helena, Arkansas, Mattie Whyte Woodridge, an educator, wrote to Eleanor Roosevelt, who persuaded congress to proclaim a National Teacher Day in 1953. The National Education Association (NEA) with some of its state affiliates lobbied congress to create a National Teacher Day for March 7, 1980, only. Meanwhile, the NEA and its affiliates continued to observe the day on the first Tuesday of March until 1985, when the National Parent Teacher Association established Teacher Appreciation Week during the first full week of May. After that was done, the NEA Representative Assembly made the Tuesday of that week National Teacher Day (National Teacher Appreciation Day) in 1985. While appreciation for teachers is shown throughout National Teacher Appreciation Week, National Teacher Day offers the opportunity for students both past and present to compliment a (former) teacher for the contributions he or she makes (made) to help students succeed in school and in life. President Joseph R. Biden, Jr., in the text above, names educators as mentors, advocates, role models, and leaders. "Education is the one field that makes all others

---

10. Biden, "A Proclamation."

possible," states Biden. "Every one of us has been shaped by someone who inspired our curiosity and helped us find our confidence, who guided us to think more clearly and pushed us to strive for better."[11] He adds, ". . . [W]e remember the tremendous debt of gratitude owed to educators everywhere who helped define us as individuals and as a country, and to all that they are doing to light the way forward for our families and our communities."[12]

During the week, but especially on Tuesday of the first full week of May, Biden calls upon all Americans "to recognize the hard work and dedication of our nation's teachers and to observe [the] day and [the] week by supporting teachers through appropriate activities, events, and program."[13] Children learn to be Americans in school, which is also where they learn the Pledge of Allegiance, the U.S. Constitution, and the unity that exists among citizens. We honor teachers and recognize the lasting contributions they make to our lives by preparing or making gifts for them, writing thank-you cards or letters, refilling their supplies, volunteering in schools, serving a meal to them, etc. Teachers, coaches, and mentors are honored on National Teacher Day, but, also, it may be someone who taught life-lessons—a friend, family member—who ought to be thanked for sharing knowledge and wisdom and inspiring a person to be a better version of himself or herself.

Journal/Meditation: Who is/was your favorite teacher? What important life lesson did he or she teach you? In what way(s) have you served as a mentor, advocate, role model, or leader for another?

Prayer: All-wise God, give teachers an abundance of your wisdom. Give them grace to share truth with all their students. And bless them with kindness and gentleness as they prepare the next generations to be the mentors, advocates, role models, and leaders who will replace them. Amen.

World Press Freedom Day

May 3

Text: "Recognizing that a free, pluralistic, and independent press is an essential component of any democratic society, . . . [the General Conference of the United Nations Educational, Scientific, and Cultural Organization (UNESCO)] invites the Director-General . . . to encourage press freedom and to promote the independence and pluralism of the media; [and] . . . to transmit to the United Nations General Assembly the wish expressed by the member states of UNESCO to have 3 May declared 'International Press Freedom Day' . . . ."[14]

11. Biden, "A Proclamation."
12. Biden, "A Proclamation."
13. Biden, "A Proclamation."
14. *Records*.

Reflection: During the twenty-sixth session of the General Conference of the United Nations Educational, Scientific, and Cultural Organization (UNESCO), held October 15 to November 7, 1991, in Paris, France, Resolution 4.3, titled "Promotion of Press Freedom in the World," was approved on November 6, 1991. As can be seen from the text above, the proposal invited the Director-General of UNESCO to transmit to the United Nations General Assembly its desire that it declare May 3 International Press Freedom Day. On December 17, 1993, the U.N. declared May 3 World Press Freedom Day. The date was chosen to honor the adoption of a statement of press freedom principles issued by African newspaper journalists in 1991. Known as the Windhoek Declaration for the Development of a Free, Independent, and Pluralistic Press or Windhoek Declaration, it has since become an affirmation of the international community's commitment to freedom of the press and a major reference in the U.N. system. Article 1 of the UNESCO Constitution states that the organization collaborates "in the work of advancing the mutual knowledge and understanding of peoples through all means of mass communication and to that end recommend[s] such international agreements as may be necessary to promote the free flow of ideas by word and image."[15] According to the U.N.s "World Press Freedom Day" webpage, UNESCO "works to foster free, independent, and pluralistic media in print, broadcast, and online. Media development in this mode enhances freedom of expression, and it contributes to peace, sustainability, poverty eradication, and human rights."[16]

The purpose of World Press Freedom Day is to raise awareness of the importance of the freedom of the press and to remind governments of their duty to respect and uphold the right to freedom of expression. According to U.N.'s "World Press Freedom Day" webpage, the day is also one "of reflection among media professionals about issues of press freedom and professional ethics. It is an opportunity to celebrate the fundamental principles of press freedom, assess the state of press freedom throughout the world, defend the media from attacks on their independence, and pay tribute to journalists who have lost their lives in the line of duty."[17] With the freedom of the press comes the responsibility of the press and all forms of communication, such as magazines, internet, and social media. In other words, freedom of the press means that media are accountable to their readers for accuracy in reporting. In the United States, the Bill of Rights (Amendment 1) states that congress can make no law abridging the freedom of speech or of the press. According to Robert Estabrook: "The press is independent of government. The founders of the United States were suspicious of the tendency of government, even the best-intentioned government, to become tyrannical at times. . . . [They] envisaged the press, despite all of its imperfections, as a kind of critic, with a role apart and distinct from that of government."[18] Estabrook ex-

15. "UNESCO Constitution," Article 1, Section 2a.
16. "World Press Freedom Day."
17. "World Press Freedom Day."
18. Estabrook, "An Unfettered Press."

plains: "... [T]he intent of the founders was that the press and government should not become institutional partners. They are natural adversaries with different functions, and each must respect the role of the other. Sometimes a free press can be a distinct annoyance and an embarrassment to a particular government, but that is one of the prices of liberty. A free press is responsible to its readers, and to them alone."[19] Thus, on World Press Freedom Day, governments are reminded of their duty to uphold the freedom of the press, journalists are reminded of their responsibility for accurate reporting, and readers are reminded of their responsibility to keep the government and the press separated from each other.

Journal/Meditation: Where do you find a free, pluralistic, and independent press where you live? How can free media contribute to peace, sustainability, poverty eradication, and human rights? As a reader, in what media do you find the press exercising its responsibility to you?

Prayer: God of the written word, through many and various people you communicate your word to me. Keep the press free, and keep journalists accountable for the truth they report. Grant that a free press enhances the liberty I enjoy now and forever. Amen.

International Firefighters' Day
May 4

Text: "The role of a firefighter in today's society—be it urban, rural, natural environment, volunteer, career, industrial, defense force, aviation, motor sport, or other—is one of dedication, commitment, and sacrifice—no matter what country we reside and work in. In the fire service we fight together against one common enemy—fire—no matter what country we come from, what uniform we wear, or what language we speak."[20]

Reflection: The words above, from J.J. Edmondson in 1999, are from the lieutenant who led the way to establish International Firefighters' Day. While there were organized firefighters in ancient Egypt and Rome, Edmondson didn't get the day established until 1999. On December 2, 1998, in Linton Community, Victoria, Australia, five men from Geelong West Fire Brigade answered a call to help others battling a large bush fire. Garry Vredeveldt, Chris Evans, Stuart Davidson, Jason Thomas, and Matthew Armstrong were on their way to help extinguish the flames when the wind suddenly switched directions and engulfed them in their truck in fire, killing all five of them. That incident inspired Edmondson, a volunteer firefighter in Victoria, to begin a petition through e-mail on January 4, 1999, to grassroots organizations and

---

19. Estabrook, "An Unfettered Press."
20. "International Firefighters' Day."

other influential people to get the day established. According to Firetech, Edmondson "felt the loss of the five men from the Geelong West Fire Brigade and believed that the world should be more aware of the dangers, sacrifice, commitment, bravery, and service that professional and volunteer firefighters around the world give to their communities."[21] There are two aspects to this day. The first is to remember firefighters of the past who have died while serving their communities or dedicating their lives to protecting the safety of countless people. The second aspect is to show support and appreciation to the firefighters around the world who continue to protect people in cities, the country, in wild areas, and who volunteer or make firefighting their career, in industry, defense, aviation, motor sport, or other venues.

The first International Firefighters' Day was celebrated on May 4, 1999. The date was chosen because it is the feast day of St. Florian, the patron saint of firefighters. Florian was born around 250 CE near a Roman town in modern-day Austria. After enlisting in the Roman army, he rose through the ranks, eventually being tasked with creating a specialized firefighting brigade. Florian died at Lauriacum (Lorch) in what is now Austria around 304 CE. After proclaiming himself a Christian, "[t]he Roman governor had him scourged, flayed, and thrown into the river Emms tied to a stone."[22] As a martyr, he is "patron of Poland, Upper Austria, and Linz and is invoked against fire because he miraculously extinguished one."[23] Some sources list him as the patron saint of chimney sweeps, too. According to legend, Roman soldiers threatened to burn Florian at the stake, but he told them that he feared no fire and would climb into it himself if they lit the pyre. Instead, as noted above, they drowned him. Thus, the day that honors the patron saint of firefighters was chosen as the day to honor the service and sacrifice of firefighters across the globe. There are a number of ways to honor St. Florian and firefighters. One of the simplest is to say "Thank You" with a card or letter to your local fire station. Another way is to share a story about the impact firefighters have had on your life or someone you know, or personally greet firefighters or fire safety personnel you meet in a store, on the street, or anywhere. Another way to celebrate the day is to make a donation to a firefighter's charity, help with a fundraiser, or volunteer at your local fire department. Place a poster or banner in your front yard, encourage local media to feature a story on the local fire department, encourage a school to sponsor activities, lessons, and presentations by and on firefighters. You can also bring food (cookies, cakes, pies) to your local fire station, practice drills with your family, and be sure that all the carbon monoxide and fire detectors in your home are working properly. You can practice safe outdoor fire, grill, and fireworks use and purchase fire extinguishers to be placed in strategic places in your home. To show your support, wear a red and blue ribbon, one of the signs of the day. Red represents fire, and blue represents water. And be sure to stop for what is called the "Sound

21. "Everything You Need to Know."
22. Walsh, "New Dictionary," 205.
23. Walsh, "New Dictionary," 205–6.

Off"—a thirty-second siren sounding at noon on May 4, followed by a sixty-second silence to honor all the firefighters and fire service personnel who have died in the line of duty over the years. Firefighters continue to lose their lives in their communities. For example on December 3, 1999, six firefighters died in the Worcester Cold Storage and Warehouse Company Fire in Worcester, Massachusetts; 343 firefighters died on September 11, 2001, in the terrorist attacks on the World Trade Center and the Pentagon; nine firefighters died in the Charleston Sofa Superstore Fire on June 18, 2007, in Charleston, South Carolina; ten firefighters died in the West Fertilizer Company Explosion on April 17, 2013, in Waco, Texas; and nineteen firefighters died in the Yarnell Hill Fire on June 30, 2013, near Yarnell, Arizona. On May 4, we honor those who have died and those who continue to risk their lives for people they don't know or to rescue defenseless animals in a burning forest.

Journal/Meditation: What word caught most of your attention in the text above from J.J. Edmondson? Explain. How will you honor firefighters where you live? Do you have smoke detectors, carbon monoxide detectors, and fire extinguishers in your home? Why? Why not?

Prayer: LORD God, you inspire men and women to volunteer or to choose a career as a firefighter. Through the intercession of St. Florina, bless those who daily risk their lives to protect me and those who live in my community and draw to yourself all those who have died in service as firefighters. Amen.

Cinco de Mayo

May 5

Text: "Whereas May 5 . . . is celebrated each year as a date of great importance by the Mexican and Mexican-American communities; whereas the Cinco de Mayo holiday commemorates May 5, 1862, the date on which the Battle of Puebla was fought by Mexicans who were struggling for their independence and freedom; whereas Cinco de Mayo . . . is celebrated annually by nearly all Mexicans and Mexican-Americans, north and south of the United States-Mexico border; . . . whereas Cinco de Mayo also serves as a reminder of the close spiritual and economic ties between the people of Mexico and the people of the United States . . . ; whereas in a larger sense Cinco de Mayo symbolizes the right of a free people to self-determination . . . ; now, therefore, be it resolved by the House of Representatives (the Senate concurring), that congress recognizes the historical struggle for independence and freedom of the Mexican people and requests the president to issue a proclamation recognizing that struggle and calling upon the people of the United States to observe Cinco de Mayo with appropriate ceremonies and activities."[24]

---

24. Congressional Record, H4150.

Reflection: On June 7, 2005, the historical significance of the Mexican holiday of Cinco de Mayo was recognized by the United States House of Representatives with the Senate concurring. As is indicated in the text above, both Mexican and Mexican-American communities had been celebrating Cinco de Mayo since 1863, after Mexico's President Benito Juarez declared it a holiday on May 9 (or September 8), 1862. After having been involved in a series of wars and discovering that the country was bankrupt, Juarez issued a moratorium on July 17, 1861, which suspended all its foreign debt payments for two years. France, Britain, and Spain sent forces to Veracruz to demand reimbursement; Britain and Spain, after negotiating with Mexico, withdrew peacefully. France, ruled by Napoleon III, decided to establish an empire in Mexico. Thus, late in 1861, a well-armed French fleet attacked Veracruz and sent Juarez and his government into retreat before continuing on toward Mexico City. Near Puebla, the 8,000 French forces battled the 4,000 Mexican forces. On May 5, 1862, the Mexicans defeated the French army. Needless to say, the Mexican victory boosted the morale of the army and the people and gave all a sense of national unity and patriotism. Of course, a year later, with more troops, the French defeated the Mexicans and captured Mexico City, a victory that lasted from 1864 to 1867, when the Mexican army arose and drove the French out of Mexico.

Even though Juarez had declared Cinco de Mayo a holiday in Mexico to commemorate the anniversary of the Battle of Puebla, it is celebrated more in the United States. Due primarily to its emphasis on independence, freedom, and self-determination—all very dear to U.S. citizens—it was transformed into a popular Mexican cultural event. After beginning in California, it made its way east across the U.S. in the 1950s and 1960s, taking root in areas with large Mexican-American populations and becoming a celebration of Mexican heritage, culture, food, music, and customs unique to Mexico. It also serves as a reminder that our neighbors to the south strive, like we do, to live lives filled with faith, family, and the hope of sharing a stronger America and a freer world. Some people mark Cinco de Mayo with banners, parades, and special events to educate students in schools as to its historical importance. Others celebrate with music, dancing, drinks, crafts, and Mexican cuisine. The holiday is noted in a variety of ways around the world. As Representative Solomon P. Ortiz stated during the U.S. House debate on June 7, 2005, "It is important to note why we celebrate this day—we celebrate the courage and the strength of a people who will fight against all odds for the things they cherish—freedom, independence, and democracy."[25]

Journal/Meditation: For what are you willing to fight against all odds? What courage and strength does that require?

Prayer: Because you desire that all people be free, O LORD, you give them courage and strength to defeat their oppressors. Grant me such courage and strength that I

---

25. Congressional Record, H4152.

may live a life filled with faith, family, and the hope of sharing a stronger America and a freer world. Amen.

NATIONAL DAY OF PRAYER
First Thursday

Text: "The president shall issue each year a proclamation designating the first Thursday in May as a National Day of Prayer on which the people of the United States may turn to God in prayer and meditation at churches, in groups, and as individuals."[26]

Reflection: While a national day of prayer was called by the first Continental Congress in 1775 and by Abraham Lincoln in 1863, it was not until 1952 that the National Day of Prayer, as we know it today, was established by a joint resolution of congress. The resolution (Public Law 82–324) stated that the president of the United States should proclaim a day each year—other than a Sunday—upon which citizens turn to God in prayer and meditation in churches, in groups, and as individuals. President Harry S. Truman signed that bill into law on April 17, 1952. Each president was given the task of choosing an appropriate date for the national observance. On May 5, 1988, congress passed Public Law 100–307, which established the National Day of Prayer as the first Thursday in May each year. On August 12, 1998, the text above was incorporated into Public law 105–225, Section 119, of Title 36 U.S. Code. The hope was that all adherents of all religions—Christians (Protestants and Catholics), Jews, Muslims, Hindus, Sikhs, etc.—would unite in prayer one day a year—in front of courthouses and state capitols, in city halls, schools, businesses, homes, churches, synagogues, mosques, temples, etc.—and bring renewed respect for God and all peoples of the world. Praying for the nation also became popular during breakfasts, luncheons, picnics, and music concerts.

On October 3, 2008, the Freedom from Religion Foundation sued to challenge the presidential designation of a National Day of Prayer. On March 1, 2010, U.S. District Judge Barbara Crabb accepted the suit, and, on April 15, 2010, ruled that the statue establishing the day of prayer was unconstitutional because it blurred the distinction between church (a religious exercise) and state (secular function). Her decision was overturned on April 14, 2011, by the Seventh Circuit Court of Appeals, which stated that the president is free to make appeals to the pubic based on many kinds of grounds—political, religious, tragedy, etc.—and that such appeals do not in any way place an obligation on citizens to comply nor do they encroach on their rights. Thus, every president since Truman has signed a National Day of Prayer proclamation. The day reminds us of our founding fathers and mothers, who issued calls for prayer and fasting in order to seek the wisdom of God when facing decisions. It is an invitation to come before God, to seek guidance for our national, state, and local leaders, and to

---

26. "Public Law 105–225," 36 U.S. Code, Section 119.

pray that divine grace will be poured on all leaders and citizens. It is a day important to all people of our nation, and should be observed by all in a spirit of unity.

Journal/Meditation: How do you observe the annual National Day of Prayer? What divine guidance is needed for leaders today? What divine guidance is needed for citizens today?

Prayer: LORD of all nations, you blessed our founding fathers and mothers with a vision in which all people could live as one in freedom and in peace. Hear my prayer for all our national, state, and local leaders and for all citizens; fill them with your grace to keep alive the vision in this land today, tomorrow, and forever. Amen.

NATIONAL NURSES DAY, NATIONAL STUDENT NURSES' DAY, AND INTERNATIONAL NURSES DAY
May 6–12

Text: "The most important practical lesson that can be given to nurses is to teach them to observe—how to observe—what symptoms indicate improvement, what the reverse—which are of importance—which are of none—which are the evidence of neglect—and what kind of neglect. If you cannot get into the habit of observation one way or another, you had better give up . . . being a nurse. In dwelling upon the vital importance of sound observation, it must never be lost sight of what observation is for. It is not for the sake of piling up miscellaneous information or curious facts, but for the sake of saving life and increasing health and comfort."[27]

Reflection: The text above, spoken by Florence Nightingale, the foundress of modern, professional nursing, are applicable not only to nurses, but to all people. Observation is the discipline of paying attention to a patient's improvement, deterioration, or neglect. As far as Nightingale is concerned, if one does not cultivate and possess the skill of observation, he or she should give up the nursing career. It is through observation that life is saved, health is increased, and comfort achieved. According to Nightingale, ". . . [E]very nurse should be one who is depended upon, in other words, capable of being a 'confidential nurse.' She [or he] does not know how soon she [or he] may find herself [or himself] placed in such a situation; she [or he] must be no gossip, no vain talker; she [or he] should never answer questions about her [or his] sick except to those who have a right to ask them."[28] In 1854, Nightingale with thirty-eight nurses went to a military camp of British soldiers, located on the outskirts of Constantinople (Istanbul), where they cleaned the patients' environment, provided medical equipment, provided clean water, and brought to a stop communicable and infectious

---

27. Nightingale, "Mother."
28. Nightingale, "Mother."

diseases. She was like a mother to the soldiers. Every night, she took her lamp and used it to see how to get to the patients' camp in order to treat them.

Since a Nurse Day was first proposed in 1953 and the first Nurse Week was held in 1954, the contributions that nurses make to society have been highlighted in various ways. International Nurses Day has been marked since 1965. Today, National Nurses Week is held from May 6 to 12. National Nurses Day (National RN Recognition Day), on May 6, begins the annual week-long attempt to raise awareness about the contributions, commitments, and vital role played by nurses in society. May 8 is designated as the annual National Student Nurses' Day; the Wednesday of National Nurses Week is designed at National School Nurse Day. The week-long celebration of nurses ends on International Nurses Day, May 12, the birthday of Florence Nightingale. During the week, nurses everywhere are recognized for the dedication and commitment to their patients and to their profession, which began with Nightingale's work with soldiers and observation.

Journal/Meditation: What kind of medical care have you recently received from a nurse? What did you notice about the nurse's observation skill? How did you thank the nurse who cared for you?

Prayer: O God, give strength and energy to all nurses, who serve you by caring for others. Grace them with compassion, understanding, and observation so that tenderness flows from their hands, listening fills their ears, comfort emerges from their lips, and hope is given to all they serve. Amen.

World Laughter Day
First Sunday

Text: "If laughter can't solve your problems, it will dissolve them by changing your body chemistry and mindset so you can face them in a better way."[29]

Reflection: Doctor Madan Kataria, founder of the Laughter Yoga movement, established World Laughter Day in Mumbai, India, on May 10, 1998. As a family doctor, Kataria was inspired by the facial feedback hypothesis, which states that a person's facial expression can have an effect on his or her emotions. Laughter changes facial expressions. According to Kataria, "When you laugh, you change. When you change, the whole world changes."[30] As noted in Kataria's words in the text above, laughter does not solve problems, but it can dissolve them by changing both the chemistry and the mindset of the person laughing, who then can face the problems in a better way. Again, according to Kataria, "We are paying [a] very high price for taking

---

29. Kataria, "Quotes."
30. Kataria, "Quotes."

life seriously; now it's time to take laughter seriously."[31] In the United States, World Laughter Day was first celebrated in Los Angeles, California, in 2005.

World Laughter Day is marked on the first Sunday of May. In more than 5,000 Laughter Yoga Clubs around the world, people are united in a non-religious, non-racial, and not-for-profit organization committed to generating good health, joy, and world peace. The celebration of people in public places with the purpose of laughing is a manifestation of world peace that can build a global consciousness of brotherhood and sisterhood and friendship. The goal of the day is to raise awareness of the many healing benefits of laughter, such as it helps to reduce pain and allows people to tolerate discomfort, it reduces blood sugar levels and increases glucose tolerance, it improves job performance, it helps blood vessels function better, it relieves stress and helps the body to relax, it boots the immune system, it burns calories, and it triggers the release of endorphins, which promotes an overall sense of wellbeing. In order to participate in this day, all one needs to do is have a good laugh, watch a funny movie, listen to a funny comedian, go to a comedy club, tell a funny joke, take a funny picture, read a funny book, or find an inspirational quote about laughter. No matter what one does, it demonstrates how much he or she cherishes the beautiful, powerful, positive emotion of laughter. Kataria states, "There is a no laughter in the medicine, but there is a lot of medicine in the laughter."[32]

Journal/Meditation: Most recently, when have your facial expressions had an effect on your emotions? How do you change, when you laugh? When have you experienced healing through laughter?

Prayer: Almighty God, pour the grace of laughter upon me, and use it to change me. Through laughter make peace and global friendship a reality in this world now and forever. Amen.

V-E Day
May 8

Text: ". . . [A]cting by authority of the German High Command, [we] hereby surrender unconditionally to the Supreme Commander, Allied Expeditionary Force, and simultaneously to the Supreme High Command of the Red Army all forces on land, sea, and in the air who are at this date under German control. The German High Command will at once issue orders to all German military, naval, and air authorities and to all forces under German control to cease active operations . . . on 8th May 1945, to remain in the positions occupied at that time, and to disarm completely,

---

31. Kataria, "Quotes."
32. Kataria, "Quotes."

handing over their weapons and equipment to the local allied commanders or officers designated by representatives of the Allied Supreme Command."[33]

Reflection: World War II came to an end with Germany's unconditional surrender on May 8, 1945, signed in Berlin, as noted in the above text. A slightly different document had been signed at Rheims, France, on May 7, 1945, by German Colonel General Alfred Jodi and accepted by Supreme Allied Commander General Dwight D. Eisenhower. After Adolf Hitler committed suicide on April 30, 1945, his successor, Grand Admiral Karl Donitz, negotiated an end to the war with the Allies. The above text, insisted upon by Soviet Premier Josef Stalin, was signed by German Field Marshal Wilhelm Keitel the next day. All German forces surrendered simultaneously to the United States supreme commander and to the Russia Red Army supreme high command. Thus, Victory in Europe Day (VE Day, V-E Day) brought the nearly six-year World War II to an end.

In the U.S., President Franklin D. Roosevelt had died of a cerebral hemorrhage on April 12, 1945, and the vice-president, Harry S. Truman, had succeeded him as president. Truman's sixty-first birthday just so happened to be May 8, 1945. He dedicated the Allied victory to Roosevelt's memory, stating that his wish was that Roosevelt had lived long enough to witness the day of victory. Because the U.S. was still mourning the passing of Roosevelt with flags at half-staff and still at war with Japan, Truman urged citizens to temper their celebrations. While a large crowd gathered in New York's Times Square, all across the country many flocked to their houses of worship to pray, maintaining a subdued observation of the first V-E Day. "The western world has been freed of the evil forces which for five years and longer have imprisoned the bodies and broken the lives of millions upon millions of freeborn men [and women]," stated Truman in his V-E Day Proclamation. "They have violated their churches, destroyed their homes, corrupted their children, and murdered their loved ones. Our armies of liberation have restored freedom to those suffering peoples, whose spirit and will the oppressor could never enslave."[34]

Journal/Meditation: From what evil force do you think the western world needs to be freed today? What prayer can you say to God to seek removal of that evil force?

Prayer: God of peace, you create all people to be free, but evil forces often arise that seek to imprison them. Give me the courage to confront suffering and to restore freedom, for those filled with your spirit and will can never be enslaved. Hear my prayer. Amen.

33. "Act of Military Surrender."
34. Truman, "V-E Day Proclamation."

Mother's Day
Second Sunday

Text: "Whereas by a Joint Resolution approved May 8, 1914, 'designating the second Sunday in May as Mother's Day . . . ,' the president is authorized and requested to issue a proclamation calling upon the government officials to display the United States flag on all government buildings, and the people of the United States to display the flag at their homes or other suitable places on the second Sunday in May as a public expression of our love and reverence for the mothers of our country, . . . I, Woodrow Wilson, President of the United States of America . . . , hereby direct the government officials to display the United States flag on all government buildings and do invite the people of the United States to display the flag at their homes or other suitable places on the second Sunday of May as a public expression of our love and reverence for the mothers of our country."[35]

Reflection: It may seem quaint that a little over one hundred years ago the public expression of love and reverence for mothers was shown by flying the United States flag! President Woodrow Wilson's proclamation of the first national Mother's Day on May 9, 1914, was the culmination of mother's day movements beginning in 1868 with Ann Jarvis, who worked to establish a Mother's Friendship Day, whose purpose was to reunite families divided during the Civil War. Previously, Jarvis had founded Mother's Day Work Clubs to improve both sanitation and health for camps of soldiers experiencing typhoid fever. While Jarvis had other ideas, she died on May 9, 1905, before having accomplished them. Jarvis's daughter, Anna Jarvis, established the present form of Mother's Day observance with the help of John Wanamaker, a Philadelphia merchant. She began with a service of worship and celebration on May 12, 1907, in Andrews Methodist Episcopal Church, Grafton, West Virginia, where her mother had taught Sunday School. On May 10, 1908, she repeated the service in the same church, but added a larger ceremony in Wanamaker Auditorium in the store in Philadelphia, where attendees received white carnations, the favorite flower of her mother. After campaigning to establish the day as a national holiday, observance of Mother's Day was taking place in all states by 1911. The emphasis on the celebration was on sentiment; the younger Jarvis wanted people to appreciate and honor their mothers with handwritten letters stating their love and gratitude. She saw the day as a personal celebration between mothers and families; she advocated wearing a white carnation and visiting one's mother or attending church services. In 1912, in an attempt to stem the tide of commercialization of the day, Jarvis trademarked "Second Sunday in May, Mother's Day, Anna Jarvis, Founder." She wanted the holiday to be a family celebration honoring its mother, not a day honoring all mothers in the country or in the world.

---

35. Wilson, "A Proclamation."

Nevertheless, the U.S. House of Representatives passed a resolution on May 10, 1913, calling upon all federal government officials to wear a white carnation on Mother's Day. On May 8, 1914, the U.S. Congress—which had rejected a proposal to make Mother's Day an official holiday in 1908—passed a law which designated the second Sunday of May as Mother's Day and requested that President Woodrow Wilson proclaim it as such. The text of that proclamation above was signed by Wilson on May 9, 1914, and it declared the first national Mother's Day. By ten years later, the holiday had become almost totally commercialized with all kinds of flowers, pink carnations if one's mother was alive and red carnations if one's mother was dead, cards, candy, brunch, jewelry, long distance telephone calls, gifts, sports events, etc. Jarvis saw all this as an abuse of the celebration, and spent her inheritance and life fighting it, until she died in 1948. Today, displaying the flag as a public expression of our love and reverence for the mothers of our country is all but forgotten in the midst of the economic commerce that now characterizes the holiday.

Journal/Meditation: If your mother is still alive, how do you express your love and gratitude to her? If your mother is deceased, how do you express your love and gratitude to her? What aspects of Mother's Day do you consider to be too commercialized?

Prayer: God, my Mother, I remember with gratitude my mother through whom you gave me birth. You exalted motherhood when your Son took flesh in the womb of his mother, Mary. Give courage and strength to all mothers in their joy of bringing forth new life today, tomorrow, and forever. Amen.

INTERNATIONAL DAY OF FAMILIES
May 15

Text: ". . . Convinced that equality between the sexes, women's equal participation in employment, and shared parental responsibility are essential elements of modern family policy; conscious of the existence of various concepts of the family in different social, cultural, and political systems; aware, at the same time, that families are the fullest reflection, at the grass-roots level, of the strengths and weaknesses of the social and developmental welfare environment, and, as such, offer a uniquely comprehensive and synthesizing approach to social issues; realizing that families, as basic units of social life, are major agents of sustainable development at all levels of society and that their contribution to that process is crucial for its success; . . . [the General Assembly of the United Nations] decides that beginning in 1994, 15 May of every year shall be observed as the International Day of Families."[36]

Reflection: On December 8, 1989, in Resolution 44/82, the General Assembly of the United Nations recognized the efforts of governments at national, regional, and local

---

36. United Nations General Assembly, A/RES/47/237.

levels in carrying out specific programs concerning the family in which the U.N. had the role of raising awareness, increasing understanding, and promoting policies that improve the position and wellbeing of the family, and it proclaimed 1994 to be the International Year of the Family. On December 14, 1990, in Resolution 45/133, the U.N. General Assembly expressed its confidence that the 1994 International Year of the Family would offer a unique opportunity for mobilizing efforts, especially at the local and national levels, to highlight the importance of the family, to promote a better understanding of its functions and problems, and to strengthen national institutions to formulate, implement, and monitor policies in respect of the family. On December 16, 1991, the General Assembly of the U.N. noted in Resolution 46/92 that an increased awareness and a highlighted importance of family issues could be detected among governments, specialized agencies, regional commissions, and intergovernmental and nongovernmental organizations in promoting a better knowledge of the economic, social, and demographic processes affecting families and their members. The U.N. also noted that there had been focused attention on the equal rights and responsibilities of all family members. On September 20, 1993, as revealed in the text above, the U.N. General Assembly declared that during the International Year of the Family, May 15 would be observed in 1994 and then every year as the International Day of Families. It saw 1994 "as a special occasion to benefit families of the world in their quest for a better life for all, based on the principle of subsidiarity, which seeks solutions to problems at the lowest level of the societal structure."[37]

The International Day of Families is designed to provide an opportunity to promote awareness of issues relating to families and to increase the knowledge of the social, economic, and demographic processes affecting families. The social aspect of family concerns its place in human society. The economic refers to the family's place in a country's economy. And the demographic refers to the characteristics of a country and how the family illustrates those characteristics. Over the years, various themes have been explored concerning families, including: poverty and homelessness; partnership; education and human rights; development; HIV/AIDS; disabilities; migration, intergenerational solidarity; gender equality; sustainable future; inclusive societies; climate change; and new technologies, to name a few. On the familial level, the International Day of Families can be marked by such activities as planting a garden together, preparing a meal together, telling and recording family stories, backyard camping, volunteering for a community project, creating a family tree, or organizing a block or community picnic. The members of a family must decide how they will promote awareness of issues relating to their family, while also increasing their knowledge of the social, economic, and demographic processes affecting them.

---

37. United Nations General Assembly, A/RES/47/237.

Journal/Meditation: What social issues affect your family? What economic issues affect your family? What demographic process affects your family? How will your family mark the International Day of Families?

Prayer: God, you created the human family so that its members could live in harmony with each other. In my family members instill a great love that results in unity. Grant that in our mutual care we may recognize you at work in our lives. Amen.

Peace Officers Memorial Day and Police Week
May 15

Text: "Resolved by the Senate and House of Representatives of the United States of America in congress assembled, that the week of May 13–19, 1962, is hereby designated as Police Week, in recognition of the contribution the police officers of America have made to our civilization through their dedicated and selfless efforts in enforcing the laws of our cities, counties, and states and of the United States regardless of the peril or hazard to themselves, and May 14th is hereby designated as Peace Officers Memorial Day in honor of the federal, state, and municipal peace officers who have been killed or disabled in [the] line of duty. Through their enforcement of our laws our country has internal freedom from fear of the violence and civil disorder that is presently affecting other nations. To this end the president is authorized and requested to issue a proclamation inviting the people of the United States to observe such period, with appropriate ceremonies and activities, as a tribute to the men and women who, night and day, stand guard in our midst to protect us through enforcement of our laws, and to honor those who have lost their lives in service to the community."[38]

Reflection: The first public law enacting Police Week and Peace Officers Memorial Day went into effect on June 21, 1961. As can be seen in the above text, the joint resolution established Police Week of May 13–19 and Peace Officers Memorial Day on May 14 of that year. The president, John F. Kennedy, issued a proclamation on April 10, 1962, doing what the congress had empowered him to do. He wrote, ". . . [O]ur law enforcement agencies play an essential role in safeguarding the rights and freedoms which have been guaranteed by the Constitution to every American citizen. . . . [T]he nation's police departments have grown to be modern and scientific law enforcement bodies which unceasingly provide a vital public service."[39] He indicated that Police Week was "in recognition of the contribution the police officers of America have made to our civilization through their dedicated and selfless efforts in enforcing our laws," and that Peace Officers Memorial Day was "in honor of the federal, state, and municipal peace officers who have been killed or disabled in [the] line of duty

---

38. "Public Law 87–54."
39. Kennedy, "Proclamation 3466."

....."[40] He invited the people of the United States to "join in commemorating police officers, past and present, who by their faithful and loyal devotion to their responsibilities have rendered a dedicated service to their communities and, in so doing, have established for themselves an enviable and enduring reputation for preserving the rights and security of all citizens."[41] On October 1, 1962, congress issued Public Law 87–726, which established May 15 of every year as Peace Officers Memorial Day—"in honor of the federal, state, and municipal officers who have been killed or disabled in the line of duty"— and the calendar week in which May 15 occurred as Police Week—"in recognition of the service given by the men and women who, night and day, stand guard in our midst to protect us through enforcement of our laws . . . ."[42] The joint resolution states that "the police officers of America have worked devotedly and selflessly in behalf of the people of this nation, regardless of the peril or hazard to themselves; and . . . these officers have safeguarded the lives and property of their fellow Americans; and . . . by the enforcement of our laws, these same officers have given our country internal freedom from fear of the violence and civil disorder that is presently affecting other nations; and . . . these men and women by their patriotic service and their dedicated efforts have earned the gratitude of the republic . . . ."[43] In response, Kennedy issued a proclamation on May 4, 1963, stating that "it is important that our people know and understand the problems, duties, and responsibilities of their police departments and the necessity for cooperating with them in maintaining law and order; and . . . it is fitting and proper that we express our gratitude for the dedicated service and courageous deeds of law enforcement officers and for the contributions they have made to the security and wellbeing of our people."[44] He also indicated that May 15 was "in honor of those peace officers who, through their courageous deeds, have lost their lives or have become disabled in the performance of duty."[45] On May 15, 1972, President Richard Nixon issued a statement about the week and day "paying tribute to the men and women of the law enforcement profession" and "honoring . . . the sacrifices of peace officers killed or disabled in the line of duty." He added: "These observances focus deserved recognition on the quiet but perilous heroism of the policemen and policewomen in communities across the land. They provide an occasion for us to thank these dedicated professions for doing an often thankless job so superbly."[46] On May 13, 1982, President Ronald Regan issued his first of four messages on Police Week and Peace Officers Memorial Day. He wrote: "Police officers shoulder the trust of their fellow citizens in their daily effort to provide the

40. Kennedy, "Proclamation 3466."
41. Kennedy, "Proclamation 3466."
42. "Public Law 87–726."
43. "Public Law 87–726."
44. Kennedy, "Proclamation 3537."
45. Kennedy, "Proclamation 3537."
46. Nixon, "Statement."

Monthly Entries for the Spiritual but not Religious through the Year

protection and service that are increasingly important to our nation. Those officers who have made the supreme sacrifice have demonstrated their devotion to the fundamental values of decency so essential to the wellbeing of American life."[47] He issued similar messages in 1984, 1985, and 1988.

Following Reagan's protocol, George Bush issued a message on May 13, 1989. In it, he stated: "Throughout the country, in each and every community, citizens expect the highest standards of conduct and character in those men and women who work in [the law enforcement] field: honor, integrity, diligence, bravery, and professionalism. Police Week is a fitting time to show our special appreciation for these individuals . . . . Police Officers' Memorial Day poignantly reminds us that law enforcement officials face great danger every day of the year."[48] He invited all citizens to join him in expressing heartfelt respect and gratitude to the nation's law enforcement officers throughout the year. In 1991, he issued a similar message. On September 13, 1994, Public Law 87–276 was amended; the officials of the government were instructed "to display at half-staff the flag of the United States on all government buildings on . . . Peace Officers Memorial Day."[49] President William J. Clinton incorporated that amendment into his May 15, 1995, proclamation. "Each year," he wrote, "we pause to remember and to honor the brave men and women whose heartfelt commitment to the law and to their fellow citizens cost them their lives." Later, in the two-page document, which consists of two paragraphs of statistics, he wrote, "America's law enforcement officers face extraordinary risks . . . ."[50] Clinton issued similar proclamations in 1996 (Proclamation 6895), 1997 (Proclamation 7000), 1998 (Proclamation 7095), 1999 (Proclamation 7195), and 2000 (Proclamation 7307). Following Clinton's lead, George W. Bush issued his first of eight Peace Officers Memorial Day and Police Week proclamations on May 8, 2001. He stated: "Police Week provides an opportunity to recognize the selfless dedication of the brave men and women who devote their lives to protecting and serving our communities. . . . We look to them to uphold the principle that no one is beyond the protection or reach of the law. . . . [O]n Peace Officers Memorial Day [we] honor those officers who made the ultimate sacrifice while performing their sworn duty. I urge all Americans to use this occasion to pay tribute to these fallen heroes by recalling their devotion, celebrating their lives, and honoring their service. Tragically, making America safer often requires great sacrifice."[51] Bush issued similar documents in 2002 (Proclamation 7558), 2003 (Proclamation 7675), 2004 (Proclamation 7784), 2005 (Proclamation 7901), 2006 (Proclamation 8014), 2007 (Proclamation 8144), and 2008 (Proclamation 8255). President Barack Obama issued a statement on National Peace Office Memorial Day, May 15, 2008, in which

47. Reagan, "Message."
48. Bush, "Message."
49. "Public Law 103–322."
50. Clinton, "Proclamation 6800."
51. Bush, G.W., "Proclamation 7435."

he acknowledged that "we honor the men and women who lost their lives making our streets safer and our families more secure . . . and our thoughts and prayers go out to their loved ones."[52] On May 11, 2009, he issued the first of eight statements. "Law enforcement officers routinely place themselves in harm's way to protect people they do not and will not know," he wrote. "They serve willingly and devotedly, and their commitment is essential for us to maintain a healthy quality of life, a strong economy, the safety of our families, and a robust national security system." Later, he added, "The benefits that peace officers provide come with great sacrifice. Every year, many give their lives in the performance of their duties."[53] Obama issued similar documents in 2010 (Proclamation 8518), 2011 (Proclamation 8676), 2012 (Proclamation 8821), 2013 (Proclamation 8979), 2014 (Proclamation 9123), 2015 (Proclamation 9277), and 2016 (Proclamation 9448). On May 15, 2017, President Donald J. Trump issued his first of four proclamations, stating: ". . . [W]e honor the men and women of law enforcement who have been killed or disabled in the course of serving our communities. Police officers are the thin blue line whose sacrifices protect and serve us every day, and we pledge to support them as they risk their lives to safeguard ours." He added, "Our liberties depend on the rule of law, and that means supporting the incredible men and women of law enforcement."[54] Trump issued similar proclamations in 2018 (Proclamation 9748), 2019 (Proclamation 9884), and 2020 (Proclamation 10032). On May 7, 2021, President Joseph R. Biden issued his first two-page Proclamation of Peace Officers Memorial Day and Police Week, stating: "Every morning, our nation's law enforcement officers pin on a badge and go to work, not knowing what the day will bring, and hoping to come home safely. . . . As we recognize Peace Officers Memorial Day and Police Week, we honor those who lost their lives in the line of duty, and thank them on behalf of this grateful nation for their service."[55] Among other points made, Biden stated, "We must . . . stop tasking law enforcement with problems that are far beyond their jurisdictions."[56] Thus, on Peace Officers Memorial Day and Police Week, the U.S. pays tribute to all police officers who have died or been disabled in the line of duty and those men and women who serve the country in law enforcement.

Journal/Meditation: Is there a difference between a Peace Officer and a Police Officer? Explain. What specific rights and privileges do law enforcement officers guarantee for you? If you know a police officer, what has he or she sacrificed?

Prayer: Father, who embrace the universe with your care, watch over all police officers. Keep them safe in their duty of making peace and protecting rights throughout my community. All glory be yours, O God, forever. Amen.

52. Obama, "Obama Statement."
53. Obama, "Proclamation 8378."
54. Trump, "Proclamation 9611."
55. Biden, "Proclamation 10208."
56. Biden, "Proclamation 10208."

Armed Forces Week and Day
Second Saturday to Third Sunday and Third Saturday

Text: "Whereas the Armed Forces of the United States serve the nation with courage and devotion both in war and in peace; and . . . whereas it is fitting and proper that we devote one day each year to paying tribute to the Armed Forces as the servants and protectors of our nation; now, therefore, I, Harry S. Truman, President of the United States of America, do hereby proclaim that Saturday, May 20, 1950, shall be known as Armed Forces Day . . . to honor the Armed Forces of the United States and the millions of veterans who have returned to civilian pursuits. As Commander in Chief of the Armed Forces . . . , I direct [that the day be marked] with appropriate ceremonies . . . . I call upon my fellow citizens to display the flag of the United States at their homes . . . and to participate in exercises expressive of our recognition of the skill, gallantry, and uncompromising devotion to duty characteristic of the Armed Forces in carrying out their missions."[57]

Reflection: Armed Forces Day was announced by Secretary of Defense Louis Johnson on August 31, 1949. It was designed to replace the individual Army, Navy, Air Force, and Marine Corps celebrations. Combining all of them into a single day would demonstrate their unification under the Department of Defense. On February 27, 1950, President Harry S. Truman noted that the Armed Forces were "a unified team, . . . performing at home and across the seas tasks vital to the security of the nation and to the establishment of a durable peace."[58] Besides demonstrating the unity of the United States Armed Forces, the day—later changed to the third Saturday of May and the week from the second Saturday to the third Sunday of May—is designed to increase awareness in citizens of the nation's Armed Forces. By expanding the public's understanding of what type of job is performed by each branch of the military and the role of the military in civilian life, more citizens can be attracted to serving in a branch of the military. "The support of an informed American people is increasingly important to the Armed Forces in these days of rapid technological advance, quick reaction time, and grave threat to our freedom," stated Robert S. McNamara, former Secretary of Defense, in 1962.[59] It is also a day to showcase to the public the modern equipment employed by the Armed Forces and to acknowledge and honor the people serving in its ranks.

Johnson declared that the day marks the combined demonstration of American's defense team towards the goal of readiness for any eventuality. "It is the first parade of preparedness by the unified forces of our land, sea, and air defense," he said.[60] General

---

57. Truman, "Proclamation 2873."
58. Truman, "Proclamation 2873."
59. "Armed Forces Day."
60. "Armed Forces Day."

Omar N. Bradley, former Chairman of the Joint Chiefs of Staff, stated, "The heritage of freedom must be guarded as carefully in peace as it was in war."[61] Admiral Forrest P. Sherman called upon all citizens to "honor the American fighting man [and woman]. For it is he [or she]—the soldier, the sailor, the airman, the marine—who has fought to preserve freedom."[62] In 1959, Neil McElroy, former Secretary of Defense, added, "The return on this investment, in terms of national strength, shows the determination of the American people to preserve our way of life and to give hope to all who seek peace with freedom and justice."[63] Originally created to honor Americans wearing the uniforms of their country and serving in the Army, Navy, Marine Corps, Air Force, and Coast Guard—today adding the Space Force—we note their determined spirit of patriotism and professionalism in the constant quest for peace and freedom, knowing that "the survival of freedom requires great cost and commitment, and great personal sacrifice," according to President John F. Kennedy in 1963.[64]

Journal/Meditation: Whom do you know who has or is serving in the Armed Forces? How does he or she display courage and devotion in service as a servant and protector of our nation? What skill does he or she employ in duty to our country?

Prayer: God of freedom and peace, keep your watchful eye on your servants in the Army, Navy, Marine Corps, Air Force, Coast Guard, and Space Force who protect our nation. Fill them with courage, give them devotion to their duty, and honor their personal sacrifice. Hear my prayer for all who wear the uniforms of our country. Amen.

World Bee Day
May 20

Text: "Recognizing . . . the urgent need to protect bees and other pollinators in a sustainable manner; . . . noting the urgent need to address the issue of the worldwide decline of pollinator diversity and the risks that this implies for agriculture sustainability, human livelihoods, and food supplies; recognizing the fundamental role and contribution of bees and other pollinators with respect to sustainable food production and nutrition, which thereby promote food security for the world's growing population and contribute to poverty alleviation, hunger eradication, and human health; recognizing also the contribution of the ecosystem services provided by bees and other pollinators to ecosystem health by safeguarding the state of biodiversity, species, and genetic diversity; expressing concern that bees and other pollinators are endangered by a range of factors, in particular the effects of human activities such as changes in land use, intensive agricultural practices, and the use of pesticides, as well

---

61. "Armed Forces Day."
62. "Armed Forces Day."
63. "Armed Forces Day."
64. "Armed Forces Day."

as pollution, pests, diseases, and climate change, which threaten their habitat, health, and development; acknowledging the urgent need to raise awareness at all levels and to promote and facilitate actions for the protection of bees and other pollinators in order to contribute to their health and development . . . ; [the General Assembly of the United Nations] decides to designate 20 May as World Bee Day . . . ."[65]

Reflection: On December 20, 2017, the General Assembly of the United Nations established World Bee Day with an over-two-page resolution which expresses the universality of bees and other pollinators in the world and all that threatens their existence. The U.N. recognized "the importance of promoting sustainable development in its three dimensions in an innovative, coordinated, environmentally sound, open, and shared manner, and the urgent need to protect bees and other pollinators in a sustainable manner" while also "taking into account [an] assessment report on pollinators, pollination, and food production."[66] It recognized "that the observance of a World Bee Day by the international community would contribute significantly to raising awareness of the importance of bees and other pollinators at all levels and would promote global efforts and collective action for their protection. . . . [T]hrough education and activities aimed at raising awareness of the importance of bees and other pollinators, the threats that they face, and their contribution to sustainable development,"[67] the U.N. sought to show the world what was happening to bees and other pollinators and the consequences if action were not taken to acknowledge the role of bees and other pollinators for the ecosystem. May 20 was chosen for World Bee Day because it is the birthday of Anton Jansa, who pioneered modern beekeeping techniques in the eighteenth century in his native Slovenia; he praised the bees for their ability to work so hard, while needing so little attention.

Now, however, bees and other pollinators need a lot of attention. The importance of bees is not focused only on the supply of honey they provide. On September 15, 2014, Slovenian beekeeper Bostjan Noc began the effort for World Bee Day. He knew that every third spoonful of the world's food relies on bees and other pollinators and that bees are increasingly endangered—in some places no longer able to survive—and human intervention was needed, and the global public needed to be made aware that it needed to preserve not only honey bees, but other pollinators, such as butterflies, bats, and hummingbirds. More than 75 percent of the world's food crops depend on pollinators. "The goal [of World Bee Day] is to strengthen measures aimed at protecting bees and other pollinators, which . . . significantly contribute to solving problems related to the global food supply and eliminate hunger in developing countries."[68] Bees and other pollinators are threatened by invasive insects, pesticides, land-use change,

---

65. United Nations General Assembly, A/RES/72/211.
66. United Nations General Assembly A/RES/72/211.
67. United Nations General Assembly, A/RES/72/211.
68. "World Bee Day."

monocropping practices, and higher temperatures associated with climate change, all of which destroy bee colonies over time. Individually, World Bee Day can be observed by planting diverse native plants, which flower at different times of the year and draw bees; by buying honey from local farms, by buying products from sustainable agriculture practices; by avoiding the use of pesticides, fungicides, or herbicides in gardens; by sponsoring a bee hive; by making a bee water fountain by leaving a water bowl outside; by help to sustain forest ecosystems; by raising awareness through sharing information with others about the decline of bees and how that affects everyone around the world. "Bees pollinate a third of what we eat and play an essential role in preserving the planet's ecosystems," states "World Bee Day."[69] Everyone in the universe needs to protect, support, and remove anything that threatens them; for whatever threatens the bees also threatens everyone in the world.

Journal/Meditation: What specific action can you take to preserve the bee population where you live? With whom can you share information about the threats that bees face and what can be done to remove those threats?

Prayer: Creator of all, you made bees to swarm and, by working together, to form a hive and to produce honeycombs of sweet delight for people to enjoy. Inspire me with a greater awareness of the role bees play in my life, give me the wisdom to know how to protect them where I live, and fill me with the courage to challenge practices that threaten their existence. Amen.

World Day for Cultural Diversity for Dialogue and Development
May 21

Text: ". . . [R]ecognizing that the United Nations should give greater weight and visibility to the theme of dialogue among civilizations, cultures, and religions, since the protection of cultural diversity is closely linked to the larger framework of the dialogue among civilizations and cultures and its ability to achieve genuine mutual understanding, solidarity, and cooperation; encouraged by . . . the promotion of dialogue and cooperation among the world's civilizations and peoples, irrespective of race, disabilities, religion, language, culture, or tradition; underlining the fact that tolerance and respect for cultural diversity and universal promotion and protection of human rights, including the right to development, are mutually supportive, and recognizing that tolerance and respect for diversity effectively promote and are supported by . . . empowerment of women; . . . [the General Assembly of the United Nations] proclaims 21 May the World Day for Cultural Diversity for Dialogue and Development . . . ."[70]

---

69. "World Bee Day."
70. United Nations General Assembly, A/RES/57/249.

Reflection: According to the United Nations General Assembly's three-page resolution of December 20, 2002, from which the above text is taken, dialogue—formal discussion that leads to understanding—is the means for sharing the diversity of cultures and for the development of them. The purpose of the day is "[t]o raise public awareness of the value and importance of cultural diversity, and, in particular to encourage, through education and the media, knowledge of the positive value of cultural diversity . . . as regards languages" and "to promote awareness of the crucial relationship between culture and development and the important role of information and communication technologies in this relationship."[71] In other words, the day provides the opportunity for communities to understand the value of cultural diversity in their midst, learn how to foster its development, and live with it in harmony. Exactly two years before the above resolution was approved (December 20, 2000), the U.N. General Assembly approved a resolution on culture and development. "Bearing in mind the importance of cultural values and cultural diversity as elements of sustainable development," the resolution stated; "underlining the fact that tolerance and respect for cultural diversity and universal promotion and protection of human rights, including the right to development, are mutually supportive; [and] emphasizing the need to enhance the potential of culture as a means of prosperity, sustainable development, and global coexistence;" the U.N. invited its members to cooperate with the United Nations Educational, Scientific, and Cultural Organization (UNESCO) by "commit[ting] themselves to promoting the dialogue among civilizations as an essential process for human development and mutual understanding and for strengthening international cooperation," while also encouraging UNESCO "to continue its work to promote a greater awareness of the crucial relationship between culture and development."[72]

In between the December 20, 2000, resolution and the December 20, 2002, resolution, the UNESCO issued its Universal Declaration on Cultural Diversity on November 2, 2001. "Culture takes diverse forms across time and space," states article 1. "This diversity is embodied in the uniqueness and plurality of the identities of the groups and societies making up humankind. As a source of exchange, innovation, and creativity, cultural diversity is as necessary for humankind as biodiversity is for nature. In this sense, it is the common heritage of humanity and should be recognized and affirmed for the benefit of present and future generations."[73] The declaration continues: "In our increasingly diverse societies, it is essential to ensure harmonious interaction among people and groups with plural, varied, and dynamic cultural identities as well as their willingness to live together. . . . [C]ultural pluralism gives policy expression to the reality of cultural diversity. . . . [C]ultural pluralism is conducive to cultural exchange and to the flourishing of creative capacity that sustain public life."[74] In Article

71. United Nations General Assembly, A/RES/57/249.
72. United Nations General Assembly, A/RES/55/192.
73. "Universal Declaration on Cultural Diversity," Article 1.
74. "Universal Declaration on Cultural Diversity," Article 2.

4, the document states: "The defense of cultural diversity is an ethical imperative, inseparable from respect for human dignity. It implies a commitment to human rights and fundamental freedoms, in particular the rights of persons belonging to minorities and those of indigenous peoples."[75] The next article explains: "Cultural rights are an integral part of human rights, which are universal, indivisible, and interdependent. The flourishing of creative diversity requires the full implementation of cultural rights . . . . All persons have therefore the right to express themselves and to create and disseminate their work in the language of their choice, and particularly in their mother tongue . . . ."[76] Article 6 continues: "Freedom of expression, media pluralism, multilingualism, equal access to art and to scientific and technological knowledge, including in digital form, and the possibility for all cultures to have access to the means of expression and dissemination are the guarantees of cultural diversity."[77] Bringing together the previous articles, Article 7 declares: "Creation draws on the roots of cultural tradition, but flourishes in contact with other cultures. . . . Heritage in all its forms must be preserved, enhanced, and handed on to future generations as a record of human experience and aspirations, so as to foster creativity in all its diversity and to inspire genuine dialogue among cultures."[78] There are many more insights worthy of reflection in the UNESCO's three-page universal declaration. In a global world, diversity needs to be respected because, through dialogue, it becomes the source of harmony and development.

Journal/Meditation: What cultural diversity do you protect through dialogue with others? What gets in the way of mutual understanding? How culturally plural is the area where you live? What does each culture contribute to creativity? What cultural rights are enjoyed by all?

Prayer: In your world, God, cultural diversity gives birth to knowledge, understanding, and respect. Out of pluralism, you create harmony. Inspire all people from various cultural backgrounds to include rather than exclude, to respect rights rather than impose prejudice, and to preserve heritage rather than destroy it. Make of me a willing instrument fostering cultural diversity where I live. Amen.

---

75. "Universal Declaration on Cultural Diversity," Article 4.
76. "Universal Declaration on Cultural Diversity," Article 5.
77. "Universal Declaration on Cultural Diversity," Article 6.
78. "Universal Declaration on Cultural Diversity," Article 7.

National Wine Day
May 25

Text: "[O LORD, my God,] you cause the grass to grow for the cattle, and plants for people to use, to bring forth food from the earth, and wine to gladden the human heart, oil to make the face shine, and bread to strengthen the human heart."[79]

Reflection: According to *Holidays Calendar*, National Wine Day on May 25 "is a day to buy wine, appreciate wine, and enjoy the history of wine" because "this alcoholic beverage has been a part of human civilization for at least 8,000 years."[80] While the buying of wine is something you, the reader, will need to do, the two verses from Psalm 104 above begin the appreciation of wine; namely, it gladdens the human heart. Wine is made from fermented grapes (or other fruits). During the process of fermentation, yeast consumes the sugars in the grapes and converts them into alcohol. Different grapes produce different wines. More complex flavors of wines are the result of winemakers combining different grapes or different wines. A wine's color is not the result of the color of the grape. The color of the wine is the result of the tannins in the grape skins that are placed in the vat during the fermentation process; the amount of time the grape skin stays in the juice is known as maceration. In general, white wines are sweeter, and red wines are drier. In general, white wines are consumed chilled, and red wines are consumed at room temperature. After uncorking an older wine, one enjoys its bouquet; however, after uncorking a younger wine, one enjoys its aroma. In the United States, the most wine that is consumed is in the states of California, Florida, and New York. In southwestern France, wine has been produced since Rome ruled the world; Romans mixed lead with wine to help preserve it and to give it a sweeter taste. Eiswein (Ice Wine), a very sweet beverage made from grapes that have frozen on the vine, was invented by the Germans. And not all wines improve with age; many are produced with the intention that they will be consumed within a few years.

The oldest winery found by archaeologists dates from 4300 BCE in a cave in Armenia. "Archaeologists call it a winery," according to National Wine Day, "because they discovered not only cups and jars for holding wine, but other equipment such as wine presses and fermentation vats that were used in the production of wine."[81] However, winemaking goes back 8,000 years; 8,000-year-old wine was found in the country of Georgia. People mark National Wine Day by pouring a glass of their favorite wine and maybe reminiscing with family and friends or enjoying it with a favorite meal. A person can visit his or her favorite winery, make wine ice-ream, wine slushies, cook with wine, or bring a bottle of wine to a friend. National Wine Day is not the only time wine is celebrated throughout the year. There are the following celebrations:

---

79. NRSV: Psalm 104:14–15.
80. "National Wine Day."
81. "National Wine Day."

International Riesling Day (March 13), International Malbec Day (April 17), International Sauvignon Blanc Day (First Friday of May), National Moscato Day (May 9), International Pinot Grigio Day (May 17), National Chardonnay Day (Thursday before Memorial Day in May), National Rose Day (Second Saturday in June), Drink Chenin Blanc Day (June 20), World Lambrusco Day (June 21), International Shiraz Day (Fourth Thursday of July), National White Wine Day (August 4), National Pinot Noir Day (August 18), National Red Wine Day (August 28), International Cabernet Sauvignon Day (August 30), National Chianti Day (First Friday in September), International Grenache Day (Third Friday of September), International Pinotage Day (Second Saturday of October), International Merlot Day (November 7), International Tempranillo Day (Second Thursday in November), National Zinfandel Day (Third Wednesday of November), International Beaujolais Nouveau Day (Third Thursday in November), International Carménère Day (November 24), International Cabernet Franc Day (December 4), National Sangria Day (December 20), and National Champagne Day (December 31).[82] The above list is not exhaustive, the date may vary from one list to another, and there is also the National Wine and Cheese Day on July 25! Celebrate National Wine Day by buying a bottle of wine to go with dinner, attend a wine tasting, or invite friends to join you for wine, cheese, and crackers.

Journal/Meditation: For what occasions do you buy wine? What do you appreciate most about wine? What history of wine is new to you?

Prayer: O LORD, my God, you bring forth wine from the grapes that grow on the earth to gladden the human heart. Give me a greater appreciation for this beverage and its history. When I drink wine, fill me with your Spirit that I may ponder all the good things that you have made. Amen.

RED NOSE DAY
Last Thursday

Text: "The iconic Red Nose . . . provides an easy way for everyone to get involved and show . . . support while capturing the essence of what Red Nose Day is all about: coming together to make a difference for children in need."[83]

Reflection: In the United States, since 2015, Red Nose Day is celebrated on the last Thursday of May. It is a campaign with the mission to end child poverty "by funding programs that keep children safe, healthy, educated, and empowered."[84] Through entertainment, people are brought together to laugh and have fun, while raising funds for children in need, poverty alleviation, and worldwide charities. The most

---

82. "Wine Holidays."
83. "What is Red Nose Day?"
84. "What is Red Nose Day?"

prominent sign of the day, as indicated in the above text, is a plastic or foam red nose, which is given in various places in exchange for a donation. People are encouraged to wear the red nose to help raise awareness of the Comic Relief charity and, of course, to make people laugh. While most people may not be aware of this fact, the design of the red nose has been changed each year. According to Becca Marsh in "30 Facts About Red Nose Day," "The idea behind Red Nose Day was to have one day of the year when everyone does something silly or comedic to raise money for Comic Relief, a non-profit organization."[85] She adds, "It is a day where everyone can have some fun, be silly and let loose, which is not only liberating for each individual, but allows everyone to laugh together and raise funds for a great cause."[86]

The charity known as Comic Relief began in England on Christmas Day 1985 as a response to famine in Ethiopia and other poverty-stricken areas around the world. Richard Curtis, a British comedy scriptwriter, and Lenny Henry, a British comedian, co-founded and co-created the charity. On February 8, 1988, Henry went to Ethiopia, where he celebrated the first Red Nose Day. In 2015, Red Nose Day came to the United States to raise funds for Comic Relief's U.S. charity, named Comic Relief, Inc., an independent organization, whose vision of a just world is one free from poverty. Comic Relief, Inc.,[87] launched Red Nose Day in 2015 in the U.S. The red nose serves as the logo and gives the day its title. The day is hosted on NBC TV.

Journal/Meditation: Why do you think it is important to laugh, have fun, and raise funds for the poor with an annual telethon? What does the red nose mean to you?

Prayer: Ever-living God, you have taught me to be mindful of those who live in poverty by acts of charity. Grant that the red nose I wear this day will remind others that there are less fortunate people in their midst and move them to laughter and a donation that is acceptable in your sight. All glory be to you, O God, forever and ever. Amen.

Memorial Day
Last Monday

Text: "The thirtieth day of May, 1868, is designated for the purpose of strewing with flowers, or otherwise decorating the grave of comrades who died in defense of their country during the late rebellion, and whose bodies now lie in almost every city, village, and hamlet churchyard in the land. . . . We should guard their graves with sacred vigilance. All that the consecrated wealth and taste of the nation can add to their

---

85. Marsh, "30 Facts."
86. Marsh, "30 Facts."
87. Comic Relief is a United Kingdom charity for the needy. Comic Relief U.S.A. was begun in 1986 and dissolved in 2011; it was focused primarily on the homeless. Comic Relief, Inc., is the U.S. sponsor of Red Nose Day, beginning May 21, 2015, a charity telethon on NBC.

adornment and security is but a fitting tribute to the memory of her slain defenders. Let pleasant paths invite the coming and going of reverent visitors and fond mourners. Let no neglect, no ravages of time, testify to the present or to the coming generations that we have forgotten as a people the cost of a free and undivided republic."[88]

Reflection: While after the end of the Civil War in 1865 various states found ways to honor their war dead, it was three years later, in 1868, that General John A. Logan, Commander in Chief of the Grand Army of the Republic—founded in 1866 and dissolved in 1956—a fraternal organization composed of veterans of the Union army, navy, and marines who served in the Civil War—issued the first call on May 5, 1868, to observe May 30, 1868, as a day to decorate the graves of those who died in defense of the country. In the text above, Logan asks citizens to strew their graves with flowers and to guard them with sacred vigilance in memory of the nation's slain defenders. He urges people not to forget the cost of freedom and the cost of a united nation. After World War I, the holiday evolved to honor military personnel who died in any war. In effect, Logan established what came to be known as Memorial Day; it was known as Decoration Day from May 30, 1868, to 1971, because that was the day the graves of military men and women were decorated with flowers and flags. While the day had often been referred to as Memorial Day as early as 1882, it was not until 1967 that its name was officially changed by federal law. On June 28, 1968, congress changed its May 30 date to the last Monday of May, effective 1971, also making it a federal holiday. On August 12, 1988, congress issued Public Law 105–225, 36 U.S. Code, Section 16, which declared the last Monday in May to be Memorial Day. That law states that the president is requested to issue a proclamation each year "(1) calling on the people of the United States to observe Memorial Day by praying, according to their individual religious faith, for permanent peace; (2) designating a period of time on Memorial Day during which the people may unite in prayer for a permanent peace; (3) calling on the people of the United States to unite in prayer at that time; and (4) calling on the media to join in observing Memorial Day and the period of prayer."[89] It is important to note that amid all other observances on Memorial Day, prayer—mentioned four times in the law—gets the most attention.

Memorial Day continued to evolve with parades, barbecues, camping, etc. until December 28, 2000, when congress enacted Public Law 106–579, known as the National Moment of Remembrance Act. "It is essential to remember and renew the legacy of Memorial Day," states the act, "which was established in 1868 to pay tribute to individuals who have made the ultimate sacrifice in service to the United States and their families."[90] It continues, "Greater strides must be made to demonstrate appreciation for those loyal people of the United States whose values, represented by their

---

88. Logan, "Memorial Day Order."
89. "Public Law 105–225," 36 U.S. Code, Section 116.
90. "Public Law 106–579."

sacrifices, are critical to the future of the United States."[91] In the morning of Memorial Day, the U.S. flag is raised to the top of the staff and then lowered to the half-staff position where it remains until noon, when it is raised to full-staff position for the rest of the day. As indicated above, the act establishes "a National Moment of Remembrance and other commemorative events [that] are needed to reclaim Memorial Day as the sacred and noble event that that day is intended to be."[92] At 3 p.m. Washington, DC, time a National Moment of Remembrance is held. The commission established by Public Law 106–579 is to "encourage the people of the United States to give something back to their country, which provides them so much freedom and opportunity."[93] The evening of Memorial Day features the National Memorial Day Concert, which takes place on the west lawn of the U.S Capitol; music is performed, and respect is paid to those who gave their lives for the nation. Many of those men and women are remembered with an artificial red poppy, adopted by the Veterans of Foreign Wars as its official memorial flower in 1922. Proceeds from the sale of the poppies assist veterans, their widows, widowers, and orphans.

Journal/Meditation: On Memorial Day, how do you honor the dead military who defended our country? When do you pray for permanent peace? How might you observe the National Moment of Remembrance? What do you give back to your country?

Prayer: Eternal God, while you desire a permanent peace among all people, there are times when values must be defended. Give rest to those who sacrificed their lives in military service for the good of my country. Guard their graves with your presence, and make me and my fellow citizens evermore grateful for our freedom. Amen.

---

91. "Public Law 106–579."
92. "Public Law 106–579."
93. "Public Law 106–579."

6

The Month of *June*

D-Day (Normandy Landings)
June 6

Text: "Soldiers, Sailors, and Airmen of the Allied Expeditionary Force! You are about to embark upon the Great Crusade, toward which we have striven these many months. The eyes of the world are upon you. The hopes and prayers of liberty-loving people everywhere march with you. In company with our brave Allies and brothers-in-arms on other fronts, you will bring about the destruction of the German war machine, the elimination of Nazi tyranny over the oppressed people of Europe, and security for ourselves in a free world. Your task will not be an easy one. . . . But this is the year 1944! . . . The tide has turned! The free men of the world are marching together to Victory! I have full confidence in your courage, devotion to duty, and skill in battle. We will accept nothing less than full Victory! . . . And let us beseech the blessing of Almighty God upon this great and noble undertaking."[1]

Reflection: The words in the above text were written and spoken on June 6, 1944, by Major General Dwight D. Eisenhower, Supreme Commander of Allied Forces, from the Supreme Headquarters of the Allied Expeditionary Force. Once the United States entered World War II, President Franklin D. Roosevelt placed Eisenhower in command of Allied forces on the Western Front: U.S., Britain, and Canada. June 6, 1944, was D-Day; multiple meanings have been assigned to the D: Designated day, Decision day, Doomsday, Death day, Disembarkation day, Debarkation day, Departed day, etc. According to the National World War II Museum, the D merely stands for Day; it is a code "for the day of any important invasion or military operation. . . . [T]he days before and after a D-Day were indicated using plus and minus signs: D-4 means four days before a D-Day, while D+7 meant seven days after a D-Day."[2] No matter what

---

1. Eisenhower, "Supreme Headquarters."
2. "What does the 'D' in D-Day mean?"

meaning is assigned to the D, June 6, 1944, was the day the landing operations and associated airborne operations began the ending of World War II. Known as Operation Overlord and technically codenamed Operation Neptune, the Normandy landing was the largest seaborne invasion in history. It laid the groundwork for the Allied victory on the Western front and the end of World War II.

The coast of Normandy was divided into five sectors: Utah Beach, Omaha Beach, Gold Beach, Juno Beach, and Sword Beach. Before troops poured onto the beaches, however, 24,000 American, British, and Canadian airborne troops began landing shortly after midnight; they were preceded by extensive aerial and naval bombardment along the coast and further inland. Then, minesweepers began to clear channels for the invasion, while naval bombardment targeted areas behind the beaches, while it was still dark. Tanks, specifically designed for the Normandy landings, prepared the way for the troops. Later, over a million troops forming thirty-nine Allied divisions would proceed to engage Nazi forces in the Battle of Normandy. Twenty-two U.S. divisions landed on Utah Beach and Omaha Beach. Twelve British divisions landed at Gold Beach and Sword Beach. Also, one French division landed at Sword Beach. Three Canadian divisions and one Polish division landed at Juno Beach. Around 5,000 landing and assault craft, 289 escort vessels, and 277 minesweepers made the Normandy landings possible. There are around 210,000 Allied casualties buried in the Normandy American Cemetery and Memorial, the Brittany American Cemetery and Memorial, the Banneville-la-Campagne War Cemetery, the Bayeux War Cemetery, the Brouay War Cemetery, the Cambes-en-Plaine War cemetery, the Fontenay-le-Pesnel War Cemetery, the Hermanville War Cemetery, the Hottot-les-Bagues War Cemetery, La Delivrande War Cemetery, the Ranville War Cemetery, the Ryes War Cemetery, the Saint-Charles-de-Percy War Cemetery, the Saint-Desir-de-Lisieux War Cemetery, the Saint-Manvieu War Cemetery, the Secqueville-en-Bessin War Cemetery, the Tilly-sur-Seulles War Cemetery, the Beny-sur-Mer Canadian War Cemetery, the Brettenville-sur-Laize Canadian War Cemetery, Les Gateys National Cemetery, and the Grainville-Langannerie Polish War Cemetery. The free people of the world demonstrated their courage, devotion to duty, and skill in battle in order to achieve victory over the German war machine and to eliminate Nazi tyranny over the oppressed peoples of Europe, while providing security for themselves and their descendants in a free world.

Journal/Meditation: What captures the hopes and prayers of liberty-loving people everywhere today? What meaning do you assign to the D in D-Day? Explain? For what freedom are you most thankful?

Prayer: Almighty God, you bestowed your blessing of freedom upon the great and noble undertaking known as D-Day and the Normandy landings. Raise your hand in blessing over the graves of those who died there. Bless all men and women who strive to overturn their oppressors, and provide security for me in a world free from tyranny of any kind. Amen.

World Food Safety Day
June 7

Text: "Noting that there is no food security without food safety and that in a world where the food supply chain has become more complex, any adverse food safety incident may have global negative effects on public health, trade, and the economy; noting also that improving food safety contributes positively to trade, employment, and poverty alleviation; taking into account that the global burden of foodborne diseases is considerable and affects individuals of all ages, in particular children under five years of age, and persons living in low-income regions of the world; cognizant of the urgent need to raise awareness at all levels and to promote and facilitate actions for global food safety, on the basis of scientific principles . . . ; [the General Assembly of the United Nations] decides to designate 7 June as World Food Safety Day."[3]

Reflection: World Food Safety Day, begun by the United Nations on December 20, 2018, should not be confused with World Food Day, another international day marked on October 16 every year since 1979. The U.N. resolution establishing World Food Safety Day, from which the above text is taken, is concerned with "setting international food standards to protect the health of consumers and in ensuring fair practices in the food trade."[4] According to the World Food Safety Day U.N. webpage, "Access to sufficient amounts of safe food is key to sustaining life and promoting good health. Foodborne illnesses are usually infectious or toxic in nature and often invisible to the plain eye, caused by bacteria, viruses, parasites, or chemical substances entering the body through contaminated food or water." Accordingly, "unsafe food is a threat to human health and economies."[5] This day attempts to raise awareness among the peoples of the world that "[f]ood safety has a critical role in assuring that food stays safe at every stage of the food chain—from production to harvest, processing, storage, distribution, all the way to preparation and consumption."[6] The aim of the day is "to draw attention and inspire action to help prevent, detect, and manage foodborne risks, contributing to food security, human health, economic prosperity, agriculture, market access, tourism, and sustainable development. . . . [It] is an opportunity to strengthen efforts to ensure that the food we eat is safe, mainstream food safety in the public agenda, and reduce the burden of foodborne diseases globally."[7]

   3. United Nations General Assembly, A/RES/73/250.
   4. United Nations General Assembly, A/RES/73/250.
   5. "World Food Safety Day."
   6. "World Food Safety Day."
   7. "World Food Safety Day."

It doesn't matter if a person grows, processes, transports, stores, distributes, sells, prepares, serves, or consumes food; everyone has a role to play in keeping it safe. It is important to comply with global food standards established by governments, scientists, the private sector, and all others who work to ensure food safety. In the United States, the food system is regulated by many federal, state, and local officials. On the federal level, the Food and Drug Administration (FDA) has established a model set of guidelines and procedures that provide a scientific, technical, and legal basis for regulating both retail and food service industries, such as restaurants, grocery stores, and institutional foodservice providers. Food safety is overseen by the U.S. Department of Agriculture (USDA) Food Safety and Inspection Service (FSIS), responsible for the safety of meat, poultry, and processed egg products, and the FDA, responsible for all other foods. State laws regulate restaurants and other retail food establishments, and local health departments inspect those to be sure they comply with specific design features, food-handling practices, and certification of food handlers. Nevertheless, as the U.N. makes clear, "Everybody has a role to play from farm to table to ensure the food we consume is safe and will not cause damages to our health."[8]

Journal/Meditation: What does "there is no food security without food safety" in the U.N. resolution mean to you? Specifically, what do you do to ensure the safety of the food you eat?

Prayer: Out of your hand you feed me abundantly, O LORD. Your earth produces food, and people harvest, process, store, distribute, prepare, and consume it. Give all harvesters, processors, storers, distributors, and preparers the wisdom to handle it safely so that it may give strength to the hungry today, tomorrow, and forever. Amen.

World Ocean Day

June 8

Text: "Recognizing the important contribution of sustainable development and management of the resources and uses of the oceans and seas to the achievement of international development goals . . . ; reiterating its concern at the adverse impacts on the marine environment and biodiversity, in particular on vulnerable marine ecosystems, including corals, of human activities, such as overutilization of living marine resources, the use of destructive practices, physical impacts by ships, the introduction of invasive alien species and marine pollution for all sources, including from land-based sources and vessels, in particular through the illegal and accidental discharge of oil and other harmful substances, the loss or release of fishing gear and the illegal or accidental release of hazardous waste such as radioactive materials, nuclear waste, and dangerous chemicals; . . . reiterating its serious concern over the current and

---

8. "World Food Safety Day."

projected adverse effects of climate change on the marine environment and marine biodiversity, and emphasizing the urgency of addressing this issue; [the General Assembly] resolves that, as from 2009, the United Nations will designate 8 June as World Oceans Day."[9]

Reflection: Only a very small part of the United Nations General Assembly Resolution 63/111 text, adopted December 5, 2008, is presented above. The resolution is twenty-nine, single-spaced pages long, set in ten-point Times-Roman font. While the first four pages of the resolution have no numbered paragraphs, pages 5 through 29 contain 177 numbered paragraphs. The first World Oceans Day was held June 8, 2009, with a general focus on the integrated management and sustainable development of the oceans and the seas. The UN called upon all countries to cooperate in every way—such as marine science, global reporting, climate change, etc.—in order to benefit from conservation and sustainable use of the oceans and the seas nationally, regionally, and globally. The resolution also addresses "transnational organized crime committed at sea, including illicit traffic in narcotic drugs and psychotropic substances, the smuggling of migrants and trafficking in persons, and threats to maritime safety and security, including piracy, armed robbery at sea, smuggling and terrorist acts against shipping, offshore installations and other maritime interests, and [notes] the deplorable loss of life and adverse impact on international trade, energy security, and the global economy resulting from such activities."[10] The resolution emphasizes "that underwater archaeological, cultural, and historical heritage, including shipwrecks and watercrafts, hold essential information on the history of humankind and that such heritage is a resource that needs to be protected and preserved."[11]

Among many other things, the resolution urges improved waste management practices, especially the impact land-based sources and marine debris has on marine pollution. It seeks information about the outer limits of the continental shelf beyond two hundred nautical miles. It recognizes the important role of international cooperation at the global, regional, subregional, and bilateral levels in combating threats to maritime security, such as piracy, armed robbery at sea, terrorist acts against shipping, and offshore installations. It calls for the protection of shipping lanes of strategic importance and significance by enhancing safety, security, and environmental protection in straits used for international navigation. Among other things, it seeks the safe maritime transport of radioactive materials; attention to hazards that may be caused by wrecks and drifting or sunken cargo to navigation or the marine environment; assistance to persons in distress at sea; control of maritime pollution through the introduction of harmful aquatic organisms and pathogens and the dumping of wastes and debris at sea; the conservation and sustainable use of marine biological diversity; the

---

9. United Nations General Assembly, A/RES/63/111.
10. United Nations General Assembly, A/RES/63/111.
11. United Nations General Assembly, A/RES/63/111.

elimination of risks to seamounts, cold water corals, hydrothermal vents, and other underwater features; and more. Because the oceans cover 70 percent of the planet, they are our source for life. They produce 50 percent of the earth's oxygen, and they are the main source of protein for thousands of people around the world. With 90 percent of big fish populations depleted, and 50 percent of coral reefs destroyed, the oceans need our support. With understanding of the oceans, we can create a new balance. Fostering pubic interest in the protection of the ocean and the sustainable management of its resources is the goal of World Oceans Day. By raising global awareness of the benefits derived from the oceans along with the challenges they face, World Oceans Day urges people around the world to foster sustainability, while meeting current needs and not compromising those of future generations.

Journal/Meditation: What can you do to foster ocean sustainability? Of all the many issues concerning the life of the oceans on the earth, which one gets most of your attention? In what specific ways can you address that issue in depth?

Prayer: Creator God, you gathered the waters of the oceans and silenced the roaring of their waves in order to make dry land appear. Living things both small and large can be found in the seas. Grant me the insight as to how I might protect the oceans on the earth. May the sea and all it contains praise you today, tomorrow, and forever. Amen.

World Day Against Child Labor
June 12

Text: "The General Conference of the International Labor Organization, . . . having met . . . on 1 June 1999, and considering the need to adopt new instruments for the prohibition and elimination of the worst forms of child labor, . . . and considering that the effective elimination of the worst forms of child labor requires immediate and comprehensive action . . . and the need to remove the children concerned from all such work . . . adopts this seventeenth day of June of the year one thousand nine hundred and ninety-nine the following Convention, which may be cited as the Worst Forms of Child Labor Convention, 1999."[12]

Reflection: On June 17, 1973, the International Labor Organization (ILO), the United Nations body that regulates the world of work, passed the "Minimum Age Convention, 1973 (No. 138)," which states, "The minimum age for admission to any type of employment or work which by its nature or the circumstances in which it is carried out is likely to jeopardize the health, safety, or morals of young persons shall not be less than eighteen years."[13] Earlier, the document declares that the minimum age shall

12. "Worst Forms."
13. "Minimum Age."

not be less than the age of completion of compulsory schooling, that is, less than fifteen years. The document makes the exception of sixteen years of age as long as the health, safety, and morals of the young person are protected and he or she has received adequate specific instruction or vocational training in the work to be done. Anyone twelve to fifteen years old may be employed to do light work, as long as it doesn't pose a harm to his or her health or development and doesn't keep the person out of school. On June 17, 1999, the ILO adopted the "Worst Forms of Child Labor Convention, 1999 (No. 182)," which apply to all persons under the age of eighteen. In an effort to eliminate the worst forms of child labor, as noted in the text above, the 1999 document identified those as "(a) all forms of slavery or practices similar to slavery, such as the sale and trafficking of children, debt bondage and serfdom and forced or compulsory labor, including forced or compulsory recruitment of children for use in armed conflict; (b) the use, procuring or offering of a child for prostitution, for the production of pornography or the pornographic performance; (c) the use, procuring, or offering of a child for illicit activities, in particular for the production and trafficking of drugs as defined in the relevant international treaties; (d) work which, by its nature or the circumstance in which it is carried out, is likely to harm the health, safety, or morals of children."[14] On June 12, 2002, the ILO launched the World Day against Child Labor in order to raise awareness concerning and to spark activism to eradicate child labor. Governments, local authorities, civil society, and international workers and employers organizations join together to identify the child labor problem and to propose guidelines to help child laborers, who are deprived of receiving an adequate education, health, leisure, and other basic freedoms, and work in hazardous environments, slavery, forced labor, drug trafficking, prostitution, or armed conflict.

Because of the pervasiveness and seriousness of the child labor problem and to highlight what can be done about it, one part of the eighth Sustainable Development Goals of the United Nations, adopted in 2015, includes a renewed global commitment to ending child labor. Goal 8.7 calls upon the global community to "[t]ake immediate and effective measures to eradicate forced labor, end modern slavery and human trafficking, and secure the prohibition and elimination of the worst forms of child labor, including recruitment and use of child soldiers, and by 2025 end child labor in all its forms."[15] Around the world, over two hundred million children work part- or full-time. They do not go to school; they have no time to play; they receive poor nutrition and care; they work in hazardous environments, slavery, forced labor, drug trafficking, prostitution, and armed conflict. The World Day against Child Labor is not against children working in areas that does not affect their health, personal development, or interfere with school attendance, such as helping parents at home, assisting in a family business, or earning pocket money outside of school hours; that kind of work contributes to a child's development and welfare and teaches skills and experience. The World

14. "Worst Forms."
15. "Sustainable Development Goals."

Day against Child Labor seeks to eliminate work that endangers a child and deprives him or her of schooling. By raising awareness, the day hopes to remove children from work that falls under the category of the worst forms of child labor, as indicated above, that is performed by a child under the minimum age, and that jeopardizes the physical, mental, or moral wellbeing of a child.

Journal/Meditation: What forms of work do you consider contribute to a child's development and welfare and teaches skills and experience? What forms of work do you consider detrimental to a child's development and welfare and falls under the category of the worst forms of child labor? How can you enhance the former kind of work while eliminating the latter kind of work?

Prayer: God, you have entrusted dignified work to all people so that they can sustain themselves with food, clothing, and shelter. Protect children from the worst forms of labor, and give to adults meaningful work that advances creation now and forever. Amen.

Flag Day

June 14

Text: "[It is] fitting that I should call your attention to the approach of the anniversary of the day upon which the flag of the United States was adopted by the congress as the emblem of the Union, and to suggest to you that it should this year and in the years to come be given special significance as a day of renewal and reminder, a day upon which we should direct our minds with a special desire of renewal to thoughts of the ideals and principles of which we have sought to make our great government the embodiment. I [, Woodrow Wilson,] suggest and request that throughout the nation and if possible in every community the fourteenth day of June be observed as Flag Day with special patriotic exercises, at which means shall be taken to give significant expression to our thoughtful love of America, our comprehension of the great mission of liberty and justice to which we have devoted ourselves as a people, our pride in the history and our enthusiasm for the political program of the nation, our determination to make it greater and purer with each generation, and our resolution to demonstrate to all the world its vital union in sentiment and purpose.... Let us on that day rededicate ourselves to the nation ... in independence, liberty, and right...."[16]

Reflection: On May 30, 1916, President Woodrow Wilson issued a proclamation, from which the above text is taken, declaring June 14, 1916, to be Flag Day. The United States entered World War I on April 6, 1917. In his June 14, 1917, "Address on Flag Day," Wilson declared that the "flag which we honor and under which we serve is the emblem of our unity, our power, our thought and purpose as a nation.... We celebrate

---

16. Wilson, "Proclamation 1335."

the day of its birth; and from its birth until now it has witnessed a great history."[17] The five-page address is Wilson's justification for entering WW I. Today, Flag Day commemorates the adoption of the flag of the U.S. on June 14, 1777, by a resolution of the Second Continental Congress. The resolution states: "Resolved, that the flag of the thirteen United States be thirteen stripes, alternate red and white; that the union of thirteen stars, white in a blue field, representing a new constellation."[18] In 1927, President Calvin Coolidge issued a proclamation. However, it was during the presidency of Harry S. Truman, who issued Flag Day Proclamations from 1945 to 1952, that on August 3, 1949, congress established National Flag Day. In his proclamations, Truman declared that the flag represents the ideal of freedom in the world, that it arouses in the hearts of Americans sentiments of gratitude for freedom, that it is a living token of human integrity and freedom, and that Flag Day is the opportunity for rededication to the ideals for which it stands. The law (63 Stat. 492), now enshrined in U.S. Code 36, Section 110 (August 12, 1998), states: "June 14 is Flag Day. The president is requested to issue each year a proclamation—calling on United States government officials to display the flag of the United States on all government buildings on Flag Day; and urging the people of the United States to observe Flag Day as the anniversary of the adoption on June 14, 1777, by the Continental Congress of the Stars and Stripes as the official flag of the United States."[19]

Since the first flag's design, sewed by Betsy Ross, a seamstress who lived in Philadelphia during the American Revolution, there have been twenty-seven official versions of the flag; as states entered the Union, more white stars were added on the blue field. The current version of the flag with fifty stars was created July 4, 1960, when Hawaii became the fiftieth state. In some cities, parades are held to mark Flag Day. The most obvious way to celebrate the day is to fly the flag and recite the Pledge of Allegiance. The week of June 14 is designated National Flag Week, when other events featuring the flag are held. The National Flag Day Foundation holds its annual observance on the second Sunday in June with a ceremonial raising of the national flag, the recitation of the Pledge of Allegiance, the singing of the national anthem, a parade, and other events. "The twenty-one days from Flag Day through Independence Day is a period to honor America," states U.S. Code 36, section 112. "Congress declares that there be public gatherings and activities during that period at which the people of the United States can celebrate and honor their country in an appropriate way."[20]

Journal/Meditation: In what specific way do you honor the United States Flag? How is the flag an emblem of Union? How do you rededicate yourself to the nation during the period from Flag Day to Independence Day?

17. Wilson, "Address on Flag Day."
18. Cohen, "What Is Flag Day?"
19. "Public Law 105–225."
20. "Public Law 105–225."

Prayer: Under you, O God, the republic of the United States is signified by the Stars and Stripes. Strengthen the devotion of all citizens who pledge allegiance to the flag and to the liberty and justice which it represents. Here my prayer this day. Amen.

Father's Day
Third Sunday

Text: "Resolved by the Senate and House of Representatives of the United States of America in congress assembled, that the third Sunday in June of each year is hereby designated as 'Father's Day.' The president is authorized and requested to issue a proclamation calling on the appropriate government officials to display the flag of the United States on all government buildings on such day, inviting the governments of the states and communities and the people of the United States to observe such day with appropriate ceremonies, and urging our people to offer public and private expressions of such day to the abiding love and gratitude which they bear for their fathers."[21]

Reflection: Before the above text became public law on April 24, 1972, Father's Day had been started by Sonora Smart Dodd in the Spokane, Washington, YMCA on June 19, 1910. She had heard about the founding of Mother's Day in 1909, and she explained to the pastor of her church that fathers should have a similar day honoring them. After the first celebration, however, not much happened. In the 1930s, Dodd tried promoting the day again, raising awareness and getting help from manufacturers of ties, tobacco pipes, men's wear, and other traditional gifts presented to fathers. With the trade groups promoting the day, by the mid-1980s the day had become a permanent holiday on the United States calendar. While a bill appeared in congress in 1913, it did not pass. President Woodrow Wilson wanted to make it official in 1916, and President Calvin Coolidge recommended that it be observed by the nation in 1924. In 1966, joint resolution 166 of the U.S. Senate and House of Representatives designated the third Sunday of that year as Father's Day. That moved President Lyndon B. Johnson on June 15, 1966, to issue "Proclamation 3730—Father's Day." After expressing the appropriateness of the congress in giving official recognition to the "well-established tradition," Johnson wrote: "In the homes of our nation, we look to the fathers to provide the strength and stability which characterize the successful family. If the father's responsibilities are many, his rewards are also great—the love, appreciation, and respect of children and spouse. It is the desire to acknowledge publicly these feelings we have for the fathers of our nation that has inspired the congress to call for the formal observance of Father's Day."[22] After requesting that government officials display the flag on all government buildings on Father's Day, Johnson wrote,

---

21. "Public Law 92-278."
22. Johnson, "Proclamation 3730."

"... I urge all our people to give public and private expression to the love and gratitude which they bear for their fathers."[23]

Six years later, Father's Day became a permanent national holiday. As the above text notes, on April 24, 1972, the U.S. Senate and House of Representatives made Public Law 92–278 effective. On May 1, 1972, President Richard Nixon issued "Proclamation 4127—Father's Day." "To have a father—to be a father—is to come very near the heart of life itself," begins Nixon's proclamation. "In fatherhood," he continues, "we know the elemental magic and joy of humanity. In fatherhood we even sense the divine, as the scriptural writers did who told of all good gifts coming 'down from the Father of lights, with whom is no variableness, neither shadow of turning'—symbolism so challenging to each man who would give his own son or daughter a life of light without shadow."[24] The biblical text comes from the Christian Bible (New Testament) Letter of James 1:17. Nixon continues eloquently, writing: "Our identity in name and nature, our roots in home and family, our very standard of manhood—all this and more is the heritage our fathers share with us. It is a rich patrimony, one for which adequate thanks can hardly be offered in a lifetime, let alone a single day.... [F]rom this year forward,... that [national] custom [of observing each year one special Sunday to honor American's fathers] carries the weight of law."[25] Nixon concludes the proclamation asking every American to make Father's Day "an occasion for renewal of the love and gratitude we bear to our fathers, increasing and enduring through all the years."[26] Public Law 105–225, issued August 12, 1998, codified Father's Day in Section 109; it designated the third Sunday in June as Father's Day, and it requested the president to issue a proclamation (a) calling all government officials to display the flag on all government buildings, (b) inviting both state and local governments and the people of the U.S. to observe Father's Day with appropriate ceremonies, and (c) urging the people of the U.S. to offer both public and private expressions of Father's Day to the abiding love and gratitude they have for their fathers.[27] Over the course of the years, Father's Day has been commercialized in the same way as Mother's Day. Families gather to celebrate the father figures in their lives and give greeting cards, electronics, tools, and watch sports on TV.

Journal/Meditation: How do you display your abiding love and gratitude for your father? What do you think of President Johnson's words about fathers providing strength and stability in the home? What do you think about President Nixon's words about fatherhood coming near to the heart of life itself? sensing the divine?

23. Johnson, "Proclamation 3730."
24. Nixon, "Proclamation 4127."
25. Nixon, "Proclamation 4127."
26. Nixon, "Proclamation 4127."
27. "Public Law 105–225."

Prayer: Father of Lights, every generous act of giving with every perfect gift comes from you in whom there is no variation or shadow due to change. I thank you, God, for my father and his abiding love and gratitude. Today, pour your blessing upon him, who reminds me of you. Amen.

Juneteenth National Independence Day
June 19

Text: ". . . [A] major general of the Union Army arrived in Galveston, Texas, [on June 19, 1865,] to enforce the Emancipation Proclamation and free the last enslaved Americans in Texas from bondage. . . . Juneteenth marks both the long, hard night of slavery and subjugation and a promise of a brighter morning to come. This is . . . a day in which we remember the moral stain, the terrible toll that slavery took on the country and continues to take, what I've long called 'America's original sin.' At the same time, I also remember the extraordinary capacity to heal and to hope and to emerge from the most painful moments and a bitter, bitter version of ourselves, but to make a better version of ourselves."[28]

Reflection: The above text represents part of the remarks made by President Joseph R. Biden on June 17, 2021, before signing the Juneteenth National Independence Day Act. "Be it enacted by the Senate and House of Representatives of the United States of America in Congress assembled: Section 1. Short Title. This Act may be cited as the 'Juneteenth National Independence Day Act.' Section 2. Juneteenth National Independence Day as a Legal Public Holiday. Section 6103(a) of title 5, United States Code, is amended by inserting after the item relating to Memorial Day the following: 'Juneteenth National Independence Day, June 19.'"[29] Senate Bill 475, which became Public Law 117–17, passed the U.S. Senate on June 15, and passed the U.S. House of Representatives on June 16. Juneteenth National Independence Day is the first new federal holiday since Martin Luther King, Jr., Day in 1983. The law commemorates the end of slavery in the U.S. According to Biden, "Great nations don't ignore their most painful moments. . . . They embrace them. . . . We come to terms with the mistakes we made. And in remembering those moments, we begin to heal and grow stronger."[30] However, according to Biden, it is also important to note that the emancipation of enslaved Black Americans did not mark the end to deliver on the promise of equality.

Juneteenth, now named Juneteenth National Independence Day, is also known as Jubilee Day, Emancipation Day, Freedom Day, and Black Independence Day. While President Abraham Lincoln had issued the Emancipation Proclamation on January 1, 1863, which outlawed slavery in all secessionist states, it was not until the end of the

---

28. Biden, "Remarks: Juneteenth."
29. "Public Law 117–17."
30. Biden, "Remarks: Juneteenth."

Civil War that Union Army General Gordon Granger proclaimed freedom to slaves in Galveston, Texas, on June 19, 1865. "The people of Texas are informed that, in accordance with a proclamation from the Executive of the United States, all slaves are free," begins Granger's General Order No. 3. He continues: "This involves an absolute equality of personal rights and rights of property between former masters and slaves, and the connection heretofore existing between them becomes that between employer and hired labor. The freedmen are advised to remain quietly at their present homes and work for wages."[31] Celebrations of African-American independence took place immediately. The next year, 1866, church-centered community gatherings were the venues for celebrating African-American culture. Over the course of the years, marking the holiday spread from state to state until the holiday was acknowledged in 1979 by forty-nine states. The holiday was marked with reading of the Emancipation Proclamation, the singing of traditional songs, and reading of works by African-American writers. In the course of the years, rodeos, baseball games, fishing tournaments, street fairs, cookouts, family reunions, park parties, historical reenactments, voter registration, and other means were added to the ways to observe the holiday, often referred to as American's second Independence Day. The day celebrates black culture; it educates through lectures and exhibitions; and it agitates against racial discrimination of any kind. As early as the 1890s, African-Americans began calling the day Juneteenth (a short form of June-nineteenth). Federal legislation had been introduced as early as 1996 along with various Senate and House resolutions, but it did not become a federal holiday until June 17, 2021. As Biden noted in his remarks before signing the bill into law: ". . . [W]e must understand that Juneteenth represents not only the commemoration of the end of slavery in American more than 150 years ago, but the ongoing work to have to bring true equity and racial justice into American society, which we can do. In short, this day doesn't just celebrate the past; it calls for action today."[32]

Journal/Meditation: What true equity and racial justice do you need to act on today? What better version of yourself do you need to make to heal American's original sin of slavery?

Prayer: I sing praises to you, O LORD, and I give thanks to your holy name. The weeping of the night of slavery was turned to the joy of the morning with the freeing of African-American slaves. Pour your grace of healing and hope upon all races in my country that every single man, woman, and child may become the best version of himself or herself and so make us a great nation. Amen.

---

31. Granger, "General Order No. 3."
32. Biden, "Remarks: Juneteenth."

Summer Solstice

June 20–22

Text: "In the Northern Hemisphere, the June solstice (aka summer solstice) occurs when the sun reaches its highest and northernmost points in the sky. It marks the start of summer in the northern half of the globe. . . . The word *solstice* comes from Latin *solstitium*—from *sol* (sun) and *stitium* (*still* or *stopped*). Due to earth's tilted axis, the sun doesn't rise and set at the same locations on the horizon each morning and evening; its rise and set positions move northward . . . in the sky as earth travels around the sun through the year. Also, the sun's track in the sky becomes higher . . . throughout the year. The June solstice is significant because the sun reaches its northernmost point in the sky at this time, at which point the sun's path does not change for a brief period of time. After the solstice, the sun appears to reverse course and head back in the opposite direction. . . . Of course, the sun itself is not moving . . . ; instead, this change in position in the sky that we on earth notice is caused by the tilt of earth's axis as it orbits the sun, as well as earth's elliptical, rather than circular, orbit."[33]

Reflection: It is very easy to forget that we live on a planet named earth that both spins on its own axis—producing night and day—and rotates around the sun in an elliptical (elongated circle) orbit that takes 365.242199 (365¼) days to complete. Because the earth's spin axis is tilted with respect to its orbital plane, when the axis points towards the sun, it is summer. At the North Pole, which never points directly at the sun—because the earth's axis is 23½ degrees—on the summer solstice it points as close as possible. With the spin axis of the earth pointing 90 degrees away from the sun, on the summer solstice at the equator day and night are almost exactly twelve hours long, more or less. After the solstice, daylight begins to shorten, and nighttime begins to lengthen. In the Northern Hemisphere, the summer solstice can occur between June 20 and 22; the date cannot be exactly and always the same because of (1) the 365.242199 days it takes to complete earth's orbit around the sun, (2) the addition of a leap year every four years, (3) the gravitational pull from the moon and other planets, and (4) the slight wobble in earth's rotation.

During the summer solstice, the sun is overhead; this means that light is falling straight upon those on the earth at the equator. More direct light from the sun means more heat. When the axis of the earth points toward the sun, the ground absorbs more heat. Astronomically, the first day of summer is calculated to be when the sun reaches its highest point in the sky, otherwise known as the summer solstice. Before the summer solstice, the direct rays of the sun are heating the earth more and more with each passing day; after the summer solstice, the direct rays of the sun begin to lose intensity more and more with each passing day and the heating diminishes gradually. Ancient people witnessed this dramatic change and marked it with festivals and rituals, which,

---

33. "Summer Solstice."

in the rhythm of farming was the midpoint of the growing season—between planting and harvest, June 24 by ancient reckoning of the solstice. It was often marked with a bonfire, feasting, dancing, singing, and preparing for the coming hot summer days. In the Christian liturgical calendar it became the birth of St. John the Baptist, who foretold the birth of Jesus which took place exactly six months later. Just as John decreased in importance, Jesus increased in importance. May 1 was a time for pairing young couples, who planned their weddings for the summer solstice in June, which is still the most popular month for weddings. Also, during the Middle Ages, ferns, which were believed to flower and produce seed only on June 23, were thought to give a person the ability to understand birds, find buried treasure, and possess abundant strength. In Latvia, people stayed awake by their bonfires in pursuit of magical fern flowers, which gave them good luck. Today, we know that ferns reproduce with spores, not flowers and seeds. Because strawberries are ripe around the summer solstice, today many people pick and eat them as the first fruits of summer. In Fairbanks and Anchorage, Alaska, because daylight lasts almost twenty-four hours on the summer solstice that far north, teams play baseball around the clock.

Journal/Meditation: What fascinates you spiritually about the summer solstice? Why do you think it is difficult for earth's creatures to realize that they are on a planet that spins on its axis while also orbiting around the sun? Why are the terms sunrise and sunset not accurate?

Prayer: O LORD, my God, you are very great. You have made the moon to mark the seasons; the sun knows its time for setting. You make darkness, and it is night. You make light, and it is day. When the sun rises, people go out to their work and to their labor until the evening. I bless you, O LORD, and praise you forever. Amen.

WORLD REFUGEE DAY

June 20

Text: "The General Assembly [of the United Nations] commends the Office of the United Nations High Commissioner for Refugees for its leadership and coordination of international action for refugees, and acknowledges the tireless efforts of the Office of the High Commissioner to provide international protection and assistance to refugees and other persons of concern and to promote durable solutions for their problems during the past fifty years; pays tribute to the dedication of United Nations humanitarian workers and associated personnel, the staff of the Office of the High Commissioner in the field, including local staff, who risk their lives in the performance of their duties; reaffirms its support for the activities of the Office of the High Commissioner, in accordance with the relevant General Assembly resolutions, on behalf of returnees, stateless persons, and internally displaced persons; . . . notes that 2001 marks the fiftieth anniversary of the 1951 Convention Relating to the Status of

Refugees, which sets out the fundamental concepts for international refugee protection; ... decides that, as from 2001, 20 June will be celebrated as World Refugee Day."[34]

Reflection: As noted in the text above, in commemoration of the 1951 Convention Relating to the Status of Refugees, which had honored refugees and both raised awareness and solicited support to those affected around the world, the General Assembly of the United Nations, on December 4, 2000, passed Resolution 55/76 naming June 20 World Refugee Day every year. The day honors refugees around the world along with raising awareness about the plight of refugees around the world. A refugee is one who has fled the conflict and persecution of his or her own country in the hope of finding safety and living a better life in a different country. A person becomes a refugee due to war, persecution, violence, conflict, poverty, drought, natural disaster, etc. A refugee can be a person who is unable to return to his or her country of origin because of what might befall him or her because of race, religion, social group, or political opinions.

World Refugee Day also seeks to raise awareness among citizens about the resilience and strength of refugees who have lost families, homes, land, and country. Others need to be reminded that refugees need their support to rebuild their lives. Refugees are fathers, mothers, sisters, brothers, and children who hope for a future different from the one they have left behind. The day seeks to build empathy and understanding of their plight among others in a country in which they seek to settle. The day shines a light on their rights, needs, and dreams with the goal of mobilizing both politics and resources so that refugees can thrive in the labor market, in society, and in the new country. Over the course of the years since 2000, the day is given a theme focused on the thriving of refugees. Such themes include access to health care, opportunity for education, justice, inclusivity, equality, solidarity, discrimination, exclusion, learning refugee stories and struggles, understanding refugee perseverance, language, etc. All refugees share a common thread of uncommon courage to survive, persevere, and rebuild their lives. Losing their homes and countries means losing their identities. By raising our awareness of all that surrounds refugees, we can help repatriate, if possible, or help them live in our country or resettle in another one. Refugees who are seen and heard are valued by the members of the community in which they live.

Journal/Meditation: What refugee do you know? From what did he or she flee? Who are the most recent refugees in your area? From what did they flee?

Prayer: Hear my prayer, O LORD, and turn your ear to hear my cry for the refugees of the world. Move the hearts of people everywhere to welcome those fleeing their homeland for whatever reason. Grant an understanding to all people that they are but passing guests in this world, like all who have gone before them. Amen.

---

34. United Nations General Assembly, A/RES/55/76.

NATIONAL AMERICAN EAGLE DAY
June 20

Text: "Whereas on June 20, 1782, the congress adopted the American bald eagle as the symbol of our nation; whereas the American bald eagle was so adopted because of its legendary strength and its single-minded commitment to the protection of its young and the defense of its home; whereas the American public has adopted the American bald eagle as a symbol of strength, courage, determination, and beauty; whereas the seals of the twelve states and the District of Columbia bear the image of the American bald eagle; . . . whereas the celebration of the Bicentennial Year of the American Bald Eagle and National Bald Eagle Day will serve to make people aware of the current plight of our country's living symbol; whereas such celebration should be conducted in a manner that encourages additional efforts to keep the American bald eagle a flying symbol of freedom: Now, therefore, be it resolved by the Senate and House of Representatives of the United States of America in congress assembled, that the year 1982 is designated as the 'Bicentennial Year of the American Bald Eagle,' and June 20, 1982, is designated as 'National Bald Eagle Day' . . . ."[35]

Reflection: In 1776, Benjamin Franklin, John Adams, and Thomas Jefferson were given the task to create a seal for the newly formed United States. Congress, however, did not accept their design. Six years passed before the design with the American Eagle was approved and became official on June 20, 1782, as noted in the above text. On December 29, 1981, the United States congress passed Public Law 97–139, from which the above text is taken. The joint resolution declared the two-hundredth anniversary year, 1982, to be a year-long celebration of the American bald eagle, and June 20, 1982, to be the first National Bald Eagle Day. The congress also acknowledged that "human encroachment on the American bald eagle's natural habitat ha[d] resulted in the designation of the American bald eagle as an endangered species throughout most of the United States" and noted that "federal, state, and local governments and private wildlife conservation groups [had] adopted programs . . . to increase the number and dispersal of nesting pairs in the United States."[36] The resolution also stated: "In order to promote and enhance efforts to inform the American people of the plight of our national bird, the American bald eagle, and to encourage additional efforts to protect and increase the population of this symbol of our nation, the president of the United States [was] authorized and requested—(1) to issue a proclamation calling upon the people of the United States, including wildlife conservation organizations and educational institutions, to observe such year and day with appropriate ceremonies and activities; (2) to send a suitable copy of such proclamation to the governor of each state and to each member of congress; and (3) to direct all federal agencies and

---

35. "Public Law 97–139."
36. "Public Law 97–139."

departments which [had] activities which affect[ed] the bald eagle to cooperate with and participate in the celebration of such year and day."[37] President Ronald Reagan issued the first and only proclamation of National Bald Eagle Day on January 28, 1982. "... [T]he bald eagle is admired as one of nature's most spectacular creatures," he wrote. "To catch a glimpse of this majestic raptor is to understand why the founding fathers chose it to represent the strength and courage of our great nation. Its grace and power in flight, its vigilance and loyalty in defending its family group, and, most of all, its courage make the eagle a proud and appropriate symbol for the United States. Its presence on the Great Seal of the United States—one talon extending the olive branch of peace, the other brandishing the arrows of defense—is a symbol of friendship and cooperation to our allies and warning to our adversaries that we are not to be trod upon."[38] Reagan recounted measures being taken to protect the eagle, and he invited U.S. citizens "to pause and reflect upon the importance of the bald eagle ... to a healthy America."[39] The only other president to acknowledge an anniversary of the American bald eagle being adopted as the symbol of the U.S. was William J. Clinton on June 20, 1995. With a White House letter he greeted "all those celebrating the 213th anniversary of the designation of the bald eagle as the national symbol of the United States of America."[40] In this letter, which is addressed to no one in particular, he mentions that "more than 4,000 pairs of adult bald eagles and perhaps as many as 5,000 juveniles now flourish." He also invited readers to renew their "dedication to protecting this irreplaceable national treasure."[41]

Thousands of bald eagles were in this country until the late 1800s, when their number began to decrease because they were seen as vermin and a threat to livestock and were shot by farmers or as game by hunters. As settlers moved west, their habitats and food sources were destroyed. In 1940, congress passed the Bald Eagle Act, which made it illegal to possess, sell, or hunt bald eagles or to possess their feathers, nests, eggs, or body parts. In 1972, the act was amended to increase the penalty a person would face for violating the act. After World War II, the pesticide DDT began to be used on mosquitoes and other pests, but it had a detrimental effect on bald eagle eggs. Eagles ate pests sprayed with DDT, and their eggs shells became thinner, causing them to break. By 1963, there were only about 417 mating pairs of bald eagles in the lower forty-eight states. In 1967, the eagle was put on the national endangered species list. The Endangered Species Acts of 1966 and 1978 helped with the restoration. Some eagles were bred in captivity and reintroduced in various places across the U.S. In 1995, eagles were removed from the endangered species list; in June 2007 their status was changed from threatened to protected. There are thousands of nesting

37. "Public Law 97–139."
38. Reagan, "Proclamation 4893."
39. Reagan, "Proclamation 4893."
40. Clinton, "Letter."
41. Clinton, "Letter."

pairs in the lower forty-eight states, but they are still threatened by the loss of habitat, contaminants, and diseases. After reaching the age of four or five, eagles mate for life. After building a very large nest—the largest of any animal species in trees—often near large bodies of open water—where they can fish and hunt for rabbits, squirrels, rats, and mice using their sharp sense of sight—the female lays two or three eggs, which both parents incubate and protect. Both parents feed the young once they hatch after thirty-four to thirty-six days. They live for thirty to thirty-five years. National American Eagle Day is sponsored primarily by American Eagle Foundation (AEF), a non-profit organization dedicated to inspiring the world to guard and protect the bald eagle, in order to raise awareness about the American Eagle, its habitats, and conservation efforts. AEF is a full-service rehabilitation and release program for eagles, also offering housing and care for permanently disabled birds. Eagle Mountain Sanctuary at Dollywood in Pigeon Forge, Tennessee, represents the largest gathering of non-releasable eagles in the world. On June 20, one can learn more about the American Eagle by reading a book, watching a documentary, or listening to a podcast. One can visit a nature preserve, a zoo, or volunteer to work with preservation groups, or fly the flag on a pole that has an eagle perched on top. Maybe the best way to celebrate the day is to find a picture of the Great Seal of the United States or to examine the back side of the one dollar bill, upon which is printed the obverse and reverse of the seal. On the obverse side of the Great Seal the eagle is at the center, holding an olive branch—a sign of peace—in its right talon and thirteen arrows, representing the original thirteen colonies, in its left talon—a sign of readiness for war. In its beak is a scroll, upon which is written the original motto in Latin: "E pluribus unum," which means "out of many, one." Again, the reference is to the thirteen colonies joining together to become a new country. National American Eagle Day is a reminder that with lots of awareness and determination we can save an endangered species in need of protection, recover its natural environment, and provide educational outreach to the people of our country.

Journal/Meditation: Which characteristic of the American bald eagle got most of your attention? Why? Why do you think the American eagle is an appropriate sign of the United States? What is the importance of the bald eagle to a healthy America? How is it an irreplaceable national treasure?

Prayer: Like the eagle who stirs its nest and hovers over its young, you protect me, O LORD. As I marvel at the way of the eagle in the sky, draw my attention to marvel at the way my country was formed and continues to be formed from many into one. Bless all in this land with peace today, tomorrow, and forever. Amen.

7

The Month of *July*

CANADA DAY
July 1

Text: "Whereas the Provinces of Canada, Nova Scotia, and New Brunswick have expressed their desire to be federally united into One Dominion under the Crown of the United Kingdom of Great Britain and Ireland, with a constitution similar in principle to that of the United Kingdom; and whereas such a union would conduce to the welfare of the provinces and promote the interests of the British Empire; and whereas on the establishment of the union by authority of Parliament it is expedient, not only that the Constitution of the Legislative Authority in the Dominion be provided for, but also that the nature of the executive government therein be declared; and whereas it is expedient that provision be made for the eventual admission into the union of other parts of British North America . . . . It shall be lawful for the queen, by and with the advice of Her Majesty's Most Honorable Privy Council, to declare by proclamation that, on and after a day therein appointed, not being more than six months after the passing of this act, the Provinces of Canada, Nova Scotia, and New Brunswick shall form and be one Dominion under the name of Canada; and on and after that day those three provinces shall form and be one Dominion under that name accordingly."[1]

Reflection: The text above is taken from the British North America Act, later renamed the Constitution Act, which brought the four separate British colonies into a union on July 1, 1867. Upper Canada (Ontario), Lower Canada (Quebec), Nova Scotia, and New Brunswick became a single Dominion within the British Empire named Canada. The holiday on July 1 was known as Dominion Day until it was renamed Canada Day on October 27, 1982. The Constitution Act, as noted above, acknowledged that the queen of England held executive power, while the seat of Canadian government was in Ottawa with one Parliament, consisting of the queen, the senate, and the house

---

1. "Constitution Act."

of commons. In 1931, the Statute of Westminster, the result of years of change and negotiation between Great Britain and Canada (and Britain's other Dominions), made Canada a country. No longer a colony, Canada's external affairs became the domain of the federal government. With the passing of the Constitution Act of 1982, Canada became completely independent from Great Britain. The Canadian Constitution took on the force of law in Canada, and no law passed by Parliament in the United Kingdom could have any effect in Canada. As noted in the text above, other parts of British North America sought entry into the new country named Canada: the Province of Manitoba was admitted in 1870; British Columbia in 1871, Prince Edward Island in 1873, Saskatchewan in 1905, Alberta in 1905, Newfoundland and Labrador in 1949 for a total of ten provinces. In addition, there are three territories: Northwest Territories admitted in 1870, Yukon in 1898, and Nunavut in 1997. The provinces and territories of Canada form the world's second-largest country by area. On Canada Day, citizens celebrate with parades, carnivals, festivals, barbecues, air shows, maritime shows, fireworks, musical concerts, and citizenship ceremonies. In the national capital in Ottawa, Ontario, concerts and cultural displays are held on Parliament Hill.

In 1980, "O Canada" was adopted as the country's national anthem, becoming effective on July 1 of that year. The anthem exists in the two official languages of Canada—English and French—neither of which is a translation of the other and both of which are in the public domain. There is also an English translation by the parliamentary translation bureau and two bilingual versions. In order to simplify things here, only the English lyrics are presented: "O Canada! / Our home and native land! / True patriot love in all of us command. / With glowing hearts we see thee rise, / The True North strong and free! / From far and wide, / O Canada, we stand on guard for thee. / God keep our land glorious and free! / O Canada, we stand on guard for thee. / O Canada, we stand on guard for thee." There are three more stanzas to the anthem, but they are seldom sung. It was not until February 15, 1965, that the National Flag of Canada made its appearance. Now celebrated annually as National Flag of Canada Day, the Maple Leaf consists of a red field with a white square at its center in the middle of which is a stylized eleven-pointed red maple leaf. Only gradually from 1867 to 1965 did Canada create for itself a national identity complete with provinces, territories, a national anthem, and a national flag. If July 1 falls on Sunday, Canada Day is observed on July 2.

Reflection: How does the line "True patriot love in all of us command" in "O Canada" apply to your country? How does the line "God keep our land glorious and free" in "O Canada" apply to your country?

Prayer: In Canada, O God, you planted pines and maples and spread great prairies with mighty rivers under shining skies from the Atlantic Ocean to the Pacific Ocean. Ruler of all, hear my humble prayer to keep Canada and all her people in your loving care today, tomorrow, and forever. Amen.

NATIONAL POSTAL WORKERS DAY, NATIONAL U.S. POSTAGE STAMP DAY

July 1

Text: "The congress shall have the power . . . to establish post offices and post roads . . . ."[2]

Reflection: July 1 both celebrates postal workers and recognizes the ease and simplicity with which mail can be sent and received using a postage stamp. As can be seen from the short text above, "The Constitution of the United States" gave congress the power to establish what is now called the United States Postal Service (USPS), also known as the Post Office, U.S. Mail, and Postal Service. Today, it is an independent agency of the executive branch of the U.S. federal government responsible for providing postal service in the U.S. Even though the first post office was established in Boston in a tavern owned by Richard Fairbanks in 1639, and the oldest operating post office is located in Hinsdale, New Hampshire, Benjamin Franklin was appointed the first postmaster general during the Second Continental Congress in 1775. After the U.S. Constitution was ratified on September 22, 1789, President George Washington appointed Samuel Osgood the first postmaster general under the Constitution. In 1792, the Post Office Department was created with the passage of the Postal Service Act. The postal system that Franklin and Osgood forged became the standard for the U.S. Post Office and is the system still used today. The department was elevated to cabinet level in 1872, then transformed by the Postal Reorganization Act of 1970 to its current USPS status. National Postal Workers Day was established by the Seattle-area postal carriers in 1997 to honor their fellow employees. Postal employees work in one of four areas. First, service clerks sell stamps and postage and help patrons pick up packages and assist with other services. Second, mail sorters physically separate the mail to where it needs to go; most mail sorting is done by machine, but people operate the machine. Third, are three types of mail carriers (also referred to as mailmen, mailwomen, postal carrier, postman, postwomen, and letter carrier): city letter carriers deliver the mail on foot in large municipalities; rural carriers deliver the mail from a car or truck over routes in the country; and highway contract route carriers are independent contractors who deliver mail over long distances in the country. Fourth, vehicle operators drive trucks carrying mail bags or pallets from one place to another. Over 653,000 men and women are employed by the USPS, which takes as its informal motto words found in Herodotus's *Histories*: "Neither snow nor rain nor heat nor gloom of night stays these couriers from the swift completion of their appointed rounds." While Herodotus (around 484–25 BCE) was referring to the courier service of the ancient Persian Empire, on National Postal Worker Day we demonstrate appreciation to all those men and women who keep the mail moving across the country.

---

2. "Constitution of the U.S.," Article 1, Section 8.

There are those who walk four to eight miles a day, those who drive many-mile routes, those who drive trucks hundreds of miles, and those who spend hours sorting mail and selling postal products in a post office. All deserve thanks with a letter, a post card, or an e-mail sent to the local post office. Where possible, thanks can be rendered after taking a tour of the local post office. While there is a National Thank a Mail Carrier Day on February 4, on July 1, we are reminded of how important all postal workers are six days a week, fifty-two weeks a year.

On July 1 every year, National U.S. Postage Stamp Day is celebrated. Not only does the day commemorate the issuance of the first postage stamp on July 1, 1847, but it also recognizes the ease and simplicity with which we can send and receive mail. A stamp on an envelope represents payment for the delivery of a letter or a package. A stamp is a unique form of currency. Before July 1, 1847, stampless letters were paid directly to the postman by the receiver; of course, there were people who refused to pay for a letter or didn't have the funds to do so. Thus, it wasn't long before post offices were full of undeliverable mail because no one would pay for it. That system was gradually phased out with the introduction of adhesive postage stamps that needed to be wetted in order to get them to stick to the envelope. With the advent of postage stamps the payment was made before the letter was mailed, and the post office delivered it whether the addressee wanted it or not! The first postage stamps issued by the U.S. government were in the denominations of five—with an engraving of Franklin—and ten cents—with an engraving of Washington; the mandatory use of postage stamps took place in 1855. By the 1890s, the post office recognized that it could increase its revenues by selling stamps as collectibles, and so it began to issue commemorative stamps. With that, philatelists (stamp collectors) and philately (the study of stamps and postal history) were born. Once self-adhesive materials were invented, the post office switched from glue that needed to be wetted to self-adhesive postage stamps. In 2007 "Forever" stamps were introduced; no matter what a person paid for them when they were purchased, they can be used on letters and cards after postage rates increase, that is, they are good forever. National U.S. Postage Stamp Day can be marked by mailing a letter, card, or post card to someone, by beginning or adding to a stamp collection, and by thanking your mail carrier for delivering your letters, cards, and bills without charge!

Journal/Meditation: Of the four types of postal employees, whom do you know is a service clerk, mail sorter, mail carrier, and vehicle operator? Is your mail carrier a city letter, rural, or contract route carrier? What is his or her name? When was the last time you visited a post office? Why did you go there?

Prayer: In times past, O LORD, you delivered news to your people through the spiritual inspiration of your prophets. Today, good news arrives in my mailbox through men and women who carry and deliver the mail. Give me a greater appreciation for this service and bless all postal employees who are diligent in service. Amen.

INDEPENDENCE DAY
July 4

Text: "When in the course of human events, it becomes necessary for one people to dissolve the political bands which have connected them with another, and to assume among the powers of the earth, the separate and equal station to which the laws of nature and of nature's God entitle them, a decent respect to the opinions of [human] kind requires that they should declare the causes which impel them to the separation. . . . Prudence, indeed, will dictate that governments long established should not be changed for light and transient causes; and accordingly all experience has shown, that [human]kind [is] more disposed to suffer, while evils are sufferable, than to right themselves by abolishing the forms to which they are accustomed. But when a long train of abuses and usurpations, pursuing invariably the same object evinces a design to reduce them under absolute despotism, it is their right, it is their duty, to throw off such government, and to provide new guards for their future security. Such has been the patient sufferance of these [thirteen] colonies; and such is now the necessity which constrains them to alter their former systems of government."[3]

Reflection: The text above consists of some of the opening words of the Declaration of Independence signed by fifty-six men representing the thirteen original British colonies: Connecticut, Delaware, Georgia, Maryland, Massachusetts, New Hampshire, New Jersey, New York, North Carolina, Pennsylvania, Rhode Island, South Carolina, and Virginia. The document to which our founding fathers signed their names was written principally by Thomas Jefferson, but prepared by a committee of five. On July 2, 1776, the Second Continental Congress voted to approve a resolution of independence. Jefferson was chosen to prepare a statement explaining the vote. He wrote that it was necessary to dissolve the colonies' political connection with Great Britain and to assume equality with her. While prudence dictated that declaring independence should not be a hasty decision, the suffering imposed by the mother country had continued to increase until it had reached a despotic level. The colonies, therefore, determined it to be their duty to throw off their tyrannical ruler's form of government. After listing all the offenses imposed by the mother country upon her thirteen colonies, the Declaration of Independence concludes by explaining that the United States of America, assembled in general congress, and "appealing to the Supreme Judge of the world for the rectitude of our intentions, do in the name, and by authority of the good people of these colonies, solemnly publish and declare that these United Colonies are, and of right ought to be, free and independent states."[4] The founding fathers absolved the colonies from all allegiance to the British crown (King George III) and dissolved all political connection between them and Great Britain. Now as free and

---

3. "Declaration of Independence."
4. "Declaration of Independence."

independent states, they had the power to levy war, conclude peace, contract alliances, establish commerce, and do everything else independent states could do. "And for the support of this Declaration," Jefferson continues, "with a firm reliance on the protection of Divine Providence, we [, the fifty-six signers,] mutually pledge to each other our lives, our fortunes, and our sacred honor."[5] The document was signed on July 4, 1776, and is commemorated every year as Independence Day (Fourth of July) in the United States of America.

Independence Day is celebrated with fireworks, parades, barbecues, carnivals, fairs, picnics, concerts, baseball games, family reunions, political speeches, patriotic displays, and red, white, and blue decorations. Fireworks are often accompanied by patriotic songs, especially "The Star-Spangled Banner," the national anthem of the United States. Originally a poem penned by Francis Scott Key named "Defence of Fort M'Henry," written on September 14, 1814, it was not made the national anthem until March 3, 1931, by a congressional resolution (Public Law 823, 46 Stat. 1508). It was codified on August 12, 1988 (Public Law 105–225), when it was designated as the official words from Key and the official music by John Stafford Smith, ironically an English composer! Key's brother-in-law, Joseph H. Nicholson, saw that the words fit Smith's music and got the first copies of the lyrics printed. However, it was Thomas Carr, who first published the lyrics and music under the title "The Star-Spangled Banner." Public Law 105–225 states that when the national anthem is played and the flag is displayed, those in uniform give the military salute throughout the playing of the anthem, those who are members of the armed forces and veterans not in uniform may render the military salute throughout the playing of the anthem, all others face the flag and stand at attention with their right hand over the heart. All with hats or caps remove them with their right hand and hold them at the left shoulder so that their right hand is over their heart. If there is no display of the flag while the anthem is being played, then all face toward the music and act as indicated if the flag were displayed. The national anthem is in the public domain; while there are four verses, usually only the first one is sung: "O say can you see, by the dawn's early light, / What so proudly we hailed at the twilight's last gleaming, / Whose broad stripes and bright stars through the perilous fights / O'er the ramparts we watched were so gallantly streaming? / And the rocket's red glare, the bombs bursting in air, / Gave proof through the night that our flag was still there; / O say does that star-spangled banner yet wave / O'er the land of the free and the home of the brave?" The last line echoes the freedom declared by the Declaration of the Independence.

Journal/Meditation: When have you had to throw off something because of absolute despotism? What is the role of God (Supreme Judge, Divine Providence) in the Declaration of Independence? To whom do you pledge your life, fortune, and sacred honor? What is your favorite line in "The Star-Spangled Banner"? What does it mean?

5. "Declaration of Independence."

Prayer: Supreme Judge, when they were oppressed, men and women from the thirteen British colonies in North America rose up and overthrew their persecutors. Give me the ability to recognize despotism and banish it from my midst, as I rely on Divine Providence for protection. Amen.

National Tattoo Day
July 17

Text: "Tattooing is the art of inserting pigment under the dermis layer of the skin to create a decorative, symbolic, or pictorial design . . . . [O]n National Tattoo Day, July 17, we set aside time to learn more about the tattooing process and its societal importance and history. If you don't have a tattoo, you're likely to know someone who does, and if you've asked [him or her] how [he or she] knew at the time when [he or she was] getting inked whether [he or she] would still want that design on [his or her] skin years or decades later, you may have just gotten a peculiar look instead of an explanation. There is certainly a fraternal connection between people who bear tattoos, a connection that those without ink can never really understand. . . .[One person] said: 'Tattoos began as a ceremony, and they're still kind of like that. Once you're under an artist's needle, it's a little like a religious experience. It's like the "Aha moment" people talk about having in business life. It illuminates something you didn't see before.'"[6]

Reflection: As can be seen from the above text, taken from *National Today's* "National Tattoo Day," getting a tattoo is a spiritual experience, if spiritual is substituted for religious. The word *tattoo* comes from the Samoan word *tatau*, which means *to strike, to tap, to mark*. Ancient Egyptians practiced tattooing, as can be seen on the skin of two mummies, dated between 3351 and 3017 BCE. The Iceman (Otzi), the natural mummy discovered in glacial ice in the Alps in 1991 and carbon-dated at 3250 BCE, bore sixty-one tattoos. Today, while most tattoos are permanent, they can be temporary; a non-permanent image is placed on the skin—a form of body painting that can be drawn, painted, airbrushed, or needled—and the ink dissolves in the blood within about six months. Permanent tattooing is a process of placing pigment into the skin's dermis, the layer under the epidermis. The most common tool used is the electric tattoo machine, which inserts the pigment into the skin using a single needle, or a group of needles, attached to an oscillating unit, which rapidly and repeatedly drives the needles in and out of the skin. The pigment is dispersed throughout a homogenized damaged layer down through the epidermis and upper dermis, in which the presence of foreign material activates the immune system's phagocytes to engulf the pigment particles. As healing takes place, the damaged epidermis flakes away, while granulation tissue forms deeper in the skin. That tissue is later converted to connective tissue by collagen growth, which mends the upper dermis, in which the pigment remains

---

6. "National Tattoo Day."

trapped and stable. In the United States, the first tattoo shop opened in New York City in 1846. Martin Hildebrandt, a German immigrant, became popular during the Civil War as both Union and Confederate soldiers and sailors sought his services.

There are three broad categories of tattoos: purely decorative, with no specific meaning for the person bearing the tattoo; symbolic, with a very specific meaning to the person bearing it; and pictorial (a depiction of a specific person or thing that has some kind of importance to the person bearing the tattoo). Five types of tattoos are recognized. Among these are (1) traumatic tattoos; when a substance, such as asphalt, gunpowder, pencil graphite, or pen ink is rubbed into a wound, the result is some kind of trauma (or accident) tattoo. Second, amateur tattoos, which may serve as a rite of passage, a mark of status or rank, a sign of religious or spiritual devotion, decoration for bravery, a pledge of love, etc. Depending upon the culture, an amateur tattoo may demonstrate how one person feels about another. Some people choose to be tattooed for artistic, cosmetic, sentimental, memorial, religious, and spiritual reasons. Third, professional tattoos often indicate identification with a particular group—ethnic, criminal, law-abiding, religious, spiritual, etc. Fourth, cosmetic tattoos serve as permanent makeup to enhance eyebrows, lips, eyes, and moles. Fifth, medical tattoos are used to ensure that instruments are properly located for repeated application of radiotherapy or other medical uses. The best time to get a tattoo is in the winter when the skin is smoother. National Tattoo Day is a good time to get a tattoo, or, minimally, investigate the possibilities if you have been thinking about it. National Tattoo Day celebrates body art; a tattoo can stimulate the mind, especially if you are thinking about getting a tattoo. Health risks need to be considered because the artist breaks the immunologic barrier formed by the skin and infections and allergic reactions can occur. A very good tattoo costs a very good price. Research is required to find a reputable artist who can create the design you may have in mind. Check the spelling if any words—English or other languages—are used. And keep in mind that there is National Tattoo Story Day, September 16, dedicated to the stories behind people's tattoos.

Journal/Meditation: If you have a tattoo, what was the spiritual experience like when you got it? If you do not have a tattoo, ask someone you know who has one to describe the spiritual experience when he or she got it. What image would you choose if you were to get a tattoo? Why?

Prayer: LORD God, you have invisibly tattooed all people and identified them as your chosen ones. Bestow skill on tattoo artists; bestow the grace of discernment upon those who seek to be tattooed; and never let us judge negatively those who display body art. Graciously hear and answer my prayer. Amen.

Nelson Mandela International Day (Mandela Day)

July 18

Text: "Recognizing the long history of Nelson Rolihlahla Mandela's leading role in and support for Africa's struggle for liberation and Africa's unity, and his outstanding contribution to the creation of a non-racial, non-sexist, democratic South Africa; recognizing also Nelson Mandela's values and his dedication to the service of humanity, as a humanitarian, in the fields of conflict resolution, race relations, promotion and protection of human rights, reconciliation, gender equality and the rights of children and other vulnerable groups, as well as the upliftment of poor and underdeveloped communities; acknowledging Nelson Mandela's contribution to the struggle for democracy internationally and the promotion of a culture of peace throughout the world; welcoming the international campaign . . . to each year observe 18 July, his birthday, as Mandela Day, . . . [the General Assembly of the United Nations] decides to designate 18 July as Nelson Mandela International Day, to be observed each year beginning in 2010."[7]

Reflection: Even before Nelson Mandela died on December 5, 2013, several groups began celebrating Mandela Day on July 18, 2009, Mandela's ninety-first birthday, with educational, art, fund-raising, and volunteer events leading to a Radio City Music Hall concert. As noted in the above text, the General Assembly of the United Nations declared July 18 to be Nelson Mandela International Day on November 10, 2009. Thus, the first U.N. Mandela Day was held on July 18, 2010. The purpose of the day is to honor the legacy of Mandela, a former president of South Africa, along with his values through volunteering and community service. The day is a global call to action; every individual person can transform the world; every individual person can make a difference. In order to emphasize the difference that a person can make, the U.N. established the Nelson Mandela Prize on June 6, 2014, with A/RES/68/275, after providing a description of it, its aim, the nomination process, and the composition of the selection committee with A/RES/69/269 on April 2, 2015. Every five years, beginning in 2015, an honorary award is given to two people—one male and one female—as a tribute to their achievements and contributions in service of humanity, while also honoring Mandela's life and legacy of reconciliation, political transition, and social transformation. The two engraved plaques acknowledge the recipients' service to humanity in the promotion of reconciliation and social cohesion, and in community development.

On December 17, 2015, after awarding the Nelson Mandela Prize for the first time earlier in the year, the U.N. General Assembly passed thirty-three-page A/RES/70/175, which extended the scope of Nelson Mandela International Day to

---

7. United Nations General Assembly, A/RES/64/13.

include and promote humane conditions of imprisonment, to raise awareness about prisoners being a continuous part of society, and to value the work of prison staff as a social service of particular importance. The resolution changed the name of the "United Nations Standard Minimum Rules for the Treatment of Prisoners" to "The Nelson Mandela Rules" "to honor the legacy of the late President of South Africa, Nelson Rolihlahla Mandela, who spent twenty-seven years in prison in the course of his struggle for global human rights, equality democracy, and the promotion of a culture of peace."[8] Mandela, who worked for liberty, unity, democracy, service to humanity, conflict resolution, race relations, human rights, reconciliation, gender equality, rights of children, rights of vulnerable adults, peace, and more, even in death continues to move people toward those goals.

Journal/Meditation: What do you honor in the legacy of Nelson Mandela? What action do you take on Nelson Mandala International Day? Which value of Nelson Mandela do you strive to imitate?

Prayer: From time to time, O God, you raise up men and women who have a passion for your values. In the last century in South Africa, you filled Nelson Mandala with a spirit of inclusivity to be manifest as liberty, unity, democracy, equality, peace, and service to humanity in many ways. Instill in me the spirit of Mandala and fill me with wisdom of your ways. Amen.

First Manned Moon Landing (Apollo 11)
July 20–21

Text: "... I believe that this nation should commit itself to achieving the goal, before this decade [of the 1960s] is out, of landing a man on the moon and returning him safely to the earth. No single space project in this period will be more impressive to [human]kind, or more important for the long-range exploration of space; and none will be so difficult or expensive to accomplish. We propose to accelerate the development of the appropriate lunar space craft. We propose to develop alternate liquid and solid fuel boosters, much larger than any now being developed, until certain which is superior. We propose additional funds for other engine development and for unmanned explorations—explorations which are particularly important for one purpose which this nation will never overlook: the survival of the man who first makes this daring flight. But in a very real sense, it will not be one man going to the moon—if we make this judgment affirmatively, it will be an entire nation. For all of us must work to put him there."[9]

---

8. United Nations General Assembly, A/RES/70/175.
9. Kennedy, "Excerpt from the 'Special Message to the Congress.'"

Reflection: On May 25, 1961, President John F. Kennedy addressed a joint session of congress. The address, known as the "Special Message to the Congress on Urgent National Needs," presents four goals Kennedy hoped to achieve before the end of the 1960s. The text above is the first of those four goals, namely, landing a man on the moon. This goal was important because during the Cold War between the United States and the Soviet Union, the latter had launched the first artificial satellite, named Sputnik 1, on October 4, 1957. Sputnik demonstrated the Soviet Union's capability of launching nuclear weapons over intercontinental distances, and, thus, it challenged the U.S.'s claims of military, economic, and technological superiority. President Dwight D. Eisenhower, Kennedy's predecessor, had responded to Sputnik by establishing the National Aeronautics and Space Administration (NASA) with the aim of launching a man into earth's orbit, but Soviet cosmonaut Yuri Gagarin became the first man in space on April 12, 1961, and the first person to orbit the earth. Alan Shepard became the first U.S. astronaut in space on May 5, 1961, completing a suborbital journey. This is what led to Kennedy's address to a joint session of congress twenty days later. Kennedy said, ". . . I am asking the congress and the country to accept a firm commitment to a new course of action, a course which will last for many years and carry very heavy costs . . . . It is a most important decision that we make as a nation. [We] have seen the significance of space and the adventures in space, and no one can predict with certainty what the ultimate meaning will be of mastery of space." Kennedy adds, "I believe we should go to the moon. . . . This decision demands a major national commitment of scientific and technical manpower, material and facilities, and the possibility of their diversion from other important activities . . . . [E]very scientist, every engineer, every serviceman, every technician, contractor, and civil servant gives his personal pledge that this nation will move forward, with the full speed of freedom, in the exciting adventure of space."[10]

The culmination of NASA's work and the fulfillment of Kennedy's goal occurred on July 20–21, 1969, when Neil Armstrong and Buzz Aldrin landed the Apollo Lunar Module (Eagle) on the moon. Armstrong was the first person to step onto the surface of the moon on July 20, voicing his now famous words: "One small step for [a] man, one giant leap for mankind." A few minutes later, on July 21, Aldrin joined him, stating, "Magnificent desolation." The flight to and the walking on the moon were a part of the Apollo 11 mission from July 16 to July 24, 1969. While Armstrong and Aldrin spent over two hours collecting lunar samples to bring back to earth, Michael Collins flew the Command Module, named Columbia, in thirty lunar orbits. This mission was the second in which all the crew members had previous spaceflight experience. Armstrong and Aldrin spent over twenty-one hours on the lunar surface at a spot named Tranquility Base, where they had taken the lunar module from Columbia and set it down. The lunar module had a stage for descent to the moon, and it had one for ascent to place the astronauts back into lunar orbit and docking with Columbia, which

---

10. Kennedy, "Excerpt from the 'Special Message to the Congress.'"

was then propelled onto a trajectory back to earth. President Richard Nixon watched from the White House, telling Armstrong and Aldrin how proud he was, how proud every citizen was, and how proud the world was. He told them that they inspired all to work hard to bring peace and tranquility to the earth. "For one priceless moment in the whole history of man all the people on this earth are truly one," stated Nixon, "one in their pride in what you have done and one in our prayers that you will return safely to earth."[11] Prayers were answered on July 24, when the astronauts splashed down in the Pacific Ocean. Apollo 11 made the U.S. victorious in the space race to put a man on the moon; it declared the U.S. superior, and it fulfilled Kennedy's 1961 goal.

Journal/Meditation: What is the spiritual significance of landing a person on the moon? How was the nation and the world connected in the Apollo 11 mission? What is the meaning of Kennedy's phrase, "the mastery of space"?

Prayer: God of the universes, you have given people the wisdom to design crafts that transport them into space, where they marvel at the vastness of your creation. Hear my prayer for all those who design, engineer, and fly into outer space. Keep them safe on their adventures and bring them safely back to the earth they call home. Amen.

Parents' Day
Fourth Sunday

Text: "Resolved by the Senate and House of Representatives of the United States of America in congress assembled, that the fourth Sunday of every July shall be established as 'Parents' Day' to be recognized as a recurring, perennial day of commemoration. All private citizens, organizations, and governmental and legislative bodies at the local, state, and federal level are encouraged to recognize Parents' Day through proclamations, activities, and educational efforts in furtherance of recognizing, uplifting, and supporting the role of parents in the rearing of their children."[12]

Reflection: On September 30, 1994, the United States House of Representatives passed the above text of what became Public Law 103–362, and on October 4, the U.S. Senate did the same. President William Clinton signed it into law on October 14, 1994. When it was codified on August 12, 1998, in 36 U.S. Code, Section 135 (Public Law 105–225), it stated: "All private citizens, organizations, and federal, state, and local governmental and legislative entities are encouraged to recognize Parents' Day through proclamations, activities, and educational efforts in furtherance of recognizing, uplifting, and supporting the role of parents in bringing up their children."[13] The law calls upon all U.S. citizens on all levels of government to accomplish three goals:

11. Nixon, "Telephone Conversation."
12. "Public Law 103–362."
13. "Public Law 105–225."

(1) to show appreciation to parents, (2) to help parents achieve a higher intellectual or spiritual level, and (3) to give encouragement to parents as they fulfill their role of rearing and caring for their children, the future population of the U.S. The law urges that the three goals be accomplished through three means: (1) proclamations about the fourth Sunday in July being Parents' Day, (2) activities, such as a family picnic, eating ice cream with a family conversation, singing favorite songs, researching the family tree and history, looking at family photographs, baking together, playing a board game together, preparing a family video, engaging in and completing a major chore (mowing, washing windows, etc.), saying "Thank You", and (3) educational efforts, like reading a book together, journaling, writing a family newsletter to share with other family members, getting more involved in school activities, etc. Parents' Day is designed for the community to assist parents in their role of raising their children.

On September 17, 2012, the General Assembly of the United Nations proclaimed "1 June the Global Day of Parents, to be observed annually, honoring parents throughout the world." It urged all its members to celebrate "in full partnership with civil society, particularly involving young people and children."[14] The U.N. resolution established the Global Day of Parents to recognize that the family is primary responsible for both nurturing and protecting children. The development of their personality relies upon a family environment of happiness, love, and understanding. The day offers the opportunity to appreciate parents' commitment to their children and honors them throughout the world for being the center of social life, education, and protection for their children. Parents are responsible for providing healthy lives, promoting the wellbeing, and ensuring educational opportunities for their children. Thus, on one day a year, parents are honored on the fourth Sunday in July in the U.S. and on June 1 globally.

Journal/Meditation: How do you mark Parents' Day? In what specific ways do you recognize, uplift, and support the role of parents in rearing their children?

Prayer: God, you are both Father and Mother to all your children. Fill me with the grace to recognize, uplift, and support the role of parents in rearing their children. Give all parents joy in their children, as they watch them achieve maturity as responsible citizens. Amen.

World War I Began
July 28

Text: "Whereas the Imperial German government has committed repeated acts of war against the government and the people of the United States of America: Therefore be it resolved by the Senate and House of Representatives of the United States of America

---

14. United Nations General Assembly, A/RES/66/292.

in congress assembled, that the state of war between the United States and the Imperial German government which has thus been thrust upon the United States is hereby formally declared; and that the president be, and he is hereby, authorized and directed to employ the entire naval and military forces of the United States and the resources of the government to carry on war against the Imperial German government; and to bring the conflict to a successful termination all of the resources of the country are hereby pledged by the congress of the United States."[15]

Reflection: On April 2, 1917, President Woodrow Wilson addressed a joint session of congress. In his speech, Wilson stated: "American ships have been sunk [by German submarines], American lives taken, in ways which it has stirred us very deeply to learn of, but the ships and people of other neutral and friendly nations have been sunk and overwhelmed in the waters in the same way. There has been no discrimination." Wilson continues: "With a profound sense of the solemn and even tragical character of the step I am taking and of the grave responsibilities which it involves, but in unhesitating obedience to what I deem my constitutional duty, I advise that the congress declare the recent course of the Imperial German Government to be in fact nothing less than war against the government and people of the United States; . . . that it take immediate steps not only to put the country in a more thorough state of defense but also to exert all its power to employ all its resources to bring the government of the German Empire to terms and end the war."[16] On April 6, 1917, as noted in the above text, the U.S. congress declared war on Germany. This war, at first called the Great War and then World War I, began on July 28, 1914, when Gavrilo Princip (one of six assassins), a Bosnian Serb Yugoslav nationalist assassinated Archduke Franz Ferdinand (and his wife Sophie), the Austro-Hungarian heir, who was visiting the Bosnian capital, Sarajevo. The political objective of the assassination of the archduke was to break off the southern Slav provinces, which Austria-Hungary had annexed from the Ottoman Empire, and combine them into Yugoslavia. The United States remained neutral until German U-boat 20 sank the British liner RMS Lusitania on May 7, 1915, with 128 Americans among the dead. Wilson demanded an end to attacks on passenger ships. However, in January 1917, Germany resumed submarine warfare; it also invited Mexico to join the war as an ally against the U.S., promising Mexico that it would help her recover the territories of Texas, New Mexico, and Arizona, which it had lost to the U.S. Wilson had no choice but to ask congress to declare war on Germany on April 2, 1917, and congress obliged on April 6, 1917. "Neutrality is no longer feasible or desirable where the peace of the world is involved and the freedom of its peoples, and the menace to that peace and freedom lies in the existence of autocratic governments

---

15. "Pubic Resolution 65–1."
16. Wilson, "Address to a Joint Session of Congress."

backed by organized force which is controlled wholly by their will, not by the will of their people," stated Wilson.[17]

World War I lasted from July 28, 1914, to November 11, 1918, although the U.S. didn't enter it until April 6, 1917. The European continent was split into two major opposing alliances named the Allied Powers and the Central Powers. The Allied Powers consisted of the United Kingdom of Great Britain and Ireland, the United States, France, the Russian Empire, Italy, Japan, Portugal, and the Balkan States (Serbia, Montenegro); the Central Powers consisted of the German Empire, the Austro-Hungarian Empire, the Ottoman Empire, and Bulgaria. While the U.S. was never a formal member of the Allied Powers, it served as an associate, especially after the passage of the Selective Service Act on May 18, 1917, which required men ages twenty-one to forty-five to register for military service; the U.S. sent 2.8 million trained soldiers to Europe. "It is a fearful thing to lead this great peaceful people into war," stated Wilson, "into the most terrible and disastrous of all wars, civilization itself seeming to be in the balance. But the right is more precious than peace, and we shall fight for the things which we have always carried nearest our hearts—for democracy, for the right of those who submit to authority to have a voice in their own governments, for the rights and liberties of small nations, for a universal dominion of right by such a concert of free peoples as shall bring peace and safety to all nations and make the world itself at least free."[18] To achieve Wilson's goals, the U.S. casualties consisted of 116,516 dead and 204,002 wounded among 8.5 million combatant deaths and 13 million civilian deaths as a direct result of the war, not counting genocides and the 1918 Spanish flu pandemic.

Journal/Meditation: What do you consider to be the best reason for entering into war? How can peace, freedom, and democracy be achieved through war?

Prayer: LORD God, you desire that all people live together in peace. When some are motivated to declare war on others, war may be the only way to preserve peace. Through the working of your Spirit, fill all men and women with a peace that eliminates all need for war today, tomorrow, and forever. Amen.

International Day of Friendship (Friendship Day)

July 30 (in the U.S., first Sunday of August)

Text: "Recognizing the relevance and importance of friendship as a noble and valuable sentiment in the lives of human beings around the world, bearing in mind that friendship between peoples, countries, cultures, and individuals can inspire peace efforts and presents an opportunity to build bridges between communities, honoring

---

17. Wilson, "Address to a Joint Session of Congress."
18. Wilson, "Address to a Joint Session of Congress."

cultural diversity, affirming that friendship can contribute to the efforts of the international community . . . towards the promotion of dialogue among civilizations, solidarity, mutual understanding, and reconciliation, [the General Assembly of the United Nations] . . . decides to designate 30 July as the International Day of Friendship; [and] invites all . . . to observe the International Day of Friendship in an appropriate manner in accordance with the culture and other appropriate circumstances or customs of their local, national, and regional communities, including through education and public awareness-raising activities."[19]

Reflection: A relationship between two people or more people is a friendship, which elicits mutual feelings of trust, affection, and behavior that typify relationships between friends. A friendship can consist of a relationship between individuals, organizations, or countries, characterized by mutual assistance, approval, and support. The United Nations resolution, as stated in the text above, established the International Day of Friendship on April 27, 2017, to be July 30 every year. While Friendship Day is celebrated on different dates in different countries around the world, in the United States it is marked on the first Sunday of August. According to the U.N. resolution, friendship is a noble and valuable sentiment that can build bridges between people, countries, and cultures; educational endeavors and awareness-raising efforts among friends can result in a greater understanding of cultural diversity.

Friendship promotes and defends a shared spirit of human solidarity. The accumulating bonds of camaraderie and the resulting development of strong ties of trust between individuals can easily spread to groups, countries, and the world. Friendships enable lasting stability in the world and provide a safety net that can protect all. They also generate passion for a better world where people are united for the common greater good. It is important to involve young people in the International Day of Friendship; they are the future leaders, who, hopefully, will respect different cultures and promote future international understanding and respect for diversity throughout the world. Besides the giving of flowers, cards, and wrist bands or taking a friend to lunch on Friendship Day, other activities might include peace education, sustainable economic and social development education, promoting respect for all human rights, fostering the equality between women and men, developing democratic participation, understanding tolerance and solidarity, etc. The building of friendship bridges connecting countries begins with the building of friendship bridges connecting individuals.

Journal/Meditation: What is your personal definition of friendship? How have your friends helped you build bridges that honor cultural diversity? Why is it important to foster understanding of cultural diversity in the world?

---

19. United Nations General Assembly, A/65/L.72.

Prayer: O God, you have made friendship a noble and valuable sentiment among your people. As an unfailing treasure, it offers pure delight to those who foster it among people, countries, and cultures. Grant that my forgiveness of others may foster friendship among all neighbors of the world. Amen.

World Day Against Trafficking in Persons
July 30

Text: "Reiterating its strong condemnation of trafficking in persons, especially women and children, which constitutes an offence and a serious threat to human dignity and physical integrity, human rights, and development; reiterating its concern that . . . trafficking in persons remains one of the grave challenges facing the international community, which also impairs the enjoyment of human rights and needs a more concerned collective and comprehensive international response; recognizing the need to continue to foster a global partnership against trafficking in persons and the need to continue to work towards an enhanced comprehensive and coordinated approach to prevent and combat trafficking and to protect and assist victims of trafficking in persons through the appropriate national, regional, and international mechanisms; . . . [the General Assembly of the United Nations,] in the context of the need for raising awareness of the situation of victims of human trafficking and for the promotion and protection of their rights, . . . designates 30 July as the World Day against Trafficking in Persons, to be observed every year . . . ."[20]

Reflection: On December 18, 2013, the General Assembly of the United Nations passed a seven-page resolution condemning trafficking in persons in its effort "to devise, enforce, and strengthen effective measures to combat and eliminate all forms of trafficking in persons, to counter the demands for trafficked victims, and to protect the victims."[21] The U.N. had passed previous resolutions in 1980, 1998, 2004, 2006, 2009, 2010, 2012, and 2013 in its efforts to combat trafficking in persons. In this resolution, it called upon all member states "to continue their efforts to criminalize trafficking in persons in all its forms, including for labor exploitation and commercial sexual exploitation of children, including by tourists, to condemn these practices and to investigate, prosecute, and penalize traffickers and intermediaries while providing protection and assistance to the victims of trafficking with full respect for their human rights . . . ."[22] The trafficking of persons is understood as the trading of humans for forced labor, sexual slavery, or commercial sexual exploitation for the trafficker or for others. The trafficking of persons includes forced marriage, removing organs or tissues for any purpose, and more. The "United Nations Convention against Transnational

---

20. United Nations General Assembly, A/RES/68/192.
21. United Nations General Assembly, A/RES/68/192.
22. United Nations General Assembly, A/RES/68/192.

Organized Crime and the Protocols Thereto," issued in 2004, defines the trafficking of persons as "the recruitment, transportation, transfer, harboring or receipt of persons, by means of the threat or use of force or other form of coercion, of abduction, of fraud, of deception, of the abuse of power or of a position of vulnerability or of the giving or receiving of payments or benefits to achieve the consent of a person having control over another person, for the purpose of exploitation. Exploitation . . . include[s], at a minimum, the exploitation of the prostitution of others or other forms of sexual exploitation, forced labor or service, slavery or practices similar to slavery, servitude, or the removal of organs."[23]

The definition also applies to children, any person under eighteen years of age: "The recruitment, transportation, transfer, harboring, or receipt of a child for the purpose of exploitation shall be considered 'trafficking in persons' even if this does not involve any of the means set forth" in the preceding quotation.[24] Children can be forced into prostitution and pornography, labor or services, illicit international adoption, early marriage, athletics, recruited as child soldiers, and used in begging. Every year millions of people are trapped in modern day slavery. In 2014, major leaders of many religions met to sign a shared commitment against modern day slavery; they called for the elimination of human trafficking. In the United States of America, January 11 is National Day of Human Trafficking Awareness. It was designated as such by the U.S. senate in 2007 to indicate that awareness is the key to the prevention of human trafficking.

Journal/Meditation: What awareness do you have of trafficking in persons that may take place where you live? What is the most horrendous aspect of this crime for you? Why?

Prayer: God, you endowed people with human dignity and integrity and gave them rights. Raise my awareness concerning the grave challenge human trafficking presents to the world. Give me the wisdom to respond to anyone who impairs the enjoyment of human rights all the days of my life. Amen.

23. "United Nations Convention," 42.
24. "United Nations Convention," 43.

8

The Month of *August*

INTERNATIONAL DAY OF THE WORLD'S INDIGENOUS PEOPLES
August 9

Text: "Recognizing the value and diversity of the cultures and the forms of social organization of the world's indigenous people; conscious of the need to improve the economic, social, and cultural situation of the indigenous people, with full respect for their distinctiveness and their own initiatives; . . . convinced that the development of indigenous people within their countries will contribute to the socio-economic, cultural, and environmental advancement of all the countries of the world; recognizing that indigenous people can and should be able through appropriate mechanisms to make their distinct contributions to humanity; . . . recognizing and strengthening the role of indigenous people and their communities; . . . determined to promote the enjoyment of the rights of indigenous people and the full development of their distinct cultures and communities; . . . [the General Assembly of the United Nations] decides that the International Day of the World's Indigenous People shall be observed every year . . . on 9 August . . . ."[1]

Reflection: The word *indigenous*, from a Latin word meaning *born in*, refers to people originating in and typical of a region or country. More specifically, the word describes ethnic groups of people who were native to a territory prior to it being incorporated into a nation and who are both politically and culturally separate from the majority ethnic identity of the state of which they are a part. Sometimes referred to as aboriginal, such native people are found in almost one hundred counties in the world. On December 23, 1994, the General Assembly of the United Nations not only established the International Day of the World's Indigenous Peoples, as noted in the text above, but also declared the first International Decade of the World's Indigenous Peoples

---

1. United Nations General Assembly, A/RES/49/214.

from 1995 to 2004. After that decade, it declared a Second International Decade from 2005 to 2015. The purpose of the twenty years' focus on native people and the yearly observance is to raise awareness and protect the rights of the world's indigenous people. For example, in 2016, the U.N. focused on the over 2,600 indigenous languages that were in danger of extinction. The day also serves as the occasion to highlight the achievements and the contributions that native people make to improve world issues, such as the environment. Indigenous people represent a vast diversity of cultures, traditions, and systems of knowledge. Usually having a close relationship with their lands, they also hold concepts about development that are based on their worldviews and priorities and not on capitalism.

Many people are not aware of how many indigenous people live in portions of the United States. In Alaska, for example, there are the Aleut, Yupik, Tlingit, and Nunavik, to name a few. In Montana, there are the Cree; in Washington State, the Makah and Quinault; in Colorado, Nevada, and Utah, the Shoshone and Paiute; in California, the Yuman-Cochimi, Miwok, Maidu, Wintu, to name a few. On the Great Plains can be found the Comanche, Osage, Sioux, Kiowa, and Omaha. The Iroquoian peoples, the Algonquian peoples, and the Shawnee peoples, all subdivided into many tribes, can be found in the northeast U.S. In the southeast are the Cherokee, Natchez, and Sioux. This list is just a sampling of indigenous peoples in the U.S. It doesn't begin to name those in Canada, Mexico, or Central America, or the over 476 million indigenous peoples living around the world. The International Day of the World's Indigenous Peoples offers the opportunity to celebrate, according to the U.N., the diversity of cultures in which we live. We can come to a deeper understanding of the economic and social situations in which indigenous peoples find themselves along with the contributions they make to the world. And, of course, focusing on the basic human rights of all people, no matter their ethnic identity, is focusing simultaneously on our own.

Journal/Meditation: Who are the indigenous people in the area where you live? What do you know about them? How can you come to a deeper understanding of their culture?

Prayer: In the beginning, O God, you created many people throughout the world and endowed them with diverse cultures and ways of life. Grant that I may come to a deeper understanding of the indigenous people who live and work around me. For in doing so, I come to a deeper understanding of you, the creator of all, who lives forever and ever. Amen.

INTERNATIONAL YOUTH DAY

August 12

Text: "[The General Assembly of the United Nations] noting especially that . . . current regional and interregional conferences of ministers responsible for youth affairs

… were invited to intensify cooperation among each other and to consider meeting regularly at the international level under the aegis of the United Nations to provide an effective forum for a focused global dialogue on youth-related issues; invites all relevant programs, funds, specialized agencies, and other bodies within the United Nations system, as well as other intergovernmental organizations and regional financial institutions, to give greater support to national youth policies and programs within their country programs . . . ; endorses the recommendation that 12 August be declared International Youth Day; [and] calls upon all states, all United Nations bodies . . . to exchange knowledge and expertise on youth-related issues . . . ; [and] reiterates the call to member states to consider including youth representatives in their delegations to the General Assembly and other relevant United Nations meetings, thus broadening the channels of communication and enhancing the discussion of youth-related issues . . . ."[2]

Reflection: The United Nations General Assembly designated August 12 as International Youth Day on December 17, 1999. Thus, the first such day was celebrated on August 12, 2000. While the day is designed to raise awareness by drawing attention to cultural and legal issues affecting youth, it serves youth throughout the world by addressing education, employment, environment, delinquency, intergenerational relations, and more. As can be seen in the above text taken from the U.N. resolution declaring August 12 International Youth Day, the goal is sharing information among those serving youth in society in order to protect them and to include them in the development of communities around the world. Young people contribute to education, employment, conflict resolution, social justice, etc., and they need to be heard by adults. That is why the U.N. invites its members to include youth representatives in the delegations to the General Assembly and other U.N. meetings so that issues facing young people can be voiced by young people themselves.

The day gives governments around the world the opportunity to draw attention to issues facing young people, who, both collectively and individually, express concerns about the environment, life, food systems, etc. A specific focus for the day is designed to recognize what youth have to contribute to the area under consideration. In the past, such topics as youth and mental health, civic engagement, peace, sustainable consumption and production, safe spaces, education, global action, and more have been addressed through concerts, workshops, cultural events, and meetings involving both national and local government officials with youth and youth organizations around the world. The U.N. recognizes that youth can be a positive force for ongoing development of their communities, when they are provided with knowledge and opportunities to contribute. They are the future, and the future is in their hands.

---

2. United Nations General Assembly, A/RES/54/120.

Journal/Meditation: How do you dialogue with youth on a local level? What are the issues facing young people where you live? In what community development are youth invited to participate where you live?

Prayer: O LORD, you have taught me from my youth according to your steadfast love. Renew all young men and women with your spirit that they may willingly contribute to the development of their communities for the common good of all. Amen.

Panama Canal Opened
August 15

Text: ". . . [T]he president is hereby authorized to acquire from the Republic of Colombia, for and on behalf of the United States, upon such terms as he may deem reasonable, perpetual control of a strip of land, the territory of the Republic of Colombia, not less than six miles in width, extending from the Caribbean Sea to the Pacific Ocean, and the right to use and dispose of the waters thereon, and to excavate, construct, and to perpetually maintain, operate, and protect thereon a canal, of such depth and capacity as will afford convenient passage of ships of the greatest tonnage and draft now in use, from the Caribbean Sea to the Pacific Ocean . . . . Such canal shall . . . be supplied with all necessary locks and other appliances to meet the necessities of vessels passing through the same from ocean to ocean; and he shall also cause to be constructed such safe and commodious harbors at the termini of said canal, and make such provisions for defense as may be necessary for the safety and protection of said canal and harbors."[3]

Reflection: On August 15, 1914, the United States opened the Panama Canal, an artificial, fifty-mile waterway in Panama that connects the Atlantic Ocean with the Pacific Ocean, across the Isthmus of Panama. France began work on the canal in 1881, but stopped in 1894 because of many problems. On June 28, 1902, the U.S. Senate and House of Representatives authorized the then-president of the U.S. Theodore Roosevelt to acquire the land from the Republic of Columbia, which owned it at that time, to complete the canal. As the text above states, the Caribbean Sea (Atlantic Ocean) was to be connected to the Pacific Ocean by a canal with locks, safe harbors, and other necessities. That congressional provision, called the Spooner Act—because it was written by U.S. Senator John Coit Spooner from Wisconsin—was signed by Roosevelt the day after it passed both houses of congress. The U.S. took over the building of the canal on May 4, 1904; in the meantime, Panama declared its independence from Columbia and became a country on November 3, 1903. In order to reduce the amount of excavation work, canal locks at each end raise ships eighty-five feet above sea level to artificial Gatum Lake and then lower the ships at the other end. The original locks

---

3. "Public Law 57–183."

were 110 feet wide, but between September 2007 and May 2016, a wider lane with new locks was built to accommodate larger ships; the new lane was opened June 26, 2016.

On September 7, 1977, President Jimmy Carter signed a treaty both guaranteeing the permanent neutrality of the canal and giving full control of it to Panama on December 31, 1999. The canal stands as one of those world-wide engineering feats. Today, it consists of artificial lakes, three improved and artificial channels, and three sets of locks. Entering from the Atlantic Ocean (Caribbean Sea), a ship enters the deep-water port of Colon (Cristobal) and travels two miles to the Gatun Locks, a three-stage flight of locks one and a fourth miles long that lifts ships to eighty-seven feet above sea level to Gatun Lake, the artificial body of water through which ships pass for fifteen miles across the Isthmus of Panama. The upper level of the lake is fed by the Chagres River about five and one-fourth miles. For seven and three-fourths miles a ship then passes through a cut through the mountain ridge forming the continental divide. Once it comes to the Pedro Miguel Lock, seven-eighths of a mile long, it begins the descent of thirty-one feet to the Pacific Ocean. Next, the ship passes through the two-stage Miraflores Locks, one and one-eighth miles long and descends fifty-four feet. After its descent, the ship is in Balboa Harbor with a channel that leads to the Pacific Ocean. With the building of the canal, ships no longer had to travel to the southernmost tip of South American to get from the Atlantic Ocean to the Pacific Ocean or vice-versa.

Journal/Meditation: In the area where you live, what engineering feat gets your attention? What does it say about human creativity and ingenuity?

Prayer: LORD God, you have shared your creativity with human beings so that when they attempt to make the world a better a place, your spirit guides their deliberations. Bless all those on ships passing through the Panama Canal every day, and keep safe the artificial waterway you have inspired people to build and to maintain. Amen.

World Humanitarian Day

August 19

Text: ". . . Reaffirming the principles of neutrality, humanity, impartiality, and independence for the provision of humanitarian assistance; emphasizing the need to mobilize adequate, predictable, timely, and flexible resources for humanitarian assistance based on and in proportion to assessed needs, with a view to ensuring fuller coverage of the needs in all sectors and across humanitarian emergencies . . . ; expressing its deep concern at the increasing challenges faced by . . . humanitarian response capacity as a result of the consequences of natural disasters, including the impact of climate change . . . ; emphasizing that enhancing international cooperation on emergency humanitarian assistance is essential . . . ; condemning the increasing number of deliberate violent attacks against humanitarian personnel and facilities and the negative implications for the provision of humanitarian assistance to populations in need; paying tribute to all humanitarian personnel . . . who have worked to promote the humanitarian cause, as well as to those who have perished in the cause of duty; [the General Assembly of the United Nations] reaffirms the obligation of all states and parties to an armed conflict to protect civilians in armed conflicts in accordance with international humanitarian law, and invites states to promote a culture of protection, taking into account the particular needs of women, children, older persons, and persons with disabilities; decides to designate 19 August as World Humanitarian Day in order to contribute to increasing public awareness about humanitarian assistance activities worldwide and the importance of international cooperation in this regard, as well as to honor all humanitarian and United Nations and associated personnel who have worked in the promotion of the humanitarian cause and those who have lost their lives in the cause of duty . . . ."[4]

Reflection: The text above is taken from the five-page resolution—A/RES/63/139—passed by the General Assembly of the United Nations on December 11, 2008. Preceding the passage of that resolution, on the same day the General Assembly passed A/RES/63/138 Safety and Security of Humanitarian Personnel and Protection of United Nations Personnel, an eight-page resolution in which it expressed its deep concern for the dangers and security risks "faced by humanitarian personnel and United Nations and associated personnel at the field level, as they operate in increasingly complex contexts, as well as the continuous erosion, in many cases, of respect for the principles and rules of international law, in particular, international humanitarian law."[5] The latter resolution commended "the courage and commitment of those who take part in humanitarian operations, often at great personal risk, especially locally recruited staff."[6] Also, it expressed "profound regret at the deaths of and violent acts against international and national humanitarian personnel and United Nations and associated personnel involved in the provision of humanitarian assistance, and strongly [deplored] the rising toll of casualties among such personnel in complex humanitarian emergencies, in particular in armed conflicts and in post-conflict situations."[7] It called upon all members to adhere to international humanitarian law and to insure the security of humanitarian and U.N. personnel along with the unhindered access to and delivery of supplies and equipment at a time when threats and attacks had escalated dramatically.

The U.N. chose August 19 as World Humanitarian Day to honor Sergio Viera de Mello, a Brazilian citizen, who over thirty years in the U.N. served in some of the most challenging humanitarian situations in the world. On August 19, 2003, a bomb

---

4. United Nations General Assembly, A/RES/63/139.
5. United Nations General Assembly, A/RES/63/138.
6. United Nations General Assembly, A/RES/63/138.
7. United Nations General Assembly, A/RES/63/138.

attack on the Canal Hotel in Baghdad, Iraq, killed him and twenty-one other humanitarian aid workers. By 2006, his family and a group of friends started a foundation to his memory and dedicated to continuing the unfinished mission of relieving the plight of humanitarian crises. The foundation, which advocates for the security and independence of humanitarian actors, pays tribute to all humanitarian personnel who have given their lives while improving the lives of other people, especially victims of humanitarian crises. The day focuses on bringing together people from all across the humanitarian system to advocate for the survival, wellbeing, and dignity of those affected by crises along with the safety and security needed by aid workers. Since World Humanitarian Day was first celebrated in 2009, particular themes are proposed by the U.N., such as the actual work and achievements of humanitarian workers in the field, inspiring the spirit of aid work in everyone, making one's mark by doing something good somewhere for someone else, etc. By having a day dedicated to recognizing humanitarian personnel and those who have lost their lives working for humanitarian causes, the U.N. hopes to inspire others to join in humanitarian endeavors.

Journal/Meditation: In what specific way can you advocate for the safety and security of humanitarian workers? Locally, how can you become a humanitarian worker? How can you honor those who have lost their lives helping others?

Prayer: God of all, you inspire some people to work for the improvement of the lives of other people. Fill me with the spirit of the humanitarian mission that I may make the world a better place. I give you thanks for the lives of all who have given their lives to the humanitarian vision of relieving the sufferings of others. Amen.

NATIONAL AVIATION DAY
August 19

Text: "Whereas the development of aeronautics in recent years has been so rapid that aviation in its many phases has come to exert a profound influence on the course of events throughout the world; and whereas American initiative and industry have contributed greatly to this development and should be encouraged to continue such contribution in order that the United States may retain its outstanding position in the field of aeronautics; and whereas . . . 'the president of the United States is authorized to designate August 19 of each year as National Aviation Day, and to issue a proclamation calling upon officials of the government to display the flag of the United States on all government buildings on that day, and inviting the people of the United States to observe the day with appropriate exercises to further and stimulate interest in aviation in the United States:' Now, therefore, I, Franklin D. Roosevelt, President of the United

States of America, do hereby designate August 19, 1939, and August 19 of each succeeding year as National Aviation Day...."[8]

Reflection: On July 25, 1939, President Franklin D. Roosevelt issue the first and only proclamation of National Aviation Day to be observed on August 19, as can be seen in the above text. The celebration was included in Public Law 105–225, Section 118, on August 12, 1998; the law states that "the president may issue each year a proclamation designating August 19 as National Aviation Day."[9] Five years before he proclaimed National Aviation Day, Roosevelt wrote a letter to Orville Wright on the thirtieth anniversary of the airplane, "the first flight of man in an airplane." In the December 16, 1933, letter, Roosevelt wrote, "It is a source of gratification to me to know that it was an American who gave the world mechanical wings, and it is an even greater satisfaction to realize the part that America has taken in the rapid development of this newest and swiftest form of transportation."[10] On August 8, 1978, President Jimmy Carter "designate[d] the year 1978, diamond jubilee anniversary of powered flight, as National Aviation Year."[11] No other presidents have made proclamations celebrating the development of aviation. What did occur was Public Law 86–304, issued September 21, 1959, designating December 17, 1959, "'Wright Brothers Day,' in commemoration of the first successful flights in a heavier-than-air mechanically propelled airplane, which were made by Orville and Wilbur Wright on December 17, 1903, near Kitty Hawk, North Carolina."[12] On the same Day, September 21, 1959, President Dwight D. Eisenhower proclaimed December 17, 1959, Wright Brothers Day, writing, "... [I]t is appropriate that the members of the Wright brothers, whose genius, courage, and enterprise wrought profound change in the lives of [human]kind, should be honored on the anniversary day of their epic flight...."[13] The pioneers of human flight were honored again in 1961 with Public Law 87–291, approved September 22, 1961, word-for-word the same as its predecessor. After stating that "December 17, 1903, marked the beginning of a revolution in the transportation and defense methods employed by all the nations of the world" and that the Wright Brothers "made the continents of this planet only hours apart," on September 22, 1961, President John F. Kennedy, declared December 17, 1961, Wright Brothers Day.[14] On December 17, 1963, congress passed a join resolution, Public Law 88–209, declaring: "... [T]he seventeenth day of December of each year is hereby designated as 'Wright Brothers Day.'"[15] Also, it requested the president to issue a proclamation annually. That is exactly with President

8. Roosevelt, "National Aviation Day," 3439.
9. "Public Law 105–225," Section 118.
10. Roosevelt, "Letter."
11. Carter, "Proclamation 4584."
12. "Public Law 86–304."
13. Eisenhower, "Proclamation 3315."
14. Kennedy, "Proclamation 3433."
15. "Public Law 88–209."

Lyndon B. Johnson did on December 17, 1963, writing: ". . . [T]he Wright Brothers' genius and their vision have revolutionized transportation and defense methods and placed the United States in the forefront of world aviation. . . . [T]he Wright brothers have brought us closer together with the other peoples of the world. . . ."[16] Johnson issued similar proclamations in 1964 (Proclamation 3628), 1965 (Proclamation 3685), 1966 (Proclamation 3757), 1967 (Proclamation 3821), and 1968 (Proclamation 3883). Working with the theme of dream, President Richard Nixon issued his first Wright Brothers Day proclamation on December 11, 1969. He began: "Over the centuries, man dreamed a great dream—to break his bondage to the earth and fly through the sky. The Greeks told of Icarus who almost succeeded, but who paid for failure with his life. The dream took shape in the mind of the Renaissance Man, da Vinci, who drew designs for a flying machine, but who never flew. But the dream was always there, and always man worked to make the dream a reality. . . . Orville and Wilbur Wright made the dream a hard scientific fact." Nixon continued: "Almost sixty-six years later, another man stepped from another craft onto another plain. His plain was the waterless Sea of Tranquility on the Moon. . . . The names of Orville Wright and Wilbur Wright symbolize America's pioneering leadership in aviation. With countless other men of all nations, they represent [human]kind's ceaseless effort to make dreams reality."[17] Nixon issued similar proclamations in 1970 (Proclamation 4024), 1971 (Proclamation 4097), 1972 (Proclamation 4174), and 1973 (Proclamation 4257). The first of President Gerald R. Ford's Wright Brothers Day proclamations was issued November 27, 1974. He stated that since the Wright Brothers' "epic flight, aviation and space technology has contributed to closer ties among the peoples of the world by igniting their imagination, promoting commerce, and encouraging travel."[18] He issued similar proclamations in 1975 (Proclamation 4404) and 1976 (Proclamation 4475).

On November 23, 1977, President Jimmy Carter remembered "Wilbur and Orville Wright" as "bicycle makers and inventors" in his first proclamation of Wright Brothers Day. "The achievement of the two brothers," he wrote, "almost unnoticed at the time, has since been recognized as one of history's most significant accomplishments. Trips that once took months now take a few hours and all the peoples of the earth have become neighbors."[19] He issued similar proclamations in 1978 (Proclamation 4584), 1979 (Proclamation 4699), and 1980 (Proclamation 4802). "Since the dawn of civilization, men have dreamed of conquering the air," began President Ronald Reagan in his first Wright Brothers Day proclamation. "History is filled with tales of those who tried to emulate the flight of birds, but not until the early days of this [twentieth] century did that dream become a reality." He explained how "aviation is vital to the American way of life and to [the] economy" and mentioned how "the pioneering

16. Johnson, "Proclamation 3565."
17. Nixon, "Proclamation 3947."
18. Ford, "Proclamation 4336."
19. Carter, "Proclamation 4541."

spirit exhibited by the Wright Brothers . . . has kept America in the forefront of innovative aeronautics," specifically, "two successful missions of the United States Space Shuttle Columbia."[20] Reagan issued similar proclamations in 1982 (Proclamation 5001), 1983 (Proclamation 5119), 1984 (Proclamation 5288), 1985 (Proclamation 5422), 1986 (Proclamation 5588), 1987 (Proclamation 5750), and 1988 (Proclamation 5919). In his first Wright Brothers Day proclamation on December 14, 1989, George Bush stated that the Wright brothers "began an exciting process of design, trial, and discovery that continue[d] . . . ." He also noted "the tremendous progress in aviation that has been made during the past . . . years."[21] In 1990 (Proclamation 6237), 1991 (Proclamation 6391), and 1992 (Proclamation 6512), he issued similar proclamations. Beginning with a short history, President William J. Clinton issued his first Wright Brothers Day proclamation on December 10, 1993. "The 'Flyer I' made its inaugural voyage on the morning of December 17, 1903," wrote Clinton. "With Orville at the controls and Wilbur on the ground, the little craft stayed aloft for only twelve seconds and covered just 120 feet." Then, he recounted how aviation technology "has evolved from propeller power to jet engine propulsion, from supersonic transport to work on hypersonic aircraft." He noted "the can-do spirit, inquisitiveness, and tenacity of the Wright Brothers" that applied "to the ongoing exploration of new aviation horizons."[22] Clinton issued similar proclamations in 1994 (Proclamation 6762), 1995 (Proclamation 6858), 1996 (Proclamation 6965), 1997 (Proclamation 7061), 1998 (Proclamation 7160), 1999 (Proclamation 7262), and 2000 (Proclamation 7387). In his first of eight Wright Brothers Day proclamations, President George W. Bush worked with the theme of the Wright Brothers critics. "Many thought powered flight impossible," Bush stated; "and skeptics called the Wrights dreamers for even entertaining the idea. . . . After many trials and errors, the Wright Brothers finally achieved a controlled flight and opened the door to a new world." Later, in the two-page document, Bush salutes "all the scientific pioneers and visionaries who despite the critics, have overcome seemingly insurmountable odds and made great advances for [humankind]. The Wright Brothers' perseverance and creativity can serve as an inspiration for those inventors who will take us to new heights in the twenty-first century."[23] Bush issued similar proclamations in 2002 (Proclamation 7635), 2003 (Proclamation 7745), 2004 (Proclamation 7856), 2005 (Proclamation 7969), 2006 (Proclamation 8091), 2007 (Proclamation 8211), and 2008 (Proclamation 8329). President Barack Obama recounts how a wooden aircraft lifted "two brothers from Dayton, Ohio, to their place in history" in his first Wright Brothers Day proclamation in 2009. "Their singular triumph triggered a revolution in transportation that would bridge the vast distance between continents and forever alter our world." He continued the history lesson,

20. Reagan, "Proclamation 4886."
21. Bush, "Proclamation 6084."
22. Clinton, "Proclamation 6638."
23. Bush, G.W., "Proclamation 7514."

using the theme of entrepreneurship, and writing: "Self-taught and financed by the proceeds of their bicycle shop, the Wright Brothers' success embodies our nation's proud tradition of entrepreneurship. . . . Orville and Wilbur Wright remind us of what can be accomplished when imagination is joined with tenacity. Their spirit lives on in every garage and basement workshop where American innovators still tinker, invent, and discover. The next Wright Brothers are among us today, working tirelessly toward a breakthrough that will spark a new industry and improve countless lives."[24] Obama issued similar proclamations in 2010 (Proclamation 8617), 2011 (Proclamation 8767), 2012 (Proclamation 8918), 2013 (Proclamation 9071), 2014 (Proclamation 9222), 2015 (Proclamation 9382), and 2016 (Proclamation 9557). President Donald J. Trump's first Wright Brothers Day proclamation is a two-page history lesson. After recounting what happened on December 17, 1903, in the first paragraph, he wrote: "Orville and Wilbur Wright shared a fascination with flight and a desire to push the limits of the possible. They were bicycle mechanics by trade, and though they lacked formal education and resources, they excelled in aviation through determination and tenacity. They built their own research facilities, learned and tested principles of engineering and aerodynamics, and endured years of failure as they improved on their designs."[25] Later, Trump recounts the July 1969 first manned mission to the Moon by Neil Armstrong, Buzz Aldrin, and Michael Collins, and Joe Sutter, who designed and built the 747 jetliner. He issued similar proclamations in 2018 (Proclamation 9833), 2019 (Proclamation 9973), and 2020 (Proclamation 10127). On December 16, 2021, President Joseph R. Biden issued his first Wright Brothers Day proclamation, writing, "The Wright Brothers' unyielding dedication, creativity, and bravery gave birth to modern aviation—skyrocketing our nation's leadership in flight, and inspiring generations of Americans to take to the skies."[26] On the second of the two-page document, Biden recounts the flight history of Amelia Earhart, the Tuskegee Airmen, astronauts, and NASA's many missions. "We were the first to break the sound barrier. The first to fly non-stop around the world," he writes.[27] In the 1994 Public Law 88–209 of December 17, 1963, Wright Brothers Day was Section 169; in the August 12, 1998, Public Law 105–225, Wright Brothers Day is Section 143. National Aviation Day, established by Roosevelt on Orville Wright's birthday, August 19, quickly moved to Wright Brothers Day, December 17. It is presented here because of the many other observances in December.

Journal/Meditation: What metaphor captures the spirit of National Aviation Day/Wright Brothers Day for you: dream, process, vision, entrepreneurship? Explain. What statement from a president caught your attention? Why?

24. Obama, "Proclamation 8466."
25. Trump, "Proclamation 9686."
26. Biden, "Proclamation 10324."
27. Biden, "Proclamation 10324."

Prayer: The spirit of inventiveness led Orville and Wilbur Wright to make the first flight in an airplane, O LORD. As I remember all the developments in aviation over the past hundred years, make be grateful for the men and women who enable me to fly across lands and oceans and for those who explore the frontiers of space. Keep safe all who board planes and bring them home to their families. Amen.

NATIONAL SENIOR CITIZEN'S DAY
August 21

Text: "Resolved by the Senate and House of Representatives of the United States of America in congress assembled, that the President is authorized and requested to issue a proclamation designating the third Sunday of August 1988 as 'National Senior Citizens Day,' and calling upon the people of the United States to observe such day with appropriate ceremonies and activities in honor of the contributions to the United States of individuals more than fifty-five years of age."[28]

Reflection: According to Public Law 100–400—the text above—passed by the U.S. House of Representatives on August 2, 1988, and by the U.S. Senate on August 8, 1988, the president was authorized and requested to proclaim the third Sunday of August 1988 as national Senior Citizens Day. The House Joint Resolution 138 became law on August 17, 1988. The third Sunday of August in 1988 was August 21. When President Ronald Reagan issued the proclamation on August 19, 1988, he designated August 21, 1988—not the third Sunday of August—as National Senior Citizens Day. That is why the day is marked on August 21 no matter what day of the week it may be. In his proclamation, Reagan stated, ". . . [O]lder people have achieved much for our families, our communities, and our country."[29] After praising improved health care, Reagan wrote: "Many older people are embarking on second careers, giving younger Americans a fine example of responsibility, resourcefulness, competence, and determination. . . . [S]enior citizens are serving as volunteers in various programs and projects that benefit every sector of society. . . . [O]lder people are making their presence felt—for their own good and that of others."[30] However, Reagan's most quoted words out of his proclamation are these: "For all they have achieved throughout life and for all they continue to accomplish, we owe older citizens our thanks and a heartfelt salute. We can best demonstrate our gratitude and esteem by making sure that our communities are good places in which to mature and grow older—places in which older people can participate to the fullest and can find the encouragement, acceptance, assistance, and services they need to continue to lead lives of independence and dignity."[31] Many

---

28. "Public Law 100–400."
29. Reagan, "Proclamation 5847."
30. Reagan, "Proclamation 5847."
31. Reagan, "Proclamation 5847."

senior citizens have been pioneers in science, medicine, psychology, civil rights, community organizers, and volunteers. The day can be marked by visiting a retirement home, taking a senior citizen relative to lunch or shopping in order to take advantage of special discounts and promotions, asking a grandparent or other relative to narrate his or her story, profiling an elderly person's life and struggles, baking a dessert for a senior citizen who has no family nearby to visit, or sending a personal note or card to an older adult who made a positive impact on your life.

Often confused with National Senior Citizen's Day is World Senior Citizen's Day, also known as International Day of Older Persons and International Day for the Elderly. The International Day for the Elderly was designated by the United Nations General Assembly on December 14, 1990, to be marked yearly on October 1. In resolution 45/106, the U.N. recognized that "the elderly are an asset to society and can contribute significantly to the development process."[32] It also recognized "the complexity and rapidity of the aging of the world's population and the need to have a common basis and frame of reference for the protection and promotion of the rights of the elderly, including the contribution that the elderly can and should make to society."[33] Like the National Senior Citizen's Day, the International Day for the Elderly is intended to increase awareness of the factors and issues that affect older adults and the need to support them through the aging process, while also recognizing their accomplishments and participation in society. The day is an opportunity to thank one's elders for everything they have done for their children and to make sure that they are not made to feel as if they are a burden to the young.

Journal/Meditation: Whom do you know who is fifty-five-years-old or older? What contribution has he or she made to the nation? What elderly person do you consider to be an asset to society? Explain.

Prayer: The days of our lives are seventy years, perhaps even eighty, if we are strong, O LORD. Make the evening of my life a homecoming, when all its elements come together in harmony, healing, unity, and peace. Speak your truth to me all the days of my life, and give me the grace to hear your words. Amen.

Women's Equality Day

August 26

Text: "The right of citizens of the United States to vote shall not be denied or abridged by the United States or by any state on account of sex."[34]

---

32. United Nations General Assembly, A/RES/45/106.
33. United Nations General Assembly, A/RES/45/106.
34. "Constitution of the U.S.," Amendment XIX.

Reflection: The above text is Amendment 19 of the United States Constitution, passed by congress on June 4, 1919, ratified on August 18, 1920, and certified on August 26, 1920. The amendment gave women the right to vote. Neither the federal government nor any state can deny the right to vote on the basis of sex. On August 26, 1972, President Richard Nixon issued Proclamation 4147, which designated that date as Women's Rights Day. In his proclamation, he called upon all citizens, "particularly those organizations concerned with the protection of human rights to observe [the] day with appropriate ceremonies and activities."[35] Nixon added: ". . . [E]very woman should have the freedom to pursue whatever career she wishes. Although women today have a great opportunity to do that, we still must do more to ensure women every opportunity to make the fullest contribution to our progress as a nation."[36]

On August 16, 1973, U.S. House of Representatives Joint Resolution 52 became Public Law 93–105. August 26 was designated Women's Equality Day, and the president was authorized and requested to issue a proclamation "in commemoration of that day in 1920 on which the women of America were first guaranteed the right to vote."[37] Nixon issued Proclamation 4236 on August 16, 1973. After recalling that the nineteenth amendment was certified as part of the U.S. Constitution on August 26, 1920, he stated that "in virtually every sector of . . . society, women are making important contributions to the quality of American life. . . . American women represent an important reservoir of ability and dedication which government must draw upon to a greater degree."[38] Then, after recalling the enactment of the Equal Opportunity Act of 1972, Nixon stated: "While we are making great strides to eliminate outright job discrimination because of sex in the federal government, we must recognize that people's attitudes cannot be changed by laws alone. There still exist elusive prejudices born of mores and customs that stand in the way of progress for women."[39] Then, for the first time, Nixon declared August 26, 1973, Women's Equality Day, and he urged all people to use the occasion "to reflect on the importance of achieving equal rights and opportunities for women and to dedicate themselves anew to that great goal." He added, "For the cause of equal rights and opportunities for women is inseparable from the cause of human dignity and equal justice for all."[40] Women's Equality Day celebrates women's struggle for suffrage and the ongoing march to full and equal participation of women in national life. Laws against sex discrimination have been passed, and they open up equal economic opportunity for women. Nevertheless, as Nixon noted in 1973, people's attitudes cannot be changed by laws alone.

35. Nixon, "Proclamation 4147."
36. Nixon, "Proclamation 4147."
37. "Public Law 93–105."
38. Nixon, "Proclamation 4236."
39. Nixon, "Proclamation 4236."
40. Nixon, "Proclamation 4236."

Journal/Meditation: How do women contribute to the progress of our nation? What do women contribute to the quality of American life? What attitude concerning women have you encountered that needs to be changed?

Prayer: In the beginning, O LORD, you made women equal to men, but an unkind history subjugated women to men. Inspire men and women around the world to respect the human dignity of all men and women and grant them equal justice for all. Hear my prayer. Amen.

School Begins
August—September

Text: "The congress [of the United States] declares it to be the policy of the United States that (1) all children enrolled in public schools are entitled to equal educational opportunity without regard to race, color, sex, or national origin; and (2) the neighborhood is the appropriate basis for determining public school assignments."[41]

Reflection: Depending upon the state, school begins in mid-August or early-September in the fifty United States of America. While the federal government does not legislate the length of attendance in school, states require children five- to eight-years-old to begin going to school and to continue until they are fifteen- to eighteen-years-old. Such compulsory education means that parents or guardians are obliged to send their children to public or private school or to homeschool them. As can be seen in the text above from Public Law 93–380, enacted August 21, 1974, the federal government is concerned about children in public schools getting an equal educational opportunity no matter their race, color, sex, or national origin. In other words, children attending public schools share equally in their free-of-charge compulsory education. All children need to master some physical skills, such as reading and writing, in order to contribute to the good of the nation. Also, compulsory education instills values, such as ethics, and social communication abilities in students. Immigrants are better able to fit into their new country. Compulsory education, which began in many places in one-room school houses, is considered a right of every citizen in the U.S., and the federal government makes it clear that they are entitled to equal educational opportunity without regard to race, color, sex, or national origin.

In general, in the U.S. children begin attending pre-school, kindergarten, and first grade, learning and progressing step-by-step to eighth grade. Then, teenagers attend four years of high school, graduating with a diploma that states they have completed the course of studies as specified by the state in which they live. If a teenager reaches the maximum age for attending school before graduating, he or she may drop out of high school and not graduate. States have a GED (General Educational

---

41. "Public Law 93–380."

Development) program in which students who did not finish high school may pass four subject tests—math, science, social studies, and reasoning through language arts—and receive a diploma that declares them to possess high-school level academic skills. Parents and guardians have the right to direct the education of their children, including the right to send them to private schools instead of public schools. There is also the option of homeschooling, which is legal in all fifty states. It requires a large time commitment on the part of parents and children. While some states require parents to register their intent to homeschool their children with the state department of education or the local district school board, others require some type of proof of yearly progress. Some states may also allow homeschooled students to attend some public-school classes and participate in other public-school activities. No matter what form of education parents choose for their children, the goal is to prepare them to take their place as literate members of the country and contribute to its common good.

Journal/Meditation: In what specific ways did your compulsory education prepare you to contribute to the common good of your town, state, and country? How did race, color, sex, or national origin affect your compulsory education? Explain.

Prayer: All-knowing God, your words are pleasant to those who listen, learn, and desire wisdom. Accompany all those beginning a new school year. Teach me prudence through insight that I may discern your ways and find great joy in keeping your statutes all the days of my life. Amen.

9

The Month of *September*

WORLD DAY OF PRAYER FOR THE CARE OF CREATION
September 1

Text: "I [, Pope Francis,] have decided to institute in the Catholic Church the 'World Day of Prayer for the Care of Creation,' which . . . is to be celebrated on 1 September. . . . As Christians we wish to contribute to resolving the ecological crisis which humanity is presently experiencing. In doing so, we must first rediscover in our own rich spiritual patrimony the deepest motivations for our concern for the care of creation. . . . The ecological crisis thus summons us to a profound spiritual conversion. . . . The annual World Day of Prayer for the Care of Creation will offer individual believers and communities a fitting opportunity to reaffirm their personal vocation to be stewards of creation, to thank God for the wonderful handiwork which he has entrusted to our care, and to implore his help for the protection of creation as well as his pardon for the sins committed against the world in which we live. . . . [T]his annual event will become a significant occasion for prayer, reflection, conversion, and the adoption of appropriate lifestyles."[1]

Reflection: On August 6, 2015, Pope Francis issued a letter announcing that September 1 every year would be the World Day of Prayer for the Care of Creation. The above text is taken from that letter in which he invoked "Saint Francis of Assisi, whose Canticle of the Creatures inspires so many men and women of goodwill to give in praise of the Creator and with respect for creation."[2] The idea was not Francis's own; he acknowledged that the Ecumenical Patriarchate of Constantinople has observed September 1, the beginning of its liturgical year, as a day of prayer for the care of creation since 1989. The new life celebrated at the beginning of a new year along with the theme of harvest taking place in the Northern Hemisphere offers much upon which

---

1. Pope Francis, "Letter."
2. Pope Francis, "Letter."

to reflect. Indeed, the World Day begins a Season of Creation ending with the Memorial of St. Francis of Assisi on October 4. During the month-long period, people are invited to engage is the most basic counter-cultural activity: pray for God's creation.

According to the pope, in order to safeguard creation, we must rediscover our spiritual approach to earthly realities, namely, we are embodied spirits, who are a part of a common home we call the earth. We have a vocation to be good stewards of creation. Our stewardship of creation can be awakened by a meditative nature walk, by reading biblical material about creation, and through singing favorite songs about the beauty of creation. Simple ways of being good stewards and combating climate change consist of changing standard light bulbs to LED ones, installing solar panels, recycling, and seeing climate change as a moral (rather than a political) issue. Taking a day for prayer for the care of creation opens us to God's guidance, inspiration, and calls to action to save our common home by taking responsibility and making a commitment to do so.

Journal/Meditation: How do you experience the ecological crisis? What do you find in your rich spiritual patrimony that motivates you to care for creation? In what specific ways are you a good steward of creation? What lifestyle change do you need to make to care for creation?

Prayer: Thank you, Creator God, for your handiwork entrusted to my care. Inspire in me ways to protect creation through transformation of my lifestyle. Hear my prayer today, tomorrow, and forever. Amen.

World War II Began

September 1

Text: "I [, Neville Chamberlain,] am speaking to you from the cabinet room at 10 Downing Street. This morning the British ambassador in Berlin handed the German government a final note stating that unless we heard from them by 11 o'clock that they were prepared at once to withdraw their troops from Poland, a state of war would exist between us. I have to tell you now that no such undertaking has been received, and that consequently this country is at war with Germany. You can imagine what a bitter blow it is to me that all my long struggle to win peace has failed. . . . But Hitler would not have it. He had evidently made up his mind to attack Poland whatever happened . . . ."[3]

Reflection: On September 1, 1939, Nazi Germany, under the leadership of Adolf Hitler, invaded Poland and began a global war that involved more than thirty countries that lasted until 1945; today it is known as World War II. Once the German Emperor Wilhelm II abdicated on November 9, 1918, the Weimar Republic was established.

3. Chamberlain, "Declaration of War."

On January 30, 1933, Adolf Hitler was appointed Chancellor of the Reich (Empire, Realm). Under his leadership, the Reichstag (home of the German parliament) turned the government into a dictatorship on March 21, 1933. It took Hitler only five years of power to begin annexing territory into Germany. First, it was Austria. Hitler's next move was to invade Poland. The United Kingdom and France had guaranteed Poland that they would declare war if Polish independence was threatened. Thus, two days later on September 3, 1939, Neville Chamberlain, prime minister of the United Kingdom, declared war on Germany at 11 a.m. As indicated in Chamberlain's radio broadcast from which the above text is taken, he had tried to avoid war by demanding that Hitler remove his troops from Poland, but Hitler had refused. "His action," according to Chamberlain, "shows convincingly that there is no chance of expecting that this man will ever give up his practice of using force to gain his will. He can only be stopped by force."[4] Later that same day, France declared war on Germany, followed by Australia, New Zealand, South Africa, and Canada.

Until December 8, 1941, the United States stayed out of World War II. President Franklin D. Roosevelt had declared that the U.S. would remain neutral, but he made efforts to help nations engaged in the struggle against Nazi Germany in order to provide the supplies they needed to fight the Germans. While many Americans opposed involving the U.S. in war, the U.S. gave the British more than fifty obsolete destroyers in exchange for leases to territory in Newfoundland and the Caribbean. The U.S. also established the Lend-Lease initiative, in which it would provide Great Britain with the supplies it needed, but would not insist on being paid immediately. When payment would finally take place, it would take the form of some consideration by Britain to the U.S. Basically, the consideration would consist of joint action towards the creation of a liberalized international economic order in the postwar world. Thus, with Lend-Lease agreements with more than thirty countries, the U.S. served its own interest in defeating Nazi Germany without entering the war until it was forced to do so. By the time World War II ended, the main combatants consisted of the Axis powers—Germany, Italy, and Japan—and the Allies—France, Great Britain, the United States, the Soviet Union, and China. In many respects, World War II was a continuation of the disputes left unsettled by World War I. One positive result of the war was the formation of the United Nations on October 24, 1945, in which the five Allies became permanent members of the U.N. Security Council.

Journal/Meditation: For what reason(s) should one nation begin a war with another nation? Why do you think dictators use force to get what they want? What do you think are the positive results that can result from war?

Prayer: God of peace, when the heart of a nation is set on war, make known your wondrous deed to make war cease. Remove the delight of war and curb the production of

4. Chamberlain, "Declaration of War."

weapons of war. Grant to me a deeper understanding of how I cannot save myself with my great strength, and give me confidence that you desire peace. Amen.

VICTORY OVER JAPAN DAY (V-J DAY)
September 2

Text: "We hereby proclaim the unconditional surrender to the Allied Powers of the Japanese Imperial General Headquarters and of all Japanese armed forces and all armed forces under Japanese control wherever situated. We hereby command all Japanese forces wherever situated and the Japanese people to cease hostilities forthwith . . . and to comply with all requirements which may be imposed by the Supreme Commander for the Allied Powers or by agencies of the Japanese government at his direction. We hereby command the Japanese Imperial General Headquarters to issue at once orders to the commanders of all Japanese forces and all forces under Japanese control wherever situated to surrender unconditionally themselves and all forces under their control. . . . The authority of the Emperor and the Japanese government to rule the state shall be subject to the Supreme Commander for the Allied Powers who will take such steps as he deems proper to effectuate these terms of surrender."[5]

Reflection: In the 1930s, Japan launched a campaign to invade all of China. In July 1937, Japan captured the former Chinese imperial capital of Peking. In battle after battle, Japanese forces pushed back Chinese forces. Shanghai fell to the Japanese, who, in December 1937, captured the capital Nanking, after which hundreds of thousands of Chinese civilians and disarmed combatants were murdered by the Japanese. This action led the United States in 1939 to notify Japan that it would not extend a trade treaty to Japan because American opinion opposed Japanese expansionism. Furthermore, exports of chemicals, minerals, and military parts to Japan were banned. In early 1941, the U.S. and Japan engaged in negotiations to improve their strained relations and to end the war in China. However, Japan's proposals were judged by the U.S. to be inadequate. Japan wanted an end to U.S. aid to China and the lifting of the oil embargo that had been placed on Japan. The U.S. required that Japan leave China. In order to prevent further U.S. intervention, Japan decided to neutralize the U.S. Pacific Fleet at Pearl Harbor. The bombing of Pearl Harbor on December 7, 1941, led the U.S. to declare war on Japan on December 8, 1941. Thus, did the U.S. enter World War II.

On August 6, 1945, the U.S. dropped an atomic bomb on Hiroshima, Japan, and on August 9, 1945, another atomic bomb on Nagasaki. This led the Japanese government to communicate its intention to surrender on August 10, 1945. On August 15, 1945, Emperor Hirohito accepted the terms of surrender, commonly known as the Potsdam Declaration, and communicated such to both the Japanese people and to Harry S. Truman, who had succeeded Roosevelt as President of the U.S. The formal

---

5. "Instrument of Surrender."

event of surrender was schedule for September 2, 1945. Onboard the battleship U.S.S. (United States Ship) Missouri in Tokyo Bay, Mamoru Shigemitsu signed the unconditional surrender document, part of which is the text above, on behalf of the emperor and government of Japan, and Yoshijiro Umezu signed it on behalf of the Japanese Imperial Headquarters along with eleven other Japanese officials. U.S. General Douglas MacArthur, both Commander in the Southwest Pacific and Supreme Commander of the Allied Forces, accepted Japan's unconditional surrender on behalf of the Allies along with nine others, one each representing the U.S., China, the United Kingdom, the Soviet Union, Australia, Canada, France, the Netherlands, and New Zealand. On September 6, 1945, Colonel Bernard Theilsen took the Instrument of Surrender to Washington, DC, and formally presented it to Truman at a ceremony in the White House the next day. And thus ended World War II.

Journal/Meditation: What are the implications of an unconditional surrender? Have you ever had to surrender unconditionally? Explain. What are the implications of dropping atomic bombs on Japan? What are the implications of dropping nuclear bombs today?

Prayer: O LORD, make the rulers of the nations wise. Keep them from declaring war by giving them a spirit of peace to solve their disagreements. Give me the same wisdom and peace in all conflicts. Amen.

INTERNATIONAL DAY OF CHARITY
September 5

Text: "Reaffirming the Universal Declaration of Human Rights, which states that recognition of the inherent dignity and of the equal and inalienable rights of all members of the human family is the foundation of freedom, justice, and peace in the world; . . . deeply concerned that poverty persists in all countries of the world, particularly in developing countries, regardless of their economic, social, and cultural situation; recognizing . . . the role of charity in alleviating humanitarian crises and human suffering within and among nations; affirming that charity may contribute to the promotion of dialogue among people from different civilizations, cultures, and religions, as well as of solidarity and mutual understanding; recognizing the efforts of charitable organizations and individuals, including the work of Mother Teresa; [the United Nations General Assembly] decides to designate 5 September as the International Day of Charity. . . ."[6]

Reflection: The United Nations General Assembly adopted the resolution in the above text declaring September 5 the International Day of Charity on December 17, 2012. The purpose of the day is to encourage charity through education and public

---

6. United Nations General Assembly, A/RES/67/105.

awareness-raising activities for individuals, charitable organizations, philanthropic organizations, and volunteer organizations on the local, national, regional, and international levels. The U.N. chose September 5 to commemorate the death of Mother Teresa of Calcutta, who, in 1950, founded the Missionaries of Charity, a Roman Catholic religious congregation, which manages homes for people dying of HIV/AIDS, leprosy, and tuberculosis. The nuns also run soup kitchens, dispensaries, mobile clinics, counselling programs, orphanages, and schools. Because St. Teresa of Calcutta was admired by many for her charitable work, the U.N. chose the day of her death, which is also her feast day in the Catholic Church, for its international-day observance.

With its own patron saint, the International Day of Charity seeks to explore the role of charity in the alleviation of poverty. Thus, while many people consider a monetary contribution to charities of their choice sufficient, the international day invites more specific activities, like providing access to clean water and sufficient sanitation. The day attempts to mobilize people around the world and sensitize them to the needs of others through volunteer activities as well as philanthropic activities. Charity promotes the rights of those who are marginalized and underprivileged, and it alleviates the effects of humanitarian crises involving health care, education, housing, and child protection. People around the world are called to spread random acts of kindness that better the human condition. Organizing any type of volunteer campaign devoted to the cause of sharing good works imitates and honors Mother Teresa of Calcutta's work with the poorest of the poor.

Journal/Meditation: What is your understanding of charity? In what charitable endeavors are you involved? How do you think charity alleviates poverty?

Prayer: Out of her endless charity, your servant Teresa of Calcutta restored human dignity to those in poverty, to those suffering, and to those dying, LORD. Fill me with her spirit that I may serve the poorest of the poor in her name, according to your will. Amen.

Labor Day
First Monday

Text: "Be it enacted by the Senate and House of Representatives of the United States of America in congress assembled, that the first Monday of September in each year, being the day celebrated and known as Labor's Holiday, is hereby made a legal public holiday, to all intents and purposes, in the same manner as Christmas, the first day of January, the twenty-second day of February, the thirtieth day of May, and the fourth day of July are now made by law public holidays."[7]

---

7. "Chapter 118."

Reflection: President Grover Cleveland signed the above text into law on June 28, 1894. The basic purpose of the law was to honor and to recognize the American labor movement along with the works and contributions of laborers to the development and achievements of the United States. The force of labor had added materially to the highest standard of living; it had also created the greatest production in the world. Labor had moved the U.S. closer to the realization of its traditional ideals of economic and political democracy. The labor movement, dedicated to the social and economic achievements of U.S. workers, wanted to honor workers who had contributed strength, prosperity, and wellbeing to the U.S.

While there are several stories about the day's origin, trade unions and labor movements wanted a day to celebrate labor. Parades, marches, and speeches became a standard way to mark Labor Day. Picnics and other types of public gatherings—such as family reunions—carnivals, firework displays, concerts, and sports—football, auto racing, tennis, etc.—not to mention retail sales, have come to dominate what has become known as Labor Day Weekend. With so many things going on, it is easy to forget that Labor Day honors the worker for his and her achievement of moving our country closer to the realization of economic stability in a political democracy.

Journal/Meditation: Who are the workers you honor on Labor Day? Make a list. What has each worker contributed to our country?

Prayer: God, you bestowed the dignity of work upon the people of the world. Give good work to those who seek it, and enable them to contribute to the good of my country through it. Bless all men and women around the world, no matter where they labor. Grant me joy in my work, no matter how important or menial it may be. Glory be to you, LORD, forever and ever. Amen.

National Grandparents Day
Sunday after Labor Day

Text: "The president is requested to issue each year a proclamation—(1) designating the first Sunday in September after Labor Day as National Grandparents Day; and (2) calling on the people of the United States and interested groups and organizations to observe National Grandparents Day with appropriate ceremonies and activities."[8]

Reflection: Marian Lucille Herndon McQuade is credited with being the force behind getting National Grandparents Day on the calendar. She, mother of fifteen children, grandmother of forty-three children, great-grandmother of ten children, and great-great grandmother of one child, worked in a nursing home and witnessed how many senior citizens had no visitors or recognition. She began her campaign in 1970, and for the next seven years got several resolutions introduced in the United States Senate and

---

8. "Public Law 105–225," Section 125; cf. "Public Law 96–62."

House of Representatives, but none of them made it through both houses. Finally, in 1977, a joint resolution was passed by both houses naming the Sunday following Labor Day as National Grandparents Day. The purpose of the day is to honor grandparents, to give them the opportunity to display love for their children's children, and to help children appreciate the strength, information, and guidance senior citizens can offer. On August 3, 1978, President Jimmy Carter proclaimed the first National Grandparents Day to be the Sunday in September after Labor Day. "Just as a nation learns and is strengthened by its history," wrote Carter, "so a family learns and is strengthened by its understanding of preceding generations. As Americans live longer, more and more families are enriched by their shared experiences with grandparents and great-grandparents."[9] According to Carter, "The elders of each family have the responsibility for setting the moral tone for the family and for passing on the traditional values of our nation to their children and grandchildren. . . . It is appropriate, therefore, that as individuals and as a nation, that we salute our grandparents for their contribution to our lives."[10] Carter concluded his proclamation by urging citizens to pause and to reflect upon the influence grandparents have had on them, especially in shaping their destiny and the legacy bestowed upon them.

The next year, on September 6, 1979, Carter issued another proclamation in which he declared the Sunday after Labor day in each year to be National Grandparents Day. In that proclamation, he wrote: "Grandparents are our continuing tie to the near-past, to the events and beliefs and experiences that so strongly affect our lives and the world around us. Whether they are our own or surrogate grandparents who fill some of the gaps in our mobile society, our senior generation also provides our society a link to our national heritage and traditions."[11] Carter stated that grandparents possess the wisdom of distilled pain and joy. He added that grandparents can reach out past pride and fear of failure to close the space between generations. In his proclamation, Carter referred to Public Law 96–62, which authorized and requested him to name the Sunday after Labor Day as the annual National Grandparents Day. The law passed the House on July 27, 1979, and the Senate on August 3, 1979. Carter signed it into law on September 6, 1979, when he issued his proclamation.

Journal/Meditation: How do you honor your grandparents? How do they display their love for you? What have you learned from grandparents (senior citizens)?

Prayer: Ever-living God, you bestow strength, information, guidance, and wisdom upon my grandparents. I ask you to continue to bless them, while you give me the grace to return to them the love they share with me. May the honor I give to them redound to your glory forever. Amen.

---

9. Carter, "Proclamation 4580."
10. Carter, "Proclamation 4580."
11. Carter, "Proclamation 4679."

National Pet Memorial Day
Second Sunday

Text: "The bond that pet parents develop over a lifetime of caring for their pet is a wonderful and rewarding experience. As pet parents share their life with another living being who happens not to be human, they experience unconditional love and a relationship like no other As their brief lives come to an end, [pet parents] want [to] ensure that [their] pet is taken care of with the same care and respect in death as in life. That is why it is important . . . to know [the] pet aftercare provider."[12]

Reflection: In 1971, the International Association of Pet Cemeteries and Crematories (IAOPCC) was founded in West Chicago by Pat Blosser. In 1972, the IAOPCC established Pet Memorial Day to be observed on the second Sunday in September. "The IAOPCC is a not-for-profit organization dedicated to advancing the standards, ethics, and professionalism of pet cemeteries and crematories worldwide."[13] It is supported by dues, donations, and other contributions from its members. The above text, taken from the IAOPCC webpage, emphasizes the relationship bond that develops between pets and humans and how it can be honored after the pet's death. Just as there are general days throughout the year for remembering the relationship bonds shared among humans, National Pet Memorial Day is the occasion to remember the unconditional love shared between humans and pets who have died.

There are many ways to remember pets who have died. If the pet was buried in a pet cemetery or if he or she was cremated and his or her ashes interred in a pet cemetery, the owner might take flowers, a wreath, a candle, or a toy with which the pet enjoyed playing to the burial site. If you are unable to visit a burial site, then lighting a candle at home to remember your pet is a good practice; the candle can also be lit on your pet's birthday and death day. Some people plant a memorial, such as a tree, a bush, or flowers. Reviewing photos and watching videos of your pet are ways to remember the bond that existed between the two of you. The photos and/or videos may spark memories of events that you have forgotten and/or inspire you to write a poem about your pet. You can open a keepsake box of the things you have kept that belonged to your pet, like tags, collars, leashes, toys, etc. Things that were important to your pet remind you of some of the experiences you shared with him or her. Pets can also be honored by volunteering at an animal shelter, volunteering at a pet park, making a donation, or fostering and/or adopting a pet from a shelter. There are many more ways to remember the bond established between you and your pet;[14] the best way for you is what is the most comfortable on National Pet Memorial Day. We never cease to grieve the passing of a human-pet relationship in which we have invested ourselves,

---

12. "International Association of Pet Cemeteries."
13. "International Association of Pet Cemeteries."
14. "Ten Ways."

our time, our home, and our resources. Therefore, it is an honor to remember the pets who have been a part of our lives on National Pet Memorial Day.

Journal/Meditation: Make a list of your deceased pets. Specifically, what did each deceased pet contribute to your life? What was the characteristics of the relationship you shared with each pet? In what way will you remember each pet on National Pet Memorial Day?

Prayer: Nothing that you have made, LORD God, ever passes out of your sight. As I remember the unconditional love of the pets with whom I have shared a relationship, I celebrate the bond established between my pets and me. And I ask you to keep them close to your heart as you hold them in the palm of your hand forever. Amen.

PATRIOT DAY AND NATIONAL DAY OF SERVICE AND REMEMBRANCE
September 11

Text: "Whereas on September 11, 2001, terrorists hijacked four civilian aircraft, crashing two of them into the towers of the World Trade Center in New York City, and a third into the Pentagon outside Washington, DC; whereas the fourth hijacked aircraft crashed in southwestern Pennsylvania after passengers tried to take control of the aircraft in order to prevent the hijackers from crashing the aircraft into an important symbol of democracy and freedom; whereas these attacks were by far the deadliest terrorist attacks ever launched against the United States, killing thousands of innocent people; and whereas in the aftermath of the attacks the people of the United States stood united in providing support for those in need: Now, therefore, be it resolved by the Senate and House of Representatives of the United States of America in congress assembled, [that] . . . September 11 [be designated] as Patriot Day."[15]

Reflection: On September 13, 2001, following the terrorist attacks mentioned above, George W. Bush declared September 14, 2001, a National Day of Prayer and Remembrance for the Victims of the Terrorist Attacks on September 11, 2001. "Civilized people around the world denounce the evildoers who devised and executed these terrible attacks," he proclaimed. "Justice demands that those who helped or harbored the terrorists be punished—and punished severely. The enormity of their evil demands it. We will use all the resources of the United States and our cooperating friends and allies to pursue those responsible for this evil, until justice is done."[16] Bush continued: "All our hearts have been seared by the sudden and senseless taking of innocent lives. We pray for healing and for the strength to serve and encourage one another in hope and faith." President Bush called upon every American to observe September 14 and

---

15. "Public Law 107–89."
16. Bush, G.W., "National Day of Prayer."

honor the memory of the 2,977 victims of the attacks and comfort those who had lost loved ones with noontime memorial services, the ringing of bells, and evening candlelight vigils. He invited all "to pray for our land."[17] On October 25, 2001, the House of Representatives passed Public Law 107–89, from which the above text comes, and on November 30, 2001, the Senate passed it. Known as Patriot Day, Bush signed it into law on December 18, 2001. The joint resolution called upon "all departments, agencies, and instrumentalities of the United States and interested organizations and individuals to display the flag of the United States at half-staff on Patriot Day in honor of the individuals who lost their lives as a result of the terrorist attacks against the United States that occurred on September 11, 2001; and the people of the United States to observe a moment of silence on Patriot Day in honor of the individuals who lost their lives as a result of the terrorist attacks against the United States that occurred on September 11, 2001."[18] Thus, the first Patriot Day was marked on September 11, 2002. The law stipulates how the day is to be observed.

On April 21, 2009, Public Law 111–13 (Serve America Act) amended Public Law 107–89. September 11 was renamed Patriot Day and National Day of Service and Remembrance. It encourages "all people of the United States, regardless of age, race, ethnicity, religion, or economic status to engage in full- or part-time national service, long- or short-term public service in the nonprofit sector or government, or volunteering."[19] President Barack Obama was the first to issue a proclamation for Patriot Day and National Day of Remembrance and Service on September 10, 2009. He wrote: "Through the twisted steel of the twin towers of the World Trade Center, the scarred walls of the Pentagon, and the smoky wreckage in a field in southwest Pennsylvania, the patriotism and resiliency of the American people shone brightly on September 11, 2001. We stood as one people, united in our common humanity and shared sorrow. We grieved for those who perished and remembered what brought us together as Americans."[20] Obama wrote: "Unthinkable acts of terrorism brought tragedy, destruction, pain, and loss for people across our nation and the world. . . . [W]e reaffirm our commitment to the ideas and ideals that united Americans in the aftermath of the attacks. . . . We must also recommit ourselves to our founding principles. . . . [O]ur fate as individuals is tied to that of our nation. Our democracy is strengthened when we uphold the freedoms upon which our nation was built: equality, justice, liberty, and democracy. These values exemplify the patriotism and sacrifice we commemorate today."[21] Obama called upon all Americans to join together in service and honor the lives lost on September 11, 2001. "Working together," he stated,

17. Bush, G.W., "National Day of Prayer."
18. "Public Law 107–89."
19. "Public Law 111–13."
20. Obama, "Patriot Day."
21. Obama, "Patriot Day."

"we can usher in a new era in which volunteering and service is a way of life for all Americans."[22]

Journal/Meditation: What do you think unites U.S. citizens today? Where do you see the founding principles of equality, justice, liberty, and democracy manifest today? How has volunteering and service become a way of life for you?

Prayer: I stand with other citizens of the United States as one nation under you, O God, as I remember and pray for those who died in the terrorist attacks of September 11, 2001. I ask you to comfort those who lost loved ones in that tragedy. Help all to find healing and recovery, and keep us strong and united as one nation. Amen.

THE STAR-SPANGLED BANNER WRITTEN
September 14

Text: "O thus be it ever, when freemen shall stand / Between their loved homes and the war's desolation. / Blest with vict'ry and peace, may the Heav'n rescued land / Praise the Power that hath made and preserved us a nation! / Then conquer we must, when our cause it is just, / And this be our motto: 'In God is our trust.' / And the star-spangled banner in triumph shall wave / O'er the land of the free and the home of the brave!"[23]

Reflection: On September 14, 1814, Francis Scott Key, a thirty-five-year-old lawyer and amateur poet, was inspired by the sign of a large United States flag flying triumphantly over Fort McHenry after British ships in Baltimore Harbor had bombed the fort but lost the Battle of Baltimore in the War of 1812. The flag displayed fifteen stars and fifteen stripes, and it was called The Star-Spangled Banner. Key wrote the poem on the back of a letter he was carrying in his pocket, and it was first published in newspapers and then made its way into *The Analectic Magazine* in 1814. The House of Representatives passed the bill to make The Star-Spangled Banner the national anthem in 1930, and the Senate passed it on March 3, 1931. It was signed into law by President Herbert Hoover on March 4, 1931.[24] It was codified along with directions for the proper posture for military, veterans, and others when it is played in Public Law 105–225 on August 12, 1998.

The official "The Star-Spangled Banner" contains four stanzas. Most people know only the first. The text above contains the fourth stanza. It differs in minor degrees from the version published in *The Analectic Magazine*: "O! thus be it ever when freemen shall stand / Between their lov'd home, and the war's desolation, / Blest with vict'ry and peace, may the heav'n-rescued land / Praise the power that hath made

---

22. Obama, "Patriot Day."
23. Key, "Defence of Fort M'Henry."
24. "Public Law 71–823."

and preserv'd us a nation! / Then conquer we must, when our cause it is just, / And this be our motto—'In God is our trust!' / And the star-spangled banner in triumph shall wave / O'er the land of the free, and the home of the brave."[25] Free people stand between home and war in order to defend their freedom. Key reflects that God rescued the United States from war and made it a nation. Therefore, with a just cause we conquer under the motto "In God is our trust," in order to keep the flag waving over the land of the free and the home of the brave.

Journal/Meditation: What line in verse four of The Star-Spangled Banner gets most of your attention? Why? What truth do you think Key captures in verse four? What does the motto "In God is our trust" mean to you?

Prayer: In you we place our trust, O God. We trust you when we leave home to face war. We trust you when we make peace. We trust you when our cause is just. Continue to preserve our nation, which you have made, and let our banner wave forever over the land of the free and the home of the brave. Amen.

National Stepfamily Day
September 16

Text: "What prompted you [, Christy Tusing-Borgeld,] to start National Stepfamily Day? A lot of heartache! Dealing with exes on both sides. At first, we all merged together just fine. After a few years, things became incredibly hard. I was on the computer one night looking for some help and support for our stepfamily, and there just wasn't a lot out there. I also noticed that night that President Clinton proclaimed 'National Parents Day.' This sparked the fire. I went to bed that night telling my husband that there should be a National Stepparents Day. But the more I thought about it, I wanted to include all the family members in such a day. So National Stepfamily Day was conceived. . . . I wasn't sure how to go about doing such a task. . . . I remember those first few years I was faxing for days. I was faxing the offices of every government official that I thought would help me and support the day. . . . I believe in this movement. I believe in second chances. I believe in supporting the family and children to be successful."[26]

Reflection: On August 3, 2017, Christy Tusing-Borgeld was interviewed by *The Stepmom Project*. The above text, taken from that interview, are her words about founding National Stepfamily Day in 1997 twenty years earlier. In the interview, Tusing-Borgeld, a stepmother herself, explains all the work it took from 1992, when she became a stepmother, to 1997 to get National Stepfamily Day recognized. As noted by *National Today*: "Families come in all shapes and sizes—small, big, biological, adoptive, and

25. Key, "Defence," *Analectic*.
26. Tusing-Borgeld, "Interview."

even step—and they all deserve to be celebrated. Unlike most types of families, members of a blended family choose to come together. Whether it is because of divorce, estrangement, death, or another reason, stepfamilies need to unite and rebuild their lives together, and that deserves recognition."[27] Cultures change through time. What had once been considered nontraditional—stepfamily—has become common. In the United States, over 30 percent of those under eighteen years of age live in stepfamily environments. This means that 114 million Americans are involved in some form of a stepfamily relationship. According to one statistic, 1,300 new stepfamilies are formed in the U.S. every day. That is why Tusing-Borgeld started National Stepfamily Day. A stepfamily is a family in which at least one parent has a child or children who are not biologically related to his or her spouse. Of course, a stepfamily may also consist of a family in which both parents have a least one child who is not biologically related to the other parent. In the latter case, it may be called a blended family. A child in a stepfamily or blended family is known as a stepson or stepdaughter to their biological parent's new spouse, who is the stepparent, stepfather, or stepmother of the child. The stepparent's (stepfather's or stepmother's) parents are step-grandparents, who have a stepgrandson(s) and/or a stepdaughter(s). Likewise, the stepparent's (stepfather's or stepmother's) brother(s) and sister(s) are step-uncle(s) and step-aunt(s). Stepsiblings (stepbrothers and stepsisters) are those children in a blended family who are the offspring of only one stepparent and are not related biologically to the other stepparent. A child born to a couple, each of whom has a child or children, is a half-sibling of stepsiblings already existing.

The prefix *step* comes from the Old English word *steop*, meaning *orphan*. Words with the prefix *step* were used originally to denote a connection resulting from the remarriage of a widowed parent. Today, *step* is used to denote a connection resulting from a remarriage of a widowed or divorced parent. No matter the reason, a stepfamily faces financial and living arrangement adjustments, feelings about the previous marriage that need resolution, and parenting changes that will be made. In *Becoming a Stepfamily*, Patricia Papernow suggested that stepfamilies pass through seven distinct stages of development. The 1993 book listed (1) fantasy, (2) immersion, (3) awareness, (4) mobilization, (5) action, (6) contact, and (7) resolution as periods of stepfamily growth. The fantasy stage is the dream of what the stepfamily can be. The immersion stage represents the struggle to live the fantasy of the perfect blended family. In the awareness stage, stepfamily members begin to gather information about what the new family really looks like. In stage 4, mobilization, the differences of stepfamily members are recognized, and in stage 5, action, reorganization of the family structure, takes place. In the contact stage, all roles of the members of the stepfamily are clearly delineated with boundaries. And in the resolution stage, the stepfamily's identity is secure; a new definition of family has emerged with roles for all. Recognizing the stage a stepfamily is in with a recognition of all its members can be celebrated on National

---

27. "National Stepfamily Day."

Stepfamily Day by cooking a meal together, sponsoring a game(s) night, watching a favorite movie, getting take-out food at a favorite place to eat, taking a family hike, eating a picnic lunch in a park, playing outdoor sports, swimming in a pool, or designing a celebration that is unique to your stepfamily and expresses the beauty of each of its members.

Journal/Meditation: If you know a stepfamily, what do you consider the members' greatest strength? If you don't know a stepfamily, what do you think is the greatest issue the members must overcome? If you are a member of a stepfamily, at which Papernow stage are you? Explain.

Prayer: As you know, O LORD, families come in all shapes and sizes. As I remember and celebrate stepfamilies today, I ask you to bless them and keep them close to you. Give other families a greater respect for those who have come together because of divorce, estrangement, death, or another reason. Unite all who rebuild their lives together. Amen.

Constitution Day and Citizenship Day

September 17

Text: "We the people of the United States, in order to form a more perfect union, establish justice, ensure domestic tranquility, provide for the common defense, promote the general welfare, and secure the blessings of liberty to ourselves and our posterity, do ordain and establish this Constitution for the United States of America."[28]

Reflection: Commonly known as the preamble, the text above explains why the eight articles of the Constitution of the United States were written and signed by thirty-eight men representing the original states on September 17, 1787. First, the desire was to form a more perfect union among the original states in order to achieve the goal of being the United States. This joining together of thirteen colonies (now states) is still a work in progress. Second, the founding fathers wanted to establish justice, which, in their estimation, had been lacking from the colonizing country. The people had determined that they were not treated with fairness or reasonableness. Third, the Constitution was written to ensure domestic tranquility, that is, to create a state of peace and calm throughout the original states that would bring about the same peace and calm for the new country as a whole. Fourth, the common defense needed to be established; defense would not be left to each state—even though each state would provide defense from the citizens living within its boundaries—but it would be the establishment of forms—such as army and navy—of defense for the whole country. Fifth, the Constitution was written to promote the general welfare, that is, the physical, social, and financial conditions under which people could live satisfactorily and

---

28. "Constitution of the U.S."

thrive. And sixth, the founders desired to secure the blessings of liberty for themselves and their posterity. Freedom from the home country was the reason the Revolutionary War was fought. Now that it was won, liberty was considered a blessing, a gift from God, to be passed on to succeeding generations in the United States of America.

This day was originally called Citizenship Day, and it was celebrated on the third Sunday of May each year. The purpose was to recognize those who by coming of age or naturalization attained the status of citizenship. Public Law 108–447 of December 8, 2004, amended Citizenship Day to Constitution Day and Citizenship Day to recognize the adoption of the United States Constitution and those who have become U.S. citizens. Section 110 of Public Law 108–447 states that "[t]he head of each federal agency or department shall (1) provide each new employee of the agency or department with educational and training materials concerning the United States Constitution as part of the orientation materials provided to the new employee; and (2) provide educational and training materials concerning the United States Constitution to each employee of the agency or department on September 17 each year."[29] Furthermore, "Each educational institution that receives federal funds for a fiscal year shall hold an educational program on the United States Constitution on September 17 of such year for the students served by the educational institution."[30] In its codified version (Pubic Law 105–225, Section 106), the day is named Constitution Day and Citizenship Day. It commemorates the formation and signing of the Constitution on September 17, 1787, and recognizes all who have become citizens. It urges the president to invite the people of the nation to observe the day in schools, churches, and other suitable places. And it urges civil and educational authorities of states, counties, cities, and towns to make plans to observe the day and "for the complete instruction of citizens in their responsibilities and opportunities as citizens of the United States and of the state and locality in which they reside."[31] In other words, the day is a teachable moment for civic education.

Journal/Meditation: Which of the following reasons for ordaining and establishing the Constitution of the United States do you think is the most important: to form a more perfect union, to establish justice, to ensure domestic tranquility, to provide for the common defense, to promote the general welfare, or to secure the blessings of liberty? Why? Which of the reasons needs the most effort today? What does citizenship mean to you?

Prayer: You have blessed the citizens of the United States of America with liberty, God; you have challenged them to be united as one in securing justice, tranquility, defense, and welfare. For all your gifts I give you thanks, and I ask your grace to continue

---

29. "Public Law 108–447."
30. "Public Law 108–447."
31. "Public Law 105–225," Section 106.

to work toward the vision the founders of my country enshrined in the Constitution. Amen.

National POW/MIA Recognition Day
Third Friday

Text: "Whereas the United States has fought in many wars; whereas thousands of Americans who served in such wars were captured by the enemy or are missing in action; whereas many American prisoners of war were subjected to brutal and inhuman treatment by their enemy captors in violation of international codes and customs for the treatment of prisoners of war and many prisoners of war died from such treatment; whereas many Americans are still listed as missing and unaccounted for and the uncertainty surrounding their fates has caused their families to suffer acute hardship; and whereas the sacrifices of American prisoners of war and Americans missing in action and their families are deserving of national recognition: Now, therefore, be it resolved by the Senate and House of Representatives of the United States of America in congress assembled, that September 18, 1987, shall be designated as 'National POW/MIA Recognition Day,' and the president is authorized and requested to issue a proclamation calling upon the people of the United States to observe such day with appropriate ceremonies and activities."[32]

Reflection: Public Law 100–102, the above text, was approved August 18, 1987. On August 21, 1987, President Ronald Reagan issued the first proclamation of National POW/MIA Recognition Day, which is not the same as National Former Prisoner of War Recognition Day on April 9. However, this was not the first public law which called upon the president to issue such a proclamation. On July 9, 1980, in a joint resolution, congress requested President Jimmy Carter to proclaim July 18, 1980, National POW/MIA Recognition Day,[33] but Carter did not do so. In his proclamation, Reagan began: "Perhaps no American could cherish our country's liberty more dearly than those who have defended it and in doing so have paid the price of capture and imprisonment." He continued, "We take solemn inspiration and resolve from the sacrifices of brave Americans who have endured captivity for their allegiance to our beloved land and our ideals. Their dignity, faith, and valor remind us of the allegiance we owe our nation and its defenders. We also take inspiration from the courage of the families of those who remain missing or unaccounted for. The fortitude they display in the face of uncertainty is heroic, like the acts of those whose fates they seek to learn."[34] On September 15, 1988, congress passed Public Law 100–431, declaring September 16, 1988, National POW/MIA Recognition Day—worded identically to the one issued the year

---

32. "Public Law 100–102."
33. "Public Law 96–307."
34. Reagan, "Proclamation 5695."

before, the above text—and Reagan responded with Proclamation 5858. On July 28, 1989, congress passed Public Law 101–65—worded identically to the two issued in the previous two years—and President George Bush responded: "The U.S. commitment to securing the release of any U.S. servicemen who may still be held against their will, to obtaining the fullest possible accounting for the missing and to repatriation of all recoverable American remains, is unshakable."[35] Except for the first designation of National POW/MIA Recognition Day in July 1980, all those that followed were for the third Friday of September, which range would be 15 through 21. Bush issued similar proclamations in 1990 (Proclamation 6180), 1991 (Proclamation 6334), and 1992 (Proclamation 6474). In his first of eight National POW/MIA Recognition day proclamations in 1993, President William J. Clinton stated: "We acknowledge a continuing obligation to [the] casualties of war, America's missing service members and civilians. Our nation remains committed to this cause, a matter of highest national priority. We renew our pledge to obtain the answer that the family members of these heroes deserve, recognizing the profound loss they have endured and their steadfast resolve to gain the peace of certainty."[36] Clinton issued similar proclamations in 1994 (Proclamation 6718), 1995 (Proclamation 6818), 1996 (Proclamation 6918), 1997 (Proclamation 7023), 1998 (Proclamation 7124), 1999 (Proclamation 7221), and 2000 (Proclamation 7340). Like Clinton before him, President George W. Bush issued his first proclamation of eight National POW/MIA Recognition Days in 2001. He wrote: "Throughout our history, American patriots have risen to answer the call when the enemies of freedom have jeopardized our liberties. . . . In answering the call to defend our ideals, generations of brave Americans have left home and family to protect our great nation, some never to return. National POW/MIA Recognition Day is notably significant for many American families. It reminds us of the men and women who withstood great hardship while imprisoned by our nation's enemies; and it reminds us of those still missing loved ones lost at war but whose fate is not yet fully known. We will not forget these patriots who were willing to give their all to preserve and protect our freedoms."[37] Similar proclamations were issued by Bush in 2002 (Proclamation 7595), 2003 (Proclamation 7707), 2004 (Proclamation 7815), 2005 (Proclamation 7930), 2006 (Proclamation 8051), 2007 (Proclamation 8177), and 2008 (Proclamation 8290). Barack Obama followed Bush as president of the U.S. Obama issued his first of eight National POW/MIA Recognition Day proclamations in 2009. He stated: "We will never cease in our mission to bring America's missing service members home; we will never forget the sacrifices they made to keep this nation free; and we will forever honor their memory. . . . [W]e pay tribute to the American men and women who have not returned from the battlefield, and we express profound gratitude to those who returned only after facing unimaginable hardship on our behalf. . . . [W]e

---

35. Bush, "Proclamation 6002."
36. Clinton, "Proclamation 6587."
37. Bush, G.W., "Proclamation 7469."

also remember the families of our prisoners of war and those missing in action and honor the sacrifices they have made."[38] Obama issued similar proclamations in 2010 (Proclamation 8563), 2011 (Proclamation 8713), 2012 (Proclamation 8867), 2013 (Proclamation 9021), 2014 (Proclamation 9169), 2015 (Proclamation 9324), and 2016 (Proclamation 9495). ". . . [W]e . . . remember our heroes who never returned home," stated President Donald J. Trump in his first of four National POW/MIA Recognition Day proclamations in 2017. ". . . [O]ur nation recognizes all American prisoners of war and service members missing in action who have valiantly honored their commitment to this great country," he continued. "It is our sacred obligation to pay tribute to the thousands of men and women of our Armed Forces who have been imprisoned while serving in conflicts and who have yet to return to American soil. . . . We do not leave our fellow man or woman behind, and we do not rest until our mission is complete."[39] Trump issued similar documents in 2018 (Proclamation 9789), 2019 (Proclamation 9930), and 2020 (Proclamation 10078). In the opening paragraph of his 2021 National POW/MIA Recognition Day proclamation, President Joseph R. Biden stated: "When service members take an oath to defend the Constitution of the United States, they do so knowing that they may be called upon to make great sacrifices to ensure and sustain our shared values. These patriots accept those risks and rush to fulfill the mission, no matter how harsh or dangerous the conditions. They embody the best of the American spirit. For the families and friends who wait at home, anxious for news of their loved ones, these sacrifices can cause great pain. For the families of the more than 81,600 service members who remain missing in action, the pain and grief is compounded by a lack of closure, and the hope that their sons and daughters, sisters and brothers, parents, and grandparents will one day return home."[40] Thus, the day is established as the third Friday of September to remind citizens to stand behind those who serve our country and to make sure we do everything possible to account for those who have never returned.

In Reagan's 1987 and 1988 National POW/MIA Recognition Day proclamations, the president stated: "To symbolize our national commitment, the POW/MIA Flag will fly over the White House, the Departments of State and Defense, the Veterans Administration, and the Vietnam Veterans Memorial . . . . It will also fly over the Vietnam Veterans Memorial on memorial Day and Veterans Day."[41] In 1971, Mary Hoff, wife of Michael Hoff—a MIA service member—contacted Norman Rivkees, vice president of Annin & Company—a flag company—to see if a flag could be made that would remind people of MIAs and POWs. Newt Heisley, an advertising agency employee and former World War II pilot, designed the flag, which is made "in black and white to represent the sorrow, anxiety, and hope symbolized by the image of the gaunt man featured on

38. Obama, "Proclamation 8419."
39. Trump, "Proclamation 9637."
40. Biden, "Proclamation 10259."
41. Reagan, "Proclamation 5695;" cf. "Proclamation 5858."

it."[42] More specifically, "The black and white POW/MIA Flag features a silhouette of a prisoner of war, with a guard tower and barbed wire in the background, and the words 'POW/MIA' at the top, and 'You are Not Forgotten' beneath."[43] In his 1989 proclamation, Bush stated the same as Reagan, but he added: "In March [1989], a POW/MIA Flag was raised in the Capitol Rotunda as a symbol of our nation's concern for those servicemen who remain missing and unaccounted for, and as an expression of our determination to obtain a full and satisfactory accounting for them. This flag shall remain on display there until the POW/MIA issue is thus resolved."[44] When congress proclaimed September 21, 1990, National POW/MIA Recognition Day, it also stated: "The National League of Families POW/MIA Flag is hereby recognized officially and designated as the symbol of our nation's concern and commitment to resolving as fully as possible the fates of Americans still prisoner, missing, and unaccounted for in Southeast Asia, thus ending the uncertainty for their families and the nation."[45] On December 5, 1991, in Public Law 102–190, congress specified that the POW/MIA Flag "shall be displayed—(1) at each national cemetery and at the National Vietnam Veterans Memorial each year on Memorial Day and Veterans Day and on any day designated by law as National POW/MIA Recognition Day; and (2) on, or on the grounds of, the buildings specified in subsection (b) on any day designated by law as National POW/MIA Recognition Day. (b) . . . The buildings referred to [above] are the buildings containing the primary offices of (1) the Secretary of State; (2) the Secretary of the Defense; (3) the Secretary of Veterans Affairs; and (4) the Director of the Selective Service System."[46] In 1994, with Public Law 103–320, congress added the White House and the Capitol Building to the list of where the flag was to be flown.[47] In the resolution, it also added a paragraph about recognizing the National League of Families POW/MIA Flag. In what is known as the Defense Authorization Act of November 18, 1997, (Public Law 105–85, Section 1082), congress required that the POW/MIA Flag "shall serve (1) as the symbol of the nation's concern and commitment to achieving the fullest possible accounting of Americans who, having been prisoners of war or missing in action, still remain unaccounted for, and (2) as the symbol of the nation's commitment to achieving the fullest possible accounting for Americans who in the future may become prisoners of war, missing in action, or otherwise unaccounted for as a result of hostile action."[48] The POW/MIA Flag is to be displayed on Armed Forces Day (third Saturday in May), Memorial Day (last Monday in May), Flag Day (June 14), Independence Day (July 4), National POW/MIA Recognition Day, and Veterans

---

42. "Four Things to Know."
43. "POW/MIA Flag Etiquette."
44. Bush, "Proclamation 6002."
45. "Public Law 101–355."
46. "Public Law 102–190."
47. "Public Law 103–320."
48. "Public Law 105–85," Section 1082.

Day (November 11). Additional places where the flag is to be displayed include the Korean War Veterans Memorial, each major military installation (as designated by the Secretary of Defense), each medical center of the Department of Veterans Affairs, and each U.S. Postal Service post office. On August 12, 1998, Public Law 105–85 was entered in 36 U.S. Code, Section 902—National League of Families POW/MIA Flag as Public Law 105–225 and, on November 3, 1998, as Public Law 105–354. On December 4, 2002, congress added the display of the POW/MIA Flag at the World War II Memorial with Public Law 107–323. On November 7, 2019, Public Law 116–67 went into effect; it states that the "POW/MIA flag [can be displayed on] all days on which the flag of the United States is displayed."[49] This means that the POW/MIA Flag can be flown at anytime and anywhere, as is often done in front of police stations, fire stations, and veterans' organizations. "When displayed on a single flagpole, the POW/MIA Flag should fly directly below, and be the same size or smaller than, the U.S. Flag."[50] If it is flown on its own pole, it is displayed to the left of the U.S. Flag (the viewer's right). If it is set flanking a speaker's podium, it should appear to the right of the U.S. Flag from the viewer's perspective. In other words, when scanning from left to right, the viewer should see the U.S. Flag first, then the POW/MIA Flag.[51] "Every day, the iconic black and white flag—a powerful symbol in recognition of the heroism and sacrifice of American POWs and MIAs—is flown above the White House," states Biden. "It is a mark of reverence and of solidarity with all those who await answers. Each day this flag flies over memorials and cemeteries, on military installations, at local post offices, and on the front lawns of homes across the nation. This flag remains a symbol of America's commitment to honor the sacrifices of all those who serve."[52]

Journal/Meditation: How does the captivity and/or the missing in action of brave Americans inspire you? How does the courage of the families of POWs and MIAs inspire you? Why do you think it is important to mark National POW/MIA Recognition Day? How do you think the POW/MIA Flag honors the sacrifices of those who serve the U.S.?

Prayer: For the men and women who have and will defend my country and who have been captured by the enemy or found missing in action, I pray this day, O God. Inspire me with their devotion to liberty, their allegiance to the United States, and their sacrificial suffering. Comfort the families of those still missing or unaccounted. Keep the best of America's spirit alive throughout the country. Amen.

---

49. "Public Law 116–67."
50. "POW/MIA Flag Etiquette."
51. "POW/MIA Flag Etiquette."
52. Biden, "Proclamation 10259."

INTERNATIONAL DAY OF PEACE

September 21

Text: "Recalling that the promotion of peace, both at an international and a national level, is among the main purposes of the United Nations . . . ; reaffirming that . . . wars begin in the minds of men [and women, and] it is in the minds of men [and women] that the defenses of peace must be construed, that a peace based exclusively upon the political and economic arrangements of governments would not be a peace which could secure the unanimous, lasting, and sincere support of the peoples of the world, and that the peace must therefore be founded, if it is not to fail, upon the intellectual and moral solidarity of [human]kind . . . ; [the General Assembly] declares that the third Tuesday of September, the opening day of the regular sessions of the General Assembly, shall be officially proclaimed and observed as International Day of Peace and shall be devoted to commemorating and strengthening the ideals of peace both within and among all nations and peoples."[53]

Reflection: The text above was passed on November 30, 1981. The first International Day of Peace was celebrated on the third Tuesday of September in 1982. The U.N. resolution called for "the promotion of peace, mainly through education in all its aspects," and the promotion of "the ideals of peace and to giving positive evidence of [the member countries'] commitment to peace in all viable ways." The U.N. hoped that "it would be possible to contribute to strengthening such ideals of peace and alleviating the tensions and causes of conflict, both within and among nations and peoples."[54] For twenty years, the International Day of Peace was marked with the opening day of the U.N. General Assembly on the third Tuesday of September.

Twenty years after the resolution on the International Day of Peace, the General Assembly of the U.N. decided to observe the International Day of Peace on September 21 each year, and it declared that it would be observed "as a day of global ceasefire and non-violence, an invitation to all nations and people to honor a cessation of hostilities for the duration of the day."[55] In its September 7, 2001, resolution, the General Assembly reaffirmed "the contribution that the observance and celebration of the International Day of Peace makes in strengthening the ideals of peace and alleviating tensions and causes of conflict."[56] It also considered "the unique opportunity [the day offered] for a cessation of violence and conflict throughout the world, and the related importance of achieving the broadest possible awareness and observance of the International Day of Peace among the global community."[57] The General Assembly invited all member states to commemorate the day with educational and public awareness

---

53. United Nations General Assembly, A/RES/36/67.
54. United Nations General Assembly, A/RES/36/67.
55. United Nations General Assembly, A/RES/55/282.
56. United Nations General Assembly, A/RES/55/282.
57. United Nations General Assembly, A/RES/55/282.

events and to cooperate in establishing a global ceasefire. The day is begun with the ringing of the U.N. Peace Bell at the U.N. Headquarters in New York; the bell, cast from coins donated by children from all continents, is inscribed with these words: "Long live absolute world peace." The bell is a sign of global solidarity.

Journal/Meditation: What does this sentence mean to you: "Wars begin in the minds of men and women, and it is in the minds of men and women that the defenses of peace must be construed"? How can you promote peace through education? What do you consider the ideals of peace to be? What other signs of global solidarity concerning peace do you know about?

Prayer: God of peace, pour your grace into the minds of world leaders in order to bring about a global solidarity among all people on earth. Show leaders the way to ceasefires and non-violence. Enable me to find ways to end conflicts with reconciliation and to bring peace upon the earth. Amen.

Autumnal Equinox

September 22–23

Text: "In mid-September each year, we greet the fall season with the arrival of the fall equinox (otherwise known as the autumnal equinox). This is the moment when the sun crosses the equator, and those of us living in the Northern hemisphere will begin to see more darkness than daylight. . . . The autumnal (fall) equinox marks the turning point when darkness begins to win out over daylight. Essentially, our hours of daylight—the period of time each day between sunrise and sunset—have been growing slightly shorter each day since the summer solstice in June, which is the longest day of the year (at least in terms of daylight). Then for the next three months our hours of daylight continue to grow shorter. At the autumnal equinox, day and night are approximately equal in length."[58]

Reflection: The autumnal or fall equinox can begin as early as September 21, as it will in 2096, or as late as September 23, as it was in 2003. Usually, however, it falls on the twenty-second or twenty-third day of September in most years. The word *equinox* is derived from two Latin words: *aequus*, meaning *equal*, and *nox*, meaning *night*. Thus, equinox describes the day when daytime and nighttime are approximately of equal duration all over the planet. The autumnal equinox is the second of two such days a year; the first occurs in March, and it is known as the spring equinox, which marks the beginning of longer days. At the time of an equinox, the sun's rays are exactly overhead at the equator in the Northern Hemisphere. Another name for an equinox is *equilux,* meaning *equal light*. While this name was coined in the 1980s, it never achieved widespread usage. After marking the autumnal equinox, the days will continue slowly to

---

58. *Farmers' Almanac*, "Fall Equinox."

get shorter over the next couple of months, as the direct rays of the sun move slowly southward until the winter solstice on December 21–22, the shortest day of the year, when the days will begin to lengthen again.

As the *Farmers' Almanac* states in the above text, the autumnal equinox marks the turning point when darkness begins to win its battle with daylight. The annual rhythm of gradually decreasing daylight (with gradually increasing darkness) and the gradually increasing daylight (with gradually decreasing darkness) caused by the earth's tilt and its elliptical orbit around the sun remind us of the points in our lives when darkness needs to increase. Darkness offers us opportunities for more rest. It gives us more time indoors for inside activities. Darkness is all about nurturing the interior or spiritual life. In darkness we develop a greater appreciation for the light. We get more comfortable with loss, grief, and death in the darkness. So, instead of bemoaning the loss of the light after the autumnal equinox, we can embrace the darkness and discover all that it has to teach us about our spiritual selves.

Journal/Meditation: How do you make use of the darkness following the autumnal equinox? How does the darkness following the autumnal equinox nourish your spiritual life?

Prayer: God of day and night, you have arranged the changing of the seasons in order to assist my spiritual growth in darkness and in light. Guide me with your grace to the fullness of day and night today, tomorrow, and forever. Amen.

Native American Day
Fourth Friday

Text: "An emphasis on freedom, justice, patriotism, and representative government have always been elements of Native American culture, and Native Americans have shown their willingness to fight and die for this nation in foreign lands. . . . Native Americans have given much to this country, and in recognition of this fact, it is fitting that [California] returns the honor by recognizing Native Americans for all their offerings to this beloved land through the establishment of a state holiday referred to as 'Native American Day' [on the Fourth Friday in September]."[59]

Reflection: On September 20, 1998, Pete Wilson, Governor of California, signed AB 1953, a bill in California making the fourth Friday in September Native American Day, a state holiday and a celebration of Native American culture. As early as 1939, Governor Culbert Olson made California the first state to honor the holiday, declaring it to be Indian Day. Governor Ronald Reagan signed a resolution in 1968 calling the holiday American Indian Day and declaring it to be observed on the fourth Friday in September. Then, in 1953, the California legislature passed AB 1953, named it Native

---

59. Bill Number: AB 1953.

American Day, and stated that it was to be observed on the fourth Friday in September. In 1997, the state of Nevada declared the fourth Friday in September as Native American Day. Since 1990, the state of South Dakota has celebrated Native American Day on the second Monday in October. The fourth Monday in September is American Indian Day in Tennessee since 1994, while the Friday following Thanksgiving Day (the fourth Thursday) in November is Native American Heritage Day in Washington state since 2014.

While the day is not observed throughout the United States, it, nevertheless, honors Native American cultures and contributions to the states that observe it and to the country as a whole. The California law acknowledges Native Americans' emphasis on freedom, justice, patriotism, and representative government. In particular it notes the armed service provided by Native Americans, their honor of the flag and veterans through song, music, and dance at powwows. The law acknowledges that Native Americans love the land, which nurtured their ancestors, and honor the earth, which gives life to people since time began. In schools, it directs educational exercises be held to commemorate and draw attention to the contributions of Native Americans to this country.

Journal/Meditation: What Native American tribes inhabit today or inhabited in the past the area in which you live? Make a list of them. What has each contributed to the culture of your area?

Prayer: God, Great Spirit of all people, long before my ancestors came to this land Native Americans honored it and lived on it. Give me the wisdom to honor the earth and to recognize their contribution to the culture in which I now live today, tomorrow, and forever. Amen.

National Good Neighbor Day
September 26

Text: "Whereas our society has developed highly effective means of speedy communication around the world, but has failed to ensure meaningful communication among people living across the globe or even across the street from one another; whereas the endurance of human values and consideration for others are critical to the survival of civilization; and whereas being good neighbors to those around us is the first step toward human understanding: Now, therefore, be it resolved [by] the Senate [of the United States] . . . that the president should designate September 26 . . . as 'National Good Neighbor Day.'"[60]

Reflection: The very first National Good Neighbor Day was proclaimed by President Gerald R. Ford on June 1, 1976, to be observed during the Bicentennial Year of the

---

60. "Senate Resolution 340."

U.S. on September 26, 1976.[61] In the proclamation, Ford reminds the nation about the "thirteen colonies [which] set aside their separate interest and united for a common purpose" and how the "nation expanded because... pioneer ancestors, though independent and self-reliant, recognized the need to work together and to extend a helping hand."[62] During the bicentennial, he wrote, that it is "only by accepting our individual responsibility to be good neighbors [that] we can survive as a strong, united nation." Furthermore, "By recognizing our dependence on each other, we preserve our independence as a people."[63] He urged citizens to teach children "to know and care about the people next door" and to "be willing to learn from each other.... Each individual American must make his or her own special effort to be a good neighbor."[64]

On June 23, 1978, Public Law 95–389 was passed by the Senate. On September 20, 1978, it passed the House of Representatives. The law authorized the president "to issue a proclamation designating September 24, 1978, as 'National Good Neighbor Day,'"[65] and call upon the citizenry to observe it. Jimmy Carter signed the law on September 29, 1978, after issuing Proclamation 4601–National Good Neighbor Day, 1978, on September 22, 1978. Carter states that "the noblest human concern is concern for others. Understanding, love, and respect build cohesive families and communities.... [T]his sense of community is nurtured and expressed in... neighborhoods."[66] Carter recognized "the importance of fostering compassion and respect... for... neighbors."[67] On April 28, 2004, the U.S. Senate passed resolution 340, from which the above text is quoted, requesting the president to designate September 26, 2004, as National Good Neighbor Day. The desire was to foster meaningful communication among neighbors, to foster the endurance of human values, and the consideration of others in order to insure the survival of civilization. According to the resolution, "... [B]eing good neighbors to those around us is the first step toward human understanding."[68]

Journal/Meditation: What do you consider the characteristics of a good neighbor? What recent meaningful communication have you had with a neighbor? Why is it important to be a good neighbor?

Prayer: Almighty God, understanding, love, and respect are ever present in your unity of Father, Son, and Holy Spirit. Fill me with the grace to spread that sense of

---

61. Ford, "Proclamation 4444."
62. Ford, "Proclamation 4444."
63. Ford, "Proclamation 4444."
64. Ford, "Proclamation 4444."
65. "Public Law 95–389."
66. Carter, "Proclamation 4601."
67. Carter, "Proclamation 4601."
68. "Senate Resolution 340."

community throughout my neighborhood by being a good neighbor and fostering human understanding among all who live near me. Amen.

INTERNATIONAL DAY FOR THE TOTAL ELIMINATION OF NUCLEAR WEAPONS

September 26

Text: "Emphasizing the importance of seeking a safer world for all and achieving peace and security in a world without nuclear weapons; . . . convinced that nuclear disarmament and the total elimination of nuclear weapons are the only absolute guarantee against the use or threat of use of nuclear weapons; . . . sharing the deep concern at the catastrophic humanitarian consequences of any use of nuclear weapons; . . . determined to work collectively towards the realization of nuclear disarmament; . . . [the General Assembly of the United Nations] declares 26 September as the International Day for the Total Elimination of Nuclear Weapons devoted to furthering this objective, including through enhancing public awareness and education about the threat posed to humanity by nuclear weapons and the necessity for their total elimination, in order to mobilize international efforts towards achieving the common goal of a nuclear-weapon-free world."[69]

Reflection: On September 28, 2013, the General Assembly of the United Nations held its first-ever high-level meeting on nuclear disarmament "with the aim to raise awareness about the threat posed to humanity by nuclear weapons and the necessity for their elimination in order to mobilize international efforts towards achieving the common goal of a nuclear-weapon-free world."[70] After that meeting, on December 5, 2013, it issued and approved a two-page resolution, from which the above text is taken, that declared September 26 International Day for the Total Elimination of Nuclear Weapons. According to the U.N. webpage: ". . . [T]he purpose of the International Day is to further the objective of the total elimination of nuclear weapons through enhancing public awareness and education about the threat posed to humanity by nuclear weapons and the necessity for their total elimination. In so doing, it is hoped that these activities will help to mobilize new international efforts towards achieving the common goal of a nuclear-weapon-free world."[71] This international day should not be confused with the International Day against Nuclear Tests observed on August 29 since December 2, 2009. The Nuclear Tests day seeks "to enhance public awareness and [provide] education about the effects of nuclear weapon test explosions or any other nuclear explosions and the need for their cessation as one of the means of achieving

---

69. United Nations General Assembly, A/RES/68/32.
70. "International Day for the Total Elimination of Nuclear Weapons."
71. "International Day for the Total Elimination of Nuclear Weapons."

the goal of a nuclear-weapon-free world."[72] According to the U.N. resolution, "every effort should be made to end nuclear tests in order to avert devastating and harmful effects on the lives and health of people and the environment," and "the end of nuclear tests is one of the key means of achieving the goal of a nuclear-weapon-free world."[73]

According to the U.N. "International Day for the Total Elimination of Nuclear Weapons" webpage, "one of humanity's greatest challenges [is] achieving the peace and security of a world without nuclear weapons."[74] To achieve a safer world without nuclear weapons, the U.N. advocates the prohibition of their possession, development, production, acquisition, testing, stockpiling, transfer, and use or threat of use. Through raising public awareness, the U.N. seeks deeper engagement on nuclear disarmament matters with the ultimate goal of "the total elimination of nuclear weapons."[75] The slow pace of disarmament raises concerns about the "catastrophic humanitarian consequences of the use of even a single nuclear weapon."[76] The day provides the occasion for the world community "to reaffirm its commitment to global nuclear disarmament as a priority." Also, "[i]t provides an opportunity to educate the public—and their leaders—about the real benefits of eliminating such weapons, and the social and economic costs of perpetuating them."[77] The two largest nuclear arsenals in the world belong to the United States and the Russian Federation. Over thirteen thousand nuclear weapons remain on the earth. The U.N. has a central role to play in the field of disarmament, but civil society, "including non-governmental organizations, academia, parliamentarians, and the mass media" play an important role "in advancing the objective of nuclear disarmament."[78] Resolution 68/32 calls upon U.N. members and civil society "to commemorate and promote the International Day [for the Total Elimination of Nuclear Weapons] through all means of educational and public awareness-raising activities."[79]

Journal/Meditation: What do you think needs to be done to make the world safer? What steps need to be taken to achieve the total elimination of nuclear weapons? What can you do to achieve the goal of a nuclear-weapon-free world?

Prayer: Creator God, you made all things good, but humanity has created weapons of mass destruction to eliminate them from the world. Pour grace upon the leaders of the world and fill them with the wisdom needed to eliminate all nuclear weapons

---

72. United Nations General Assembly, A/RES/64/35.
73. United Nations General Assembly, A/RES/64/35.
74. "International Day for the Total Elimination of Nuclear Weapons."
75. United Nations General Assembly, A/RES/68/32.
76. "International Day for the Total Elimination of Nuclear Weapons."
77. "International Day for the Total Elimination of Nuclear Weapons."
78. United Nations General Assembly, A/RES/68/32.
79. United Nations General Assembly, A/RES/68/32.

so all people can live in safety, security, and peace. Inspire me with the knowledge of what I can do to further the goal of a nuclear-weapon-free world. Amen.

World Tourism Day
September 27

Text: "The General Assembly [of the United Nations World Tourism Organization] . . . decides to institute a World Tourism Day to be observed on 27 September of each year, beginning in 1980, by appropriate celebrations on the themes chosen for the purpose by the Assembly on the proposal of the Executive Council . . . ."[80]

Reflection: During the third session of the United Nations World Tourism Organization (UNWTO), held in Torremolinos, Spain, from September 17 to 28, 1979, the General Assembly accepted the proposal for the World Tourism Day submitted by the Secretary-General of the UNWTO and set its annual commemoration on September 27, as can be seen in the resolution from which the above text is taken. Since the first time World Tourism Day would be celebrated was 1980, it also accepted the theme proposed—"tourism's contribution to the preservation of the cultural heritage and to peace and mutual understanding"—along with the theme for 1981—"tourism and the quality of life."[81] According to the proposal, the date was chosen because it was "the anniversary of the adoption of the WTO Statutes by the Extraordinary General Assembly of IUOTO [International Union of Official Travel Organizations], held at Mexico City from 17 to 28 September 1970."[82] ". . . [T]he purpose of the [day]," according to the proposal, is ". . . to make official, private, and commercial bodies, and the public at large, more aware of the real values of tourism, travel, and leisure activities." It is "essentially an information action, carried out at every level and through all available media, centered on the date chosen, and accompanied wherever possible by concrete measures concerning tourism promotion and facilitation on the part of government authorities and the travel trade itself."[83] Furthermore, "[a] world tourism day . . . provide[s] a specific frame of reference and carr[ies] a symbolic meaning: the continuing commitment of WTO member states . . . to their undertaking to promote tourism . . . with a view to contributing to economic development, peace, prosperity, and universal respect for, and observance of, human rights and fundamental freedoms."[84]

At the UNWTO General Assembly in Santiago, Chile, from September 27 to October 1, 1999, the WTO adopted a six-page "Global Code of Ethics for Tourism"

---

80. United Nations World Tourism Organization, A/RES/76 (III).
81. United Nations World Tourism Organization, A/RES/76 (III).
82. United Nations World Tourism Organization, A/3/14, par. 7.
83. United Nations World Tourism Organization, A/3/14, par. 9.
84. United Nations World Tourism Organization, A/3/14, par. 5.

on October 1, 1999. Consisting of a preamble and ten articles, the document seeks to promote and develop "tourism with a view to contributing to economic development, international understanding, peace, prosperity, and universal respect for, and observance of, human rights and fundamental freedoms for all without distinction as to race, sex, language, or religion."[85] Furthermore, "tourism represents a vital force for peace and a factor of friendship and understanding among the people of the world." The aim of the "Global Code" is "to promote responsible, sustainable, and universally accessible tourism in the framework of the right of all persons to use their free time for leisure pursuits or travel with respect for the choices of society of all peoples."[86] The reason for issuing the "Global Code" was to provide "a number of principles and a certain number of rules [to be] observed" and the fact that "responsible and sustainable tourism is by no means incompatible with the growing liberalization of the conditions governing trade in services and under whose aegis the enterprises of this sector operate and that it is possible to reconcile in this sector economy and ecology, environment and development, openness to international trade and protection of social and cultural identities."[87] The document states that it is the wish of the UNWTO "to promote an equitable, responsible, and sustainable world tourism order, whose benefits will be shared by all sectors of society in the context of an open and liberalized international economy . . . ."[88] On December 21, 2001, the U.N. accepted the "Global Code," "which outlines principles to guide tourism development and to serve as a frame of reference for the different stakeholders in the tourism sector, with the objective of minimizing the negative impact of tourism on environment and on cultural heritage, while maximizing the benefits of tourism in promoting sustainable development and poverty alleviation as well as understanding among nations."[89] Thus, the World Tourism Organization, the leading United Nations agency in the field of tourism, has the mission of promoting tourism as a driver of economic growth, inclusive development, and environmental sustainability and offers leadership and support to the tourism sector in advancing knowledge and tourism policies around the world.[90] According to the U.N.'s World Tourism Day webpage, "Tourism creates jobs, promotes local culture and products, works in the sustainable use and management of the environment, . . . and improves measures to make tourism an inclusive experience for all."[91]

85. "Global Code," Preamble.
86. "Global Code," Preamble.
87. "Global Code," Preamble.
88. "Global Code," Preamble.
89. United Nations General Assembly, A/RES/56/212.
90. "World Tourism Day."
91. "World Tourism Day."

Journal/Meditation: When have you most recently been a tourist? Where did you go? About what culture did you learn? How did you contribute to the economy, peace, prosperity, human rights and freedoms, and protection of the environment?

Prayer: You have created a diversity of cultures upon the earth, O LORD, to display the possibilities of humanity. When I travel, give me a deeper understanding of culture, a greater respect for human rights and freedoms, and a genuine awareness of environmental protection. Hear my prayer for peace in the world. Amen.

National Coffee Day, International Coffee Day
September 29, October 1

Text: "Coffee's journey to ubiquity began in Ethiopia, where it was first cultivated. From the fifteenth century Yemeni traders exported it to Sufi monasteries in order to help worshippers remain wakeful during their all-night devotions. Coffee then spread to Mecca and Medina, and on to Cairo, Aleppo, and Damascus. In the 1550s coffee houses began to appear in Constantinople; by the end of the century they were everywhere in the city. . . . Coffee houses transformed Constantinople because they provided a new space in the city for meeting and talking outside the traditional confines of the mosque and home. English traders in cities such as Aleppo, Smyrna, and Constantinople began to drink the beverage and, like billions more in years to come, got addicted to the stuff."[92]

Reflection: Because of their proximity, National Coffee Day on September 29 and International Coffee Day on October 1 are treated together. In the above text, taken from Ben Wilson's *Metropolis: A History of the City, Humankind's Greatest Invention*, the author spends five pages narrating the effect coffee had on cities of the world. According to *National Today's* "International Coffee Day," ". . . Coffee is originally from Ethiopia . . . . Around the 700s [CE], a herd of goats started acting strangely, almost as if they were dancing. Their owner, Kaldi, discovered that they were eating a sort of red bean and concluded that was the cause of their behavior. Kaldi decided to share his findings with a monk who required something that could help him to stay awake all night as he prayed; but another story claims that the monk refused and threw the beans into the fire and the pleasing aroma that come from it was just wonderful."[93] Other accounts place the goat herder's experience in the ninth century. Nevertheless, coffee drinking became popular in the Arab world around the fifteenth century in Yemen. Around 1560, it made its way through Europe, after passing through Egypt, Persia, and Turkey. In 1670, coffee beans were smuggled out of the Middle East and taken to Mysore, India, and from there they traveled to Europe, Indonesia, and the

---

92. Wilson, *Metropolis*, 194–5.
93. "International Coffee Day."

Americas. As Wilson notes in the above text, coffee houses in Constantinople became the new locations for business transactions; Venice had a coffee house in 1645; in London, coffee houses became the new locations for intelligent, engaging, in-depth discussions. James Folger introduced coffee to gold miners in California in 1865, and the J.A. Folger & Company was born in 1872. It wasn't long before Maxwell House and Hills Brothers entered the coffee market. In the United States, a new coffee market took hold in the 1960s, and Seattle's Starbucks changed everything in 1971. Today, Brazil produces more coffee in the world than any other country, with Columbia closely behind. The second largest traded commodity right after crude oil is coffee. That is why it is important to buy ethically grown coffee.

Coffee is made from coffee beans, which are pits found in the coffee berry or cherry; thus, a coffee bean is a fruit which grows on a bush. A cup of coffee is judged using four components: aroma, body, acidity, and flavor. The aroma is the fragrance smelled when a fresh bag of roasted, whole coffee beans or ground coffee beans is opened. The way the beans are roasted, ground, and brewed are factors in determining the body of the coffee. According to *National Day's* "National Coffee Day:" "The bean affects the texture of the coffee, whether its silky, creamy, thick, or thin on the tongue and throat. However, the darker the roast and how we brew it will alter the feel of a coffee's body. . . . Where a coffee bean grows determines its acidity. The higher the elevation the coffee grows, the higher the quality and the acidity."[94] The flavor is the overall taste of the brewed coffee, which can be prepared basically in one of four ways: decoction (through boiling), infusion (through steeping), gravitational feed (through percolating and drip), and pressurized percolation (such as espresso). If kept hot, brewed coffee deteriorates rapidly; if kept in an oxygen-free environment in a sealed container, it can last indefinitely even at room temperature. Coffee, a natural source of caffeine—itself a natural substance—gives the body an energy boost. Coffee can also help burn fat, increase metabolic rate, and includes some essential nutrients, such as niacin, magnesium, potassium, manganese, panthothenic acid, and riboflavin. It helps our brains produce dopamine and adrenaline, improving our memories. The purpose of both National Coffee Day and International Coffee Day—begun by the International Coffee Organization (ICO)[95] in 2014—is to create awareness about the process that implicates coffee's production and to promote heathy and safe methods and procedures not only for humans, but also for the planet. According to the ICO:

---

94. "National Coffee Day."

95. "The International Coffee Organization (ICO) is the main intergovernmental organization for coffee, bringing together exporting and importing governments to tackle the challenges facing the world coffee sector through international cooperation. . . . The ICO's mission is to strengthen the global coffee sector and promote its sustainable expansion in a market-based environment for the betterment of all participants in the coffee sector. It makes a practical contribution to the development of a sustainable world coffee sector and to reducing poverty in developing countries . . . . The ICO was set up in London in 1963 under the auspices of the United Nations because of the great economic importance of coffee." Cf. https://internationalcoffeeday.org/copy-of-about-2020 for more information.

"International Coffee Day is a celebration of the coffee sector's diversity, quality, and passion. It is an opportunity for coffee lovers to share their love of the beverage and support the millions of farmers whose livelihoods depend on the aromatic crop."[96] Thus, on either day, enjoy a cup or two of your favorite coffee or try coffee from another country. Gather with some friends at a favorite coffee shop for conversation. Try a different brewing method. Buy a cup of coffee for a coworker, friend, family member, etc. Gather information about coffee from a book, a magazine, a documentary. Bake a coffee dessert for an older person, make a batch of homemade coffee ice cream, or purchase a container of your favorite coffee and give it to someone you know who loves coffee. These are but two among many days celebrating coffee throughout the year: January 18, National Gourmet Coffee Day; January 25, National Irish Coffee Day; February 17, National Cafe Au Lait Day; May 16, National Coffee Day; July 24, Coffee Day; July 26, National Milkshake Day; September 7, National Frappe Day; November 8, National Cappuccino Day; November 24, National Espresso Day; December 3, National Peppermint Latte Day; and December 15, National Gingerbread Latte Day, are a few among many more.

Journal/Meditation: What is the spiritual experience you associate with coffee? What are the ethical implications of the coffee you purchase? What is your favorite aspect of brewing coffee? Why?

Prayer: Creator God, I acknowledge that my cup of coffee puts me in solidarity with the one who planted the seedlings, the one who nurtured the soil, the one who watered the bushes, the one who harvested the beans, the one who brought the beans to market, the one who roasted the beans, and the one (or: with me) who brewed this cup of coffee. I pray that justice has been given to everyone in the chain of production and that the pleasure I receive gives you praise now and forever. Amen.

---

96. International Coffee Organization.

10

The Month of *October*

INTERNATIONAL DAY FOR OLDER PERSONS
October 1

Text: "Recognizing that the elderly are an asset to society and can contribute significantly to the development process; . . . recognizing also the complexity and rapidity of the aging of the world's population and the need to have a common basis and frame of reference for the protection of the rights of the elderly, including the contribution that the elderly can and should make to society; . . . [the General Assembly of the United Nations] designates 1 October as International Day for the Elderly."[1]

Reflection: On December 14, 1990, the General Assembly of the United Nations, passed resolution 45/106, from which the above text is taken, on the implementation of the international plan of action on aging and related activities. In that resolution, as can be seen above, the U.N. designated October 1 as International Day for the Elderly. The day was observed for the first time in 1991, but by December 16, 1991, the name of the day had been changed to International Day for Older Persons. This can be seen in the "United Nations Principles for Older Persons," a resolution passed by the General Assembly of the U.N. on December 16, 1991. The purpose of the day is to raise awareness about issues affecting the elderly and to appreciate the contributions that older persons make to society. In that regard, it is similar to National Grandparents Day, celebrated in the United States on the Sunday after Labor Day. The document reaffirms "fundamental human rights, . . . the dignity and worth of the human person, . . . [and] the equal rights of men and women." It appreciates "the tremendous diversity in the situation of older persons, not only between countries but within countries and between individuals, which requires a variety of policy responses." It acknowledges "that in all countries, individuals are reaching an advanced age in greater numbers and in better health than ever before." And, it is "[c]onvinced that in a world characterized

---

1. United Nations General Assembly, A/RES/45/106.

by an increasing number and proportion of older persons, opportunities must be provided for willing and capable older persons to participate in and contribute to the ongoing activities of society."[2] Then, the document encourages governments to incorporate eighteen principles into their national programs. Here the focus is on the principles contained in the U.N. resolution.

Eighteen numbered principles are divided into five categories: independence, participation, care, self-fulfillment, and dignity. Six principles are listed in the independence category. "(1) Older persons should have access to adequate food, water, shelter, clothing, and health care through the provision of income, family, and community support and self-help. (2) [They] should have the opportunity to work to have access to other income-generating opportunities, (3) . . . be able to participate in determining when and at what pace withdrawal from the labor force takes place, (4) . . . have access to appropriate educational and training programs, . . . (5) be able to live in environments that are safe and adaptable to personal preferences and changing capacities; [and] (6) . . . be able to reside at home for as long as possible."[3] Three principles are presented in the participation category. "(7) Older persons should remain integrated in society, participate actively in the formulation and implementation of policies that directly affect their wellbeing, and share their knowledge and skills with younger generations. (8) [They] . . . should be able to seek and develop opportunities for service to the community and to serve as volunteers in positions appropriate to their interest and capabilities, [and] (9) . . . be able to form movements of associations of older persons."[4] Under the category of care, five principles are presented. " (10) Older persons should benefit from family and community care and protection in accordance with each society's system of cultural values. (11) [They] . . . should have access to health care to help them to maintain or regain the optimum level of physical, mental, and emotional wellbeing and to prevent or delay the onset of illness, (12) . . . have access to social and legal services to enhance their autonomy, protection, and care, (13) . . . be able to utilize appropriate levels of institutional care providing protection, rehabilitation, and social and mental stimulation in a humane and secure environment, (14) . . . be able to enjoy human rights and fundamental freedoms when residing in any shelter, care, or treatment facility, including full respect for their dignity, beliefs, needs, and privacy and for the right to make decisions about their care and the quality of their lives."[5] Only two principles are presented in the category of self-fulfillment: "(15) Older persons should be able to pursue opportunities for the full development of their potential [and] (16) . . . have access to the educational, cultural, spiritual, and recreational resources of society."[6] Likewise, two principles are present-

2. United Nations General Assembly, A/RES/46/91.
3. United Nations General Assembly, A/RES/46/91, pars. 1–6.
4. United Nations General Assembly, A/RES/46/91, pars. 7–9.
5. United Nations General Assembly, A/RES/46/91, pars. 10–14.
6. United Nations General Assembly, A/RES/46/91, pars. 15–16.

ed in the category of dignity: "(17) Older persons should be able to live in dignity and security and be free of exploitation and physical or mental abuse and (18) . . . should be treated fairly regardless of age, gender, racial or ethnic background, disability, or other status, and be valued independently of their economic contribution."[7] When marking the International Day for Older Persons, the goal is to create awareness and empathy for the wellbeing of the elderly by spending time with them, visiting nursing homes, cooking or baking something for them, and sending greeting cards to them.

Journal/Meditation: Of the eighteen principles presented in the United Nations Principles for Older Persons, which one got the most of your attention? Why? What older person you know can you join in marking the International Day for Older Persons?

Prayer: Heavenly Father, you have given special gifts to older persons which bring wisdom to their years. Through the privilege of a long life, give the elderly the dignity and respect due them and grant me a greater appreciation for all they have to share with me. Throughout their seniority, give them joy in your presence. Amen.

WORLD TEACHERS' DAY
October 5

Text: "Recalling that the right to education is a fundamental human right; . . . recognizing the essential role of teachers [, those persons in schools who are responsible for the education of pupils,] in educational advancement and the importance of their contribution to the development of [humans] and modern society; . . . convinced that . . . similar questions arise in all countries with regard to the status of teachers [that] call for the application of a set of common standards and measures . . . ; [the Special Intergovernmental Conference on the Status of Teachers adopts the Recommendation Concerning the Status of Teachers]."[8]

Reflection: Also known as International Teachers' Day, World Teachers' Day was established in 1994 to commemorate the signing of UNESCO's (United Nations Educational, Scientific, and Cultural Organization) October 5, 1966, "Recommendation Concerning the Status of Teachers." This twelve-page document, from where the above text comes, set the standard for addressing the status and situations of teachers around the world in both public and private schools from the beginning of education to the completion of the secondary stage. One of the document's guiding principles states: "Education from the earliest school years should be directed to the all-around development of the human personality and to the spiritual, moral, social, cultural, and economic progress of the community, as well as to the inculcation or deep respect for

---

7. United Nations General Assembly, A/RES/46/91, pars. 17–18.
8. "Recommendation: Status of Teachers."

human rights and fundamental freedoms...."[9] According to the document, "[I]t is the fundamental right of every child to be provided with the fullest possible educational opportunities...."[10] The Recommendation states, "Teaching should be regarded as a profession; it is a form of public service which requires of teachers expert knowledge and specialized skills, acquired and maintained through rigorous and continuing study...."[11] The rest of the document addresses twelve educational objectives and policies; how teachers, "who possess the necessary moral, intellectual, and physical qualities and who have the required professional knowledge and skills,"[12] should be prepared for their profession through a program of study, "the main elements [being] philosophy, psychology, sociology as applied to education, the theory and history of education, and of comparative education, experimental pedagogy, school administration, and methods of teaching the various subjects."[13] The document addresses teacher preparation institutions, the need for further education for teachers, employment, teaching as a career, along with the rights and responsibilities of teachers, the conditions for effective teaching and learning, salaries, and the teacher shortage.

On November 11, 1997, UNESCO approved "Recommendation Concerning the Status of Higher-Education Teaching Personnel." The preamble states that the organization is "conscious that higher education and research are instrumental in the pursuit, advancement, and transfer of knowledge and constitute an exceptionally rich cultural and scientific asset."[14] This document states "that the right to education, teaching, and research can only be fully employed in an atmosphere of academic freedom and autonomy for institutions of higher education and that the open communication of findings, hypotheses, and opinions lies at the very heart of higher education and provides the strongest guarantee of the accuracy and objectivity of scholarship and research."[15] This eleven-page document defines higher education as "programs of study, training or training for research at the post-secondary level provided by universities or other educational establishments that are approved as institutions of higher education by the competent state authorities, and/or through recognized accreditation systems."[16] The document provides guiding principles—global objectives being international peace, understanding, and cooperation—along with eleven sections explaining educational objectives and policies; institutional rights, duties, and responsibilities; rights and freedoms of higher-education teaching personnel; duties and responsibilities of higher-education teaching personnel; preparation for a career in higher education;

9. "Recommendation: Status of Teachers," par. 3.
10. "Recommendation: Status of Teachers," par. 10a.
11. "Recommendation: Status of Teacher," par. 6.
12. "Recommendation: Status of Teachers," par. 11.
13. "Recommendation: Status of Teachers," par. 20.
14. "Recommendation: Status of Higher-Education Teaching Personnel."
15. "Recommendation: Status of Higher-Education Teaching Personnel."
16. "Recommendation: Status of Higher-Education Teaching Personnel," par. 1a.

employment, evaluation, salary, and time for research. The document states that scholars have an obligation to base research on an honest search for truth.[17]

Journal/Meditation: What specific aspects of your personality were developed by your education? Which teacher(s) contributed the most to your growth? Explain.

Prayer: God, you teach people through your word. Help me to learn from your Son, called teacher, not only to seek wisdom, but to seek self-knowledge, which brings me to an awareness of your presence. Bless all teachers today, tomorrow, and forever. Amen.

LEIF ERIKSON DAY
October 9

Text: "Resolved by the Senate and House of Representatives of the United States of American in congress assembled, that the president of the United States is authorized to officially proclaim October 9 in each year as Leif Erikson Day."[18]

Reflection: On September 2, 1964, Public Law 88–566, which is quoted above in its entirety, was approved by the congress and the president of the United States. On August 12, 1998, when it entered into Public Law 105–225, Section 114, it was modified: "The president may issue each year a proclamation designating October 9 as Leif Erikson Day."[19] Even though its later form states that the president *may* issue an annual proclamation, every president from Lyndon B. Johnson to the present has done so. In his first proclamation, issued September 2, 1964, Johnson stated, "Leif Erikson, Norseman, son of Erik the Red and great seafarer, in the year 1000 valiantly explored the shores of the American Continent; and . . . the intrepid exploits of the Vikings of Erikson's time strike a responsive chord in the hearts of all the American people, who as a nation are today embarked upon an adventurous exploration of the unfathomed realms of space . . . ."[20] Johnson issued similar proclamations in 1965 (Proclamation 3666), 1966 (Proclamation 3745), 1967 (Proclamation 3808), and 1968 (Proclamation 3872). More of the history concerning Erikson was presented by President Richard Nixon in his first proclamation of the day on September 11, 1969. "Leif Erikson and his crew of adventurous Norse seafarers sailed across the northern seas nearly a thousand years ago and landed on the shores of North America," he began. "These resourceful explorers opened new horizons to the west—a truly courageous and historic achievement." He added: "The spirit of Leif Erikson has continued to inspire millions of people, particularly the ten million Americans whose ancestors

---

17. "Recommendation: Status of Higher-Education Teaching Personnel," par. 33.
18. "Public Law 88–566."
19. "Public Law 105–225," Section 114.
20. Johnson "Proclamation 3610."

came from the Viking lands. It is especially appropriate that we recognize Leif Erikson's explorations in 1969, the year in which a new kind of explorers landed on the moon and returned home to inspire all [human]kind from now on."[21] Nixon issued similar proclamations in 1970 (Proclamation 4003), 1971 (Proclamation 4081), 1972 (Proclamation 4146), and 1973 (Proclamation 4233). President Gerald R. Ford issued his first Leif Erikson Day proclamation on October 3, 1974. He wrote: "Today most of the world's frontiers have been explored, but there are still personal frontiers that are no less challenging and forbidding than those faced so many years ago. . . . [L]et us draw inspiration from the indomitable spirit and undaunting determination of Leif Erikson."[22] In 1975 (Proclamation 4392) and in 1976 (Proclamation 4450), Ford issued similar documents. President Jimmy Carter stated, "The United States [owes a] debt to that courageous Norseperson, Leif Erikson, . . . and recalls a distant age when brave adventurers sailed forth into the unknown," in his first Leif Erikson Day proclamation on September 23, 1977. "As a people," he wrote, "we continue to embody this spirit of bold discovery, and we take pride in his historical exploits."[23] Carter issued similar proclamations in 1978 (Proclamation 4592), 1979 (Proclamation 4677), and 1980 (Proclamation 4777). "Nordic stories passed through the ages tell us of the Viking Leif Erikson and his explorations across the North Atlantic," begins President Ronald Reagan in his October 6, 1981, proclamation. He continues: "One of the most daring of the great Norse adventurers, he may have been the first European to discover our continent. Scandinavian tales tell us of a cargo of timber and wild grapes he brought from North America to his home in Greenland more than four centuries before Columbus. . . . Leif Erikson was an explorer, and he has come to symbolize [human]kind's efforts to push back . . . frontiers, master the elements, and conquer . . . fear of the unknown."[24] Reagan issued similar proclamations in 1982 (Proclamation 4961), 1983 (Proclamation 5097), 1984 (Proclamation 5238), 1985 (Proclamation 5374), 1986 (Proclamation 5547), 1987 (Proclamation 5722), and 1988 (Proclamation 5871).

In the first of four Leif Erikson Day proclamations, on October 6, 1989, President George Bush wrote that each year we "commemorate the life and legacy of this courageous Norse missionary and explorer" and "we also celebrate our nation's Nordic heritage." Bush noted that "Erikson was commissioned by King Olaf Tryggvason (Olaf I) to return to Greenland as a missionary."[25] Bush issued other Leif Erikson Day proclamations in 1990 (Proclamation 6183), 1991 (Proclamation 6342), and 1992 (Proclamation 6479). In his first Leif Erikson Day proclamation on October 8, 1993, President William J. Clinton noted the "outstanding contributions that Nordic Americans have made to the United States" and how "the bonds that Leif Erikson—son of Iceland,

21. Nixon, "Proclamation 3928."
22. Ford, "Proclamation 4321."
23. Carter, "Proclamation 4524."
24. Reagan, "Proclamation 4871."
25. Bush, "Proclamation 6041."

grandson of Norway—forged continue unbroken today. We maintain an impressive exchange of people and ideas with the Nordic countries." Later in the proclamation, Clinton states: ". . . [T]he Nordic countries retain their important role in fostering democracy, transatlantic cooperation, and an open trading system. Their many contributions to international diplomacy, humanitarian assistance, and peace-keeping in the world's trouble spots set a high standard that the rest of the world greatly admires." Clinton identifies the Nordic Countries as "Denmark, Finland, Iceland, Norway, and Sweden."[26] In 1994 (Proclamation 6735), 1995 (Proclamation 6837), 1996 (Proclamation 6934), 1997 (Proclamation 7035), 1998 (Proclamation 7135), 1999 (Proclamation 7236), and 2000 (Proclamation 7358), Clinton made similar proclamations. On October 9, 2001, President George W. Bush issued his first of eight Leif Erikson Day proclamations, in which he stated, "The Nordic and American peoples share the virtues of courage, resourcefulness, and self-reliance, and they have built nations based on the principles of liberty, justice, and equality." Then, reflecting upon "Erikson's groundbreaking achievements," Bush recognized "that achieving difficult goals requires people who are courageous and willing to sacrifice, who take action and take risks." He then recounts some of those actions: ". . . American researchers and entrepreneurs, including many of Nordic descent, are making landmark discoveries in the fields of genetics, information technology, biotechnology, and renewable energy."[27] Bush issued similar proclamations in 2002 (Proclamation 7605), 2003 (Proclamation 7718), 2004 (Proclamation 7828), 2005 (Proclamation 7943), 2006 (Proclamation 8063), 2007 (Proclamation 8187), and 2008 (Proclamation 8303). In his first of eight Leif Erikson Day proclamations, October 7, 2009, President Barack Obama begins by explaining why October 9 was chosen for the date: "On this day in 1825, the ship Restauration landed in New York City after sailing for three months from Stavanger, Norway. The fifty-two passengers aboard represented the first organized emigration of Norwegians to America." Later, he adds, "Our nation's founding history is marked by millions of individuals who faced great hardship and difficulty as they pursued a brighter future abroad." He notes that the spirit that lived with Leif Erickson "has inspired countless others who venture from their homes in search of opportunity, uncertain of the possibilities and challenges that await them."[28] In 2010 (Proclamation 8581), 2011 (Proclamation 8734), 2012 (Proclamation 8885), 2013 (Proclamation 9037), 2014 (Proclamation 9189), 2015 (Proclamation 9344), and 2016 (Proclamation 9519), Obama issued similar documents. In his first of four Leif Erikson Day proclamations, issued October 6, 2017, President Donald J. Trump refers to Erikson and his crew as "intrepid explorers" who "were likely the first Europeans to reach our great home, North America." Then, he adds, ". . . [W]e celebrate their remarkable journey and the brave Viking culture that lies at the core of the New World's passion

26. Clinton, "Proclamation 6607."
27. Bush, G.W., "Proclamation 7483."
28. Obama, "Proclamation 8435."

for discovery and determination to tackle unimaginable challenges." Trump also notes "Nordic accomplishments," such as attributing "our hamburgers to Danish-American Louis Lassen, . . . the famed St. Louis Arch to Finnish-American Eero Saarinen, . . . [Charlies Brown, Snoopy, and the Peanuts comic strip to] Norwegian-American and cartoonist Charles M. Schulz . . . , [and] Finnish-American John Morton [, who] signed the Declaration of Independence."[29] Trump issued similar proclamations in 2018 (Proclamation 9802), 2019 (Proclamation 9946), and 2020 (Proclamation 10097). President Joseph R. Biden's first Leif Erikson Day proclamation, issued October 8, 2021, is two-pages long. Like Obama, he recounts the reasons the day is marked on October 9: "Eight centuries after Leif Erikson's expedition, on October 9, 1825, six Norwegian families arrived in New York City in search of freedom and opportunity. This first group of organized Norwegian immigrants to the United States blazed a new path that fellow Norwegians—as well as Danes, Finns, Icelanders, and Swedes—soon followed. . . . These Northern European settlers have become a part of America's rich tapestry, and through service, sacrifice, and countless contributions they have fortified America's culture, society, and economy." Later, Biden adds that we "honor Leif Erikson, son of Iceland and grandson of Norway, and . . . celebrate our Nordic-American heritage . . . ."[30] Thus, on Leif Erikson Day, we remember the Viking explorer who discovered America and continues to inspire countless people through the years to explore the world in which they live. We also honor those of Nordic heritage who continue to contribute to U.S. culture.

Journal/Meditation: In what specific way does Leif Erikson inspire you to be an explorer? What personal frontiers have you explored? Explain. What important fact about Leif Erikson did you learn that is inspiring you now?

Prayer: God of explorers, throughout human history you have summoned men and women to search the world for liberty, justice, and equality. Share with me the same spirit you gave to Leif Erikson that I may venture into my world through service and sacrifice to appreciate ever more deeply the heritage that others have left to me. Amen.

World Mental Health Day
October 10

Text: "World Mental Health Day, celebrated every year on October 10, is aimed at raising awareness and spreading education about mental health issues across the globe. . . . 'In recent years, there has been increasing acknowledgement of the important role mental health plays in achieving global development goals, as illustrated by the inclusion of mental health in the Sustainable Development Goals,' according to [the] World

---

29. Trump, "Proclamation 9657."
30. Biden, "Proclamation 10280."

Health Organization (WHO). People with mental health conditions are at higher risk of dying prematurely. Depression, one of [the] commonest mental health illness[es,] is one of the leading causes of disability, while suicide is the second leading cause of death among fifteen– to twenty-nine-year-old[s], as per WHO."[31]

Reflection: Before there was World Mental Health Day, there was the World Health Organization (WHO), whose first Director-General, George Brock Chisolm, suggested that the World Federation for Mental Health (WFMH) be created as an international nongovernmental body to provide a link to mental health organizations and United Nations agencies. The WFMH was born on August 21, 1948; John Rawlings Rees, Chisolm, four psychiatrists, and one anthropologist presented the idea to the congress of the International Committee for Mental Hygiene, whose members agreed to change the name to the WFMH in order to promote among people and nations the highest possible level of mental health in its broadest biological, medical, educational, and social aspects. The World Federation for Mental Health, led by the deputy Secretary-General Richard Hunter, sponsored the first World Mental Health Day on October 10, 1992, to raise awareness of mental health issues around the world and to mobilize efforts in support of mental health care. In 1994, under the leadership of Secretary-General Eugene Brody, specific themes were chosen for each year, such as women and mental health, children and mental health, mental health and human rights, depression, mental health and older adults, dignity in mental health, mental health in the workplace, etc. According to WHO, depression is the most common mental health illness, while suicide is the second leading cause of death among those fifteen to twenty-nine years old.

Educating about mental health and raising awareness among people around the world about mental health has resulted in some people taking a mental health day. An employee, athlete, or volunteer takes a sick day for reasons other than physical illness. A mental health day is a person's true need to have a day to reset his or her mental health rather than a day to skip work. Such mental health days may be caused by major depressive disorder, bipolar disorder, or other mental illness that cause severe impairment on a person's ability to function in the workplace, in the field or on the court, or in other roles. In fact, the workplace, the game, or the anxiety can be the stressors that exacerbate episodes of depressions, mania, and other illnesses. A day away to reset focus and to treat oneself well can be the best medicine taken on a mental health day and raise awareness concerning mental health issues.

Journal/Meditation: What do you know about mental health issues? Whom do you know has been treated for mental health? Have you ever taken a mental health day? Explain.

---

31. "World Mental Health Day."

Prayer: LORD God, you created people from the dust of the earth and breathed into them the breath of life. Fill all people with your Spirit that they may enjoy mental health in your presence. Give me the wisdom to know when I need a mental health day and the courage to take it. Amen.

Columbus Day
Second Monday

Text: "The president is requested to issue each year a proclamation—(1) designating the second Monday in October as Columbus Day; (2) calling on United States government officials to display the flag of the United States on all government buildings on Columbus Day; and (3) invite the people of the United States to observe Columbus Day, in schools and churches, or other suitable places, with appropriate ceremonies that express the public sentiment befitting the anniversary of the discovery of America."[32]

Reflection: On April 30, 1934, the congress of the U.S. authorized and requested the president to designate October 12 of each year as Columbus Day. That is what Franklin D. Roosevelt did on September 30, 1934.[33] On June 28, 1968, Columbus Day became a federal holiday, effective January 1, 1971; at the same time, it was to be celebrated on the second Monday in October.[34] On August 12, 1998, the legislation concerning Columbus Day—the text above—was incorporated into Public Law 105–225. On Columbus Day 1971, the first time it was a legal federal holiday and the first time it was marked on the second Monday in October, President Richard Nixon proclaimed that the U.S. was honoring "the memory of the great captain whose historic voyages led to the migration of peoples to the New World and brought fresh promises of liberty and freedom to the Old."[35] Nixon wrote, "An intrepid explorer, a supreme navigator, but above all a man of unshakeable faith and courage, this son of Italy sailed in service of the Spanish crown on a mission that forever broadened [hu]man's hopes and horizons."[36]

While there began a practice of replacing Columbus Day with Indigenous Peoples' Day in 1992 and by 2018 had spread to some U.S. cities, the celebration of the Genovese-born explorer's arrival in the Dominican Republic, where he first set foot on October 12, 1492, continues today. With the Santa Maria, the Nina, and La Pinta ships, Columbus spent three months voyaging to the New World. His landing initiated the colonization of the Americas by Spain, followed by other European powers.

32. "Public Law 105–225," Section 107.
33. Roosevelt, "Proclamation 2101."
34. "Public Law 90–363."
35. Nixon, "Proclamation 4078."
36. Nixon, "Proclamation 4078."

In 1968, President Lyndon B. Johnson proclaimed one of the last October 12 Columbus Day observances writing that the U.S. honored "the memory of the great Italian navigator, Christopher Columbus, who sailed forth on uncharted seas in a voyage that was to change the history of the world."[37] He stated, "The breadth of his imagination, the force of his determination, and the magnitude of his achievement have not dimmed with the passing of time. We are all spiritual heirs of Christophe Columbus. His unbounded faith and courage are a part of the patrimony of every American."[38]

Journal/Meditation: What of your faith and courage is like that of Christopher Columbus? How are you a spiritual heir of Christopher Columbus?

Prayer: Holy Father, you inspired your servant Christopher Columbus with the courage to sail to the New World in service to his country. As a spiritual heir of Columbus, grant me the wisdom and courage to navigate my path to the future. All glory be to you now and forever. Amen.

National Farmer's Day

October 12

Text: ". . . National Farmer's Day . . . offers much-deserved praise to the hard-working farmers across the nation. In the midst of harvest-season, the day prays tribute to the men, women, and families who put food in the grocery stores and on our tables every day. . . . From very early in American culture, farmers set an example with their endless hard work. Not only do they provide a nation with the food we eat, but they also contribute to our economy in numerous ways. Before seeds even find their way into the ground, farmers supply a stream of jobs."[39]

Reflection: Formerly known as Old Farmer's Day, records of the events marking National Farmer's Day go back to the 1800s, but no one in particular has determined the exact origins of the day. Most likely the day began as a celebration at the end of the harvest. Now, the day is set aside for people "to give thanks to farmers, both past and present, for their hard work in producing the food and fiber which feeds and clothes people all over the world."[40] Because the day is celebrated in October, many farmers are able to take a day off from labor and join in celebrating a holiday in their honor. The day also pays tribute to ranchers, who, with farmers, plow, sow, grow, and harvest to feed the nation and get fresh food on the nation's tables. It is important to realize that about 2% of us feed and sustain the rest of us.

---

37. Johnson, "Proclamation 3873."
38. Johnson, "Proclamation 3873."
39. "National Farmer's Day."
40. Winters, "National Farmers Day."

Most consumers are not aware that farmers and ranchers contribute to manufacturing, marketing, and tourism. Both small and large communities are kept strong by farmers and ranchers. Leather, apparel, restaurants, grocery stores, beverages, textiles, trucking, railroad, forestry, fisheries, pharmaceuticals, and transportation represent some of the products and areas that rely on agriculture. Even those who visit farmer's markets may not realize how much all the products and areas represented at such venues rely on farming and ranching.

Journal/Meditation: Where do you encounter farming or ranching or both? What do farmers and ranchers contribute to the economy where you live? What can you do today to mark National Farmer's Day?

Prayer: You commissioned people to till the ground, LORD God, in order to provide plants from the earth as food to sustain their lives. When I am hungry, I look to you for food in due season, which you give to me out of your steadfast love. I thank you for all your gifts that sustain me. Amen.

White Cane Safety Day, Blind Americans Equality Day

October 15

Text: "Resolved by the Senate and House of Representatives of the United States of America in congress assembled, that the president is hereby authorized to issue annually a proclamation designating October 15 as White Cane Safety Day; and calling upon the people of the United States to observe such day with appropriate ceremonies and activities."[41]

Text: On October 6, 1964, White Cane Safety Day became Public Law 88-628 in the United States. On August 12, 1998, it was incorporated into Public Law 105-225, Section 142. The first president to issue a proclamation was Lyndon B. Johnson on October 6, 1964. He began the proclamation by giving a short history of the use of a white cane by the blind: "A white cane in our society has become one of the symbols of a blind person's ability to come and go on his [or her] own. Its use has promoted courtesy and special consideration for the blind on our streets and highways."[42] In fact, by the 1930s, the white cane had become a standard object used by people around the world to indicate blindness or impaired vision. The white color was used because it was seen easily in the darkness. The cane was also a sign of independence; "[t]he blind were able to go, to move, to be, and to compete with all others in society."[43] Johnson wrote: "To make our people more fully aware of the meaning of the white cane, and

---

41. "Public Law 88-628."
42. Johnson, "Proclamation 3622."
43. Maurer, "White Cane."

of the need for motorists to exercise special care for the blind persons who use it, the congress . . . approved . . . White Cane Safety Day."⁴⁴ He called upon all U.S. citizens "to make every effort to promote the safety and welfare of [all] blind persons on the streets and highways, and thereby to contribute to their independence of spirit and their capability for self-management."⁴⁵ Johnson issued similar proclamations in 1965 (Proclamation 3679), 1966 (Proclamation 3749), 1967 (Proclamation 3787), and 1968 (Proclamation 3846). President Richard Nixon issued his first White Cane Safety Day proclamation on May 20, 1969, writing: "A symbol of the blind person's determination to help himself [or herself] and to live a normal life is the white cane. . . . [T]he white cane helps the blind person to help himself [or herself] by increasing the range of his [or her] activities."⁴⁶ He issued similar proclamations in 1970 (Proclamation 3992), 1971 (Proclamation 4062), 1972 (Proclamation 4141), 1973 (Proclamation 4226), and 1974 (Proclamation 4301). President Gerald R. Ford issued his first proclamation on June 23, 1975, writing: "The white cane is universally recognized as one of the simplest yet most effective aids to the independent mobility of the blind." It has become a sign "of their capacity to contribute meaningfully to the progress of all Americans."⁴⁷ Later, he added, "Motorists and bicyclists should . . . be particularly alert for pedestrians using white canes and respond to their presence with an extra measure of care and caution."⁴⁸ Ford issued a similar proclamation in 1976 (Proclamation 4452). The first of President Jimmy Carter's four proclamations of White Cane Safety Day in 1977 began, "The white cane, an ingeniously simple device in an age of complex technology, helps assure that those with impaired or lost vision can lead rich and useful lives. . . . [B]lindness need not be a barrier to full participation in social and economic life, and the white cane is responsible for some of this progress."⁴⁹ He issued three more proclamations in 1978 (Proclamation 4583), 1979 (Proclamation 4678), and 1980 (Proclamation 4783). "For blind Americans, the white cane is an important sign of independence, symbolizing their ability to travel in our nation's cities and towns with great confidence and safety," began President Ronald Reagan in his first of eight proclamations. "For motorists, the white cane symbolizes caution, and reminds them that their courtesy and consideration insure the safety of the visually disabled."⁵⁰ He exhorted citizens to "extend every courtesy to those who carry [the white cane]" for by doing so, they "respect and ensure the right to independence of the visually disabled as they pursue a productive and fulfilling life."⁵¹ Reagan issued similar proclamations

44. Johnson, "Proclamation 3622."
45. Johnson, "Proclamation 3622."
46. Nixon, "Proclamation 3913."
47. Ford, "Proclamation 4380."
48. Ford, "Proclamation 4380."
49. Carter, "Proclamation 4528."
50. Reagan, "Proclamation 4863."
51. Reagan, "Proclamation 4863."

in 1982 (Proclamation 4963), 1983 (Proclamation 5091), 1984 (Proclamation 5259), 1985 (Proclamation 5382), 1986 (Proclamation 5550), 1987 (Proclamation 5730), and 1988 (Proclamation 5881). Reagan was followed by President George Bush, who issued his first White Cane Safety Day proclamation in 1989. He called the white cane, "the staff that gives blind individuals greater freedom of movement as they pursue their daily activities." He said that it enabled "its users to travel more safely in the public environment." And he stated that observing the day was "an occasion to renew . . . determination to eliminate barriers that continue to hinder the full participation of blind Americans in . . . society . . . , [and] to acknowledge the accomplishments of people who are blind . . . ."[52] He issued three more similar proclamations in 1990 (Proclamation 6200), 1991 (Proclamation 6344), and 1992 (Proclamation 6481).

Following in the footsteps of his predecessors, President William J. Clinton issued eight White Cane Safety Day proclamations. His first was in 1993. ". . . [T]he white cane means freedom," he stated in the opening paragraph, "freedom to move safely and independently through [visually impaired Americans'] daily lives, participating fully in the activities of their homes, places of employment, and communities." He added that the day "recognizes our nation's commitment to remove any physical or attitudinal barriers that Americans with disabilities may still face."[53] He issued similar proclamations in 1994 (Proclamation 6741), 1995 (Proclamation 6840), 1996 (Proclamation 6941), 1997 (Proclamation 7037), 1998 (Proclamation 7140), 1999 (Proclamation 7240), and 2000 (Proclamation 7367). Likewise, George W. Bush issued eight proclamations, his first in 2001. He stated that the observance of White Cane Safety Day represented "a declaration of freedom. It also signifie[d] a commitment by the sighted community to improve access to basic services for blind and visually impaired persons," whose white cane enabled them "to participate in the facets of daily life." He called upon Americans to join him in opening "the doors of opportunity further and making the American dream a reality for all blind and visually impaired citizens of [the] nation."[54] Bush issued similar proclamations in 2002 (Proclamation 7610), 2003 (Proclamation 7722), 2004 (Proclamation 7833), 2005 (Proclamation 7949), 2006 (Proclamation 8069), 2007 (Proclamation 8191), and 2008 (Proclamation 8307). President Barack Obama, who followed Bush as president of the U.S., issued his first of two White Cane Safety Day proclamations in 2009. "For blind Americans, the white cane is a potent symbol of . . . freedom," he wrote, "affording them greater independence and mobility." He renewed the U.S.'s "commitment to provide full inclusion and equal opportunities for those . . . who are blind or have low vision," also stating, that the "white cane is just one of a wide range of tools that sustain independence and productivity."[55] Obama noted that 2009 was the forty-fifth anniversary of the first White Cane Safety Day;

52. Bush, "Proclamation 6047."
53. Clinton, "Proclamation 6612."
54. Bush, G.W., "Proclamation 7486."
55. Obama, "Proclamation 8439."

"Americans who are blind or have low vision have achieved substantial progress," he said, also noting the "remarkable contributions to [the] nation" made by the visually impaired, "proving that sight is no requisite for success."[56] He issued his second similar proclamation in 2010 (Proclamation 8588). In 2011, Obama changed the name of the day to Blind Americans Equality Day.[57] "Generations of blind and visually impaired Americans have dedicated their passion and skills to enhancing our national life," he began, "leading as public servants, penning works of literature, lending their voice to music, and inspiring as champions of sport. . . . [W]e celebrate the achievements of blind and visually impaired Americans and reaffirm our commitment to advancing their complete social and economic integration."[58] In the proclamation, he mentioned White Cane Safety Day, but proclaimed October 15 Blind Americans Equality Day. He issued five more similar proclamations in 2012 (Proclamation 8889), 2013 (Proclamation 9042), 2014 (Proclamation 9195), 2015 (Proclamation 9349), and 2016 (Proclamation 9575). Following Obama's lead, President Donald J. Trump issued four Blind Americans Equality Day proclamations. His first, in 2017, stated, ". . . [W]e celebrate the achievements of our blind and visually impaired citizens. These individuals make meaningful contributions every day to our country, enhancing and strengthening our communities and our culture. . . . [W]e rededicate our efforts and continue working to ensure all Americans, including those who are blind or visually impaired, have every opportunity to achieve success."[59] He issued similar proclamations in 2018 (Proclamation 9807), 2019 (Proclamation 9950), and 2020 (Proclamation 10102). In his first Blind American Equality Day proclamation, President Joseph R. Biden, stated, ". . . [W]e recognize the rights, talents, and contributions of blind and visually impaired Americans who represent every segment of our diverse population." He added, ". . . [W]e recommit to ensuring freedom, equality, and opportunity for all blind and visually impaired Americans, whose contributions continue to make our nation stronger."[60] In his two-page proclamation, Biden mentions that what is now named Blind Americans Equality Day—"to honor the contributions of blind and visually impaired Americans"[61]—was formerly named White Cane Safety Day. Thus, on October 15, the achievements of blind and visually impaired people are celebrated, and the sign of their blindness—the tool of independence—is the white cane.

Journal/**Reflection**: If there is a visually impaired person in your neighborhood, or if you know one, who uses a white cane, how is the white cane a sign of mobility, independence, freedom, participation, contribution, and useful life? If there is no visually

---

56. Obama, "Proclamation 8439."
57. "Blind Americans, 125 Statute 2104."
58. Obama, "Proclamation 8739."
59. Trump, "Proclamation 9662."
60. Biden, "Proclamation 10288."
61. Biden, "Proclamation 10288."

impaired person in your neighborhood, or if you do not know one, who uses a white cane, what one statement by a U.S. president got most of your attention? Why?

Prayer: O LORD, you open the eyes of the blind and visually impaired by giving them hope of freedom, independence, and the opportunity to participate in society and live a right and useful life. Open my blind eyes to see the needs of the blind and visually impaired, and give me grace to treat them with respect, human dignity, and honor in your sight. Amen.

World Food Day
October 16

Text: "Considering that food is a requisite of human survival and wellbeing and a fundamental human right; . . . being concerned that the problem of providing a balanced adequate diet for the world's population is greater than ever and that on the basis of most criteria the world food situation has deteriorated; . . . believing in the necessity to mobilize and sustain interest and support for the necessary long-term effort to overcome widespread malnutrition; further believing that a material stimulus and incentive in this regard would be the establishment of a World Food Day; [the conference of the United Nations Food and Agriculture Organization] decides to establish a World Food Day to be observed annually on 16 October, the anniversary of the founding of the Food and Agriculture Organization of the United Nations . . . ."[62]

Reflection: In 1945, the Food and Agriculture Organization (FAO) of the United Nations was founded on October 16. On November 28, 1979, the FAO initiated World Food Day to be observed on October 16 annually to mark its founding. In the resolution establishing World Food Day, six objectives were presented. First, the FAO wanted to raise public awareness of both the nature and dimensions of the long-term world food problem and to develop a national and international sense of solidarity in the struggle against hunger, malnutrition, and poverty. Second, it hoped to bring greater attention to world agricultural production and stimulate efforts toward that end on all levels of government and non-government. Third, the FAO wanted to foster the sharing of science and technology among countries for the benefit of small farmers and landless laborers in the hope of an agricultural revolution through new biological approaches. It wanted to draw attention to successes achieved in food and agricultural development, according to its fourth objective. Objectives five and six promoted participation by the rural masses in decisions and measures affecting their development, and encouraged economic and technical cooperation among developing countries in agriculture, forestry, and fisheries and in nutrition and rural development.

---

62. Resolution 1/79, Food and Agriculture Organization.

In order to accomplish its objectives, FAO leads international efforts to defeat hunger with the goal to achieve food security for all people. In general, food security exists when all people at all times are free from hunger. In more technical terms, when all people at all times have physical, social, and economic access to sufficient, safe, and nutritious food, which meets their dietary needs and food preferences for an active and healthy life, food security exists.[63] World Food Day was first celebrated in the United States in 1982; it is sponsored by 450 national, private voluntary organizations. The day is focused on the World Food Day theme, which has been provided by the FAO since 1981. The theme highlights an area that needs action and provides a common focus for those marking the day. Such themes as women in agriculture, rural poverty, food and the environment, fighting hunger and malnutrition, water for life, the right to food, family farming, ending world hunger, etc. have been employed. George-Andre Simon notes four dimensions of food security: availability (the amount of food present), access (ability to acquire food physically, financially, and socio-culturally), utilization (safe and nutritious food which meets dietary needs), and stability (permanent basis with sustainability).[64] Consequently, "a situation where some people do not have access to sufficient quantities of safe and nutritious food and hence do not consume the food that they need to grow normally and conduct an active and healthy life" is defined as food insecurity.[65] Thus, World Food Day attempts to raise awareness of the issues behind poverty and hunger.

Journal/Meditation: In general, what is the status of food security and food insecurity where you live? How can you combat hunger?

Prayer: Once you opened your hand and fed your people with mana, quail, and water in the desert, O LORD. Your Son, Jesus Christ, taught his followers to feed each other with the little bit of food each possessed. Inspire me to do all I can to remove food insecurity where I live today, tomorrow, and forever. Amen.

National Boss's Day
October 16

Text: "Patricia Bays Haroski laid the groundwork for national Boss's Day while working as a secretary for her father at State Farm Insurance Company, in Deerfield, Illinois. She honored her father on his birthday, October 16, by registering the secular holiday with the U.S. Chamber of Commerce in 1958. In 1962, Illinois Governor Otto Kerner proclaimed the day an official holiday. By 1979, National Boss's Day was generally

---

63. Simon, "Food Security," Section 2.1.
64. Simon, "Food Security," Section 2.2.
65. Simon, "Food Security," Section 3.1.

recognized throughout the United States. Within the past decade, the day has been celebrated to some extent in Australia, India, Ireland, South Africa, and the U.K."[66]

Reflection: Also known as National Boss Day and Bosses Day, National Boss's Day recognizes the boss, who supervises the workplace. The day, marked on October 16 (on a weekend the celebration is moved to Friday or Monday), employees have the opportunity to show appreciation and thankfulness to their bosses and to remember the boss's kindness and fairness throughout the year. Haroski, as noted in the above text, desired to honor her father, but she also wanted to improve the relationship between employees and supervisors; she understood that younger employees did not often know about the challenges their bosses faced in running a business. Employees may give their supervisors cards, gift certificates, flowers, coffee, host a potluck, share the boss's accomplishments, etc. The goal is to work on the boss-employee relationship by fostering mutual trust and respect which results in good communication.

Alison Green provides five reasons why the day should not be celebrated. She states, first, that the boss's position is one of power that makes it very inappropriate to solicit recognition from employees, "especially to make them feel it's obligatory. Obligatory appreciation doesn't count for much."[67] Second, "one of the problems with Boss's Day is that it makes all appreciation offered up under its auspices suspect."[68] Third, "[i]t creates inappropriate monetary pressure on employees. . . . Employees should never feel pressured to dip into their own funds to pay for a gift to the boss."[69] This is because, fourth, "[g]ood bosses don't want gifts from their subordinates. Good bosses . . . don't want employees feeling even slightly obligated to shell out for this type of thing."[70] And, fifth, the day "flies in the face of etiquette. Traditional etiquette says . . . that any gift-giving in the workplace should be from a boss to an employee and not the other way around."[71] Because this day is an observance and not a nationwide public holiday, it was not celebrated until Kerner proclaimed the day an official holiday in 1962. While it is marked by some businesses, others choose to ignore it.

Journal/Meditation: If you have a boss, what do you specifically value about him or her? If you are a boss, what do you consider your greatest strength to be? If you are self-employed, what does this day mean to you?

Prayer: Creator God, in your sight all men and women share equality. In my sight, some men and women serve as bosses and some as employees. Grant bosses a great deal of kindness and fairness toward employees; and grant employees a great deal of

---

66. Wilkie, "Challenges."
67. Green, "5 Reasons."
68. Green, "5 Reasons."
69. Green, "5 Reasons."
70. Green, "5 Reasons."
71. Green, "5 Reasons."

trust and respect toward their bosses. May bosses and employees work together for the greater good of the nation. Amen.

INTERNATIONAL DAY FOR THE ERADICATION OF POVERTY
October 17

Text: "The General Assembly [of the United Nations], noting that the eradication of poverty and destitution in all countries, in particular in developing countries, has become one of the priorities of development . . . , and considering that the promotion of the eradication of poverty and destitution requires public awareness, . . . decides to declare 17 October International Day for the Eradication of Poverty, to be observed beginning in 1993; . . . [and] invites all states to devote the day to presenting and promoting, as appropriate in the national context, concrete activities with regard to the eradication of poverty and destitution . . . ."[72]

Reflection: On December 22, 1992, the General Assembly of the United Nations passed a resolution to observe annually October 17 as the International Day for the Eradication of Poverty beginning in 1993. According to the U.N. Homepage for the International Day for the Eradication of Poverty, the observance began on October 17, 1987, in Paris, where over one hundred thousand people gathered where the Universal Declaration of Human Rights was signed in 1948, to honor victims of extreme poverty, violence, and hunger. "They proclaimed that poverty is a violation of human rights and affirmed the need to come together to ensure that these rights are respected."[73] The convictions of those gathered in Paris were put into words, inscribed on a memorial stone, and unveiled in 1987: "Wherever men and women are condemned to live in extreme poverty, human rights are violated. To come together to ensure that these rights are respected is our solemn duty."[74] Observing the day promotes dialogue and understanding between people who live in poverty and their communities. Those who live in poverty and destitution are given the opportunity to have their voices heard about their efforts and struggles. The day "reflects the willingness of people living in poverty to use their expertise to contribute to the eradication of poverty."[75] According to the U.N., "In a world characterized by an unprecedented level of economic development, technological means, and financial resources, that millions of persons are living in extreme poverty is a moral outrage. Persons living in poverty experience many interrelated and mutually reinforcing deprivations that prevent them from realizing their rights and perpetuate their poverty, including: dangerous work conditions,

---

72. United Nations General Assembly, A/RES/47/196.
73. "International Day . . . Poverty—Homepage."
74. "International Day for Eradication of Poverty," Wikipedia.
75. "International Day . . . Poverty—Homepage."

unsafe housing, lack of nutritious food, unequal access to justice, lack of political power, and limited access to health care."[76]

In these (post) COVID-19 pandemic days, it is important to be aware that between 88 and 115 million people are being pushed into poverty as a result of the crisis, creating a new extreme poor. The measures imposed to limit the spread of the pandemic, although necessary, have further pushed the new poor even further into poverty. In other words, the economy which enabled many people in poverty to survive was shut down in many countries. According to the U.N. web page about the day, those pushed into extreme poverty by the pandemic do not want to build back better to what they were before. "They do not want a return to the endemic structural disadvantages and inequalities. Instead, people living in poverty propose to build forward. Building forward means transforming our relationship with nature, dismantling structures of discrimination that disadvantage people in poverty, and building on the moral and legal framework of human rights that places human dignity at the heart of policy and action."[77] The web page states, "Building forward means not only that no one is left behind, but that people living in poverty are actively encouraged and supported to be in the front, engaging in informed and meaningful participation in decision-making processes that directly affect their lives."[78]

Journal/Meditation: How do you think poverty is a violation of human rights? Do you think poverty is a moral outrage? Explain. How can you help the poor build forward where you live?

Prayer: LORD God, throughout history the poor have always been your special concern. With your Spirit as my guide, raise my awareness concerning what perpetuates poverty and give me the courage to participate in decision-making processes that enhance human rights. Amen.

Missouri Day
Third Wednesday

Text: "The third Wednesday of October of each year is known and designated as 'Missouri Day' and is set apart as a day commemorative of Missouri history to be observed by the teachers and pupils of schools with the appropriate exercises. The people of the state of Missouri, and the educational, commercial, political, civic, religious, and fraternal organizations of the state of Missouri are requested to devote some part of the day to the methodical consideration of the products of the mines, fields, and forests of the state and to the consideration of the achievements of the sons and daughters of

---

76. "International Day for the Eradication of Poverty—U.N."
77. "International Day for the Eradication of Poverty—U.N."
78. "International Day for the Eradication of Poverty—U.N."

Missouri in commerce, literature, statesmanship, science and art, and in other departments of activity in which the state has rendered service to [human]kind."[79]

Reflection: Originally, Missouri Day was held on the first Monday in October, but it was moved to the third Wednesday of October on August 28, 1969. Native Missourian and Trenton schoolteacher Anna Lee Brosius Korn was instrumental in getting Missouri Day established in 1915 to teach students about Missouri history. Missouri Day in October is not the same as National Missouri Day on January 4, established in 2017 by National Day Calendar. As can been concluded from the above text, there are three aspects to the day: (1) Missouri history, (2) Missouri products, and (3) important Missouri people. First, Missouri history: Missouri entered the union as the twenty-fourth sate on August 10, 1821, at the same time as Maine; Missouri entered as a slave state, and Maine entered as a free state; it was called the Missouri Compromise. During the Civil War, Missouri was divided; the north served the Union, and the south served the Confederacy. The state capital is in Jefferson City, while the most populated cities are: Kansas City, St. Louis, Springfield, Independence, and Columbia. Missouri is known as the "Show Me" state. The Missouri State bird is the Eastern Bluebird;[80] the state game bird is the Northern Bobwhite Quail;[81] the Missouri State Flag consists of three horizontal stripes of red, white, and blue with the Missouri coat of arms centered over the stripes and encircled by a blue band containing twenty-four stars;[82] the state floral emblem is the hawthorn;[83] the state arboreal emblem is the flowering dogwood;[84] the state lithologic (rock) emblem is Mozarkite;[85] the state mineral is galena;[86] the state song is the "Missouri Waltz;"[87] the great seal of the state, whose center is composed of two parts: on the right is the United States coat of arms containing the bald eagle with arrows and olive branches in its claws signifying war and peace, and on the left is a grizzly bear and a silver crescent moon from the Missouri coat of arms; the arms is encircled by a belt inscribed with "United We Stand, Divided We Fall;" two grizzly bears on either side of the arms signify strength and bravery, and they stand on top of a scroll bearing the state motto: "Salus Populi Suprema Lex Esto" ("Let the good of the people be the supreme law") with 1820 below the scroll, the year Missouri

---

79. Revisor of Missouri, 9.040.
80. Revisor of Missouri, 10.010.
81. Revisor of Missouri, 10.012.
82. Revisor of Missouri, 10.020.
83. Revisor of Missouri, 10.030.
84. Revisor of Missouri, 10.040.
85. Revisor of Missouri, 10.045.
86. Revisor of Missouri, 10.047.

87. Revisor of Missouri, 10.050. The "Missouri Waltz" contains two stanzas which mention Missouri: (2) "Way down in Missouri where I heard this melody / When I was a little child upon my Mommy's knee; / The old folks were hummin'; their banjos were strummin'; / So sweet and low." (6) "Way down in Missouri where I learned this lullaby, / When the stars were blinkin' / and the moon was climbin' high; / Seems I hear voices low, as in days long ago, / Singin' hush-a-bye."

began functioning as a state; above the bears are twenty-three smaller stars and one larger one, indicating that Missouri was the twenty-fourth state to enter the Union; the whole seal is enclosed by a scroll bearing the words "The Great Seal of the State of Missouri;[88] the state musical instrument is the fiddle;[89] the state fossil is the crinoid, commonly known as a sea lily;[90] the state dinosaur is the *Parrosaurus missouriensis*;[91] the state tree nut is the eastern black walnut;[92] the state fruit tree is the Pawpaw;[93] the state animal is the Missouri mule;[94] the state historical dog is Old Drum;[95] the state wonder dog is Jim;[96] the state exercise is jumping jacks;[97] the state American Folk Dance is the Square Dance;[98] the state invertebrate is the crayfish;[99] the state aquatic animal is the paddlefish;[100] Missouri's state fish is the channel catfish; [101] the state horse is the Missouri Fox Trotting Horse;[102] the state's purple martin capital is Adrian;[103] the state grass is the Big Bluestem;[104] the state grape is the Norton (Cynthiana) Grape;[105] the state insect is the honeybee;[106] the state amphibian is the American Bullfrog;[107] the state reptile is the three-toed box turtle;[108] the state dessert is the ice cream cone;[109] the state child abuse prevention sign is a blue ribbon;[110] the state tartan features a design of crisscrossing blue, red, brown, and white lines on a field of dark blue and green;[111] the state's official endangered species is the hellbender salamander;[112] the St. Louis

88. Revisor of Missouri, 10.060.
89. Revisor of Missouri, 10.080.
90. Revisor of Missouri, 10.090.
91. Revisor of Missouri, 10.095.
92. Revisor of Missouri, 10.100.
93. Revisor of Missouri, 10.105.
94. Revisor of Missouri, 10.110.
95. Revisor of Missouri, 10.112.
96. Revisor of Missouri, 10.113.
97. Revisor of Missouri, 10.115.
98. Revisor of Missouri, 10.120.
99. Revisor of Missouri, 10.125.
100. Revisor of Missouri, 10.130.
101. Revisor of Missouri, 10.135.
102. Revisor of Missouri, 10.140.
103. Revisor of Missouri, 10.141.
104. Revisor of Missouri, 10.150.
105. Revisor of Missouri, 10.160.
106. Revisor of Missouri, 10.170.
107. Revisor of Missouri, 10.170.
108. Revisor of Missouri, 10.175.
109. Revisor of Missouri, 10.180.
110. Revisor of Missouri, 10.185.
111. Revisor of Missouri, 10.190.
112. Revisor of Missouri, 10.200.

Blues is the official state hockey team;[113] and the Gateway Arch is Missouri's official state monument.[114]

Second, Missouri's major products include livestock (beef cattle and hogs), poultry (chickens and turkeys), forest products, dairy products, and crops (soybeans, corn, cotton, rice, wheat, and hay). Fruit crops include apples, peaches, grapes, and watermelons. Vegetable crops include potatoes, tomatoes, pumpkins. When it comes to mining, lead and limestone are the most important. Missouri is also home to a variety of manufacturing businesses. Third, some famous Missourians include Maya Angelou, a poet; Josephine Baker, an entertainer; Thomas Hart Benton, an artist; George Caleb Bingham, an artist; Susan Elizabeth Blow, an educator; Daniel Boone, an adventurer; Omar N. Bradley, a military leader; George Washington Carver, a scientist; Christopher (Kit) Carson, an adventurer; William Clark, an explorer; Samuel Clemens (Mark Twain), an author; Walt Disney, a cartoonist; St. Rose Philippine Duchesne, a sainted missionary; Eugene Field, a children's author; Phoebe Apperson Hearst, a volunteer and children's activist; Edwin Powell Hubble, an astronomer; James Langston Hughes, a musician; Jesse James, an outlaw; Scott Joplin, a musician; Emmett Kelly, a clown; James Cash (J.C.) Penny, a businessman; John J. Pershing, a military leader; Joseph Pulitzer, a newspaperman; Stuart Symington, a public official; Harry S. Truman, president of the U.S.; and Laura Ingalls Wilder, an author. Thus, on the third Wednesday of October we celebrate Missouri history, Missouri products, and remember outstanding Missouri people.

Journal/Meditation: What one bit of history about Missouri did you learn from the above reflection? What one item produced in Missouri surprised you? Who do you think is the most outstanding Missourian?

Prayer: Heavenly Father, you inspired the founding fathers and mothers of Missouri to remember that united they stood, but divided they fell. Inspire all state citizens with a spirit of unity, and fill all state government leaders with the will to let the good of the people always be the supreme law today, tomorrow, and forever. Amen.

Sweetest Day
Third Saturday

Text: "Sweetest Day began in Cleveland in 1922[115] when a man named Herbert Birch Kingston decided to bring a little happiness into the lives of orphans, shut-ins, and others who were often forgotten. With the help of friends, he distributed candy and small gifts to Cleveland's underprivileged. On the very first Sweetest Day, actress Ann

---

113. Revisor of Missouri, 10.225.
114. Revisor of Missouri, 10.240.
115. Various sources have various dates for the first Sweetest Day: October 8, 1921 (most likely); October 10, 1921; October 18, 1921; the second Sweetest Day was October 14, 1922.

Pennington . . . presented 2,200 Cleveland newspaper boys with boxes of candy to express gratitude for their service to the public. Another popular actress, Theda Bara, . . . gave away ten thousand boxes of candy to patients in Cleveland hospitals and to those who came to watch her film in a local Cleveland theater. . . . Sweetest Day has its roots in random acts of kindness . . . ."[116]

Reflection: The forerunner of Sweetest Day was Candy Day, which came into existence on May 10, 1916, when the National Confectioners' Association (NCA) members approved a motion to designate a Saturday in October as Candy Day. The first such celebration occurred on October 14, 1916. In 1917, the October 6 observance was cancelled due to Herbert Hoover's reminder to the NCA that it would be contrary to the World War I effort to conserve sugar. And that would have been the end of it except for Herbert Birch Kingston, who was either president of the Kingston Co. (a Cleveland advertising company)[117] or a Cleveland candy company employee and philanthropist.[118] Kingston renamed the day and retooled it to serve as motivation to help the less fortunate. His goal was to bring a little happiness into the lives of orphans, shut-ins, and others who were often forgotten. He got eight Cleveland confectioners to come together in 1921 to form the Sweetest Day in the Year Committee chaired by Carleton C. Hartzell. October 8, 1921, was chosen to be Sweetest Day, whose purpose was to bring happiness to everyone. Kingston wanted the day to be one of philanthropy, an occasion to express kindness and tenderness especially to those often forgotten. According to Mitch Allen, "Kingston's goal was to encourage each of us to express a more spiritual love that so often goes unexpressed—the love we have for strangers."[119]

The October 2, 1921, issue of the *Cleveland Plain Dealer* featured a four-page special section about the first Sweetest Day. The front page featured stories about remembering friends, wives, and loved ones, the eight confectioners who designed the day, and the large number of candy manufacturers in Cleveland, Ohio. The second page was filled with candy ads. Stories about candy's food value for energy dominated page 3. And page 4 carried stories about orphans getting boxes of candy, the making of fudge, and a long list of candy dealers in Cleveland. The October 2, 1922, special section of the *Cleveland Plain Dealer* carried headlines about the Sweetest Day being named for everyone, and doctors were the first to introduce candies. Page 2 featured the photos of the members of the committee, which had grown from eight to twelve, along with a story about eating candy as part of a meal and dates being the oldest of sweets. Modern candy makers were declared to be skilled laborers on page 3, and page 4 was a full-page ad about the Sweetest Day in the year being Saturday, October 14,

---

116. Allen, "Origins." In Allen, "Origins (Updated)," the first day is listed as October 8, 1921.
117. Allen, "Origins (Updated)."
118. Oatman, "What is Sweetest Day?"
119. Allen, "Origins (Updated)."

1922.[120] Kingston's goal of encouraging each of us to express a more spiritual love that so often goes unexpressed is found in the opening line of the ad: "Love is always the dominant motif in a successful life. Most of us have love in our hearts, but too often it remains there, never manifesting itself before those who inspire it. . . . On this day, . . . steal enough time from the turmoil of routine affairs to bring a bit of good sheer to those you love. A present, perhaps, and more than that add a loving word—a smile—a kiss. . . . The Sweetest Day is worthy of our attention. Regard its observance as a sacred duty—and a rare opportunity."[121] While a romantic element has entered into the observance of this day (making it a type of Valentine's Day in October), it is still possible to give a card with a sweet message to someone you appreciate, candy, other sweets, flowers, trinkets, etc. One can also invite friends for a candy-making session, share favorite candy recipes, surprise someone with a special coffee, invite a friend for dinner, or share doughnuts. Any kind of a token of spiritual love will be appreciated by the postal carrier, the grocery store clerk, and coworkers.

Journal/Meditation: What has been your most recent random act of kindness? To whom have you brought a little happiness recently? How is spiritual love a dominant motif in your life?

Prayer: God, out of your abundant kindness you provided your people with the sweetest of honey from the rock. Fill me with spiritual love that my random acts of kindness may be sweet to you and demonstrate that my generosity flows from you and gives your glory now and forever. Amen.

UNITED NATIONS DAY
October 24

Text: "The General Assembly, conscious of the need to enhance the purposes and principles of the Charter of the United Nations, mindful that in its resolution 168 (II) of 31 October 1947 the General Assembly declared 24 October, the anniversary of the coming into force of the Charter, as 'United Nations Day,' believing that the anniversary of the United Nations should be an occasion for governments and peoples to reaffirm their faith in the purposes and principles of the Charter, declares that 24 October, United Nations Day, shall be an international holiday and recommends that it should be observed as a public holiday by all states, members of the United Nations."[122]

Reflection: As indicated in the above text, issued December 6, 1971, the General Assembly of the United Nations had on October 31, 1947, declared that October 24, "the

---

120. For pictures of *Cleveland Plain Dealer's* two special sections, visit Exner, "Sweetest Day," https://cleveland.com/news/2021/10/what-is-sweetest-day-unofficial-holiday-has-cleveland-roots.html.
121. Exner, "Sweetest Day."
122. United Nations General Assembly, A/RES/2782(XXVI).

anniversary of the coming into force of the Charter of the United Nations," would "officially [be] called 'United Nations Day' and . . . be devoted to making known to the peoples of the world the aims and achievements of the United Nations and to gaining their support for the work of the United Nations . . . ."[123] The 1971 resolution encouraged member nations to observe it as a public holiday. The purpose of the day is for member states of the U.N. to amplify their common agenda and to reaffirm the purposes and principles of the U.N. Charter. Around the world, U.N. Day is celebrated with meetings, discussions, and exhibits about achievements and goals of the U.N. In honor of the twenty-fifth anniversary of the U.N. poet W.H. Auden of the United Kingdom wrote a poem, and Pablo Casals of Spain set it to music. Titled "A Hymn to the United Nations," it is often played during the annual concert held in the General Assembly Hall of the U.N. Headquarters in New York on U.N. Day. "Let music for peace / Be the paradigm, / For peace means to change At / the right time, as the World- / Clock / Goes Tick- and Tock. / So may the story / Of our human city / Presently move / Like music, when / Begotten notes / New notes beget / Making the flowing / of time a growing / Till what it could be / At last it is, / Where even sadness / In a form of gladness, / When fate is freedom, / Grace and Surprise."[124] The annual U.N. Day serves as a call to strengthen international cooperation in the interest of both nations and peoples for a more peaceful and prosperous future for all.

In the United States, every year the president issues a proclamation for United Nations Day. The first was issued by Harry S. Truman on September 9, 1948. Truman noted that ". . . [T]he people of the United States are united in a firm resolve to cooperate effectively with other countries, through the medium of the United Nations, to the end that a future of peace, freedom, and justice may prevail upon the earth."[125] Truman continues, ". . . [I]t is fitting that the devotion of the American people to the ideals expressed in the Charter of the United Nations should be reaffirmed in our inmost hearts and expressed in public ceremonies. . . . [I]t is our desire that our support of the United Nations be given added strength and positive affirmation through the activities of an informed public."[126] Truman urged U.S. citizens to observe the day with exercises exemplifying their recognition of the achievements of the U.N., their support of its aims, and their determination to strive for the realization of those aims. He also called upon officers at all levels of government, civic, educational, and religious organizations and institutions, and the media "to cooperate in programs designed to give public expression to . . . devotion to the United Nations and to make more effective [the citizens'] participation in the work of the United Nations . . . ."[127]

123. United Nations General Assembly, A/RES/168(II).
124. "Does the U.N.?"
125. Truman, "Proclamation 2811."
126. Truman, "Proclamation 2811."
127. Truman, "Proclamation 2811."

Journal/Meditation: What do you consider to be the greatest achievement of the United Nations? What truth does the portion of Auden's "A Hymn to the United Nations," quoted above, reveal to you? How can you participate in the work of the United Nations?

Prayer: Father and Mother of all peoples, I give you thanks for the work done by men and women who lead the United Nations. I pray that all your children reaffirm the dignity and worth of every person and that your grace ensure life for all now and forever. Amen.

National Mother-in-Law Day
Fourth Sunday

Text: "Maybe you've heard it before: You marry the family. When you say 'I do,' you inherit a new set of siblings, parents, and cousins, and that includes your spouse's mom. National Mother-in-Law Day celebrates the woman who raised your significant other and made [him or her] the person [he or she is] today."[128]

Reflection: When two people enter into marriage, each of them gets a mother-in-law, the mother of one's spouse. The first Mother-in-Law Day was marked on March 5, 1934, in Amarillo, Texas. It was begun by the editor of a local newspaper, Gene Howe, to atone for belittling his own mother-in-law in his editorial column. After that, holidays honoring mothers-in-law were held on various dates around the country until 1975, when the National Mothers-in-Law Day Council set the date as the last Sunday of October. Two floral organizations got involved in promoting the day in 1977: Society of American Florists and Florists' Transworld Delivery (FTD). Since 1977, mothers-in-law have been honored for their contributions to the success of families on National Mother-in-Law Day on the fourth Sunday in October.

Mothers-in-law can be honored with love and thanksgiving for help and support with a message written in a card or letter. A gift of flowers, chocolates, or lunch is also appropriate. Dinner at a favorite restaurant, performing a task for her in her home, playing her favorite card game, or asking her to teach something only she knows how to do are other ways to observe the day. If one's mother-in-law has died, a visit to her grave will honor her on this day. National Mother-in-Law Day celebrates the other mother in many people's lives.

Journal/Meditation: Specifically, what do you recognize in your spouse as coming from your mother-in-law? What has your mother-in-law contributed to the success of your family?

---

128. "National Mother-in-Law Day."

Prayer: Ever-loving God, you bestow your grace upon all people. Pour your gift upon my mother-in-law that it may be seen in every facet of her life. Grant that the deep love you have for her may, through her daily life, reveal your love for all today, tomorrow, and forever. Amen.

National Chocolate Day
October 28

Text: "Chocolate is a confection made from cacao seeds, which grow on cacao trees in the tropics. Seeds are removed from their pods and then dried, roasted, and ground into cacao powder or paste, which is then mixed with other ingredients such as butters, oils, sweeteners, milk, and flour to produce chocolate."[129]

Reflection: The above text, taken from the *WinCalendar* webpage on "National Chocolate Day," serves as a fitting introduction for one of three national chocolate days (July 7,[130] October 28,[131] December 28[132]), World (International) Chocolate Day (July 7[133]), and International Chocolate Day (September 13[134]). Chocolate, coming from the Aztec word *xocolatl*—meaning *bitter water*—is made from the seed of the tropical Theobrama cacao tree. *Theobrama* means *food of the gods*. After picking the cacao pods, they are cleaned of the pithy white material from the fruit and dried. Then, they are fermented to develop the flavor and remove the bitter taste. After fermenting, processors dry, clean, and roast the beans. "The papery shell is removed and cacao nibs are revealed. Chocolatiers then grind them into cacao mass, separate them into cacao solids and cacao butter, combine them with milk and sugar, or in the case of white chocolate, just the chocolate butter with milk and sugar."[135] Cocoa beans are about 50 percent cocoa butter and 50 percent chocolate liquid. Historians document the earliest use of cacao seeds from around 1900 BCE. According to *Holidays Calendar*: "The Olmecs made a drink out of chocolate and placed it in special jars known as *tecomates*. They most likely passed down this preparation of chocolate to the Mayans, who enjoyed drinking the chocolate drink from tall cylinder beakers. The Aztecs also had special cups just for drinking chocolate drinks, and some historians believe this was because drinking chocolate was a status symbol, and so drinking chocolate was a

---

129. "National Chocolate Day," *WinCalendar*.
130. Chocolate was brought to Europe on July 7, 1550.
131. National Chocolate Day was created by the National Confectioners Association.
132. National Chocolate Candy Day.
133. Chocolate was brought to Europe on July 7, 1550. The first World (International) Chocolate Day was celebrated on July 7, 2009.
134. The National Confectioners Association began International Chocolate Day to coincide with the birthday of Milton Hershey on September 13, 1857.
135. "National Chocolate Day," *National Today*.

way to show off social status or wealth."[136] According to *National Today*: "Aztecs loved their newly discovered liquid chocolate to the extent that they believed Quetzalcoatl, the god of wisdom, literally bestowed it upon them. Cacao seeds acted as a form of currency."[137] Hernando Cortes (1485–1547), the Spanish conquistador who led the expedition that caused the fall of the Aztec Empire in Mexico, brought cocoa beans to Spain, where a chocolate drink with sugar became popular. By 1550 chocolate spread across Europe, with the word *chocolate* first appearing in print in England in 1604.

Chocolate came to what would become the United States in 1765, with the first chocolate factory opening in 1780. It was not until the 1860s when chocolate creams—candies with sugar-cream centers—were eaten by Americans. In England, John Cadbury opened a shop in Birmingham in 1824 and sold drinking chocolate and cocoa in his shop. He began making chocolate bars in 1842. Henri Nestle, who opened a chocolate shop in Vevey, Switzerland, in 1866, grew into one of the largest food conglomerates in the world. Meanwhile, milk chocolate was invented in Switzerland in 1875, when Daniel Peter added his chocolate to the newly-discovered sweetened condensed milk of Nestle. That inspired Milton S. Hershey to purchase chocolate processing equipment at the World's Columbian Exposition in Chicago in 1893 and make and sell chocolate-covered caramels. He was producing his own milk chocolates in 1900, erecting a large factory in Derry Township, Pennsylvania, in 1905, and inventing the famous Hersey Kiss in 1907 with its trademark foil wrapper added in 1924. On the West Coast, Franklin C. Mars was inspired to begin Mars Candy Factory in Tacoma, Washington, in 1911, and to make a variety of chocolate candy bars. Today, many people prefer dark chocolate because it contains less sugar than milk chocolate. Nevertheless, chocolate is sold in four basic common types: (1) unsweetened chocolate for baking, (2) sweet chocolate for cocoa solids and cocoa butter, (3) milk chocolate for sweet candy, and (4) white chocolate with no cocoa solids. In addition to the chocolate days listed above, there are also: National Chocolate Covered Cherry Day (January 3), National Bittersweet Chocolate Day (January 10), National Chocolate Cake Day (January 27), National Hot Chocolate Day (January 31), Dark Chocolate Day (February 1), National Chocolate Fondue Day (February 5), World Nutella Day (February 5), Cream Cheese Brownie Day (February 10), National Cream-Filled Chocolates Day (February 14), National Chocolate Mint Day (February 19), National Chocolate Covered Nuts Day (February 25), National Chocolate Souffle Day (February 28), National Oreo Cookie Day (March 6), National White Chocolate Cheesecake Day (March 6), National Chocolate Caramel Day (March 19), National Chocolate Covered Raisin Day (March 24), National Black Forest Cake Day (March 28), National Chocolate Mousse Day (April 3), National Chocolate Covered Cashews Truffle Day (April 21), National Devil Dog Cakes Day (April 27), National Chocolate Parfait Day (May 1), National Truffles Day (May 2), National Chocolate Custard Day

---

136. "National Chocolate Day," *Holidays Calendar*.
137. "National Chocolate Day," *National Today*.

(May 3), National Nutty Fudge Day (May 12), National Chocolate Chip Day (May 15), National Devil's Food Cake Day (May 19), National Rocky Road Ice Cream Day (June 2), National Chocolate Macaroons Day (June 3), National Chocolate Ice Cream Day (June 7), National German Chocolate Cake Day (June 11), National Fudge Day (June 16), National Eat an Oreo Day (June 19), National Chocolate Éclair Day (June 22), National Chocolate Pudding Day (June 26), National Chocolate Wafer Day (July 3), National Milk Chocolate with Almonds Day (July 8), Peanut Butter and Chocolate Day (July 23), National Hot Fudge Sundae Day (July 25), National Milk Chocolate Day (July 28), National Ice Cream Sandwich Day (August 2), National Chocolate Chip Cookie Day (August 4), National S'mores Day (August 10), National Chocolate Pecan Pie Day (August 20), National Chocolate Milkshake Day (September 12), National White Chocolate Day (September 22), National Chocolate Milk Day (September 27), National M & M Day (October 13), National Chocolate Covered Insects Day (October 14), National Chocolate Cupcake Day (October 18), Office Chocolate Day (October 20), National Candy Day (November 4), National Bittersweet Chocolate with Almonds Day (November 7), Chocolates Day (November 29), National Mousse Day (November 30), National Sacher Torte Day (December 5), National Chocolate Brownie Day (December 8), National Cocoa Day (December 13), and National Chocolate-Covered Anything Day (December 16), to name a few! Anyone of these chocolate days can be celebrated by eating a chocolate bar or a chocolate dessert, by drinking hot chocolate or chocolate milk or a chocolate milkshake, by making truffles, by touring a local chocolatier, by hosting a chocolate tasting party, etc. Eaten in moderation, chocolate can improve blood flow. It triggers the production of serotonin in nerve cells which stabilize mood, reduce depression, and regulate anxiety. Dark chocolate, which is high in flavonoids, provides antioxidants which can lower blood pressure, and, while in the mouth, can kill bacteria that cause tooth decay. National and international chocolate days are dedicated to all things chocolate and provide the opportunities to reflect on how much chocolate we eat and how important it is to our lives.

Journal/Meditation: For you, what is the spirituality of eating chocolate? What type(s) of chocolate do you buy? Why? What is your favorite day for celebrating chocolate? Why?

Prayer: Chocolate is one of your many gifts to your people, O LORD. Either in its dark, white, or milk chocolate form, it brings delight to those who savor it. Grant to me a deeper appreciation for this many-used gift, accept my thanksgiving for it, and hear my praise now and forever. Amen.

World Cities Day

October 31

Text: ". . . [I]t is recognized that cities [and human settlements] are engines of economic growth, which, if well planned and developed, . . . can promote economically, socially, and environmentally sustainable societies; [therefore the General Assembly of the United Nations] . . . decides to designate 31 October, beginning in 2014, as World Cities Day, [and] invites states, the United Nations system, in particular UN-Habitat, relevant international organizations, civil society, and all other relevant stakeholders to observe and raise awareness of the day, and . . . welcomes the commitments of member states and the efforts of other stakeholders to promote an integrated approach to planning and building sustainable cities and urban settlements; encourages governments and Habitat Agenda partners to use planned city extension methodologies to guide the sustainable development of cities experiencing rapid urban growth, in order to prevent slum proliferation, enhance access to urban basic services, support inclusive housing, enhance job opportunities, and create a safe and healthy living environment; recognizes the significance of equitable and adequate access to urban basic services as a foundation for sustainable urbanization and, therefore, to overall social and economic development; . . . [and] invites member states and Habitat Agenda partners to formulate and implement sustainable development policies that promote just, resilient, and inclusive cities . . . ."[138]

Reflection: World Cities Day was established by the United Nations General Assembly on December 27, 2013, with the first celebration held on October 31, 2014. The day is organized by the U.N. Human Settlements Program (U.N.-Habitat[139]) in coordination with each year's selected host city. The day marks the end of a month-long program—Urban October, launched in 2014 to emphasize the world's urban challenges and engage the international community towards the New Urban Agenda[140]—and begun with World Habitat Day established December 17, 1985, on "the first Monday of October of every year."[141] The goal of World Cities Day is to promote the international community's interest in global urbanization, while seeking cooperation among

---

138. United Nations General Assembly, A/RES/68/239.

139. "U.N. Habitat . . . promote[s] transformative change in cities and human settlements through knowledge, advice, technical assistance, and collaborate action. [Its] mission embodies the four main roles of the organization, which can be summarized as think, do, share, and partner" (https://unhabitat.org/about-us).

140. "The New Urban Agenda was adopted at the United Nations Conference on Housing and Sustainable Urban Development (Habitat III) . . . on 20 October 2016. It was endorsed by the United Nations General Assembly . . . on 23 December 2016. The New Urban Agenda represents a shared vision for a better and more sustainable future. If well-planned and well-managed, urbanization can be a powerful tool for sustainable development for both developing and developed countries" (https://habitat3.org/the-new-urgan-agenda/).

141. United Nations General Assembly, A/RES/40/202. The goal of the day is to reflect on the state of habitats and on the basic right of all to adequate shelter.

countries in both meeting opportunities and addressing challenges of urbanization. Hopefully, the realization is sustainable urban development around the world. While there is a specific theme for each year—such as climate resilience, innovations, governance, inclusivity, transformations, etc.—the general theme of every year is "Better City, Better Life." According to the World Cities Day U.N. webpage: "Urbanization provides the potential for new forms of social inclusion, including greater equality, access to services, and new opportunities and engagement and mobilization that reflects the diversity of cities, countries, and the globe. . . . Inequality and exclusion abound, often at rates greater than the national average, at the expense of sustainable development that delivers for all."[142]

The observance of World Cities Day ties into Goal 11 of the U.N.'s "Transforming Our World: The 2030 Agenda for Sustainable Development," passed by the General Assembly on September 25, 2015: "Make cities and human settlements inclusive, safe, resilient, and sustainable."[143] By 2030, the first three subgoals state that "access for all to adequate, safe, and affordable housing and basic services and upgrade[d] slums" should be ensured; that "access to safe, affordable, accessible, and sustainable transport systems" should be provided for all, "improving road safety, notably by expanding public transport, with special attention to the needs of those in vulnerable situations, women, children, persons with disabilities, and older persons;" and "inclusive and sustainable urbanization and capacity for participatory, integrated, and sustainable human settlement planning and management in all countries" should be enhanced.[144] Furthermore, "efforts to protect and safeguard the world's cultural and natural heritage" are to be strengthened by 2030; "the number of deaths and the number of people affected" are to be significantly reduced; "the direct economic losses relative to global gross domestic product caused by disasters, including water-related disasters, with a focus on protecting the poor and people in vulnerable situations" are to be substantially decreased; "the adverse per capita environmental impact of cities, including by paying special attention to air quality and municipal and other waste management" are to be reduced; and "universal access to safe, inclusive, and accessible, green and public spaces, in particular for women and children, older persons, and persons with disabilities" are to be provided.[145] The final three subgoals include supporting "positive economic, social, and environment links between urban, peri-urban, and rural areas by strengthening national and regional development planning;" substantially increasing "the number of cities and human settlements adopting and implementing integrated policies and plans towards inclusion, resource efficiency, mitigation and adaptation to climate change, resilience to disasters, and develop and implement . . . holistic disaster risk management at all levels;" and supporting "least developed

---

142. "World Cities Day."
143. United Nations General Assembly, A/RES/70/1.
144. United Nations General Assembly, A/RES/70/1, Sections 11.1–3.
145. United Nations General Assembly, A/RES/70/1, Sections 11.4–7.

countries, including through financial and technical assistance, in building sustainable and resilient buildings utilizing local materials."[146] Thus, in order to have a better life, people around the world need better cities.

Journal/Meditation: Which of the subgoals mentioned above got most of your attention? Why? Which of the subgoals mentioned above do you think is the hardest to achieve? Why? Which of the subgoals mentioned above do you think is the easiest to achieve? Why?

Prayer: Blessed are you, O LORD, for you guard the cities where you have chosen to live, and you have shown your steadfast love to those who live in cities. Fill with your Spirit all who work to make cities and human settlements inclusive, safe, resilient, and sustainable. Hear my prayer today, tomorrow, and forever. Amen.

REFORMATION DAY
October 31

Text: "Out of love for the truth and the desire to bring it to light, the following propositions will be discussed at Wittenberg, under the presidency of the Reverend Father Martin Luther, Master of Arts and of Sacred Theology, and Lecturer in Ordinary on the same at that place. Wherefore he requests that those who are unable to be present and debate orally with us, may do so by letter. In the name of our Lord Jesus Christ. Amen. . . . 36. Every truly repentant Christian has a right to full remission of penalty and guilt, even without letters of pardon. 37. Every true Christian, whether living or dead, has part in all the blessings of Christ and the Church; and this is granted him by God, even without letters of pardon. . . . 43. Christians are to be taught that he [or she] who gives to the poor or lends to the needy does a better work than buying pardons. 44. Because love grows by works of love, and man [and woman] becomes better, but by pardons man [and woman] does not grow better, only more free from penalty. 45. Christians are to be taught that he [or she] who sees a man [or woman] in need, and passes him [or her] by, and gives [his or her money] for pardons, purchases not the indulgence of the pope, but the indignation of God. 46. Christians are to be taught that unless they have more than they need, they are bound to keep back what is necessary for their own families, and by no means to squander it on pardons. 47. Christians are to be taught that the buying of pardons is a matter of free will, and not of commandment."[147]

Reflection: On October 31, 1517, Martin Luther, in accord with the statutes of the University of Wittenberg, posted the "Ninety-Five Theses" on every church door in the city. The only church usually mentioned concerning the theses-posting is that of All

---

146. United Nations General Assembly, A/RES/70/1, Sections 11a–c.
147. Luther, "Disputation."

Saints. The theses, more accurately titled the "Disputation on the Power and Efficacy of Indulgences," are written propositions meant to be argued in a formal academic disputation. That is why the opening paragraph of the "Disputation," presented in the above text, begins by inviting interested scholars to attend the event and participate orally in the discussion; those who are unable to attend are invited to participate by writing letters. In this usual form of academic inquiry, Luther, as an academic doctor, has the privilege of hosting such a debate. Retrospectively, October 31, 1517, signals the beginning of the Reformation or the birth of Protestantism in what was once an all-Catholic world. Luther, a German monk, belonged to the religious order known as the Augustinian Hermits. His theses, some of which are found in the above text, advanced his position against what he saw as the abuse of the clergy selling plenary indulgences, certificates that were believed to reduce the temporal punishment of souls in purgatory for sins committed before death, purchased either by an individual for future redemption or on behalf of deceased loved ones. According to Luther, "They preach [vanity] who say that so soon as the penny jingles into the money-box, the soul flies out [of purgatory]."[148] In the Catholic Church, indulgences were a part of the economy of salvation. When Christians confessed their sins, they were forgiven and no longer liable to receive eternal punishment in hell. However, they may still have been liable to temporal punishment in a place between earth and heaven called purgatory. Such temporal punishment in purgatory could be mitigated by performing works of mercy before death or by indulgence (a type of kindness) after death. The clergy abused the system by selling indulgences, and the pope, Leo X, granted a plenary indulgence in 1515 intended to finance the construction of the new St. Peter Basilica in Rome. Luther thought that indulgences cheapened grace by not requiring repentance for sins. In other words, people had come to believe that they could buy their way out of purgatory.

While all 95 theses cannot be presented here, we see Luther's basic idea reflected in theses 36 and 37 above. Every truly repentant person has already been forgiven, according to Luther, and full remission of penalty and guilt has been received—without an indulgence document. Furthermore, in thesis 37, he states that letters of pardon (indulgence documents) are not necessary to share in the blessings of Christ and the Church (the treasury of grace), because it is given freely by God to both the living and the dead. In theses 43 through 47, as presented in the above text, Luther critiques the practice of buying indulgences because they keep Christians from giving to the poor, lending to the needy, growing through works of love, or caring for their families. In other words, there is no reason for works of charity if the grace received from such works can be bought as indulgences. Luther states that there is no commandment about the need to buy indulgences; to do so squanders money, and buying them purchases God's indignation. For Luther, "The true treasure of the Church is the

---

148. Luther, "Disputation, 27."

Most Holy Gospel of the glory and the grace of God."[149] In other words, the treasure cannot be bought; it is a free gift from God. Thus, the indulgence controversy began the Reformation, but it pales when placed beside more important matters, such as justification by faith alone and the bondage of the will. Nevertheless, in 1668, October 31 was declared to be Reformation Day, an annual holiday in Wittenburg, Electorate of Saxony, in the Holy Roman Empire (now Germany). Without Luther, without the Reformation, there would be no spiritual but not religious people around the world today.

Journal/Meditation: For you, what is the meaning of "Reformation Day"? What works of charity do you perform? Why do you perform them? Would you have bought an indulgence? Why or why not?

Prayer: Through the suffering, death, and resurrection of your Son, Eternal Father, you have bestowed upon the human race a mighty grace that frees all from sin and punishment. Grant me full appreciation of your freely-given gift, keep me from taking it for granted, and never let me think that I can buy it. Amen.

HALLOWEEN I

October 31

Text: "... [U]nderstanding the meaning of Halloween is made easier by the archetypal nature of the holiday. It is fair to say that virtually every ancient and modern culture has had some festival or rituals dealing with the dead, together with various troublesome or evil spirits from the supernatural world. . . . [T]he nature of Halloween is based upon archetypal structures within our psyche which evoke themes that underlie our emotional and spiritual life."[150]

Reflection: October 31, Halloween, is intimately connected to November 1, All Saints Day, and November 2, All Souls Day. The verb *to hallow* means *to make someone or something holy*. The noun *hallow* is a synonym for *saint*. The adjective *hallowed* means sanctified or kept for religious use. On Halloween, a contraction of All Hallows Eve, ancient people began praying, asking the saints to intercede with God for the souls of the dead. In other words, the three days of October 31, November 1, and November 2 was Christianity's way of dealing with the dead. Those living on the earth sought the help of those living in heaven for those living in liminal purgatory; the concept, based on a three-storied universe, is commonly known as the communion of saints. Based on the shorter days, falling leaves, and colder temperatures—death and decay—those three days, representing the transition from summer to winter, were the logical time for this to take place. Ancient people thought that on November 1 the veil between

---

149. Luther, "Disputation, 62."
150. George, *Mythology*, 150.

this world and the Otherworld was very thin. According to Arthur George, "The portals between this world and the Otherworld were most commonly mounds of earth, . . . hills, . . . the bottoms of lakes, caves, waterfalls, and some streams. [On November 1] these portals were open so that both the inhabitants of this world and those of the Otherworld could go back and forth."[151] The interaction between the worlds brought about transformation, specifically, regeneration.

Transformation and regeneration were enacted using fire. All home fires were extinguished, and a large bonfire was lit. Fire is a transforming agent; it incinerates the old in order to make way for the new. Transformation was also enacted by eating pork. Because pigs were associated with the Otherworld, eating supernatural pork was though to give immortality to people. Likewise, drinking beer, wine, and mead—collectively called spirits—brought about intoxication, an experience of the divine! Finally, ancient people enacted the transformation through their costumes; they dressed in imitation of the spirits in the Otherworld. Thus, the barriers between this world and the Otherworld, between the natural and the supernatural, between the living and the dead were broken. Halloween, bringing together this world and realms beyond everyday life, became popular in the United States in the late-nineteenth century.

Journal/Meditation: What emotional or spiritual theme of Halloween most resonates with you? How are fire, food, drink, and costume used today on Halloween to enact transformation?

Prayer: You, O LORD, are in communion with everything and everyone you have created. From your perspective earth, heaven, and the underworld are one; the living and the dead are not separated. Give me the wisdom to understand deeply the unity that exists among all you have made. Amen.

Halloween 2
October 31

Text: "Halloween is probably our most confusing holiday . . . . We have symbols of the fruits of harvest (cornstalks and corn, pumpkins, and other squash) celebrating the fertility of the earth juxtaposed with symbols of decay and death: autumn leaves, skeletons, ghosts, the Grim Reaper, gravestones, Dracula, and the dead rising from their graves . . . . Other symbols of the holiday more generally evoke the supernatural, such as haunted houses, fairies, and witches. . . . [T]he costumes themselves are a hodgepodge of themes . . . of death or the supernatural, some parody celebrities, some allude to current events, some make social or political statements, and others are sick jokes. . . . We encounter pirates, plants, hot dogs, garbage cans, vending machines, rockets, sperm, tubes of toothpaste, Monica Lewinsky in her stained blue dress—the variety is

---

151. George, *Mythology*, 159.

endless. And the holiday is celebrated universally across the population, regardless of age, gender, religion, nationality, ethnicity, political affiliation, or sexual preference."[152]

Reflection: For most people Halloween is all about trick-or-treating, and even more about being treated without the tricks. As costumed trick-or-treaters walk from house to house, they see pumpkins, representing the fertility of the earth, while walking through dead leaves and around trees full of ghosts and front yards turned into cemeteries. Some pumpkins are carved with all types of faces and illuminated from within by candles or battery-fueled lights. Few people know the origin of Jack-o'-lanterns, originally carved from turnips—not pumpkins because pumpkins are native to North America—and developed to frighten away evil spirits. Jack-o'-lanterns are the result of a folktale about a man named Jack and the devil, who have a drink together. After Jack convinces the devil to turn himself into a coin to pay for the drinks, Jack puts the coin in his pocket next to a silver cross, which keeps the devil from changing back to his previous form. Eventually, Jack frees the devil on the condition that he will not bother Jack for a year, nor will he claim Jack's soul should Jack die. Next, Jack tricks the devil into climbing a tree to pick some fruit, but Jack carves a cross on the tree, and the devil cannot come down until he promises to leave Jack alone for ten years. Jack dies. God will not allow him into heaven, but the devil will not allow him into hell. Jack goes off with only a burning coal, which he places in a carved turnip, and he has been roaming the earth ever since. He was known as Jack of the Lantern, now simply Jack-o'-lantern. Scary faces were also carved into potatoes and beets and placed in windows and near doors to frighten away Jack and any other evil spirits. In America, immigrants discovered that pumpkins made perfect Jack-o'-lanterns.[153]

Another way to protect oneself from evil spirits was to wear a disguise. Some people disguised themselves as the evil spirits, blackening their faces with ashes from a fire. Believing that the dead in churchyards rose on this one night of year, those costumed as corpses from various classes of society participated in the death dance to remind themselves not to forget the fate of all earthly life. Because most of that is now forgotten, people merely attend costume parties! To get to the party they may have to pass through a front-yard cemetery to be reminded of the transitory nature of life, but today the mock burial ground is meant merely to frighten them while white sheets, representing souls, are now known as ghosts, and skeletons doting the landscape are reminders of biology class. Other costumes portray supernatural figures, such as vampires, witches, and superpowers gathered from comic books and TV shows, like superman, batman, wonder woman, etc. Haunted houses, corn mazes, and even hayrides to some degree are designed to evoke fear. In order to protect children from harm, trunk-or-treating now takes place; children are offered treats from the trunks of cars parked in church or school lots. Long forgotten spirituality supports

---

152. George, *Mythology*, 149.
153. "The Legend of 'Stingy Jack.'"

apple bobbing or apple dunking; apples were associated with the other world. An apple pealed in a long strip and tossed over the should would reveal the first letter of one's future spouse. Two hazelnuts, associated with divine wisdom, roasted near a fire could foretell a bad match if they jumped away from the heat or a good match if they didn't move. Modern Halloween observances remain a mixture of practices.

Journal/Meditation: What is your favorite Halloween practice? What spiritual meaning does it have for you?

Prayer: Heavenly Father, you give special days to all people. On this Halloween, protect all who trick-or-treat, wear costumes, and make or carry lanterns. When I cannot see the way before me, awaken trust in me that I may play before you all my days and dance in your presence eternally. Amen.

11

The Month of *November*

ALL SAINTS' DAY
November 1

Text: "The communion of saints is the church. Since all the faithful form one body, the good of each is communicated to the others. . . . [T]here exists a communion of goods in the church. . . . [T]he riches of Christ are communicated to all the members. As this church is governed by one and the same Spirit, all the goods she has received necessarily become a common fund. The term 'communion of saints' therefore has two closely linked meanings: communion in holy things . . . and among holy persons . . . ."[1]

Reflection: Known as All Hallows' Day, Hallowmas, Feast of All Saints, and Solemnity of All Saints, All Saints' Day on November 1 is the middle day of a triduum (three days)—often called Allhallowtide—consisting of Halloween (October 31), All Saints' Day (November 1), and All Souls' Day (November 2). In Christianity this day honors all the saints, both those who are known and those who are not known. It also includes those who are no longer celebrated individually. Roman Catholics, Anglicans, Lutherans, Methodists, and many unchurched people mark this day in some way. In some countries, this day is a national holiday to remember saints of the past and present and to give thanks to God for the lives and deaths of saints, both those who may be or may have been famous and those who may be or may have been unknown.

The underlying basis for the day stems from the belief that there is a powerful spiritual bond between those in heaven and those living on the earth. Using the concept of the Pauline metaphor of the body of Christ[2] leads to the belief that there exists a communion of goods shared by all the members of the body. It is called the communion of saints, and it is like a common fund from which all become holy persons

---

1. *Catechism*, pars. 946–8.
2. Cf. NRSV: Romans 12:4–8; 1 Corinthians 12:12–27.

in communion through the Spirit. Those named and unnamed saints in the past share communion with those named and unnamed saints in the present.

Journal/Meditation: With what saint—named or not named—in the past do you share a spiritual bond? With what saint—named or not named—in the present do you share a spiritual bond? In your speech, whom do you often refer to as a saint?

Prayer: Ever-living God, you never cease to draw men and women to your holiness so that you can make them saints. Bestow upon me an abundance of your grace that I may be a living saint today in the hope of living in your presence forever. Amen.

ALL SOULS' DAY
November 2

Text: ". . . [T]he term 'soul' often refers to human life or the entire human person. . . . [S]oul also refers to the innermost aspect of [men and women], that which is of greatest value in him [or her], that by which he [or she] is most especially in God's image: 'soul' signifies the *spiritual principle* in man [and woman]. The human body shares in the dignity of 'the image of God' . . . [E]very spiritual soul is created immediately by God . . . and . . . it is immortal; it does not perish when it separates from the body at death . . . ."[3]

Reflection: All Souls' Day, also referred to as the Commemoration of All the Faithful Departed and the Day of the Dead, is the last day of a triduum (three days)—often called Allhallowtide—consisting of Halloween (October 31), All Saints' Day (November 1), and All Souls' Day (November 2). On this day Roman Catholics, Anglicans, Lutherans, Methodists, and many unchurched people remember their deceased loved ones by visiting their graves, cleaning and repairing tombs and headstones, offering prayers, and placing flowers, candles, and food near or on graves.

The underlying basis for the day stems from the belief that there is a powerful spiritual bond between those in heaven (saints), those living on the earth, and those who have died (and are in purgatory). "All who die in God's grace and friendship, but still imperfectly purified, are indeed assured of their eternal salvation," states the *Catechism*, "but after death they undergo purification, so as to achieve the holiness necessary to enter the joy of heaven."[4] The name given to that process is purgatory. Using the concept of the Pauline metaphor of the body of Christ[5] leads to the belief that there exists a communion of goods shared by all the members of the body living and dead. It is called the communion of saints, and it is like a common fund from which all become holy persons in communion through the Spirit. Each individual

---

3. *Catechism*, pars. 363–4, 366.
4. *Catechism*, par. 1030.
5. Cf. NRSV: Romans 12:4–8; 1 Corinthians 12:12–27.

person is given a spiritual and immortal soul by God; it makes the person the image of God; it is a share in God's Spirit that gives life; it is the spiritual principle which all humankind share. In other words, the spiritual soul cannot perish when the body dies because it is divine. If it is not yet perfect in holiness, it is purified instantly by God and received into heaven. The common fund shared by saints, the living, and the dead can be accessed by the living in order to seek the assistance of God, the Blessed Virgin Mary, or saints for anyone deceased. That is why on All Souls' Day, the living assist the dead with their prayers, Masses, and good works. What the dead cannot do for themselves, the living either can do for them or get the assistance of God, Mary, and the saints.

Journal/Meditation: Who are the deceased members of your family or friends? How are you connected spiritually to them? How do you assist them on their journey to perfect holiness?

Prayer: Life-giving God, through your Spirit you draw men and women to your holiness so that they may enjoy eternal salvation. Bestow upon the deceased members of my family and my deceased friends an abundance of your grace to make them perfect in holiness. Grant that I may one day join them in beholding your presence forever. Amen.

Election Day
Tuesday after the First Monday

Text: "Be it enacted by the Senate and House of Representatives of the United States of America in congress assembled, that Title 3 of the United States Code, entitled 'The President,' is codified and enacted into positive law and may be cited as '3 U.S.C., [Section]', as follows: . . . [Section 1]. The electors of President and Vice President shall be appointed, in each state, on the Tuesday next after the first Monday in November, in every fourth year succeeding every election of a President and Vice President."[6]

Reflection: The legalese presented in the text above indicates that the general election of federal public officials takes place on the Tuesday after the first Monday in November; that means that it occurs within November 2 to 8. Every four years a president and a vice president are elected. Members of the House of Representatives are elected every two years to serve two-year terms. Members of the Senate are elected every two years to serve six-year terms; one third of the senators are elected every two years. When a general election is held for representatives and senators and not for a president and vice-president, it is referred to as a midterm election. As a matter of convenience, many state and local government positions are also chosen on election day so that election officials can save money. Ten states and two territories have made

---

6. "Public Law 80-771."

election day a public holiday; other states require that workers be given time off with pay to go to their polling place and vote. Most states permit early voting, and most have some kind of absentee ballot procedure.

Setting election day in November was done by the congress to make voting convenient in the earliest days of the United States. By the second Tuesday in November, the harvest was gathered and the severest of winter weather piling highways with snow and ice had not yet arrived. Furthermore, those elected would be able to take office at the beginning of the new year. Voters could attend church on Sunday, traveling to their polling place on Monday—think in terms of either driving a horse and buggy or horses and wagon to the county seat—vote on Tuesday, and travel home so farmers could sell their produce in the markets on Wednesday. With that lifestyle quickly disappearing, it behooves lawmakers to reconsider when to hold election day. On election day, after careful evaluation, citizens vote for candidates who best represent their values and what is the common good of the country.

Journal/Meditation: What do you think are the responsibilities of voters to candidates running for election? In the last federal election, what values caused you to vote for the candidates for whom you voted? In the last local election, what role did the common good play in your choice for candidates?

Prayer: Fill both voters and candidates with your Spirit, LORD God, that they choose those who hold in reverence the common good of my country. Fill me with the Spirit of discernment that I may take my responsibility to vote with all seriousness and the wisdom to support values representing what is good for all. Amen.

Daylight Saving Time Ends
First Sunday

Text: "Section 3(a) of the Uniform Time Act of 1966 (15 U.S.C. 260(a)) is amended—by . . . striking 'last Sunday of October' and inserting 'first Sunday of November.'"[7]

Reflection: On August 8, 2005, Public Law 109–58 was enacted by congress. Known as the Energy Policy Act of 2005, Section 110 amended the Uniform Time Act of April 13, 1966, by changing the beginning (first Sunday of April) and ending (last Sunday of October) of Daylight Savings Time. From 2 a.m. on the second Sunday of March to 2 a.m. on the first Sunday of November, most U.S. citizens advance their clocks by one hour. On the first Sunday of November, they retreat their clocks by one hour. A catchy phrase was coined to remind people what to do: "Spring forward, Fall back." The Uniform Time Act of 1966 was itself an amendment of the Standard Time Act of 1918. The goal of those laws was to create a uniform start date and a uniform end date for Daylight Savings Time (DST). The law does not require that all states observe DST.

---

7. "Public Law 109–58." The beginning of DST is covered in The Month of March, chapter 3.

In the United States, Arizona and Hawaii do not observe Daylight Savings Time, as some U.S. territories do not.

The purpose of retreating clocks is to enable more hours of work or school in the morning daylight. Even though the hours of daylight are fewer from the first Sunday of November to the second Sunday of March, most of the daylight hours occur when most people are going to work or to school. Using the hours of standard time, energy is conserved and traffic accidents are reduced along with some incidents of crime. More hours of natural sunlight are able to be used. Changing the clock for only four months, however, affects one's circadian clock, an internal clock that informs us when to go to sleep and when to awake. Melatonin is produced by the body when it is time to sleep, and its production is stopped by the body when it is time to awaken. Ending Daylight Savings Time after eight months causes the body to get out of sync, and this can cause interrupted sleep and, consequently, health problems. Sleep enables the body to heal and repair itself; interrupted sleep can lead to an increased risk of stroke, heart disease, and cancer. An out of sync circadian rhythm can cause cognition functions, like learning, problem solving, decision-making, creativity, inattention, poor focusing, the inability to monitor behavior, to regulate emotions, to perceive consequences, depression, etc. This is why there are people who advocate either staying all year on Daylight Savings Time or staying all year on Standard Time to avoid the disruption of the circadian clock.

Journal/Meditation: What happens to you when Daylight Savings Time ends on the first Sunday of November and Standard Time resumes? Do you advocate year-long Daylight Savings Time or year-long Standard Time? Why?

Prayer: God of light and darkness, you created the sun and moon for light to work and the night for darkness to sleep. As I enter more deeply into the period of the shortest days of the year, shed the light of your grace upon me to give me good health and sound judgment all the hours of my life. Amen.

WORLD FREEDOM DAY
November 9

Text: "The fall of the Berlin Wall on November 9, 1989, stands as the turning point of the Cold War and a significant landmark in freedom's victory over tyranny. The Wall stood as a grim symbol of the separation of free people and those living under dictatorships. We honor the spirit and perseverance of those who strived for freedom in East Germany and under other repressive regimes. Since the fall of the Berlin Wall, many countries have achieved freedom via the ballot box, through political pressure rising from their citizens, or as a result of the settlement of internal or regional conflicts. We celebrate the new freedom in which much of the world lives today."[8]

Reflection: The federal observance named World Freedom Day was first proclaimed on November 9, 2001, by United States President George W. Bush to commemorate the fall of the Berlin Wall—a barrier that surrounded West Berlin and prevented access to it from East Berlin and adjacent areas of East Germany from 1961 to 1989—on November 9, 1989, and the end of communist rule in Central and Eastern Europe. In his proclamation of the first World Freedom Day, from which the above text is taken, Bush stated: "During the Cold War, freedom and authoritarianism clashed. Countries and entire regions suffered under repressive ideologies that sought to trample human dignity."[9] Later, he added: "On World Freedom Day, we . . . recognize that more than two billion people still live under authoritarian regimes. . . . [C]itizens of many countries suffer under repressive governments. . . . In every oppressive nation, pro-democracy activities are working to stoke the fires of freedom, often at great risk."[10] He encouraged all Americans to support those who sought to lead their people out of oppression and to honor those who fight for freedom anywhere in the world. Bush issued seven more proclamations of World Freedom Day in 2002 (Proclamation 7625), 2003 (Proclamation 7732), 2004 (Proclamation 7845), 2005 (Proclamation 7960), 2006 (Proclamation 8081), 2007 (Proclamation 8202), and 2008 (Proclamation 8318). President Barack Obama continued proclaiming November 9 to be World Freedom Day. In his first (2009) of eight proclamations, he wrote in the opening paragraph: "Twenty years ago today, the Wall came down in Berlin and both a country and a continent came together. . . . The Iron Curtain that divided Europe for decades finally fell, ushering in a new era of freedom and cooperation. On this anniversary, we are reminded that no challenge is too great for a world united in common purpose. After the Berlin Wall fell, oppressive regimes across the globe gave way. . . . [P]rison camps closed and democracy's doors were unlocked for millions who had known only tyranny."[11] Later, he added: "Today, the barriers that challenge our world are not walls of cement and iron, but ones of fear, irresponsibility, and indifference. . . . [W]e must work with all nations to strengthen civil societies, support democratic institutions and the rule of law, and promote free and fair electoral processes."[12] Then, in very profound words he recalled: "From our first days as a nation, Americans have felt a sense of urgency and determination to promote liberty and release the potential within each individual to contribute to the common good. On World Freedom Day, we celebrate the thriving democracies of Central and Eastern Europe, and we honor their citizens'

---

8. Bush, G.W., "Proclamation 7499."
9. Bush, G.W., "Proclamation 7499."
10. Bush, G.W., "Proclamation 7499."
11. Obama, "Proclamation 8452."
12. Obama, "Proclamation 8452."

right to choose their own destinies and contribute to their nations' future success."[13] Obama called upon the people of the U.S. to reaffirm their dedication to freedom and democracy. He issued similar proclamations in 2010 (Proclamation 8599), 2011 (Proclamation 8752), 2012 (Proclamation 8903), 2013 (Proclamation 9056), 2014 (Proclamation 9209), 2015 (Proclamation 9364), and 2016 (Proclamation 9538).

". . . [W]e celebrate the day on November 9, 1989, when people of East and West Germany tore down the Berlin Wall and freedom triumphed over Communism," stated President Donald J. Trump in his first World Freedom Day proclamation. "We loud the courage of all people who insist on a better future for themselves, their families, and their country, as we reflect on the state of freedom in our world today and those who have made the ultimate sacrifice defending it," he wrote. "The fall of the Berlin Wall spurred the reunification of Germany and the spread of democratic values across Central and Eastern Europe. Through democratic elections, and a strong commitment to human rights, these determined men and women ensured that their fellow and future citizens could live their lives in freedom. Today, we are reminded that the primary function of government is precisely this, to secure precious individual liberties."[14] He added, "When nations work together, we have and we will secure and advance freedom and stability throughout our world. On World Freedom Day, we recommit to the advancement of freedom over the forces of repression and radicalism."[15] Trump issued similar proclamations in 2018 (Proclamation 9821), 2019 (Proclamation 9965), and 2020 (Proclamation 10117). President Joseph R. Biden issued his first World Freedom Day proclamation on November 8, 2021. The two-page document begins with a recounting of history: "For nearly three decades, the Berlin Wall stood as a physical symbol of the Cold War, dividing democratic West Berlin from communist East Berlin. Today, we remember the East Germans who escaped and those who died attempting to attain a life of freedom. We recognize the irrepressible human spirit that no wall could contain, which fueled the civil resistance, sacrifice, and courageous defiance of people across Central and Eastern Europe. We recall the euphoria and the hope of the East and West Berliners who gathered at the wall on November 9, 1989, chanting, "Tor Auf!"—"Open the gate!"[16] Biden continued: "It was the aspirations for freedom of the people of Central and Eastern Europe that ultimately brought down the Berlin Wall and overcame the Soviet Union's attempts to keep Europe divided by force. On World Freedom Day, we commemorate this historic event and honor all those who peacefully rose up and claimed their freedom and all those who continue their legacy by peacefully working to end tyranny and oppression in our world today."[17] Later, he added: ". . . [W]e have seen great progress to advance hu-

13. Obama, "Proclamation 8452."
14. Trump, "Proclamation 9673."
15. Trump, "Proclamation 9673."
16. Biden, "Proclamation 10304."
17. Biden, "Proclamation 10304."

man rights and fundamental freedoms as well as to build and consolidate democratic institutions across the formerly communist countries of Central and Eastern Europe and around the world. However, democracy is still fragile, and in too many places it remains under threat."[18] He continued: "In the face of resurgent authoritarianism and attacks on human rights around the globe, the United States is working to support democratic renewal and resilience at home and abroad. It remains as important as ever to counter the range of threats to democracy—and, ultimately, peace and stability—including transnational repression, corruption, cyberattacks, disinformation, digital authoritarianism, inequality and injustice, voter suppression, and economic coercion."[19] He concluded the proclamation by reaffirming the U.S.'s "commitment to the ideal that democracy—a government of the people, by the people, and for the people—is how we best safeguard the rights, freedoms, and dignity that belong to every person. Together, with other free nations, the United States remains committed to the vital work of strengthening our democratic institutions, defending civil society, advancing human rights, and holding those who commit abuses and foster corruption accountable."[20] We mark World Freedom Day to reaffirm our dedication to freedom and democracy.

Journal/Meditation: Do you think it is easy to take freedom and democracy for granted? How? After choosing a single sentence from the proclamation of any president above, ask yourself: Where have I seen this occur? How can I further freedom and democracy around the world from where I live?

Prayer: You endowed all people with equal human rights, O LORD, and bestowed upon them the freedom to live their lives in security and peace. For all the work toward freedom and democracy, I give you thanks today; for the work remaining to be done, I seek your grace to carry the banner of freedom and democracy and pass it on to the fellow men and women with whom I share this world. Hear my heartfelt prayer. Amen.

Veterans Day
November 11

Text: "Whereas it has long been our custom to commemorate November 11, [1918,] the anniversary of the ending of World War I, by paying tribute to the heroes of that tragic struggle and by rededicating ourselves to the cause of peace; . . . and whereas the congress passed a concurrent resolution on June 4, 1926 (44 Stat. 1982), calling for the observance of November 11 with appropriate ceremonies, and later provided in an act approved May 13, 1938 (52 Stat. 351), that the eleventh of November should

---

18. Biden, "Proclamation 10304."
19. Biden, "Proclamation 10304."
20. Biden, "Proclamation 10304."

be known as Armistice Day; and whereas in order to expand the significance of that commemoration and in order that a grateful nation might pay appropriate homage to the veterans of all its wars who have contributed so much to the preservation of this nation, the congress, by an act approved June 1, 1954 (68 Stat.168), changed the name of the holiday to Veterans Day."[21]

Reflection: As President Dwight D. Eisenhower explains in his proclamation of the first Veterans Day to be held November 11, 1954, the end of World War I had been commemorated as Armistice Day since November 11, 1918. While the Treaty of Versailles was not signed until June 28, 1919, as the official end of World War I, the fighting ceased when an armistice—a temporary cessation of hostilities—between the Allied forces and Germany went into effect on the eleventh hour of the eleventh day of the eleventh month in 1918. To announce the armistice, President Woodrow Wilson addressed a joint session of congress on November 11, 1918. A year later, Wilson had a statement published in *The New York Times* declaring November 11, 1919, Armistice Day. On June 4, 1926, congress declared that November 11 should be marked annually with thanksgiving and prayer and exercises that perpetuate peace through good will and mutual understanding between nations. Congress requested the president of the United States to issue a proclamation calling upon government officials to display the flag on all government buildings and to invite the citizens to observe Armistice Day in schools, churches, and other suitable places. On May 13, 1938, congress made Armistice Day a legal holiday, and on June 1, 1954, changed the name of the holiday to Veterans Day. Because of the June 28, 1968, congressional act that made certain legal holidays fall on floating Mondays in order to ensure three-day weekends, Veterans Day became a Monday celebration. However, because of the confusion it caused, Veterans Day was returned to November 11 annually with a congressional act on September 18, 1975.[22] On October 7, 2016, congress enacted Public Law 114–240, which added a practice to Veterans Day: "The president shall issue each year a proclamation calling on the people of the United States to observe two minutes of silence on Veterans Day in honor of the service and sacrifice of veterans throughout the history of the nation, beginning at 3:11 p.m. Atlantic standard time; 2:11 p.m. eastern standard time; 1:11 p.m. central standard time; 12:11 p.m. mountain standard time; 11:11 a.m. Pacific standard time; 10:11 a.m. Alaska standard time; and 9:11 a.m. Hawaii-Aleutian standard time."[23]

Anyone who has served in the armed forces of the United States—Air Force, Army, Coast Guard, Marine Corps, Navy, Space Force—is a veteran. He or she has had the experience of being a member of the armed forces and may have fought in one of the U.S. wars. On November 11, citizens honor veterans who have served in

---

21. Eisenhower, "Proclamation 3071."
22. Gaylord, "Documentary History."
23. "Public Law 114–240."

any branch of the armed forces. They pay tribute to them and thank them for their service to their country; a grateful nation pays homage to them. In his proclamation, Eisenhower calls upon all citizens to "remember the sacrifices of all those who fought so valiantly, on the seas, in the air, and on foreign shores, to preserve our heritage of freedom . . . ."[24] He also asks citizens to reconsecrate themselves "to the task of promoting an enduring peace so that [veterans'] efforts shall not have been in vain."[25] Thus, while we honor the men and women who have served our country in the armed forces on November 11, we also rededicate ourselves to the cause of peace.

Journal/Meditation: How can you observe two minutes of silence on Veterans Day? Specifically, whom do you honor on Veterans Day for his or her or their service in the armed forces? How do you honor him or her or them? What do you do to foster enduring peace?

Prayer: God of peace, bless the veterans of this country; they are worthy men and women who have given their best when they served and protected this land. Accept our thanks for them, as this grateful nation pays homage to them. Watch over them, bless them with happiness, and give us peace. Amen.

National Philanthropy Day
November 15

Text: "Whereas philanthropic organizations are largely responsible for enhancing the quality of life for Americans and other people throughout the world; whereas our nation owes a great debt to the schools, churches, museums, art and music centers, and organizations which aid and comfort the elderly, the disadvantaged, and the sick; and whereas the people of the United States should demonstrate their gratitude and support for philanthropic organizations and the efforts, skills, and resources of individuals who carry out their missions: Now, therefore, be it resolved by the Senate and House of Representatives of the United State of America in congress assembled, that November 15, 1986, is designated as 'National Philanthropy Day,' and the president is authorized and requested to issue a proclamation calling upon the people of the United States to observe such day with appropriate ceremonies and activities."[26]

Reflection: In order to honor national philanthropists, the joint resolution—passed by the Senate on October 25, 1985, amended and passed by the House on June 11, 1986, and concurred by the Senate on September 18, 1986—became Public Law 99-436, from which the above text is taken, on October 2, 1986. The first National Philanthropy Day was proclaimed by President Ronald Reagan on November 14, 1986, to

---

24. Eisenhower, "Proclamation 3071."
25. Eisenhower, "Proclamation 3071."
26. "Public Law 99-436."

be the next day. "The literal meaning of 'philanthropy,' began Reagan, "is 'affection for [human]kind.'" Then, he explained: "Throughout our history, we Americans have displayed this trait through our generous charitable giving and our spirit of neighbor helping neighbor. We help each other, and we reach out to help people all over the world. Our tradition of voluntarism embodies a great deal of caring, initiative, and ingenuity in solving problems and improving our communities. It is one of our greatest strengths as a people."[27] Reagan added: "We can be very grateful to the philanthropic individuals and organizations who have contributed so much to our social welfare, our cultural life, and the improvement of our communities. We can be grateful as well for our American spirit of giving from the heart."[28] With several updates and some slight rewording of Public Law 99-436, congress passed Public Law 101-138 on November 3, 1989, and declared November 18, 1989, National Philanthropy Day. President George Bush issued the second proclamation of National Philanthropy Day on November 15, 1989, stating: "[The] spirit of voluntary association and service to others continues to be a proud portion of the American character. Today, nonprofit philanthropic organizations in the United States number in the hundreds of thousands. These organizations employ millions of people, many of them volunteers. The American people give generously to all of them—not only through financial contributions but also through regular donations of their time, talents, and material resources." He added, "... [W]e recognize and salute the outstanding work done by members of our nation's philanthropic organizations."[29] With updated statistics, on October 31, 1990, congress passed Public Law 101-489, which proclaimed November 16, 1990, National Philanthropy Day. Bush responded with a proclamation, which began: "Henry David Thoreau once observed that 'the virtue we appreciate, we to some extent appropriate.' We therefore do well to recognize the thoughtfulness and generosity of all those Americans who devote their time, talent, and material resources to philanthropic organizations and activities. By celebrating their many contributions to society, we reaffirm the spirit of voluntary giving and service to others that is one of our nation's greatest strengths."[30] Later, he added: "On National Philanthropy Day, we proudly express our respect and appreciation for all those Americans who devote their time, energy, and material resources to philanthropic endeavors. Our entire country benefits from their magnanimity and hard work, and all of us can be inspired by their example."[31] The last Public Law (102-165) designating a National Philanthropy Day was passed on November 18, 1991. It declared the date for the celebration to be November 19, 1991. Except for updated statistics, it was similar in wording to its three predecessors. As in his two previous proclamations, Bush began by stating, "Public philanthropy has long

27. Reagan, "Proclamation 5571."
28. Reagan, "Proclamation 5571."
29. Bush, "Proclamation 6071."
30. Bush, "Proclamation 6225."
31. Bush, "Proclamation 6225."

been a hallmark of American life."[32] Later, he added, ". . . [V]oluntary service remains essential to solving our nation's most serious social problems. . . . Pubic philanthropy is not just about money. Millions of Americans—people of every age, race, and walk of life—give of their time and their talents in voluntary community service. . . . These Americans are demonstrating that you don't have to be wealthy to be a philanthropist; you just have to care."[33] November 19, 1991, marks the end of public laws and presidential proclamations about National Philanthropy Day.

However, National Philanthropy Day continues today under the auspices of the Association of Fundraising Professionals (AFP). The day continues to support and celebrate charitable activities that take the form of financial donations and volunteered efforts. Besides recognizing the contributions that philanthropy makes to society, the day also honors individuals, businesses, and support organizations that are active in the philanthropic community. At the same time as the U.S. congress was enacting the first National Philanthropy Day legally, Philanthropist Douglas Freeman of Orange County, California, was enacting it for the AFP. Before the AFP came into existence, the American Association of Fund Raising Counsel (AAFRC) was created in 1940. In 1960, by the common vision of Benjamin Sklar, William R. Simms, and Harry Rosen, the National Society of Fund Raisers (NSFR) was born with the purpose and mission "to aid fundraisers in the performance of their professions duties; to unite those engaged in the profession of fundraising; to formulate, promote, and interpret to organizations, agencies, and the public the objectives of fundraising and the role of those who practice it; to promote and maintain high standards of public service and conduct; to exchange ideas and experiences and to collect and disseminate information of value to fundraisers and the public; to promote, sponsor, and encourage study, research, and instruction in the field of fundraising by means of courses in established institutions of learning and by other means; and to encourage and sponsor the granting of awards and fellowships in recognized institutions of learning for study and research in the field of fundraising."[34] In 1977, NSFR changed its name to the National Society of Fund Raising Executives (NSFRE). As the organization continued to grow, amassing 22,000 members in 1999 with 157 chapters, its name was changed in January 2001 to AFP and its global headquarters located in Arlington, Virginia. In 1986, Marvin Hamlisch wrote a song—"Now, More Than Ever,"—which carries the spirit of the annual National Philanthropy Day. "Now more than ever we must stand united," the lyrics begin. "We must give all that we can give, and now more than ever we must help our brother. With one another we will succeed. You and me, we know what our goal is. Let's prove that we can pull through. Now more than ever we need love. With love there's nothing we can't do. With love more than ever we'll give more than ever.

32. Bush, "Proclamation 6376."
33. Bush, "Proclamation 6376."
34. "History of the AFP."

We'll live to see our dreams come true."[35] The lyrics and music can be downloaded and duplicated for any type of philanthropic event.

Journal/Meditation: With what philanthropic organization are you involved? How does it enhance the quality of life for others? Of all the purposes and missions of the AFP listed above, which one gets most of your attention? Why? What do the lyrics of Hamlisch's "Now, More Than Ever," mean to you?

Prayer: Now, more than ever, heavenly Father, I ask you to bring people together to give from their time, talent, and treasure to show their love and help others. With your grace motivate all men and women to see that not only are they brothers and sisters, but that when they help each other, they are helping themselves and living to see their dreams come true. Amen.

America Recycles Day
November 15

Text: "Recycling is one of the great success stories in America's crusade to protect our environment and preserve our natural resources. Americans have undergone a fundamental change in attitude about recycling during the past four decades. Where most Americans and many industries were once unmindful of our resources and careless in disposing of waste materials, people across our country now recognize the importance of recycling and have made it part of their daily routines. . . . Nonetheless, the recycling process is complete only when recovered materials return to the market as new products for purchase by consumers. The most effective way we can ensure the continued success of recycling in America is to expand markets for products that contain recycled materials. Buying recycled products conserves resources, reduces water and air pollution, saves energy, and creates jobs."[36]

Reflection: The first America Recycles Day—sometimes called National Recycling Day—was proclaimed by President William J. Clinton on November 15, 1999. The above text is taken from the two-page proclamation in which Clinton explains: "America Recycles Day unites business and industry, environmental and civic groups, and local, state, and federal government agencies to encourage recycling. This partnership challenges all businesses and consumers in America to increase their purchases of recycled products, to boost their recycling efforts, and to start new recycling programs." Later, he added, "I urge all Americans . . . to take personal responsibility for the environment not only by recycling, but also by choosing to purchase and use products made from recycled materials."[37] Clinton issued a similar proclamation in 2000 (Proc-

---

35. Hamlisch, "Now, More Than Ever."
36. Clinton, "Proclamation 7250."
37. Clinton, "Proclamation 7250."

lamation 7377). It is important to note that America Recycles Day is managed and promoted by Keep America Beautiful—a non-profit organization founded in 1953 and based in Stamford, Connecticut—which took ownership of the observance in 2009, after it was started as Texas Recycles Day in 1994, and taken over by the Nation Recycling Coalition in 1997. The day both promotes and celebrates recycling and the importance of recycling through the use of an annual theme. Keep American Beautiful aims to end littering to improve recycling and to beautify communities across the United States.

Following Clinton, President George W. Bush issued the first of eight America Recycles Day proclamations on November 15, 2001. "We must preserve our natural heritage by serving as good stewards of our land," he began. "Recycling helps to serve this important function by conserving our natural resources as we reuse them where we can. Recycling safeguards our environment and helps keep America beautiful for present and future generations."[38] Later, he added: "Successful recycling includes not only the collection of materials, but also the manufacture of new products and the purchase of recycled content products. Buying products made of recycled materials contributes to domestic energy conservation and, ultimately, a cleaner environment."[39] Bush issued similar proclamations in 2002 (Proclamation 7627), 2003 (Proclamation 7734), 2004 (Proclamation 7846), 2005 (Proclamation 7962), 2006 (Proclamation 8083), 2007 (Proclamation 8203), and 2008 (Proclamation 8319). "Every day, Americans who recycle conserve valuable recourses while reducing our nation's carbon footprint," began President Barack Obama in his first of eight America Recycles Day proclamations. "The reprocessing of materials is fundamental to our future prosperity," he continued, "as recycling helps preserve our natural environment and sustain our economy. . . . On America Recycles Day, we celebrate the individuals, communities, local governments, and businesses that recycle their waste and continually think of innovative ways to use materials that might otherwise be discarded."[40] According to Obama: "Recycling improves our daily lives and helps to protect our planet for the future. Through recycling, we conserve energy, consume less of our precious natural resources, decrease the amount of waste deposited in landfills, and reduce greenhouse gas emissions. Communities across America also benefit by avoiding the pollution associated with the extraction of raw materials and their processing into finished products. . . . Curbside recycling, electronics collection drives, community composting programs, and other similar methods contribute to the success of our efforts."[41] Similar proclamations were issued by Obama in 2010 (Proclamation 8601), 2011 (Proclamation 8754), 2012 (Proclamation 8905), 2013 (Proclamation 9057), 2014 (Proclamation 9211), 2015 (Proclamation 9368), and 2016 (Proclamation

---

38. Bush, G.W., "Proclamation 7503."
39. Bush, G.W., "Proclamation 7503."
40. Obama, "Proclamation 8453."
41. Obama, "Proclamation 8453."

9543). In his first observance of America Recycles Day, on November 15, 2017, President Donald J. Trump issued only a single-page statement, which began: "On America Recycles Day, we recognize the importance of minimizing waste by reusing and recycling. Recycling supports American manufacturing and conserves valuable resources, protecting our nation's economic and environment health."[42] He added: "... [W]e celebrate Americans whose recycling habits help maintain our global leadership and competitiveness. . . . Rather than throwing away valuable resources, we should return them back into our economy, to rebuild our nation's infrastructure and create innovative new products."[43] In 2018, 2019, and 2020, Trump issued only a one-page short "Message on America Recycles Day." President Joseph R. Biden resumed the proclamation of America Recycles Day with his two-page document on November 12, 2021. He stated: "By reducing, reusing, and recycling, we can decrease waste and the greenhouse gasses that fuel the climate crisis while protecting our communities and our environment. On America Recycles Day, we celebrate efforts across the country to manage our resources responsibly and creatively, and we recommit ourselves to building a brighter and more sustainable future for all people."[44] On the second page of the proclamation, Biden stated: "To improve our national recycling system and manage our precious resources equitably and sustainably, it is going to take all of us—including federal, state, tribal, and local governments, our partners in the private sector, and individual Americans making a difference in their communities. We must continue to work together to properly recycle and manage materials throughout their lifecycles and ensure that every American's right to a healthy environment is fulfilled and protected."[45] Then, he concluded, "As we continue to pursue bold action to tackle climate change, we can all do our part to create a more sustainable future by making simple changes in our own lives."[46] By making simple changes in our own lives, we can be dedicated to recycling and buying products made from recyclables instead of tossing everything into the trash can.

Journal/Meditation: Do you recycle? If so, why? If not, why not? Choose a sentence from one of the presidential proclamations above that got your attention and ask yourself: What does that sentence mean to me?

Prayer: Creator God, you entrusted all you created to humankind as their heritage and taught men and women how to be good stewards and safeguard their environment. Help me to learn all the ways that I can conserve, recycle, and manage resources responsibly and creatively for future prosperity. All glory be to you in all that you have made now and forever. Amen.

42. Trump, "Statement on America Recycles Day."
43. Trump, "Statement on America Recycles Day."
44. Biden, "Proclamation 10308."
45. Biden, "Proclamation 10308."
46. Biden, "Proclamation 10308."

WORLD PHILOSOPHY DAY
Third Thursday

Text: "Recalling that philosophy is a discipline that encourages critical and independent thought and is capable of working towards a better understanding of the world and promoting tolerance and peace; . . . convinced that the institutionalization of Philosophy Day at UNESCO as world philosophy day would win recognition for and give strong impetus to philosophy and in particular to the teaching of philosophy in the world; . . . [the General Conference of UNESCO] proclaims the third Thursday of November every year 'World Philosophy Day,' [and] invites . . . active participation of National Commissions for UNESCO, non-governmental organizations and the public and private institutions concerned (schools, universities, institutes, municipalities, cities, communities, philosophical associations, cultural associations, and so on) . . . ."[47]

Reflection: During its General Conference held in Paris October 3–21, 2005, the United Nations Educational, Scientific, and Cultural Organization (UNESCO), declared the third Thursday of November annually to be World Philosophy Day. As can be seen in the text above, it did so in order to encourage critical thinking, which, hopefully, leads to better understanding of the world and promoting tolerance and peace among its inhabitants. It is important to understand that UNESCO is not advocating speculative philosophy (a philosophy professing to be founded upon intuitive or a priori insight and especially insight into the nature of the Absolute or Divine broadly; a philosophy of the transcendent or one lacking empirical bases; theoretical as opposed to demonstrative philosophy—logical and methodological reasoning or proof that is necessarily true and absolutely certain) or normative philosophy (the phenomenon in human societies of designating some actions or outcomes as good, desirable, or permissible, and others as bad, undesirable, or impermissible; a standard for evaluating or making judgments about behavior or outcomes). UNESCO is more properly focused on critical thinking or critical questioning which explores the various meanings of life in various individuals and peoples around the world. Critical thinking or critical questioning means the exercise of careful investigation or the rendering of judicious information that leads to deeper understanding. Instead of thinking that confirms what has always been done in the past or the way it was done in the past, critical thinking questions presuppositions and seeks creative understanding, solutions, and perspectives. As Benjamin Franklin is often quoted as saying, "If we all think alike, no one is thinking."

According to the World Philosophy Day page on the UNESCO webpage, "Philosophy is an inspiring discipline as well as an everyday practice that can transform societies."[48] It enables the discovery of "diversity of the intellectual currents in the

---

47. "Proclamation of World Philosophy Day," Section 37.
48. "World Philosophy Day."

world" and it "stimulates intercultural dialogue. By awakening minds to the exercise of thinking and the reasoned confrontation of opinions, philosophy helps to build a more tolerant, more respectful society. It thus helps to understand and respond to major contemporary challenges by creating the intellectual conditions for change."[49] World Philosophy Day fosters an international exercise in free, reasoned, and informed thinking on the major challenges of the time. Through philosophical dialogues, debates, conferences, workshops, cultural events, and presentations around a theme proposed for the day, philosophers and scientists from all branches of natural and social sciences, educators, teachers, students, press journalists, other mass media representatives, and the general public participate in critical thinking and questioning that foster the development of human thought.

Journal/Meditation: When has your critical and independent thinking brought you a better understanding about something in the world? about another culture? about a specific practice within a culture different from your own?

Prayer: Heavenly Father, you have bestowed upon humankind the ability to seek wisdom through reasoning. Inspire me through informed thinking that transforms me and contributes to the intellectual currents in the world that lead to greater understanding, tolerance, respect, and peace. With others enable me to create change that leads to growth for all. Amen.

GETTYSBURG ADDRESS ANNIVERSARY
November 19

Text: "Four score and seven years ago our fathers brought forth on this continent a new nation, conceived in liberty, and dedicated to the proposition that all men [and women] are created equal. Now we are engaged in a great civil war, testing whether that nation, or any nation so conceived and so dedicated, can long endure. We are met on a great battlefield of that war. We have come to dedicate a portion of that field, as a final resting place for those who here gave their lives that that nation might live. It is altogether fitting and proper that we should do this."[50]

Reflection: Abraham Lincoln, sixteenth president of the United States, delivered the Gettysburg Address in Gettysburg, Pennsylvania, on November 19, 1863, as a small part of the program at the dedication of the Soldiers' National Cemetery. The speech was given about four and a half months after Union armies defeated Confederacy armies at the Battle of Gettysburg. Following the July 1–3, 1863, battle, the bodies of Union soldiers were buried in the battlefield. On October 17, 1863, exhumation of those bodies and reburial in the National Cemetery began; on November 19, 1863,

---

49. "World Philosophy Day."
50. Lincoln, "Gettysburg Address."

the process was less than half complete. It wasn't long before Lincoln's short speech was recognized as one of the most influential statements of the purpose of the United States. Just like scholarly biblical literature begins with the premise that there is no original text, there is no original text of the Gettysburg Address. There are five manuscripts; a draft copy was given to each of his two private secretaries and three copies, written by Lincoln for charitable purposes and well after November 19, were given to three different men. Keeping in mind that copy machines had not yet been invented, a copy had to be hand written; this leaves lots of room for changes and mistakes. Since the copy given to Colonel Alexander Bliss is the only one to which Lincoln affixed his signature, it is considered to be the standard version of the speech.

The text above represents the standard first two paragraphs of the Gettysburg Address. Lincoln begins his narrative by remembering the signing of the Declaration of Independence eighty-seven years before 1863 or 1776. All men and women are created equal; according to the Declaration of Independence, that is a self-evident truth. He uses the imagery of conception, birth, and purpose to remind his hearers about the nation of the United States. The conception took place in liberty; it was born on the continent of North America; and its purpose was to demonstrate that all people are created equal. Lincoln understood that the Civil War was a test of endurance for the United States or any nation conceived in liberty, born through Revolutionary War, and dedicated to the equality of all. How long can it endure? It is a test because the U.S. is an experiment in government that continues. It is important for the reader to remember that this speech is given at a cemetery, where bodies are being exhumed and reburied. In other words, those listening to this speech are surrounded by death. On the Gettysburg Battlefield, Lincoln is part of the dedication of a section of it as final resting place for those who died that the nation might live. This is nothing other than the Christian Bible (New Testament) understanding that Jesus' death gave life to the world. Those buried in that field bear witness that the test was passed. The nation will endure. That is why in the next paragraph (not printed above) Lincoln explains that those gathered on the field cannot dedicate, consecrate, or hallow the ground; only those who died there can do that.

Journal/Meditation: How do you see the self-evident truth that all men and women are created equal being applied today? How is the U.S. still testing that concept? How have you experienced death giving birth to life?

Prayer: Blessed be you, O God, Father of Jesus Christ. You have inspired my ancestors to bring forth the United States on the North American continent, conceived in liberty, and dedicated to the proposition that in your sight all men and women are equal. When war tests this purpose, give me and my fellow citizens the strength to endure today, tomorrow, and forever. Amen.

INTERNATIONAL MEN'S DAY
November 19

Text: "The six pillars of International Men's Day: 1. To promote positive male role models; not just movie stars and sports men but every day, working class men who are living decent, honest lives. 2. To celebrate men's positive contributions to society, community, family, marriage, child care, and to the environment. 3. To focus on men's health and wellbeing; social, emotional, physical, and spiritual. 4. To highlight discrimination against men; in areas of social services, social attitudes and expectations, and law. 5. To improve gender relations and promote gender equality. 6. To create a safer, better world; where people can be safe and grow to reach their full potential."[51]

Reflection: Thomas Oaster, Director of the Missouri Center for Men's Studies and Associate Professor at the University of Missouri at Kansas City, Missouri, began to develop the idea of a men's day in 1991. On February 7, 1992, Oaster sponsored the first International Men's Day, "conceived as a day of the type of activity which indicates the most comprehensive and enduring respect for men of all ages everywhere on earth."[52] From its inception on February 8, 1991, to the first ever International Men's Day on February 7, 1992, Oaster wrote a booklet of over fifty-nine pages in which he presented his ideas about the day and invited others to join him. He wanted to thank men for their contributions to society. He successfully promoted the event again in 1993 advertising it as a day of respect for men in cooperation with the Missouri Center for Men's Studies. The 1994 event was successful, too, but by 1995 the event was poorly attended, and Oaster made no more plans to continue it. Jerome Teelucksingh, a lecturer from the History Department in the University of the West Indies, revived International Men's Day in 1999, and he chose to celebrate it on November 19 to honor his father's birthday. Teelucksingh promoted the day as one where all issues affecting men and boys could be addressed. While the observance of the day spread to approximately seventy countries, by 2009 only the Maltese Association of Men's Rights continued to observe it in February. The members of the Maltese committee voted in 2009 to move the event to November 19. In November 2009, Teelucksingh and members of the coordination committee for International Men's Day ratified the objectives presented in the text above. While the day is not officially recognized by the United Nations, it is marked annually by as many as forty countries around the world.

The day is designed to celebrate boys' and men's achievements and contributions, while noting issues that are unique to boys' and men's experiences. Both boys and girls need positive male role models of ordinary, decent, honest men. Today, men contribute to society, community, family, child care, and the environment. What once was divided between work for only women or for only men has become a career for

---

51. "Objectives."
52. "Kansas Stream."

anyone who wants it, such as doctors, nurses, elementary school teachers, etc. While the tough man physique still exists, health issues unique to men and boys and health care socially, emotionally, physically, and spiritually is more prominent. In many careers, men experience discrimination, especially socially, and that is an important issue of which many people are not aware. Improving gender relations and gender equality takes a lot of awareness that leads to change emotionally and spiritually. And fostering growth to one's full potential requires a safe environment, for which men share responsibility. Annually, a theme is chosen to help focus on the six pillars. In the past, yearly themes have touched on the importance of giving boys a good start in life, health issues for men and boys, safety, reproduction options for men, male suicide, diversity, positive male role models, and better relations between men and women, to name a few.

Journal/Meditation: Of the six pillars of International Men's Day, which one do you consider the most important? Why? Which man in your life has been a positive role model? To which man in your life do you show the most respect? Why?

Prayer: You made men and women in your image, God, creating them male and female. You blessed them equally giving them dominion over all things. Pour your grace on the boys and men in my life that they may live decent and honest lives, making positive contributions to society, staying healthy and safe, and growing spiritually in your presence forever. Amen.

WORLD TOILET DAY
November 19

Text: "Deeply concerned by the slow and insufficient progress in providing access to basic sanitation services, . . . and conscious of the impact of the lack of sanitation on people's health, poverty reduction, economic and social development, and the environment, in particular water resources, [the General Assembly of the United Nations] . . . decides to designate 19 November as World Toilet Day in the context of Sanitation for All; [and] urges all member states, the organizations of the United Nations system, and all other relevant stakeholders to encourage behavioral change, together with policies for increasing access to sanitation among the poor, complemented by a call to end open defecation as a practice that is extremely harmful to public health; encourages [the same groups] to approach the sanitation issue in a much broader context and to encompass all its aspects including hygiene promotion, the provision of basic sanitation services, sewerage and wastewater treatment and reuse in the context of integrated water management; [and] invites all . . . to observe World Toilet Day in the context of Sanitation for All in an appropriate manner, including through education and activities to raise public awareness on the importance of access to sanitation for all . . . ."[53]

Reflection: At first glance, a person may giggle when seeing that the United Nations celebrates World Toilet Day, which resolution was adopted on July 24, 2013. However, after reading the above text, which is taken from the resolution, one begins to see that World Toilet Day is less about toilets and more about complete sanitation. According to the U.N.'s World Toilet Day webpage, "The observance celebrates toilets and raises awareness of the 3.6 billion people living without access to safely managed sanitation." It continues, "When some people in a community do not have safe toilets, everyone's health is threatened. Poor sanitation contaminates drinking-water sources, rivers, beaches, and food crops, spreading deadly diseases among the wider population."[54] In other words, access to a safe functioning toilet impacts public health, human dignity, and personal safety. When there are no working sanitation systems, feces are not treated and disease spreads. Soil-transmitted diseases along with water-borne-transmitted disease infect millions of people around the world. World Toilet Day was chosen as the name for the observance because World Sanitation Day didn't offer lots of understanding for the general public. While toilets are only the first stage of sanitation systems, they lead to awareness concerning hygiene, handwashing, basic sanitation services, sewerage and wastewater treatment, fecal sludge management, municipal solid waste management, stormwater management, and integrated water management. According to the U.N.'s World Toilet Day webpage, ". . . [S]anitation systems [around the world] are underfunded, poorly managed or neglected . . . , with devastating consequences for health, economics, and the environment, particularly in the poorest and most marginalized communities."[55]

World Toilet Day is designed to inspire action to tackle the global sanitation crisis. It falls under U.N. Sustainable Development Goal 6: "Ensure availability and sustainable management of water and sanitation for all."[56] That goal, among many others, was adopted by the General Assembly of the United Nations on September 25, 2015, in a resolution titled "Transforming Our World: The 2030 Agenda for Sustainable Development." Several of the subgoals of Goal 6, specifically apply to World Toilet Day. For example, 6.2 states, "By 2030, achieve access to adequate and equitable sanitation and hygiene for all and end open defecation . . . ."[57] 6.3 states, "By 2030, improve water quality by . . . halving the proportion of untreated wastewater . . . ."[58] And 6a and 6b state: "By 2030, expand international cooperation and capacity-building

---

53. United Nations General Assembly, A/RES/67/291.
54. "World Toilet Day."
55. "World Toilet Day."
56. United Nations General Assembly, A/RES/70/1.
57. United Nations General Assembly, A/RES/70/1.
58. United Nations General Assembly, A/RES/70/1.

support to developing countries in water- and sanitation-related activities and programs, including . . . wastewater treatment . . . . Support and strengthen the participation of local communities in improving water and sanitation management."[59] In other words, adequate sanitation is a human right for the millions of people who have no toilets. "At the current rate of progress," according to the U.N.'s World Toilet Day webpage, "it will be the twenty-second century before sanitation for all is a reality."[60] Thus, World Toilet Day attempts to mobilize people around the world to encourage governments and other organizations to plan activities that get people involved in sanitation issues in order to make progress on Sustainable Goal 6.

Journal/Meditation: What connection do you understand sanitation to have to health, the economy, and the environment? How can you promote World Toilet Day? What sanitation issues are present where you live?

Prayer: O God, you created people to be healthy and to live long lives proclaiming your praise. Bestow your Spirit of wisdom upon leaders in communities where adequate sanitation is not available in order foster people's health, the economy, and the environment. Help all to make sustainable sanitation available for all. Amen.

World (Universal, International) Children's Day

November 20

Text: "Whereas the peoples of the United Nations have, in the charter, reaffirmed their faith in fundamental human rights and in the dignity and worth of the human person, and have determined to promote social progress and better standards of life in larger freedom; whereas the United Nations has, in the Universal Declaration of Human Rights, proclaimed that everyone is entitled to all the rights and freedoms set forth therein, without distinction of any kind, such as race, color, sex, language, religion, political or other opinion, national or social origin, property, birth, or other status; whereas the need for such special safeguards has been stated in the Geneva Declaration of the Rights of the Child of 1924, and recognized in the Universal Declaration of Human Rights and in the statutes of specialized agencies and international organizations concerned with the welfare of children; whereas [human]kind owes to the child the best it has to give, now, therefore, the General Assembly proclaims this Declaration of the Rights of the Child to the end that he [or she] may have a happy childhood and enjoy for his [or her] own good and for the good of society the rights and freedoms herein set forth, and calls upon parents, upon men and women as individuals, and upon voluntary organizations, local authorities, and national governments to

---

59. United Nations General Assembly, A/RES/70/1.
60. "World Toilet Day."

recognize these rights and strive for their observance by legislative and other measures progressively taken in accordance with the . . . principles."[61]

Reflection: As noted in the text above, World Children's Day—also referred to as Universal Children's Day and International Children's Day—was established by the United Nations in 1954 after having acquired the League of Nations 1924 document on children's rights. The 1924 document states: "1. The child must be given the means requisite for its normal development, both materially and spiritually. 2. The child [who] is hungry must be fed, the child [who] is sick must be nursed, the child [who] is backward must be helped, the delinquent child must be reclaimed, and the orphan and the waif must be sheltered and succored. 3. The child must be the first to receive relief in times of distress. 4. The child must be put in a position to earn a livelihood and must be protected against every form of exploitation. 5. The child must be brought up in the consciousness that [his or her] talents must be devoted to the service of [his or her] fellow men [and women]."[62] On November 20, 1959, the General Assembly of the United Nations adopted Resolution 1836, the Preamble of which is the text above. That resolution contains ten principles, first, ensuring that all children enjoy all the rights in the declaration without distinction or discrimination based on race, color, sex, language, religion, political or other opinion, national or social origin, property, birth or social status. Second, the child enjoys special protection to enable him or her to develop physically, mentally, morally, spiritually, and socially. Third, from birth a child is entitled to a name and a nationality. Fourth, children enjoy social security—to grow and develop in health, to have special protection provided by their mothers, and to have the right to adequate nutrition, housing, recreation, and medical services. Fifth, a physically, mentally, or socially handicapped child is to be given special treatment, education, and care. Six, for full and harmonious development of personality, children need love and understanding, an atmosphere of affection, and of moral and material security. Seventh, every child is entitled to receive education within his or her own culture to develop his or her abilities, judgment, sense of moral and social responsibility, and to become a useful member of society. Principle 8 states that children in all circumstance are the first to receive protection and relief. Nineth, children are to be protected against all forms of neglect, cruelty, and exploitation—they are not to be employed until they reach a minimum age; they are not to work in any occupation that may harm their health or keep them from being educated; their physical mental, or moral development cannot be compromised. And tenth, children are to be protected from practices which foster racial, religious, and any other form of discrimination; they are to be raised in a spirit of understanding, tolerance, friendship, peace, and with full consciousness that talents should be devoted to the service of fellow men and women.

61. United Nations General Assembly, A/RES/1386 (XIV).
62. "History of Universal Children's Day."

To commemorate the November 20, 1959, document, the General Assembly of the United Nations issued the Convention on the Rights of the Child on November 20, 1989.[63] That over-seven-page work expands the 1959 declaration with a more extensive preamble and fifty-four articles. The convention defines a child as "every human being below the age of eighteen years, unless under the law applicable to the child, majority is attained earlier."[64] The document makes clear that "the best interests of the child shall be a primary consideration."[65] Other highlights of the 1989 convention include the child's "right to freedom of expression,"[66] the right "to freedom of thought, conscience, and religion,"[67] the rights "to freedom of association and to freedom of peaceful assembly."[68] According to Article 16, "No child shall be subjected to arbitrary or unlawful interference with his or her privacy, family, home, or correspondence, nor to unlawful attacks on his or her honor and reputation."[69] Other articles in the convention cover parents' responsibilities for a child's upbringing; the government's responsibility to protect the child from all forms of physical or mental violence, injury or abuse, neglect or negligent treatment, maltreatment or exploitation, including sexual abuse; the treatment of mentally or physically disabled children; the right of a child to health care; the right to a standard living adequate for the child's physical, mental, spiritual, moral, and social development; the right to education; the right to rest and leisure; and more. World (Universal, International) Children's Day gives people an inspirational entry to advocate, to promote, and to celebrate children's rights. Hopefully, both dialogue and action result in building a better world for children, while promoting international togetherness and awareness among children universally.

Journal/Meditation: Out of all the rights of children mentioned above, which one do you think is the most important? Why? What do you think is meant by normal spiritual development of children? How do you teach children that their talents are to be devoted to serving other people?

Prayer: O LORD, you have compassion on all your children. Turn to me, and be gracious to me. Give me strength to serve you in my dedication to the children of the world. Remember that all of us are your children, Most High, now and forever. Amen.

NOTE: Because of the complicated history of National Children's Day and National Child's Day in the United States, four entries narrating that complicated history of each of these observances are presented below. What began as National Children's

63. United Nations General Assembly, A/RES/44/25.
64. United Nations General Assembly, A/RES/44/25, Article 1.
65. United Nations General Assembly, A/RES/44/25, Article 3.
66. United Nations General Assembly, A/RES/44/25, Article 13.
67. United Nations General Assembly, A/RES/44/25, Article 14.
68. United Nations General Assembly, A/RES/44/25, Article 15.
69. United Nations General Assembly, A/RES/44/25, Article 16.

Day on August 8, 1982, was moved to the second Sunday in October from 1989 to 1992, then to the third Sunday in November in 1993, back to the second Sunday in October from 1994 to 2000, then renamed National Child's Day and set for the first Sunday of June from 2001 to 2008, returned to the third Sunday of November for 2009, then from 2010 to 2021 set on November 20.

NATIONAL CHILDREN'S DAY 1
November 20

Text: "Whereas America's children represent new life and new hope for the future of the nation and the world; whereas children should be regarded as this nation's most precious resource, and be assured of proper guidance and opportunity to be prepared to become productive citizens and responsible leaders of tomorrow; whereas children have a right to quality education, freedom from hunger, freedom from poverty, freedom from discrimination, and the legacy of a world at peace . . . ; . . . August 8, 1982, is designated as 'National Children's Day' . . . ."[70]

Reflection: While the first Children's Day was celebrated on the second Sunday of June in 1857 by Rev. Dr. Charles Leonard, pastor of the Universalist Church of the Redeemer in Chelsea, Massachusetts, who held a special service for and dedicated to children—called Rose Day, then Flower Sunday, then Children's Day—the first official and legal celebration of National Children's Day didn't occur in the United States until August 8, 1982, as noted in the text above. Ronald Reagan was the first U.S. president to proclaim it. "National Children's Day," he wrote, "provides a time for us to recognize the value, vitality, and potential of our young people. It is a day to recommit ourselves to nurturing our youth and to helping them achieve a healthy and happy future." He concludes his proclamation, stating, ". . . [T]he manner in which our children grow and learn will dramatically affect how our nation is able to meet its future challenges."[71] After 1982, resolutions were introduced in the House of Representatives in 1982 (Res. 500), 1983 (Res. 294), 1984 (Res. 634), and 1988 (Res. 631), and in the Senate in 1989 (Res. 15), but it was not until July 6, 1989, that congress passed Public Law 101-52. The new law repeated much of the 1982 law, but it added that "adults in the United States should have an opportunity to reminisce on their youth to recapture some of the fresh insight, innocence, and dreams that they may have lost through the years," that "the designation of a day to commemorate the children of the United States . . . provide(s) an opportunity to emphasize to children the importance of developing an ability to make the choices necessary [in life]," and that "the people of the United States should emphasize to children the importance of family life, education,

---

70. "Public Law 97-29."
71. Reagan, "Proclamation 4951."

and spiritual qualities . . . ."[72] Public Law 101–52 designated the second Sunday in October of 1989 as National Children's Day. President George Bush proclaimed October 8, 1989, National Children's Day. "Children are a great and precious blessing," he wrote. "Parents have no greater responsibility than to ensure that the young stranger God brings into their lives is welcomed, loved, nourished, and protected." In his two-page proclamation, he also states: "Fascinated by the countless little miracles of creation, which we grown-ups so often overlook as we rush to meet the demands of the adult world, children help us to see the world around us as if it were fresh and new. Filled with imagination and dreams, they take us into the future—and inspire us to be responsible for it." Bush cautions, "We must . . . remember the importance of teaching them the difference between liberty and license, for one is rooted in respect for human dignity, while the other only diminishes it."[73]

On August 9, 1990, the same resolution as that issued in 1989 became Public Law 101–349.[74] Again, Bush issued a two-page proclamation declaring October 14, 1990, National Children's Day. "The importance of parents' example cannot be overstated," he wrote, "because without trust in God and a firm belief in what is right and good, a child is much like a ship without an anchor or compass." He added, ". . . [E]ach and every child is a treasure from God."[75] Public Law 102–116 was passed by congress on October 3, 1991; while it did not differ from its two predecessors, it did remind "parents, teachers, and community and religious leaders [to] celebrate the children of the United States, whose questions, laughter, and tears are important to the existence of the United States."[76] Bush issued another two-page proclamation, declaring October 13, 1991, National Children's Day, stating, "Because the person who enjoys a healthy, happy childhood is most likely to become a healthy, well-adjusted adult, we do well to recall our obligation—as parents and as a nation—to protect, nurture, and provide for our children." He adds, ". . . [P]arents also have a responsibility to nurture the spiritual and intellectual development of the child whom God has entrusted to their care. . . . Filling a child's emotional and spiritual needs and material demands requires faith, sacrifice, fortitude, and commitment—virtues that are the measure of love and the strength of families."[77] October 11, 1992, was proclaimed National Children's Day by Bush in response to Public Law 102–425.[78] Bush stated that children's "future and the future of the United States depend on our efforts to ensure that every child receives the material, emotional, and spiritual support that he or she needs to become a healthy, well-adjusted, and responsible adult." He added, "Religious congregations, schools,

72. "Public Law 101–52."
73. Bush, "Proclamation 6039."
74. "Public Law 101–349."
75. Bush, "Proclamation 6197."
76. "Public Law 102–116."
77. Bush, "Proclamation 6355."
78. "Public Law 102–425."

and community organizations all have a role in maintaining an environment in which families can thrive and in which young people can enjoy the security of childhood, while also learning about the meaning of love and responsibility."[79]

Journal/Meditation: In what specific ways do children give new life and new hope for the future of our nation and the world? What does "the manner in which children grow and learn dramatically affect how our nation is able to meet its future challenges" mean to you. Which one of Bush's remarks catches most of your attention? Why?

Prayer: God, the birth of children gives both our nation and our work new life and new hope. Help all parents to give the material, emotional, and spiritual support to their children so that they grow into healthy, well-adjusted, responsible adults. As the son/daughter of my parents, I praise you now and forever. Amen.

National Children's Day 2

November 20

Text: "Whereas the designation of a day to commemorate the children of the nation will emphasize to the people of the United States the importance of the role of the child within the family; whereas the people of the United States should emphasize to children the importance of family life, education, and spiritual qualities; ... the third Sunday in November of 1993 is designated as 'National Children's Day,' and the president of the United States is authorized and requested to issue a proclamation calling upon the people of the United States to observe the day with appropriate ceremonies and activities."[80]

Reflection: On November 17, 1993, the United States congress passed Public Law 103–147, from which the above text is taken. While the law resembles its predecessors, it moves the observance of National Children's Day from the second Sunday in October to the third Sunday in November. Resolutions concerning the day had been introduced in the House of Representatives in 1990 (Res. 481), 1991 (Res. 183), 1992 (Res. 469), and 1993 (Res. 226), but they never made it to the Senate. Dutifully, President William J. Clinton proclaimed the third Sunday in November, the twenty-first, National Children's Day for 1993. "America's children are at once our most precious national resource and our most weighty responsibility," Clinton wrote. "They represent our future hopes and aspirations," he said. Later, in his two-page proclamation, he added, "This is an issue that all Americans can and should support and promote."[81] In 1994, congress moved National Children's Day to the second Sunday in October by passing Public Law 103–361. Except for the change in the date for the observance,

---

79. Bush, Proclamation 6490."
80. "Public Law 103–147."
81. Clinton, "Proclamation 6626."

the text of the law was the same as its predecessor.[82] Clinton declared October 9, 1994, National Children's Day, writing: "With every baby born in America, our nation reaffirms its hope for the future.... Our most solemn obligation to our children cannot be merely that we hold a torch to guide their way around every dark and treacherous corner. Rather, we must strive to kindle a spark within each child—a spark that will become the flame of knowledge and imagination, the fire of justice and compassion."[83] After this law, resolutions were introduced in the Senate in 1994 (Res. 211), 1995 (Res. 178), 1996 (Res. 292), and 1998 (Res. 260 and 275), but none of them made it to the House. Clinton, however, continued to proclaim the second Sunday in October as National Children's Day. For the most part, his proclamations are the occasion for him to explain what he and the Democratic Party accomplished in passing legislation that aided children. Setting politics aside, the statements from Clinton's proclamations present some matter for reflection.

In his proclamation declaring Sunday, October 8, 1995, National Children's Day, he quotes Ralph Waldo Emerson: "We find a delight in the beauty and happiness of children that makes the heart too big for the body."[84] In 1996, he wrote: "Our nation benefits when every American child is truly valued and cherished.... Only when we reaffirm our commitment to our children's wellbeing can we truly say that we are prepared for the challenges that await us in the next century." Later, in the proclamation of October 13, 1996, National Children's Day, Clinton added, "Because safety, health, a clean environment, quality education, and economic security are the keys to a brighter future, they are necessary investments in the healthy growth and development of our children."[85] Before spending two paragraphs on what his administration had accomplished to help parents and children, Clinton, in his proclamation of October 12, 1997, wrote: "With the birth of every child, the world becomes new again. Within each new infant lies enormous potential—potential for loving, for learning, and for making life better for others." He continued: "But this potential must be nurtured. Just as seeds need fertile soil, warm sunshine, and gentle rain to grow, so do our children need a caring environment, the security of knowing they are loved, and the encouragement and opportunity to make the most of their God-given talents." He called upon U.S. citizens to recommit themselves "to creating a society where parents can raise healthy, happy children; where every newborn is cherished, where every child is encouraged to succeed, and where all [the] young people are free to pursue their dreams."[86] In declaring October 11, 1998, National Children's Day, Clinton stated: "Children are our greatest blessing, and raising them well is the most challenging and rewarding task any of us will ever undertake. On National Children's Day, let us recommit ourselves—as

82. "Public Law 103–361."
83. Clinton, "Proclamation 6734."
84. Clinton, "Proclamation 6833."
85. Clinton, "Proclamation 6939."
86. Clinton, "Proclamation 7040."

loving parents and caring citizens—to ensure that all of America's children grow up in truly nurturing environments where their needs are met and where they have every opportunity to make the most of their lives."[87] In his October 10, 1999, two-page proclamation of National Children's Day, most of which concerns what his administration has done for children and families, he writes: "Children bring so much hope, joy, and love to our lives; in return, we owe them our time, our attention, the power of our example, and the comfort of our concern. It is a fair trade, and one that enriches the lives of us all."[88] In his last proclamation of National Children's Day to be observed on October 8, 2000, Clinton wrote: "Children hold a special place in our lives, and raising healthy, happy children is the greatest success any parent can hope to achieve; it should also be an important goal of every member of society, because children are profoundly influenced by the people and environment around them."[89] After narrating in three long paragraphs the achievements of his administration for parents and children, he wrote: "As we observe National Children's Day this year, let us recommit ourselves to using every resource in this time of unprecedented prosperity to build a bright future for all our children. Let us show our love for them not only through our words, but also by making the tough decisions and important investments necessary to give them the opportunity to achieve their dreams."[90]

Journal/Meditation: How does the birth of a child make the world new again? What do you think you owe the children of your nation? Which one of Clinton's remarks catches most of your attention? Why?

Prayer: Heavenly Father, just as seeds need fertile soil, warm sunshine, and gentle rain to grow, give the children of this country a caring environment, the security of being loved, and the encouragement and opportunity to make the most of the talents you have given them. Grant me the knowledge to contribute to a nation full of healthy, happy children. Amen.

NATIONAL CHILD'S DAY 1
November 20

Text: "Whereas June 3, 2001, the first Sunday of June, falls between Mother's Day and Father's Day; whereas each child is unique, is a blessing, and holds a distinct place in the family unit; . . . whereas encouragement should be given to families to set aside special time for all family members to engage together in family activities; . . . whereas the designation of a day to commemorate our children will emphasize to the people of the United States the importance of the role of the child within the family and society:

87. Clinton, "Proclamation 7139."
88. Clinton, "Proclamation 7238."
89. Clinton, "Proclamation 7356."
90. Clinton, "Proclamation 7356."

Now, therefore, be it resolved, that the Senate designates June 3, 2001, as 'National Child's Day'...."[91]

Reflection: On May 25, 2001, the Senate of the United States passed Resolution 90, part of which is the text above, declaring June 3, 2001, National Child's Day. The resolution changed the date for honoring children from the second Sunday of October to what seems to be the first Sunday of June, and it also changed the name from National Children's Day to National Child's Day. In general, the three-page resolution contains the same language as its predecessors, some of the exceptions being presented in the above text. President George W. Bush accepted the resolution, understanding that the U.S. Senate was naming the first Sunday of June every year National Child's Day. In his two-page proclamation, Bush declared, "This special occasion gives us a unique opportunity to remember the joys and wonder of our own childhood and to reflect on how positive and healthy experiences in one's early years significantly influence later achievements and happiness." He continued: "Our nation must reaffirm its commitments to loving and caring for our children.... Because many youngsters now grow up in single-parent homes, we must promote responsible fatherhood, in all its aspects, including spiritual leadership, emotional security, and financial support.... We must also provide [young people] with a quality education, so that no child is left behind in our fast-paced global economy."[92] The "no child left behind" phrase becomes a trademark of Bush's administration concerning education. Deviating from the first Sunday of June for his 2002 proclamation of National Child's Day on June 9, Bush writes: "From the excitement of watching a toddler take a first step to the satisfaction of seeing [him or her] mature into adulthood, we are blessed to share our lives and experiences with children. Their thoughts, ideas, and unique perspectives renew our appreciation for life." Later, he writes, "... [W]e must use the resources of our families, communities, schools, and government to ensure that no child is left behind." After several paragraphs explaining what his administration is doing for families and children, Bush states: "I encourage all community leaders, educators, faith-based organizations, and citizens to seek opportunities to mentor, encourage, and listen to our children. As we observe National Child's Day, we should also communicate to young people that their dreams, aspirations, happiness, and wellbeing are important to us and to our future."[93] The 2003 National Child's Day was set for June 1, which returned it to the first Sunday in June for the rest of Bush's presidency. "Parents are a child's first teachers, and they can be the most effective instructors," states the president in his proclamation. "One of the most helpful activities parents can do with their children is read with them. Children who develop a love for reading expand their imaginations and cultivate a thirst for learning that lasts a lifetime.... Summertime... is also a time for parents to

---

91. "Senate Resolution 90."
92. Bush, G.W., "Proclamation 7446."
93. Bush, G.W., "Proclamation 7571."

strengthen their ties to their children by spending time with them and helping them to broaden their experiences." After mentioning the greater opportunities given to children by his administration, Bush urges "parents to spend more time with their children, read to them, listen to their concerns, offer guidance and love, and encourage their dreams."[94] "Children need our guidance and support," states Bush in his June 6, 2004, proclamation of National Child's Day. "During this time in America's history, teaching our children to love our nation and its values remains a critical responsibility," he writes. "We need to help young people understand that freedom is God's gift to every man and woman and that America's legacy is one of ensuring liberty for all. Our children also need to know about what other generations have done to build and preserve this great country, including the service and sacrifice of the men and women who have defended our nation."[95] Most of the two-page 2004 document explains what Bush's administration is doing in the area of education, including his signing of the No Child Left Behind Act of 2001. Nevertheless, he ends the proclamation by writing, "On National Child's Day, we recognize the importance of working together to create a society that is safe for our children, and we renew our commitment to helping families build a bright future for young people and our nation."[96]

The focus of Bush's June 5, 2005, National Child's Day proclamation is on family. "Family is the most important influence in a child's life," write Bush. "Parents are teachers, disciplinarians, advisors, and role models. By providing hope and stability, parents help children to understand the consequences of their actions and to recognize that the decisions they make today can affect the rest of their lives."[97] After family, Bush lists teachers. "Teachers also make a real difference in children's lives. America's educators help our students build character and acquire the skills and knowledge they need to succeed as adults."[98] The rest of the proclamation details what Bush's administration is doing to ensure that young people have a foundation of love and respect and insisting upon accountability in public schools. "On National Child's Day," writes Bush, "we underscore our commitment to supporting children and to helping them realize a bright and hopeful future."[99] There is a relatively short proclamation of June 4, 2006, as Bush begins, "A hopeful society ensures that its children are provided with the knowledge, skills, and opportunities to succeed." Then, Bush adds: "The character of a child is formed in the earliest years through the love and guidance of family members and other caring individuals. A parent, teacher, or mentor can help improve a child's academic achievement, encourage right choices, and help [him or her] to

---

94. Bush, G.W., "Proclamation 7683."
95. Bush, G.W., "Proclamation 7793."
96. Bush, G.W., "Proclamation 7793."
97. Bush, G.W., "Proclamation 7909."
98. Bush, G.W., "Proclamation 7909."
99. Bush, G.W., "Proclamation 7909."

understand the importance of serving a cause greater than self."[100] The June 3, 2007, proclamation of National Child's Day is about the administration's educational efforts, especially the reauthorization of the No Child Left Behind Act. "Today's children are tomorrow's leaders," states Bush, "and our nation has a responsibility to ensure that they develop the character and skills needed to succeed."[101] Bush's last proclamation of National Child's Day was June 1, 2008. "On National Child's Day," he wrote, "we underscore the importance of fostering the love, encouragement, and protection that empowers our children to become happy and successful adults."[102] Themes similar to Bush's previous proclamations are stated again along with the No Child Left Behind Act and other administration accomplishments in education. It also needs to be noted that during the Bush presidency, two resolutions concerning National Children's Day were introduced in the House of Representatives—Resolution 736 in 2004 and Resolution 103 in 2005—but neither of them was ever sent to the Senate. As early as 1979 (Resolution 174), legislation for National Child's Day was introduced in the House of Representatives and again in 2001 (Resolution 231) and 2008 (Resolution 1296), but never moved forward. Likewise, National Child's Day legislation was introduced in the Senate in 1999 (Resolution 111), 2000 (Resolution 296), 2001 (Resolution 90), and 2003 (Resolution 644), but never moved forward.

Journal/Meditation: What does "no child left behind" mean to you. What has been your experience of that philosophy (slogan)? Which one of Bush's remarks catches most of your attention? Why?

Prayer: LORD God, you provide parents, educators, and community leaders as mentors for the nation's children. Pour your grace upon them, and help them to communicate to children that their dreams, aspirations, happiness, and wellbeing are important to all citizens and to their future. Amen.

National Child's Day 2

November 20

Text: "America's children deserve every opportunity to reach their fullest potential, and it is our responsibility to ensure they have the tools required to grow and flourish. This includes providing our young people with access to affordable, high-quality health care and an education that both informs and inspires. On National Child's Day, we celebrate the promise living within every child."[103]

---

100. Bush, G.W., "Proclamation 8026."
101. Bush, G.W., "Proclamation 8152."
102. Bush, G.W., "Proclamation 8267."
103. Obama, "Proclamation 8457."

Reflection: Following Public Law 103–147 of 1993, which established the third Sunday in November as National Children's Day before Public Law 103–361 of 1994 moved it to the second Sunday in October, President Barack Obama proclaimed the third Sunday in November (22) 2009 as National Child's Day, the name for the day established by Senate Resolution 90 in 2001, when the observance of the day was set as the first Sunday of June. Most of Obama's proclamation is focused on the direction his administration is taking for parents and children. The basic outline for his future work is found in the above text taken from that first proclamation. Obama does declare: "Across America, countless individuals selflessly provide their time and energy in our homes, schools, and community organizations to ensure our sons and daughters may one day realize their dreams. Today, we recommit ourselves to the vision of our founders to give all our children a fair chance and an equal start in life."[104] In 2010, Obama proclaimed National Child's Day to be November 20, the same day as the United Nations' World (Universal, International) Children's Day. "On National Child's Day," he wrote, "we celebrate America's children and rededicate ourselves to helping them reach for their dreams and realize their full potential." He continued, "To build a strong foundation for our children's future, we must support their health and development and ensure that they receive a high-quality education that will prepare them to lead in the twenty-first century."[105] Obama, like George Bush, William Clinton, and George W. Bush before him spends most of this and his future proclamations on National Child's Day emphasizing his administration's themes of education, affordable health care, healthy eating, and exercise. Investing in children's education is given a long paragraph in the 2010 proclamation. He states that children's education, which is "a key to success and a prerequisite to opportunity," along with early childhood programs "can greatly influence learning capabilities later in life...." Obama writes: "Teachers are the most important resource to a child's learning, and countless children benefit from the experience and enthusiasm that teachers bring to the classroom. These individuals instill in our youth the knowledge that will enable them to grow into active and engaged adults." He concludes, "This Child's Day, let us recommit to instilling the values, vision, and knowledge that will allow our children to realize a future of opportunity and prosperity."[106] The theme of providing children with a future of opportunity and prosperity continues in the 2011 National Child's Day proclamation. "As a nation, we carry a fundamental responsibility to unlock the potential within every child," Obama writes. "Today, we celebrate our sons and daughters, and we recommit to giving them the future they deserve." Again, "On National Child's day, we remember that the promise of a brighter tomorrow is fulfilled by what we do for our children today."[107] Two very long paragraphs explain what his

104. Obama, "Proclamation 8457."
105. Obama, "Proclamation 8604."
106. Obama, "Proclamation 8604."
107. Obama, "Proclamation 8758."

administration is doing for children. The 2012 proclamation consists of a report on what Obama's administration is doing for children in the areas of education, healthy eating, and exercise. The opening paragraph, however, states: "All children deserve the chance to follow their passions, chase their dreams, and pursue their fullest measure of happiness. On National Child's Day, we celebrate the innumerable ways our sons and daughters have enriched our lives, and we rededicate ourselves to helping them achieve excellence in everything they do."[108] Obama's 2013 proclamation of National Child's Day being November 20 continues to reflect upon the theme of education: "In the United States of America, no matter where you come from, who you are, or how you look, you should have a chance to succeed," he writes. "That is why we must build ladders of opportunity for all children—including high-quality preschool, strong education in key fields like math and science, and nutritious meals that give young people the energy to focus." Later, he adds, "With the support of a nation and the guidance of parents and mentors, our children can lead America into a bright new age. Today, let us strengthen our resolve to provide the opportunities their energy and creativity demand."[109]

The opening paragraph for the 2014 National Child's Day proclamation, while lengthy, deserves reflection. "In the faces of today's children we see tomorrow's leaders and innovators," begins Obama. "Like their parents and grandparents before them, they have the potential to unearth new discoveries, pioneer bold inventions, and unlock groundbreaking solutions to longstanding problems. Every generation has sought to reach beyond the limits of the known world and push the boundaries of human imagination. But to realize what we know is possible for our daughters and sons, we must harness their talents and abilities." He concludes the opening paragraph, writing, "On National Child's Day, we recognize that success is built on a foundation of opportunity, and we continue our work to build a society where every child can seize his or her future."[110] After again focusing on education, healthy food, exercise, and affordable health care, he states: "As we celebrate the limitless potential of a generation born in an era of tremendous possibility, let us join with parents, professionals, and community members and renew our commitment to supporting the dreams of all our daughters and sons."[111] The phrase "daughters and sons"—instead of "sons and daughters"—continues to be used in the November 20, 2015, National Child's Day proclamation. The opening paragraph states: "Our greatest obligation is to our daughters and sons. With unbound imagination and limitless dreams, today's young Americans will carry forward our country's legacy and shape the contours of the twenty-first century and beyond. On National Child's Day, we reaffirm our support for them in all they do, and we uphold our commitment to enabling them with the tools and

---

108. Obama, "Proclamation 8907."
109. Obama, "Proclamation 9059."
110. Obama, "Proclamation 9212."
111. Obama, "Proclamation 9212."

resources necessary to write the next great chapter of our nation's story."[112] The work Obama's administration has done for children is recounted in the next three lengthy paragraphs. Nevertheless, Obama states, "Our children must have every opportunity to pursue their greatest aspirations—regardless of their background, their circumstances, or what zip code they were born into." Then, he calls upon citizens: "Today, let us rededicate ourselves to upholding the ideal that with hard work and dedication, America's children can make of their lives what they will. By supporting our youth and encouraging them to never give up on their dreams, we can forge a brighter future for them, their children and grandchildren, and all future generations."[113] Obama's last presidential proclamation of National Child's Day took place in 2016. Material from his 2015 proclamation is echoed in the opening paragraph: "No matter what zip code they are born into, every young child in America deserves the opportunity to learn, grow, and realize their dreams in a safe and healthy environment. From ensuring they are cared for and nourished to helping them become educated participants in our democracy, we must all do our part to support the next generation of leaders. Today, let us lift up every child in need and strive to leave behind a world that we are proud of for children across our country."[114] Later, after several paragraphs recounting his administration's accomplishments for children and parents, he states, "We know that when we invest in young children, the outcomes are significant—and by investing in early education and preschool for all, we can set children up for success later in life." Words worthy of reflection are found near the end of the proclamation: "Our journey is not complete until all our children are cared for, cherished, and safe from harm. On National Child's Day, let us forge a future of greater opportunity and prosperity for every young person, and let us seek to reach our greatest potential as a nation by ensuring our daughters and sons can live up to theirs."[115] Donald Trump made no proclamations designating National Child's Day observances. However, President Joseph R. Biden chose to follow Obama's lead and proclaimed November 20, 2021, National Child's Day. Echoing Obama, Biden wrote in the opening paragraph: "Our nation's children are the kite strings that hold our national ambitions aloft—and it is our shared responsibility to make sure that they have every opportunity to thrive. On National Child's Day, we recommit ourselves to ensuring that every child in America has a fair shot at a bright future, regardless of the gender, race, ethnicity, or the zip code [he or she is] born into."[116] After recounting his administration's plans for children and families in the future in three lengthy paragraphs, Biden states: "We owe every child the opportunity to dream and flourish, supported by adults helping to make their dreams a reality. On National Child's Day, we reaffirm our commitment

112. Obama, "Proclamation 9370."
113. Obama, "Proclamation 9370."
114. Obama, "Proclamation 9545."
115. Obama, "Proclamation 9545."
116. Biden, "Proclamation 10312."

to uplift the children in our lives and in our communities. Their future is our future, and our nation's success tomorrow relies on the care and investment we provide for our children today."[117]

Journal/Meditation: For you, what are the necessary ingredients for a successful childhood? To you what is the difference between the phrase "sons and daughters" and the phrase "daughters and sons"? Which one of Obama's or Biden's remarks catches most of your attention? Why?

Prayer: Heavenly Father, you create your children so that they can follow their passions, chase their dreams, and pursue their fullest measure of happiness in your presence. Stretch out your hand in blessing over all children, and give their parents and mentors the wisdom and imagination to guide the future leaders of our nation to carry forward the legacy of our country today, tomorrow, and forever. Amen.

GREAT AMERICAN SMOKEOUT
Third Thursday

Text: "The Great American Smokeout is an opportunity for people who smoke to commit to healthy, smoke-free lives—not just for a day, but year round. The Great American Smokeout provides an opportunity for individuals, community groups, businesses, health care providers, and others to encourage people to use the date to make a plan to quit or plan in advance and initiate a smoking cessation plan on the day of the event. The Great American Smokeout event challenges people to stop smoking and helps people learn about the many tools they can use to help them quit and stay quit."[118]

Reflection: There is a difference between a smoke out—to drive somebody or something from a hiding place by using smoke—and a smokeout—a day during which smokers are encourage to abstain from smoking as part of a campaign to emphasize the hazards of the practice. In 1970, Arthur P. Mullaney asked people in Randolph, Massachusetts, to give up cigarettes for a day and donate the money they would have spent on cigarettes to a high school scholarship fund. Lynn R. Smith, editor of the *Monticello Times* in Minnesota led the first Don't Smoke Day in 1974. By 1976, the idea had caught on, and on November 18 of that year, the California Division of the American Cancer Society got close to a million people to quit smoking for the day. The next year the American Cancer Society made the event national. As a result, smoking was limited in restaurants in Berkeley, California, as early as 1977. San Francisco eliminated smoking in private workplaces in 1983. Smoke-free domestic flights of six hours of less became federal law in 1990. By 1994, states began to file lawsuits seeking

---
117. Biden, "Proclamation 10312."
118. "History of the Great American Smokeout."

millions of dollars from tobacco companies to pay for the cost of smoking-related illnesses. Also in 1994, ABC News aired a report revealing how cigarette companies manipulated the nicotine in their products to cause and sustain addiction in people who smoke. The U.S. Food and Drug Administration began an investigation on the manipulation of nicotine and how children were being targeted through advertising and promotion in 1994. By 1999, the Department of Justice filed suit against cigarette manufacturers, charging the industry with defrauding the public by lying about the risks of smoking. Also in 1999, a settlement was passed which required tobacco companies to cover Medicaid costs of treating people who smoke.

The Great American Smokeout Event is held annually on the third Thursday of November by the American Cancer Society. Because addiction to nicotine in cigarettes is one of the strongest and most deadly addictions one can have, research shows that people who smoke are most successful in their efforts to stop smoking when they have support from telephone hotlines, American Cancer Society programs, Nicotine Anonymous meetings, self-help books and materials, smoking counselors or coaches, and encouragement and support from friends and family members. The annual event has changed the attitudes of many people about smoking, and those changes have been manifested in community programs and smoke-free laws that save lives. In the 1970s when all this began, smoking was common, and secondhand smoke was everywhere. The event draws attention to preventing deaths and chronic illnesses caused by smoking, manifested in banning smoking in many places, raising taxes on cigarettes, limiting cigarette promotions, discouraging teen cigarette use, and other actions that counter smoking, the leading cause of cancer death—lung cancer, larynx cancer, mouth cancer, sinuses cancer, throat cancer, esophagus cancer, bladder cancer—in the United States. It also seems to be linked to pancreas, cervix, ovary, colon, kidney, and stomach cancers, and some types of leukemia. The journey to a smoke-free life begins with a plan; quitting is a process. Because smoking is the single largest preventable cause of death and illness in the world, the first step toward a healthier life and reducing one's cancer risk may begin with a rally, a parade, gathering information about quitting-smoking programs, etc. on the Great American Smokeout. Anything that highlights the dangers of smoking and challenges people to stop using tobacco—including the Collegiate Smokeout, which takes place on college campus the same day as the Great American Smokeout—can lead to a healthier and longer life for those who act on what they learn.

Journal/Meditation: What attitude change is necessary for a person to commit to arrive at a smoke-free life? Do you know anyone who quit smoking? What plan did he or she employ to quit smoking? If you are a person who smokes, why have you not quit?

Prayer for Smokers: LORD God, you are an always-close helper in time of need. Give me the strength to stop smoking. Because smoking does not benefit me financially, physically, emotionally, or spiritually, hear my cry and deliver me from my nicotine addiction. Amen.

Prayer for Non-Smokers: LORD God, you are an always-close helper in time of need. Pour your grace upon the members of my family and friends, and give them strength to overcome their addiction to nicotine. Make them living temples of your glory now and forever. Amen.

World Television Day

November 21

Text: "Recalling . . . that the United Nations cannot achieve its purposes unless the peoples of the world are fully informed of its aims and activities; recalling also its resolutions concerning information in service of humanity and United Nations public information policies and activities; reaffirming its commitment . . . to the principles of freedom of information, as well as to those of the independence, pluralism, and diversity of the media; underlining that communications have become one of the today's central international issues, not only for their relevance for the world economy, but also for their implications for social and cultural development; recognizing the increasing impact that television has on decision-making by alerting world attention to conflicts and threats to peace and security and its potential role in sharpening the focus on other major issues, including economic and social issues; underlining . . . that television, as one of today's most powerful communications media, could play a role in presenting these issues to the world; noting with satisfaction the holding . . . on 21 and 22 November 1996 of the first World Television Forum, where leading media figures met under the auspices of the United Nations to discuss the growing significance of television in today's changing world and to consider how they might enhance their mutual cooperation; [the General Assembly of the United Nations:] 1. Decides to proclaim 21 November World Television Day, commemorating the date on which the first World Television Forum was held; 2. Invites all member states to observe World Television Day by . . . focusing, among other things, on such issues as peace, security, economic and social development, and the enhancement of cultural exchange . . . ."[119]

Reflection: On December 17, 1996, the General Assembly of the United Nations declared November 21 to be the annual commemoration of World Television Day. The resolution, from which the above text is taken, decided on November 21 because on November 21 and 22, 1996, the U.N. had held the first World Television Forum, which is mentioned in the above text. "U.N. leaders recognized that television could bring attention to conflicts, raise awareness of threats to peace and security, and sharpen focus

---

119. United Nations General Assembly, A/RES/51/205.

on social and economic issues," states *National Today*. "Television was acknowledged as a major tool in informing, channeling, and affecting public opinion, having an undoubtable presence and influence on world politics." The General Assembly of the U.N. chose "not to celebrate the object itself [(the TV)], but the symbol for communication and globalization in the contemporary world that it represents."[120] In other words, "Television is a symbol of communication and globalization that educates, informs, entertains, and influences our decisions and opinions."[121] According to *Days of the Year*, ". . . World Television Day is not meant to be so much a celebration of the electronic tool itself, but rather of the philosophy which it represents—a philosophy of openness and transparency of world issues."[122]

The first broadcasts on the monochrome screen from only three studios (ABC, CBS, NBC) advanced quickly to color, hundreds of channels, larger and larger TVs, and ongoing sophisticated optics and digital enhancements. "Television continues to be the single largest source of video consumption," states the U.N.'s World Television Day webpage. "Though screen sizes have changed, and people create, post, stream, and consume content on different platforms, the number of households with television sets around the world continues to rise. The interaction between emerging and traditional forms of broadcast creates a great opportunity to raise awareness about the important issues facing our communities and our planet."[123] U.N. Web TV is the official streaming video platform for live and on-demand coverage of U.N. meetings and events. UNTV provides live feeds and HD broadcast-quality files on demand. U.N. videos from around the world are produced for news and social media platforms, as well as for broadcast partners in the six official languages of the UN: French, Spanish, English, Chinese, Arabic, and Russian. The U.N. Audio-Visual Library archives video and audio that mark iconic and historic moments from the last seventy years. On World Television Day, we remember that television helped to bring the reality of a rapidly changing world into homes and changed forever the way people perceived the world. It is a good day to sit in front of the television (meaning *vision at a distance*) and notice how it informs and changes both your world view, your politics, and your spirituality.

Journal/Meditation: How does television affect the decisions you make about the world, economy, politics, and spirituality? What recent world issue did television help you understand better?

Prayer: Through the ongoing development of the technology of television, the world can see at a distance what is taking place around the globe, O God. Grant as I see and understand that I may also grow in deeper compassion for people who suffer in all

---

120. "World Television Day," *National Today*.
121. "World Television Day," *National Today*.
122. "World Television Day," *Days of the Year*.
123. "World Television Day," United Nations.

kinds of ways. Also, grant that my spirituality may be enhanced through the news that streams into my home through the television. Amen.

THANKSGIVING DAY
Fourth Thursday

Text: "Whereas it is the duty of all nations to acknowledge the providence of Almighty God, to obey his will, to be grateful for his benefits, and humbly to implore his protection and favor; and whereas both Houses of Congress have . . . requested me 'to recommend to the people of the United States a day of public thanksgiving and prayer, to be observed by acknowledging with grateful hearts the many and signal favors of Almighty God, especially by affording them an opportunity peaceably to establish a form of government for their safety and happiness:' I [, George Washington,] recommend and assign Thursday, the twenty-sixth day of November [, 1789,] . . . to be devoted by the people of these states to the service of that great and glorious Being who is the beneficent author of all the good that was, that is, or that will be; that we may then all unite in rendering unto him our sincere and humble thanks for his kind care and protection of the people of this country previous to their becoming a nation; for the signal and manifold mercies and the favorable interpositions of his providence in the course and conclusion of the late [Revolutionary] war; for the great degree of tranquility, union, and plenty which we have since enjoyed; for the peaceable and rational manner in which we have been enabled to establish constitutions of government for our safety and happiness, and particularly the national one now lately instituted; for the civil and religious liberty with which we are blessed, and the means we have of acquiring and diffusing useful knowledge; and in general, for all the great and various favors which he has been pleased to confer upon us."[124]

Reflection: When George Washington was commander of the Continental Army, he agreed with the Continental Congress that December 18, 1777, should be set aside as the first national thanksgiving day of the recently-formed United States of America. After the Revolutionary War was won, the Constitution prepared, and Washington became the first president of the U.S., he accepted congress' recommendation and declared November 26, 1789, a day of public thanksgiving and prayer, offering "supplications to the great Lord and Ruler of Nations . . . to enable us all, whether in public or private stations, to perform our several and relative duties properly and punctually; . . . to promote the knowledge and practice of true religion and virtue, and the increase of science . . . ; and, generally, to grant unto all [human]kind such a degree of temporal prosperity as he alone knows to be best."[125] The text above forms a list of what citizens should thank God. In 1795, Washington issued another proclamation

124. Washington, "Proclamation."
125. Washington, "Proclamation."

about the "circumstances which peculiarly mark our situation with indications of the Divine beneficence toward us" along with another list leading citizens "to acknowledge [their] many and great obligations to Almighty God and to implore him to continue and confirm the blessing [they] experience."[126] Washington called upon "all persons whomsoever, within the United States, to set apart and observe Thursday, the nineteenth day of February [1795], as a day of public thanksgiving and prayer . . . to the Great Ruler of Nations for the manifold and signal mercies which distinguish [their] lot as a nation . . . ."[127] Thereafter follows a long list of blessings for which people should be thankful. After Washington, presidents continued to issue Thanksgiving Proclamations, but the dates and the months varied. Standardization of Thanksgiving Day began with President Abraham Lincoln, who issued two proclamations "in the midst of a Civil War of unequaled magnitude and severity."[128] In 1863, he asked his fellow citizens "to set apart and observe the last Thursday of November . . . as a day of thanksgiving and praise to [their] beneficent Father who dwell[s] in the heavens." He wrote about the year having "been filled with the blessings of fruitful fields and healthful skies." He added, "To these bounties, which are so constantly enjoyed that we are prone to forget the source from which they come, others have been added which are of so extraordinary a nature that they cannot fail to penetrate and soften even the heart which is habitually insensible to the ever-watchful providence of Almighty God."[129] After presenting a list of blessings for which citizens should be thankful, Lincoln wrote: "No human counsel ha[s] devised nor ha[s] any mortal hand worked out these great things. They are the gracious gifts of the Most High God . . . ."[130] In 1864, he again appointed and set apart "the last Thursday in November . . . as a day of thanksgiving and praise to Almighty God, the beneficent Creator and Ruler of the Universe."[131] Lincoln lists the blessing from the Heavenly Father that have come to citizens in their homes, soldiers in their camps, and sailors on the seas as: health, emancipation, immigration, wealth, and labor's rewards. "Moreover," states Lincoln, "he has been pleased to animate and inspire our minds and hearts with fortitude, courage, and resolution sufficient for the great trial of civil war into which we have been brought by our adherence as a nation to the cause of freedom and humanity, and to afford to us reasonable hopes of an ultimate and happy deliverance from all our dangers and afflictions."[132]

After 1864, presidents continued to issue proclamations of a Thanksgiving Day being usually the last Thursday of November. However, there were some proclamations of it taking place in October and December. President Franklin D. Roosevelt

126. Washington, "Proclamation 6."
127. Washington, "Proclamation 6."
128. Lincoln, "Proclamation 106."
129. Lincoln, "Proclamation 106."
130. Lincoln, "Proclamation 106."
131. Lincoln, "Proclamation 118."
132. Lincoln, "Proclamation 118."

proclaimed the fifth (last) Thursday of November—the thirtieth—of 1933 to be a day of thanksgiving for people to "give humble thanks for the blessings bestowed upon [them] during the year past by Almighty God."[133] In 1934, he proclaimed November 29 a Day of Thanksgiving, writing, ". . . [T]o set aside in the autumn of each year a day on which to give thanks to Almighty God for the blessings of life is a wise and reverent custom, long cherished by our people."[134] In 1935, he proclaimed the last (fourth) Thursday to be a Day of National Thanksgiving. "We can well be grateful that more and more of our people understand and seek the greater good of the greater number," he wrote. He urged all citizens to show their "appreciation [for] the blessings that Divine Providence ha[d] bestowed upon [them] in America."[135] The last (fourth) Thursday in November 1936 was designated a day of national thanksgiving by Roosevelt. ". . . [I]t is our right to express our gratitude that Divine Providence has vouchsafed us wisdom and courage to overcome adversity," he wrote.[136] "The custom of observing a day of public thanksgiving began in Colonial times," wrote Roosevelt in his proclamation that the last (fourth) Thursday in November 1937 was a day of National Thanksgiving, "and has been given the sanction of national observance through many years. It is in keeping with all of our traditions that we, even as our father [and mothers] in olden days, give humble and hearty thanks for the bounty and the goodness of Divine Providence."[137] In 1938, Roosevelt proclaimed November 24 (the last or fourth Thursday) as a day of general thanksgiving. In his proclamation he mentions George Washington's thanksgiving proclamations along with Abraham Lincoln's thanksgiving proclamations. ". . . [F]rom our earliest recorded history, American's have thanked God for their blessings," he wrote.[138] In 1939, Roosevelt did not proclaim the last (fifth) Thursday of November as Thanksgiving Day; he changed it to the fourth Thursday, November 23. He invited citizens "on the day set aside for [the] purpose [of general thanksgiving to] give thanks to the Ruler of the Universe for the strength which he has vouchsafed [them] to carry on [their] daily labors and for the hope that lives within [them] of the coming of a day when peace and the productive activities of peace shall reign on every continent."[139] In 1940[140] and in 1941,[141] Roosevelt moved the national day of thanksgiving to the third (out of four) Thursday in November, specifically November 21, 1941, and November 20, 1941. On December 26, 1941, Roosevelt signed Public Law 77–379, which stated 'that the fourth Thursday

133. Roosevelt, "Proclamation 2062."
134. Roosevelt, "Proclamation 2107."
135. Roosevelt, "Proclamation 2146."
136. Roosevelt, "Proclamation 2208."
137. Roosevelt, "Proclamation 2260."
138. Roosevelt, "Proclamation 2310."
139. Roosevelt, "Proclamation 2373."
140. Roosevelt, "Proclamation 2441."
141. Roosevelt, "Proclamation 2522."

of November in each year after the year 1941 be known as Thanksgiving Day, and is hereby made a legal public holiday."[142] Since 1942, when Roosevelt issued his proclamation, which "solemnly express[es] . . . dependence upon Almighty God," when the United States is "waging a battle on many fronts for the preservation of liberty . . . in this time of national emergency," Thanksgiving Day was celebrated (on November 26) and continues to be celebrated on the fourth Thursday in November.[143] Over the course of the years, Thanksgiving Day lost its focus on God's providence for the nation and shifted to individual homes with a meal of turkey, dressing, potatoes, green-bean casserole, and pumpkin pie. Instead of being celebrated as a public holiday, it has morphed into a day of parades, football games, and other sports events.

Journal/Meditation: In your lifetime, what changes in the observance of Thanksgiving Day have you witnessed? George Washington referred to the "glorious Being (God) who is the beneficent author of all the good that was, that is, or that will be." For what in the past, in the present, and in the future do you thank Almighty God? What president's words in the above reflection get most of your attention? Why?

Prayer: Almighty God, I humbly beseech you that all citizens of the United States prove themselves to be a nation mindful of your bountiful favors. Defend our liberties, and continue to fashion us into one united people. Fill with your Spirit of wisdom those we elect to serve us. Fill our hearts with thankfulness and praise to you now and forever. Amen.

BLACK FRIDAY

Friday after Thanksgiving

Text: "Black Friday: The Day after Thanksgiving, regarded as the first day of the traditional Christmas shopping season, on which retailers offer special reduced prices. Origin: . . . The shopping sense dates from the 1960s and was originally used with reference to congestion created by shoppers; it was later explained as a day when retailers' accounts went from being 'in the red' to 'in the black.'"[144]

Reflection: As the above Oxford-powered English dictionary entry states, the first popular use of the phrase "Black Friday" was by traffic-weary Philadelphia officers in the early 1960s. Before that in 1951, it was used to describe the high worker absenteeism on the Friday after Thanksgiving giving them a four-day weekend. Philadelphia police officers revived its use to describe the traffic jams caused by shoppers. Philadelphia merchants disliked the term because it seemed to them to describe a negative situation. Indeed, it had been used to describe the St. Valentine's Day massacre of

---

142. "Public Law 77–379."
143. Roosevelt, "Proclamation 2571, Proclamation 2600, Proclamation 2629."
144. "Black Friday."

mobsters in Chicago and financial panics of 1869 and 1873! The merchants proposed other names, but nothing seemed to work. One solution was that the black in black Friday referred to the profits made by stores (in the black) as opposed to being in the red (loss) until Black Friday, when they posted profits. In other words, this was an attempt by merchants to rebrand the day with positive connotations.[145]

Black Friday, no matter what its connotations, has come to be regarded as the beginning of the Christmas shopping season. The next major holiday after Thanksgiving is Christmas, so it would only make sense that, since most people mark the Friday after Thanksgiving as the second of a four-day weekend, the Christmas shopping season would begin with an increase in the number of potential shoppers. Retailers cater to shoppers by hosting all kinds of sales, including limited items for those who get to the stores early. This serves to create a sense of urgency among shoppers; they want to begin shopping early in order to have access to the doorbuster sales. Joining the many other shoppers on the day after Thanksgiving has a spiritual aspect, too. All those on crowded streets and in crowded stores and overflowing malls are engaged in the same enterprise: shopping. There can be generated a sense of unity of purpose as shoppers help merchants switch from red ink to black ink.

Journal/Meditation: Have you shopped on Black Friday? If yes, did you feel a sense of urgency? Describe it. If not, what do you do on the Friday after Thanksgiving?

Prayer: I give thanks to you, Heavenly Father, for my home, my clothes, and my food. I give thanks to you for my family, my friends, and my neighbors. Bless those who labor on Black Friday with patience. Bless those who shop on Black Friday with joy. Keep all safe on this busy shopping day. Amen.

Small Business Saturday
Saturday after Thanksgiving

Text: ". . . [W]hereas small businesses focus on two key strategies: deepening relationships with customers and creating value for customers; whereas . . . consumers in the United States agree that the success of small businesses is critical to the overall economic health of the United States; . . . that small businesses contribute positively to the local community by supplying jobs and generating tax revenue; consumers . . . have small businesses in their community that the consumers would miss if the small businesses closed; [and] whereas . . . consumers . . . agree that it is important to support the small businesses in their community, . . . the Senate . . . supports efforts—(a) to encourage consumers to shop locally; and (b) to increase awareness of the value of

---

145. Zimmer, "Origins of 'Black Friday.'"

locally owned small businesses and the impact of locally owned small businesses on the economy of the United States."[146]

Reflection: Small Business Saturday is a shopping holiday on the Saturday after Thanksgiving—that is, the Saturday after Black Friday—falling between November 24 and November 30. The day was created by American Express in 2010, as a result of the recession of 2008, in an effort to spotlight small businesses and encourage consumers to shop locally both in person and online. The first Small Business Saturday took place on November 27, 2010. In partnership with the National Trust for Historic Preservation and American Express, the day was promoted nationwide through radio and television advertising campaigns. The goal of the day is to highlight the importance of small businesses in local communities and increase their sales during the Christmas shopping season. It is easy for larger companies to receive all the focus on Black Friday; Small Business Saturday encourages shoppers to visit small and locally owned businesses, such as restaurants, salons, specialty grocery stores, service-based businesses, etc. and give them a revenue boost, which, in turn, promotes a healthier local economy. When families and friends visit local brick-and-mortal businesses—and/or shop online—they are fostering the growth of their local economy. Usually, small businesses offer special sales events, discounts, and other incentives to encourage shoppers to visit their stores. Neighborhood Champions, organizations that promote Small Business Saturday, assist in advertising the day. Local libraries, visitor centers, and chambers of commerce use posters, message boards, and other means to call attention to the day. Small Business Saturday is a registered trademark of American Express Marketing & Development Corporation; the words "Shop Small" in a circle within a square identifies a business as one observing Small Business Saturday under the auspices of American Express.

On November 10, 2011, in preparation for the second Small Business Saturday, the U.S. Senate issued Resolution 320, from which the above text is taken. After designating November 26, 2011, as Small Business Saturday, the senate expressed its support to increase awareness of the value of locally owned small businesses. According to the resolution, small businesses represent 99.7 percent of all businesses having employees in the U.S. They employ one half of the employees in the private sector; they pay 44 percent of the total payroll of the employees in the private sector in the U.S.; they are responsible for more than 50 percent of the private, nonfarm product of the gross domestic product; they generated 65 percent of net new jobs during the last 17 years [previous to 2011]; and they generate 60 to 80 percent of all new jobs annually.[147]

Journal/Meditation: Why is it important to you to have a good relationship with small business owners in your community? What is the spiritual dimension of shopping

---

146. "Senate Resolution 320."
147. "Senate Resolution 320."

locally in small businesses? What guidelines do you use when determining whether to shop in a small business or in a large box store?

Prayer: Holy God, send your Spirit of Wisdom to guide me and all shoppers during this holiday season. Bless all small business owners with grateful shoppers from their communities. And grant that both business owners and shoppers are filled with gratitude and hope this day, tomorrow, and forever. Amen.

Cyber Monday
Monday after Thanksgiving

Text: "12 Tips to Stay Safe on Cyber Monday: Tip 1: Check the URL in the browser bar. Some fraud sites will mirror the real site and put it on a URL that is very similar . . . . Tip 2: Make sure your antivirus software is up to date and doing regular scans of your computer. Tip 3: If you try to visit a site and a malware warning page appears, do not visit the site, even if it is a reputable site, until the warning page is removed. Tip 4: Do not open or click on any links within e-mails that seem suspicious. If you are concerned, get in contact with the site you believe the e-mail is from and confirm with [it]. Tip 5: When on the checkout pages, make sure at the start of the web address there is an https:// . . . . And there should be a small padlock icon in the address also. [This] indicates it's a safe and secure connection. Tip 6: Choose a strong password and mix it up for every site. . . . Tip 7: Only visit reputable sites that you know are safe. Tip 8: Keep your online receipts and check them against your statement. If you think you've spotted an unauthorized payment, contact your bank. Tip 9: Never share private information, such as card details and passwords, with anyone online. If you're having problems with the payment steps or have forgotten your password, etc., either contact the site in question, or ask someone you trust offline—never online. Tip 10: If you try to bid for an item on an auction site and the buyer tries to get you to trade off-site, be very careful. If you agree to do this, you will not be covered. Tip 11: Keep your web browser up to date. Tip 12: If using a mobile device, be extra cautious. Mobile [may not have yet] caught up with all the built-in safety features desktops [and laptops] currently have."[148]

Reflection: On November 21, 2005, Shop.org published a press release, stating, ". . . [O]nline retailers have set their sights on something different: Cyber Monday, the Monday after Thanksgiving, which is quickly becoming one of the biggest online shopping days of the year."[149] With that line from the news release, the term "Cyber Monday" was born. According to John Sutter, "Ellen Davis, vice president of the National Retail Federation, which owns CyberMonday.com (and Shop.org), said

---

148. "Twelve Tips."
149. Sutter, "Why."

the 'Cyber Monday' term originated organically as retailers noticed that consumers turned to the internet to shop on the Monday after Thanksgiving."[150] According to Robert Hof, "[t]he idea was born when a few people at the organization were brainstorming about how to promote online shopping, says Shop.org Executive Director Scott Silverman. . . ."[151] The trend to shop online on the Monday after Thanksgiving—between November 26 and December 2—had actually started earlier in 2002 and 2003. As workers returned to their offices after a four-day Thanksgiving weekend, they began to use the better computer connections there (in opposition to those they had at home) to do the shopping they did not finish on Black Friday or Small Business Saturday. All the National Retail Federation did was to put a name on the day workers shopped online. Hof quotes Silverman as stating, ". . . [I]t was an opportunity to create some consumer excitement."[152] Merchants post once-a-year deals online for those workers using their employers' computers and for those at home to tackle their shopping lists. As a result, online shopping on the Monday following Thanksgiving has grown steadily since 2005.

The text above presents twelve tips when shopping international online retailers, no matter if one is shopping from work or at home. Merchants, both operating large and small businesses, offer more and more deals. Cyber Monday offers people the opportunity to buy gifts that family members cannot know about. This has made the day an annual event for online holiday shoppers. While some employers have put an end to employees' use of company equipment, there is still plenty of time to shop from home by taking precautions, like checking the URL in the browser bar, updating antivirus software, paying attention to malware, avoiding links, being sure of secure checkout sites, making sure passwords are strong and changed often, visiting only reputable sites, checking online receipts against credit or debit card statements, never sharing private information online, not trading offsite when bidding on an auction, keeping an up-to-date browser, and being sure that all devices used for shopping are protected. Employing the tips in the above text can provide a good experience for finding bargains on Cyber Monday.

Journal/Meditation: Out of the twelve tips presented above, which one most needs your improvement? What do you need to do? What is the spiritual dimension of shopping online on Cyber Monday?

Prayer: Almighty God, on this Cyber Monday fill me with the Spirit of Wisdom to judge wisely what I purchase online for those I love. Keep me generous, yet keep me frugal, so that I do not spend beyond my means. Keep me safe today. Amen.

---

150. Sutter, "Why."
151. Hof, "Cyber Monday."
152. Hof, "Cyber Monday."

Giving Tuesday
Tuesday after Thanksgiving

Text: "Giving Tuesday is a movement that unleashes the power of radical generosity around the world. Giving Tuesday reimagines a world built upon shared humanity and generosity. [Its] global network collaborates year-round to inspire generosity around the world, with a common mission to build a world where generosity is part of everyday life. Whether it's making someone smile, helping a neighbor or stranger . . . , showing up for an issue or people . . . care[d] about, or giving some of what [one has] to those who need . . . help, every act of generosity counts, and everyone has something to give."[153]

Reflection: On what has come to be known as Giving Tuesday, the Tuesday after Thanksgiving—falling between November 27 to December 3—began November 27, 2012. Henry Timms at the 92nd Street Y and its Belfer Center for Innovation & Social Impact in New York City along with the United Nations Organization began the day with the simple idea of encouraging people to do good by donating to charity after they finished Cyber Monday shopping. The founders wanted to "[d]evise a way to spread the values of the Y beyond its Upper East Side confines, and give people a way to pivot back to the values of community and gratitude celebrated on Thanksgiving after Black Friday and Cyber Monday."[154] Now as an independent nonprofit and global movement, it inspires millions of people to give, collaborate, and celebrate generosity. According to Zoe Fox on *Mashable*, a technology website, the "new annual celebration is less about buying gifts and more about giving back."[155] In addition to *Mashable*, the original founding partners include Skype, DoGoodBuy.Us, Ampush, Pencils of Promise, and Cisco. The goal is "to drive the energy of the connected generation toward creating positive change in the world. [I]t's not a day focused on spreading awareness for one cause or raising money for one charity. The goal is to channel the giving spirit of the Holiday Season into a powerful day of action. This is about improving . . . community and taking action where [one] find[s] it most needed."[156] In 2012, Giving Tuesday raised $10.1 million, which continued to increase year by year to 2021's $2.7 billion. In 2022, Giving Tuesday, which has grown into a global movement, marks its tenth anniversary.

According to John Otis and Remy Tumin, "The branding was meant to go viral, to inspire widespread fund-raising for all kinds of nonprofit groups: everything from clothing to food and blood drives to random acts of kindness. . . . [I]t would celebrate many different ways of getting involved and helping others."[157] In other words, in 2015,

- 153. "About Giving Tuesday."
- 154. Otis and Tumin, "On Giving Tuesday."
- 155. Fox, "Inspiring."
- 156. Fox, "Inspiring."
- 157. Otis and Tumin, "On Giving Tuesday."

the goal was achieving name recognition, which would ensure continued growth in money, volunteering, and other incentives to encourage people to donate on the day and get involved in the movement. According to Asha Curran, "... [G]enerosity must be at the heart of the society we rebuild together, unlocking dignity, opportunity, and equity around the globe."[158] "What we need," states Curran, "is not incremental but radical generosity—generosity not as a benevolence that the haves show to the have-nots, but rather an expression of mutuality, solidarity, and reciprocity." She continues, "Radical generosity transcends simply giving money—which unfortunately has yet to stop wars, suffering, and inequity through the ages—and focuses our efforts to love, help, understand, offer hope, and find new ways of healing at the root of our issues."[159] Curran, co-founder and CEO of Giving Tuesday, continues: "When we act collectively, ... we can make massive change happen. We know it can work and our collective action has so much potential still untapped. ... [W]e see people across all borders, sectors, and beliefs come together as a global movement in shared moments to give, mobilizing communities, and strengthening the ties that bind us together as a society. ... Our goal is to uncover grassroots innovation, emerging opportunities for collaboration, and analyzing data to understand how radical generosity is happening and mobilize more people to act on this idea, just as we have with Giving Tuesday throughout its nearly ten-year history."[160] In her *Newsweek* opinion, Curran explains that radical generosity "illustrates that our neighbors should be clothed, fed, cared for, and included, and this should not be restricted to the realm of nonprofits, governments, large corporations, or wealthy individuals." She writes: "Philanthropic power is something each of us holds, even if we haven't discovered it yet." It "is within the capacity of every single human to practice, and the intentional practicing of it brings healing, forges strong bonds between people, and strengthens communities. ... By actively caring for our fellow humans—through acts of kindness, mutual aid, volunteering, outreach, conversation, or financial giving—we can build connections, bring forth equity, and exercise empathy."[161] In order to help "amplify the next generation of young leaders to be organizers, thought-leaders, and campaign managers for a more generous world," Giving Tuesday launched Giving Tuesday Spark! for "youth shaking up and spearheading many of the major movements on key issues facing our world today, from climate change to healthcare to student debt."[162] Young people all over the world are challenged "to participate in service projects, volunteer activities, and acts of kindness in honor of Giving Tuesday."[163]

158. Curran, "We Must Embrace Radical Generosity."
159. Curran, "We Must Embrace Radical Generosity."
160. Curran, "We Must Embrace Radical Generosity."
161. Curran, "We Must Embrace Radical Generosity."
162. "Introducing."
163. "Introducing."

Journal/Meditation: How do you think Giving Tuesday is an antithesis of consumer culture and a way for people to give back? In what radical generosity have you engaged? What everyday life generosity do you have to give that expresses mutuality, solidarity, and reciprocity?

Prayer: God of all that is good, fill me and all people with the spirit of radical generosity. Inspire all to join together to share our riches, no matter how small, with others to create a more generous world through acts of kindness, mutual aid, volunteering, outreach, conversation, and financial giving that equity and empathy may abound to your glory. Amen.

12

The Month of *December*

WORLD AIDS DAY
December 1

Text: "The stigma that surrounded AIDS was actually twofold. One . . . , was what you could easily argue had to do with homophobia. But also there was a stigma of fear. There was a lot that people felt they did not know about the epidemic, and they were afraid. And they were right to be afraid because of the things that they were hearing. So, I think the stigma that surrounded [AIDS] made it something that people didn't want to talk about. . . . [I]t was something that they didn't know what to say, if it came into their lives. And . . . for people who were affected by it, they did not want to bring up whatever it was that their experience was with it because in those days, people were being fired from their job. They were being denied Social Security benefits. They were being ostracized by their families. They were being evicted from their homes because they were sick and dying. . . . [P]eople were integrating . . . fear into their lives. And we've seen that change now. You don't see that same kind of thing. . . . I think the symbolism is not insignificant, and I think it's not without substance. The fact that . . . conversation occurs on an annual basis on World AIDS day is significant."[1]

Reflection: In the above text, James W Bunn, then-president of Global Health Communications and one of the founders of World AIDS Day with Thomas Netter, spoke with Melissa Block on National Public Radio on December 1, 2011, about the beginning of World AIDS Day on December 1, 1988. This international day is dedicated to raising awareness of the acquired immunodeficiency syndrome (AIDS) caused by the spread of the human immunodeficiency virus (HIV) and the life-threatening conditions that result. Basically, the virus attacks the immune system and reduces the person's resistance to other diseases. AIDS is the final stage of a person living with HIV. In August 1987, Bunn and Netter, who were public information officers for the Global

---

1. Block, "How World AIDS Day Began."

Program on AIDS at the World Health Organization (WHO) in Geneva, Switzerland, took their idea to Jonathan Mann, then the Director of the Global Program on AIDS, who liked the concept, approved it, and agreed that the first observance of World AIDS Day should be December 1, 1988. That date was chosen because it was long enough after the elections in the United States and long enough before the Christmas holidays began to attract attention by newspapers, radio, TV, and other forms of communication. The worldwide observance was for those who had died from AIDS, since it had first been discovered in 1984, and those living with the disease in 1988. Now, World AIDS Day is the longest-running disease awareness and prevention initiative of its kind in the history of public health. Today, with proper medical help, people can live healthy lives while being HIV positive without developing AIDS. December 1 is an occasion to educate the public on issues of concern about HIV/AIDS, to mobilize political will and resources to address global problems, and to celebrate and reinforce achievements of humanity.

In the United States in 1989, President George Bush issued a statement on the observance of World AIDS Day, declaring that there was "a commemoration in Washington to remember all those with HIV infection and all who [had] died from it."[2] Bush wrote about the resources that had been committed to research. "At the same time," he stated, "we must also educate and prevent. The disease is spread through known ways, and it is clear that education on the facts is our best means of combating AIDS at this time." He concluded, ". . . [W]e . . . remember those Americans who have become infected with the virus, including some who may be unaware of their infection. These people need our help and our compassion."[3] Beginning in 1993, U.S. Presidents started issuing proclamations about World AIDS Day on December 1. William J. Clinton was the first to do so. In his first of eight proclamations, he wrote: "The extent of HIV infection is overwhelming, but we must not allow ourselves to despair in the face of these daunting statistics. Instead, we must accelerate our efforts to find effective treatments, a vaccine, and an eventual cure for this scourge that haunts us."[4] He added, "Education is our most effective tool in preventing the spread of HIV/AIDS. . . . We . . . must look deep within our souls to find the compassion, the values, the spirit, and the commitment that will allow us to conquer this modern-day plague." He called upon "every American to join in the effort to fight the spread of HIV and to treat those living with HIV with dignity and respect."[5] Clinton issued similar proclamations from 1994 to 2000.[6] Following Clinton, George W. Bush issued nine World AIDS Day proclamations. His first marked the twentieth "year that the world [had] been fighting the disease." He stressed "that every individual [had] both the

2. Bush, "Statement."
3. Bush, "Statement."
4. Clinton, "Proclamation 6632."
5. Clinton, "Proclamation 6632."
6. "Proclamations 6759, 6854, 6959, 7056, 7153, 7256, and 7382."

responsibility and the opportunity to help prevent the spread of HIV/AIDS and to assist those suffering from the disease.[7] Bush issued similar proclamations from 2002 to 2009.[8] In 2010, in his first World AIDS Day Proclamation, Barack Obama wrote about the release of the "first comprehensive National HIV/AIDS Strategy for the United States." He proclaimed, "Its vision is an America in which new HIV infections are rare, and when they do occur, all persons—regardless of age, gender, race or ethnicity, sexual orientation, gender identity, or socio-economic circumstance—will have unfettered access to high-quality, life-extending care." In his three-page proclamation, he stated, "Tackling this disease requires a shared response that builds on the successes achieved to date." Then, he added, "On World AIDS Day, we mourn those we have lost and look to the promise of a brighter future and a world without HIV/AIDs."[9] Obama issued similar proclamations from 2011 to 2016.[10] For each of the four years of his presidency, Donald J. Trump commemorated World AIDS Day with a proclamation. "The first documented cases of the human immunodeficiency virus infection (HIV) and acquired immune deficiency syndrome (AIDS) thirty-six years ago became the leading edge of an epidemic that swept across the United States and around the globe, devastating millions of individuals, families, and communities," he stated in his first proclamation.[11] "In the decades since—through public and private American leadership, innovation, investment, and compassion—we have ushered in a new, hopeful era of prevention and treatment," he stated. ". . . [O]n World AIDS Day, we honor those who have lost their lives to AIDS, we celebrate the remarkable progress we have made in combatting this disease, and we reaffirm our ongoing commitment to end AIDS as a public health threat."[12] Trump issued similar proclamations from 2018 to 2020.[13] ". . . World AIDS Day has been recognized as an opportunity for people around the world to stand together in the fight against HIV," begins Joseph R. Biden in his 2021 proclamation of World AIDS Day.[14] ". . . [W]e are focused on addressing health inequities and inequalities and ensuring that the voices of people with HIV are at the center of our work to end the HIV epidemic globally," he added. He noted that "700,000 Americans . . . have tragically died from AIDS-related illness since the start of the epidemic," and that he and his administration are "committed to helping the world end the AIDS epidemic as a public health threat by 2030." He concluded his over-two-page proclamation, stating, ". . . [W]e rededicate ourselves to building on the progress of the last four decades; upholding and advancing human rights; supporting

7. Bush, G.W., "Proclamation 7510."
8. "Proclamations 7631, 7740, 7850, 7967, 8087, 8207, 8325, and 8459."
9. Obama, "Proclamation 8609."
10. "Proclamations 8762, 8909, 9064, 9216, 9374, and 9548."
11. Trump, "Proclamation 9680."
12. Trump, "Proclamation 9680."
13. "Proclamations 9829, 9970, and 10123."
14. Biden, "Proclamation 10317."

research, science, and data-driven solutions; expanding access to housing, education, and economic empowerment; and fighting stigma and discrimination."[15] According to the Joint United Nations Program on HIV/AIDS (UNAIDS), begun in 1996, "Economic, social, cultural, and legal inequalities must be ended as a matter of urgency if we are to end AIDs by 2030."[16]

Journal/Meditation: Do you fear HIV/AIDS? If so, why? If not, why not? How well educated are you about HIV/AIDS? Why should age, gender, race or ethnicity, sexual orientation, gender identity, or socio-economic circumstances not affect care for HIV/AIDS patients?

Prayer: God of Healing, keep me mindful of my sisters and brothers suffering from HIV and AIDS. Help me make a safe haven in the world for those who are abandoned, discriminated against, and rejected on account of their illness. When they are in pain, send your Spirit to be salve for their wounds. With your Son, grant them compassion when they face death, and give them the assurance of eternal life in your presence forever. Amen.

INTERNATIONAL DAY OF DISABLED PERSONS: PART 1
December 3

Text: "Considering that the United Nations Decade of Disabled Persons has been a period of awareness-raising and of action-oriented measures aimed at the continued improvement of the situation of persons with disability and the equalization of opportunities for them; aware of the need for more vigorous and broader action and measure at all levels to fulfill the objectives of the Decade and the World Program of Action concerning Disabled Persons; . . . [the General Assembly of the United Nations] 1. invites all member states and organizations concerned to intensify their efforts aimed at sustained effective action with a view to improving the situation of persons with disabilities; 2. Proclaims 3 December as the International Day of Disabled Persons . . . ."[17]

Reflection: On December 16, 1976, the General Assembly of the United Nations proclaimed "the year 1981 International Year for Disabled Persons, with the theme 'full participation,'" and the objectives of "helping disabled persons in their physical and psychological adjustment to society;" ". . . providing disabled persons with proper assistance, training, care, and guidance, to make available to them opportunities for suitable work and to ensure their full integration in society; encouraging study and research projects designed to facilitate the practical participation of disabled persons

---

15. Biden, "Proclamation 10317."
16. "End Inequalities."
17. United Nations General Assembly, A/RES/47/3.

in daily life, for example, by improving their access to public buildings and transportation systems; [and] educating and informing the public of the rights of disabled persons to participate in and contribute to various aspects of economic, social, and political life...."[18] In the United States, on February 6, 1981, President Ronald Reagan proclaimed 1981 the International Year of Disabled Persons, writing: "We seek... an era of national renewal, an era that will set loose again the energy and ingenuity of the American people. Today there are thirty-five million disabled Americans who represent one of our most underutilized national resources. Their will, their spirit, and their hearts are not impaired, despite their limitations. All of us stand to gain when those who are disabled share in America's opportunities.... [W]e can expand the opportunities for disabled Americans to make a fuller contribution to our national life."[19] On February 26, 1982, the Senate and House of Representatives of the United States issued Public Law 97–149, which, in part, states: "Whereas the designation by the United Nations of 1981 as the International Year of Disabled Persons has stimulated new progress toward achieving the full participation in national and community life of the thirty-five million Americans who have disabilities;... whereas further progress should be made in the United States toward achieving the following long-term goals of and for disabled persons promoted during the International Year of Disabled Persons: (1) expanded educational opportunity; (2) improved access to housing, buildings, and transportation; (3) expanded employment opportunity; (4) expanded participation in recreational, social, and cultural activities; (5) expanded and strengthened rehabilitation programs and facilities; (6) purposeful application of biomedical research aimed at conquering major disabling conditions; (7) reduction in the incidence of disability by expanded accident and disease prevention; (8) expanded application of technology to minimize the effects of disability; and (9) expanded international exchange of information and experience to benefit all disabled persons;... resolved by the Senate and House of Representatives of the United States of American in congress assembled, that 1982 hereby is designated the 'National Year of Disabled Persons,' and the president of the United States is authorized and requested to issue a proclamation calling upon the elected officials and people of the United States to observe such year through activities in support of the long-term goals for disabled persons promoted during the International Year of Disabled Persons."[20] On April 26, 1982, Regan responded by issuing a proclamation declaring 1982 the National Year of Disabled Persons. He wrote: "... [W]e were made aware of the many accomplishments of disabled people," during the 1981 International Year of Disabled Persons, "and we rejoiced at the number of lives that were made richer and more productive through education, rehabilitation, and employment."[21] He continued, "We must seize

18. United Nations General Assembly, A/RES/31/123.
19. Reagan, "Proclamation 4818."
20. "Public Law 97–149."
21. Reagan, "Proclamation 4935."

the opportunities afforded by the International Year of Disabled Persons to increase our national awareness of what remains to be done in order to assure all disabled Americans full and active participation our society."[22] He concluded by proclaiming 1982 the National Year of Disabled Persons.

On December 3, 1982, the General Assembly of the United Nations passed a resolution adopting the "World Program of Action Concerning Disabled Persons," prepared by the U.N. Department of Economic and Social Affairs. "Recognizing that the International Year of Disabled Persons contributed to the acceptance by the community of the right of disabled persons to participate fully in the social life and development of their societies and to enjoy living conditions equal to those of their fellow citizens," stated the resolution; "convinced that the International Year of Disabled Persons gave a genuine and meaningful impetus to activities related to equalization of opportunities for disabled persons, as well as prevention and rehabilitation at all levels;" and "expressing its satisfaction with the efforts of member states during the International Year of Disabled Persons to improve the conditions and wellbeing of disabled persons and their willingness to involve disabled persons and their organizations in all matters of concern to them,"[23] the U.N. adopted the World Program of Action Concerning Disabled Persons. The eleven-page document "is a global strategy to enhance disability prevention, rehabilitation, and equalization of opportunities, which pertains to full participation of persons with disabilities in social life and national development."[24] It emphasizes "the need to approach disability from a human rights perspective. Its three chapters provide an analysis of principles, concepts, and definitions relating to disabilities, an overview of the world situation regarding persons with disabilities, and sets out recommendations for action at the national, regional, and international levels."[25] The over-arching goal of the document is full participation of the then-estimated 500 million disabled persons in the world by offering them opportunities equal to those of the whole population and an equal share in the improvement in living conditions resulting from social and economic development. Also passed on December 3, 1982, was a resolution by the U.N. General Assembly about the implementation of the World Program of Action Concerning Disabled Persons. The resolution stated that the General Assembly was convinced that the International Year of Disabled Persons "gave a genuine and meaningful impetus to activities related to equalization opportunities for disabled persons, as well as prevention and rehabilitation at all levels."[26] The resolution called upon member states "to develop plans for the equalization of opportunities for disabled persons, as well as for prevention and rehabilitation, and thereby ensure early implementation of the World Program of

22. Reagan, "Proclamation 4935."
23. United Nations General Assembly, A/RES/37/52.
24. "World Program of Action."
25. "World Program of Action."
26. United Nations General Assembly, A/RES/37/53.

Action Concerning Disabled Persons."[27] It also proclaimed "the period 1983–92 United Nations Decade of Disabled Persons as a long-term plan of action" and encouraged "governments to proclaim national days for the disabled."[28] In March 1983 in the United States Senate and in July 1983 in the U.S. House of Representatives, congress expressed "that the president should implement, within the United States, the objectives of the United Nations Decade for Disabled Persons (1983–92)." Both houses required "the president to report annually to congress, in accordance with United Nations General Assembly Resolution 37/53 on executive branch plans to implement the objectives of the United Nations Decade of Disabled Persons."[29] On November 22, 1983, the General Assembly of the United Nations noted "the emergence of organizations of disabled persons in all parts of the world and their positive influence on the image and conditions of persons with disabilities."[30] It was "concerned that developing countries [were] experiencing increasing difficulties in mobilizing adequate resources for meeting pressing needs in the field of disability prevention, rehabilitation, and equalization of opportunities for the millions of persons with disabilities."[31] Thus, it recommended "that the resources of the Trust Fund—established by the General Assembly for the International Year of Disabled Persons—should be geared . . . towards the implementation of the World Program of Action and towards helping persons with disabilities to organize themselves, towards assisting in implementing support and consultative services for technical cooperation, and inter-organizational task forces . . . ." It also appealed "to governments and private sources for continuing generous voluntary contributions to the Trust Fund."[32] On November 28, 1983, U.S. President Ronald Reagan proclaimed "the years 1983 through 1992 as the National Decade of Disabled Persons." In his proclamation, he stated: "We . . . gained vast new insights into the significant impact that access to education, rehabilitation, and employment have on [disabled persons'] lives. The progress we have made is a tribute to the courage and determination of our disabled people, to innovative research and development both in technology and training techniques to assist the disabled, and to those—whether in the private or public sectors—who have given so generously of their time and energies to help enrich the lives of disabled persons. . . . For only through opportunities to use the full range of their potential will our disabled citizens attain the independence and dignity that are their due."[33] Thus, both internationally and nationally there was a ten-year focus on persons with disabilities. "A person is handicapped when he or she is denied the opportunities generally available in the community that are necessary

27. United Nations General Assembly, A/RES/37/53.
28. United Nations General Assembly, A/RES/37/53.
29. "Senate Concurrent Resolution 22," "House Concurrent Resolution 39."
30. United Nations General Assembly, A/RES/38/28.
31. United Nations General Assembly, A/RES/38/28.
32. United Nations General Assembly, A/RES/38/28.
33. Reagan, "Proclamation 5131."

for the fundamental elements of living, including family life, education, employment, housing, financial and personal security, participation in social and political groups, religious activity, intimate and sexual relationships, access to public facilities, freedom of movement, and the general style of daily living,"[34] stated the "World Program of Action Concerning Disabled Persons."

Journal/Meditation: In his 1981 International Year of Disabled Persons proclamation, Reagan stated that disabled persons' will, spirit, and hearts were not impaired, despite their limitations. Where have you discovered that to be true? In Public Law 97–149, congress established nine long-term goals of and for disabled persons: (1) expanded educational opportunity; (2) improved access to housing, buildings, and transportation; (3) expanded employment opportunity; (4) expanded participation in recreational, social, and cultural activities; (5) expanded and strengthened rehabilitation programs and facilities; (6) purposeful application of biomedical research aimed at conquering major disabling conditions; (7) reduction in the incidence of disability by expanded accident and disease prevention; (8) expanded application of technology to minimize the effects of disability; and (9) expanded international exchange of information and experience to benefit all disabled persons. Which of those do you think have been achieved? Explain.

Prayer: Loving God, you create every living person in your image and likeness. Give me the sight to recognize you in all persons with disabilities and to welcome them into my life. Pour your grace upon all who work to enable the full participation of disabled persons in daily life equal to those of other members of the human family. Amen.

INTERNATIONAL DAY OF DISABLED PERSONS: PART 2
December 3

Text: "Considering that the United Nations Decade of Disabled Persons has been a period of awareness-raising and of action-oriented measures aimed at the continued improvement of the situation of persons with disabilities and the equalization of opportunities for them; aware of the need for more vigorous and broader action and measures at all levels to fulfil the objectives of the Decade and the World Program of Action Concerning Disabled Persons; [the General Assembly of the United Nations] . . . 1. Invites all member states and organizations concerned to intensify their efforts aimed at sustained effective action with a view to improving the situation of persons with disability; [and] 2. Proclaims 3 December as the International Day of Disabled Persons."[35]

---

34. "World Program of Action."
35. United Nations General Assembly, A/RES/47/3.

The Month of December

Reflection: During the Decade of Disabled Persons, the congress of the United States passed the "Americans with Disabilities Act of 1990,"[36] the fifty-two-page Public Law 101–336, which prohibits discrimination based on disabilities. President George Bush signed the bill into law on July 26, 1990. The purpose of the law is "(1) to provide a clear and comprehensive national mandate for the elimination of discrimination against individuals with disability; (2) to provide clear, strong, consistent, enforceable standards addressing discrimination against individuals with disabilities; (3) to ensure that the federal government plays a central role in enforcing the standards established in the Act on behalf of individuals with disabilities; and (4) to invoke the sweep of congressional authority, including the power to enforce the fourteenth amendment and to regulate commerce, in order to address the major areas of discrimination faced day-to-day by people with disabilities."[37] The Americans with Disabilities Act was amended on September 25, 2008, and signed by President George W. Bush. The law, which became effective January 1, 2009, states, "[P]hysical or mental disabilities in no way diminish a person's right to fully participate in all aspects of society, yet many people with physical or mental disabilities have been precluded from doing so because of discrimination; others who have a record of a disability or are regarded as having a disability also have been subjected to discrimination."[38] At the end of the 1983–92 United Nations Decade of Disabled Persons, the U.N. proclaimed December 3 to be the annual International Day of Disabled Persons, on October 14, 1992, as noted in the above text. On December 13, 2006, the U.N. issued the "Convention on the Rights of Persons with Disabilities," a thirty-one-page text with a preamble and fifty articles, effective May 3, 2008.[39] The Convention recognizes "the inherent dignity and worth and the equal and inalienable rights of all members of the human family as the foundation of freedom, justice, and peace in the world." It recognizes "that everyone is entitled to all the rights and freedoms set forth therein, without distinction of any kind" and it reaffirms "the universality, indivisibility, interdependence, and interrelatedness of all human rights and fundamental freedoms and the need for persons with disabilities to be guaranteed their full enjoyment without discrimination." It also recognizes "that disability is an evolving concept and that disability results from the interaction between persons with impairments and attitudinal and environmental barriers that hinders their full and effective participation in society on an equal basis with others." It emphasizes "the importance of mainstreaming disability issues as an integral part of relevant strategies of sustainable development," and recognizes "that discrimination against any person on the basis of disability is a violation of the inherent dignity and worth of the human person, . . . the diversity of

---

36. "Public Law 101–336."
37. "Public Law 101–336."
38. "Public Law 110–325."

39. "Convention on the Rights of Persons with Disabilities," United Nations General Assembly, A/RES/61/106.

persons with disabilities, . . . and the need to promote and protect the human rights of all persons with disabilities, including those who require more intensive support." It notes that "persons with disabilities continue to face barriers in their participation as equal members of society and violations of their human rights in all parts of the world," recognizing "the importance of international cooperation for improving the living conditions of persons with disabilities, . . . the valued existing and potential contributions made by persons with disabilities to the overall wellbeing and diversity of their communities, and that the promotion of the full employment by persons with disabilities of their human rights and fundamental freedoms and of full participation by persons with disabilities will result in their enhanced sense of belonging and in significant advances in the human, social, and economic development of society and the eradication of poverty." The Convention recognizes "the importance for persons with disabilities of their individual autonomy and independence, including the freedom to make their own choices," while considering "that persons with disabilities should have the opportunity to be actively involved in decision-making processes about policies and programs, including those directly concerning them." Also, it is concerned "about the difficult conditions faced by person with disabilities who are subject to multiple or aggravated forms of discrimination on the basis of race, color, sex, language, religion, political or other opinion, national, ethnic, indigenous or social origin, property, birth, age, or other statue." The Convention highlights "that the majority of persons with disabilities live in conditions of poverty" and recognizes "the importance of accessibility to the physical, social, economic, and cultural environment, to health and education, and to information and communication, in enabling persons with disabilities to fully enjoy all human rights and fundamental freedoms." It notes "that persons with disabilities and their family members should receive the necessary protection and assistance to enable families to contribute towards the full and equal enjoyment of the rights of persons with disabilities."[40] Article 1 states that the purpose of the Convention "is to promote, protect, and ensure the full and equal enjoyment of all human rights and fundamental freedoms by all persons with disabilities, and to promote respect for their inherent dignity. Persons with disabilities include those who have long-term physical, mental, intellectual, or sensory impairments which in interaction with various barriers may hinder their full and effective participation in society on an equal basis with others."[41]

On July 30, 2009, the United States signed the United Nations Convention on the Rights of Persons with Disabilities.[42] On December 2, 2009, President Barack Obama proclaimed December 3 as International Day of Persons with Disabilities. After mentioning that there were "650 million people living with disabilities worldwide" in his

40. "Convention on the Rights of Persons with Disabilities," Preamble, Sections 1–3, 5, 7–16, 20, 22, 24.
41. "Convention on the Rights of Persons with Disabilities," Article 1.
42. United Nations Treaty Collection.

proclamation, he wrote: ". . . [W]e celebrate the skills, achievement, and contributions of persons with disabilities in America and around the world. We recognize the progress we have made toward equality for all, and we rededicate ourselves to ensuring individuals with disabilities can reach their greatest potential. . . . The International Day of Persons with Disabilities is a time to renew our commitment to the principles of empowerment, dignity, and equality. . . . We must continue to embrace diversity and reject discrimination in all its forms, and insist on equality of opportunity and accessibility for all."[43] He issued similar proclamations in 2010 (Proclamation 8612), 2011 (Proclamation 8763), 2012 (Proclamation 8913), 2013 (Proclamation 9066), 2014 (Proclamation 9217), 2015 (Proclamation 9376), and 2016 (Proclamation 9550). From 2018 to 2019, the United Nations published its "Disability Inclusion Strategy," "to strengthen system-wide accessibility for persons with disabilities and the mainstreaming of their rights. . . . The policy establishes the highest levels of commitment and a vision for the United Nations system on disability inclusion for the next decade and is aimed at creating an institutional framework for the implementation of the Convention on the Rights of Persons with Disabilities and the 2030 Agenda for Sustainable Development."[44] The twenty-five-page strategy "includes two aligned components: (a) an entity accountability framework, with fifteen common-system indicators, focused on four areas: leadership, strategic planning and management inclusiveness; programming; and organizational culture, and (b) a United Nations country team accountability scorecard on disability inclusions . . . ."[45] In the summary, the document states: "Through the Strategy, the United Nations system will systematically embed the rights of persons with disabilities into its work, both externally, through programming, and internally, and will build trust and confidence among persons with disabilities to ensure that they are valued and their dignity and rights are respected and that, in the workplace, they find an enabling environment in which to fully and effectively participate on an equal basis with others."[46] The U.N. called the strategy an "urgent need . . . to improve its performance with regard to disability inclusion." Its comprehensive strategy "provides a foundation for sustainable and transformative change towards disability inclusion throughout all pillars of the organization's work." According the International Day of Persons with Disabilities webpage, "Disability inclusion is an essential condition to upholding human rights, sustainable development, and peace and security. . . . The commitment to realizing the rights of persons with disabilities is not only a matter of justice; it is an investment in a common future."[47] President Joseph R. Biden issued his first proclamation of the International Day of Persons with Disabilities on December 2, 2021. After recalling the passage of the

43. Obama, "Proclamation 8462."
44. "United Nations Disability Inclusion Strategy."
45. "United Nations Disability Inclusion Strategy."
46. "United Nations Disability Inclusion Strategy."
47. "International Day of Persons with Disabilities."

Americans with Disabilities Act, he stated: ". . . [W]e have made profound progress to advance the rights, opportunities, full participation, and economic self-sufficiency of people with disabilities—both here at home and in nations around the world. . . . [W]e reaffirm the full promise of dignity, equity, and respect due to all disabled people and recognize the work that still remains to fully deliver on that promise."[48] Later, in the two-page document, he stated, "Today and every day, we reaffirm our commitment to ensuring dignity, equity, and respect for all people with disabilities."[49] On December 3, we "affirm that a government of, by, and for the people—including those with disabilities—remains humanity's most enduring means to advance peace, prosperity, and security."[50]

Journal/Meditation: Where do you find people with disabilities participating in all aspects of society where you live? Where do you find people with disabilities discriminated because of their disabilities where you live? What specific words from the above reflection got your attention? Why?

Prayer: We have achieved great progress in advancing the rights, opportunities, full participation, and economic self-sufficiency of people with disabilities, O God. But we have lots of work yet to do to fully affirm the dignity, equity, and respect due to all disabled people. Guide my efforts to advance peace, prosperity, and security for all those with disabilities. Amen.

INTERNATIONAL VOLUNTEER DAY FOR ECONOMIC AND SOCIAL DEVELOPMENT

December 5

Text: "Considering that volunteer service . . . is making an important contribution to socio-economic development activities; recognizing the desirability of stimulating the work of all volunteers both in the field and in organizations—multilateral, bilateral or national, non-governmental or government-supported—and of giving encouragement to those volunteers, many of whom engage in volunteer service at considerable personal sacrifice, [the General Assembly of the United Nations] invites governments to observe annually, on 5 December, an International Volunteer Day for Economic and Social Development, and urges them to take measures to heighten awareness of the important contribution of volunteer service, thereby stimulating more people in all walks of life to offer their services as volunteers both at home and abroad; invites also specialized agencies, other organizations of the United Nations system and non-governmental organizations that provide, are affiliated with, or benefit from volunteer

---

48. Biden, "Proclamation 10318."
49. Biden, "Proclamation 10318."
50. Biden, "Proclamation 10318."

service to undertake and promote activities to stimulate greater awareness of the contribution to their work made by volunteers . . . ."[51]

Reflection: On December 17, 1985, the General Assembly of the United Nations instituted the International Volunteer Day for Economic and Social Development, commonly referred to as the International Volunteer Day. As can be gleaned from the above text, the goal of the day was to promote volunteerism, to encourage world governments to support volunteers, and to recognize their contributions at both national and international levels. The day provides a chance for organizations, communities, and individuals to volunteer with private institutions, academic establishments, community groups, not-for-profit organizations, media outlets, faith groups, sports teams, recreational clubs, and government agencies to combat poverty, hunger, disease, health, environmental degradation, and gender inequality. In other words, the day celebrates active volunteers while attracting new ones. The annual International Volunteer Day was so successful that the U.N. General Assembly proclaimed 2001 the International Year of Volunteers on November 20, 1997.[52] After a very successful International Year of Volunteers, on December 5, 2001, the U.N. General Assembly adopted a resolution supporting volunteering along with a five-page annex consisting of recommendations on ways both governments and the U.N. system could support volunteering.[53] The resolution recalls how governments have developed "comprehensive strategies and programs by raising public awareness about the value and opportunities of volunteerism and by facilitating an enabling environment for individuals and other actors of civil society to engage in voluntary activities, and the private sector to support such activities," before "recognizing the valuable contribution of volunteering, [which includes] traditional forms of mutual aid and self-help, formal service delivery, and other forms of civic participation, to economic and social development, benefiting society at large, communities, and the individual volunteer." The resolution also recognizes "that volunteerism is an important component of any strategy aimed at . . . such areas as poverty reduction, sustainable development, health, disaster prevention and management and social integration, and, in particular, overcoming social exclusion and discrimination." It "commends the ongoing contributions of all volunteers to society, including in extraordinary conditions such as disasters" and "encourages all people to become more engaged in volunteer activities."[54]

There is not enough space here to present all the ideas in the annex that are worthy of reflection. The recommendations are divided into three sections: general considerations, government support, and support by the U.N. system. Those three sections are subdivided, and the subdivisions are often subdivided in order to present

---

51. United Nations General Assembly, A/RES/40/212.
52. United Nations General Assembly, A/RES/52/17.
53. United Nations General Assembly, A/RES/56/38.
54. United Nations General Assembly, A/RES/56/38.

as clear as possible a process to support volunteers and to create favorable environments to attract new volunteers. ". . . [T]he terms volunteering, volunteerism, and voluntary activities," states the annex, "refer to a wide range of activities, including traditional forms of mutual aid and self-help, formal service delivery, and other forms of civic participation, undertaken of free will, for the general public good and where monetary reward is not the principal motivating factor."[55] It makes clear, "There is not one universal model of best practice, since what works well in one country may not work in another with very different cultures and traditions."[56] The annex warns, "Neglecting to factor volunteering into the design and implementation of policies could entail the risk of overlooking a valuable asset and undermine traditions of cooperation that bind communities together."[57] The general considerations end by stating that it is important "to ensure that opportunities for volunteering in all sectors are open both to women and men, given their different levels of participation in different areas, and recognizing the potential effect of volunteering on the empowerment of women."[58] The annex urges governments to create favorable environments that support voluntary activities; to highlight the contributions of volunteers; to encourage media to support volunteers in public awareness-raising activities; to encourage and facilitate preparation, training, and recognition of volunteers; to introduce enabling legislation; etc.[59] Within the U.N. itself, the annex encourages more volunteerism; research that documents volunteerism and major global concerns; recognition of volunteers; long-term planning that involves all segments of society in volunteering; assisting governments in promoting volunteerism, etc.[60] On November 26, 2002, in a follow-up to the International Year of Volunteers, the U.N. General Assembly issued another resolution that repeated many of the same points stated in earlier ones. However, it did note "with appreciation the efforts to increase awareness of volunteerism through global information sharing and education, including efforts to develop an effective network for volunteers through . . . the International Year of Volunteers website and linked national sites."[61] In its three pages, it called upon governments "to implement further the recommendations contained in the annex to its resolution 56/38, keeping in mind the economic significance of volunteering," to actively support the observance of December 5 as International Volunteer Day for Economic and Social Development, "to recognize and promote all forms of volunteerism as an issue that involves and benefits all segments of society, including children, young persons, older persons, persons with disabilities, minorities and immigrants, and those who remain

55. United Nations General Assembly, A/RES/56/38, Annex 1.1.
56. United Nations General Assembly, A/RES/56/38, Annex 1.3.
57. United Nations General Assembly, A/RES/56/38, Annex 1.6.
58. United Nations General Assembly, A/RES/56/38, Annex 1.7.
59. United Nations General Assembly, A/RES/56/38, Annex 2.1.
60. United Nations General Assembly, A/RES/56/38, Annex 3.1.
61. United National General Assembly, A/RES/57/106.

excluded for social or economic reasons," and "to support volunteerism as a strategic tool to enhance economic and social development, including by expanding corporate volunteering."[62] On December 18, 2008, another two-page resolution follow-up to the International Year of Volunteers was issued by the U.N. General Assembly. Among many other things, it noted "the momentum created by the International Year has contributed to the vibrancy of volunteerism globally with the involvement of more people, from a broader cross-section of societies," and it reaffirmed the need "to raise awareness of the contributions of volunteerism to peace and development . . . ."[63]

Journal/Meditation: In your experience, what does volunteer service contribute to socio-economic development where you live? What are the volunteer opportunities in your area? In which do you serve? In what ways is awareness raised about volunteer contributions where you live?

Prayer: LORD, on this International Volunteer Day, I give you thanks for all those you call to give of their time, talent, and service to others. May I always remember that every gift comes from you and is meant to be shared. Inspire others to join in service to their brothers and sisters by volunteering somewhere in the community of the world. Amen.

St. Nicholas Day

December 6

Text: "As dry leaves that before the wild hurricane fly, / When they meet with an obstacle, mount to the sky; / So up to the house-top the courses they[64] flew, / With the sleigh full of toys, and St. Nicholas too."[65]

Reflection: In his "A Visit from St. Nicholas," Clement Clarke Moore refers to "St. Nicholas" three times and to "St. Nick" one time. In 1823, when the poem was first published, St. Nicholas or St. Nick referred to the fourth-century bishop of Myra in Asia Minor (now Turkey). He was very popular throughout Europe, and he was known for his secret, generous gift-giving. He rescued three girls from one poor family by dropping a sack of gold coins through the window of their home for three nights so their father would have a dowry for each one of them; thus, he kept the three young women out of prostitution! In popular iconography, St. Nicholas displaying a long white beard wears a long red cape (liturgical cope) or chasuble (liturgical Mass vestment) over a white alb (long white underdress) with a red stole (long strip of cloth hung around the neck); on his head is a red miter (pointed bishop's hat), on his

---

62. United National General Assembly, A/RES/57/106.
63. United National General Assembly, A/RES/63/153.
64. Eight tiny reindeer.
65. Moore, "A Visit."

right ring finger is a ruby ring over a white glove, and in his left gloved hand is a gold crosier (bishop's staff with a crook at the top). In his left hand he either carries three bags of gold or holds a plate displaying three bags of gold, that often look like three gold balls,[66] to emphasize his gift-giving. In the Dutch-speaking countries, he rides a white horse over the rooftops at night, delivering gifts through the chimneys, and he is known as Sinterklaas. Because St. Nicholas is credited with raising three children, who had been murdered and pickled in brine in a barrel by a butcher planning to sell them as pork during a famine, people came to think of him as the patron saint of children. Thus, in the Netherlands, Belgium, Luxembourg, and northern France, he carries a big, red book in which he records whether children have been good (nice) or naughty in the past year. Before going to bed on December 5, children place their shoes next to the fireplace chimney with a carrot, hay, or sugar cubes for St. Nicholas's horse and a bowl of water nearby. The next morning, December 6, they find candy, oranges, pastry, chocolate, or some other treat.

When Dutch-speaking immigrants arrived in the United States, they brought Sinterklaas with them. It is not difficult to see how the name *Sinterklaas* (St. Nicholas) became *Santa Claus*. His long red cape became a red coat with a black belt over red pants. His red miter's stiffness was removed, the point at the top sewed together with a tassel added, and the red nightcap placed on his head with the long top leaned to one side. White trim was added to the coat and hat, and white gloves covered his hands. Over his left shoulder he held a large bag of gifts—"A bundle of Toys he had flung on his back, / And he looked like a peddler just opening his pack."[67]—which he extracted from his "sleigh full of Toys," before coming down the chimney with a bound, filling the stockings, "And laying his finger aside of his nose, / And giving a nod, up the chimney he rose."[68] Instead of a white horse, Santa Claus rides in a winter sleigh pulled by eight reindeer, and instead of shoes placed by the fireplace chimney into which are put gifts, Santa Claus deposits gifts in stockings, which become large socks, hung on or by the fireplace to dry. He remains the patron of nice children, keeping mental records or long scrolls that record the names of both nice and naughty little ones. Moore added further description to St. Nicholas turned Santa Claus: "He was dressed all in fur, from his head to his foot, / And his clothes were all tarnished with ashes and soot; / . . . His eyes—how they twinkled! his dimples how merry! / His cheeks were like roses, his nose like a cherry! / His droll little mouth was drawn up like a bow / and the beard of his chin was as white as the snow; / . . . He had a broad face

---

66. In the Low Countries, the gold balls were thought to be oranges, which came from Spain. This led to the understanding that St. Nicholas lived in Spain and came to visit every winter bringing oranges. On Saturday after November 11, Sinterklaas returns to the Low Counties riding in a steamboat. After it anchors, he disembarks and parades through the streets on his white horse. Between then and December 6, he visits schools, hospitals, and shopping centers, while keeping records of nice and naughty children. On December 7, he returns to Spain to get oranges for the next year.

67. Moore, "A Visit."

68. Moore, "A Visit."

and a little round belly, / That shook when he laughed, like a bowlful of jelly. / He was chubby and plump, a right jolly old elf, / And I laughed when I saw him, in spite of myself."[69] That is how St. Nicholas of Asia Minor on December 6 became Santa Claus of the United States on December 25.

Journal/Meditation: What elements of St. Nicholas continue after he became Santa Claus? What gift-giving do you practice that echoes St. Nicholas's ministry to the poor? to children?

Prayer: God of St. Nicholas, you filled your bishop with your own Spirit of gift-giving. As I remember his generosity today, instill in me the same Spirit that I may be motivated to share with others what you have so graciously bestowed upon me today, tomorrow, and forever. Amen.

National Pearl Harbor Remembrance Day
December 7

Text: "Whereas, on December 7, 1941, the Imperial Japanese Navy and Air Force attacked units of the armed forces of the United States stationed at Pearl Harbor, Hawaii; whereas more than 2,000 citizens of the United States were killed and more than 1,000 citizens of the United States were wounded in the attack on Pearl Harbor; whereas the attack on Pearl Harbor marked the entry of the United States into World War II; . . . whereas commemoration of the attack on Pearl Harbor will instill in all people of the United States a greater understanding and appreciation of the selfless sacrifice of the individuals who served in the armed forces of the United States during World War II; now, therefore, be it resolved . . . that December 7 of each year is designated as 'National Pearl Harbor Remembrance Day'. . . ."[70]

Reflection: As noted in the above text, on December 7, 1941, the Japanese Navy and Air Force attacked United States Armed Forces stationed at Naval Station Pearl Harbor in what was then the Territory of Hawaii, established April 30, 1900. On Sunday morning, December 7, 1941, 2,403 Americans were killed and more than 1,178 were injured. The surprise attack sank four U.S. Navy battleships, damaged four others, damaged three cruisers, three destroyers, and one minelayer. In addition 188 aircraft were destroyed and 159 were damaged. The next day, December 8, 1941, President Franklin Roosevelt addressed a joint session of the U.S. Senate and House of Representatives, referring to the previous day as "a date which will live in infamy."[71] After stating that "the United States of America was suddenly and deliberately attacked by naval and air forces of the Empire of Japan," Roosevelt explained that the U.S. "was at

---

69. Moore, "A Visit."
70. "Public Law 103–308."
71. Roosevelt, "Address to Congress."

peace with that nation" and was "in conversation . . . looking toward the maintenance of peace." He added, ". . . [T]he distance of Hawaii from Japan makes it obvious that the attack was deliberately planned many days or even weeks ago. During the intervening time, the Japanese government has deliberately sought to deceive the United States by false statements and expressions of hope for continued peace."[72] He continued to narrate Japan's other attacks and asked congress to declare war on the Japanese Empire. Congress did so that same day, and the U.S. entered World War II on the side of the Allies.

House Joint Resolution 131, from which the above text is taken and which became Public Law 103-308 on August 23, 1994, when President William J. Clinton signed it into law—and was included in a simpler form in Public Law 105-225 on August 12, 1998—created National Pearl Harbor Remembrance Day, also referred to as Pearl Harbor Remembrance Day and Pearl Harbor Day. Clinton issued the first Proclamation of National Pearl Harbor Remembrance Day on November 29, 1994, to be observed on December 7. In his proclamation, he recalled the surprise attack by the Japanese as marking "the beginning of America's involvement in World War II," which "involved America in a worldwide battle against the forces of fascism and oppression." He continued, "Those Americans who remember World War II have a profound responsibility to pass on the lessons of that conflict to the generations that have followed."[73] He devotes one paragraph to World War II, reminding citizens that "more than 400,000 Americans made the ultimate sacrifice to ensure the continued survival of our nation and the precious gift of peace." He continues, "On this day, we give thanks to the noble veterans of World War II for the priceless liberty they helped to secure." He urges all Americans to observe the day "in honor of the Americans who served at Pearl Harbor."[74] Since 1994, presidents have issued yearly proclamations calling on the people of the U.S. to observe the day and "all departments, agencies, and instrumentalities of the United States government, and interested organizations, groups, and individuals, to fly the flag of the United States at half-staff each December 7 in honor of the individuals who died as a result of their service at Pearl Harbor."[75] Memorial services are held at venues in Pearl Harbor, wreaths are laid, speeches are given, luncheons are held, and survivors' recollections are also part of this non-federal holiday.

Journal/Meditation: How does National Pearl Harbor Remembrance Day instill in you a greater understanding and appreciation of the selfless sacrifice of individuals who served in the armed forces during World War II? What lessons learned from

72. Roosevelt, "Address to Congress."
73. Clinton, "Proclamation 6758."
74. Clinton, "Proclamation 6758."
75. "Public Law 105-225."

World War II do you think need to be passed on to current generations? How do you mark National Pearl Harbor Remembrance Day?

Prayer: Mighty God, as I recall the tragedy of Pearl Harbor today, through your Spirit bestow upon me a greater understanding and appreciation for the selfless sacrifice of the men and women who served this country during World War II. Guide all world leaders to peace so that war can be eliminated from this world. Shower your blessings upon this country and her citizens and preserve us in freedom. Amen.

Green Monday
Second Monday

Text: "Green Monday refers to one of the retail industry's busiest shopping days, occurring on the second Monday in December. Green Monday represents the day many shoppers rush to purchase last-minute holiday gifts and take advantage of deals. . . . E-bay claims it created the phrase in 2007 after it realized that the most profitable sales day was the second Monday of [December] that year."[76]

Reflection: The second Monday in December was named Green Monday by the web shopping site e-bay in 2007 after it realized that it was one of its most profitable sales days. In 2007, shoppers had estimated that by then it was getting late to purchase an item online and get it shipped to one's home in time for Christmas. Of course, that problem has subsequently been addressed by the U.S. Post Office, UPS, FedEx, and others. Sometimes also called Cyber Monday 2 or Manic Monday, Green Monday features a high volume of online shoppers seeking deals. Many retailers offer deals from a percent off regular prices, to a certain number of dollars off a minimum order, to doorbuster deals, to free shipping. For shoppers who did not take advantage of the sales on Black Friday or Cyber Monday, Green Monday presents a chance to take advantage of big savings.

The word *green* in Green Monday has three references. First, green refers to the money shoppers will simultaneously save from sales online, yet spend on merchandise. Second, green refers to the money retailers will bank from the sales made to shoppers. Third, green refers to the environment, which is protected by online shopping—a more eco-friendly endeavor—than driving to brick and mortar stores for sales. Once e-bay began Green Monday, it didn't take long for other retailers to capitalize on the idea for another shopping holiday.

Journal/Meditation: Morally, how much profit can a store make before it is too much profit? What is the best percent off a regularly priced item you ever received? Explain. How do you practice eco-friendly shopping before Christmas? For you, what is the spiritual dimension of shopping?

76. Green, "Green Monday."

Prayer: Almighty God, as I engage in exchanging "green" for gifts, keep me aware of how I treat the earth you created. Grant me safe travels on the internet and help me find good deals for those I love. Accept my shopping on this Green Monday as glory and praise of you. Amen.

Human Rights Day
December 10

Text: "Considering that on 10 December 1948 the General Assembly [of the United Nations] proclaimed the Universal Declaration of Human Rights as a common standard of achievement for all peoples and all nations; considering that the Declaration marks a distinct forward step in the march of human progress; considering that the anniversary of this event should be appropriately celebrated in all countries as part of a common effort to bring the Declaration to the attention of the peoples of the world; . . . the United Nations . . . invites all states and interested organizations to adopt 10 December of each year as Human Rights Day, to observe this day to celebrate the proclamation of the Universal Declaration of Human Rights by the General Assembly on 10 December 1948 and to exert increasing efforts in this field of human progress."[77]

Reflection: As can be read in the above text, On December 4, 1950, the United Nations General Assembly established the annual celebration of the signing of the Universal Declaration of Human Rights which occurred on December 10, 1948. According to the Preamble of the Declaration, ". . . [R]ecognition of the inherent dignity and of the equal and inalienable rights of all members of the human family is the foundation of freedom, justice, and peace in the world."[78] The Preamble continues: ". . . [D]isregard and contempt for human rights have resulted in barbarous acts which have outraged the conscience of [human]kind, and the advent of a world in which human beings shall enjoy freedom of speech and belief and freedom from fear and want has been proclaimed as the highest aspiration of the common people. . . . [I]t is essential . . . that human rights should be protected by the rule of law."[79] Therefore, "The General Assembly [of the United Nations] proclaims this Universal Declaration of Human Rights as a common standard of achievement for all peoples and all nations, to the end that every individual and every organ of society . . . shall strive by teaching and education to promote respect for these rights and freedoms and by progressive measures, national and international, to secure their universal and effective recognition and observance . . . ."[80] The Declaration consists of thirty articles, of which only a few can be highlighted here. "All human beings are born free and equal in dignity

---

77. United Nations General Assembly, 423 (V).
78. "Universal Declaration of Human Rights."
79. "Universal Declaration of Human Rights."
80. "Universal Declaration of Human Rights."

and rights," states Article 1. "Everyone is entitled to all the rights and freedoms set forth in this Declaration, without distinction of any kind, such as race, color, sex, language, religion, political or other opinion, national or social origin, property, birth or other status," states Article 2. And, states Article 3, "Everyone has the right to life, liberty, and the security of person."[81] On Human Rights Day, reading the Declaration, which can be found easily on the internet by typing "Universal Declaration of Human Rights" in one's browser on a computer, is a must-read for everyone.

In the United States, the first president to proclaim Human Rights Day was Lyndon B. Johnson on December 10, 1963, "the fifteenth anniversary of the adoption by the United Nations of the Universal Declaration of Human Rights as a common standard of achievement for all peoples and nations...."[82] In his proclamation, Johnson asked citizens to rededicate themselves to the humanitarian precepts enumerated in that document and "to devote [their] full energy to the task of assuring that each human being—regardless of his [or her] race,... creed, color, or place of national origin—shall be afforded a meaningful opportunity to enjoy fully the rights and benefits embodied in [that instrument] of liberty and to enjoy fully [the] heritage of justice under law."[83] In 1964, 1965, 1966, 1967, and 1968, Johnson issued similar proclamations.[84] In 1968, he mentions that the "United Nations has designated 1968 as International Human Rights Year" and he proclaims it as such.[85] President Richard Nixon proclaimed Human Rights Day in 1969, 1970, 1971, 1972, and 1973,[86] as did President Gerald R. Ford in 1974, 1975, and 1976.[87] After quoting Benjamin Franklin's prayer that God granted the love of liberty and a thorough knowledge of the rights of humankind to all the nations of the earth, Ford wrote in 1974: "Franklin's spirit of universality has found rich modern expression in the Universal Declaration of Human Rights."[88] President Jimmy Carter stated that the Universal Declaration of Human Rights of the United Nations General Assembly was a great event "in the long struggle for the rights of human beings" in his 1977 proclamation of Human Rights Day.[89] He issued similar proclamations in 1978, 1979, and 1980.[90] In his first of eight proclamations of Human Rights Day, President Ronald Reagan declared that the Universal Declaration of Human Rights secured "basic human rights for the people of all nations."[91] He

81. "Universal Declaration of Human Rights."
82. Johnson, "Proclamation 3563."
83. Johnson, "Proclamation 3563."
84. "Proclamations 3631, 3691, 3758, 3814, and 3882."
85. Johnson, "Proclamation 3814."
86. "Proclamations 3946, 4022, 4096, 4173, and 4256."
87. "Proclamations 4337, 4408, and 4479."
88. Ford, "Proclamation 4337."
89. Carter, "Proclamation 4542."
90. "Proclamations 4609, 4705, and 4804."
91. Reagan, "Proclamation 4885."

stated, "... [H]uman rights are rights of individuals: rights of conscience, rights of choice, rights of association, rights of emigration, rights of self-directed action, and the right to own property."[92] Regan's proclamation of Human Rights Day continued from 1982 to 1988.[93] In his first declaration of Human Rights Day in 1989, George Bush stated that the U.N.'s Universal Declaration of Human Rights "established a common standard of conduct for all peoples and all governments."[94] In his two-page proclamation, he mentions a number of the rights in the Declaration. He issued similar proclamations in 1990, 1991, and 1992.[95] "This year [1993] marks the forty-fifth anniversary of the Universal Declaration of Human Rights," stated President William J. Clinton in his 1993 proclamation.[96] He writes about "the universality of these rights and the common duty of all governments to uphold them," and how the Declaration "transcends socio-economic conditions, as well as religious and cultural traditions, for no circumstance of birth, gender, culture, or geography can limit the yearnings of the human spirit for the right to live in freedom and dignity. These longings to improve the human condition ... are innate desires of humankind." He adds, "When we speak about human rights, we are talking about real people in real places."[97] In subsequent years, 1994 to 2000, Clinton issued similar proclamations.[98] George W. Bush's proclamation of Human Rights Day 2001 was tempered by "[t]he terrible tragedies of September 11," which "served as a grievous reminder that the enemies of freedom do not respect or value individual human rights," he stated. "Civilized people everywhere have recognized that terrorists threaten every nation that loves liberty and cherishes the protection of individual rights."[99] From 2002 to 2008, Bush issued similar proclamations of Human Rights Day.[100] From 2009 to 2016,[101] President Barack Obama proclaimed Human Rights Day on December 10. In his first proclamation in 2009, he stated, "Although every country and culture is unique, certain rights are universal: the freedom of people—including women and ethnic and religious minorities—to live as they choose, speak their minds, organize peacefully, and have a say in how they are governed, with confidence in the rule of law."[102] In his first proclamation of the day in 2017, President Donald J. Trump stated that the U.N. Universal Declaration of Human Rights "is grounded in the recognition that just governments must respect the

92. Reagan, "Proclamation 4885."
93. "Proclamations 5003, 5135, 5287, 5420, 5589, 5752, and 5921."
94. Bush, "Proclamation 6082."
95. "Proclamations 6238, 6390, and 6513."
96. Clinton, "Proclamation 6637."
97. Clinton, "Proclamation 6637."
98. "Proclamations 6761, 6855, 6964, 7089, 7158, 7258, and 7386."
99. Bush, G.W., "Proclamation 7513."
100. "Proclamations 7634, 7744, 7854, 7968, 8090, 8210, and 8328."
101. "Proclamations 8464, 8616, 8765, 8915, 9069, 9219, 9380, and 9553."
102. Obama, "Proclamation 8464."

fundamental liberty and dignity of their people."[103] Trump issued three more proclamations for Human Rights Day from 2018 to 2020.[104] In 2021, not following in the steps of his predecessors who issued one proclamation covering both Human Rights Day and Bill of Rights Day, President Joseph R. Biden issued two proclamations: one for Human Rights Day and one for Bill of Rights Day. In the proclamation for Human Rights Day he expresses "thanks to the moral leadership and service of Eleanor Roosevelt as the first Chairperson of the Commission on Human Rights," adding that "the world took an enormous step forward with the creation of the Universal Declaration of Human Rights (UDHR)." He continued: "The UDHR enshrines the human rights and fundamental freedoms inherent in all people—no matter who they are, where they come from, or whom they love. It is a foundational document that proclaims a truth too often overlooked or ignored—that 'all human beings are born free and equal in dignity and rights.'" Later in the over-two-page proclamation, he stated, ". . . [T]he United States today remains steadfast in our commitment to advancing the human rights of all people—and to leading not by the example of our power but by the power of our example."[105] It is worthy to note that, other than the Bible, the Universal Declaration of Human Rights holds the world record as the most translated document.

Journal/Meditation: What do you think keeps some people from recognizing the inherent dignity and the equal and inalienable rights of all members of the human family? What do you think is the most important human right? Where you live, what step can you take to dedicate yourself to assuring that every human being can enjoy the full rights and benefits accorded him or her under the law? What individual rights have you ever been denied? Why?

Prayer: You have bestowed human rights and fundamental freedoms on all people, O LORD. No matter who they are, from where they come, or whom they love, their universal human rights cannot be denied or taken away. Awaken me to a deeper understanding of that truth so that I will always treat all members of the human family with dignity. Amen.

Human Rights Week

December 10–17

Text: "Whereas fundamental rights and freedoms—freedom of speech and of the press, freedom of assembly and association, freedom of conscience and religious worship, the right to fair trial and equal treatment under the law—are being sought by peoples everywhere; and whereas we must press forward to achieve these fundamental rights and freedoms for all persons equally; now, therefore, I, Dwight D. Eisenhower,

   103. Trump, "Proclamation 9685."
   104. "Proclamations 9832, 9972, and 10124."
   105. Biden, "Proclamation 10321."

President of the United States of America, do hereby proclaim the period of December 10 to December 17, 1958, as Human Rights Week; and I call upon the citizens of the United States to observe this week by rereading and studying the Bill of Rights in the Constitution of the United States and the Universal Declaration of Human Rights of the United Nations, that we may all be reminded of our many responsibilities and privileges as a people blessed by a heritage of freedom and equality. Let us firmly rededicate ourselves to the achievement of the goals of liberty and equal opportunity, for ourselves and for our neighbors throughout the world."[106]

Reflection: The first Human Rights Week in the United States was proclaimed by President Dwight D. Eisenhower on November 20, 1958. It began on Human Rights Day, December 10, included Bill of Rights Day on December 15 (see below) and concluded on December 17. Part of Eisenhower's proclamation is the text above. The president did not proclaim Human Rights Day nor Bill of Rights Day; he proclaimed a week-long period calling upon U.S. citizens to read the United Nations Universal Declaration of Human Rights and the United States Bill of Rights. In 1959 and 1960, Eisenhower issued similar proclamations.[107] Likewise, President John Kennedy mentioned the December 10 anniversary of the Universal Declaration of Human Rights and the December 15 anniversary of the Bill of Rights and proclaimed Human Rights Week from December 10 to 17, 1961. Kennedy, who issued a similar proclamation in 1962,[108] called upon citizens "to honor [their] heritage by study of [those] great documents."[109] In 1963, President Lyndon B. Johnson proclaimed "December 10 . . . as Human Rights Day and December 15 . . . as Bill of Rights Day and call[ed] upon the people of the United States to observe the week December 10–17 as Human Rights Week."[110] He asked citizens to rededicate themselves "to the humanitarian precepts enumerated in those documents and" to be resolved "to devote [their] full energy to the task of assuring that each human being—regardless of his race, . . . creed, color, or place of national origin—. . . be afforded a meaningful opportunity to enjoy fully the rights and benefits embodied in [those] instruments of liberty and to enjoy fully [their] heritage of justice under law."[111] Johnson issued similar proclamations in 1964, 1965, 1966, and 1968;[112] in 1967, "in honor of the adoption by the General Assembly of the United nations of the Universal Declaration of Human Rights, December 10, 1948," and "in honor of the ratification of the American Bill of Rights, December 15, 1791," Johnson proclaimed the week of December 10 through 17, 1967, to be Human Rights

106. Eisenhower, "Proclamation 3265."
107. "Proclamations 3327 and 3381."
108. "Proclamation 3508."
109. Kennedy, "Proclamation 3442."
110. Johnson, "Proclamation 3563."
111. Johnson, "Proclamation 3563."
112. "Proclamations 3631, 3691, 3758, and 3882."

Week and the year 1968 to be Human Rights Year."[113] He called upon all Americans and all government agencies "to use [the] occasion to deepen [their] commitment to the defense of human rights and to strengthen [their] efforts for their full and effective realization both among [their] own people and among all the peoples of the United Nations."[114] President Richard Nixon, proclaimed "December 10, 1969, as Human Rights Day and December 15, 1969, as Bill of Rights Day, and call[ed] upon the people of the United States of America to observe the Week of December 10-17, 1969, as Human Rights Week."[115] He stated that the two documents—Universal Declaration of Human Rights and Bill of Rights—"are close in spirit although widely separated in time."[116] In 1970, 1971, 1972, and 1973, Nixon issued similar proclamations.[117] Nixon's successor, President Gerald R. Ford, continued to proclaim Human Rights Day, Bill of Rights Day, and call upon the people of the U.S. "to observe the week beginning December 10, 1974, as Human Rights Week" and to "draw on [the] values" contained in the Universal Declaration of Human Rights and the Bill of Rights "to promote peace, justice, and civility at home and around the world."[118] Ford issued similar proclamations in 1975 and 1976.[119] For four years, President Jimmy Carter continued to do what his predecessors had done, stating in his first proclamation "that the promotion of respect for human rights is the shared responsibility of the world community."[120] He did not specify the end of the observance of the Human Rights Week, only that it began on December 10, 1977. His three subsequent proclaims in 1978, 1979, and 1980 followed the same pattern.[121] He indicated that the Human Rights Week "should be a time set apart for the study of our own rights, so basic to the working of our society, and for a renewal of our efforts on behalf of the human rights of all peoples everywhere."[122]

After being elected president in November 1980, Ronald Reagan issued his proclamation concerning Human Rights Week in 1981. Like Carter, he only stipulated the beginning date for the week: December 10. He invited each person to give "special thought to the blessing . . . enjoy[ed] as a free people and . . . [to] dedicate [his or her] efforts to making the promise of [the] Bill of Rights a living reality for all Americans, and, where possible for all [human]kind."[123] For the next seven years—1982 through

113. Johnson, "Proclamation 3814."
114. Johnson, "Proclamation 3814."
115. Nixon, "Proclamation 3946."
116. Nixon, "Proclamation 3946."
117. "Proclamations 4022, 4096, 4173, and 4256."
118. Ford, "Proclamation 4337."
119. "Proclamations 4408 and 4479."
120. Carter, "Proclamation 4542."
121. "Proclamations 4609, 4705, and 4804."
122. Carter, "Proclamation 4804."
123. Reagan, "Proclamation 4885."

1988—he issued similar proclamations.[124] In 1986, he announced that Human Rights Week began December 8.[125] George Bush proclaimed Human Rights Week beginning December 10, 1989. In his first of four two-page proclamations for 1989 and 1990 through 1992,[126] he stated, "Safeguarding individual liberty and fundamental human rights is not only the duty of any legitimate government, but also the key to economic prosperity and lasting peace among nations."[127] In 1993, President William J. Clinton issued the first of eight proclamations of Human Rights Week. After declaring December 10 Human Rights Day and December 15 Bill of Rights Day, he noted that Human Rights Week began on December 10. "The Bill of Rights and Universal Declaration of Human Rights enshrine this timeless truth for all people and all nations: respect for human rights is the foundation of freedom, justice, and peace."[128] From 1994 through 2000, he continued to issue two-page proclamations, stating that Human Rights Week began December 10, but giving no ending date.[129] In 1995, he specified that the week began December 10 and extended through December 16.[130] Except for his first proclamation of Human Rights Week[131] in 2001—beginning December 9—all of President George W. Bush's usually short proclamations from 2002 to 2008 indicate that it began December 10, but, as his predecessors did, he gave no date as to when the week ended.[132] In his 2001 words, he called "upon the people of the United States to honor the legacy of human rights passed down . . . from previous generations and to resolve that such liberties . . . prevail in [the] nation and throughout the world as [all] move[d] into the twenty-first century."[133] ". . . Human Rights Week must be our call to action," stated President Barack Obama in his first proclamation of the observance.[134] He added, ". . . [W]e will never waver in our pursuit of the rights, dignity, and security of every human being."[135] In his next seven proclamations of Human Rights Week, following in the steps of his predecessors, he gave December 10 as the beginning of the week of observance, but he did not give an ending date.[136] In his first two-page proclamation of Human Rights Week in 2017, President Donald J. Trump wrote, ". . .

---

124. "Proclamations 5003, 5135, 5287, 5420, 5589, 5752, and 5921."
125. Reagan, "Proclamation 5589."
126. "Proclamations 6238, 6390, and 6513."
127. Bush, "Proclamation 6082."
128. Clinton, "Proclamation 6637."
129. "Proclamations 6761, 6855, 6964, 7089, 7158, 7258, and 7386."
130. Clinton, "Proclamation 6855."
131. Bush, G.W., "Proclamation 7513."
132. "Proclamations 7634, 7744, 7854, 7968, 8090, 8210, and 8328."
133. Bush, G.W., "Proclamation 7513."
134. Obama, "Proclamation 8464."
135. Obama, "Proclamation 8464."
136. "Proclamations 8616, 8765, 8915, 9069, 9219, 9380, and 9553."

[W]e rededicate ourselves to steadfastly and faithfully defending . . . human rights."[137] Trump issued similar proclamations from 2018 through 2020.[138] However, he changed the beginning date for all three subsequent years: In 2018, Human Rights Week began December 9; in 2019, December 8; and in 2020, December 6. Unlike his predecessors, who issued one proclamation that covered Human Rights Day on December 10 and Bill of Rights Day on December 15 and Human Rights Week beginning December 10, President Joseph R. Biden issued two proclamations. The one that concerns us here is for Human Rights Day and Human Rights Week beginning December 10. In that proclamation, Biden stated that global leaders "working together" recommit themselves "to promoting respect for human rights and combating growing threats to democracy, including authoritarianism and corruption."[139] In that two-and-a-half-page document, Biden asked all Americans to dedicate themselves "to bringing [the] nation and [the] world closer to a future in which every human being is free to pursue [his or her] highest dreams and unleash [his or her] full potential."[140] In his remarks at the opening session of the Summit for Democracy on December 9, 2021, Biden spoke to fellow leaders, members of civil society, activists, advocates, and citizens, stating: "We stand at an inflection point in our history. . . . The choices we make . . . in this moment are going to fundamentally determine the direction our world is going to take in the coming decades. Will we allow the backward slide of rights and democracy to continue unchecked? Or will we together—together—have a vision and the vision—not just 'a' vision, 'the' vision—and courage to once more lead the march of human progress and human freedom forward?"[141] Those are the questions to be pondered during Human Rights Week.

Journal/Meditation: What do you consider to be your fundamental rights? Make a list. What human right do you think is threated the most at home and around the world? What words of what presidential proclamation above got most of your attention? If you haven't read the Universal Declaration of Human Rights and the Bill of Rights, what is keeping you from doing so during Human Rights Week? Both can be found online.

Prayer: God of justice and mercy, you created every human being with dignity and bestowed upon every one rights and freedoms that enhance their dignity. During this Human Rights Week, grant me a deeper understanding that neither race, creed, color, sex, or place of national origin affect the divine dignity you have bestowed upon all people. In your eyes, all are brothers and sisters enjoying a heritage of justice now and forever. Amen.

137. Trump, "Proclamation 9685."
138. "Proclamations 9832, 9972, and 10124."
139. Biden, "Proclamation 10321."
140. Biden, "Proclamation 10321."
141. Biden, "Remarks at Summit."

International Mountain Day
December 11

Text: "The General Assembly [of the United Nations] . . . welcomes the success achieved during the International Year of Mountains; . . . recommends that the experience gained during the International Year of Mountains be valued in the context of an appropriate follow-up; . . . notes with appreciation the work undertaken by the Food and Agriculture Organization of the United Nations as the lead agency for the International Year of Mountains . . . ; decides to designate 11 December as International Mountain Day, as from 11 December 2003, and encourages the international community to organize on this day events at all levels to highlight the importance of sustainable mountain development . . . ."[142]

Reflection: On December 20, 2002, the General Assembly of the United Nations established International Mountain Day to be December 11, beginning in 2003. At first, one might begin to think that this day has to do with recreation, such as hiking, backpacking, climbing, camping, skiing, snowshoeing, snowboarding, etc. However, as the U.N. resolution notes, the day is about "sustainable mountain development."[143] As can be inferred from the above text, on November 10, 1998, the U.N. proclaimed "the year 2002 as the International Year of Mountains."[144] In that resolution, it acknowledged "the work already undertaken to achieve sustainable mountain development by the Food and Agriculture Organization of the United Nations," and it encouraged "all governments, the United Nations system, and all other actors to take advantage of the International Year of Mountains in order to increase awareness of the importance of sustainable mountain development."[145] On December 20, 2000, the U.N. passed another resolution related to the International Year of Mountains. In this one, it encouraged "all states, the United Nations system, and all other actors to take advantage of the International Year of Mountains to ensure the present and future wellbeing of mountain communities by promoting conservation and sustainable development in mountain areas; to increase awareness and knowledge of mountain ecosystems, their dynamics and functioning, and their overriding importance in providing a number of crucial goods and services essential to the wellbeing of both rural and urban, highland and lowland people, in particular water supply, food security, and to promote and defend the cultural heritage of mountain communities and societies."[146] The success achieved in sustainable mountain development during the 2002 International Year of Mountains is what led the U.N. to establish the annual International Mountain Day beginning December 11, 2003.

142. United Nations General Assembly, A/RES/57/245.
143. United Nations General Assembly, A/RES/57/245.
144. United Nations General Assembly, A/RES/53/24.
145. United Nations General Assembly, A/RES/53/24.
146. United Nations General Assembly, A/RES/55/189.

According to the U.N.'s International Mountain Day webpage: "Mountains are home to 15 percent of the world's population and host about half of the world's biodiversity hotspots. They provide freshwater for everyday life to half of humanity.... Unfortunately, mountains are under threat from climate change and overexploitation. As the global climate continues to warm, mountain people—some of the world's poorest—face even greater struggles to survive. The rising temperatures also mean that mountain glaciers are melting at unprecedented rates, affecting freshwater supplies downstream for millions of people."[147] The webpage also notes that "[o]f the twenty plant species that supply 80 percent of the world's food, six originated and have been diversified in mountains: maize, potatoes, barley, sorghum, tomatoes, and apples."[148] Mountain conservation is a key factor for sustainable development. Three mountain targets are among the seventeen among the United Nations Sustainable Development Goals. "By 2030, protect and restore water related ecosystems, including mountains, forests, wetlands, rivers, aquifers, and lakes," states goal 6.6.[149] "By 2030, ensure the conservation, restoration, and sustainable use of terrestrial and inland freshwater ecosystems and their services, in particular forests, wetlands, mountains, and drylands, in line with obligations under international agreements," declares goal 15.1.[150] And, "By 2030, ensure the conservation of mountain ecosystems, including their biodiversity, in order to enhance their capacity to provide benefits that are essential for sustainable development," states goal 15.4.[151] Samuel Elzinga writes: "Regardless of where we live, mountains play an integral role in the daily lives of much of the world population. Much of the world's usable freshwater supply originates from mountain areas. Mountainous ecosystems additionally host a variety of climates, ranging from rainforests to high-altitude deserts. According to the FAO-UN [Food and Agriculture Organization of the United Nations], more than 90 percent of the world's mountain dwellers live in developing countries, including 634 million people living in rural areas where the vast majority live below the poverty line, and more than one in two face food insecurity. Modern challenges, such as climate change and migration, make their situation even worse."[152] Every December 11, the world takes note about mountain communities around the world and raises its awareness about the importance of sustainable mountain development.

Journal/Meditation: What one thing have you learned about sustainable mountain development? What do you think is the number one threat to mountains today?

---

147. "International Mountain Day."
148. "International Mountain Day."
149. United Nations General Assembly, A/RES/70/1.
150. United Nations General Assembly, A/RES/70/1.
151. United Nations General Assembly, A/RES/70/1.
152. Elzinga, "Celebrate."

Which of the three sustainable goals mentioning mountains gets most of your attention? Why? What role do mountains play in your daily life?

Prayer: In ancient times, you were believed to live on a mountain top, O God. Through the help of your grace, give me greater awareness of how mountains play an integral role in my daily life. Then, give me the strength to work toward sustainable mountain development that benefits all people today, tomorrow, and forever. Amen.

Bill of Rights Day
December 15

Text: "Congress shall make no law respecting an establishment of religion, or prohibiting the free exercise thereof; or abridging the freedom of speech, or of the press; or the right of the people peaceably to assemble, and to petition the government for a redress of grievances. . . . [T[he right of the people to keep and bear arms shall not be infringed. The right of the people to be secure in their persons, houses, papers, and effects, against unreasonable searches and seizures, shall not be violated . . . . No person shall be held to answer for a capital, or otherwise infamous crime, unless on a presentment or indictment of a grand jury . . . ; nor shall any person be subject for the same offence to be twice put in jeopardy of life or limb; nor shall be compelled in any criminal case to be a witness against himself [or herself], nor be deprived of life, liberty, or property, without the process of law; nor shall private property be taken for public use, without just compensation. In all criminal prosecutions, the accused shall enjoy the right to a speedy and public trial, by an impartial jury . . . . Excessive bail shall not be required, nor excessive fines imposed, nor cruel and unusual punishments inflicted. The enumeration in the Constitution, of certain rights, shall not be construed to deny or disparage others retained by the people. The powers not delegated to the United States by the Constitution not prohibited by it to the states, are reserved to the states respectively, or to the people."[153]

Reflection: The Bill of Rights, from which the above text is taken, consists of the first ten amendments to the Constitution which were ratified on December 15, 1791. Once the Constitution was adopted, a number of states expressed a desire, in order to prevent abuse of its powers, to add declaratory and restrictive clauses to it. In order to accomplish this, twelve amendments to the Constitution of the United States were prepared. On December 15, 1791, ten of the twelve amendments were ratified and called the U.S. Bill of Rights; the document contains the fundamental rights of citizens and guarantees equal protection for them under the law. It was not until 1941 that Public Law 243 (House Joint Resolution 120) passed the U.S. House on June 16 and the U.S. Senate on August 14, that President Franklin D. Roosevelt signed

---

153. "Bill of Rights."

into law a bill that provided "for the proper observance of the one hundred and fiftieth anniversary of the adoption of the first ten amendments to the Constitution, known as the Bill of Rights." The president was authorized and requested to issue a proclamation designating December 15, 1941, as Bill of Rights Day. The flag was to be displayed on all government buildings and the people of the U.S. were invited "to observe the day with appropriate ceremonies and prayer."[154] Roosevelt did as he was asked and proclaimed the first Bill of Rights Day. In his two-page proclamation, he stated, "The first ten amendments, the great American charter of personal liberty and human dignity, became a part of the Constitution of the United States on the fifteenth day of December, 1791."[155] Later, he wrote, "It is especially fitting that this anniversary should be remembered and observed by those institutions of a democratic people which owe their very existence to the guarantees of the Bill of Rights.... The fifteenth day of December, 1941, is therefore set apart as a day of mobilization for freedom and for human rights, a day of remembrance of the democratic and peaceful action by which these rights were gained, a day of reassessment of their present meaning and their living worth."[156] Five years later, on May 29, 1946, congress approved Public Law 392 (House Joint Resolution 273) authorizing and requesting President Harry S. Truman to honor the one hundred and fifty-fifth anniversary of the Bill of Rights by proclaiming December 15, 1946, Bill of Rights Day.[157] In his proclamation, Truman acknowledged that it was "fitting ... [to] set aside a day for solemn contemplation of ... liberties and of the recent world-wide battle [World War II] to protect them from annihilation."[158] He issued the proclamation again in 1947, stating, "Since to comprehend and value our liberties is the first condition of remaining free, I urge the people of the nation to reexamine and to reflect upon the provisions of our Constitution which secure our freedom under law—particularly the guarantees of freedom of religion, speech, the press, and assembly, as well as the pledges of fair trial and of security against unreasonable searches and seizures, and against the deprivation of life, liberty, or property without due process of law."[159] In 1955, President Dwight D. Eisenhower issued a single-page statement about the Bill of Rights: "[The] Bill of Rights Day ranks in the forefront of our days of commemoration," he wrote. "By the Bill of Rights our people are guaranteed the most precious of liberties...." He expressed his hope "that citizens throughout [the] land [would] renew in their hearts and minds a devotion to these freedoms and a determination to defend them against all forms of attack."[160] In his 1958 proclamation of a Human Rights Week, he mentioned both the Bill of Rights

154. "Public Law 243."
155. Roosevelt, "Proclamation 2524."
156. Roosevelt, "Proclamation 2524."
157. "Public Law 392."
158. Truman, "Proclamation 2713."
159. Truman, "Proclamation 2761."
160. Eisenhower, "Statement."

and the Universal Declaration of Human Rights of the United Nations, but he did not proclaim a Bill of Rights Day.[161]

President John F. Kennedy followed Eisenhower's lead in 1961, acknowledging December 15 as marking the anniversary of the adoption of the Bill of Rights and December 10 as the adoption of the Universal Declaration of Human Rights. However, he did not proclaim a Bill of Rights Day.[162] On October 9, 1962, congressed passed Public Law 87–759, which designated "December 15, 1962, as Bill of Rights Day" and called "upon the people of the United States to observe such day with appropriate ceremonies and activities. . . ."[163] Kennedy proclaimed December 15, 1962, Bill of Rights Day. He stated, ". . . [T]he principles of freedom and justice in our Bill of Rights are embodied in the Universal Declaration of Human Rights." He added, "Let us shoulder our responsibilities, as trustees of freedom, to make the Bill of Rights a reality for all our citizens."[164] Following Kennedy's lead, President Lyndon B. Johnson proclaimed Bill of Rights Day in 1963, 1964, 1965, 1966, and 1968.[165] In 1967, he remembered December 15 as the ratification date for the Bill of Rights, but he did not proclaim Bill of Rights Day.[166] In his first proclamation of Bill of Rights Day in 1963, he stated that December 15 had "long been celebrated in gratitude for the guarantees of individual rights and liberties set forth" in the Bill of Rights.[167] President Richard Nixon proclaimed Bill of Rights Day for December 15 in 1969, 1970, 1971, 1972, and 1973.[168] In his first proclamation in 1969, he stated that the founders of the Republic "sought to ensure that the power of the government would not abridge the rights of citizens" and so wrote the first ten amendments to the Constitution.[169] "We should take the opportunity, whenever possible," stated President Gerald R. Ford, in his first proclamation of Bill of Rights Day in 1974, "to strengthen the liberties which have been assured us in the Bill of Rights."[170] He did the same in 1975 and 1976.[171] According to President Jimmy Carter in his first proclamation of Bill of Rights Day in 1977, "The Bill of Rights culminated the Founders' [of the country] efforts to create for their new country a national life grounded in liberty and respect for individual rights."[172] In 1978, 1979, and 1980, Carter continued to proclaim December 15 Bill of Rights

---

161. Eisenhower, "Proclamation 3265."
162. Kennedy, "Proclamation 3442."
163. "Public Law 87–759."
164. Kennedy, "Proclamation 3508."
165. "Proclamations 3563, 3631, 3691, 3758, and 3882."
166. Johnson, "Proclamation 3814."
167. Johnson, "Proclamation 3563."
168. "Proclamations 3946, 4022, 4096, 4173, and 4256."
169. Nixon, "Proclamation 3946."
170. Ford, "Proclamation 4337."
171. "Proclamations 4408 and 4479."
172. Carter, "Proclamation 4542."

Day.[173] For the eight years of his presidency, Ronald Reagan proclaimed Bill of Rights Day from 1981 to 1988.[174] In 1981, he invited U.S. citizens to give "special thought to the blessings [they] enjoy[ed] as a free people and [to] . . . dedicate [their] efforts to making the promise of [the] Bill of Rights a living reality for all Americans . . . ."[175] Following Reagan, George Bush proclaimed Bill of Rights Day from 1989 through 1992.[176] In his first proclamation in 1989, Bush stated, ". . . [T]he principles enshrined in our Bill of Rights have proved to be not only guiding tenets of American government, but also a model for the world."[177] In his first of eight proclamations of Bill of Rights Day in 1993, President William J. Clinton stated, "Our Bill of Rights guarantees our fundamental liberties, including freedom of religion, speech, and the press. . . . We continue to commemorate Bill of Rights Day because ensuring respect for human rights in the United States is never ending—it is a work in progress."[178] In a similar way, he proclaimed Bill of Rights Day from 1994 to 2000.[179] Overshadowed by "the terrible tragedies of September 11," 2001, George W. Bush proclaimed December 15, 2001, Bill of Rights Day; he reminded Americans that they stood "united with those who love democracy, justice, and individual liberty" and were "committed to upholding [those] principles, embodied in . . . [t]he Bill of Rights, that have safeguarded [them] through [their] history . . . ."[180] Likewise, from 2002 through 2008, Bush continued to proclaim Bill of Rights Day.[181] In 2009, President Barack Obama issued his first proclamation of Bill of Rights Day, writing, "[The fundamental rights at the core of the Bill of Rights] are the values that define us as a people, the ideals that challenge us to perfect our union, and the liberties that generations of Americans have fought to preserve at home and abroad."[182] In a similar vein, he issued Bill of Rights Day proclamations from 2010 through 2016.[183] In his first of four proclamations of Bill of Rights Day—all of which are over two pages long—President Donald J. Trump stated that the Bill of Rights is a "sustaining bulwark," which "has formed the bedrock of the constitutional protections every American holds dear as [his or her] birthright." He explains how the Bill of Rights, "a specific enumeration of fundamental rights that would prevail even against a future government inclined to abuse the power it has over the lives of

---

173. "Proclamations 4609, 4705, and 4804."
174. "Proclamations 4885, 5003, 5135, 5287, 5420, 5589, 5752, and 5921."
175. Reagan, "Proclamation 4885."
176. "Proclamations 6082, 6238, 6390, and 6513."
177. Bush, "Proclamation 6082."
178. Clinton, "Proclamation 6637."
179. "Proclamations 6761, 6855, 6964, 7059, 7158, 7258, and 7386."
180. Bush, G.W., "Proclamation 7513."
181. "Proclamations 7634, 7744, 7854, 7968, 8090, 8210, and 8328."
182. Obama, "Proclamation 8464."
183. "Proclamations 8616, 8765, 8915, 9069, 9219, 9380, and 9553."

citizens," enhances the Constitution.[184] In 2018, 2019, and 2020, Trump issued similar proclamations.[185] The only president to issue a separate proclamation for Bill of Rights Day since Franklin D. Roosevelt in 1941 is President Joseph R. Biden in 2021. After narrating some of the history about the Bill of Rights in his two-page proclamation, Biden states, "These amendments protect some of the most indispensable rights and liberties that define us as Americans. Though we have often struggled to live up to the promises they contain, 230 years after the ratification of the Bill of Rights, respect for human rights and fundamental freedoms remains at the center of our democracy." He adds, "[A]mending the Constitution illustrates that improving our democracy is the shared and constant duty of all Americans. Democracy's greatest strength is the ability it provides its citizens to improve their system of government, which is why democracy is uniquely suited to face the challenges of a changing world."[186] Since the first ten amendments were incorporated into the Bill of Rights in 1791, seventeen more amendments—for a total of twenty-seven amendments—have been added to the document.

Journal/Meditation: What do you think is the most important right you have in the Bill of Rights? Explain. Which statement by a U.S. president got most of your attention? Why? What does it mean to you? What liberty from the Bill of Rights do you contemplate the most?

Prayer: On this Bill of Rights Day, O God, I join in a prayer of thanksgiving for the countless freedoms and liberties you have bestowed upon the United States of America through the Bill of Rights. On this day of remembrance, deepen my appreciation for the gifts I enjoy in this democracy and grant peace within our borders and throughout all the countries of the world. Amen.

International Migrants Day

December 18

Text: "Considering that the Universal Declaration of Human Rights proclaims that all human beings are born free and equal in dignity and rights and that everyone is entitled to all the rights and freedoms set forth therein, without distinction of any kind, in particular as to race, color, or national origin; encouraged by the increasing interest of the international community in the effective and full protection of the human rights of all migrants, and underling the need to make further efforts to ensure respect for the human rights and fundamental freedoms of all migrants; [the General Assembly of the United Nations] . . . decides to proclaim 18 December International Migrants Day [and] invites members states, as well as intergovernmental and non-governmental

---

184. Trump, "Proclamation 9685."
185. "Proclamations 9932, 9972, and 10124."
186. Biden, "Proclamation 10323."

organizations to observe International Migrants Day, through . . . the dissemination of information on the human rights and fundamental freedoms of migrants, the sharing of experience, and the design of actions to ensure their protection."[187]

Reflection: The Universal Declaration on Human Rights was issued by the United Nations on December 10, 1948. It was, as the above text makes clear, a declaration that all people are born free, equal in dignity, and equal in rights no matter to what race they belong, what their skin color may be, or from what country they come. It only follows logically that migrants, persons moving from place to place, would share in universal rights. However, in order to focus for a day on the rights of migrants, the need to protect those rights, and the need to ensure respect for them, the U.N. established International Migrants Day on December 4, 2000, to be marked every year on December 18. December 18 was chosen because that was the date when the U.N. General Assembly passed the "International Convention on the Protection of the Rights of All Migrant Workers and Members of Their Families" in 1990. That twenty-eight-page document contains ninety-three articles specifying how to respect and protect the rights of migrants. According to the U.N. webpage on International Migrants Day, "Today, more people than ever live in a country other than the one in which they were born. While many individuals migrate out of choice, many others migrate out of necessity."[188]

The "International Convention on the Protection of the Rights of All Migrant Workers and Members of Their Families" is "convinced that the rights of migrant workers and members of their families have not been sufficiently recognized everywhere and therefore require appropriate international protection."[189] A migrant worker, according to the Convention, "refers to a person who is to be engaged, is engaged, or has been engaged in a remunerated activity in a state of which he or she is not a national."[190] A member of the family "refers to persons married to migrant workers or having with them a relationship that, according to applicable law, produces effects equivalent to marriage, as well as their dependent children and other dependent persons who are recognized as members of the family."[191] Thus, the Convention makes clear that it applies "to all migrant workers and members of their families without distinction of any kind, such as sex, race, color, language, religion or conviction, political or other opinion, national, ethnic, or social origin, nationality, age, economic position, property, marital status, birth, or other status."[192] It also makes clear that the Convention applies "during the entire migration process of migrant workers and members

---

187. United Nations General Assembly, A/RES/55/93.
188. "International Migrants Day."
189. United Nations General Assembly, A/RES/45/158, Preamble.
190. United Nations General Assembly, A/RES/45/158, Article 2.1.
191. United Nations General Assembly, A/RES/45/158, Article 4.
192. United Nations General Assembly, A/RES/45/158, Article 1.1.

of their families, which comprises preparation for migration, departure, transit, and the entire period of stay and remunerated activity in the state of employment as well as return to the state of origin or the state of habitual residence."[193] Migrant workers and their families may be considered as documented or non-documented.[194] The human rights shared by all migrant workers and their families include—among many more in the Convention—the freedom to leave any state, including their country of origin; the right to life; the right not to be tortured or subjected to cruel, inhuman, or degrading treatment or punishment; the right not to be held in slavery or servitude; the right to freedom of thought, conscience, and religion; the right to hold opinions without interference; the right not to be subjected to arbitrary or unlawful interference with privacy, family, home, correspondence, or other communications, or not to have honor and reputation unlawfully attacked; the right not to be arbitrarily deprived of property; the right to liberty and security of person; the right to be treated with humanity and with respect for the inherent dignity of the human person and for cultural identity; the right to equality with nationals of the state with concern before the courts and tribunals; the right not to be held guilty of any criminal offence on account of any act or omission that does not constitute a criminal offence under national or international law; the right not to be imprisoned on the ground of failure to fulfill a contractual obligation; the right not to have identity documents, documents authorizing entry, residence, or work permits confiscated, destroyed, or attempted to be destroyed; the right not to be subject to measures of collective expulsion; the right to have recourse to the protection and assistance of the consular or diplomatic authorities of the state of origin; the right to recognition everywhere as a person before the law; the right to enjoy treatment no less favorable than that which applies to nationals of the state of employment in respect or remuneration; the right to participate in trade unions and other associations; the right to be treated the same as nationals when employed; the rights of children to a name, birth registration, and nationality; the right to education; the right of respect for cultural identity; the right, upon termination of work, to transfer earnings, savings, and personal property; and more.[195] According to the U.N. webpage on International Migrants Day: "A broad range of factors continue to determine the movement of people. They are either voluntary or forced movements as a result of the increased magnitude and frequency of disasters, economic challenges, and extreme poverty or conflict. All these will significantly affect the characteristics and scale of migration in the future and determine the strategies and policies countries must develop in order to harness the potential of migration while ensuring the fundamental human rights of migrants are protected."[196] That is why the focus of International Migrants Day is the sharing of information on the human rights and

---

193. United Nations General Assembly, A/RES/45/158, Article 1.2.
194. United Nations General Assembly, A/RES/45/158, Article 5 (a) and (b).
195. United Nations General Assembly, A/RES/45/158, Articles 8–27, 29–32.
196. "International Migrants Day."

fundamental freedoms of migrants and their families and taking action to ensure their protection.

Journal/Meditation: Which human right of migrants presented in the above list got most of your attention? Why? In your opinion and/or experience, in the past what has been the major distinction made between migrants and nationals? Why do you think it is easy to make distinctions between migrants and nationals?

Prayer: In your sight, O God, all people are migrant workers traveling with their families through this life. Instill in people around the world a greater awareness that all migrant workers and members of their families without distinction of any kind are born free and equal in dignity and rights and that all are entitled to all the rights and all the freedoms. Help me to realize, LORD, that all people are your people. Amen.

INTERNATIONAL HUMAN SOLIDARITY DAY
December 20

Text: "The General Assembly [of the United Nations] . . . acknowledges that sustained economic growth, supported by rising productivity and a favorable environment, including for private investment and entrepreneurship, is necessary to eradicate poverty, achieve the internationally agreed development goals, . . . and realize a rise in living standards; . . . recognizes that . . . it is imperative that developing countries be integrated into the world economy and share equitably in the benefits of globalization; . . . reaffirms that, within the context of overall action for the eradication of poverty, special attention should be given to the multidimensional nature of poverty and the national and international conditions and policies that are conducive to its eradication, fostering . . . the social and economic integration of people living in poverty and the promotion and protection of all human rights and fundamental freedoms for all, including the right to development; . . . reaffirms that the eradication of poverty should be addressed in a multisectoral and integrated way, . . . taking into account the importance of the need for the empowerment of women and sectoral strategies in such areas as education, development of human resources, health, human settlements, rural, local, and community development, productive employment, population, environment, and natural resources, water, and sanitation, agriculture, food security, energy, and migration, and the special needs of disadvantaged and vulnerable groups in such a way as to increase opportunities and choices for people living in poverty and to enable them to build and to strengthen their assets so as to achieve development, security, and stability, and, in that regard, encourages countries to develop their national poverty reduction policies in accordance with their national priorities, including, where appropriate, through poverty reduction strategy papers; . . . recalls that . . . the heads of state and government . . . identified solidarity as one of the fundamental and universal values that should underlie relations between peoples in the twenty-first century, and in that regard decides to proclaim 20 December of each year International Human Solidarity Day; invites governments and relevant stakeholders to utilize entrepreneurship, taking fully into account national interests, priorities, and development strategies, to contribute to poverty eradication."[197]

Reflection: On December 22, 2005, the General Assembly of the United Nations passed an eleven-page resolution with fifty-six numbered paragraphs and two pages of non-numbered paragraphs. The above text is taken from that resolution. While the focus of the resolution is poverty eradication in all its many forms, the means to achieve that goal is building "on a foundation of global cooperation and solidarity."[198] Literally, solidarity means "harmony of interests and responsibilities among individuals in a group, especially as manifested in unanimous support and collective action for something."[199] In the U.N., solidarity is identified "as one of the fundamental values of international relations in the twenty-first century, wherein those who either suffer or benefit least deserve help from those who benefit most."[200] That is why the U.N. promotes a culture of solidarity; the spirit of sharing is important for combating poverty. Indeed, according to the U.N.'s International Human Solidary Day webpage: "The concept of solidarity has defined the work of the United Nations since the birth of the organization. The creation of the United Nations drew the peoples and nations of the world together to promote peace, human rights, and social and economic development. The organization was founded on the basic premise of unity and harmony among its members, expressed in the concept of collective security that relies on the solidarity of its members to unite 'to maintain international peace and security.'"[201] As can be seen in the text above, the U.N. identifies "solidarity as one of the fundamental and universal values that should underlie relations between peoples in the twenty-first century."[202] Because "the number of people living in extreme poverty in many countries continues to increase, with women and children constituting the majority and the most affected groups," the U.N. reiterates "that eradicating poverty is the greatest global challenge facing the world today and an indispensable requirement for sustained development, in particular for developing countries."[203] In other words, the way to eradicate poverty is in global solidarity.

The human solidarity envisioned by the U.N. begins with "good governance at the international level," which "is fundamental for achieving poverty eradication and sustainable development." However, "in order to ensure a dynamic and enabling

---

197. United Nations General Assembly, A/RES/60/209, pars. 4, 6–7, 25, 43–4.
198. "International Human Solidarity Day."
199. *Encarta*.
200. "International Human Solidarity Day."
201. "International Human Solidarity Day."
202. United Nations General Assembly, A/RES/60/209, par. 43.
203. United Nations General Assembly, A/RES/60/209.

international economic environment, it is important to promote global economic governance through addressing the international finance, trade, technology, and investment patterns that have an impact on the development prospects of developing countries." Furthermore, "sound economic policies, solid democratic institutions responsive to the needs of the people and improved infrastructure are the basis for sustained economic growth, poverty eradication, and employment creation." Also, "freedom, peace, and security, domestic stability, respect for human rights, including the right to development, and the rule of law, gender equality, market-oriented policies, and an overall commitment to just and democratic societies are . . . essential and mutually reinforcing."[204] Solidarity, also referred to as international cooperation, "is essential in supplementing and supporting the efforts of developing countries to utilize their domestic resources for development and poverty eradication."[205] The U.N. notes that "debt relief can play a key role in liberating resources that should be directed towards activities consistent with poverty eradication, sustained economic growth, and sustainable development, and the achievement of the internationally agreed development goals"—solidarity.[206] ". . . [T]he potential of information and communication technologies . . . serve as a powerful tool for development and poverty eradication and . . . help the international community to maximize the benefits of globalization."[207] The result of the resolution, in part, links "poverty eradication and improving access to safe drinking water," "adequate housing," and "rural poverty and hunger."[208] This annual International Human Solidarity Day recognizes the universal value of solidarity by reminding U.N. member states of their global objectives and initiatives to eradicate poverty and to share their poverty eradication strategies with each other around the world. According to the U.N. webpage, this is a day "to celebrate our unity in diversity, . . . to remind governments to respect their commitment to international agreements, . . . to raise public awareness of the importance of solidarity, . . . to encourage debate on the ways to promote solidarity for the achievement of the Sustainable Development Goals including poverty eradication . . . [and] to encourage new initiatives for poverty eradication."[209]

Journal/Meditation: When have you experienced solidarity? unity in diversity? Explain. How is solidarity a fundamental and universal value? With what is your solidarity threatened?

Prayer: While I am an individual, Creator God, and all other people are individuals, you, our common source, are our unity in our diversity. Draw people internationally

---

204. United Nations General Assembly, A/RES/60/209, pars. 9, 11.
205. United Nations General Assembly, A/RES/60/209, par. 14.
206. United Nations General Assembly, A/RES/60/209, par. 21.
207. United Nations General Assembly, A/RES/60/209, par. 24.
208. United Nations General Assembly, A/RES/60/209, pars. 35–7.
209. "International Human Solidary Day."

into human solidarity so that what we cannot do alone we can accomplish together to give our world freedom, peace, and security today, tomorrow, and forever. Amen.

SUPER SATURDAY
Saturday before Christmas

Text: "Super Saturday, also known as Panic Saturday, is the last Saturday before Christmas, a major revenue-generating day for retailers, and shoppers' traditional last chance for serious gift buying. As such, Super Saturday features big discounts, extended store hours, and, for many retailers, one of the best sales days of the entire year."[210]

Reflection: Because Christmas moves from one day of the week to another, the Saturday before it, known as Super Saturday or Panic Saturday, can be as close as one day or as far away as seven days. The use of the name "Super Saturday" has no clear reference; it was used as early as 2007 to designate a major revenue day for retailers, while offering shoppers, who had waited until the last day or few days to get their buying done, last-minute bargains. Because Super Saturday often falls only a day or a few days before Christmas, it has become a major source of revenue for brick-and-mortar stores due to the amount of foot traffic it generates in distinction to online ordering, which cannot usually be delivered in a day or a few days before Christmas. Thus, according to Jim Probasco, "The top five Super Saturday shopping destinations, in order, are discount department stores, department stores, wholesale clubs, electronic stores, and dollar stores."[211] A lot of people—last-minute shoppers—visit such stores in order to complete Christmas shopping on Super Saturday, the last of a string of special shopping days before Christmas.

Because the end of the shopping season is upon them, shoppers witness retailers vying with each other for their business by offering one-day sales with deep discounts, extending store hours, and attempting to clear shelves of merchandise—all in an effort to get shoppers into their stores. Usually, by the middle of December, more than half of United States shoppers still have buying to do; this makes them the easy target of retailers, who want the end-of-the-year sales to push them from red ink to black ink in their accounting ledger. Of course, retailers also know that if they make the deal sweet enough, they can spark impulse buying even from those who have already finished their Christmas shopping. While the moniker "Super Saturday" can also be used for any Saturday where a large number of related events take place, in December it refers to the last Saturday for serious shopping before Christmas.

---

210. Probasco, "Super Saturday."
211. Probasco, "Super Saturday."

Journal/Reflection: Do you finish your Christmas shopping early, or do you wait until your last chance to complete it? Why? What are the Super Saturday advantages and disadvantages for shoppers? What are the Super Saturday advantages and disadvantages for retailers?

Prayer: Help me to keep in mind the purpose of Christmas gift-giving, O God. Guide me to a present that will express my love for another and will extend through me your love for him or her. Bless all shoppers with patience and joy as they prepare to celebrate Christmas. Amen.

Winter Solstice
December 21–22

Text: "The winter solstice . . . is the astronomical first day of winter in the Northern Hemisphere and the shortest day of the year. . . . For the northern half of Earth (the Northern Hemisphere), the winter solstice occurs annually on December 21 or 22. . . . The winter solstice is the day with the fewest hours of sunlight in the whole year, making it the 'shortest day' of the year. . . . [A]fter we reach the winter solstice, the days begin once again to grow longer and longer until we reach the summer solstice—the first day of summer and the longest day of the year."[212]

Reflection: At a precise moment on December 21 or 22 every year, the winter solstice occurs. While most people think of it as a day or several-day event, it is the moment when the earth is tilted as far away from the sun as possible before it begins to tilt the opposite direction. At that moment, the sun's path across the sky is as low in the sky as it can be; during the winter, the sun arcs lower or closer to the horizon. Standing outside in the sun, a person casts the longest shadow he or she can cast all year on the winter solstice. In other words, at the precise moment of the winter solstice, the sun's path reaches its most southerly point in the sky, and astronomical winter begins and lasts until the spring equinox. Astronomical seasons are determined by the position of the earth in relation to the sun. The moment is called a solstice, a word composed of two Latin words: *sol* meaning *sun*, and *sistere* meaning *to stand still*. Thus, the winter solstice is when the sun appears to stand still for a few days before and after the specific time of the event. Because the noontime elevation of the sun is so slight, the sun's path seems to stay the same or to stand still. And because the sun's path is so low in the sky, the shortest day of the year occurs; the least amount of daylight, which begins to lengthen the moment the solstice is over, has led to different celebrations of dark (death) and light (birth). At the North Pole there is no daylight on the winter solstice, but the number of hours of daylight gradually increases to the equator.

212. "When Is?"

The first day of winter was honored by Druids, who, according to the *Farmers' Almanac*, "thought of [the winter solstice] as a time of death and rebirth when nature's powers and . . . [peoples] souls [were] renewed." The winter solstice marked "the moment in time when the Old Sun die[d] (at dusk on the twenty-first of December) and when the Sun of the New Year [was] born (at dawn on the twenty-second of December), framing the longest night of the year. The birth of the New Sun is thought to revive the earth's aura in mystical ways, giving a new lease on life to spirits and souls of the dead."[213] Germanic peoples honored the winter solstice with a holiday named Yule, during which fires were lit to represent the heat, light, and life-giving properties of the sun. A Yule log was burned in the fireplace in honor of the god Thor, whose responsibility it was to bring back the sun's warmth. A part of the log was kept as a token of good luck and to serve as kindling for the next winter solstice. In some European countries, the ashes of the Yule log were spread on the dead fields as fertilizer to give them life in the spring, while in other countries the ashes were placed under one's bed to protect the house from lightning and thunder. In Rome, the holiday was called Saturnalia, which began on December 17 and ended on the Winter Solstice. It honored Saturnus, the god of agriculture and harvest, by thanking him for the harvest (the result of sunlight) which was sustaining life and petitioning him to give another good harvest (as the result of sunlight) for the next year. Because the Romans could detect that the days were getting longer by December 25, they marked a holiday called Sol Invictus, the Unconquered Sun or Invincible Sun. As will be seen below, Sol Invictus, along with Yule, was Christianized and became Christmas.

Journal/Meditation: How is the winter solstice a time of death and rebirth for you? What do winter fires—especially one in your fireplace or outdoor fire pit—mean to you? What do winter fires engender among those who gather around them?

Prayer: Creator God, you formed the universe in magnificence with its millions of solar systems. On the earth, you place people, who observe the times for the rising and the setting of the sun, the changing length of days, and equinoxes and solstices. As I mark the winter solstice, give me a deeper appreciation for the cycle of death and life that occurs in the seasons and in my own life. Amen.

Festivus

December 23

Text: "**Frank Costanza (Jerry Stiller)**: Many Christmases ago, I went to buy a doll for my son. I reached for the last one they had, but so did another man. As I rained blows upon him, I realized there had to be another way. **Cosmo Kramer (Michael Richards)**: What happened to the doll? **Constanza**: It was destroyed. But out of that a

---

213. "Winter Solstice."

new holiday was born . . . a Festivus for the rest of us! **Kramer**: That must have been some kind of doll. **Constanza**: She was."[214]

Reflection: The above text is some of the dialogue from "The Strike" episode of the ninth season of *Seinfeld*, which was first broadcast on December 18, 1997. In the above dialogue, Constanza (Stiller) explains to Kramer (Richards) how he created the secular holiday as an alternative statement against the commercialization, consumerism, and the pressures of Christmas. Festivus is celebrated on December 23. One holiday observer greets another, saying, "Happy Festivus." The slogan for the holiday is "A Festivus for the rest of us!" While the holiday made its public debut on *Seinfeld*, it was originally created by Daniel O'Keefe, an author, editor, and father of TV writer Dan O'Keefe, who marked it in his family as early as 1966. Daniel named the day using the Latin word *Festivus*, meaning *excellent, jovial, lively*. The Latin word is derived from *festus*, meaning *joyous; holiday, feast day*. Dan wrote about Festivus as he had experienced it as a child, depicting it in the Seinfeld episode noted above. Everything about the holiday seems to be a parody and a form of playful consumer resistance to Christmas. There are four main components.

First, in the room where the celebration takes place is an unadorned aluminum pole. "The pole was chosen in opposition to the highly decorated, commercialized Christmas trees . . . ."[215] The pole, stuck in a Christmas-tree stand, is in direct contrast to normal holiday materialism. Second, before beginning to eat the Festivus dinner—traditionally meatloaf on a bed of lettuce with no alcohol served—the Airing of Grievances, the third component, takes place. "At the beginning of the Festivus dinner, each participant tells friends and family all the times they have disappointed him or her the past year."[216] Fourth, once the dinner is finished, the Feats of Strength occurs. ". . . [T]he head of the household tests his or her strength against one participant of the head's choosing."[217] This is usually a wrestling match; Festivus is over once the head of the household is pinned. If he or she is not pinned, then Festivus continues until the requirement is meant. According to Allison Hope, Festivus is "a holiday that allows us to maintain a healthy dose of grumpiness." It is "for all who feel that the normal holiday traditions don't quite fit the bill . . . ." It is for those who "want to embrace their inner 'bah humbug' than their Christmas spirit."[218]

Journal/Meditation: How do you resist the commercialization, consumerism, and pressures of Christmas? How do you deal with grumpiness? How do you enhance the Christmas spirit?

---

214. "Happy Festivus."
215. "Happy Festivus."
216. "Happy Festivus."
217. "Happy Festivus."
218. Hope, "Festivus."

Prayer: Every year, O Lord, the festival of Christmas is celebrated around the world. Bestow upon those with whom I celebrate the feast a moderation in all things, forgiveness for all wrongs, hurts, and disappointments, and strength to celebrate together as one family. Amen.

CHRISTMAS EVE
December 24

Text: "'Twas the night before Christmas, when all through the house / Not a creature was stirring, not even a mouse. / . . . When out on the lawn there arose such a clatter, / I sprang from the bed to see what was the matter. / Away to the window I flew like a flash, / Tore open the shutters and threw up the sash. / The moon on the breast of the new-fallen snow / Gave the luster of mid-day to objects below. / . . . As I drew in my head, and was turning around, / Down the chimney St. Nicholas came with a bound."[219]

Reflection: Until Clement Clarke Moore's "A Visit from St. Nicholas"—published on December 23, 1823, in the *Sentinel*, a newspaper of Troy, New York—everything about St. Nicholas took place on St. Nicholas Eve, December 5, when gifts were given in imitation of the saint who had saved the three daughters of a poor man by providing him with dowries for them for marriage. Without the bags of gold tossed through the window (in some accounts, tossed down the chimney), the daughters would have been forced into prostitution, sold into slavery, or have to marry undesirable husbands. In time, as the story continued to circulate, the gold was described as landing in stockings or shoes hung by the fireplace to dry. As a result, children began hanging their stockings on the fireplace or placing their shoes there or elsewhere in the hope that St. Nicholas would leave gifts on the eve of his feast, December 5, to be enjoyed on his feast day, December 6. After having been attributed with raising three murdered and innocent children, St. Nicholas also gained a reputation of knowing who was naughty and who was nice and recording such information in a large book he carried. In Holland, he rode a white horse, a sign of his deification and transformation, while in the United States, he rode in a wagon pulled by a horse—until Moore transformed and placed him into a sleigh with eight reindeer. Basically, Moore's poem, from which the above text comes, took St. Nicholas away from his December 5 evening activity and placed his reincarnated form—Santa Claus or Father Christmas—on Christmas Eve, where he has remained for a hundred years. Thus, on Christmas Eve Santa Claus departs from the North Pole to begin his annual journey of delivering gifts to nice children around the world.

While more information about the transformation of St. Nicholas to Sinterklaas can be found above for the Feast of St. Nicholas on December 6, we do well to

---

219. Moore, "A Visit."

reflect upon Christmas Eve, the entire day before Christmas Day. In the mind of some people, Christmas Eve has been limited to the evening before Christmas Day, a type of anticipation of Christmas Day. Indeed, according to Jewish tradition, the new day begins with the evening before. Christian liturgical time, likewise, begins at sunset or more specifically at 4 p.m. on the evening before. On Christmas Eve family and friends may gather for a meal, sing Christmas carols, exchange Christmas cards, erect or enjoy previously erected Christmas trees, lights, and other decorations, or wrap, exchange, and open gifts in imitation of the gift-bearing Santa Claus. In those and many other activities, transformation among family and friends occurs. Many of even the spiritual but not religious attend a candlelight Christ-Mass (Christmas) Eve service of carols and Scripture, a Roman Catholic Mass during the Night—formerly called Midnight Mass—a Nativity play, or other type of congregational service. Thus, just as there has taken place in history a transition from St. Nicholas to Santa Claus, and just as Christmas Eve night is a transition to Christmas Day, the spirituality of Christmas gathering and gift-giving is taking some of one's self (represented by a gift or food) and giving it to or sharing it with another. To do so, one must make a transition. It is during the night, when parents and children are in bed, that the narrator of Moore's poem sees the moon shining on fresh snow which lights up the night as if it were the middle of the day! What a transition!

Journal/Meditation: What spiritual transition takes place in you from Christmas Eve to Christmas Day? In what transforming activities do you participate with others on Christmas Eve? In the above text, Moore mentions the transition from the quiet in the house to the noise outside the house; which—quiet or noise—fosters better spiritual reflection for you?

Prayer: Father of Jesus, you chose your Son by anointing him with the oil of the Holy Spirit. His birth in the flesh signaled the potential for me to be born spiritually over and over again. Awaken me to this reality that I may experience your divinity and one day be deified with your Christ forever and ever. Amen.

Twelve Days of Christmas

Christmas Day 1

December 25

Text: "Joseph . . . went from the town of Nazareth in Galilee to Judea, to the city of David called Bethlehem, because he was a descended from the house and family of David. He went to be registered with Mary, to whom he was engaged and who was expecting a child. While they were there, the time came for her to deliver her child.

And she gave birth to her first-born son and wrapped him in bands of cloth, and laid him in a manger, because there was no place for them in the inn."[220]

Reflection: As well as can be determined, Jesus was probably born sometime between 6 and 4 BCE. Joseph and Mary, his parents, were Jews of modest means. The place of his birth was most likely Nazareth—not Bethlehem—since he was known as Jesus of Nazareth.[221] The author of Matthew's Gospel and the author of Luke's Gospel place his birth in Bethlehem "in order to fulfill the prophecy in Micah 5:2,[222] in order to substantiate the claim that he was the Messiah."[223] Before birth narratives were created, one of the earliest declarations of his divinity is focused on his resurrection. In his letter to the Romans, Paul states that Jesus "was declared to be Son of God with power according to the spirit of holiness by resurrection from the dead."[224] As oral stories concerning "the extraordinary character of Jesus' life, death, and reported resurrection" circulated, the resurrection "was projected backwards to his conception and birth."[225] This is seen primarily in iconography depicting his birth. He was wrapped in bands of cloth, like one would wrap a dead body in a shroud! He was placed in a manger, a trough from which livestock eat. According to Arthur George, "The earliest view was that Jesus became divine at his resurrection," when God breathed the breath of life, the animating divine force, into his dead body to raise him from the dead. . . . [T]hen in Mark['s Gospel] Jesus became divine at his baptism. Matthew and Luke made him divine as of his conception, while at the farthest extreme in John Jesus exists as a divine being in heaven before the creation of the cosmos."[226] Another development in iconography occurred when Jesus' birth was depicted as taking place in a cave. While there may be some faint allusion to Isaiah 33:16,[227] like the bands of cloth in which the baby is wrapped, the cave prefigures his entombment after his death on the cross. Easter, the resurrection of Jesus from the dead through the power of the Spirit, being the primary Christian festival, was read backwards into his birth, the actual date which is not known. As the understanding that one's true birthday was his or her death day, when he or she entered into eternal bliss in heaven, it became important for the Messiah to have an entry into the world as well as an exit to

---

220. NRSV: Luke 2:4-7.

221. Cf. Mark 1:9, 24; 10:47; 14:67; 16:6; Matthew 2:23; 4:13; 21:11; 26:71; Luke 2:4, 39, 51; 4:16, 34, 37; 24:19; John 1:45; 18:5, 7; 19:19; Acts 2:22; 3:6; 4:10; 6:14; 10:38; 22:8; 26:9.

222. "But you, O Bethlehem of Ephrathah, who are one of the little clans of Judah, from you shall come forth for me one who is to rule in Israel, whose origin is from of old, from ancient days."

223. George, *Mythology*, 199.

224. NRSV: Romans 1:4.

225. George, *Mythology*, 198.

226. George, *Mythology*, 213.

227. "Those who walk righteously and speak uprightly, who despise the gain of oppression, who wave away a bribe instead of accepting it, who stop their ears from hearing of bloodshed and shut their eyes from looking on evil, they will live on the heights; their refuge will be the fortresses of rocks; their food will be supplied, their water assured."

manifest his divinity. Thus, the birth narrative was created to serve that purpose. In Luke's extensive narrative about conception and birth, from which the text above is taken, the Holy Spirit is at work and God is anointing Jesus in the womb. What began with resurrection has been predicated of conception, birth, and baptism. According to Luke, Jesus is Son of God at the moment of his conception in the womb of his mother, Mary, nine months before he is born.

The message of Christmas is that there is both a fleshly birth of Jesus and a spiritual birth of him. Out of the animal known as humankind (Mary), there comes the spiritual (Jesus Christ). The mediating force, the creative divine power or energy that connects God to humanity—that causes the incarnation—is the Holy Spirit. "[T]he Holy Spirit," according to George, "is a link to God and yields an experience of the divine."[228] ". . . [T]he incarnation of the divine in Jesus marks the dawn of . . . higher consciousness, resulting quite literally in a spiritual birth."[229] The Spirit, who continues to work through creation and provides guidance to people, has a deifying effect on people. The Spirit is the psychic energy that brings divine unconscious to consciousness; it is an overwhelming numinous experience; it is incarnation; it is the awareness that people are divine. As George states so eloquently, ". . . [I]ncarnation can occur in any and all of us, and repeatedly. . . . As a result, [we are] . . . able to live more spiritually integrated lives. . . . [T]he incarnation of the divine in Jesus marks the dawn of . . . higher consciousness, resulting quite literally in a spiritual birth . . . ."[230] That is the same message that the depiction of the nativity taking place in a cave delivers. According to George, "Caves often symbolize the dark, undifferentiated, timeless, primordial state before the creation occurred and hence become the place of creation, including birth, especially since they resemble the womb and were often thought of as such. Similarly, . . . they are places of re-creation and transformation . . . . The cave is therefore a place of a spiritual quest and rebirth. The image of Jesus' birth in it thus further symbolizes a spiritual birth, and spiritual potential for anyone."[231]

Journal/Meditation: When is your fleshly birthday? When was your most recent spiritual birth? How did it occur? How many spiritual births have you experienced? Make a list of them.

Prayer: Father of Jesus, you chose your Son by anointing him with the oil of the Holy Spirit. His birth in the flesh signaled the potential for me to be born spiritually over and over again. Awaken me to this reality that I may experience your divinity and one day be deified with your Christ forever and ever. Amen.

---

228. George, *Mythology*, 243.
229. George, *Mythology*, 245.
230. George, *Mythology*, 245.
231. George, *Mythology*, 236–7.

Christmas Day 2
December 25

Text: "... [T]he church father Sextus Julius Africanus (ca. 160–ca. 240 CE) argued that ... Jesus' conception ... occurred on March 25, which meant that he was born nine months later, on December 25. His rationale was that the real and important creation of Jesus was on the date of his incarnation as divine (virginal conception), not that of his subsequent earthly birth. It was this December 25 date for Jesus' birth which took hold and endured.... This idea conveniently put Jesus' birth right on the winter solstice, which in Rome under the Julian calendar was observed on December twenty-fifth. The ancients viewed the winter solstice as the birthday of the sun, because it marks the annual turnaround when the sun, like a newborn child, begins to grow, and points toward spring and renewal. Further, Roman Emperors in this period identified themselves with the sun ...."[232]

Reflection: In Rome, the winter solstice was celebrated on December 25 because, by then, the people could tell that the days were getting longer. It was called the *Sol Invictus* (Unconquered Sun); it was introduced in Rome on December 25, 274, by the Roman Emperor Aurelian (270–5), even though an inscription exists from 158 CE. On that date, Aurelian, who had a new temple built for *Sol Invictus*, dedicated it, instituted games in his honor to be held every four years, and noted that the new temple was the fourth in honor of the god in Rome. From Aurelian to Constantine I (306–37), *Sol Invictus* was of supreme importance. However, once Constantine converted to Christianity, the sun god began to dim as the Son of God grew brighter. Before that, however, on March 7, 321, Constantine had decreed that the first day of the week would be known as *Dies Solis*, the Day of the Sun, Sunday, the Roman day of rest. The last inscription referring to *Sol Invictus* is 387 CE. Once the first Christian Roman Emperor was seated on his throne, it didn't take long for the Unconquered Sun to become the Unconquered Son. In other words, the annual celebration of the Sun's birthday became the annual celebration of the Son's birthday. Christianity had its own biblical solar imagery from which to draw. For example, the prophet Malachi had written, "... [F]or you who revere my name the sun of righteousness shall rise, with healing in its wings;"[233] Jesus was the sun of righteousness who arose on December 25 to overcome all evil in the world. The author of Matthew's Gospel had described Jesus' transfigured (a prelude to resurrection) face as shining "like the sun,"[234] and the author of the book of Revelation had described "his face" as being "like the sun shining with full force."[235] Add to the repertoire the note in Mark's Gospel that at Jesus' death at

---

232. George, *Mythology*, 230.
233. NRSV: Malachi 4:2a.
234. NRSV: Matthew 17:2.
235. NRSV: Revelation 1:16.

noon "darkness came over the whole land until three in the afternoon"[236]—the sun disappeared—coupled with the multiple times the Johannine Jesus declares himself to be the light of the world,[237] and add in the reference to "very early on the first day of the week, when the sun had risen,"[238] as the three women make their way to Jesus' tomb to discover that he has been raised from the dead, and it is easy to see how Jesus became the Unconquered Son! In other words, as Christianity grew and Rome declined, Jesus' nativity took over the winter solstice holiday on December 25. The transfigured, resurrected Christ was projected back to the Jesus born December 25.

The transition from the Unconquered Sun to the Unconquered Son, projected backward from his transfiguring resurrection to his birth, was assisted by the Roman *Saturnalia*, another Roman festival held December 17 to the 23. *Saturnalia* was a festival of dissolution (reversal, inversion), which "normally occurs during a seasonal transition from one state of being into another, whether astronomical in nature (e.g., solstice, equinox) or in terms of human activity (e.g., sowing, harvest)."[239] *Saturnalia* was the dissolution of the light and its being replaced with dark, but soon it would begin to be light again (solstice). During *Saturnalia*, the entrances of temples were adorned with new green foliage, signifying the continuation of life and fertility. Candles were given, received, and burned, signifying the returning power of the sun's light. It is not difficult to see the connection between birth and light, especially if a few verses from the prologue to John's Gospel are considered: "What has come into being in [the Word, who was God,] was life, and the life was the light of all people. The light shines in the darkness, and the darkness did not overcome it. The true light, which enlightens everyone, was coming into the world."[240] Eventually, Christmas both absorbed and extinguished *Sol Invictus* and *Saturnalia*. What were left were Christmas wreaths, trees, mistletoe, holly, "the Yule log that protects the household; candles; . . . and eventually whole Christmas trees" decorated with burning candles and fruit (making them trees of life). According to George, "[Christmas trees] have nothing to do with the birth of Jesus and everything to do with pagan winter solstice festivals, symbolizing the continuation of life and the sun through the winter."[241]

Journal/Meditation: In what ways are the winter solstice and the birth of Jesus connected? Make a list. Which one gets most of your attention? Why? In what ways is *Saturnalia* still celebrated in your home? Make a list. Which one is the most important to you? What does it mean to you? What does it signify?

236. NRSV: Mark 15:33; cf. Matthew 27:45.
237. Cf. NRSV: John 8:12; 9:5; 12:46.
238. NRSV: Mark 16:2.
239. George, *Mythology*, 60.
240. NRSV: John 1:3b–5, 9.
241. George, *Mythology*, 241.

Prayer: God of life and light, from the beginning your Word was with you; he was a light shining in darkness. Your Word became flesh and lived among us and died and you raised him from the dead, like the sun that rises reborn on the winter solstice. See in the wreath, mistletoe, holly, and tree in my home the life and light in which I hope to share with you eternally. Amen.

Kwanzaa Begins

December 26 (to January 1)

Text: "As an African American and Pan-African holiday celebrated by millions throughout the world African community, Kwanzaa brings a cultural message which speaks to the best of what it means to be African and human in the fullest sense. . . . The holiday [is] . . . engaged as an ancient and living cultural tradition which reflects the best of African thought and practice in its reaffirmation of the dignity of the human person in community and culture, the wellbeing of family and community, the integrity of the environment and . . . kinship with it, and the rich resource and meaning of a people's culture."[242]

Reflection: Kwanzaa, derived from a Swahili word meaning *first*—referring to the first fruits of the harvest—is an annual celebration of African heritage in African-American culture that begins December 26 and ends on January 1. The Swahili word meaning *first* is *kwanza*. Maulana Karenga, who created this African-American holiday in 1996 in California to bring African-Americans together as a community, added another a on the end to lengthen the word to seven letters to represent the seven days of the festival. While at first it was meant to be an alternative to Christmas, it quickly became a celebration in addition to Christmas to reclaim important African-American values. According to Stephanie King, its "seven-day celebration of African roots, observed by people of all faith backgrounds, since it's not tied to any religion, . . . is anchored by seven principles . . . which aim to inspire Black people to be united, self-determined, accountable for their communities, financially invested in Black-owned businesses, purposeful with their lives, creative, and full of faith."[243] Karenga focused on seven principles as ways to empower people to rediscover their African heritage and concretize their value system. Thus, the first principle is unity; Black culture strives for and maintains unity in the family, the community, the nation, and the race. Second, self-determination is the ability to define oneself by name, creativity, and speech. Collective work and responsibility is the third principle; the focus is on building and maintaining community together and making others' problems those of the community to be solved together. Fourth, cooperative economics builds and maintains stores, shops, and other businesses owned by African-Americans and profits from them

---

242. "Founder's Welcome."
243. King, "Principles."

together. The fifth principle is purpose, making the collective vocation the building and development of community in order to restore people to their traditional greatness. Sixth, creativity, is the value of doing as much as possible in order to leave the community more beautiful and beneficial than when it was inherited. And seventh is faith—not any specific religion—belief in people, such as parents, teachers, leaders, and the righteousness and victory of the African-American struggle. Along with the seven principles, there are seven signs. First, there is a place mat upon which everything else is set. The mat represents the historical and traditional foundation upon which people stand and upon which they build their lives. Second, crops, the result of collective planning and work and the resulting joy, sharing, unity, and thanksgiving that are part of African harvest festivals. In the United States, nuts, fruits, and vegetables representing crops and the work of the harvest are placed on the mat. The third item on the mat is an ear or stalk of corn, which represents fertility of the people and the idea that through children, the future hopes of the family are brought to life. The fourth item on the mat is a candleholder with places for seven candles. The candelabra represents African ancestry and the origin of black culture. Collectively, the seven candles, fifth, represent the sun's power as it returns after the solstice; in addition, each candle represents one of the seven principles. The three red candles, the three green candles, and the one black candle, the colors of African-American people, signify light. In the candelabra, three red candles, placed on the left, represent the blood of the ancestors; the black candle, located in the middle of the candelabra, signifies African people everywhere; and the three green candles, placed on the right, represent the earth, life, and the promise of the future. On December 26, the black candle is lit, and the principle of unity is discussed. On December 27, the red candle on the left of the black candle is lit, and the principle of self-determination is discussed. The green candle closest to the black candle is lit on December 28, and the principle of collective work and responsibility is discussed. On December 29, the middle of the three red candles is lit, and cooperative economics is the topic for discussion. On December 30, the middle of the three green candles is lit, and purpose is discussed. On December 31, the last of the red candles is lit, and creativity is discussed; food, drink, dance, and music may be a part of day six. And on January 1, the last of the green candles is lit, and faith is the topic of discussion. The sixth item on the mat is the unity cup, used on the sixth day of the celebration; a libation of wine or juice placed in the cup honors ancestors. Every family member drinks from the cup as both a sign of unity and in remembrance of ancestors. And the seventh ritual item on the mat consists of gifts given to encourage growth, achievement, and success. Handmade gifts are preferred because they promote self-determination, purpose, and creativity.

In the United States, the first president to send a message to those observing Kwanzaa was William J. Clinton in 1993. He wrote that Kwanzaa invited "people to embrace their African heritage . . . [by gathering] together with loved ones to enjoy [the] special holiday based on the rich cultural traditions of Africa." He added, ". . .

Kwanzaa encourages us to rebuild [neighborhoods] and gives . . . the opportunity to celebrate the strengths of the African American community. The seven principles of Kwanzaa . . . provide young people with the pride, direction, and inner strength to work for a brighter future."[244] In 1994, Clinton issued a "Statement on the Observance of Kwanzaa," but returned to sending a "Message" from 1995 through 2000. George W. Bush followed Clinton's messages with his own from 2001 through 2008. In 2001, he wrote: "Kwanzaa provides an opportunity for people of African heritage, regardless of their religious background or faith, to come together and to show reverence for their Creator and creation, to commemorate the past, to recommit to high ideals, and to celebrate the good in life."[245] From 2009 through 2016, President Barack Obama issued statements on the observance of Kwanzaa. "This is . . . a time of reflection and renewal," he wrote in his first statement, "as we come to the end of one year and the beginning of another. The Kwanzaa message tells us that we should recall the lessons of the past even as we seize the promise of tomorrow." After mentioning the seven principles of the festival, he wrote, "These same principles have sustained us as a nation during our darkest hours and provided hope for better days to come."[246] And while they were extremely brief, President Donald J. Trump issued statements from 2017 through 2020. In 2017, he invited citizens to "celebrate during this joyous time the richness of the past and look with hope toward a brighter future."[247] Thus, what began in California in 1966, has become a U.S.-wide and a world-wide celebration of African-American heritage and culture. In the words of the holiday greeting, "Joyous Kwanzaa."

Journal/Meditation: For you, what does it mean to celebrate African culture? Of the seven principles of Kwanzaa, which one do you think is the most important? Why? What do the messages and statements of U.S. presidents say to you about Kwanzaa?

Prayer: Heavenly Father, who created people with white, red, brown, yellow, and black skin, bestow upon all your creation unity, self-determination, collective work and responsibility, cooperative economics, purpose, creativity, and faith. Fill me with the mystery of the spirit of diversity in life, especially African culture and heritage, as I celebrate Kwanzaa and give thanks to you for the freedom and justice you bestow on all people today, tomorrow, and forever. Amen.

---

244. Clinton, "Message."
245. Bush, G.W., "Message."
246. Obama, "Statement."
247. Trump, "Statement."

Third Day of Christmas: Christmas Tree

December 27

Text: "1. O Christmas Tree, O Christmas Tree, / How lovely are your branches! / O Christmas Tree, O Christmas Tree, / How lovely are your branches! / Not only green in summer's heat, / But also winter's snow and sleet. / O Christmas Tree, O Christmas Tree, / How lovely are your branches! / 2. O Christmas Tree, O Christmas Tree, / Of all the trees most lovely! / O Christmas Tree, O Christmas Tree, / Of all the trees most lovely! / Each year you bring to us delight / With brightly shining Christmas light! / O Christmas Tree, O Christmas Tree, / Of all the trees most lovely! / 3. O Christmas Tree, O Christmas Tree, / We learn from all your beauty; / O Christmas Tree, O Christmas Tree, / We learn from all your beauty; / Your bright green leaves with festive cheer, / Give hope and strength throughout the year. / O Christmas Tree, O Christmas Tree, / We learn from all your beauty."[248]

Reflection: The three verses of the song "O Christmas Tree" in the above text are one translation from the German "O Tannenbaum" into English. The music is a traditional folk song having nothing to do with Christmas until Ernst Anschutz wrote new lyrics in 1824. Anschutz's lyrics praise the fir tree for its evergreen quality representing constancy and faithfulness, but by the middle of the nineteenth century they began to be sung as a Christmas carol in praise of the Christmas Tree. Because the English translation attempts to capture what the German says, there are several possibilities in English, based on the translator's rhyming scheme. For example, an alternate to the first verse is: "Your branches green delight us. . . . / They are green when summer days are bright / They are green when winter snow is white."[249] Another English translation of the first verse states: "Thy leaves are so unchanging. / Not only green when summer's here, / But also when 'tis cold and drear."[250] Literally, the verse is about the loyalty of the leaves or needles, which are green in summer and in winter, when it snows.

Until the evergreen tree came into use in the sixteenth century, various people—Egyptians, Chinese, Hebrews, Romans—used them to represent eternal life. It wasn't until the second half of the nineteenth century that Christians began to celebrate Christmas by bringing a fir, spruce, or pine evergreen conifer into the home and decorating it with colored paper, apples and other fruits, wafers, tinsel, sweets, gingerbread, chocolates, and candles, which were replaced by electric lights once such power became widespread. On the top could be found an angel, representing the angel of the Lord who appeared to shepherds in Luke's Gospel,[251] or a star, representing the luminary followed by the magi in Matthew's Gospel.[252] Thus, gradually, the tree used

---

248. "O Christmas Tree."
249. "O Tannenbaum."
250. "O Christmas Tree: Lyrics."
251. Cf. NRSV: Luke 2:9.
252. Cf. NRSV: Matthew 2:2b.

by other religions was Christianized and referenced as the tree in paradise from which the man and woman ate the forbidden fruit;[253] it was even decorated with apples, since many thought that the forbidden fruit was an apple! Once ornaments were made from wood, glass, metal, ceramic, plastic, etc., the use of apples, nuts, dates, pretzels, and other eatables gave way to artificial objects. By the early nineteenth century, the Christmas tree was common in homes across the United States. The species of tree used most for Christmas is fir, because it does not shed its needles as it dries. Also used are spruce and pine in a variety of species. Around the world, various cultures have adapted the tree to meet its needs; thus, there are living Christmas trees that can be planted after they are used, there are rentable living Christmas trees which are returned after the holidays to be rented again, there are aluminum trees, and there are all types of artificial trees. It was not until 1982 that Vatican City erected a Christmas Tree! Pope St. John Paul II introduced the custom. On December 19, 2004, he explained the meaning of the tree. "In winter the evergreen becomes a sign of undying life. In general, the tree is decorated and Christmas gifts are placed under it. The symbol is also eloquent from a typically Christian point of view: It reminds us of the 'tree of life,'[254] representation of Christ, God's supreme gift to humanity." The pope continued: "The message of the Christmas tree, therefore, is that life is 'ever green' if one gives: not so much material things, but of oneself; in friendship and sincere affection, and fraternal help and forgiveness, in shared time and reciprocal listening."[255]

Journal/Meditation: What does your Christmas tree mean to you? Does it speak more of constancy, faithfulness, undying life, or the gift of God? Explain. What do its ornaments signify for you?

Prayer: Father of Jesus, you created the evergreen tree to be one most lovely and bring delight to young and old with its shining Christmas lights. May the tree in my home give hope and strength with festive cheer to all who see it throughout this year and into eternity. Amen.

Fourth Day of Christmas: Charlie Brown Christmas Tree

December 28

Text: "**Lucy**: We need a Christmas tree. . . . Charlie Brown, you get the tree. **Charlie Brown**: Okay. I'll take Linus with me. . . . Well, I guess we'd better concentrate on finding a nice Christmas tree. **Linus**: Gee, do they still make wooden Christmas trees? **Charlie Brown**: This little green one here seems to need a home. **Linus**: I don't know,

---

253. Cf. NRSV: Genesis 3:1-6.

254. Cf. NRSV: Genesis 2:9; 3:22, 24; Proverbs 11:30; 15:4; 2 Esdras 8:52; 4 Maccabees 18:16; Revelation 2:7; 22:2, 14, 19.

255. John Paul II, "Christmas Tree."

Charlie Brown. . . . This doesn't seem to fit the modern spirit. **Charlie Brown**: I don't care. We'll decorate it, and it'll be just right for our play. Besides, I think it needs me. . . . **Lucy**: What kind of a tree is that? You were supposed to get a good tree. Can't you even tell a good tee from a poor tree? . . . **Charlie Brown**: I guess you were right, Linus. I shouldn't have picked this little tree. . . . I guess I really don't know what Christmas is all about. . . . I won't let all this commercialism ruin my Christmas. I'll take this little tree home and decorate it . . . . I never thought it was such a bad little tree. It's not bad at all, really. Maybe it just needs a little love. Charlie Brown is a blockhead, but he did get a nice tree."[256]

Reflection: The dialogue above comes from "A Charlies Brown Christmas" a 1965 animated television special based on the comic strip named "Peanuts" by Charles M. Schulz. The Charlie Brown Christmas Tree was about a two-foot-long branch from a pine tree stuck upright into two crisscrossed boards. Because it was a branch, it was slightly curved to one side. It was decorated with a single red spherical ornament, and Linus's blue blanket draped over the crisscrossed wood. This poor-looking, unattractive, or malformed tree—because it was a pine branch—was a protest against the commercialization of Christmas, as represented in the show by aluminum Christmas trees popular in the United States in the early 1960s. Throughout the thirty-minute show, Charlie Brown is attempting to find the true meaning of Christmas.

Charlie Brown's non-commercialized Christmas tree is contrasted to Snoopy's decorating of his doghouse for a neighborhood lights and display contest. As Charlie Brown walks by Snoopy's doghouse, he says: "What's going on here? What's this? Find the true meaning of Christmas. Win money, money, money. Spectacular, super-colossal neighborhood Christmas-lights-and-display contest. Lights-and-display contest? Oh, no. My own dog gone commercial. I can't stand it."[257] Later, walking past Snoopy's doghouse again, he sees that his dog has won first place in the contest, and he says: "First prize? Oh, well! This commercial dog is not going to ruin my Christmas."[258] As Charlie Brown searches for the true meaning of Christmas, Linus tells him what it is all about. After quoting Luke 2:8–14,[259] Linus states, "That's what Christmas is all about, Charlie Brown."[260]

---

256. "Charlie Brown Christmas."

257. "Charlie Brown Christmas."

258. "Charlie Brown Christmas."

259. "In that region there were shepherds living in the fields, keeping watch over their flock by night. Then an angel of the Lord stood before them, and the glory of the Lord shone around them, and they were terrified. But the angel said to them, 'Do not be afraid; for see—I am bringing you good news of great joy for all the people: to you is born this day in the city of David a Savior, who is the Messiah, the Lord. This will be a sign for you: you will find a child wrapped in bands of cloth and lying in a manger.' And suddenly there was with the angel a multitude of the heavenly host, praising God and saying, 'Glory to God in the highest heaven, and on earth peace among those whom he favors!'"

260. "Charlie Brown Christmas."

Journal/Meditation: What is Christmas all about for you? Does your Christmas tree need you, like Charlie Brown's needed him? Explain. Does your Christmas tree need a little love, like Charlie Brown's needed his? Explain.

Prayer: Lord, like the animated character Charlie Brown, I often find myself searching for the true meaning of Christmas. Help me to find it not in the glitter and lights, but in the peace and calm of the season. Amen.

Fifth Day of Christmas: Candles

December 29

Text: "Then the kingdom of heaven will be like this. Ten bridesmaids took their lamps and went to meet the bridegroom. Five of them were foolish, and five were wise."[261]

Reflection: The Romans began making candles around 500 BCE; they used tallow wax, which they got from the meat of cows and sheep. Using a strand of twine for a wick, they dipped the string in the tallow, allowed it to dry, and dipped it again, allowed it to dry, and continued to repeat the process until the candle was the size they wanted. While such candles were popular, they were a luxury item. In China, as early as 221 BCE, candles were made from whale fat or beeswax. In ancient India, candles were made from boiled cinnamon and yak butter. However, olive oil lamps were more prevalent because olive oil was readily available. The oil was poured into a small central hole in various sizes of round clay lamps. At one side was a handle, and opposite it was a larger hole in which was placed a cloth wick or reed, which was set on fire. In the story narrated above, the five foolish bridesmaids brought no extra olive oil for their lamps, while the wise ones brought extra flasks of olive oil for their lamps. While the foolish bridesmaids went off to the store to buy more oil, the wedding party arrived, and the wise bridesmaids went into the reception. When the foolish ones returned, they found the door closed and locked, and they were not admitted to the wedding party.

While candles and olive oil lamps were used for light, they also highlighted the focus of a room. In the dark, people are drawn to a candle burning brightly. Once the Roman Empire fell and olive oil became a scarce commodity, a surge in demand for candles arose. At first tallow was used, but it produced an unpleasant odor. Beeswax was used, but it was expensive. By the nineteenth century, paraffin, distilled from coal and oil shales, was used to make candles; stearic acid was added to make the candles last longer. Once the incandescent light bulb was invented, candles became a luxury item with cleaner burning ingredients, such as soy, palm, and flax-seed oil, being used to make them. At Christmastime, red, green, and white candles appear in centerpieces on tables, grouped together on mantels of fireplaces, or set elsewhere in

---

261. NRSV: Matthew 25:1-2.

the home. While they are no longer used as a source of light, in a darkened room they draw attention to themselves and at the same time draw people together. Today, many candles are powered by 2 AA batteries, which cause the bright, flickering LED bulb in the center to be flameless and easily turned on and off with a remote control. They give a warm, natural-looking light that is not easily recognized as artificial by others. Nevertheless, like their predecessors of all kinds and oil lamps, too, they draw together people to celebrate the twelve days of Christmas.

Journal/Meditation: If you use candles in your home, where are they placed? How are they used? What do they accomplish? What feelings, spoken or unspoken, do they elicit?

Prayer: God of light, as I continue to celebrate this Christmas Season, keep your grace burning within me that I may be light for others even as they are light for me. Hear this prayer through the light of the world, your Son, Jesus, who is Lord forever and ever. Amen.

Sixth Day of Christmas: Reindeer

December 30

Text: "When, what to my wondering eyes should appear, / But a miniature sleigh, and eight tiny reindeer. / With a little old driver, so lively and quick, / I knew in a moment it must be St. Nick. / More rapid than eagles his coursers they came. / And he whistled, and shouted, and called them by name; / 'Now, Dasher! now Dancer! now Prancer and Vixen! / On, Comet! on Cupid! on Donder and Blitzen! / To the top of the porch! to the top of the wall! / Now dash away! dash away! dash away all.' . . . He sprang to his sleigh, to his team gave a whistle, / And away they all flew like the down of a thistle . . . ."[262]

Reflection: According to Clement Clarke Moore's "A Visit from St. Nicholas," the jolly old elf, who has since come to be named Santa Claus, rides in a sleigh pulled by eight flying reindeer through the night sky on Christmas Eve to deliver gifts to children. Before Moore's poem was published in 1823, St. Nicholas delivered gifts on December 5, the eve of his own feast day celebrated on December 6. In Moore's poem, however, he arrives on Christmas Eve in a sleigh pulled by reindeer. And that has become the tradition in the United States. Reindeer, also known as caribou in North America, vary in size, color, and species, and are associated with the far northern part of the northern hemisphere. Reindeer is the European name for the species, while caribou is the North American name for the species. Both males (bulls) and females (cows) grow antlers annually, although bull antlers are typically larger. Bulls begin to grow antlers in March or April, and females begin to grow them in May or June. After the

262. Moore, "A Visit."

autumn rut, bulls lose their antlers, while cows keep theirs until they calve. Reindeer have been domesticated by peoples living in the far north, and they are used for food, clothing, milking, as draught animals, beasts of burden, and pack animals. Not only did Moore indicate that St. Nicholas's sleigh was pulled by reindeer, but he also named all eight of them. First, Dasher, one who dresses or acts flamboyantly or stylishly. Second, Dancer, one who dances, that is, one who moves rhythmically to music, who jumps up and down or leaps and skips. Third, Prancer, one who moves around in a lively and carefree way, a horse who raises the front legs and jumps forward on the back legs or walks with lively springing steps, a mettlesome or fiery horse. Fourth, Vixen, a spirited or fierce woman. Fifth, Comet, a celestial object made of a nucleus of ice and dust which, when near the sun, has a tail of gas and dust particles. Sixth, Cupid, a winged boy with a bow and arrows. Seventh, Donder (Dunder), meaning thunder, and Blitzen (Blixem), meaning lightning. The first four named reindeer are like stylishly, well-dressed, spirited, lively dancers—"The prancing and pawing of each little hoof," writes Moore. The last four named reindeer are like objects seen in the sky—"And away they all flew like the down of a thistle," writes Moore. Thus, the eight named reindeer dance or fly through the sky.

In 1939, Robert L. May introduced reindeer number 9 to the world: Rudolph. May, an ad man for the Montgomery Ward chain of department stores, was asked by his boss to produce a little book that would be given to children who came to the store at Christmastime. *Rudolph the Red-Nosed Reindeer* came into existence with copious illustrations created by Denver L. Gillen. The story is about a socially outcast reindeer, who is taunted by other reindeer: "Ha ha! Look at Rudolph! His nose is a sight! / It's red as a beet! Twice as big! Twice as bright!"[263] May explains: "Where most reindeer noses are brownish and tiny, / Poor Rudolph's was red, very large, and quite shiny."[264] One year, as Santa Claus prepared for his world-wide sleigh flight, a world-encompassing fog rolled in. "'This fog,' he complained, 'will be hard to get through.' / He shook his round head. (And his tummy shook too.)"[265] "And Santa was right (as he usually is) / The fog was as think as a soda's white fizz."[266] Santa begins his travels through the fog, and arrives at the house where Rudolph lives and is in bed asleep. After going down the chimney, Santa enters the reindeer's room: "And there lay . . . but wait now! What would you suppose? / The glowing (you've guessed it) was Rudolph's red nose!"[267] Santa has an idea. So, he awakens Rudolph: "And Rudolph could scarcely believe his own eyes! / You can just imagine his joy and surprise."[268] "'I'll need you,'

---

263. May, *Rudolph*, 3.
264. May, *Rudolph*, 4.
265. May, *Rudolph*, 7.
266. May, *Rudolph*, 8.
267. May, *Rudolph*, 14.
268. May, *Rudolph*, 16.

said Santa, 'to help me tonight / To lead all my deer on the rest of our flight!'"[269] "So Rudolph pranced out through the door very gay / And took his proud place at the head of the sleigh."[270] The narrator of the story continues: "And 'brilliant' was almost no word for the way / That Rudolph directed the deer and the sleigh. / In spite of the fog, they flew quickly and low / And made such use of the wonderful glow . . . ."[271] Santa finishes delivering toys around the world and his flight with Rudolph's guidance. Then, Santa brings back Rudolph to his home town. "(The funny-faced fellow they'd [other reindeer] always called names / And practically never allowed in their games) / Was now to be envied by all, far and near. / For no greater honor can come to a deer / Than riding with Santa and guiding his sleigh, / The number-one job on the number-one day!"[272] After Rudolph is hailed as a hero by all the reindeer who had previously taunted him, the narrator concludes, "And that's why whenever it's foggy and gray, / It's Rudolph the Red-nose who guides Santa's sleigh."[273] And thus, in popular culture, Rudolph became the ninth reindeer pulling Santa Claus's sleigh. Rudolph's place was cemented in place by Johnny Marks's 1949 "Rudolph the Red-Nosed Reindeer" song, based on May's story, the animated TV special of the same name in 1964, the feature film of the same name in 1998, and more. Reindeer with holiday bows around their necks of all kinds appear in yards; they are male, female, and baby, often lighted from within or from without. The message about the social outcast being the most important and useful member of a community continues to resonate in United States culture.

Journal/Meditation: Which named reindeer is your favorite? Why? What great honor has come to a social outcast you know?

Prayer: All of your creation praises you, Holy One. Give me the style, steps, spirit, flight, and light of your reindeer in my work, play, and prayer. Open my eyes to see that the most important member of my community may be him or her who seems to be outcast. Hear my prayer on this sixth day of Christmas. Amen.

New Year's Eve
December 31

Text: "Should old acquaintance be forgot, / And never brought to mind? / Should old acquaintance be forgot, And long, long ago. / And for long, long ago, my dear / For long, long ago, / We'll take a cup of kindness yet, / For long, long ago."[274]

269. May, *Rudolph*, 18.
270. May, *Rudolph*, 19.
271. May, *Rudolph*, 20–21.
272. May, *Rudolph*, 25.
273. May, *Rudolph*, 29–30.
274. "History and Words." "Should auld acquaintance be forgot, / And never brought to mind? /

Reflection: The above text are the first verse and chorus from "Auld Lang Syne," a poem written by Robert Burns in 1788 and set to music in 1799. Because Burns incorporated Scottish into the poem-become-song, the title itself along with its use in the first line of the chorus have been translated into English as "Old Long Since," "Long, Long Ago," "Days Gone By," "Times Long Past," "Old Times," or "For the Sake of Old Times." The usually sung version bidding farewell to the old year at the stroke of midnight on New Year's Eve is found in the footnote below. Most people know the first verse and chorus, but most don't know the other four verses of the song. Like the chorus' "take a cup of kindness," the second verse states, "surely you'll buy your pint-jug and I'll buy mine, and we'll take a cup of kindness yet, for long, long ago," and the third verse contains the line "we'll take a deep draught of good-will." As such the song is a fitting toast to the old year—365 or 366 days have passed—and a fitting greeting to the new course of 365 or 366 days. Drinking alcoholic beverages is one way that people in the United States—and elsewhere—dispose of the chaos of the previous year, while simultaneously greeting the recreated order of the new year. According to Arthur George, "Our contemporary tradition of excessive drinking on New Year's Eve fits [the] pattern, which of course is experienced as disorder!"[275] The pattern is simple: chaos or disorder becomes order or a new beginning. Hence, the practice of New Year's resolutions. This is a proactive approach to controlling our own destiny; in other words, we are recreating ourselves, and, hopefully, the world in which we live. According to George: ". . . [T]he occasion provides us an opening and special opportunity to shape our future. And it starts by cycling out the bad. New Year's addresses our psychological need to have a second chance and fashion a renewed self that we can feel good about. . . . New Year's has a liminal character, and as such is an occasion to reflect upon where we are going in our lives, consider what changes may be in order, and plan accordingly."[276] It is no accident that this takes place ten days after the winter solstice; out of the darkness of the past year comes new light. The old is dissolved, and the new emerges. It is why we acknowledge the first baby's birth in the new year.

"Auld Lang Syne" asks if old acquaintances should be forgotten? Should we forget those with whom we have traveled? with those whom we have sailed? with those whom we lock hands? with those whom we have been drinking? While our first response to all the questions is "No, we should not forget them," the fact on New Year's Eve is that we will forget them. Some of them will have died, moved, lost interest, etc. as another year slips by. The people with whom we are drinking this New Year's Eve will most likely not be the same folks next New Year's Eve. And even if they are some of the same people, they will not be the same psychologically. Like us, they will have changed, if they have kept their New Year's resolutions from long, long ago.

Should auld acquaintance be forgot, / And auld lang syne. / For auld lang syne, my jo, / For auld lang syne, / We'll take a cup o' kindness yet, / For auld lang syne."

275. George, *Mythology*, 20.

276. George, *Mythology*, 39.

Journal/Meditation: From what chaos are you emerging? To what new beginning are you headed? What acquaintance or companion have you forgotten in the past year? What difference has that made in your life?

Prayer: While I like to think that I hold onto long, long ago, O God, I realize that I am always changing and only you are ever the same. Guide me through this New Year's Eve to the New Year of new experiences and opportunities. Help me offer kindness to all I encounter as I make my way to you today, tomorrow, and forever. Amen.

Bibliography

"About Giving Tuesday." https://givingtuesday.org/about/.

"Act of Military Surrender." Definitive German Instrument of Surrender (8 May 1945). http://en.wikisource.org/wiki/Definitive_German_Instrument_of_Surrender_(8_May_1945).

"All Amendments to the United States Constitution." http://hrlibrary.umn.edu/education/all_amendments_usconst.htm.

Allen, Mitch. "The Origins of Sweetest Day." *Mimi Magazine*, n.d. https://directory.mimivanderhaven.com/articles/the-origins-of-sweetest-day.

———. "The Origins of Sweetest Day (Updated). *Mimi Magazine*, n.d. https://directory.mimivanderhaven.com/articles/the-origins-of-sweetest-day-updated.

The Analects by Confucius. Translated by James Legge. Global Grey, 2018. http://globalgreybooks.com/analects-ebook.html.

"Armed Forces Day." https://afd.defense.gov/.

Biden, Joseph R., Jr. "A Proclamation on National Teacher Appreciation Day and National Teacher Appreciation Week, [April 30,] 2021." https://www.whitehouse.gov/briefing-room/presidential-actions/2021/04/30/a-proclamation-on-national-teacher-appreciation-day-and-national-teacher-appreciation-week.

———. "Proclamation 10176—National Former Prisoner of War Recognition Day, 2021." https://presidency.ucsb.edu/documents/proclamation-10176-national-former-prisoner-war-recognition-day-2021.

———. "Proclamation 10208—Peace Officers Memorial Day and Police Week, 2021." https://presidency.ucsb.edu/documents/proclamation-10208-peace-officers-memorial-day-and-police-week-2021.

———. "Proclamation 10259—National POW/MIA Recognition Day, 2021. https://presidency.ucsb.edu/documents/proclamation-10259-national-powmia-recognition-day-2021.

———. "Proclamation 10280—Leif Erikson Day, 2021." https://presidency.ucsb.edu/documents/proclamation-10280-leif-erikson-day-2021.

———. "Proclamation 10288—Blind Americans Equality Day, 2021. https://presidency.ucsb.edu/documents/proclamation-10288-blind-americans-equality-day-2021.

———. "Proclamation 10304—World Freedom Day, 2021." https://presidency.ucsb.edu/documents/proclamation-10304-world-freedom-day-2021.

———. "Proclamation 10308—America Recycles Day, 2021." https://presidency.ucsb.edu/documents/proclamation-10308-america-recycles-day-2021.

———. "Proclamation 10312—National Child's Day, 2021." https://presidency.ucsb.edu/documents/proclamation-10312-national-childs-day-2021.

———. "Proclamation 10317—World AIDS Day, 2021." https://presidency.ucsb.edu/documents/proclamation-10317-world-aids-day-2021.

———. "Proclamation 10318—International Day of Persons with Disabilities, 2021. https://presidency.ucsb.edu/documents/proclamation-10318-international-day-persons-with-disabilities-2021.

———. "Proclamation 10321—Human Rights Day and Human Rights Week, 2021." https://presidency.ucsb.edu/documents/proclamation-10321-human-rights-day-and-human-rights-week-2021.

———. "Proclamation 10323—Bill of Rights Day, 2021." https://presidency.ucsb.edu/documents/proclamation-10323-bill-rights-day-2021.

———. "Proclamation 10324—Wright Brothers Day, 2021." https://presidency.ucsb.edu/documents/proclamation-10324-wright-brothers-day-2021.

———. "Remarks by President Biden at the Summit for Democracy Opening Session." https://www.whitehouse.gov/briefing-room/speeches-remarks/2021/12/09/remarks-by-president-biden-at-the-summit-for-democracy-opening-session/.

———. "Remarks on Signing the Juneteenth National Independence Day Act." https://presidency.ucsb.edu/documents/remarks-signing-the-juneteenth-national-independence-day-act.

Bill Number: AB 1953. http://leginfo.ca.gov.

"The Bill of Rights." https://archives.gov/founding-docs/bill-of-rights-transcript.

"Black Friday." https://lexico.com/en/definition/black_friday.

"Blind Americans Equality Day, 125 Statute 2104." https://www.govinfo.gov/app/details/STATUTE-125/STATUTE-125-Pg2104.

Block, Melissa. "How World AIDS Day Began." *NPR*, December 1, 2011. https://npr.org/2011/12/01/143017936/how-world-aids-day-began.

Bodhi, Bhikkhu. "Introduction." In *The Dhammapada: The Buddha's Path of Wisdom*. Translated by Acharya Buddharakkhita. Kandy, Sri Lanka: Buddhist Publication Society, 1985.

The Book of Mormon. Translated by Joseph Smith. Salt Lake City, UT: The Church of Jesus Christ of Latter-Day Saints, 1976.

Borg, Marcus J. "Jesus: A Sketch." In *Profiles of Jesus*, edited by Roy W. Hoover, 129–136. Santa Rosa, CA: Polebridge, 2002.

Brown, Lillian. "Tooth Fairy." *Chicago Daily Tribune*, September 27, 1908, 37. https://newspapers.com/newspage/354963876/.

Brussat, Frederic, and Mary Ann Brussat. Review of *Belief without Borders: Inside the Minds of the Spiritual but not Religious*. https://spiritualityandpractice.com/books/reviews/view/26773.

Buck, Christopher. "World Religion Day (January)." In *Religious Celebrations: An Encyclopedia of Holidays, Festivals, Solemn Observances, and Spiritual Commemorations*, edited by J. Gordon Melton, et al., 1:936–9. Santa Barbara, CA: ABC-CLIO, 2011.

Burton, Tara Isabella. "'Spiritual but not Religious': Inside America's Rapidly Growing Faith Group." https://vox.com/identities/2017/11/10/16630178/study-spiritual-but-not-religious.

Bush, George. "Message on the Observance of Police Week and Police Officers' Memorial Day, May 1989." https://presidency.ucsb.edu/ocuments/message-the-observance-police-week-and-police-officers-memorial-day-may-1989.

———. "Proclamation 5951—National Former Prisoners of War Recognition Day, 1989." https://presidency.ucsb.edu/documents/proclamation-5951-national-former-prisoners-war-recognition-day-1989.

———. "Proclamation 6002—National POW/MIA Recognition Day, 1989." https://presidency.ucsb.edu/documents/proclamation-6002-national-powmia-recognition-day-1989.

———. "Proclamation 6039–National Children's Day, 1989." https://presidency.ucsb.edu/documents/proclamation-6039-national-childrens-day-1989.

———. "Proclamation 6041—Leif Erikson Day, 1989." https://presidency.ucsb.edu/documents/proclamation-6041-leif-erikson-day-1989.

———. "Proclamation 6047—White Cane Safety Day, 1989." https://presidency.ucsb.edu/documents/proclamation-6047-white-cane-safety-day-1989.

———. "Proclamation 6071—National Philanthropy Day, 1989." https://presidency.ucsb.edu/documents/proclamation-6071-national-philanthropy-day-1989.

———. "Proclamation 6082—Human Rights Day, Bill of Rights Day, and Human Rights Week, 1989." https://presidency.ucsb.edu/documents/proclamation-6082-human-rights-day-bill-rights-day-and-human-rights-week-1989.

———. "Proclamation 6084—Wright Brothers Day, 1989." https://presidency.ucsb.edu/documents/proclamation-6084-wright-brothers-day-1989.

———. "Proclamation 6090—National Sanctity of Human Life Day, 1990." https://presidency.ucsb.edu/documents/proclamation-6090-national-sanctity-human-life-day-1990.

———. "Proclamation 6113—National Former Prisoners for War Recognition Day, 1990." https://presidency.ucsb.edu/documents/proclamation-6113-national-former-prisoners-for-war-recognition-day-1990.

———. "Proclamation 6197—National Children's Day, 1990." https://presidency.ucsb.edu/documents/proclamation-6197-national-childrens-day-1990.

———. "Proclamation 6225—National Philanthropy Day, 1990." https://presidency.ucsb.edu/documents/proclamation-6225-national-philanthropy-day-1990.

———. "Proclamation 6267—National Former Prisoner of War Recognition Day, 1991 and 1992." https://presidency.ucsb.edu/documents/proclamation-6267-national-former-prisoner-war-recognition-day-1991-and-1992.

———. "Proclamation 6355—National Children's Day, 1991." https://presidency.ucsb.edu/documents/proclamation-6355-national-childrens-day-1991.

———. "Proclamation 6376—National Philanthropy Day, 1991." https://presidency.ucsb.edu/documents/proclamation-6376-national-philanthropy-day-1991.

———. "Proclamation 6490—National Children's Day, 1992." https://presidency.ucsb.edudocuments/proclamation-6490-national-childrens-day-1992.

———. "Statement on the Observance of World AIDS Day." https://presidency.ucsb.edu/documents/statement-the-observance-world-aids-day.

Bush, George W. "Message on the Observance of Kwanzaa." https://presidency.ucsb.edu/documents/message-the-observance-kwanzaa-0.

———. "National Day of Prayer and Remembrance for the Victims of the Terrorist Attacks on September 11, 2001." https://georgewbush-whitehouse.archives.gov/news/releases/2001/09/print/20010913-7.html.

———. "Proclamation 7421—National Former Prisoner of War Recognition Day, 2001." https://presidency.ucsb.edu/documents/proclamation-7421-national-former-prisoner-war-recognition-day-2001.

———. "Proclamation 7435—Peace Officers Memorial Day and Police Week, 2001." https://presidency.ucsb.edu/documents/proclamation-7435-peace-officers-memorial-day-and-police-week-2001.

———. "Proclamation 7446—National Child's Day, 2001." https://presidency.ucsb.edu/documents/proclamation-7446-national-childs-day-2001.

———. "Proclamation 7469—National POW/MIA Recognition ay, 2001." https://presidency.ucsb.edu/documents/proclamation-7469-national-powmia-recognition-day-2001.

———. "Proclamation 7483—Leif Erikson Day, 2001." https://presidency.ucsb.edu/documents/proclamation-7483-leif-erikson-day-2001.

———. "Proclamation 7486—White Cane Safety Day 2001." https://presidency.ucsb.edu/documents/proclamation-7486-white-cane-safety-day-2001.

———. "Proclamation 7499—World Freedom Day, 2001." https://presidency.ucsb.edu/documents/proclamation-7499-world-freedom-day-2001.

———. "Proclamation 7503—America Recycles Day, 2001." https://presidency.ucsb.edu/documents/proclamation-7503-america-recycles-day-2001.

———. "Proclamation 7510—World AIDS Day, 2001. https://presidency.ucsb.edu/documents/proclamation-7510-world-aids-day-2001.

———. "Proclamation 7513—Human Rights Day, Bill of Rights Day, and Human Rights Week, 2001." https://presidency.ucsb.edu/documents/proclamation-7513-human-rights-day-bill-rights-day-and-human-rights-week-2001.

———. "Proclamation 7514—Wright Brothers Day, 2001." https://presidency.ucsb.edu/documents/proclamation-7514-wright-brothers-day-2001.

———. "Proclamation 7520—National Sanctity of Human Life Day, 2002." https://presidency.ucsb.edu/documents/proclamation-7520-national-sanctity-human-life-day-2002.

———. "Proclamation 7571—National Child's Day, 2002." https://presidency.ucsb.edu/documents/proclamation-7571-national-childs-day-2002.

———. "Proclamation 7683—National Child's Day, 2003." https://presidency.ucsb.edu/documents/proclamation-7683-national-childs-day-2003.

———. "Proclamation 7793—National Child's Day, 2004." https://presidency.ucsb.edu/documents/proclamation-7793-national-childs-day-2004.

———. "Proclamation 7909—National Child's Day, 2005." https://presidency.ucsb.edu/documents/proclamation-7909-national-childs-day-2005.

———. "Proclamation 8026—National Child's Day, 2006." https://presidency.ucsb.edu/documents/proclamation-8026-national-childs-day-2006.

———. "Proclamation 8152—National Child's Day, 2007." https://presidency.ucsb.edu/documents/proclamation-8152-national-childs-day-2007.

———. "Proclamation 8267—National Child's Day, 2008." https://presidency.ucsb.edu/documents/proclamation-8267-national-childs-day-2008.

Cardy, Glynn. "When the Dust Settles: A Tribute to John Shelby Spong." *The Fourth R* 35:1 (2022) 10, 23.

Carter, Jimmy. "Proclamation 4524—Leif Erikson Day, 1977." https://presidency.ucsb.edu/documents/proclamation-4524-leif-erikson-day-1977.

———. "Proclamation 4528—White Cane Safety Day, 1977." https://presidency.ucsb.edu/documents/proclamation-4528-white-cane-safety-day-1977.

———. "Proclamation 4541—Wright Brothers Day, 1977." https://presidency.ucsb.edu/documents/proclamation-4541-wright-brothers-day-1977.

———. "Proclamation 4542—Bill of Rights Day, Human Rights Day and Week, 1977." https://presidency.ucsb.edu/documents/proclamation-4542-bill-rights-day-human-rights-day-and-week-1977.

———. "Proclamation 4580—National Grandparents Day, 1978." https://presidency.ucsb.edu/documents/proclamation-4580-national-grandparents-day-1978.

———. "Proclamation 4584—National Aviation Year and Wright Brothers Day, 1978." https://presidency.ucsb.edu/documents/proclamation-4584-national-aviation-year-and-wright-brothers-day-1978.

———. "Proclamation 4601—National Good Neighbor Day, 1978." https://presidency.ucsb.edu/documents/proclamation-4601-national-good-neighbor-day-1978documents/proclamation-4601-national-good-neighbor-day-1978.

———. "Proclamation 4679—National Grandparents Day." https://presidency.ucsb.edu/documents/proclamation-4679-national-grandparents-day.

———. "Proclamation 4804—Bill of Rights Day, Human Rights Day and Week, 1980." https://presidency.ucsb.edu/documents/proclamation-4804-bill-rights-day-human-rights-day-and-week-1980.

Casey, Michael. *Balaam's Donkey*. Collegeville, MN: Liturgical, 2019.

Catechism of the Catholic Church. Washington, DC: United States Catholic Conference, 1994.

Cathcart, Thomas. *There is no God and Mary is His Mother: Rediscovering Religionless Christianity*. Minneapolis: Fortress, 2020.

Chamberlain, Neville. "Declaration of War: Chamberlain's Radio Broadcast, 3 September 1939, 11 a.m." https://www.theguardian.com/world/2009/sep/06/second-world-war-declaration-chamberlain.

"Chapter 118—An Act Making Labor Day a Legal Holiday." https://tile.loc.gov/storage-services/service/ll/llsl//llsl-c53/llsl-c53.pdf.

"A Charlie Brown Christmas (1965) Transcript." https://tvshowtranscripts.ourboard.org/viewtopic.php?f=150&t=32381.

Chaucer, Geoffrey. "The Parliament of Fowls." Translated by A.S. Kline, 2007. https://poetryintranslation.com/PITBR/English/Fowls.php#highlightthe+parliament+of+fowls.

Cheah, S.G. "Women in Red: The Surprising History of International Women's Day." https://eviemagazine.com/search?query=Women%20in%20Red&page=1.

"Chinese New Year and the Legend of Nian." https://ancient-origins.net/news-general/chinese-new-year-001289.

Clark, Corrie E. and Lynn J. Cunningham. "Daylight Saving Time." Congressional Research Service (May 29, 2018), ii. https://crsreports.congress.gov/product/pdf/R/R45208.

Clinton, William J. "Letter, June 20, 1995." https://eagles.org/wp-content/uploads/2019/05/clinton-AED.pdf.

———. "Message on the Observance of Kwanzaa [, 1993]." https://presidency.ucsb.edu/documents/message-the-observance-kwanzaa-2.

———. "Proclamation 6541—National Former Prisoner of War Recognition Day, 1993." https://presidency.ucsb.edu/documents/proclamation-6541-national-former-prisoner-war-recognition-day-1993.

———. "Proclamation 6587—National POW/MIA Recognition Day, 1993." https://presidency.ucsb.edu/documents/proclamation-6587-national-powmia-recognition-day-1993.

———. "Proclamation 6607—Leif Erikson Day, 1993." https://presidency.ucsb.edu/documents/proclamation-6607-leif-erikson-day-1993.

———. "Proclamation 6612—White Cane Safety Day, 1993." https://presidency.ucsb.edu/documents/proclamation-6612-white-cane-safety-day-1993.

———. "Proclamation 6626—National Children's Day, 1993." https://presidency.ucsb.edu/documents/proclamation-6626-national-childrens-day-1993.

———. "Proclamation 6632—World AIDS Day, 1993." https://presidency.ucsb.edu/documents/proclamation-6632-world-aids-day-1993.

———. "Proclamation 6637—Human Rights Day, Bill of Rights Day, and Human Rights Week, 1993." https://presidency.ucsb.edu/documents/proclamation-6637-human-rights-day-bill-rights-day-and-human-rights-week-1993.

———. "Proclamation 6638—Wright Brothers Day, 1993." https://presidency.ucsb.edu/documents/proclamation-6638-wright-brothers-day-1993.

———. "Proclamation 6734—National Children's Day, 1994." https://presidency.ucsb.edu/documents/proclamation-6734-national-childrens-day-1994.

———. "Proclamation 6758—National Pearl Harbor Remembrance Day, 1994." https://presidency.ucsb.edu/documents/proclamation-6758-national-pearl-harbor-remembrance-day-1994.

———. "Proclamation 6800—Peace Officers Memorial Day and Police Week, 1995." https://presidency.ucsb.edu/documents/proclamation-6800-peace-officers-memorial-day-and-police-week-1995.

———. "Proclamation 6833—National Children's Day, 1995." https://presidency.ucsb.edu/documents/proclamation-6833-national-childrens-day-1995.

———. "Proclamation 6855—Human Rights Day, Bill of Rights Day, and Human Rights Week, 1995." https://presidency.ucsb.edu/documents/proclamation-6855-human-rights-day-bill-rights-day-and-human-rights-week-1995.

———. "Proclamation 6939—National Children's Day, 1996." https://presidency.ucsb.edu/documents/proclamation-6939-national-childrens-day-1996.

———. "Proclamation 7040—National Children's Day, 1997." https://presidency.ucsb.edu/documents/proclamation-7040-national-childrens-day-1997.

———. "Proclamation 7139—National Children's Day, 1998." https://presidency.ucsb.edu/documents/proclamation-7139-national-childrens-day-1998.

———. "Proclamation 7238—National Children's Day, 1999." https://presidency.ucsb.edu/documents/proclamation-7238-national-childrens-day-1999.

———. "Proclamation 7250—America Recycles Day, 1999." https://presidency.ucsb.edu/documents/proclamation-7250-america-recycles-day-1999.

———. "Proclamation 7356—National Children's Day, 2000." https://presidency.ucsb.edu/documents/proclamation-7356-national-childrens-day-2000.

Cohen, Jennie. "What Is Flag Day?" http://history.com/news/what-is-flag-day.

Commoner, Barry. "Earth Day: A Question of Survival." New York: CBS News, April 22, 1970. https://paleycenter.org/collection/item/?q=Earth+Day&p=1&item=T:39446.

Congressional Record 109th Congress (2005–2006). "Recognizing Historical Significance of the Mexican Holiday of Cinco De Mayo (House of Representatives, June 7, 2005)," H4150–52. http://web.archive.org/web/20140902181814/http://thomas.loc.gov.cgi-bin/query/R?r109:FLD001:H04151.

"Constitution Act, 1867." https://laws-lois.justice.gc.ca.

"The Constitution of the United States." http://archives.gov/founding-docs/constitution-transcript.

"Constitution of the World Health Organization." https://who.int/governance/eb/who_constitution_en.pdf.

"Convention on the Rights of Persons with Disabilities." https://un.org/development/desa/disabilities/convention-on-the-rights-of-persons-with-disabilities/convention-on-the-rights-of-persons-with-disabilities-2.html.

Curran, Asha. "We Must Embrace Radical Generosity with or without COVID." *Newsweek* (December 30, 2021). https://newsweek.com/we-must-embrace-radical-generosity-without-covid-opinion-1571485.

"The Declaration of Independence." https://archives.gov/founding-docs/declaration-transcript.

"Department of Public Information to Launch 'Language Days at the United Nations.'" Press Release (February 19, 2010). https://un.org/press/en/2010/obv853.doc.htm.

Dimbleby, Richard. "The Swiss Spaghetti Harvest." London: British Broadcasting Corporation, Panorama (April 1, 1957). http://hoaxes.org/archive/permalink/the_swiss_spaghetti_harvest.

"A Document on Human Fraternity for World Peace and Living Together." https://press.vatican.va/content/salastampa/en/bollettino/pubblico/2019/02/04/190204f.html.

"Does the UN have a Hymn or National Anthem?" https://ask.un.org/loader?fid=8279&type=1&key=52dfabb4fe2753e1f6a37eda8de69d7e.

Eisenhower, Dwight D. "Proclamation 3071—Veteran's Day, 1954." https://presidency.ucsb.edu/documents/proclamation-3071-veterans-day-1954.

———. "Proclamation 3091—Loyalty Day." https://presidency.ucsb.edu/documents/proclamation-3091-loyalty-day-1955.

———. "Proclamation 3265—Human Rights Week, 1958." https://presidency.ucsb.edu/documents/proclamation-3265-human-rights-week-1958.

———. "Proclamation 3315—Wright Brothers Day, 1959." https://presidency.ucsb.edu/documents/proclamation-3315-wright-brothers-day-1959.

———. "Statement by the President: Bill of Rights Day." https://presidency.ucsb.edu/documents/statement-the-president-bill-rights-day.

———. "Statement by the President on the Observance of World Health Day." https://presidency.ucsb.edu/documents/statement-the-president-the-observance-world-health-day.

———. "Supreme Headquarters Allied Expeditionary Force." https://eisenhowerlibrary.gov/research/online-documents/world-war-ii-d-day-invasion-normandy.

Elzinga, Samuel. "Celebrate International Mountain Day: Mountains and Biodiversity. *UNA-USA Store* (October 30, 2019). https://unausa.org/celebrate-international-mountain-day-mountains-matter-for-youth/#:~:text=International%20Mountain%20Day%20is%20celebrated,57%2F245%20in%20December%202002.

Encarta: World English Dictionary. New York: St. Martin, 1999.

"End Inequalities. End AIDS. End Pandemics." https://un.org/en/observances/world-aids-day.

"English Language Day." https://daysoftheyear.com/days/english-language-day/.

"English Language Day U.N." https://un.org/en/observances/english-language-day.

Estabrook, Robert E. "An Unfettered Press: Right and Responsibilities." https://usa.usembassy.de/etexts/media/unfetter/press07.htm.

BIBLIOGRAPHY

"Everything You Need to Know about International Firefighters' Day." https://firetechglobal.com/everything-you-need-to-know-about-international-firefighters-day-blog-firetech-global/.

Exner, Rich. "Sweetest Day and its Cleveland Roots." (May 19, 2019). https://cleveland.com/news/2021/10/what-is-sweetest-day-unofficial-holiday-has-cleveland-roots.html.

Farmers' Almanac. "Fall Equinox—When is the First Day of Fall? (2021)." https://www.farmersalmanac.com/fall-equinox-first-day-of-fall.

"First Ever Official World Creativity and Innovation Day Supported by United Nations Being Observed." *Merinews* (April 22, 2018). https://merinews.com/article/first-ever-official-world-creativity-and-innovation-day-supported-by-united-nations-being-observed/15930138.shtml.

Ford, Gerald R. "Proclamation 4321—Leif Erikson Day, 1975." https://presidency.ucsb.edu/documents/proclamation-4321-leif-erikson-day-1974.

———. "Proclamation 4336—Wright Brothers Day, 1974." https://presidency.ucsb.edu/documents/proclamation-4336-wright-brothers-day-1974.

———. "Proclamation 4337—Bill of Rights Day, Human Rights Day and Week." https://presidency.ucsb.edu/documents/proclamation-4337-bill-rights-day-human-rights-day-and-week.

———. "Proclamation 4380—White Cane Safety Day, 1975." https://presidency.ucsb.edu/documents/proclamation-4380-white-cane-safety-day-1975.

———. "Proclamation 4444—National Good Neighbor Day, 1976. https://presidency.ucsb.edu/documents/proclamation-4444-national-good-neighbor-day-1976.

"The Founder's Welcome." https://officialkwanzaawebsite.org/.

"Four Things to Know about POW/MIA Recognition Day." https://military.com/history/4-things-know-pow-mia-recognition-day.html.

Fox, Zoe. "Six Inspiring Organizations Joining in #Giving Tuesday" *Mashable* (October 23, 2012). https://mashable.com/archive/giving-tuesday-skype-cisco.

"Franklin D. Roosevelt Presidential Library." https://fdrlibrary.tumblr.com/post/8035795743/i-think-this-would-be-a-good-time-for-beer.

Gaylord, Tom. "A Documentary History of Veterans Day." Pritzker Legal Research Center Blog. https://library.blog.law.northwester.edu/2015/11/11/a-documentary-history-of-veterans-day/.

Geisel, Theodor Seuss. *How the Grinch Stole Christmas*. New York: Random House, 1957.

George, Arthur. *The Mythology of America's Seasonal Holidays: The Dance of the Horae*. Cham, Switzerland: Palgrave Macmillan, 2020.

Ghosh, Basab. "The Legend of Frosty the Snowman." https://bedtimeshortstories.com/the-legend-of-frosty-the-snowman.

"Global Code of Ethics for Tourism." https://webunwto.s3.eu-west-1.amazonaws.com/imported_images/37802/gcetbrochureglobalcodeen.pdf.

Goldberg, Philip. "Namaste: Let's Keep it After the Pandemic." *Spirituality and Health* 24:3 (2021) 12–13.

———. "Holy Places Everywhere." *Spirituality and Health* 23:5 (2020) 24–25.

Granger, Gordon. "General Order No. 3." https://tsl.texas.gove/ref/abouttx/juneteenth.html.

Green, Alison. "5 Reasons Boss's Day is Total BS." *U.S. News and World Report* (October 12, 2015). https://money.usnews.com/money/blogs/outside-voices-careers/2015/10/12/4-reasons-boss-day-is-total-bs.

Green, Laura. "Green Monday." *Investopedia* (November 22, 2021). https://investopedia.com/terms/g/green-monday.asp.

Hamlich, Marvin. "Now, More Than Ever." https://npdoc.org/wp-content-uploads/2021/05/Now-More-Than-Ever-Music-and-yrics.pdf.

Hansen, Michael. *The First Spiritual Exercises: Four Guided Retreats*. Notre Dame, IN: Ave Maria, 2013.

"Happy Festivus . . . for the Rest of Us." https://festivusweb.com/.

Hendler-Voss, Amanda. "Restore Justice." *U.S. Catholic* 84:8 (2019) 32–7.

"The History and Words of Auld Lang Syne." https://scotland.org/features/the-history-and-words-of-auld-lang-syne.

"History of the Association of Fundraising Professionals." https://afpglobal.org/history-association-fundraising-profssionals.

"History of the Great American Smokeout Event." https://cancer.org/healthy/stay-away-from-tobacco/great-american-smokeout/history-of-the-great-american-smokeout.html.

"History of Universal Children's Day." https://nationaltoday.com/universal-childrens-day/.

Hof, Robert D. "Cyber Monday, Marketing Myth." https://web.archive.org/web/20120629055913/http://www.businessweek.com/bwdaily/dnflash/nov2005/nf20051129_9946_db016.htm.

Hollywood, Amy. "Spiritual but not Religious: The Vital Interplay between Submission and Freedom." https://bulletin.hds.harvard.edu/winter-spring-2010/.

Hope, Allison. "Festivus, the 'Seinfeld' Holiday Focused on Airing Grievances, is for Everyone." *CNN Health* (December 22, 2021). https://cnn.com/2021/12/22/health/festivus-seinfeld-wellness/index.html.

"House Concurrent Resolution 39." https://congress.gov/bill/98th-congress/house-concurrent-resolution/39?r=75&s=1.

Hubl, Thomas. "Lean into Wisdom." https://spiritualityhealth.com/articles/2020/08/17/collective-trauma-thomas-hubl.

"Instrument of Surrender." https://archivesfoundation.org/documents/japanese-instrument-surrender-1945/.

"International Association of Pet Cemeteries & Crematories." https://iaopc.com/page/pet-owners.

"International Coffee Day." https://nationaltoday.com/international-coffee-day/.

International Coffee Organization. "International Coffee Day." https://ico.org/international-doffee-day.asp.

"International Convention on the Protection of the Rights of All Migrant Workers and Members of Their Families [A/RES/45/158]." https://un.org/en/development/desa/population/migration/generalassembly/docs/globalcompact/A_RES_45_158.pdf.

"International Day for the Eradication of Poverty." https://un.org/en/observances/day-for-eradicating-poverty.

"International Day for the Eradication of Poverty." Wikipedia. https://en.wikipedia.org/wiki/International_Day_for_the_Eradication_of_Poverty.

"International Day for the Eradication of Poverty—Homepage." United Nations. https://un.org/development/desa/socialperspectiveondevelopment/.

"International Day for the Total Elimination of Nuclear Weapons." https://un.org/en/observances/nuclear-weapons-elimination-day.

"International Day of Conscience." https://un.org/en/observances/conscience-day.

Bibliography

"International Day of Conscience: Commemorating the Importance of the Human Conscience." https://codecacy.org/post/international-day-of-conscience.

"International Day of Forests." https://un.org/en/observances/forests-and-trees-day.

"International Day of Human Fraternity." https://un.org/en/observances/human-fraternity.

"International Day of Persons with Disabilities." https://un.org/en/observances/day-of-persons-with-disabilities.

"International Event Day: International Day of Conscience." https://internationaleventday.com/event/international-day-of-conscience/.

"International Firefighters' Day." https://firefightersday.org/.

"International Human Solidarity Day." https://un.org/en/observances/human-solidarity-day.

"International Migrants Day." https://un.org/en/observances/migrants-day.

"International Mountain Day." https://un.org/en/observances/mountain-day.

"Introducing Giving Tuesday for Kids." https://givingtuesday.org/blog/introducing-givingtuesdaykids/.

John Paul II. "Christmas Tree is Symbol of Christ, Says Pope." *Zenit* (December 19, 2004). https://web.archive.org/web/20071208101926/http://www.zenit.org/article-11828?l=english.

Johnson, Lyndon B. "Proclamation 3563—Bill of Rights Day—Human Rights Day." https://presidency.ucsb.edu/documents/proclamation-3563-bill-rights-day-human-rights-day.

———. "Proclamation 3565—Wright Brothers Day, 1963." https://presidency.ucsb.edu/documents/proclamation-3565-wright-brothers-day-1963.

———. "Proclamation 3610—Leif Erikson Day, 1964." https://presidency.ucsb.edu/documents/proclamation-3610-leif-erikson-day-1964.

———. "Proclamation 3622—White Cane Safety Day, 1964." https://presidency.ucsb.edu/documents/proclamation-3622-white-cane-safety-day-1964.

———. "Proclamation 3730—Father's Day, 1966." https://presidency.ucsb.edu/documents/proclamation-3730-fathers-day-1966.

———. "Proclamation 3814—Human Rights Week and Human Rights Year." https://presidency.ucsb.edu/documents/proclamation-3814-human-rights-week-and-human-rights-year.

———. "Proclamation 3873—Columbus Day, 1968." https://presidency.ucsb.edu/documents/proclamation-3873-columbus-day-1968.

Jones, Robert. "The Twelve Theses of John Shelby Spong." *The Fourth R* 35:1 (2022) 11–14.

Kachtick, Keith. "Circles and Synchronicities." *Spirituality and Health* 24:5 (2021) 24–27.

"'Kansas Stream' 1991–92." http://internationalmensday.co/kansas-stream-1991-92/.

Kataria, Madan. "Quotes from Dr. Madan Kataria!" https://prezi.com/xgkxrkiva2ol/quotes-from-drmadan-kataria/.

Kennedy, John F. "Excerpt from the 'Special Message to the Congress on Urgent National Needs.'" https://nasa.gov/vision/space/features/jfk_speech_text.html.

———. "Proclamation 3433—Wright Brothers Day, 1961." https://presidenty.ucsb.edu/documents/proclamation-3433-wright-brothers-day-1961.

———. "Proclamation 3442—Human Rights Week, 1961." https://presidency.ucsb.edu/documents/proclamation-3442-human-rights-week-1961.

———. "Proclamation 3466—Police Week and Peace Officers Memorial Day, 1962." https://presidency.ucsb.edu/documents/proclamation-3466-police-week-and-peace-officers-memorial-day-1962.

———. "Proclamation 3508—Bill of Rights Day, Human Rights Day." https://presidency.ucsb.edu/documents/proclamation-3508-bill-rights-day-human-rights-day.

———. Proclamation 3537—Peace Officers Memorial Day and Police Week." https://presidency.ucsb.edu/documents/proclamation-3537-peace-officers-memorial-day-and-police-week.

Key, Francis Scott. "Defence of Fort M'Henry." https://www.poetryfoundation.org/poems/47349/defence-of-fort-mhenry.

Key, Francis Scott. "Defence of Fort M'Henry." *The Analectic Magazine* 4 (1814) 433–4. https://babel.hathitrust.org/cgi/pt?id=umn.31951000925404p&view=1up&seq=7&skin=2021.

Kiesling, Stephen. "The New American Love Revolution: A Conversation with Marianne Williamson." *Spirituality and Health* 21:6 (2018) 62–7.

King, Martin Luther, Jr. "I Have a Dream Speech." https://kr.usembassy.gov/martin-luther-king-jr-dream-speech-1963/?_ga=2.93968733.1975122296.1652976260-1800523453.1651070358.

King, Stephanie L. "The Principles and Meaning of Kwanzaa." *Oprah Daily* (December 7, 2020). https://oprahdaily.com/life/a34894866/kwanzaa-principles-candles-meaning/.

Kitchener, Caroline. "What It Means to be Spiritual but not Religious." https://theatlantic.com/membership/archive/2018/01/what-it-means-to-be-spiritual-but-not-religious/550337/.

Krattenmaker, Tom. "Come Together." *Spirituality and Health* 25:3 (2022) 43–4.

"Labor Unions Start Fight for Universal Eight-Hour Day." *The Day Book* (February 22, 1916). https://chroniclingamerica.loc.gov.

"Law Enforcement Oath of Honor." International Association of Chiefs of Police. https://theiacp.org/sites/default/files/all/i-j/IACP_Oath_of_Honor_En_8.5x11_Web.pdf.

"The Legend of 'Stingy Jack." https://history.com/news/history-of-the-jack-o-lantern-irish-origins.

Lincoln, Abraham. "The Gettysburg Address." http://144.208.79.222/~abraha21/alo/lincoln/speeches/gettysburg.htm.

———. "Proclamation 106—Thanksgiving Day 1863." https://presidency.ucsb.edu/documents/proclamation-106-thanksgiving-day-1863.

———. "Proclamation 118—Thanksgiving Day 1864." https://presidency.ucsb.edu/documents/proclamation-118-thanksgiving-day-1864.

Lipka, Michael, and Claire Gecewicz. "More Americans now Say They're Spiritual but not Religious." https://pewresearch.org/fact-tank/2017/09/06/more-americans-now-say-theyre-spiritual-but-not-religious/.

Logan, John A. "Memorial Day Order: General Orders No. 11, May 5, 1868." http://web.archive.org/web/20100527152857://http://www.cem.va.gov/hist/memdayorder.asp.

Longfellow, Henry Wadsworth. "Paul Revere's Ride." https://paulreverehouse.org/longfellows-poem/.

Luther, Martin. "Disputation of Doctor Martin Luther on the Power and Efficacy of Indulgences." (October 31, 1517). https://gutenberg.org/cache/epub/274/pg274.txt.

Maher, Dennis. "Soul and Spirit at Westar." *The Fourth R* 34:3 (2021) 10–14.

Marsh, Becca. "30 Facts about Red Nose Day." https://thefactsite.com/facts-about-red-nose-day/.

Maurer, Marc. "What Cane Safety Day: A Symbol of Independence." *Future Reflections* 2:5 (1983). https://nfb.org/sites/dafault/files/images/nfb/publications/fr/fr02/issue5/fo20507.html.

May, Robert L. *Rudolph the Red-Nosed Reindeer*. Chicago: Montgomery Ward, 1939. https://npr.org/2013/12/25/256579598/writing-rudolph-the-original-red-nosed-manuscript.

McInerney, Andy. "May Day, The Worker's Day, Born in the Struggle for the Eight-Hour Day." *Liberation & Marxism* 27 (1996) 92–100. https://journals.co.za/doi/10.10520/AJA15955753_276.

"Meet the 'Spiritual but not Religious.'" https://barna.com/research/meet-spiritual-not-religious/.

Mercadante, Linda A. "Are the Spiritual but not Religious Turning East?" https://huffpost.com/entry/are-the-spiritual-eastern-religion_b_5161316.

"Minimum Age Convention, 1973 (No. 138)." International Labor Organization. https://ilo.org/dyn/normlex/en/f?p=NORMLEXPUB:12100:0::NO::P12100_ILO_CODE:C138.

Missouri Revised Statutes Title V. Military Affairs and Police, Section 44.115. Persons Employed by or Associated with Civil Defense Agencies—Qualifications—Oath Required. https://codes.findlaw.com/mo/title-v-military-affairs-and-police/mo-rev-st-44-115.html#:~:text=%E2%80%9CI%2C%20_____%2C%20do%20solemnly,obligation%20freely%2C%20without%20any%20mental.

Moore, Clement Clarke. "A Visit from St. Nicholas." https://poets.org/poem/visit-st-nicholas.

"Multilingualism." https://un.org/sg/en/multilingualism/index.shtml.

"National Chocolate Day." https://holidayscalendar.com/event/national-chocolate-day/.

"National Chocolate Day." https://nationaltoday.com/national-chocolate-day/.

"National Chocolate Day." https://wincalendar.com/Chocolate-Day.

"National Coffee Day." https://nationaldaycalendar.com/national-coffee-day-september-29/.

"National Doctors Day." https://doctorsday.org.

"National Farmer's Day." https://NationalDayCalendar.com/national-farmers-day-october-12/.

"National Law Enforcement Appreciation Day." https://nationaltoday.com/national-law-enforcement-appreciation-day/.

"National Mother-in-Law Day." https://nationaldayarchives.com/day/national-mother-in-law-day/.

"National Pet Day." *National Today*. https://nationaltoday.com/national-pet-day/.

"National Pet Day." *Days of the Year*. https://daysoftheyear.com/days/pet-day/.

"National Pet Day: Life Upgraded." https://nationalpetday.co/.

"National Stepfamily Day." https://nationaltoday.com/national-stepfamily-day/.

"National Tattoo Day." https://nationaltoday.com/national-tattoo-day/#:~:text=Tattooing%20is%20the%20art%20of.its%20societal%20importance%20and%20history.

"National Wine Day." https://holidayscalendar.com/event/national-wine-day/.

New Revised Standard Version Bible. New York: National Council of the Churches of Christ in the U.S.A., 1989.

Nightingale, Florence. "Some Sentences of Florence." In "Florence Nightingale: The Mother of Nursing." By Hosein Karimi and Negin Masoudi Alavi. *Nursing and Midwifery Studies* (June 4, 2015). https://ncbi.nlm.nih.gov/pmc/articles/PMC4557419.

Nixon, Richard. "Proclamation 3913—White Cane Safety Day, 1969." https://presidency.ucsb.edu/documents/proclamation-3913-white-cane-safety-day-1969.

———. "Proclamation 3928—Leif Erikson Day, 1979." https://presidenty.ucsb.edu/documents/proclamation-3928-leif-erikson-day-1969.

———. "Proclamation 3946—Bill of Rights Day, Human Rights Day." https://presidency.ucsb.edu/ documents/proclamation-3946-bill-rights-day-human-rights-day.

———. "Proclamation 3947—Wright Brothers Day, 1969." https://presidency.ucsb.edu/documents/proclamation-3947-wright-brothers-day-1969.

———. "Proclamation 4078—Columbus Day, 1971." https://presidency.ucsb.edu/documents/proclamation-4078-columbus-day-1971.

———. "Proclamation 4127—Father's Day." https://presidency.ucsb.edu/documents/proclamation-4127-fathers-day.

———. "Proclamation 4147—Women's Rights Day." https://presidency.ucsb.edu/documents/proclamation-4147-womens-rights-day.

———. "Proclamation 4236—Women's Equality Day." https://presidency.ucsb.edu/documents/proclamation-4236-womens-equality-day.

———. "Statement about Peace Officers Memorial Day and Police Week, 1972." https://presidency.ucsb.edu/ documents/statement-about-peace-officers-memorial-day-and-police-week-1972.

———. "Telephone Conversation with the Apollo 11 Astronauts on the Moon." https://presidency.ucsb.edu/ people/president/richard-nixon.

Oatman, Alexis. "What is Sweetest Day? Unofficial Holiday has Cleveland Roots." (October 16, 2021). https://cleveland.com/news/2021/10/what-is-sweetest-day-unofficial-holiday-has-cleveland-roots.html.

Obama, Barack. "Obama Statement on the National Peace Officer Memorial Day." https://presidency.ucsb.edu/ documents/obama-statement-the-national-peace-officer-memorial-day.

———. "Patriot Day and National Day of Service and Remembrance, 2009." https://obamawhitehouse.archives.gov/the-press-office/presidential-proclamation-patriot-day-and-national-day-remembrance-and-service.

———. "Proclamation 8360—National Former Prisoner of War Recognition Day, 2009." https://presidency.ucsb.edu/ documents/proclamation-8378-peace-officers-memorial-day-and-police-week-2009.

———. "Proclamation 8378—Peace Officers Memorial Day and Police Week, 2009." https://presidency.ucsb.edu/ documents/proclamation-8378-peace-officers-memorial-day-and-police-week-2009.

———. "Proclamation 8419—National POW/MIA Recognition Day, 2009." https://presidency.ucsb.edu/ documents/proclamation-8419-national-powmia-recognition-day-2009.

———. "Proclamation 8435—Leif Erikson Day, 2009." https://presidency.ucsb.edu/documents/proclamation-8435-leif-erikson-day-2009.

———. "Proclamation 8439—White Cane Safety Day, 2009." https://presidency.ucsb.edu/documents/proclamation-8439-white-cane-safety-day-2009.

———. "Proclamation 8452—World Freedom Day, 2009." https://presidency.ucsb.edu/documents/proclamation-8452-world-freedom-day-2009.

———."Proclamation 8453—America Recycles Day, 2009." https://presidency.ucsb.edu/documents/proclamation-8453-america-recycles-day-2009.

———. "Proclamation 8457—National Child's Day, 2009." https://presidency.ucsb.edu/documents/proclamation-8457-national-childs-day-2009.

———. "Proclamation 8462—International Day of Persons with Disabilities, 2009." https://presidency.ucsb.edu/ documents/proclamation-8462-international-day-persons-with-disabilities-2009.

———. "Proclamation 8464—Human Rights Day, Bill of Rights Day, and Human Rights Week, 2009." https://presidency.ucsb.edu/ documents/proclamation-8464-human-rights-day-bill-rights-day-and-human-rights-week-2009.

———. "Proclamation 8466—Wright Brothers Day, 2009." https://presidency.ucsb.edu/ documents/proclamation-8466-wright-brothers-day-2009.

———. "Proclamation 8604—National Child's Day, 2010." https://presidency.ucsb.edu/ documents/proclamation-8604-national-childs-day-2010.

———. "Proclamation 8609—World AIDS Day, 2010." https://presidency.ucsb.edu/ documents/proclamation-8609-world-aids-day-2010.

———. "Proclamation 8739—Blind Americans Equality Day, 2011." https://presidency.ucsb.edu/ documents/proclamation-8739-blind-americans-equality-day-2011.

———. "Proclamation 8758—National Child's Day, 2011." https://presidency.ucsb.edu/ documents/proclamation-8758-national-childs-day-2011.

———. "Proclamation 8907—National Child's Day, 2012." https://presidency.ucsb.edu/ documents/proclamation-8907-national-childs-day-2012.

———. "Proclamation 9059—National Child's Day, 2013." https://presidency.ucsb.edu/ documents/proclamation-9059-national-childs-day-2013.

———. "Proclamation 9212—National Child's Day, 2014." https://presidency.ucsb.edu/ documents/proclamation-9212-national-childs-day-2014.

———. "Proclamation 9370—National Child's Day, 2015." https://presidency.ucsb.edu/ documents/proclamation-9370-national-childs-day-2015.

———. "Proclamation 9545—National Child's Day, 2016." https://presidency.ucsb.edu/ documents/proclamation-9545-national-childs-day-2016.

———. "Statement on the Observance of Kwanzaa." https://presidency.ucsb.edu/ documents/statement-the-observance-kwanzaa-1.

"Objectives of International Men's Day." https://internationalmensday.com/objectives-of-imd/.

"O Christmas Tree." https://christmasmusicsongs.com/lyrics/o-christmas-tree-lyrics.html.

"O Christmas Tree: Lyrics." https://carols.org.uk/o_christmas_tree.htm.

O'Day, Gail R., and David Peterson, eds. *The Access Bible: New Revised Standard Version with the Apocryphal/Deuterocanonical Books*. New York: Oxford University Press, 1999.

"O Tannenbaum." https://www.google.com/search?q=o+christmas+tree+lyrics&rlz=1C1GCEB_enUS892US892&ei=xy3kYYnpLbO9oPEPs6SN0A0&ved=0ahUKEwjJ6LTcv7b1AhWzHjQIHTNSA90Q4dUDCA4&uact=5&oq=o+christmas+tree+lyrics&gs_lcp=Cgdnd3Mtd2l6EAMyBAgAEEMyBQgAEIAEMgUIABCABDIFCAAQgAQyBQgAEIAEMgUIABCABDIFCAAQgAQyBQgAEIAEMgUIABCABDIFCAAQgAQ6BwgAEEcQsAM6BwgAELADEEM6BwguELADEEM6CggAEOQCELADGAA6DAguEMgDELADEEMYAToHCC4QsQMQQzoFCC4QgAQ6BAguEEM6CAguEIAEELEDOgsILhCABBDHARCvATOICAAQgAQQsQM6DgguEIAEELEDEMcBEKMCSgUIIlU4YAUoECEEYAE0ECEYYAU0FCEQY_AVKBQhEGPgcSgQIQxgDUOQJWKI2YMQ3aAFwAngAgAFZiAH3EJIBAjMxmAEA0AEByAEPwAEB2gEGCAAQARgJ2gEGCAEQARgI&sclient=gws-wiz.

Otis, John and Remy Tumin. "On Giving Tuesday, 'No Act of Giving is too Small.'" *The New York Times* (Nov. 24, 2018). https://nytimes.com/2018/11/24/neediest-cases/giving-tuesday.html.

Paige, Colleen. "About Colleen and Her Work." https://colleenpaige.com/about.

———. "National Pet Day: Life Upgraded." https://nationalpetday.co/.

Patterson, Stephen J. "Dirt, Shame, and Sin in the Expendable Company of Jesus." In *Profiles of Jesus*, edited by Roy W. Hoover, 195–222. Santa Rosa, CA: Polebridge, 2002.

Pelikan, Jaroslav, ed. *Sacred Writings: Volume 3: Islam: The Qur'an*. Translated by Ahmed Ali. New York: Book-of-the-Month Club, 1992.

Pinchot (Pixchor), Gifford. "Forest Service Circular 96." In *Report of the Farmers' Institutes Held under the Auspices of the West Virginia State Board of Agriculture, Report No. 5*, 10–14. Charleston: Tribune Printing, 1907.

Pope Francis. "Letter of His Holiness Pope Francis for the Establishment of the 'World Day of Prayer for the Care of Creation' [1st September]." https://vatican.va/content/francesco/en/letters/2015/documents/papa-francesco_20150806_lettera-giornata-cura-creato.html.

Poust, Mary DeTurris. *Everyday Divine*. New York, NY: Alpha, 2012.

"POW/MIA Flag Etiquette." Gettysburg Flag Works. East Greenbush, NY. https://gettysburgflag.com/pow-mia-flag-etiquette.

Probasco, Jim. "Super Saturday." *Investopedia* (November 30, 2021). https://investopedia.com/super-saturday-definition-5210183.

"Proclamation of World Philosophy Day." *United Nations Educational, Scientific, and Cultural Organization, Records of the General Conference, Volume 1: Resolutions* (October 3–21, 2005). https://unesdoc.unesco.org/ark:/48223/pf0000142825.page=86.

"Public Law 57–183." https://uslaw.link/citation/stat/32/481.

"Public Law 71–823." https://govtrackus.s3.amazonaws.com/legislink/pdf/stat/46/STATUTE-46-Pg1508.pdf.

"Public Law 73–3." https://govtrackus.s3amazonaws.com/legislink/pdf/stat/48/STATUTE-48-Pg16.pdf.

"Public Law 77–379." https://govtrackus.s3.amazonaws.com/legislink/pdf/stat/55STATUTE-55-Pg862b.pdf.

"Public Law 80–771." https://law.cornell.edu/uscode/text/3/1.

"Public Law 85–529." https://time.com/wp-content/uploads/2015/05/statute-72-pg369-2.pdf.

"Public Law 86–304." https://govinfo.gov/content/pkg/STATUTE-73/pdf/STATUTE-73-Pg583-3.pdf#page=1.

"Public Law 87–54." https://govinfo.gov/contents/pkg/STATUTE-75/pdf/STATUTE-75-Pg94-3.pdf#page=2.

"Public Law 87–726." https://govinfo.gov/contents/pkg/STATUTE-76/pdf/STATUTE-76-Pg676.pdf.

"Public Law 87–759." https://govinfo.gov/content/pkg/STATUTE-76/pdf/STATUTE-76-Pg755.pdf.

"Public Law 88–209." https://govinfo.gov/content/pkg/STATUTE-77/pdf/STATUTE-77-Pg402.pdf#page=1.

"Public Law 88–566." https://govinfo.gov/content/pkg/STATUTE-78/pdf/STATUTE-78-Pg849.pdf.

"Public Law 88-628." https://govtrack.us/congress/bills/88/hjres753/text.

"Public Law 90–363." https://govinfo.gov/content/pkg/STATUTE-82/pdf/STATUTE-82-Pg250-3.pdf.

"Public Law 92–278." https://govinfo.gov/content/pkg/STATUTE-86/pdf/STATUTE-86-Pg124-2.pdf.

"Public Law 93–105." https://govinfo.gov/content/pkg/STATUTE-87/pdf/STATUTE-87-Pg350.pdf.

"Public Law 93–380." https://law.cornell,edu/uscode/text/20/chapter-39.

"Public Law 95–389." https://govinfo.gov/content/pkg/STATUTE-87/pdf/STATUTE-87-Pg350.pdf.

"Public Law 96–62." https://congress.gov/bill/96th-congress/house-joint-resolution/244/text.

"Public Law 96–307." https://congress.gov/96/statute/STATUTE-94/STATUTE-94-Pg938.pdf.

"Public Law 97–29." https://congress.gov/bill/97th-congress/house-joint-resolution/191/text.

"Public Law 97–139." https://congress.gov/bill/97th-congress/senate-joint-resolution/121/text?r=53&s=1.

"Public Law 97–149." https://congress.gov/bill/97th-congress/senate-joint-resolution/134/text.

"Public Law 99–16." https://congress.gov/bill/99th-congress/senate-joint-resolution/50/text/pl?overview=closed.

"Public Law 99–268." https://congress.gov/bill/99th-congress/senate-joint-resolution/226/text/pl?overview=closed.

"Public Law 99–436." https://congress.gov/bill/99th-congress/senate-joint-resolution/207/text.

"Public Law 100–102." https://govinfo.gov/content/pkg/STATUTE-101/pdf/STATUTE-101-Pg719.pdf.

"Public Law 100–269." https://www.congress.gov/100/statute/STATUTE-102/STATUTE-102-Pg43.pdf.

"Public Law 100–400." https://govinfo.gov/content/pkg/STATUTE-102/pdf/STATUTE-102-Pg1010.pdf.

"Public Law 101–52." https://congress.gov/101/statute/STATUTE-103/STATUTE-103-Pg142.pdf.

"Pubic Law 101–336." https://govinfo.gov/content/pkg/STATUTE-104/pdf/STATUTE-104-Pg327.pdf.

"Public Law 101–349." https://govinfo.gov/content/pkg/STATUTE-104/pdf/STATUTE-104-Pg401.pdf.

"Public Law 101–355." https://congress.gov/bill/101st-congress/house-joint-resolution/467/text?r=84&s=1.

"Public Law 101–473." https://govinfo.gov/content/pkg/STATUTE-104/pdf/STATUTE-104-Pg1096.pdf

"Public Law 102–116." https://congress.gov/102/statute/STATUTE-105/STATUTE-105-Pg583.pdf.

"Public Law 102–190." https://govinfo.gov/content/pkg/STATUTE-105/pdf/STATUTE-105-Pg1290.pdf.

"Public Law 102–425." https://congress.gov/102/statute/STATUTE-106/STATUTE-106-Pg2172.pdf.

"Public Law 103–147." https://congress.gov/103/statute/STATUTE-107/STATUTE-107-Pg1500.pdf.

"Public Law 103–308." https://govinfo.gov/content/pkg/BILLS-103hijres131enr/pdf/BILLS-103hjres131enr.pdf.

"Public Law 103–320." https://congress.gov/103/statute/STATUTE-108/STATUTE-108-Pg1791.pdf.

"Public Law 103–322." https://govinfo.gov/content/pkg/STATUTE-108-pdf/STATUTE-108-Pg1796.pdf.

"Public Law 103–361." https://www.congress.gov/103/statute/STATUTE-108/STATUTE-108-Pg3463.pdf.

"Public Law 103–362," https://www.govinfo.gov/content/pkg/STATUTE-108/pdf/STATUTE-108-Pg3465.pdf.

"Public Law 105–85." https://congress.gov/bill/105th-congress/house-bill/1119/text.

"Public Law 105–225." https://govinfo.gov/content/pkg/PLAW-105publ225/pdf/PLAW-105publ225.pdf.

"Public Law 106–579." https://govinfo.gov/content/pkg/PLAW-106publ229/pdf/PLAW-106publ229.pdf.

"Public Law 107–89." http://gpo.gov/fdsys/pkg/PLAW-107publ89/pdf/PLAW-107publ89.pdf.

"Public Law 108–447." https://www.govinfo.gov/content/pkg/PLAW-108publ447/pdf/PLAW-108publ447.pdf.

"Public Law 109–58." https://www.govinfo.gov/content/pkg/PLAW-109publ58/pdf/PLAW-109publ58.pdf.

"Public Law 110–325." https://govinfo.gov/content/pkg/PLAW-110publ325/pdf/PLAW-110publ325.pdf.

"Public Law 111–13." https://www.govinfo.gov/content/pkg/PLAW-111publ13/pdf/PLAW-111publ13.pdf.

"Public Law 114–240." https://uscode.house.gov/statviewer.htm?volume=130&page=974.

"Public Law 116–67." https://congress.gov/116/plaws/publ67/PLAW-116publ67.pdf.

"Public Law 117–17." https://congress.gov/bill/117th-congress/senate-bill/475/text?q=%7B"search"%3A%5B"%5C"Public+Law+117-17%5C""%2C"%5C"Public"%2C"Law"%2C"117-17%5C""%5D%7D&r=1&s=1.

"Public Law 243." https://www.google.com/books/edition/United_States_Statutes_at_Large/5DO2zVxP2dgC?hl=en&gbpv=1&dq=Public+Law+243,+August+21,+1941,+Bill+of+Rights&pg=PA665&printsec=frontcover.

"Public Law 392." https://books.google.com/books?id=gGFO084y_uAC&pg=PA229&lpg=PA229&dq=May+29,+1946+Bill+of+Rights+Day&source=bl&ots=9fMAmBM1RF&sig=ACfU3U2gNdh_5Gowe5s4C0B0EPWBzwDWgw&hl=en&sa=X&ved=2ahUKEwj8jrD-gaP1AhVJXcoKHSxQA7EQ6AF6BAg1EAM#v=onepage&q=May%2029%2C%201946%20Bill%20of%20Rights%20Day&f=false.

"Public Resolution 65–1, 40 Statue 1. A Joint Resolution of April 6, 1917, Declaring that a State of War Exists Between the Imperial German Government and the Government and the People of the United States and Making Provision to Prosecute the Same." https://catalog.archives.gov/id/5916620.

"Random Acts of Kindness." https://randomactsofkindness.org/.

Reagan, Ronald. "Message on the Observance of Police Week, Peace Officers' Memorial Day, May 1982." https://presidency.ucsb.edu/documents/message-the-observance-police-week-peace-officers-memorial-day-may-1982.

———. "Proclamation 4818—International Year of Disabled Persons." https://presidency.ucsb.edu/documents/proclamation-4818-international-year-disabled-persons.

———. "Proclamation 4863—White Cane Safety Day." https://presidency.ucsb.edu/documents/proclamation-4863-white-cane-safety-day.

———. "Proclamation 4871—Leif Erikson Day, 1981." https://presidency.ucsb.edu/documents/proclamation-4871-leif-erikson-day-1981.

———. "Proclamation 4885—Bill of Rights Day, Human Rights Day and Week, 1981." https://presidency.ucsb.edu/documents/proclamation-4885-bill-rights-day-human-rights-day-and-week-1981.

———. "Proclamation 4886—Wright Brothers Day, 1981." https://presidency.ucsb.edu/documents/proclamation-4886-wright-brothers-day-1981.

———. "Proclamation 4893—Bicentennial Year of the American Bald Eagle and National Bald Eagle Day." https://presidency.ucsb.edu/documents/proclamation-4893-bicentennial-year-the-american-bald-eagle-and-national-bald-eagle-day.

———. "Proclamation 4935—National Year of Disabled Persons." https://presidency.ucsb.edu/documents/proclamation-4935-national-year-disabled-persons.

———. "Proclamation 4951—National Children's Day, 1982." https://presidenty.ucsb.edu/documents/proclamation-4951-national-childrens-day-1982.

———. "Proclamation 5131—National Decade of Disabled Persons." https://presidency.ucsb.edu/documents/proclamation-5131-national-decade-disabled-persons.

———. "Proclamation 5147—National Sanctity of Human Life Day, 1984." https://presidency.ucsb.edu/documents/proclamation-5147-national-sanctity-human-life-day-1984.

———. "Proclamation 5316—World Health Week and World Health Day, 1985." https://presidency.ucsb.edu/documents/proclamation-5316-world-health-week-and-world-health-day-1985.

———. "Proclamation 5454—World Health Week and World Health Day, 1986." https://presidency.ucsb.edu/documents/proclamation-5454-world-health-week-and-world-health-day-1986.

———. "Proclamation 5571—National Philanthropy Day, 1986." https://presidency.ucsb.edu/documents/proclamation-5571-national-philanthropy-day-1986.

———. "Proclamation 5589—Human Rights Day, Bill of Rights Day, and Human Rights Week, 1986." https://presidency.ucsb.edu/documents/proclamation-5589-human-rights-day-bill-rights-day-and-human-rights-week-1986.

———. "Proclamation 5695—National POW/MIA Recognition Day, 1987." https://presidency.ucsb.edu/documents/proclamation-5695-national-powmia-recognition-day-1987.

———. "Proclamation 5788—National Former Prisoners of War Recognition Day, 1988." https://presidency.ucsb.edu/documents/proclamation-5788-national-former-prisoners-war-recognition-day-1988.

———. "Proclamation 5847—National Senior Citizens Day, 1988." https://presidency.ucsb.edu/documents/proclamation-5847-national-senior-citizens-day-1988.

"Recommendation Concerning the Status of Higher-Education Teaching Personnel." Legal Instruments. UNESCO: Office of International Standards and Legal Affairs. (November 11, 1997). http://portal.unesco.org/en/ev.php-UR_ID=13144&URL_DO=DO_TOPIC&url_section=201.HTML.

"Recommendation Concerning the Status of Teachers." Legal Instruments. UNESCO: Office of International Standards and Legal Affairs. (October 5, 1966). http://portal.unesco.org/en/ev.php-URL_OD=13084&URL_DO=DO_topic&URL_SECTION=201.html.

Records of the General Conference [of UNESCO]: Twenty-Sixth Session, Vol. 1: Resolutions. Paris, France: UNESCO, 1992.

Resolution 1/79, Food and Agriculture Organization of the United Nations. https://fao.org/3/x5565E/x5565e05.htm#wfd.

Revisor of Missouri. https://revisor.mo.gov/main/OneSection.aspx?section=9.040&bid=268&hl=Missouri%u2044Day.

The Rig Veda. Translated by Ralph T. H. Griffith. NY: Book-of-the-Month-Club, 1992.

Rohr, Richard. "A Big Experiment." Center for Action and Contemplation. August 16, 2019. https://cac.org/daily-meditations/a-big-experiment-2019-08-16/.

———. "A Communion of Subjects." Center for Action and Contemplation. June 26, 2020. https://cac.org/daily-meditations/a-communion-of-subjects-2020-06-26/.

———. "Community as Alternative Consciousness." Center for Action and Contemplation. June 1, 2020. https://cac.org/daily-meditations/community-as-alternative-consciousness-2020-06-01/.

———. "God Uses Everything." Center for Action and Contemplation. September 14, 2020. https://cac.org/daily-meditations/god-uses-everyting-2020-09-14/.

Roosevelt, Franklin D. "Address to Congress Requesting a Declaration of War with Japan, December 8, 1941." http://docs.fdrlibrary.marist.edu/tmirhdee.html.

———. "A Letter on the Thirtieth Anniversary of the Airplane." https://presidency.ucsb.edu/documents/letter-the-thirtieth-anniversary-the-airplane.

———. "National Aviation Day." *Federal Register: The National Archives of the United States* 4:144 (1934) 3439. https://govinfo.gov/content/pkg/FR-1939-07-28/pdf/FR-1939-07-28.pdf.

———. "Proclamation 2062—Thanksgiving Day—1933." https://presidency.ucsb.edu/documents/proclamation-2062-thanksgiving-day-1933.

———. "Proclamation 2101—Columbus Day." https://presidency.ucsb.edu/documents/proclamation-2101-columbus-day.

———. "Proclamation 2107—Thanksgiving Day." https://presidency.ucsb.edu/documents/proclamation-2107-thanksgiving-day.

———. "Proclamation 2146—Thanksgiving Day." https://presidency.ucsb.edu/documents/proclamation-2146-thanksgiving-day.

———. "Proclamation 2208—Thanksgiving Day." https://presidency.ucsb.edu/documents/proclamation-2208-thanksgiving-day.

———. "Proclamation 2260—Thanksgiving Day." https://presidency.ucsb.edu/documents/proclamation-2260-thanksgiving-day.

———. "Proclamation 2310—Thanksgiving Day." https://presidency.ucsb.edu/documents/proclamation-2310-thanksgiving-day.

———. "Proclamation 2373—Thanksgiving Day." https://presidency.ucsb.edu/documents/proclamation-2373-thanksgiving-day.

———. "Proclamation 2441—Thanksgiving Day." https://presidency.ucsb.edu/documents/proclamation-2441-thanksgiving-day.

———. "Proclamation 2522—Thanksgiving Day." https://presidency.ucsb.edu/documents/proclamation-2522-thanksgiving-day.

———. "Proclamation 2524—Bill of Rights Day." https://presidency.ucsb.edu/documents/proclamation-2524-bill-rights-day.

———. "Proclamation 2571—Thanksgiving Day." https://presidency.ucsb.edu/documents/proclamation-2571-thanksgiving-day.

———. "Proclamation 2600—Thanksgiving Day, 1943." https://presidency.ucsb.edu/documents/proclamation-2600-thanksgiving-day-1943.

———. "Proclamation 2629—Thanksgiving Day, 1944." https://presidency.ucsb.edu/documents/proclamation-2629-thanksgiving-day-1944.

Roosevelt, Theodore. "Arbor Day Proclamation to the School Children of the United States." In *Report of the Farmers' Institutes Held under the Auspices of the West Virginia State Board of Agriculture, Report No. 5*, 9. Charleston: Tribune Printing, 1907.

"*Rosarium Virginis Mariae*: On the Most Holy Rosary." In *The Liturgy Documents*: Volume 4: Supplemental Documents for Parish Worship, Devotions, Formation, and Catechesis, 525–50. Chicago: Liturgy Training, 2013.

"Saint Patrick's Breastplate." https://irishcentral.com/roots/st-patricks-breastplate-prayer-irelands-patron-saint.

Scobey, Annmarie. "Keep Prayer in Mind." *U.S Catholic* 83:5 (2018) 43–4.

"Senate Concurrent Resolution 22." https://congress.gov/bill/98th-congress/senate-concurrent-resolution/22.

"Senate Resolution 90." https://congress.gov/107/bills/sres90/BILLS-107sres90ats.pdg.

"Senate Resolution 138." https://congress.gov/115/bills/sres138;BILLS-115sres138is.pdf.

"Senate Resolution 320." https://congress.gov/bill/112th-congress/senate-resolution/320/text.

"Senate Resolution 340." *Congressional Record—Senate*. April 28, 2004. https://govinfo.gov/content/pkg/BILLS-108sres340ats/pdf/BILLS-108sres340ats.pdf.

Shapiro. Rami. "Roadside Assistance for the Spiritual Traveler." *Spirituality and Health* 25:2 (2022) 11–12.

———. "Roadside Assistance in the Holy Land." *Spirituality and Health* 22:1 (2019) 46–50.

Sheldrake, Philip. *The Spiritual Way: Classic Traditions and Contemporary Practice*. Collegeville, MN: Liturgical, 2019.

Simon, George-Andre. "Food Security: Definition, Four Dimensions, History." Rome, Italy: University of Roma Tre, 2012. https://www.fao.org/fileadmin/templates/ERP/uni/F4D.pdf.

"The Skinny on Administrative Professionals Day." http://happyworker.com/magazine/culture/the-skinny-on-administrative-professionals-day-week#.YoaVr6jMIdU.

"Solstices and Equinoxes: 2001 to 2100." http://astropixels.com/ephemeris/soleq2001.html.

"Summer Solstice 2021: The First Day of Summer." *The Old Farmer's Almanac*. https://almanac.com/content/first-day-summer-summer-solstice.

"Sustainable Development Goals." https://un.org/sustainabledevelopment/sustainable-development-goals/.

Sutter, John D. "Why 'Cyber Monday' is Mostly Myth." http://edition.cnn.com/2010/TECH/web/11/29/cyber.monday.hoax/.

Tarkki, Jarmo. "John Shelby Spong in Memoriam." *The Fourth R* 35:1 (2022) 18–22.

"Ten Ways to Honor Your Pet on National Pet Memorial Day." *Richell International*. https://richellusa.com/10-ways-to-honor-your-pet-on-national-pet-memorial-day/.

Truman, Harry S. "Proclamation 2713—Bill of Right Day, 1946." https://presidency.ucsb.edu/documents/proclamation-2713-bill-rights-day-1946.

———. "Proclamation 2761—Bill of Rights Day, 1947." https://presidency.ucsb.edu/documents/proclamation-2761-bill-rights-day-1947.

———. "Proclamation 2811—United Nations Day, 1948." https://presidency.ucsb.edu/documents/proclamation-2811-united-nations-day-1948.

———. "Proclamation 2873—Armed Forces Day, 1950." http://presidency.ucsb.edu/documents/proclamation-2873-armed-forces-day-1950.

———. "V-E Day Proclamation." In "Interesting Facts about Victory in Europe Day (VE Day)." https://asomf.org/interesting-facts-about-victory-in-europe-day/.

Trump, Donald J. "Message on World Health Day." https://presidency.ucsb.edu/documents/message-world-health-day.

———. "Proclamation 9591—National Former Prisoner of War Recognition Day, 2017." https://presidency.ucsb.edu/documents/proclamation-9591-national-former-prisoner-war-recognition-day-2017.

———. "Proclamation 9611—Peace Officers Memorial Day and Police Week, 2017. https://presidency.ucsb.edu/documents/proclamation-9611-peace-officers-memorial-day-and-police-week-2017.

———. "Proclamation 9637—National POW/MIA Recognition Day, 2017." https://presidency.ucsb.edu/proclamation-9637-national-powmia-recognition-day-2017.

———. "Proclamation 9657—Leif Erikson Day, 2017." https://presidency.ucsb.edu/documents/proclamation-9657-leif-erikson-day-2017.

———. "Proclamation 9662—Blind Americans Equality Day, 2017." https://presidency.ucsb.edu/documents/proclamation-9662-blind-americans-equality-day-2017.

———. "Proclamation 9673—World Freedom Day, 2017." https://presidency.ucsb.edu/documents/proclamation-9673-world-freedom-day-2017.

———. "Proclamation 9680—World AIDS Day, 2017." https://presidency.ucsb.edu/documents/proclamation-9680-world-aids-day-2017.

———. "Proclamation 9685—Human Rights Day, Bill of Rights Day, and Human Rights Week, 2017." https://presidency.ucsb.edu/documents/proclamation-9685-human-rights-day-bill-rights-day-and-human-rights-week-2017.

———. "Proclamation 9686—Wright Brothers Day, 2017." https://presidency.ucsb.edu/documents/proclamation-9686-wright-brothers-day-2017.

———. "Proclamation 9691—National Sanctity of Human Life Day, 2018." https://presidency.ucsb.edu/documents/proclamation-9691-national-sanctity-human-life-day-2018.

———. "Statement on America Recycles Day." https://presidency.ucsb.edu/documents/statement-america-recycles-day.

———. "Statement on the Observance of Kwanzaa." https://presidency.ucsb.edu/documents/statement-the-observance-kwanzaa-8.

Tusing-Borgeld, Christy. "Interview with the Founder of National Stepfamily Day: Christy Tusing-Borgeld." *The Stepmom Project*. https://thestepmomproject.com/interview-founder-national-stepfamily-day-christy-tusing-borgeld/.

"Twelve Tips to Stay Safe on Cyber Monday." https://web.archive.org/web/20140913055413/http://www.cybermondaysniper.com/safety/.

"United Nations Convention against Transnational Organized Crime and the Protocols Thereto." https://www.unodc.org/documents/middleeastandnorthafrica/organised-crime/UNITED_NATIONS_CONVENTION_AGAINST_TRANSNATIONAL_ORGANIZED_CRIME_AND_THE_PROTOCOLS_THERETO.pdf.

"United Nations Disability Inclusion Strategy." https://un.org/en/content/disabilitystrategy/documentation/UN_Disability_Inclusion_Strategy_english.pdf.

BIBLIOGRAPHY

"UNESCO [United Nations Educational, Scientific, and Cultural Organization] Constitution." http://portal.unesco.org/en/ev.php-URL_ID=15244&URL_DO=DO_TOPIC&URL_SECTION=201.html.

United Nations General Assembly. A/RES/31/123 International Year of Disabled Persons. https://un-documents.net/a31r123.htm.

———. A/RES/34/24 Implementation of the Program for the Decade for Action to Combat Racism and Racial Discrimination. https://documents-dds-ny.un.org/doc/RESOLUTION/GEN/NR0/376/51/IMG/NR037651.pdf?OpenElement.

———. A/RES/36/67 International Year of Peace and International Day of Peace. https://undocs.org/A/RES/36/67.

———. A/RES/37/52 World Program of Action Concerning Disabled Persons. https://un-documents.net/a37r52.htm.

———. A/RES/37/53 Implementation of the World Program of Action Concerning Disabled Persons. https://documents-dds-ny.un.org/doc/RESOLUTION/GEN/NR0/425/31/IMG/NR042531.pdf?OpenElement.

———. A/RES/38/28 Implementation of the World Program of Action Concerning Disabled Persons. https://un.org/depts/dhl/resguide/r38_resolutions_table_eng.htm / File:///C/Users/OWNER/Downloads/A_RES_38_28-EN.pdf. https://undocs.org/en/A/RES/38/28.

———. A/RES/40/202 Human Settlements. https://undocs.org/en/A/RES/40/202.

———. A/RES/40/212 International Volunteer Day for Economic and Social Development. https://undocs.org/A/RES/40/212.

———. A/RES/44/25 Convention on the Rights of the Child. https://undocs.org/A/RES/44/25.

———. A/RES/45/106 Implementation of the International Plan of Action on Aging and Related Activities. https://documents-dds-ny.un.org/doc/RESOLUTION/GEN/NR0/564/95/IMG/NR056495.pdf?OpenElement.

———. A/RES/45/158 International Convention on the Protection of the Rights of All Migrant Workers and Members of Their Families. https://un.org/en/development/desa/population/migration/generalassembly/docs/globalcompact/A_RES_45_158.pdf.

———. A/RES/46/91 United Nations Principles for Older Persons." https://ohechr.org/Documents/ProfessionalInterest/olderpersons.pdf.

———. A/RES/47/3 International Day of Disabled Persons. https://documents-dds-ny.un.org/doc/RESOLUTION/GEN/NR0/023/71/IMG/NR002371.pdf?OpenElement.

———. A/RES/47/193 Observance of World Day for Water. https://undocs.org/A/RES/47/193.

———. A/RES/47/196 Observance of an International Day for the Eradication of Poverty. https://undocs.org/A/RES/47/196.

———. A/RES/47/237 International Year of the Family. http://undocs.org/A/RES/47/237.

———. A/RES/49/214 International Decade of the World's Indigenous People. https://undocs.org/A/RES/49/214.

———. A/RES/51/205 Proclamation of 21 November as World Television Day." https://undocs.or/en/A/RES/51/205.

———. A/RES/52/17 International Year of Volunteers. https://undocs.org/A/RES/52/17.

———. A/RES/53/24 International Year of Mountains. https://documents-dds-ny.un.org/doc/UNDOC/GEN/N98/776/23/PDF/N9877623.pdf?OpenElement.

BIBLIOGRAPHY

———. A/RES/54/120 Policies and Programs Involving Youth. https://undocs.org/A/RES/54/120.

———. A/RES/55/76 Fiftieth Anniversary of the Office of the United Nations High Commissioner for Refugees and World Refugee Day. https://undocs.org/A/RES/55/76.

———. A/RES/55/93 Proclamation of 18 December as International Migrants Day. https://documents-dds-ny.un.org/doc/UNDOC/GEN/N00/564/97/PDF/N0056497.pdf?OpenElement.

———. A/RES/55/189. https://documents-dds-ny.un.org/doc/UNDOC/GEN/N00/570/67/PDF/N0057067.pdf?OpenElement.

———. A/RES/55/192 Culture and Development. https://undocs.org/en/A/RES/55/192.

———. A/RES/55/282 International Day of Peace. https://undocs.org/A/RES/55/192.

———. A/RES/56/38 Recommendations on Support for Volunteering. https://undocs.org/A/RES/56/38.

———. A/RES/56/212 Global Code of Ethics for Tourism." https://undocs.org/en/A/RES/56/212.

———. A/RES/56/262 Multilingualism. https://undocs.org/A/RES/56/262.

———. A/RES/57/106 Follow-up to the International Year of Volunteers. https://undocs.org/A/RES/57/106.

———. A/RES/57/245 International Year of Mountains, 2002. https://documents-dds-ny.un.org/doc/UNDOC/GEN/N02/555/58/PDF/N0255558.pdf?OpenElement.

———. A/RES/57/249 Culture and Development. https://undocs.org/en/A/RES/57/249.

———. A/RES/60/7 Holocaust Remembrance. https://undocs.org/A/RES/60/7.

———. A/RES/60/209 Implementation of the First United Nations Decade for the Eradication of Poverty (1997–2006). https://documents-dds-ny.un.org/doc/UNDOC/GEN/N05/500/14/PDF/N0550014.pdf?OpenElement.

———. A/RES/61/106 Convention on the Rights of Persons with Disabilities. https://un.org/en/development/desa/population/migration/generalassembly/docs/globalcompact/A_RES_61_106.pdf.

———. A/RES/61/193 International Year of Forests. https://documents-dds-ny.un.org/doc/UNDOC/GEN/N06/506/01/PDF/N0650601.pdf?OpenElement.

———. A/RES/62/10 World Day of Social Justice." https://undocs.org/en/A/RES/62/10.

———. A/RES/63/111 Oceans and the Law of the Sea. https://undocs.org/A/RES/63/11.

———. A/RES/63/138 Safety and Security of Humanitarian Personnel and Protection of United Nations Personnel. https://undocs.org/A/RES/63/138.

———. A/RES/63/139 Strengthening of the Coordination of Emergency Humanitarian Assistance of the United Nations. https://undocs.org/A/RES/63/139.

———. A/RES/63/153 Follow-up to the Implementation of the International Year of Volunteers. https://undocs.org/A/RES/63/153.

———. A/RES/64/13 Nelson Mandela International Day. https://undocs.org/A/RES/64/13.

———. A/RES/64/35 International Day against Nuclear Tests." https://undocs.org/A/RES/64.35.

———. A/RES/66/281 International Day of Happiness. https://undocs.org/A/RES/66/281.

———. A/RES/66/292 Global Day of Parents. https://undocs.org/A/RES/66/292.

———. A/RES/67/105 International Day of Charity. https://undocs.org/A/RES/67/105.

———. A/RES/67/124 A-B Questions Relating to Information, United Nations Public Information Policies and Activities. https://undocs.org/en/A/RES/67/124.

———. A/RES/67/200 International Day of Forests. https://un.org/en.ga/search/view_doc.asp?symbol=A/RES/67/200.

———. A/RES/67/291 Sanitation for All. https://undocs.org/en/A/RES/67/291.

———. A/RES/67/292 Multilingualism. https://undocs.org/A/RES/67/292.

———. A/RES/68/32 Follow-up to the 2013 High-level Meeting of the General Assembly on Nuclear Disarmament. https://undocs.org/en/A/RES/68/32.

———. A/RES/68/192 Improving the Coordination of Efforts against Trafficking in Persons. https://undocs.org/A/RES/68/192.

———. A/RES/68/205 World Wildlife Day. https://undocs.org/A/RES/68.205.

———. A/RES/68/239 Implementation of the Outcome of the United Nations Conference on Human Settlements (Habitat II) and Strengthening of the United Nations Human Settlements Program (UN-Habitat). https://undocs.org/A/RES/68/239.

———. A/RES/69/250 Pattern of Conferences. https://undocs.org/en/A/RES/69/250.

———. A/RES/70/1 Transforming Our World: The 2030 Agenda for Sustainable Development. https://www.un.org/en/development/desa/population/migration/generalassembly/docs/globalcompact/A_RES_70_1_E.pdf.

———. A/RES/70/175 United Nations Standard Minimum Rules for the Treatment of Prisoners (the Nelson Mandela Rules). https://undocs.org/A/RES/70/175.

———. A/RES/71/284 World Creativity and Innovation Day. https://undocs.org/en/A/RES/71/284.

———. A/RES/71/328 Multilingualism. https://undocs.org/en/A/RES/71/328.

———. A/RES/72/211 World Bee Day. https://undocs.org/en/A/RES/72/211.

———. A/RES/73/250 World Food Safety Day. https://undocs.org/en/A/RES/73/250.

———. A/RES/73/329 Promoting the Culture of Peace with Love and Conscience. https://undocs.org/en/A/RES/73/329.

———. A/RES/75/200 International Day of Human Fraternity. https://undocs.org/en/A/RES/75/200.

———. A/RES/168 (II) United Nations Day. https://un.org/ga/search/view_doc.asp?symbol=A/RES/168(II).

———. A/RES/1386 (XIV) Declaration of the Rights of the Child. https://undocs.org/A/RES/1386%20(XIV).

———. A/RES/2142 (XXI) Elimination of All Forms of Racial Discrimination. https://un.org/ga/search/view_doc.asp?symbol=A/RES/2142%20(XXI).

———. A/RES/2782 (XXVI) Proclamation of United Nations Day as an International Holiday. https://un.org/ga/search/view_doc.asp?symbol=A/RES/2782(XXVI).

———. A/65/L.72 International Day of Friendship. https://documents-dds-ny.un.org/doc/UNDOC/LTD/N11/314/00/PDF/N1131400.pdf?OpenElement.

———. A/67/62 Questions Relating to Information. https://undocs.org/en/A/67/62.

———. 423 (V) Human Rights Day. https://un.org/ga/search/view_doc.asp?symbol=A/RES/423(V).

United Nations Treaty Collection. Chapter IV: Human Rights. "15. Convention on the Rights of Persons with Disabilities." https://treaties.un.org/Pages/ViewDetails.aspx?src=TREATY&mtdsg_no=IV-15&chapter=4&clang=_en.

United Nations World Tourism Organization. A/RES/76 (III) World Tourism Day. https://.e-unwto.org/doi/epdf/10.18111/unwtogad.1979.1.rg33t8x5l2221252.

———. A/3/14 Proposal to Institute World Tourism Day. https://e-unwto.org/doi/pdf/10.18111/unwtogad.1979.1.q551504q782j2l54.

BIBLIOGRAPHY

"Universal Declaration of Human Rights [A/RES/217 (III)]." https://un.org/sites/un2.un.org/files/udhr.pdf.

"Universal Declaration on Cultural Diversity." https://portal.unesco.org/en/ev.php-URL_ID=13179&URL_DO=DO_PRINTPAGE&URL_SECTION=201.html.

Walsh, Michael. *A New Dictionary of Saints: East and West*. Collegeville, MN: Liturgical, 2007.

Washington, George. "First Inaugural Address: Final Version, 30 April 1789." https://founders.archives.gov/?q=%20First%20Inaugural%20Address%3A%20Final%20Version&s=1111311111&r=1.

———. "Proclamation—Day of National Thanksgiving." https://presidency.ucsb.edu/documents/proclamation-day-national-thanksgiving.

———. "Proclamation 6—Day of Public Thanksgiving." https://presidency.ucsb.edu/documents/proclamation-6-day-public-thanksgiving.

"What does the 'D' in D-Day mean?" The National World War II Museum. https://army.mil/e2/downloads/rv7/d-day/the-meaning-of-dday-fact.pdf.

"What is Red Nose Day?" https://rednoseday.org/what-is-red-nose-day.

"What to Name the Super Bowl? Rozelle Asks Newsmen to Help." *The Fort Scott Tribune* (May 25, 1967) 9. https://news.google.com/newspapers?id=MtgfAAAAIBAJ&pg=3999%2C1286543.

"When is the First Day of Winter?" https://almanac.com/content/first-day-winter-winter-solstice.

Wilkie, Dana. "The Challenges of Show Appreciation on Boss's Day." https://shrm.org/resourcesand tools/hr-topics/employee-relations/pages/the-challenges-of-showing-appreciation-on-boss-day.aspx.

Wilson, Ben. *Metropolis: A History of the City, Humankind's Greatest Invention*. New York: Anchor, 2020.

Wilson, Woodrow. "Address on Flag Day." https://presidency.ucsb.edu/documents/address-flag-day.

———. "Address to a Joint Session of Congress Requesting a Declaration of War Against Germany." https://presidency.ucsb.edu/documents/address-joint-session-congress-requesting-declaration-war-against-germany.

———. "A Proclamation." (May 9, 1914). https://archives.gov/historical-docs/todays-doc/?dod-date=509#:~:text=On%20May%209%2C%201914%2C%20President,the%20mothers%20of%20our%20country.

———. "Proclamation 1335—Flag Day." https://presidency.ucsb.edu/documents/proclamation-1335-flag-day.

"Wine Holidays of the Year (Official Wine Day Calendar)." *Wine Folly*. https://winefolly.com/lifestyle/national-wine-day/.

Winters, Amie. "National Farmers Day Celebrated October 12." https://weau.com/2021/10/12/national-farmers-day-celebrated-october-12/.

"Winter Solstice 2021: When is It, and What is It?" https://farmersalmanac.com/winter-solstice-first-day-winter.

"World Bee Day." https://un.org/en/observances/bee-day.

"World Cities Day." https://un.org/en/observances/cities-day.

"World Creativity and Innovation Day." https://un.org/en/observances/creativity-and-innovation-day.

"World Food Safety Day." https://un.org/en/observances/food-safety-day.

"World Health Organization." https://un.org/youthenvoy/2013/09/who-world-health-organisation/.

"World Mental Health Day: All about History, Significance, and Theme for This Year." New Delhi, India: *Hindustan Times* (December 5, 2021). https://www.hindustantimes.com/lifestyle/health/world-mental-health-day-2021-all-about-history-significance-and-theme-101633785903784.html.

"World Philosophy Day." https://en.unceso.org/commemorations/philosophy-day.

"World Poetry Day, 30 C/Resolution 29." *Records of the General Conference, 30th Session, Parish, 26 October to 17 November 1999, Vol. 1: Resolutions.* https://unesdoc.uncesco.org/ark:/48223/pf0000118514.page=70.

"World Poetry Day, UNESCO." https://en.unesco.org/commemorations/worldpoetryday.

"World Press Freedom Day." https://un.org/en/observances/press-freedom-day.

"World Program of Action Concerning Disabled Persons. https://un.org/development/desa/disabilities/resources/world-programme-of-action-concerning-disabled-persons.html.

"World Radio Day." https://un.org/en/observances/radio-day.

"World Television Day." https://daysoftheyear.com/days/world-television-day/.

"World Television Day." https://un.org/en/observances/world-televison-day.

"World Television Day." https://nationaltoday.com/world-television-day/.

"World Toilet Day." https://un.org/en/observances/toilet-day.

"World Tourism Day." https://un.org/en/observances/tourism-day.

"Worst Forms of Child Labor Convention, 1999 (No. 182)." International Labor Organization. https://ilo.org/Search5/search.do?sitelang=en&locale=en_EN&consumercode=ILOHQ_STELLENT_PUBLIC&searchWhat=Worst+Forms+of+Child+Labor+Convention%2C+1999&searchLanguage=en.

Young, Robin, and Karyn Miller-Medzon. "Can Spirituality Exist without God? A Growing Number of Americans Say Yes." https://wbur.org/hereandnow/2020/01/13/spirituality-krista-tippett.

Zimmer, Ben. "The Origins of 'Black Friday.'" https://visualthesaurus.com/cm/wordroutes/the-origins-of-black-friday/.

Index

Note: Because many entries begin with *Day, International, National,* or *World,* they have not been used in this index. For example, National Aviation Day is indexed under Aviation Day, National.

Abraham Lincoln's Birthday, 25
Administrative Professionals Week and Administrative Professionals Day, 86
Administrative Professionals Day, Administrative Professionals Week and, 86
Against Child Labor, World Day, 130
Against Trafficking in Persons, World Day, 160
AIDS Day, World, 299
All Saints' Day, 249
All Souls' Day, 250
American Eagle Day, National, 141
American Revolutionary War Began, 79
American Smokeout, Great, 284
America Recycles Day, 261
(Apollo 11), First Manned Moon Landing, 153
April Fool's (Fools') Day, 60
Arbor Day, 88
Armed Forces Week and Day, 114
Autumnal Equinox, 200
Aviation Day, National, 168

Bee Day, World, 115
Beer Day, National, 64
Bill of Rights Day, 328
Black Friday, 291
Blind Americans Equality Day, White Cane Safety Day, 222
Boss's Day, National, 227

Canada Day, 144
Candles, 354
Candy Cane, 3
(Carnival) Mardi Gras, 39
Charity, International Day of, 182
Charlie Brown Christmas Tree, 352
Child Labor, World Day Against, 130

Children's Day 1, National, 273
Children's Day 2, National, 275
Children's Day, World (Universal, International), 270
Child's Day 1, National, 277
Child's Day 2, National, 280
Chinese New Year, 32
Chocolate Day, National, 238
Christmas Day 1, 343
Christmas Day 2, 346
Christmas Day 3, 6
Christmas Eve, 342
Christmas Tree, 351
Christmas Tree, Charlie Brown, 352
Cinco de Mayo, 100
Cities Day, World, 241
Citizenship Day, Constitution Day and, 192
Coffee Day, International, National Coffee Day, 208
Coffee Day, National, International Coffee Day, 208
Columbus Day, 220
Conscience, International Day of, 61
Constitution Day and Citizenship Day, 192
Creativity and Innovation Day, World, 80
Cultural Diversity for Dialogue and Development, World Day for, 117
Cyber Monday, 294

D-Day (Normandy Landings), 125
Daylight Saving Time Begins, 44
Daylight Savings Time Ends, 252
Development, World Day for Cultural Diversity for Dialogue and, 117
Dialogue and Development, World Day for Cultural Diversity for, 117
Disabled Persons: Part 1, International Day of, 302

387

Index

Disabled Persons: Part 2, International Day of, 306
Doctors Day and National Physicians Week, National, 57

Eagle Day, National American, 141
Earth Day, 83
Easter Sunday, 73
Economic and Social Development, International Volunteer Day for, 310
Election Day, 251
Eleventh Day of Christmas, 4
Elimination of Racial Discrimination, International Day for the, 49
English Language Day, 84
Epiphany, 6
Equinox, Spring, 46
Equinox, Autumnal, 200
Eradication of Poverty, International Day for the, 229
Erickson Day, Leif, 215

Families, International Day of, 108
Farmer's Day, National, 221
Father's Day, 134
Festivus, 340
Fifth Day of Christmas, 354
Firefighters Day, International, 98
Fireplace, 2
First Manned Moon Landing (Apollo 11), 153
Flag Day, 132
Food Day, World, 226
Food Safety Day, World, 127
Forests, International Day of, 53
Former Prisoner(s) of War Recognition Day, National, 68
Fourth Day of Christmas, 352
Freedom Day, World, 253
Freedom Day, World Press, 96
Friendship (Friendship Day), International Day of, 158
(Friendship Day) International Day of Friendship, 158
Frosty the Snowman, 5

Gettysburg Address Anniversary, 265
Giving Tuesday, 296
Good Neighbor Day, National, 202
Grandparents Day, National, 184
Great American Smokeout, 284
Green Monday, 317
Grinch, The, 4
Groundhog Day, 20

Halloween 1, 245
Halloween 2, 246
Happiness, International Day of, 47
Health Day, World, 66
Health Day, World Mental, 218
Holocaust Remembrance Day, International, 17
Human Fraternity, International Day of, 21
Humanitarian Day, World, 166
Human Rights Day, 318
Human Rights Week, 321
Human Solidarity Day, International, 335

Inauguration Day, 14
Income Tax Day, 77
Independence Day, 148
Independence Day, Juneteenth National, 136
Indigenous Peoples, International Day of the World's, 162
Innovation Day, World Creativity and, 80

Jefferson's Birthday, Thomas, 75
Juneteenth National Independence Day, 136

King, Martin Luther, Jr., Day, 11
Kwanzaa Begins, 348

Labor Day, 183
Labor, World Day Against Child, 130
Laughter Day, World, 104
Law Enforcement Appreciation Day, National, 8
Leif Erikson Day, 215
Lincoln's Birthday, Abraham, 25
Love Your Pet Day, National, 36
Loyalty Day, 94

(Mandela Day), Nelson Mandela International Day, 152
Mandela International Day (Mandela Day), Nelson, 152
Manned Moon Landing (Apollo 11), First, 153
Mardi Gras (Carnival), 39
Martin Luther King, Jr., Day, 11
May Day, 91
Memorial Day, 122
Men's Day, International, 267
Mental Health Day, World, 218
Migrants Day, International, 332
Missouri Day, 230
Moon Landing (Apollo 11), First Manned, 153
Mother-in-Law Day, National, 237
Mother's Day, 107

Index

Mountain Day, International, 326

Native American Day, 201
Neighbor Day, National Good, 202
Nelson Mandela International Day (Mandela Day), 152
New Year, Chinese, 32
New Year's Day, 1
New Year's Eve, 357
Nicholas Day, St., 313
Nineth Day of Christmas, 2
(Normandy Landings), D-Day, 125
Nose Day, Red, 121
Nuclear Weapons, International Day for the Total Elimination of, 204
Nurses' Day, National, National Student Nurses' Day, International Nurses Day, 103
Nurses' Day, International, National Nurses Day, National Student Nurses' Day, 103

Ocean Day, World, 128
Older Persons, International Day for, 211

Panama Canal Opened, 165
Parents' Day, 155
Passover, 55
Patrick's Day, St., 45
Patriot Day and National Day of Service and Remembrance, 187
Patriots' Day, 78
Peace, International Day of, 199
Peace Officers Memorial Day and Police Week, 110
Pearl Harbor Remembrance Day, National, 315
Persons, International Day for Older, 211
Persons, International Day of Disabled: Part 1, 302
Persons, International Day of Disabled: Part 2, 306
Persons, World Day Against Trafficking in, 160
Pet Day, Love Your, 36
Pet Day, National, 72
Pet Memorial Day, National, 186
Philanthropy Day, National, 258
Philosophy Day, World, 264
Physicians Week, National Doctors Day and National, 57
Poetry Day, World, 51
Police Week, Peace Officers Memorial Day and, 110
Postage Stamp Day, National U.S., National Postal Workers Day, 146

Postal Workers Day, National U.S. Postage Stamp Day, National, 146

Poverty, International Day for the Eradication of, 229
POW/MIA Recognition Day, National, 194
Prayer, National Day of, 102
Prayer for the Care of Creation, World Day of, 178
President's Day (Washington's Birthday), 29
Press Freedom Day, World, 96
Prisoner(s) of War Recognition Day, National Former, 68

Racial Discrimination, International Day for the Elimination of, 49
Radio Day, World, 26
Ramadan, 89
Random Acts of Kindness Day, National, 31
Recycles Day, America, 261
Red Nose Day, 121
Reformation Day, 243
Refugee Day, World, 139

Reindeer, 355
Religion Day, World, 10
Religious Freedom Day, National, 13
Revolutionary War Began, American, 79

St. Nicholas Day, 313
St. Patrick's Day, 45
Saints' Day, All, 249
Sanctity of Human Life Day, National, 15
School Begins, 176
Senior Citizen's Day, National, 173
Service and Remembrance, National Day of, Patriot Day, 187
Sixth Day of Christmas, 355
Small Business Saturday, 292
Smokeout, Great American, 284
Social Development, International Volunteer Day for Economic and, 310
Social Justice, World Day for, 34
Solstice, Summer, 138
Solstice, Winter, 339
Souls' Day, All, 250
Spring Begins, 46
Star Spangled Banner Written, The, 189
Stepfamily Day, National, 190
Student Nurses' Day, National, International Nurses Day, National Nurses' Day, 103
Summer Solstice, 138
Super Bowl Sunday, 24
Super Saturday, 338
Sweetest Day, 233

389

Index

Tattoo Day, National, 150
Teacher Appreciation Day, National, National Teacher Appreciation Week, 95
Teacher Appreciation Week, National, National Teacher Appreciation Day, 95
Teachers' Day, World, 213
Television Day, World, 286
Tenth Day of Christmas, 3
Thanksgiving Day, 288
Third Day of Christmas, 351
Thomas Jefferson's Birthday, 75
Toilet Day, World, 268
Tooth Fairy Day, 37
Tourism Day, World, 206
Trafficking in Persons, World Day Against, 160
Twelfth Day of Christmas, 5

United Nations Day, 235
U.S. Postage Stamp Day, National, National Postal Workers Day, 146

Valentine's Day, 28
V-E Day, 105

Veterans Day, 256
(V-J Day), Victory Over Japan Day, 181
Victory Over Japan Day (V-J Day), 181
Volunteer Day for Economic and Social Development, International, 310

(Washington's Birthday) President's Day, 29
Water Day, World, 54
Weapons, International Day for the Total Elimination of Nuclear, 204
White Cane Safety Day, Blind Americans Equality Day, 222
Wildlife Day, World, 41
Wine Day, National, 120
Winter Solstice, 339
Women's Day, International, 42
Women's Equality Day, 174
Workers' Day, International, 92
World War I Began, 156
World War II Began, 179
Wright Brothers Day, 168

Youth Day, International, 163

Recent Books by Mark G. Boyer published by Wipf & Stock

Nature Spirituality: Praying with Wind, Water, Earth, Fire

A Spirituality of Ageing

Weekday Saints: Reflections on Their Scriptures

Human Wholeness: A Spirituality of Relationship

A Simple Systematic Mariology

Praying Your Way through Luke's Gospel and the Acts of the Apostles

An Abecedarian of Animal Spirit Guides: Spiritual Growth through Reflections on Creatures

Overcome with Paschal Joy: Chanting through Lent and Easter—Daily Reflections with Familiar Hymns

Taking Leave of Your Home: Moving in the Peace of Christ

An Abecedarian of Sacred Trees: Spiritual Growth through Reflections on Woody Plants

Divine Presence: Elements of Biblical Theophanies

Fruit of the Vine: A Biblical Spirituality of Wine

Names for Jesus: Reflections for Advent and Christmas

Talk to God and Listen to the Casual Reply: Experiencing the Spirituality of John Denver

Christ Our Passover Has Been Sacrificed: A Guide through Paschal Mystery Spirituality—Mystical Theology in The Roman Missal

Rosary Primer: The Prayers, The Mysteries, and the New Testament

RECENT BOOKS BY MARK G. BOYER PUBLISHED BY WIPF & STOCK

From Contemplation to Action: The Spiritual Process of Divine Discernment Using Elijah and Elisha as Models

Love Addict

All Things Mary: Honoring the Mother of God—An Anthology of Marian Reflections

Shhh! The Sound of Sheer Silence: A Biblical Spirituality that Transforms

What is Born of the Spirit is Spirit: A Biblical Spirituality of Spirit

Very Short Reflections—for Advent and Christmas, Lent and Easter, Ordinary Time, and Saints—through the Liturgical Year

Living Parables: Today's Versions

My Life of Ministry, Writing, Teaching, and Traveling: The Autobiography of an Old Mines Missionary

300 Years of the French in Old Mines: A Narrative History of the Oldest Village in Missouri

Journey into God: Spiritual Reflections for Travelers

www.ingramcontent.com/pod-product-compliance
Lightning Source LLC
Chambersburg PA
CBHW060505300426
44112CB00017B/2552